KU-510-321

Pro Tools® 10 Power!: The Comprehensive Guide

Frank D.Cook

Course Technology PTR
A part of Cengage Learning

COURSE TECHNOLOGY
CENGAGE Learning

Australia • Brazil • Japan • Korea • Mexico • Singapore • Spain • United Kingdom • United States

Pro Tools® 10 Power!: The Comprehensive Guide
Frank D. Cook

Publisher and General Manager, Course Technology PTR: Stacy L. Hiquet

Associate Director of Marketing: Sarah Panella

Manager of Editorial Services: Heather Talbot

Senior Marketing Manager: Mark Hughes

Acquisitions Editor: Orren Merton

Project Editor/Copy Editor: Cathleen D. Small

Technical Reviewer: Eric Kuehnl

Interior Layout Tech: MPS Limited, a Macmillan Company

Cover Designer: Mike Tanamachi

Indexer: Broccoli Information Management

Proofreader: Sue Boshers

© 2013 Course Technology, a part of Cengage Learning.

ALL RIGHTS RESERVED. No part of this work covered by the copyright herein may be reproduced, transmitted, stored, or used in any form or by any means graphic, electronic, or mechanical, including but not limited to photocopying, recording, scanning, digitizing, taping, Web distribution, information networks, or information storage and retrieval systems, except as permitted under Section 107 or 108 of the 1976 United States Copyright Act, without the prior written permission of the publisher.

For product information and technology assistance, contact us at
Cengage Learning Customer & Sales Support, 1-800-354-9706

For permission to use material from this text or product, submit all requests online at **www.cengage.com/permissions**

Further permissions questions can be emailed to
permissionrequest@cengage.com

Pro Tools is a registered trademark of Avid Technology, Inc. All other trademarks are the property of their respective owners.

All images © Cengage Learning unless otherwise noted.

Library of Congress Control Number: 2011940300

ISBN-13: 978-1-133-73253-2

ISBN-10: 1-133-73253-4

Course Technology, a part of Cengage Learning

20 Channel Center Street

Boston, MA 02210

USA

Cengage Learning is a leading provider of customized learning solutions with office locations around the globe, including Singapore, the United Kingdom, Australia, Mexico, Brazil, and Japan. Locate your local office at:
international.cengage.com/region

Cengage Learning products are represented in Canada by Nelson Education, Ltd.

For your lifelong learning solutions, visit **courseptr.com**

Visit our corporate website at **cengage.com**

SHREWSBURY COLLEGE LIBRARY

Inv No. T- 1365023 Date 12-10-12

Ord No. 39638 Date 5-10-12

Class No. 781.34536 COO

Price £28-99 Checked P

065432

Printed in the United States of America
1 2 3 4 5 6 7 14 13 12

Acknowledgments

I wish to thank my wife and kids for putting up with my long work hours, the staff at Avid and Digidesign who have afforded me endless opportunities to learn Pro Tools in depth and who have tirelessly answered my many questions, my fellow Pro Tools instructors who have inspired me and provided invaluable input, and all of the industry professionals that I have had the good fortune to interact with and learn from.

I must also acknowledge the authors of the previous books in the *Pro Tools Power!* series—Colin MacQueen, Steve Albanese, and Christopher R. Burns—whose excellent work is the foundation upon which this book is built. This latest edition is truly a mere update to the detailed and comprehensive coverage they have provided for earlier versions covering Pro Tools 5, 6, 7, and 8.

Lastly, I'd like to offer special thanks to my friend and colleague, Eric Kuehnl, for his excellent technical review of the manuscript and numerous last-minute catches, and to my editor, Cathleen Small, for her keen eye and attention to detail. It has been a pleasure to work with you both.

About the Author

Frank D. Cook works as an independent consultant, trainer, and course developer for the Avid Learning Partner Program. His company, Insource Writing Solutions, has partnered with Avid Technology, Inc. for more than six years to develop certification courses in Pro Tools, ICON integrated console systems, and VENUE live sound systems.

Frank is a bass guitarist, a longtime Pro Tools user, and an Avid Master Instructor. Frank has worked in the technical publications and education industries for more than 15 years. As a writer, editor, technical publications manager, and business owner, Frank has authored and contributed to hundreds of guides, manuals, reports, and other publications for clients in a wide variety of industries. His writing and consulting company, Insource Writing Solutions, specializes in documentation for the digital audio industry. His new venture, NextPoint Training, focuses on advanced training in Pro Tools, VENUE, digital media, and related products and technologies.

Frank teaches Pro Tools courses as an adjunct professor at American River College in Sacramento, California.

Contents

Chapter 3
Your System Configuration

Chapter 4
Creating Your First Pro Tools Session

Chapter 5
The Transport Window

127

Chapter 6
The Edit Window

145

Chapter 7
The Mix Window

Chapter 8
Menu Selections: Highlights

Chapter 9
Plug-Ins, Inserts, and Sends

315

Chapter 10
MIDI   351

Chapter 11
Synchronization   391

Chapter 12
The Pro Tools Groove

407

Chapter 13
A Multitrack Music Session

433

Chapter 17
The Score Editor Window
521

Chapter 18
Pro Tools Power: The Next Step
529

Appendix D
Power Tips and Loopy Ideas 577

Appendix E
Signal Flow in Pro Tools 593

Introduction

Since it arrived on the scene, Pro Tools has consistently set the standard for reliability and features that meet the real-world needs of audio production enthusiasts and professionals alike.

Pro Tools has been an industry standard since it was introduced in 1991. It is used in a wide variety of industries and applications: multimedia, music production, video post-production, journalism, game audio, broadcast, live sound, and many others. Many excellent learning resources exist for Pro Tools users, including books, support and educational material on the Avid website, Avid Learning Partner locations, and university and recording-school programs.

This book seeks to pull together a comprehensive overview of Pro Tools operation, the currently available configurations, the most common ways in which Pro Tools is used, and the essential technical information necessary to get your Pro Tools rig working with the rest of your studio gear. This book is intended to serve the following purposes:

- Jumpstart Pro Tools users, both those with a solid audio background and those who are more or less new to hands-on audio production.
- Help more-experienced users get deeper into the program and into areas that they may be unfamiliar with.
- Provide some interesting and thought-provoking tips for Pro Tools users at all levels.

You will find that the book communicates on several different levels simultaneously, reviewing general concepts, providing step-by-step instructions, and covering technical details to clarify concepts. In addition, you will find suggestions for peripherals and techniques that will save you time.

The book starts by reviewing the currently available Pro Tools configurations (which are revisited in more detail in Chapter 3, "Your System Configuration"). Next, it walks through basic concepts, reviewing the essential functions in the main Pro Tools windows and menus. The objective here is to help you become productive in Pro Tools in as little time as possible. For that reason, you will find any theoretical discussions or descriptions of Pro Tools functions grounded with real-world examples.

How to Use This Book

You can read this book from start to finish, jump directly to specific chapters if you prefer, or graze throughout. Although I prefer plain, straightforward language (and try to write that way), some of the technical information can be a little dense. If you run into sections that are a bit hard to grasp at first, don't sweat the technical details. Just focus on the big picture for now; you can always review later for further depth.

I recommend that all users take a moment to review the basic information in Chapter 2, "Pro Tools Terms and Concepts," however. This chapter establishes background concepts and vocabulary that are essential for understanding how Pro Tools works. If you're new to *all* of this, including audio and MIDI in general, be sure to read Chapter 1, "About Pro Tools," to get a jumpstart.

Who Can Benefit

Aside from covering Pro Tools 10 configurations on Mac and Windows, this book also provides useful information for the following:

- New Pro Tools users.

- Experienced users seeking to broaden their knowledge, get up to date on recent versions, or branch into other areas of production.

- Veteran users. (Even those who have been using Pro Tools for years can find some interesting tips and techniques when they study the application anew.)

Quick Start for You Impatient Types

Okay, so you just cranked up Pro Tools, and you're not even sure where to start. Well, the *Pro Tools Reference Guide* PDF document and/or the online help (both included with the program) can definitely be worth your time. You might print out some sections of the *Reference Guide* (as well as the *Keyboard Shortcuts* guide, also included) and lug them around with you for the next few weeks. You will find that Avid's manuals are well written and thorough.

If you're a first-time user and are anxious to get started with Pro Tools, you might go straight to Chapter 4, "Creating Your First Pro Tools Session." This chapter walks you through creating a session, creating tracks, recording and editing audio, inserting effects plug-ins, and performing simple mix automation.

Once you've gotten beyond your first session, you can push ahead through the chapters covering the Transport, Edit, and Mix windows. Even better, check out Chapter 2. This chapter will help you with the basic functions and terminology that you absolutely must understand to work sensibly with Pro Tools.

Conventions Used in This Book

This book covers standard Pro Tools 10 software, Pro Tools HD 10 software, Pro Tools|HD hardware, Pro Tools|HD-Native hardware, and Pro Tools|HDX hardware. The software and hardware features covered in this book are equally applicable to systems on both Windows and Macintosh platforms, unless otherwise noted.

Keyboard Shortcuts (Macintosh/Windows)

Rather than focusing exclusively on either Macintosh or Windows keyboard shortcuts, I've opted to always include keyboard equivalents for both. Macintosh keyboard shortcuts are listed first, followed by the Windows equivalent in parentheses.

The following Mac/Window key equivalents apply throughout Pro Tools, with a few exceptions where operating system–level conflicts occur:

- The Mac Command key corresponds to the Ctrl key in Windows.
- The Mac Option key corresponds to the Alt key in Windows.
- The Mac Control key corresponds to the Start key in Windows. (For Mac users, Control-click is also often an alternative to right-clicking the mouse.)

Note, though, that these Mac/Windows key equivalents are not universal and do not necessarily apply when working in other applications.

Pro Tools Versions

This first edition of *Pro Tools 10 Power!* is directed toward all users of Pro Tools 10 and Pro Tools HD 10 software and builds off of earlier books in the series. Previous books in the *Power!* series for Pro Tools covered version 8 (ISBN 1-59863-898-x), version 7 (ISBN 1-59863-473-9), and version 6 (ISBN 1-59200-505-5).

Avid is doing a great job of steadily evolving the Pro Tools platform. Pro Tools was introduced in 1991 as a four-in, four-out system with a handful of built-in effects—no plug-ins or TDM existed at the time. Pro Tools was (and remains) *the* product in the hard-disk recording category that literally revolutionized the recording industry. Since then, top-end configurations have progressed to hundreds of potential I/O channels, a depth of signal routing and plug-in processing capability that's mind-boggling, with 32-bit floating-point audio at sample rates up to 192 kHz. Pro Tools systems are used around the world for every conceivable audio application: music, film, television, spoken-word, research, forensics, restoration, sound design, and so on.

Current versions of the Pro Tools software support a wide range of audio hardware, including Avid's Pro Tools interfaces (Mbox family, 003 family, and Eleven Rack), numerous M-Audio interfaces, compatible third-party interfaces, Pro Tools|HD and HD-Native hardware, and the recently announced Pro Tools|HDX hardware.

The discontinued Pro Tools 24|Mix, Pro Tools|24, and Pro Tools III systems were based on an earlier TDM architecture that is no longer in use. Likewise, the Digi 001 and first-generation Mbox systems used previous LE versions of Pro Tools. None of these systems is compatible with Pro Tools 10 software. Accordingly, this edition of *Pro Tools 10 Power!* does not address this legacy hardware.

Where appropriate, I point out features that are available only in Pro Tools HD software or that rely on Pro Tools|HD or HDX hardware. For the most part, Pro Tools HD 10 software includes all software features of standard Pro Tools 10 software. Any restrictions or changes applicable to HD software are identified in the text.

What's *Not* in This Book

Every effort has been made to make this edition of *Pro Tools 10 Power!* a thoroughly comprehensive and multilevel book. However, the Pro Tools program is so powerful and feature-rich that there is seemingly no limit to the time one could devote to exploring its functions in various specialized fields, so some advanced nuances have certainly escaped coverage here.

At the other end of the spectrum, the book assumes a certain level of basic knowledge in computer fundamentals as well as recording and mixing technology on the part of the reader (that's you). If you are lacking in these areas, you might want to supplement this book with one or more additional resources.

Computer Fundamentals

The nature of this book doesn't afford space to cover basic computer concepts. If you are unfamiliar with tasks such as how to empty your Trash or Recycle Bin, how to open a menu, or how to access a Control Panel, or if you don't know the difference between a folder and a file, you should seek out one of the many excellent resources available to learn about such things. You really *do* need to understand how your computer works as well as how to maintain your operating system, drives, files, and so on to get the most out of your Pro Tools system—there's just no getting around it. Your computer, as the platform for Pro Tools, is one of the tools of your craft. Just as you have to change the strings on your instrument, replace the batteries in stompboxes, and clean the heads on your tape recorders (as we did in the good old days), you have to be able to navigate your computer system and keep it in good working condition.

In Chapter 3, we review computer and hard-drive requirements for Pro Tools specifically and the basic peripherals most users need (such as MIDI and SMPTE interfaces, mixers and microphone preamps, and a good system for monitoring audio playback).

Older "Legacy" Versions of Pro Tools

It is true that many discontinued Pro Tools systems are still quite functional today. For example, even though Digi 001 and Mix|24 models were discontinued back in 2004, they deliver excellent performance on an adequate computer system of the same vintage, and continue in production at many facilities.

Nevertheless, those systems are well documented elsewhere, including in previous versions of this book. Thus, they are not covered in this Pro Tools 10 edition, in order to make space to cover the many recent developments in the world of Pro Tools and the currently supported configurations.

Pro Tools 6 Power! (ISBN 1-59200-505-5) and *Pro Tools 7 Power!* (ISBN 1-59863-473-9) cover the 6.*xx* and 7.*xx* versions of Pro Tools, respectively, and are ideal resources for users of these systems. Those books also distinguish features that are different in the 6.4 and earlier software versions for 24|Mix, Digi 001, and ToolBox systems.

Users of older systems (including Pro Tools III hardware configurations) should be *very* cautious about upgrading computer hardware or operating systems. Never assume that a newer operating system, even if it *is* compatible with your older computer, is compatible with an older version of Pro Tools. For example, no release of Pro Tools 5 software will work under Macintosh OS X, even in Classic mode, and no version prior to 6.9.2 will work under Mac OS X 10.4 or later.

For complete system requirements and a list of qualified computers, operating systems, hard drives, and third-party devices, refer to the latest information on Avid's website: www.avid.com.

Future Versions of Pro Tools, TBA Next Week/Month/Year...

In all likelihood, the content of this book will continue to be meaningful even as new releases of Pro Tools appear. The descriptions herein are based on currently shipping versions of Pro Tools 10. Minor upgrades are always coming out, usually to address bug fixes or to support new hardware options. Farther down the road, more significant upgrades are certain to introduce additional features. Most actual operational changes will probably be minor to moderate for the next several releases, but it is entirely possible that discrepancies will exist in certain screenshots and/or functions. Again, the basic concepts explained in this book will remain valid despite new features that may be added in the future.

Other Programs

This book covers some stereo editing programs for checking, tweaking, or converting bounced files, as well as common CD-burning software. But it does not dedicate pages to walking through step-by-step operations in these audio programs or utilities. Many users find Norton SystemWorks (Norton Utilities) extremely useful for maintaining a Pro Tools rig. Some Macintosh users prefer the Tech Tool or DiskWarrior programs, which also do a great job of keeping your hard disks free of errors that can interfere with Pro Tools' performance. These applications are not covered in this text, but information on their use is readily available on the web.

Similarly, feature comparisons with other multitrack audio/MIDI programs don't fit within the space of this book. Current versions of Logic Pro, Cubase, Nuendo, Digital Performer, SONAR, Reason, Record, ACID, Ableton Live, and others are all fine programs—each, like Pro Tools, with its strengths and weaknesses. Many of these applications are commonly found cohabitating with Pro Tools in both hobbyist and professional systems. Several can even operate concurrently with Pro Tools, linked together via ReWire. Whether any of these is right for your needs really depends on your working style and personal preference. Sometimes one program is more suited to certain projects than others.

However, Pro Tools is a powerful production environment; you can do just about anything with it. And that is the focus of the book you hold in your hands: how to use Pro Tools to achieve your recording, editing, mixing, and automation goals. So, if you are ready, let's get started exploring Pro Tools 10!

Thank You!

If you are new to Pro Tools or to digital audio workstations (DAWs) in general, you're in for a treat. The hands-on, nonlinear audio experience you are undertaking with this program will completely transform your creative process. For that matter, it may change your entire perception of audio. If you *already* know your way around the program, prepare to dive much deeper into this powerful production environment. Even if you are already a veteran user, you're likely to find some tips and applications in these pages that will get you thinking in new directions.

Before going on, though, let me take the opportunity here to say thank you for considering this book. I sincerely hope that the content herein energizes your learning experience, enriches your creative process, and furthers your success with Pro Tools.

1 About Pro Tools

I f you're just getting started in the digital-audio production world, this chapter and the next will be particularly useful. These two chapters focus on basic concepts in Pro Tools and provide an overview of the digital-recording process, some common digital-audio file formats, and the MIDI protocol.

Users who are new to Pro Tools and computer-based recording will find the experience to be quite different from traditional audio production. When using linear tools for working with music and audio (such as digital and analog tape recorders, for instance), all the audio components must be assembled and mixed in real time. You can't change the order of recorded events without creating a new copy or, worse yet, destructively cutting up the tape and splicing bits together in a different order.

Digital-audio workstations such as Pro Tools, on the other hand, allow you to alter the order of audio events on any track, at any time—from initial recording to the final phases of mixdown. Pro Tools provides extremely granular editing precision (down to the sample level). This makes it easy to create seamless edits almost anywhere within your recorded audio. The editing power of Pro Tools is limited only by your perseverance.

While Pro Tools unleashes new editing possibilities for your audio, its mixing power will likewise transform the methods and practices you use to polish your sounds. Traditionally, mixing down from multiple source tracks to a stereo master was essentially a live performance, often requiring multiple sets of hands. Audio engineers could repeat the same song or scene dozens of times, attempting to perfect the mix or just improve upon mixing moves from the previous pass. With Pro Tools, you can start to build your mix even while still recording tracks. And of course, every aspect of the Pro Tools mix can be automated down to a microscopic level of precision, so your creative ambitions will increase correspondingly.

And of course, Pro Tools offers a vast amount of control for shaping and processing your sound. Not only are high-quality signal processors and effects included with all versions of Pro Tools, but its open architecture accommodates plug-in software from third parties—everything from emulations of "vintage" compressors and reverbs to amp and tape simulators and much more.

Because the entire virtual signal-processing environment is in the digital domain, the noise-floor problems associated with analog devices and cables in a traditional studio are things of the past.

1

Here again, the capabilities of Pro Tools are limited not as much by your system (which, budget permitting, can always be upgraded) as by how maniacal, ambitious, or just plain creative *you* want to be.

What Is Pro Tools?

In a nutshell, Pro Tools is computer software for Macintosh and Windows computers that is used to create audio projects through recording, editing, and automated mixing of hard disk–based digital audio and MIDI data. Though originally developed by Digidesign, Pro Tools software and related hardware (cards, audio interfaces, and peripheral equipment) are now products of Avid Technology. Digidesign merged with Avid in 1995, operating as an independent division of the company until 2010, when the company consolidated operations under the Avid name.

The first Pro Tools system was introduced in 1991, originally supporting just four tracks of digital audio. Since then, numerous updates to the Pro Tools software and hardware have brought about revolutionary changes in the audio industry. The latest version of Pro Tools—Pro Tools 10—was unveiled in October 2011 and furthered some of the radical modifications in features and configurations that were first introduced a year earlier with Pro Tools 9.

By way of recap, the configurations available for Pro Tools 9 include the following:

■ Pro Tools 9 software with any Pro Tools, M-Audio, or compatible third-party audio interface. In these configurations, Pro Tools runs as host-based software with standard functionality. The software functionality can be enhanced with the addition of the Complete Production Toolkit add-on.

■ Pro Tools HD 9 software with a Pro Tools|HD Native card and one or more HD-series audio interfaces. In this configuration, Pro Tools runs as host-based software with the enhanced functionality of Pro Tools HD software and improved I/O capacity afforded by HD-series interfaces.

■ Pro Tools HD 9 software with one or more HD-series DSP cards and one or more HD-series audio interfaces. In this configuration, the Pro Tools mix engine runs on the card-based DSP, with the enhanced functionality of Pro Tools HD software, complemented by the enhanced processing power of the HD card(s) and expandable I/O capacity.

With Pro Tools 10, Avid has expanded on the available hardware configurations. Current system configurations include the following:

■ Pro Tools 10 software with any Pro Tools, M-Audio, or compatible third-party audio interface. In these configurations, Pro Tools runs as host-based software. As with Pro Tools 9, the software functionality can be enhanced with the addition of the Complete Production Toolkit.

■ Pro Tools HD 10 software with a Pro Tools|HD Native card and one or more HD-series audio interfaces. In these configurations, Pro Tools HD runs as host-based software with the improved I/O capacity afforded by HD-series interfaces.

- Pro Tools HD 10 software with one or more HD-series DSP cards and one or more HD-series audio interfaces. As in earlier versions, the Pro Tools mix engine runs on the card-based DSP, providing enhanced processing power and expandable I/O capacity.

- Pro Tools HD 10 software with one or more Pro Tools|HDX PCIe cards and one or more qualified HD-series audio interfaces. In this configuration, the Pro Tools mix engine runs on DSP on the HDX card(s), providing higher voice counts, dramatically increased processing power, and maximum I/O expandability.

Most Pro Tools systems require both an audio interface and the Pro Tools software. These can often be purchased as a bundle at a discounted price; however, the Pro Tools software and interface can also be purchased separately. Standard Pro Tools 10 software gives users a great deal of flexibility to work with the audio interface of their choice.

Pro Tools 10 is compatible with legacy audio interfaces (such as those supported in Pro Tools M-Powered 8 and Pro Tools LE 8), as well as current Pro Tools and M-Audio branded interfaces (such as the third-generation Mbox family and the M-Audio Venom) and any Core Audio or ASIO audio interface with supported drivers.

In addition, beginning with version 9.0, Pro Tools provides an Aggregate I/O option for using the built-in audio on a Mac computer, allowing the software to be run with *no* connected interface. In this configuration, Pro Tools will record and play back through the computer's onboard audio ports.

To any of these systems you can also add peripherals—MIDI or synchronization interfaces, mixers or control surfaces for hands-on control of the software, and so on. On systems with Pro Tools|HD or HDX hardware, you can expand the Pro Tools configuration with additional cards to increase your processing power and available input/output channels.

Following is a brief overview of some currently supported hardware options. Chapter 3, "Your System Configuration," discusses the Pro Tools software versions in greater detail. Chapter 18, "Pro Tools Power: The Next Step," also provides more information about expansion options for the various Pro Tools hardware configurations.

- **Pro Tools Mbox Family.** The audio interfaces in this product line were introduced in September 2010 as the third-generation Mbox products. Pro Tools Mbox interfaces are compatible with Pro Tools LE 8, Pro Tools 9, and Pro Tools 10 software, as well as all Core Audio– and ASIO-compatible software packages, including Logic, Live, Record, Reason, Digital Performer, Fruity Loops, Cubase, Nuendo, SONAR, and more. The Pro Tools Mbox family includes the following interfaces:
  - **Mbox Mini.** Mbox Mini is an ultra-portable USB audio interface that provides 2 × 2 simultaneous channels of I/O and up to 24-bit/48-kHz audio resolution. Input options include one XLR mic/line combo input with a mic preamp and 48V phantom power and two 1/4-inch instrument inputs (one DI, one line-level/DI). Outputs include two balanced 1/4-inch monitor outputs and a 1/4-inch stereo headphone output.

- **Mbox.** The professional-grade Mbox audio interface provides 4 × 4 simultaneous channels of I/O and up to 24-bit/96-kHz audio resolution with bus-powered USB 2.0 connectivity. Analog input options include two XLR mic/line combo inputs with mic preamps and 48V phantom power and two 1/4-inch DI inputs on the front panel. Analog outputs include two balanced 1/4-inch monitor outputs and a 1/4-inch stereo headphone output. The Mbox also provides stereo S/PDIF digital I/O, as well as both MIDI input and MIDI output ports.

- **Mbox Pro.** The Mbox Pro is a high-resolution, high-performance 8 × 8 audio interface providing up to 24-bit, 192-kHz audio resolution via FireWire connectivity. Analog inputs include four mic inputs (two XLR mic/DI combo, two XLR) with mic preamps, 48V phantom power, and high-pass filters; four 1/4-inch TRS line-level inputs; and two unbalanced Alt line-level inputs (two RCA, one stereo mini 1/8-inch). Analog outputs include six balanced 1/4-inch TRS line-level outputs and two 1/4-inch stereo headphone outputs with discrete volume controls. The Mbox Pro also provides stereo S/PDIF digital I/O, as well as both MIDI input and MIDI output ports and word-clock I/O.

- **Mbox 2 Family.** The audio interfaces in this product line were sold from 2005 through 2010, bundled with the current version of Pro Tools LE software. Although discontinued, these interfaces are compatible with Pro Tools LE (through version 8), Pro Tools 9, and Pro Tools 10 software. The Mbox 2 family includes the following interfaces:
  - **Mbox 2.** The successor to the original Mbox, the Mbox 2 was introduced by Digidesign in the fall of 2005. This external desktop audio interface connects to the computer's USB port. In addition to two analog input/output (I/O) channels—each of which has separate input jacks for microphone, line (1/4-inch balanced TRS), and instrument levels—the Mbox 2 supports using the S/PDIF digital I/O simultaneously, allowing up to four inputs with a digital mirror of the analog outputs. It also features one MIDI input and one MIDI output.

  - **Mbox 2 Mini.** This compact USB audio interface provides two channels of analog I/O: Input 1 offers both XLR and unbalanced TS (1/4-inch phone, tip-sleeve) jacks, while Input 2 offers an unbalanced 1/4-inch TS phone jack that is compatible with line- or instrument-level sources. The two analog monitor outputs also use unbalanced 1/4-inch jacks.

  - **Mbox 2 Micro.** This extremely compact USB audio interface was added to the Mbox 2 family in the fall of 2007. Unlike other Pro Tools audio interfaces, the Mbox 2 Micro has no audio inputs. The only I/O provided is a single stereo analog output, with a 1/8-inch TRS connector (compatible with either headphone or line output connections) for which a volume dial is provided on the end of the unit.

  - **Mbox 2 Pro.** The top of the line in the Mbox 2 family, this audio interface connects to the host computer via FireWire. It supports sample rates up to 96 kHz. Four analog inputs are provided: mic/line inputs 1–2 can be switched between combo jacks (compatible with both XLR and 1/4-inch phone) and front-panel DI inputs for guitar, bass, etc., while Aux In line inputs 3–4 can be switched between balanced TRS (1/4-inch phone, tip-ring-sleeve) jacks and RCA phono jacks where a turntable can be connected. In addition to the dedicated monitor output pair on the rear panel (for outputs 1–2 from Pro Tools), six analog line outputs are provided: 1–4 are mono with balanced 1/4-inch TRS jacks, while 5–6 share a single unbalanced stereo TRS jack. When all analog and digital I/O is utilized, the Mbox 2 Pro can function as a 6 × 8 audio interface.

- **003 Family (discontinued).** Interfaces in this product line are compatible with Pro Tools LE (through version 8), Pro Tools 9, and Pro Tools 10 software. The 003 family includes the following interfaces:

  - **003.** The successor to the Digi 002 (see below), this multichannel audio interface/control surface connects to the computer's FireWire port. The 003 supports up to 18 channels of audio input/output (16- or 24-bit recording at sample rates up to 96 kHz) from a combination of eight analog I/O channels, stereo S/PDIF, and eight-channel ADAT Lightpipe digital I/O. Four XLR microphone preamp inputs with phantom power and individual trim controls are included on the first four input channels. The 003 also provides one MIDI input and two MIDI output ports, two headphone outputs, dedicated monitor output for channels 1–2 from Pro Tools plus an additional Alternate Monitor output, and an Aux Input pair for a CD player, iPod, or similar device. In addition to the audio I/O, this unit provides a control surface for Pro Tools, including Transport switches, touch-sensitive motorized faders, Solo/Mute switches, assignable rotary encoders, data displays, and other dedicated switches for Pro Tools functions. The 003 also offers BNC connectors for word-clock input/output (used for synchronizing the internal sample clock with other digital devices in your studio).

  - **003 Rack.** This interface has the same I/O as the 003 interface, but in a rack-mountable format without the control surface.

  - **003 Rack+.** This interface is essentially the same as the 003 Rack with four additional XLR preamp inputs, for a total of eight microphone inputs.

- **Digi 002/Digi 002 Rack (discontinued).** The Digi 002 and Digi 002 Rack have the same I/O configuration as their successors the 003 and 003 Rack. The Digi 002 combines the I/O of its audio interface with an 8-channel control surface.

- **Eleven Rack.** The Eleven Rack is a guitar recording and effects processing system designed for Pro Tools and live performance. Eleven Rack provides a high-resolution, dual DSP-powered audio interface to eliminate latency when recording with its built-in amp/cabinet/effects tones. Using Eleven Rack with Pro Tools lets you record both dry and processed guitar signals simultaneously, allowing you to re-amplify later without patching a single cable. Additionally, the Eleven Rack amp, cabinet, and effects settings are embedded into the audio tracks you record, enabling you to automatically recall those settings from your audio files on any Pro Tools system with Eleven Rack. When used as a standalone amp tone and effects signal processor, Eleven Rack allows you to access its classic collection of effects—from must-have stompboxes to world-class rackmount studio processors—and integrate them into your existing rig, closing the gap between studio and stage. Eleven Rack also offers powerful control options using affordable MIDI controllers and expression pedals, giving you full foot control over everything from vintage wah effects to tempo-driven delays and more.

- **M-Audio systems.** These configurations are supported by Pro Tools M-Powered, Pro Tools 9, and Pro Tools 10 software and use one of the many available audio interface options from M-Audio. Among the M-Audio hardware options are PCI cards (with either breakout cables or external interfaces) and external audio interfaces that connect to the computer's USB or FireWire port. The number and type of audio, MIDI, and word-clock inputs/outputs vary according to the model, and some offer internal mixing capabilities of their own. Chapter 3 discusses the M-Audio hardware options for Pro Tools in more detail.

- **Pro Tools|HD Native.** These systems consist of Pro Tools HD 9 or Pro Tools HD 10 software, combined with the Pro Tools|HD Native PCIe card, and one or more Pro Tools HD-series interfaces. The HD Native card supports up to four HD interfaces, for up to 64 channels of I/O in large sessions (playback/recording on up to 192 audio tracks with Pro Tools HD 9 or up to 256 audio tracks with Pro Tools HD 10). This configuration allows you to run Pro Tools HD software in a host-based environment (meaning the software runs off of the processing power of the host computer).

- **Pro Tools|HD.** These systems consist of Pro Tools HD software, one or more PCIe cards (or PCI/PCI-X), and one or more Pro Tools HD-series audio interfaces. The HD cards incorporate specialized DSP processors to enable the TDM plug-in and signal-routing architecture. Adding more HD cards expands the system's DSP capabilities—to support a more intensive use of plug-ins, for example. While the audio hardware options for standard Pro Tools systems (and older LE and M-Powered systems) have a fixed number of input/output channels, HD system configurations are expandable. Adding more cards permits you to attach more audio interfaces, which increases the available number of audio I/O channels. (Each card supports up to 32 I/O channels—and up to two audio interfaces—with a maximum of 160 I/O channels on the entire Pro Tools|HD system.) HD|2 and HD|3 configurations from Avid consist of an HD Core card with one or two additional HD Accel cards, respectively. Pro Tools|HD configurations are discussed in more detail in Chapter 3.

- **Pro Tools|HDX.** These systems consist of Pro Tools HD software, one or more Pro Tools|HDX PCIe cards, and one or more supported Pro Tools HD-series audio interfaces. Like the older Pro Tools|HD hardware, HDX hardware provides dedicated DSP for high-definition digital audio recording, editing, signal processing, mixing, and I/O capabilities. However, HDX cards are far more powerful than HD cards. Each HDX card provides recording and playback for up to 256 tracks at 44.1 kHz or 48 kHz, up to a maximum of 768 simultaneous tracks. Each card supports up to 64 I/O channels—and up to four audio interfaces—with a maximum of 192 channels of I/O on the entire Pro Tools|HDX system.

Note Refer to Chapter 3 for more detailed descriptions of the various audio interface options for Pro Tools.

Photo courtesy of Avid.

Figure 1.1 This Pro Tools rig features Pro Tools|HD hardware, a D-Control worksurface, and surround monitors.

Users often add other hardware devices (from Avid and third parties) to complete these configurations. Hardware add-ons may include MIDI interfaces, synchronization peripherals for SMPTE time code or video sync, external MIDI controllers, keyboards and modules, digital-audio routers and mixers, microphone preamps, external control surfaces (such as the one shown in Figure 1.1), and interfaces for multitrack digital-audio recorders from Alesis, Tascam, and others. Some of these are discussed in Chapter 3.

Older Generations of Pro Tools (Versions 8, 7, 6, and 5) This book doesn't recount the entire Pro Tools history back to 1991, when version 1 hit the street. However, it may be useful to understand the general characteristics of recent versions of Pro Tools; many of these older systems are still in use today in both professional and project studio settings.

- **Pro Tools version 8.** Introduced in late 2008, version 8 represented a major overhaul of the graphical user interface and introduced a multitude of new functions and instruments for music production. Major additions included a new Score Editor, Elastic Pitch, track compositing, and Quick Start when launching Pro Tools. Enhancements included customizable toolbars, a revamped Track List, a new MIDI Editor window, better-resolution waveform displays, and the ability to host multiple audio file formats in the same host-based session. Numerous new plug-ins were added as standard components of Pro Tools, including a variety of virtual instruments.

- **Pro Tools version 7.** First introduced in the fall of 2005, version 7 boasted a reorganized menu structure and new features such as region looping, region grouping, real-time properties for MIDI tracks, sends doubled to 10 per track, enhancements to the Separate Region and Strip Silence functions, REX/Acid file support, Instrument tracks, use of RTAS plug-ins on any track type in Pro Tools HD, support for multi-processor computers and multi-core processors, enhanced support for ICON worksurfaces, and multiple video file support in HD systems, plus drag-and-drop enhancements for the Regions List and the Workspace browser. Additional key features were added in subsequent releases. Version 7.3 added continuously resizable track heights; mixer reconfiguration during playback; automation and MIDI enhancements, such as diatonic transposition; key signature events; and window configurations. Version 7.4 added Elastic Audio features, including Elastic Audio markers, Analysis and Warp views for tracks, and related features for conforming audio regions to the session tempo.

■ **Pro Tools version 6.** Introduced at the end of 2002, this version marked a major upgrade from previous generations of Pro Tools and was the first version for Macintosh OS X and Windows XP. Along with other updates to the user interface, the Project and Workspace browsers were new, as were Groove templates, Groove Quantize, many features in the MIDI Operations window, the Click plug-in, iLok support for plug-in and software authorizations, and use of Core MIDI services on Mac OS X (instead of OMS, used in previous Macintosh versions).

■ **Pro Tools version 5.** Introduced in 2000, this was the first generation of Pro Tools to offer an LE version (host-based plug-in processing, not requiring TDM hardware). Pro Tools 5 ran on Macintosh OS 9, Windows 98/Me, or Windows 2000, and Windows NT for TDM systems. The Digi 001 audio interface (now discontinued) was introduced with version 5 as the first hardware option for Pro Tools LE. The DigiTranslator option for OMF transfers between Pro Tools and Avid video-editing systems (among others) was introduced. Also new was the ability to record/edit MIDI events within Pro Tools, with all the associated features in MIDI tracks. Multiple ruler formats and markers in the Edit window timeline were also introduced, as were marker memory locations and the Trim tool's time compression/expansion mode.

How It Works

Pro Tools records digital audio and MIDI data and provides software tools for editing both. It's important to have a clear understanding of the differences between the two types of data.

Digital Audio Data Represents Audio Waveforms

In digital-audio recording, an input signal from an analog source (a varying voltage from a microphone or other device) arrives at an analog-to-digital (A/D) converter (often abbreviated as ADC). This converter periodically measures the level (amplitude) of the incoming audio signal and stores a numerical value representing this measurement in a file or encodes it onto a tape. This is the digitizing process, where a continuous, real-world phenomenon is converted into a series of numbers (samples) at a fixed rate over time. When audio is recorded digitally, the continuous variations of the audio waveform are captured at a fixed resolution, converted into a series of numbers, and then saved within a file.

The goal is to measure the constant fluctuations within the original incoming audio signal often enough (at a sufficient sample rate) and precisely enough (at a sufficient bit depth) that when the measurements are played back (converted back into an analog signal by the digital-to-analog converter, or DAC), they closely resemble the original source waveform. Figure 1.2 provides a signal-flow diagram for the hard disk–recording process.

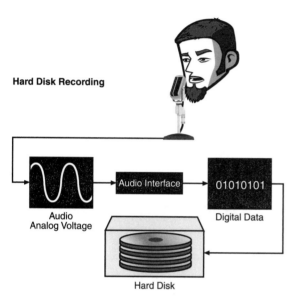

Figure 1.2 Hard disk recording: signal flow.

MIDI Data Represents Performance Events and Controller Data

MIDI, or *Musical Instrument Digital Interface*, is a communications protocol originally developed for transmitting and receiving (and later recording or playing back) performance events. MIDI events contain information about the notes that are triggered, when they are triggered, and at what velocity; the movement of pedals, sliders, and knobs; and so on. MIDI keyboards, controllers, and sound modules speak a common "language" so that they can be connected or so that a performance originally created on one device can be played back on another.

Although Pro Tools also offers many features that allow MIDI-compatible musical instruments and effects to be incorporated into the same recording/editing environment as audio, MIDI data is *not* audio. Sometimes, an external MIDI module is selected as the destination for events sent from a MIDI track, and that module is what actually produces sound—in response to the MIDI event messages received. When using an external MIDI device, the audio from the device must be routed back into Pro Tools through the audio interface in order to be incorporated into your Pro Tools mix, as shown in Figure 1.3. Typically, this might be done through an Aux Input or Instrument track that monitors the physical audio inputs where the device is connected.

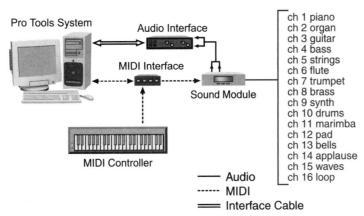

Figure 1.3 A basic MIDI configuration, with an external MIDI keyboard controller and sound module.

On the other hand, many users prefer software-based instruments—either separate programs or plug-ins that are enabled (instantiated) on Pro Tools tracks. In this case, the virtual instrument is chosen as the destination from one or more MIDI tracks, in much the same way as an external module would be. Version 7 introduced Instrument tracks, which combine aspects of an Aux Input track and a single MIDI track. Instrument tracks save screen space and offer other conveniences. Instrument tracks are covered in more detail in Chapter 6, "The Edit Window," and Chapter 7, "The Mix Window."

More about MIDI   The MIDI standard was developed in the early 1980s by audio and musical-instrument manufacturers to allow synthesizers, drum machines, and similar devices to be interconnected. The MIDI specification describes both a serial communications protocol and a standardized set of data messages for the events that these devices generate (or receive). For example, MIDI messages might specify the press of a certain key at a certain velocity, a movement of the pitch bend or modulation wheel, a press or release of the sustain pedal, and so on. MIDI tracks do *not* record or transmit sound; they record and transmit performance *events* as data.

Dedicated computer programs for recording and reproducing MIDI data, known as MIDI sequencers, have been around for decades. Like Pro Tools, these programs capture MIDI events (with the appropriate time references) from an external MIDI keyboard or other controller via a MIDI interface that converts the MIDI protocol into a data format that the computer can understand. Sequencers also provide software-editing tools to modify and play back MIDI events.

Where Audio and MIDI Data Are Stored in Pro Tools   The basic Pro Tools document is called a *session file*. It contains the mix configuration, references to external audio files and clip (region) definitions, automation data, track names, and other parameters. The session file also contains all MIDI data you record or create in that session (including all MIDI clips/regions). In contrast, the audio clips/regions you deal with in Pro Tools are actually pointers (references) to separate audio files on the hard disk.

Multitrack Recording, Mixdown, and Mastering: An Overview

In most audio recordings, numerous channels are separately recorded from multiple microphones, electric instruments, synthesizers, and other sources. These might be recorded onto separate tracks of a tape in a traditional studio or, in the case of Pro Tools, into separate audio files, which are arranged as playlists within tracks in the Edit window. Having each sound source available on a separately recorded track allows for subsequent manipulation of the sounds, such as changing their relative volumes and panning, plus correcting of any mistakes. You can record additional tracks as you listen to previously recorded material.

Mixdown (often called *remix* in the United Kingdom) is the final stage in the recording process, when multiple sources of audio are combined into a standard playback format—one mono channel, a stereo channel pair, or a multi-channel format in surround mixing. This might be done in real time, as when a stereo mix is recorded to a DAT or other mastering recorder. In the case of Pro Tools, however, quite often the mix is bounced to disk as a new file. During mixdown, the audio engineer balances volume levels, establishes the spatial placement of each sound source, and applies equalization, dynamics processing, and other types of signal processing to alter sounds. Additionally, sounds can be routed to other locations (either external or internal), where additional effects processing (such as delay or reverb) might be applied. Obviously, as a performer, Pro Tools offers you unprecedented control over your finished mix. As anyone who has followed commercial music over the past years has observed, creative mixing techniques are often as much a part of the artistic process as the initial performances. For that matter, many musically interesting pieces are being created with Pro Tools that don't directly involve any live performers at all, further blurring the distinction between performer and engineer.

Mastering is the processing and transferring of finished audio mixes to a medium suitable for duplication. This can range from simple sequencing of songs and trimming beginnings/endings to applying signal processing to improve uniformity of the material (especially when recorded at different times and places) and using sophisticated effects processing (dynamics processing and equalization in particular) that compensates for the characteristics of the final playback medium.

Many of the onscreen objects in Pro Tools resemble traditional elements in this process—the controls in the Mix and Transport windows, for example. But although it is convenient to think of Pro Tools as a virtual studio—and certainly, many of the metaphors from traditional audio production do apply—working in this environment does require adjusting to a new mindset; many things simply have no counterpart in a traditional studio. The segmentation of functions and project phases, the linearity, and the relative lack of editing precision that typify tape-based recording (whether analog or digital) disappear with Pro Tools.

Back when digital audio workstation technology was still relatively new, we commonly drew parallels to traditional recording technology to explain the Pro Tools work process (effects racks and patchbays, source/tape switches on mixer channels, gain stages, sync mode, two-track mastering recorders, and so on). With time, however, more and more users are coming to Pro Tools who have never used or even heard of the hardware and processes of a traditional studio. All they've ever known is computer-based digital audio. The stock metaphors that Pro Tools supposedly emulates are losing their meaning for today's audio gearheads; they wouldn't know a splicing block from a wood planer! So if you *are* an audio-production veteran, and this is your first experience with a nonlinear audio production system, be prepared to adopt some new habits and a new mental geometry for your work process.

Digital Audio Basics

This section summarizes in a few paragraphs a major subject that can easily fill entire books. The intent here is simply to set up the context in which Pro Tools exists, not to get you up to speed on the ins and outs of digital audio at large. If all this is brand new to you, and you would like to learn more, please check out one of the many excellent resources on sound recording and digital audio. A few are listed in Appendix A, "Further Study and Resources on the Web."

Introduction: Analog Recording

Electronic audio recording consists of three basic phases: First, a sound occurs in the environment—a disturbance of the air caused by an actual mechanical (acoustical) phenomenon. Second, a transducer—a microphone, for instance—converts this acoustical energy to an electrical signal, translating the sound wave into corresponding variations in voltage. Lastly, the voltage variations produced by the transducer are stored or recorded so that they can be played back afterward.

On traditional (analog) tape recorders, an electromagnet realigns magnetic particles (or domains) on the surface of a moving tape, varying the intensity of its magnetic field in response to variations in the incoming voltage. This is a fairly continuous process—at least as far as the density of the magnetic coating and the speed of the tape permit. When the magnetically stored level variations on the tape are converted back into voltages through an amplifier and speakers, the result is comparable, or analogous, to the original signal. This is analog recording. A real-time chain of physical components directly converts energy from acoustic (mechanical) to electrical to magnetic form and then back again.

Sampling Theory Overview

Digital audio recording proceeds a little differently. Through sampling, the incoming audio voltage is measured at fixed time intervals. Each measurement (or sample) is stored as a digital word (a binary number with a fixed number of digits) in RAM, on tape, or on a computer disk. In the case of conventional audio CDs, the sample rate is 44,100 times per second (44.1 kHz) in stereo. A sample rate of 48,000 times per second (48 kHz) is the norm for digital audio tracks incorporated in videotape formats, such as BetaCam, D1, D2, and DVCAM (as well as camcorders in Mini DV and DVCAM format). The standard for DVD-Audio discs is 96 kHz.

Most Pro Tools configurations enable you to choose between several different sample rates and bit depths, both as the recording format for your session and for any mixdown files you eventually record or bounce to disk. Both options affect audio quality in very different ways; your best choice for a given situation depends on many factors. You don't *always* want to burden your system's processing capacity or waste disk space by simply choosing the highest possible resolution for each parameter. For now, just keep these two basic principles in mind:

■   The more times per second an incoming audio signal is measured, the higher the upper limit for high-frequency sound that can be captured. (Higher sample rate = higher frequency range.) See Figure 1.4.

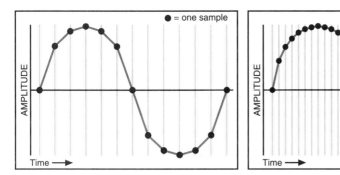

Figure 1.4   A sine wave captured at two different sample rates.

■   The more binary digits (bits) in the digital word representing each sample (that is, the bigger the number used to represent the sample's amplitude), the more precise the measurement. (Higher bit depth = lower quantization error, a kind of distortion.) This in turn translates to a greater dynamic range in the recording. However, don't get the idea that progressively increasing the bit depth will endlessly improve audio quality. For one thing, our hearing has limitations for dynamic range and for our capacity to distinguish minute level variations in a given frequency range. Many experts will argue that, for practical purposes, a 16-bit audio recording at consistently high levels can sound as "good" as 24-bit recording. Nonetheless, if you record material at very low levels (either to allow headroom or to capture a performance with a large or unpredictable dynamic range), recording at 24 bits can be a prudent habit. See Figure 1.5.

Hard disk–recording systems such as Pro Tools record digital audio and store the sample data on hard disk as audio files. Although higher sample rates and bit depths can capture more details in the source signal, the resultant audio files are also proportionately larger. This places greater demands on the host computer, requires more disk space, and so on—and it's important to recognize that the effects on audio quality become imperceptible beyond a certain practical limit. The impact on quality will center on how the digital signals are edited, combined, and processed in the software environment. One of the reasons the audio CD standard was established at

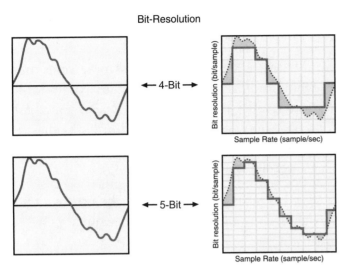

Figure 1.5 A sound wave captured at two different bit depths (higher bit depth = less rounding in the measured values for each sample).

44.1 kHz (44,100 cycles per second, or Hertz) was that this sampling rate easily allows maximum fundamental frequencies of up to 20 kHz to be captured, roughly corresponding to the upper limit of adult human hearing. At 16 bits per stereo sample, good-sounding streams of audio data can be reliably played back on consumer CD players. For initial recording of audio tracks, however, 24-bit audio is currently the most common practice—regardless of the final resolution of the delivery medium.

Higher Sample Rate = Higher Frequency Range   The *Nyquist Frequency* (the highest sine-wave frequency you theoretically can represent when sampling audio) corresponds to half the current sample rate. The *Shannon-Nyquist Theorem* states that the sample rate must be at least twice that of the highest-frequency sound you want to record so that both negative and positive excursions of a periodic waveform can be captured. If only a portion of a high-frequency waveform is captured, digital artifacts are created by a phenomenon called *aliasing*. Aliasing consists of spurious frequencies present when a digital-audio recording is played back due to erroneous capture of high-frequency information (beyond the Nyquist Frequency). To eliminate the possibility of any incoming frequencies higher than the Nyquist limit hitting the analog-digital audio converters, digital audio devices incorporate some sort of low-pass filter. This typically eliminates high frequencies starting substantially below half the sample rate (due to cost considerations and physical limitations on filter design). Thus the audio CD standard, with a 44.1-kHz sampling rate, reaches frequencies up to approximately 20,000 Hz rather than the theoretical 22,050-Hz Nyquist limit (half the sample rate).

Until recently, 44.1 kHz and 48 kHz were the most common sample rates for professional audio applications, with bit depths of 16, 20, 24, and occasionally 32 bits. High-end Pro Tools|HD systems pushed the envelope a little further, supporting 24-bit audio at sample rates of 88.2, 96, 176.4, or 192 kHz. Today, many Avid audio interfaces support sample rates of 96 kHz or higher, with some supporting up to 192 kHz with standard Pro Tools software.

Digital Audio File Formats   Numerous file formats are used for storing data representing digital audio waveforms. Here are some of the more common ones that will be relevant to your work in Pro Tools:

- **WAV.** Native to Microsoft Windows and supported by most Macintosh programs (including Pro Tools), the WAV (pronounced "wave") format is similar to the AIF format, described below. Some Windows multimedia programs *only* support audio files in WAV format. Pro Tools can import and convert WAV files or bounce to disk in WAV format, even while using AIF as the session's recording file format (or SDII format, in older Mac versions). Pro Tools 8 and later support sessions with mixed file formats, as long as the bit depth and sample rate match, allowing WAV files to live harmoniously with other file formats without requiring conversion. (Pro Tools 10 also supports audio files with mixed *bit depths*.)

- **Broadcast WAV Format (BWF).** This is an extension of the WAV format, which you can select in Pro Tools as a new session's recording format. Broadcast WAV allows ownership information to be embedded in audio files. More importantly, Broadcast WAV files support embedded time-code information, which can be useful for correctly spotting files to their original location—even in other programs, such as video editors or other digital audio workstations. This audio file format is the best choice when compatibility between Windows and Mac versions of Pro Tools is a potential concern. Using Broadcast WAV may also improve compatibility or, at the very least, eliminate a conversion step when sharing audio, OMF, or MXF files with video-editing systems across platforms. In fact, Broadcast WAV is the audio file format that the Audio Engineering Society (AES) recommends for submission and long-term archival of music projects.

- **Audio Interchange File Format (AIF or AIFF).** A mono/stereo file format originally developed by Apple, AIF has been extensively supported in interactive and electronic media applications for both Macintosh and Windows platforms. However, many video editors and interactive content developers are migrating toward Broadcast WAV for long-term compatibility; be sure to check before starting a project of this type. The AIF format supports loop points for samplers or sample playback programs (although you have to create these loop points in a program other than Pro Tools). Loop points within an AIF file are recognized by Adobe Director and some other interactive applications. Note: Director and Flash developers may use markers, or cue points, to tag specific locations within an AIF (or WAV) audio file. Cue points can be added using programs such as Peak (Mac), WaveLab (Windows), or Sound Forge (Windows).

■ **Sound Designer II (SDII or SD2).** Early Macintosh versions of Pro Tools recorded audio to disk exclusively in Sound Designer II format. Sound Designer was Digidesign's groundbreaking Macintosh audio editing program, introduced in the 1980s. From its beginnings as a simple mono editing program for samplers (transmitting sample data—slowly—via MIDI), it evolved into a robust stereo hard disk recording and editing environment based on Digidesign's Sound Tools II hardware, the precursor to Pro Tools that became an industry standard for editing and mastering stereo audio. SDII files can be mono or stereo, with bit depths of 16, 20, or 24 bits. They can include loop points (for samplers) and region (clip) definitions (more about this in Chapter 2, "Pro Tools Terms and Concepts"). Beginning with version 9, Pro Tools no longer natively supports the SDII format. However, if compatibility with legacy Pro Tools systems is required, Mac users with older systems can choose this format. SDII files don't support sample rates higher than 48 kHz.

■ **QuickTime.** The player for this digital video file format developed by Apple is included in the Mac operating system and is also available as a free download for Windows. Audio-only QuickTime files are essentially AIF files designated for QuickTime playback; these will sometimes be requested by interactive developers. The audio tracks within QuickTime movies are also often AIF format. You can import QuickTime movies into Pro Tools sessions as your video master for post-production and then bounce Pro Tools audio mixes directly back out into a new copy of the QuickTime movie file.

■ **MPEG Audio, Layer 3 (MP3).** This compressed audio format uses a lossy compression method in which some amount of the original information is permanently lost. The lower the bit rate (the amount of data per second, measured in kilobits, required to play back the audio file), the more noticeable the compromise in audio quality will be. MP3 encoding offers substantial size reduction before drastic degradation occurs, however—on the order of 5:1 or greater. Of course, the MP3 format is enormously popular for exchanging music on the Internet. It is also increasingly common in audio files for interactive media because MP3 compression yields much better sonic results than other methods of decreasing file size, such as reducing sample rate and performing drastic bit-depth reduction. Pro Tools users involved with interactive developers (or with bands trying to promote themselves on the Internet) commonly need to save out mixes as MP3 files.

■ **MPEG Audio, Layer 4 (MPEG-4).** Though formalized in 1998, this format did not become an official international standard until 2000. This compression standard builds upon digital-television technology. Apple's QuickTime file format was adapted as the basis for the MPEG-4 file format, and Apple has played an active role in its development. The more advanced audio encoding used in MPEG-4 produces smaller files and better audio quality than MP3.

■ **Advanced Audio Coding (AAC).** AAC is implemented as a variant of MPEG-4 that has been popularized by Apple for online purchasing and download of audio files at its iTunes Music Store. This format is much more efficient at audio data compression than MP3, producing comparable results at file sizes as much as 30 percent smaller.

- **RealAudio.** Developed by Real Networks, this streaming, compressed audio file format is often used on the Internet. Because RealPlayer is available to all users as a free download (and also supports streaming video files), some companies and media organizations use this technology to deliver audio and video content over the web. As a result, Pro Tools engineers are occasionally asked to deliver mixes in RealAudio format. Audio can be reduced to various throughputs (with audible compression artifacts at more extreme compression levels) according to requirements. SureStream technology allows several different versions of the audio to be incorporated into a single RealAudio file link, with the appropriate density being selected for playback according to the bandwidth available for each user's Internet connection. However, for all of its benefits, many users resist installing RealPlayer on their systems because of the invasive nature of the software (changing preferences for media file types, difficult uninstalls on Windows systems, and so on), which can be a major inconvenience—especially for audio and other media-production professionals.

- **ReCycle (REX).** This audio format is optimized for time-sliced loops—that is, audio files that have been analyzed and broken down into their rhythmic components. The REX format was developed for the ReCycle program by Propellerhead Software and has since been superseded by the REX2 format. Many loop-oriented programs, such as Reason and Cubase, support using REX2 files in their editing/mixing environment. REX-based loops can be played at any tempo without pitch changes. Also, having individual rhythmic components automatically sliced up makes it easy to rearrange them into new rhythmic patterns. You can import REX files into Pro Tools by dragging them from the Workspace browser or desktop directly into the Clip List (or Region List in Pro Tool 9 and earlier). Depending on your audio preferences in Pro Tools, time slices within source REX files can be imported either as individual clips (regions) within a clip group (region group) or, in versions 7.4 and higher, consolidated into a single clip (region) for Elastic Audio analysis.

- **ACID.** This is another format optimized for time-sliced loops and allowing for transformation to new tempos and keys. It's named for the ACID program by Sony (originally developed by Sonic Foundry). Like REX files, you can bring ACID files into Pro Tools by dragging into the Clip List (Region List) from the Workspace browser or desktop. Elastic Audio analysis markers are automatically added for any time-slice information contained in the ACID file.

Note In Pro Tools 10, the term *clip* replaces the term *region* throughout the Pro Tools user interface. Thus, the term *Clip List* replaces *Region List*, and the term *clip group* replaces *region group*.

MIDI Basics

As mentioned above, MIDI stands for *Musical Instrument Digital Interface*. To reiterate: MIDI is a communications protocol (with a standard data structure, cabling, DIN-5 connectors, and interfaces) for transmitting, receiving, and storing performance events. MIDI events are control (and timing) messages—they are *not* audio! The reception of a MIDI event may cause devices to emit audio, such as when a note-on event is transmitted from a Pro Tools MIDI track to a synth module (connected through a MIDI interface or USB port) or to a software instrument plug-in. Of course, MIDI also has many other applications. It's used, for example, to change parameters on external effects, to edit internal patches in sound modules, to control lighting, and to automate mixing boards.

When you arm a MIDI (or Instrument) track for recording in Pro Tools, it responds to incoming MIDI event data from the selected MIDI interface/port for that track. When you press a key on your synth keyboard, for example, a note-on message is transmitted to Pro Tools. This note-on event includes two parameters: the number of the note you pressed and the velocity with which the key was struck, as shown in Figure 1.6. Likewise, when you release each key, a note-off event is sent, specifying the note number and its release velocity. The pitch bend, modulation, aftertouch (channel pressure), and other interpretive moves you perform on the MIDI controller are transmitted in a similar fashion.

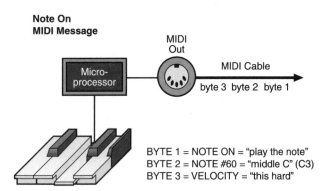

Figure 1.6 MIDI is a language for transmitting performance information (events). Here, a note-on MIDI event is transmitted when a key is pressed on a MIDI keyboard.

MIDI Connections MIDI is a serial communications protocol. MIDI-compatible devices have 5-pin DIN connectors for MIDI. Computers require a MIDI interface to translate between this protocol and their hardware/software (or a corresponding USB connection). Fortunately, Pro Tools can recognize any MIDI interface that fits your needs and budget. Many of Avid's current audio interfaces, including the Pro Tools Mbox and 003, provide MIDI input and output on the interface itself.

Consumer-level Windows soundcards commonly include a built-in MIDI in/out port, which usually requires the separate purchase of a short adapter cable that splits out to two 5-pin DIN in/out connectors. Macintosh computers require an external MIDI interface, generally connected to the USB port. Windows users requiring *multiple* MIDI inputs/outputs or more sophisticated features also use an external USB MIDI interface.

MIDI interfaces range from simple one-in, one-out models, through 2 × 2, 4 × 4, 8 × 8, 10 × 10, and more. You can even network certain multiport MIDI interfaces for dozens of MIDI inputs/outputs. Many also provide real-time routing and filtering between their inputs and outputs (handy for larger configurations with multiple MIDI controllers) and synchronization for SMPTE time code. (More about this in Chapter 11, "Synchronization.")

Many current musical keyboards, pads, control surfaces, and such use direct USB connections to the host computer. Users of these controllers may not require a MIDI interface at all, especially if their sound sources for MIDI tracks are all software based.

MIDI File Formats

Like MIDI sequencers (Digital Performer, Logic Pro, Cubase, SONAR, and others), Pro Tools records standard MIDI events into its own proprietary file format. Each of these programs offers a wealth of display options for MIDI data (for both musical and mixing applications) and many real-time functions that affect how MIDI events are played back. In the case of Pro Tools, all the MIDI performance data that you record or create is incorporated into the session file itself (unlike audio, which is stored into separate files on disk).

Importing Standard MIDI Files into Pro Tools   The Pro Tools File > Import > MIDI command brings Standard MIDI File (SMF) format files into your session, either to the Clip List (Region List) only or directly to tracks. An appropriate number of new MIDI clips (regions) (and new tracks, if you choose that option in the MIDI Import Options dialog box) are created as required by the contents of the MIDI file. In Pro Tools 7 and later, MIDI files can be managed and imported directly from DigiBase browser windows. You can use the Workspace browser to navigate to a MIDI file on disk and then drag either directly into the Clip List (Region List) or into the track display area of the Edit window, where an appropriate number of new MIDI tracks will automatically be created. Yet another option is to simply drag an SMF format file directly into Pro Tools from the Finder (Mac) or Explorer (Windows).

Occasionally, users need to transfer an entire MIDI file (consisting of multiple tracks, with their note events, controller data, program settings, volume, and other data) from one program to another. The Standard MIDI File (SMF) format was defined to facilitate this process. SMF files (which typically have the .mid filename extension) use an interchange format, which includes all MIDI events, track names, volume and pan settings, and many other parameters. If you properly prepare before exporting a file, none of the necessary MIDI performance data will be lost or misinterpreted when transferring files between different applications. In Pro Tools, you can import or export files in SMF format (including tempo map and key signature information). This ensures compatibility not only with other MIDI sequencing software, but also with multimedia applications (such as applications on the web or interactive CDs and DVDs), which can play back these SMF format files.

Standard MIDI Files and General MIDI   If you are creating SMF format files for multimedia (in Windows, these must always have the .mid filename extension to be properly recognized), be sure to use General MIDI (GM) program numbers for designating the sounds you want for each track. (Many current synths and modules have a General MIDI bank. GM is also the norm for assigning sounds to MIDI program numbers on soundcards for Windows, as well as QuickTime Musical Instruments for Macs. However, these may not actually offer unique sounds for each of the 128 program numbers defined in General MIDI. Instead, they may use the same timbre for several different acoustic pianos or drum sets, for example.) By using General MIDI program numbers, if you choose sound #14 for your xylophone part, it will still be a xylophone sound of some type when played back by QuickTime Musical Instruments, Windows Media Player, or standard interactive applications. It may not *sound* quite as good as the xylophone sound you used to compose the piece, but at least it won't be, say, a tuba!

Routing External MIDI Gear into Pro Tools   If you have sufficient audio inputs on your Pro Tools hardware (for example, with any 003, Mbox Pro, or HD system, and certain M-Audio interfaces), you might connect the outputs from your external synthesizer to an input pair on your audio interface and create individual stereo Aux Input tracks to monitor them in Pro Tools. Having the synth's audio output routed through the Pro Tools mixing environment, as shown in Figure 1.7, offers many advantages. You can apply automation and real-time plug-in processing to these external sound sources and, of course,

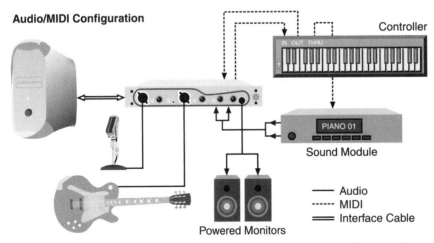

Figure 1.7 A typical configuration with an 003 or M-Audio interface with MIDI inputs/outputs. The audio outputs of the external MIDI sound module enter the audio inputs on the interface. MIDI data sent from Pro Tools is passed through the MIDI keyboard to the module.

incorporate their audio as you bounce your mix to disk as a stereo file. However, in some cases, the number of channels required for multiple external modules will exceed the available inputs on the audio hardware—especially considering that while recording, you might want at least an input or two free for your microphones and guitar preamps. Another alternative is to use the M-Audio NRV10 or a small mixer (or even a clean-sounding line mixer) to combine some external sources into a stereo submix prior to the audio inputs on your interface, and then monitor this via a single stereo Aux Input track.

Software-Based Virtual Instruments for MIDI

For the Pro Tools composer, software instruments are one of the most exciting technical developments of recent years. In very simple terms, these are either some sort of plug-in (a software construct activated within the host application) or a separate program whose audio outputs stream into Pro Tools through a software-routing technology called ReWire. You can assign the output from any MIDI track (or Instrument track) to any currently enabled software instruments in the Pro Tools session using MIDI channel assignments. Additionally, Instrument tracks can be used like MIDI tracks with associated Aux Inputs, hosting virtual instrument plug-ins directly on each track. Each virtual instrument presents a software interface for altering its parameters and selecting presets according to the kind of sound generator being modeled (sampler; analog, FM, or wavetable synthesizer; drum machine; and so on).

Re-opening a Pro Tools session instantly recalls all settings, effects, and signal-routing configurations for each of its active software instruments. (Of course, if you're using an additional program slaved to Pro Tools via ReWire, its configuration must be saved and recalled separately, in that program's own format.) If you've ever managed a complex MIDI configuration with multiple external modules, you'll recognize the benefit of storing settings within a session—without this convenience, you must keep detailed documentation of the setup for each song. Even then, reproducing a given configuration and gain structure months later is often nearly impossible. But with Pro Tools, settings and signal routing recall exactly as they were no matter how much time has passed. Better yet, because all the routing is within the computer, it is all done with no added noise!

Summary

This chapter provided a broad overview of what Pro Tools is and the kinds of system configurations that are possible, a basic introduction to core digital audio and MIDI concepts, and a general look at the recording process. As mentioned, any one of these subjects alone can fill entire books (some good options for further study are listed in Appendix A), so the intent of this review was to provide some context and a basic vocabulary for understanding how things work in digital workstations, such as Pro Tools.

Chapter 2 covers additional fundamental concepts—especially the key terms that all users must understand to effectively use Pro Tools. For more information about MIDI and its applications within Pro Tools, see Chapter 10, "MIDI."

2 Pro Tools Terms and Concepts

Whether you're new to Pro Tools or you have an extensive audio background, you may find it helpful to explore the basic concepts in this chapter. These conceptual building blocks will provide a good grounding for your exploration of non-linear audio and the virtual studio. Some of the terms defined in this chapter have specific meanings in the Pro Tools environment (for example, tracks versus channels), so even experienced audio users can benefit from taking a moment to review this material. If this is your first time around with digital audio workstations and with Pro Tools in particular, this chapter should help you get up to speed quickly.

Pro Tools Data and Files

Each Pro Tools session consists of multiple files and folders that contain the media and other data used in the session. Therefore, when it comes to managing your Pro Tools configuration, it's very important that you know where the various components are located. Let's take a look at the master session document where you store your work, the audio files that Pro Tools creates, and how you actually view and edit these within the Pro Tools software.

Session

The session file is the basic document of Pro Tools. After you open the Pro Tools program and select File > New Session, a dialog box will appear, allowing you to select between creating a blank session with no tracks or creating a session based on one of several templates that Pro Tools offers. These templates provide a prearranged selection of plug-ins, signal routings, and even MIDI files to jumpstart your progress on a session, all of which can be added to or altered. You can also select the sample rate and bit depth of the new session, as well as the audio file type you want to use within the session.

Next, you will need to choose a location on your hard drive to create and save the session files and folders, and you'll need to name the session. A new session folder of the same name will be created in the location you specify, within which the Pro Tools document resides (see Figure 2.1).

The session file includes information about the name and appearance of any tracks you create; all mix settings and the appearance of the onscreen mixer; routing of audio between tracks, sends,

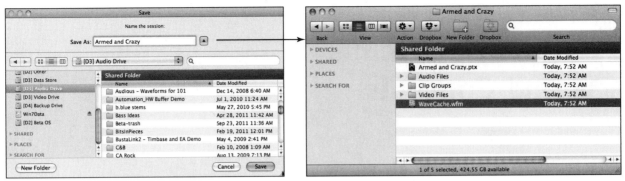

Figure 2.1 A Pro Tools session document (inside a session folder of the same name), with the Audio Files folder and other needed files and folders.

inserts, plug-in effects, and audio inputs/outputs; and other parameters. Any MIDI data you record or create in Pro Tools is also stored within the session document.

By contrast, the audio that you record and edit from within the session is actually stored separately on your hard disk. When you record or import audio in a Pro Tools session document, the files are stored in the Audio Files subfolder within the session folder. The audio segments, or *clips*, that you work with in Pro Tools are merely pointers to areas within the parent audio files on the hard disk.

Note In earlier versions of Pro Tools, clips were known as *regions*. This terminology was changed in Pro Tools 10 to align more closely with Avid Media Composer software.

The session document is essentially where you work—recording audio and MIDI, creating a signal-routing and effects-processing structure, editing your audio, creating a mix, automating the movement of faders, and so on. Session files remain relatively small because they don't actually contain any audio. They *refer* to much larger audio files, portions of which are used within the Pro Tools session. The audio waveforms can be viewed where they have been placed within Pro Tools Audio tracks.

Audio Files

The digital audio data you record to disk from each Audio track in a Pro Tools session is stored in a file (within the session's Audio Files folder—see Figure 2.2). Each filename inherits the name of the track where it was recorded, so it's a good idea to give your Audio tracks meaningful names as you prepare to record in them. (You can also change the name of an audio file later, by right-clicking or double-clicking on the clip.)

Pro Tools can also import existing audio files into the current session (and convert their format, sample rate, and/or bit depth if necessary). A single audio file may be used in several different Pro Tools sessions—this is commonly done with frequently used items, such as test tones, station IDs,

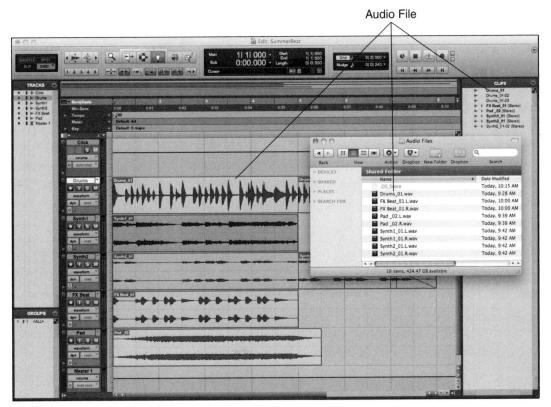

Figure 2.2 Audio recordings in Pro Tools create new audio files on disk (and new audio clips in the Pro Tools session). Clips that correspond to whole audio files appear in bold type in the Clip List.

drum sounds, stock sound effects, and so on. Typically, as you record in Pro Tools, you end up creating a large number of audio files. By default, audio recording is non-destructive—*all* the takes are retained from every track. Because multiple digital audio files can potentially take up a lot of hard-disk space, file management is an important issue in Pro Tools. It can be helpful to selectively eliminate unneeded audio as your project progresses; the sheer size of these audio files can introduce some pretty hefty data-storage issues. (More about this in Appendix C, "Archive and Backup.")

Clips

An audio clip is a segment of audio data of any length—a guitar riff, a four-bar drum phrase, a sound effect, or a phrase of dialog. Audio clips represent a portion of audio within a longer audio file that is external to the Pro Tools session document itself.

In contrast, the data in MIDI clips is included within the session document, whether the data is recorded or created within Pro Tools or imported from some existing file.

New clips are created automatically when you record to any track. When you record audio to a track, audio files are created on your hard disk. The audio clips appear in the Clip List, along with any MIDI or video clips in your session. (Each type of clip has a distinctive icon to represent its content.) Entire audio files—whether they are recorded in Pro Tools or are imported from another disk location—appear in the Clip List, along with other audio clips that represent only specific portions within the parent sound files. (Whole-file audio clips are displayed in boldface type in the Clip List; clips representing only a portion of the parent file are displayed in plain type.)

Once you place existing audio or MIDI files and clips in Pro Tools tracks, you can capture or separate additional clip definitions for any selected range via commands in the Edit menu. Many of the edits you perform on clips in tracks (for example, eliminating the middle portion of a longer clip) create new, additional clip definitions, as do various processing operations in the Pro Tools menus.

Because audio clips are only pointers to external files (or portions within the external files), you can string clips together in any order by dragging, cutting/copying, pasting, or duplicating within tracks. Pro Tools handles the seamless, non-linear playback of all these segments within many separate audio files via the system's read-ahead buffer. This is the essential non-linear (and usually non-destructive) nature of digital audio workstations such as Pro Tools—no matter how much you chop up and reorder the clips in your tracks, the original audio files are not altered.

Creating additional audio-clip definitions occupies only a negligible amount of extra disk space. Multiple clip definitions within the same audio file or MIDI clip can overlap or coincide in any manner that is convenient. For example, you could define 16 bars of a recorded bass track as a clip named Verse2 and substitute it for the bass in Verse3, where the bass player made some mistake. Or, you could select a smoothly looping eight-bar section of a drum recording, separate a clip called DrumGroove, and loop or duplicate this clip as many times as necessary to build up a layered dance track. (Separating and capturing a new clip involve very similar commands. Both add a new clip definition to the Clip List, but Edit > Separate Clip actually replaces the current track selection with the new clip definition, while Clip > Capture adds the new clip definition to the Clip List without replacing the current selection.) No matter how many times you repeat the drum loop, its audio data only occupies those eight bars worth of space within its source audio file on the hard disk.

Clips that are duplicated or copied and pasted in an Edit window Track Playlist can also keep associated automation information, which includes volume, mute, solo, pan, sends, and plug-in parameter changes. So, for example, if you love the timing of a quick boost in volume automation that is associated with a clip that you want to use elsewhere in the session, you have the option of copying the volume automation along with the clip's audio data.

Figure 2.3 shows how audio clips appear in the Edit window, both as waveforms within Audio tracks and as items in the Clip List (the bin at the right side of the Edit window). During playback, Pro Tools retrieves all the appropriate sections of audio in multiple files. All clips in a track will play back at the correct time—even if they point to sections within audio files that reside on physically separate sections of the disk(s).

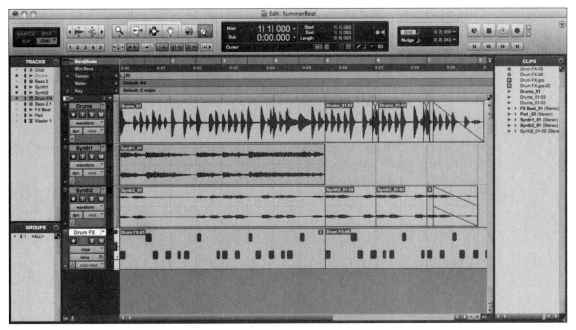

Figure 2.3 Clips are segments of audio or MIDI data; audio clips can represent entire files or portions within files. Some clip definitions are created automatically by Pro Tools in the course of editing.

Tracks

An Audio, MIDI, or Instrument track is where clips are recorded or strung together. Each horizontal strip in the Edit window (into which you record or drag audio and MIDI clips) represents one of these virtual tracks. The Mix window displays the same Audio, MIDI, and Instrument tracks as the Edit window, but as vertical mixer strips. (Instrument tracks are a sort of hybrid track type, combining the functions of Aux Input tracks, as seen in the Mix window, with the functions of MIDI tracks, as seen in the Edit window. MIDI clips can be recorded and edited on Instrument tracks the same as on MIDI tracks.)

Each Audio, MIDI, or Instrument track has its own playlist of clips (see the next section), plus an automation playlist for volume faders, pan, sends, and plug-in parameters. Tracks can be assigned any convenient name and dragged into any convenient order as you work. (On systems with Pro Tools|HD hardware, when tracks are manually assigned to voices rather than assigned using the default dynamic voice allocation mode, track positions also affect playback priority. Leftmost tracks in the Mix window or topmost tracks in the Edit window always have priority access to manually assigned voices.) Each track can be muted, soloed, assigned to any audio input/output available on the system, or routed to another destination through Pro Tools' internal mixing busses.

Two other classes of tracks that do not contain clips also offer many similar features to Audio tracks: Aux Input tracks and Master Fader tracks. (See the definitions for these terms later in this chapter.) Lastly, if you import QuickTime movies or digital video file types as references for a post-production project, a Video track is created. Chapter 7, "The Mix Window," explores the various classes of tracks in Pro Tools.

Playlists

In general terms, an Edit Playlist is a list of audio (or MIDI) clips strung together in a specific order on a Pro Tools track. Recorded audio used by an Audio track is stored within files on the hard disk; a playlist is a list of clips (pointers to audio data within those audio files) indicating which are to be read for playback, at what time, and in what order.

In Pro Tools, each track you see in the Edit window consists of a graphic playlist that may contain one or more clips. Clips can be viewed as blocks within each track or, when Waveform view is selected, as visual representations of the audio waveform in the file on disk.

Let's say you import a few dozen sound effects from a CD library and then place them onto an Audio track in the Pro Tools Edit window. You can trim their beginnings and ends, create fade-ins and fade-outs on the clip boundaries (see the "Fades and Crossfades" section later in this chapter), and resize the clips in other ways. When you click Play, Pro Tools will play the specific sections of the files represented by your clips, with seamless fades on the ends. Pro Tools follows every Audio track's playlist, pre-loading all appropriate audio data from disk into the playback buffer for timely playback.

Each Audio, MIDI, or Instrument track includes a pop-up Playlist selector (small down arrow to the right of each track name in the Edit window), which can be used to switch between alternate playlists for the track (as shown in Figure 2.4).

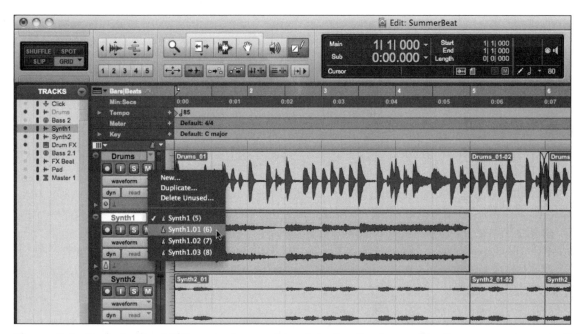

Figure 2.4 Each Audio, MIDI, or Instrument track in Pro Tools graphically represents a playlist of clips arranged in a specific order. You can switch between multiple playlists for each track, using the pop-up Playlist selector shown here.

Playlists are useful for experimentation; you can duplicate the current playlist so that you can experiment, knowing you can always go back to the original playlist. (Users familiar with video-editing systems will note that the playlist for each Pro Tools track is comparable to an Edit Decision List, or EDL for short.) Unlike with audio tape, playback order is not restricted to the original physical order of the source material on the recording medium.

Track Automation Playlists versus Edit Playlists of Clips   Each Pro Tools track has only one automation playlist for a given parameter, regardless of which Edit Playlist (clip order) is selected. This is extremely important to keep in mind when experimenting with audio clips within alternate playlists on the same Audio track. By default, any automation data (for example, volume, pan, or effects parameters) associated with any clips you copy or move will also be copied/moved. Sometimes the resulting automation changes may not be appropriate when you switch to a different Edit Playlist. If you want to experiment not only with audio-clip order but also with automation within a track, it may be better to duplicate the entire Audio track than to use alternate playlists.

MIDI and Instrument tracks also allow you to view and edit automation, of course. However, most of the playlist graphs in MIDI tracks actually represent MIDI controller messages for parameters that are transmitted along with the note events on the track's MIDI channel (sustain pedal, mod wheel, breath controller data, or MIDI volume and pan, for example). Instrument tracks include both MIDI controller graphs and automation playlists. The appearance of MIDI volume, pan, and other controller graphs in MIDI and Instrument tracks is similar to automation on Audio tracks; however, it is handled quite differently by Pro Tools. All MIDI controller automation—for volume, pan, pedals, modulation, aftertouch, and so on—is actually contained within the MIDI clips themselves. Therefore, on MIDI and Instrument tracks, you can freely edit the MIDI volume, pan, and other controller data in each alternate playlist without affecting the other Edit Playlists on the same track.

Note   In Pro Tools 10, each audio clip also has an associated Clip Gain Line, which can be edited to dynamically adjust the amplitude of the associated audio, similar to editing volume automation. For details on Clip Gain, see "Working with Clip-Based Gain" in Chapter 6, "The Edit Window."

How Pro Tools Handles Audio

Using conventional mixing boards and tape recorders, it's fairly easy to see where your audio enters and exits individual channels, auxiliary inputs or outputs, and so on. For the sake of convenience, Pro Tools uses mixer strips and tracks as familiar metaphors, but in fact the Pro Tools mixer is much more flexible than a traditional console. If you approach Pro Tools with a traditional tape-based mindset, you might think, for example, that to have functionality equivalent to a 24-track recorder, you need 24 channels of input/output (I/O) on your Pro Tools audio interfaces. However, this is not the case!

If you're coming to this program from a traditional MIDI or audio background, you need to adjust your thinking about voices, tracks, and, in particular, channels to truly understand the power of Pro Tools.

Voice, Track Priority

The number of voices in a digital audio workstation determines the number of separate audio tracks it can play at any given moment. Voices in Pro Tools are like a pool of digital-audio converters, which Audio tracks must use to play back the audio clips (regions) they contain. By default, Pro Tools dynamically assigns voices to tracks (via the Dyn setting in the Voice Assignment selector for each track) to avoid conflicts. On Pro Tools systems without Pro Tools|HD hardware, this is the only option for managing voice allocation—other than setting a track's voice assignment to "off" so that it doesn't play at all, as shown in Figure 2.5.

Figure 2.5 A track's voice selector in the Edit window. Choices are Dynamic, where Pro Tools automatically handles voice allocation, and Off, which silences the track.

With Pro Tools|HD hardware, however, you can *manually* assign a voice number to each Pro Tools track. Whenever two tracks want to use the same manually assigned voice at the same moment, the one with the highest playback priority will be voiced. The scheme for managing voice allocation is very simple: Whichever track is higher in the Edit window—or further left in the Mix window—gets priority. Wherever the higher-priority track contains an audio clip, it will play, even if that means cutting off a clip already sounding in another lower-priority track assigned to the same voice number. If you drag tracks into a different order, you also change their priority. Multiple tracks can be assigned to the same voice as long as their clips don't overlap at any point in time. Each can play back all required audio. This effectively gives you much more polyphony out of the fixed number of voices your Pro Tools system provides. Each track maintains its own completely independent routing, effects, automation, and so on, which is unaffected by that of any other tracks assigned to the same voice.

Bear in mind that multichannel tracks (stereo and surround) utilize a corresponding number of voices. This is why high-end configurations support such high voice counts. For complex soundtrack mixes with many surround submixes, stereo tracks, and so on, the number of voices required for playback can get large very quickly. Also, on systems with HD or HDX hardware, each active ReWire channel in your Pro Tools session can consume one of your available voices. See "ReWire (and the ReWire Plug-In)" later in this chapter for more information on ReWire. As explained in Chapter 7, on Pro Tools|HD or HDX systems, using Native plug-ins on a track can increase voice usage—for example, adding two more voices for a mono track or four more for a stereo track.

In the early days of Pro Tools, voice assignment was quite an art form. (Systems with fewer than 16 voices were common, whereas today up to 768 voices are supported.) On current Pro Tools systems, though, most users can leave the default Dyn (Dynamic) setting for track voice assignment and let the software automatically handle allocation. Therefore, unless you specifically assign two tracks to the same voice manually, voice assignment won't necessarily be an issue. Exceptions could occur when you're specifically using this voice-stealing feature to assemble a composite (comp) track or to bleep out certain words in a voice recording or lyric. In the latter case, you would place the bleep sounds into a higher-priority track that's assigned to the same voice as the track you want to bleep.

Channels

Although the mixer strips in the Pro Tools Mix window are sometimes called *mixer channels*, this term is really more of a holdover from traditional analog mixing boards, where each channel actually does correspond to an audio input. In the Pro Tools realm, we generally reserve the term *channel* strictly for describing the I/O capabilities of the audio hardware itself. For example, the Avid HD I/O audio interface offers up to 16 discrete channels of Pro Tools input and output in a standard configuration. The Mbox Mini is a two-channel system: two inputs (one of which can be switched between microphone and line/instrument jacks on the rear of the interface) and two line-level outputs.

Nevertheless, you will occasionally see colloquial references to the channels or channel strips in the Pro Tools Mix window. Indeed, an Audio track *is* a virtual signal path whose input(s) and output(s) can be configured to any physical input/output or internal mixing bus within the software mixing environment.

In Pro Tools, the number of Audio tracks playing back simultaneously can be significantly greater than the number of audio channels that the hardware interface provides, as shown in Figure 2.6. The number of output channels on the interface determines your options for the main mix output assignment, for additional sends to external effects or headphone mixes, for looping audio through external audio devices, and so on. The number of input channels on your audio hardware determines the number of discrete external audio sources that can be recorded simultaneously (and the return capabilities from external effects devices, whether these are monitored via Aux Inputs or used as hardware I/O inserts).

Figure 2.6 In the Pro Tools environment, channel refers to an audio input or output (analog and/or digital) on the audio interface. The number of input channels on the hardware determines how many audio sources you can record simultaneously, even though a much larger number of tracks may play back audio.

Avid Audio Interfaces—Past and Present   In the past, model numbers given to the external Pro Tools audio interfaces described their input/output capabilities. For example, 882 I/O interfaces had 8 analog inputs, 8 analog outputs, and 2 channels of digital I/O; the 1622 I/O had 16 analog inputs, 2 analog outputs, and 2 digital channels; the 888 I/O interfaces had 8 analog inputs, 8 analog outputs, and 8 channels of digital I/O. At a certain point, however, this nomenclature was abandoned.

The Digi 001 (now discontinued) had eight analog inputs and outputs, plus ADAT Lightpipe digital I/O and two channels of S/PDIF digital I/O. It also provided a headphone output, MIDI in/out, and two microphone preamplifiers.

The Digi 002 family and 003 family (both now discontinued) were the next steps up in hardware for Pro Tools LE. Like the Digi 001, they included eight analog inputs/outputs plus ADAT Lightpipe and S/PDIF digital I/O. Four high-quality mic preamps were provided. These interfaces also offered a dedicated monitor output, a second MIDI output, and a footswitch jack. The Digi 002/003 audio interfaces also included a control surface with motorized faders, while the Digi 002 Rack and 003 Rack versions consisted of a rackmountable unit with the same I/O connections, minus the control surface. The 003

Rack+ offers eight mic/line/DI inputs, eight line outputs, and two aux inputs, plus ADAT Lightpipe and S/PDIF digital I/O.

The original Mbox interface connected to a computer's USB port, offering two channels of audio I/O with inputs switchable between analog and digital connectors. The second-generation Mbox 2 model also connected to the host computer via USB, adding the capability to use both the analog and digital I/O simultaneously for 4 × 2 operation. It also featured MIDI input and output (as did the Mbox 2 Pro, which connected via FireWire and offered expanded I/O capabilities). The Mbox 2 Mini provided analog stereo I/O via a USB connection, while the Mbox 2 Micro provided stereo analog output *only*.

The current Avid interfaces for non-HD Pro Tools systems include the third-generation Pro Tools Mbox family (Mbox Mini, Mbox, and Mbox Pro) and the Eleven Rack. The Mbox Mini is an ultra-compact 2 × 2 audio interface offering audio resolutions up to 24-bit, 48-kHz. The standard Mbox provides a 4 × 4 audio interface with audio resolutions up to 24-bit, 96-kHz. The Mbox Pro is a high-performance 8 × 8 audio interface, featuring four mic inputs with professional grade preamps, four TRS line-level inputs, S/PDIF in/out, MIDI in/out, and audio resolutions up to 24-bit, 192-kHz.

Eleven Rack is a guitar recording and effects processing system that functions as a DSP-accelerated high-resolution audio interface for Pro Tools. It features emulations of classic guitar amp tones inspired by Fender, Vox, Marshall, and others; a collection of sought-after classic stompbox tones inspired by effects from MXR, Electro-Harmonix, Ibanez, and more; a powerful collection of studio-quality rack-mount effects processors; convolution-based cabinet and microphone emulations; and other attributes that allow guitarists to fine-tune their live and studio sound. Eleven Rack supports up to eight simultaneous channels of high-resolution recording up to 24-bit/96-kHz. The unit includes an XLR mic input, two 1/4-inch line-level inputs, stereo balanced XLR outputs and dedicated 1/4-inch outputs, AES/EBU and S/PDIF digital I/O, and MIDI input and output.

The names of audio interfaces originally introduced with Pro Tools|HD highlighted their capacity for high-resolution audio. The 96 I/O and 96i I/O offered 24-bit conversion at sample rates up to 96 kHz. The 192 I/O also offered 24-bit audio, supporting sample rates up to 192 kHz, while the 192 Digital I/O was a digital-only version without the analog input or output sections. Most of these interfaces also incorporated AES/EBU and S/PDIF digital connections, plus simultaneous ADAT Lightpipe for interconnection with digital multitrack recorders and other devices. In contrast, the 96i I/O had no Lightpipe or TDIF connectors but offered 16 channels of analog input and stereo analog output, plus a single stereo S/PDIF digital I/O.

Current HD-series audio interfaces include the HD OMNI, HD I/O, and HD MADI, all of which support high-resolution audio up to 24-bit/192-kHz. HD OMNI is an all-in-one Pro Tools HD series interface. It provides two digitally controlled mic preamps, four line inputs, eight line outputs, eight channels of ADAT digital I/O, 2 × 8 channels of AES/EBU I/O, and two channels of S/PDIF I/O. (The maximum number of usable I/O channels in any configuration is 8 × 8.) HD OMNI provides full routing, mixing, and monitoring control for Pro Tools|HD, Pro Tools|HDX, and Pro Tools|HD Native systems in a single, one rack-space unit.

HD I/O is a redesigned and upgraded version of the earlier 192 I/O. Available in one of three configurations, HD I/O provides a balance of analog and digital I/O with the 8 × 8 × 8 option, a maximum configuration of analog or digital I/O with the 16 × 16 Analog or 16 × 16 Digital options, and the ability to expand or customize your I/O with analog or digital option cards.

HD MADI is an all-digital interface for Pro Tools that can send and receive up to 64 channels of digital audio per interface, providing direct digital connections between a Pro Tools|HD, Pro Tools|HDX, or Pro Tools|HD Native system and other MADI devices.

Chapter 18, "Pro Tools Power: The Next Step," provides more detailed information about hardware options for Pro Tools|HD, Pro Tools|HDX, and Pro Tools|HD Native systems.

Virtual Tracks versus Physical Tracks

On a traditional multitrack tape recorder (analog *or* digital), audio information is recorded physically onto the tape, at a location directly corresponding to its playback time. When recording with Pro Tools, however, audio data entering a track is written to a hard disk; the Track Playlist then controls the triggering of audio playback at the appropriate time. The Audio tracks in Pro Tools are virtual tracks. Instead of residing at adjacent physical locations, the source audio files for the audio clips on the track can sometimes actually reside at widely scattered locations on your computer's hard disk(s). At any moment, you can move audio events from one location or Audio track to another, regardless of where they were originally recorded or the disk location where they currently reside. This gives you tremendous freedom to experiment with different arrangements.

On most multitrack tape recorders, the assignment of outputs or playback voices to tape tracks is fixed. The physical audio inputs and outputs 1–8 correspond to tape tracks 1–8, and that's it. In Pro Tools, however, the inputs and outputs on the audio interface are available to many different tracks for diverse purposes during all phases of a project. One or more voices may handle playback for several of the Audio tracks that you edit on screen, but each of these can be independently assigned to different inputs and outputs (any physical input or output or an internal mixing bus). Simply put, voices act as a pool of audio converters enabling tracks to play. Each voice is available to play back a single channel of any Audio tracks assigned to it, but it can only enable one channel (for example, one side of a stereo track) at any given moment.

Standard Pro Tools software offers a maximum of 96 mono or stereo Audio tracks of simultaneous playback, and voice allocation is dynamically handled by Pro Tools to avoid conflicts. In systems with Pro Tools|HD hardware, voice allocation can be dynamic or assigned manually, and the total number of tracks can exceed the number of voices. Figure 2.7 provides a simple representation of this concept. Many tracks are assigned to share the same voice, but as long as

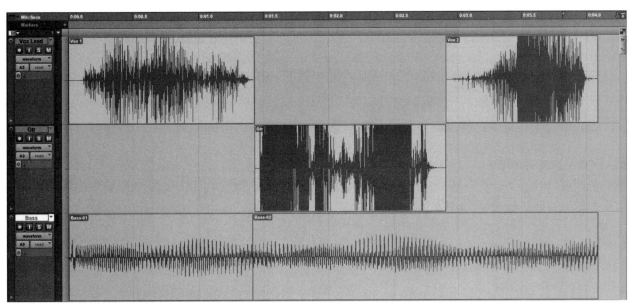

Figure 2.7 The virtual Audio tracks in Pro Tools are graphic representations of playlists that determine when audio clips are played. In systems with Pro Tools|HD hardware, for an audio clip to be heard, the voice assigned to the track must be available.

no two clips of audio within these tracks ever coincide, each can play all its required audio. Where they do overlap, whichever track is highest in the Edit window or leftmost in the Mix window has priority to play the clips it contains, even cutting in on another previously sounding track if necessary and stealing the voice.

Voice allocation lets you use more channels of audio than the number of voices (or audio polyphony) on your system. This is what is meant by virtual tracks—unlike on a multitrack tape recorder, the number of available, mixable tracks actually exceeds the number of voices in the mixer. Again, the selected input and output of each track—and its routing, plug-ins, automation, and other parameters—are completely independent of any other tracks assigned to the same voice.

Destructive versus Non-Destructive Editing

Destructive editing is what happens when you cut and splice audio tape. In this scenario, the editing process permanently alters the actual recording medium in order to make changes. Recording on traditional multitrack tape recorders (even digital) is likewise destructive; if you record a new take of a solo or voiceover, the audio previously recorded on that same tape track is gone forever.

In contrast, the non-linear access provided by Pro Tools and other digital audio workstations permits playing back clips (segments) of audio in any order, without altering the original recorded data. Therefore, hard-disk editing is non-destructive by nature. No matter how many clips and fades you create or how much you alter their playback order, the original recorded take remains intact on the disk. Even process-based effects (such as the AudioSuite version of pitch shifting, for example) are non-destructive by default. They create new audio files to contain the result of the audio processing you apply.

As you record a solo or voiceover in Pro Tools, unless you specifically enable Destructive Recording mode (Options > Destructive Recording), each take is separately recorded to disk. Sequential numbers are automatically assigned to each clip name so you can tell which takes are most recent. You can even composite together an ideal version using sections of various takes, all recorded on the same Pro Tools track (perhaps in Loop Record mode, in which case all your loop-recorded takes are actually clips within a single audio file).

Fades and Crossfades

A fade gradually increases the audio volume from zero at the beginning of an audio clip or decreases it to zero at the end. Pro Tools offers a variety of shapes that determine how audio will fade from or to silence at the beginning or end of an audio clip. These include a variety of equal power and equal gain curves, linear fades, S-curves, and so on. A crossfade is created by overlapping the fade-in and fade-out for two adjacent clips in the same track across the immediate boundary between them.

To create a fade, you would highlight a portion of audio at the beginning or end of an audio clip in a track and select Edit > Fades > Create.

The Fades dialog box (shown in Figure 2.8) allows you to audition and select various fade-in or fade-out shapes. When two clips are adjacent to each other on the same track, and you create a fade across the boundary between them, the resultant crossfade overlaps each clip, using material in each parent audio file beyond each clip's boundaries in the track. (If insufficient additional material is available because the selection extends beyond the beginning or end of a parent audio file, Pro Tools will display a dialog box and allow you to automatically adjust the fade boundaries.)

Figure 2.8 When you create a crossfade between two adjacent audio clips, a portion of the underlying audio within the parent files is played before and after the transition. This figure shows the Fades dialog box, where fade-in and fade-out shapes are displayed.

Crossfades are very useful for overlapped effects. They can also smooth out edits—for example, where the decay of a cymbal needs to overlap the beginning of the next drum clip in order to sound natural, when you're duplicating a short section of background ambience to fill a given amount of time and don't want the splices to be obvious, or when you're slicing up a stereo mix to create a new arrangement.

Note Pro Tools 10 introduces real-time fades for all fade-ins, fade-outs, and crossfades. Earlier Pro Tools versions used rendered fade files. Since Pro Tools 10 calculates and plays back fades in real time, Pro Tools no longer requires a Fade Files folder inside the Session folder.

Mixing Concepts

Chapter 7, "The Mix Window," and Chapter 9, "Plug-ins, Inserts, and Sends" go into depth about mixing and signal routing in Pro Tools. The discussion in this chapter is limited to a few key terms that have specialized meanings in the Pro Tools environment (versus traditional analog mixers).

Grouping Tracks

In Pro Tools, a Mix or Edit group is formed when multiple tracks are linked; in this way, volume faders (and volume automation) can be ganged together. Also, selections and edits made in one track can be mirrored in the other tracks in the group. For example, after selecting four related tracks (backing vocal tracks, drum tracks, or sound-effects tracks), you can use the Track > Group command to create a Mix group and/or Edit group so that all four tracks can be treated as a unit. (Each group you create can be active in either the Mix or Edit window, in both windows, or in neither window.) When a group is active, all changes made to the volume, selections, and view on one track in the group will apply to the others as well (as will the solos, mutes, send levels, and send mutes, if enabled for the group).

As you change the volume for any one of the tracks in an active group, *all* their faders will move up and down together, maintaining the relative volume levels of each individual fader. Output assignment and panning for each of the tracks in a group remain independent, as do voice-assignment and plug-in settings. By default, mute status and send levels from individual tracks in a group are also independent. However, for each group, you can also link mutes and send-level adjustments by enabling these attributes when creating the group.

As shown in Figure 2.9, a track can belong to more than one group. Grouping tracks in Pro Tools can also make it easier to manage sessions; for example, you can select all tracks belonging to a specific group by clicking next to the group name in the Group List. Pro Tools provides a Group List in both the Mix and Edit windows for enabling, modifying, deleting, and renaming groups. You can also assign custom colors to each group to more easily identify member tracks. Pro Tools currently supports up to 104 group IDs, arranged in four banks of 26 each.

Figure 2.9 Grouping tracks can simplify mixing and editing. As shown in this figure, clicking on the Group ID pop-up displays the tracks included in the Mix group.

Grouping Clips   Pro Tools also allows you to group clips in the Edit window (via the Clip > Group command). For example, you might select several clips on a single track (segments of a guitar solo you've edited together, for example) and then group them so that you can manipulate them as a single unit. These clip groups are unrelated to the Mix and Edit groups shown in the Group List.

A small icon appears in the lower-left corner of a clip group to indicate that the object contains multiple source clips. You can even create clip groups across multiple tracks. (More about this in Chapter 6.) Fades can be applied to clip groups, even if they span source clip boundaries or consist of multiple tracks. You can also ungroup clips at any time for further editing.

Busses

A bus is an audio pipeline (or virtual audio cable) used to route signals within Pro Tools and can be used for many different purposes. You can use busses individually, in stereo pairs, or in multi-channel groups. You can set the input or output of any Audio, Aux Input, or Instrument track to one of the many busses that Pro Tools provides, and you can assign each of the track's sends to a bus. You can use busses in mono, as stereo pairs, or as multichannel paths in surround mixing.

Busses are frequently used to mix signals from multiple sources. For example, you could assign the main outputs from multiple tracks to a common stereo bus pair where they are combined and then create an Aux Input track (covered later in this chapter) to monitor the bus pair as its selected input source. The Aux Input's level fader then provides a single volume control for all tracks assigned to the bus pair. In turn, its own inserts and sends also allow you to use effects that will apply to the entire submix. (In conventional mixing boards, this is also sometimes known as a *subgroup*; this book, however, uses the term *submix* to avoid any potential confusion with Edit and Mix groups in Pro Tools.) In Pro Tools 8.1 and later, output paths for the physical audio ports on your audio interface are also associated with busses. To avoid confusion, this book uses the terms *internal mix bus* and *output bus* to distinguish between the two types of busses.

Busses in Pro Tools are also commonly used as destinations for sends from multiple tracks, combining their signals on their way to an Aux Input track used as an effects return, with a reverb or delay insert, for example (similar to main Aux Send outputs on a live mixing console). Pro Tools 10 software and Pro Tools HD 10 software systems provide up to 256 internal mix busses.

Sends

Also known as an *auxiliary send* (or *aux send*) on traditional mixers, a send is a secondary audio signal pathway from a channel or track. In Pro Tools, sends are used to route signals from any Audio, Aux Input, or Instrument track to another destination, independently from the source track's main output assignment. You can route the 10 sends on each track either to a physical output on the audio hardware (for a performer's cue mix or an external effects processor, for example) or to any one of Pro Tool's internal mix busses. Sends are frequently used from multiple tracks to a single destination—for instance, to apply a reverb or delay effect by selecting the mix bus as the audio input for an Aux Input track where a plug-in effect has been inserted. Unlike inserts, where a track's entire signal passes through the processor (a typical way to, for example, use a compressor or EQ plug-in), sends are *additional*, parallel destinations for a track's signal and have no effect on its main output. So if you've created a send from your vocal track to an Aux Input track where a reverb plug-in is inserted, both the dry (unprocessed) signal from the source track and the reverb's wet output from the Aux Input track can be present in the main mix from Pro Tools. Sends can be mono, stereo, or multichannel. Of course, the level, pan, and muting of each send can be automated.

Aux Input Tracks

Aux Input tracks have a similar appearance to Audio tracks in the Pro Tools mixing environment, but they cannot contain audio clips. They can be mono, stereo, or multichannel. The input selector on each Aux Input track allows you to select its audio source: actual, physical audio inputs on the hardware interface—as defined by the Input paths in the I/O Setup dialog box—or one of the internal mixing busses in Pro Tools. Alternatively, you can instantiate a virtual instrument plug-in on an Aux Input track and use that as the source of the audio presented at its output. As with Audio tracks, you can also insert plug-in effects on Aux Inputs, create sends to other destinations, and automate their volume, pan, sends, or plug-in parameters. The output of each Aux Input can be assigned to any internal mix bus or to an output path for one or more physical outputs on the audio hardware. Common uses of Aux Input tracks include the following:

- **Effects busses.** You might insert a reverb or delay plug-in on a stereo Aux Input and set its input source to stereo bus 1–2. You would then route stereo sends from various Audio tracks to bus 1–2 so that you can feed some of their signal into the reverb or delay effect.

- **Submixes.** You could assign the outputs of multiple tracks (such as multitrack drums) to a bus pair and then create a stereo Aux Input track with that bus pair selected as its input. Not only does this provide a single volume fader for the entire stereo drum (or other) submix, it also provides a convenient way to apply a processor, such as a stereo compressor, to the submix.

- **Monitoring external sources.** The output of an external synthesizer or module that you are using as a sound source for MIDI tracks can be fed into the Pro Tools mixer via an Aux Input track. This allows you to incorporate the device's audio output when you bounce your mix to disk as a new file. (However, it is often preferable to record the device's output onto an Audio track for this same purpose.) Of course, you can also place insert effects (for example, reverb, compression, and EQ) on the Aux Input or Audio track where an external source is being monitored. You could also use Aux Inputs to monitor (and process) audio channels from a multitrack tape recorder within the Pro Tools mixing environment.

- **Click track.** The Click plug-in, used to provide a metronome for your Pro Tools session, is usually instantiated on a mono Aux Input track. (This will be the case if you use the Track > Create Click Track command or set your preferences so that a click track is automatically created in all new sessions.)

- **Virtual instrument plug-ins.** Aux Input tracks have traditionally been used for instantiating software instrument plug-ins in Pro Tools. Although Aux Input tracks can still be used for this purpose, Instrument tracks (discussed in the next section) provide another option.

- **ReWire.** When you use this virtual signal-routing technology—see the section "ReWire (and the ReWire Plug-In)" later in this chapter—to stream audio channels from virtual-synthesizer or sampler programs into Pro Tools, their outputs can also be monitored via Aux Input tracks (although, here again, Instrument tracks provide another option).

Instrument Tracks

Instrument tracks were introduced in version 7 of Pro Tools. An Instrument track can be described as a combination of an Aux Input with a single, incorporated MIDI track. As seen in the Mix window, an Instrument track is very similar to an Aux Input track, with an additional Instrument section that can be displayed at the top of its channel strip. In the Edit window, however, an Instrument track looks and acts more like a MIDI track. It contains MIDI notes and clips and provides breakpoint editing for volume and pan automation, as well as MIDI controller graphs. (Details about MIDI track elements are provided in Chapters 6 and 7.) It is still possible to instantiate virtual-instrument plug-ins on an Aux Input or Audio track, as in previous versions of Pro Tools. In fact, for multi-timbral plug-ins (plug-ins that respond to incoming MIDI data on more than one channel simultaneously), this may still be your preferred method. However, when a single MIDI playlist is used for a mono-timbral instrument, managing the MIDI data and virtual instrument together on a single, combined Instrument track is easier, reducing onscreen clutter. Instrument tracks have a distinctive icon in the Mix window, making it easier to distinguish them at a glance from Aux Inputs being used for other purposes—especially in larger sessions.

Master Fader Tracks

Master Fader tracks act as the last stage before audio signals are sent to the physical outputs on your system. When a Master Fader is created and assigned to one or more physical outputs, all audio signals routed to that output path can be boosted or attenuated by the Master Fader. Like Audio and Aux Input tracks, Master Fader tracks enable you to insert plug-in effects into the signal chain for any of the output paths or internal mix busses in your Pro Tools session and automate volume and plug-in parameters, if desired. On Master Fader tracks, however, the Inserts section is post-fader only, as opposed to pre-fader on Audio, Aux Input, and Instrument tracks. Master Fader tracks appear in the Edit and Mix windows alongside Audio, Aux Input, MIDI, and Instrument tracks and have a similar appearance and behavior, except that, like Aux Input tracks, they cannot contain clips. Master Fader tracks can be mono, stereo, or multichannel. They have no Sends; no Record, Solo, or Mute buttons; no pan controls; and no input source selector (because, by definition, Master Fader tracks represent *only* the output stage of the selected physical output path or bus).

Adding Master Fader tracks has a negligible impact on system performance because in the Pro Tools software mixing environment, this object *already exists* in the signal path for all busses and output paths. Making this stage visible by creating a Master Fader track allows you to apply gain control, plug-in processing, automation, and so on to the selected mono, stereo, or multichannel signal path.

A typical use of a Master Fader track is to provide a final monitoring and control stage for your main mix output. For example, you might use Outputs 1 and 2 on your audio interface as your main stereo output. Creating a Master Fader track for that output pair provides a level meter, so you can confirm that your mix output isn't overloading. When recording to an external device and even when bouncing a mixdown file to disk—as described later in this chapter and in Chapter 16, "Bouncing to Disk, Other File Formats"—clipping can be a problem. You might also apply final EQ, dynamics processing, dithering (when bouncing a higher bit-depth session down to a 16-bit mix, for example), and other finishing effects (again, as post-fader effects) at this last output stage of your mix.

Master Fader tracks have many other uses, however. Many users create a Master Fader track for each bus they're using for send effects—using its volume fader or dynamics plug-ins to avoid clipping due to signals being combined from many source tracks, for example. Others find Master Fader tracks useful simply for applying inserts post-fader, meaning that the audio signal reaches the inserts after it passes through the fader stage and can be boosted or attenuated by the fader.

Depending on the sound you're after and how you want the effect to interact with any volume-fader automation prior to it in the signal chain, this can also be a powerful technique.

Before starting work on a stereo project, you may find it helpful to create a Master Fader track—at the very least so that you can see what's going on with your output levels. (As you will learn in Chapter 7, if you open an Output window for your main output's Master Fader track, it will be visible even when you're working in the Edit window—*very* handy.) Other potential uses are limited only by your imagination and creativity.

Unity Gain   When you create a new Master Fader track to monitor and/or control the path to an audio output or mixing bus in Pro Tools, its volume fader defaults to 0 dB. This setting for a volume fader doesn't apply any gain change to audio signals passing through it. (That is, the signal volume isn't increased or decreased.) In professional audio, this is also known as *unity gain*.

Plug-Ins

The Pro Tools software architecture is flexible and fairly open, allowing you to enhance your software mixing environment with additional processing modules according to your needs. One of the significant innovations Pro Tools introduced in the digital audio editing field was the ability to incorporate additional effects-processing plug-ins at insert points in the mixing/signal-routing environment. Most commonly, plug-ins are used for applying real-time effects to audio signals (similar to using an insert point on an analog mixing board to patch in a compressor, for example). Pro Tools also allows you to apply non–real-time process-based AudioSuite plug-ins. Instead of working in real time, these plug-ins render their results as new audio files that store the results of the selected effect settings. In Pro Tools, non–real-time effects are accessed via the AudioSuite menu.

Generally speaking, a plug-in is an algorithm or auxiliary software program that functions as an add-in module within another program; it cannot work by itself. Plug-ins add functionality to the host application and may be provided by the manufacturer or by third parties.

Third-Party Plug-Ins   When Digidesign introduced the plug-in concept in Pro Tools' stereo predecessor, Sound Tools II, the company made the then-revolutionary choice to make the programming code available so that third parties could develop their own compatible plug-ins and market them to Digidesign users. Today, scores of companies offer plug-in software modules that are compatible with Pro Tools, some of which are virtual musical instruments, in addition to a wealth of sophisticated effects processors. Not only does this increase the variety of special-purpose effects available, it also allows different plug-in developers to tailor the tonal quality, parameters, and user interface of their processors to suit different tastes.

Many plug-in software modules are included with Pro Tools (in AudioSuite, Native, and/or DSP format, depending on the system you're using), including ones for equalization, dynamics processing, reverb, modulation, harmonic processing, and delays. Naturally, the more effects-processing plug-ins you use simultaneously, the more demands are made on your system's audio-signal–processing capabilities.

Note   Native plug-ins run on the host processor, whereas DSP plug-ins run on the DSP chips included on an HD- or HDX-series card. Prior to Pro Tools 10, Native plug-ins were limited to the RTAS format; likewise, DSP plug-ins were limited to the TDM format. Pro Tools 10 introduces a new plug-in format, AAX, which supports both Native and DSP processing.

Consequently, in the Insert selectors on Pro Tools 10, the term *Native* replaces the term *RTAS* for host-based plug-ins, and the term *DSP* replaces the term *TDM* for card-based plug-ins.

One of the great advantages of using plug-in software processing is that signal-degradation problems associated with the traditional analog studio setup are a thing of the past. Also, from a user's perspective, having a reasonably consistent interface for working with all of your effects processors means that you spend a lot less time wading through manuals, proprietary technology, and jargon. Adding effects processing via plug-ins tends to be less expensive in the long run, too, because you aren't buying stacks of redundant boxes, each with its own inputs/outputs, displays, and so on. The ability to automate plug-in parameters opens up a whole new world of creative possibilities. Furthermore, a single plug-in can be used simultaneously at several locations in the same mix, so you're getting more processing capacity for your money. Figure 2.10 represents the signal flow in an Audio track, showing the location of the Inserts section where plug-in effects are instantiated.

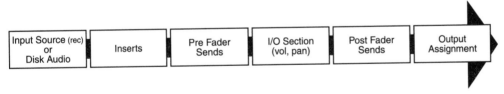

Figure 2.10   Signal flow of an Audio track. While recording, an Audio track's volume fader has no effect on the recorded level from the input. However, you can apply a gain change to the monitoring level.

Instantiate   Just what does it mean to instantiate a plug-in? When you select a plug-in on an insert slot, you're creating an "instance" of this software process at that point within the host program's virtual signal-routing environment—a software object called EQ III, for example—that now demands some portion of your system's available processing power. You might instantiate numerous EQ, compressor, and other types of plug-ins on individual tracks.

Inserts

An insert, also known as an *insert point*, is a feature found in mixing consoles (and in the Pro Tools mix environment). Simply put, an insert is a break in the signal chain—an access point allowing a track's audio to be routed through an external device or through a plug-in processor. Each Audio track, Aux Input track, Instrument track, or Master Fader track in Pro Tools offers an Inserts section, with two sets of five slots where plug-ins can be instantiated. The pop-up menus for each slot in the Inserts section of a track are used to select and "patch in" a software plug-in—the audio signal passes completely through the plug-in before proceeding through successive plug-in slots and eventually to the track's volume/pan controls and output assignment. In Pro Tools, insert points are all pre-fader except on Master Fader tracks, where they are always post-fader.

Hardware I/O inserts can also be created at these same insert points. You can use the inserts to pass the audio signal out to an external device and back to the track via real physical audio inputs/outputs—either analog or digital—on your audio interface. This is how you might incorporate some specialized external effects processor into the Pro Tools mixing environment, for example. However, if you're using a 2 × 2 system like the Mbox Mini (or an M-Audio interface such as the Fast Track USB, M-Audio Transit, or Ozone), this isn't a practical option because your main outputs will already be in use for your stereo mix.

Bouncing to Disk

When you execute the File > Bounce to > Disk command, a new audio file is created in real time, incorporating all the editing and automation information in the current session that affects the selected output pair. What you hear during the bounce process (muted/unmuted tracks, automation, and anything else affecting the mix) is exactly what you will get in the resultant audio file. Bouncing to disk is comparable to the traditional studio practice of mixing down multitrack recordings to a stereo master recorder, except that it's a completely digital process, of course; no superfluous noise or audio degradation is introduced, as is common when recording to an analog master tape. If you make any selection within the timeline of your Pro Tools session, only that portion will be included in the bounced file; otherwise, the bounce will include the entire session from beginning to end. To burn an audio CD from your Pro Tools mix or save out a stereo file when collaborating with a video editor or multimedia author, you can use the File > Bounce to > Disk command.

If you're running out of playback voices or your computer's performance has begun to suffer from too many tracks and plug-ins, you can bounce down a stereo submix of multiple backing tracks (with effects) so that those voices are again available for recording/playback of additional tracks. Of course, you can always retrieve the original backing tracks and revise that submix; like so many things in Pro Tools, it's a non-destructive process.

If you have external MIDI modules being triggered by MIDI tracks in your Pro Tools session, their audio output will need to be routed into Pro Tools in order to be incorporated into your bounced mix, usually through Aux Inputs.

Using Audio from Pro Tools in Other Programs   The File > Bounce to > Disk command is one way to export selections of audio for use with other audio-capable programs. As noted, you might bounce out stereo files in order to create an audio CD with Mac programs such as Roxio's Jam or Toast or Apple's iTunes, or with Windows programs such as Steinberg's WaveLab, Roxio's Media Creator, Sony/Sonic Foundry's CD Architect or Sound Forge, and so on. Converting clips or bounced mixes to AIF, WAV, or MP3 files at various resolutions is also a frequent intermediate step when producing audio for interactive media (CD-ROM, Internet, interactive DVD, video games, and so on) with programs and technologies such as Adobe Director, Flash, and Premiere; Microsoft PowerPoint and Visual Basic; ToolBook; 3D Game Studio; and others.

The Bounce to Disk dialog box allows you to choose an audio file format, including AIF, SD2, Broadcast WAV, QuickTime audio, MP3, and others. You can also choose the number of channels, bit depth, and sample rate for the bounced file. Although you may be able to select a resolution of 8-bit, 16-bit, 24-bit, or 32-bit float (new in Pro Tools 10) for the bounced file, you may wonder why you would ever want to bounce to a lower resolution. One extreme example would be in order to produce 8-bit files for interactive media (multimedia CD-ROMs and such) in situations where disk limitations or system throughput don't permit playback of full CD-quality 16-bit, 44.1-kHz stereo audio. For music production, you might bounce from a 96-kHz, 24-bit session down to 44.1-kHz, 16-bit files as required to burn an audio CD. For in-depth information about this process, see Chapter 16.

Note   Pro Tools 10 provides new options in the Bounce to Disk dialog box that enable you to quickly add your bounced file to your iTunes library and/or upload the file to your SoundCloud account. These bounce options are covered in depth in Chapter 16.

Avid Technology

The following sections discuss several key technical terms that are commonly used in Avid manuals and other documentation. More than simply marketing constructs, these terms refer to important technical innovations by Avid/Digidesign and are enabling technologies for Pro Tools in general.

DAE (Digidesign Audio Engine)

An operating-system extension for real-time digital-audio processing, DAE automatically operates in the background when you launch Pro Tools. It mediates access between the Pro Tools software and the audio hardware. It also handles the pre-loading of digital-audio data from disk into the DAE playback buffer for smooth playback at the proper time. You may occasionally need to change the size of this buffer in the Playback Engine dialog box (Pro Tools 9 and earlier), depending on your hardware configuration and how fragmented or slow your hard disks are.

If something about your system is producing a performance error in Pro Tools, an alert box may appear with a numerical reference to a "DAE error." Typing this error code into the Avid Knowledge Base, found in the Support area of the company's website (http://www.avid.com), will often yield useful information about possible causes and solutions for your problem.

TDM (Time-Division Multiplexing)

TDM is a multichannel signal-routing matrix implemented within the Pro Tools environment (systems with Pro Tools|HD or Pro Tools|HDX hardware only). TDM operates at a much higher multiple of the audio sample rate so that more than one stream of audio can be routed and processed within a single data bus cycle. TDM requires specific hardware configurations, all of which feature dedicated digital signal processing (DSP) chips on PCI cards in the host computer.

TDM is also a plug-in architecture that requires a TDM-capable hardware configuration. TDM plug-ins can often be much more robust and processor intensive than host-based (Native) effects because they can rely on dedicated DSP chips on the PCI cards rather than sharing the host CPU's processing power with the operating system and Pro Tools itself. The TDM plug-in architecture is used in Pro Tools|HD configurations (although these also support both Native plug-ins and Audio-Suite plug-in formats). (The predecessor systems—24|Mix, Pro Tools|24, and Pro Tools III—were also TDM-based; these systems don't support current versions of the Pro Tools software.)

The TDM II bus architecture was introduced with Pro Tools|HD hardware. TDM II doubled the number of time slots from previous TDM systems (from 256 to 512), which has been essential for handling the higher sampling rates supported by HD-series interfaces. This architecture also makes much more efficient use of the available TDM resources.

Note   Pro Tools|HDX systems use a TDM architecture that is different from that used in Pro Tools|HD systems. HDX TDM offers 1536 time slots for communication between multiple HDX cards. Note, however, that Pro Tools|HDX systems *do not* support TDM plug-ins.

More about Signal Processing and Routing in Pro Tools   For more information about how Pro Tools routes audio within its virtual mixing and processing environment, see Chapter 9, which discusses DSP and Native plug-ins, ReWire, and other features of the integrated virtual studio provided by Pro Tools.

ReWire (and the ReWire Plug-In)

ReWire is a technology developed by Propellerhead Software (developers of the Reason and Record applications) for routing digital audio, MIDI, tempo, and transport commands between multiple programs running on the same computer. A ReWire application (such as Sibelius, Reason, or Ableton Live, for example) is slaved to Pro Tools. Any sequences, loops, or drum patterns in the slaved ReWire program will start and stop under the control of the Pro Tools Transport and tempo. Likewise, you can assign the output from any Pro Tools MIDI track to one of the active MIDI-compatible modules within the ReWire program.

After enabling a ReWire program such as Reason on a track in Pro Tools, you can then choose which of the virtual output audio channels from that program will route to that particular track. Because many ReWire programs have their own mixing capabilities, the channel(s) from the ReWire program that you enable for routing into Pro Tools could represent a single instrument module or a submix that sums many modules together. The routing is enabled in Pro Tools by the ReWire plug-in (see Figure 2.11).

 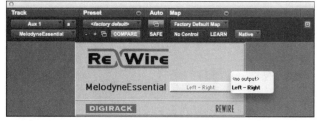

Figure 2.11 Examples of a mono and stereo ReWire plug-in.

Elastic Audio

Elastic Audio is Avid's term for a set of audio-processing features introduced in version 7.4 of Pro Tools. Elastic Audio combines beat and tempo analysis, transient detection, and sophisticated, non-destructive algorithms for real-time time compression and expansion of audio clips in Pro Tools tracks. Among other things, because the "native" tempo and rhythm within an audio clip are detected (via detected transient events), it is possible to conform clips to the session tempo and reposition ("quantize") its audio events to a given rhythmic value—1/8 notes, for example. Event markers identify the transients and other audio events within the clip. Another type of marker, called a *Warp marker*, can be used to drag an audio event to a given position in the Pro Tools Timeline, stretching or compressing the surrounding audio to accommodate this shift.

An important aspect of Elastic Audio, which is explained in more detail in Chapter 12, "The Pro Tools Groove," is its ability to audition drum loops and other audio files in a DigiBase browser window at the current session tempo. In Figure 2.12, Analysis view is displayed in the lower track, revealing Event markers as vertical bars superimposed over the audio, while Warp view is displayed in the upper track, showing Warp markers as vertical bars with a triangle at their base used to realign portions of the audio waveform. You can add, move, or remove Event markers and Warp markers as necessary.

Elastic Pitch, introduced with Pro Tools 8, allows real-time pitch transposition over a two-octave range. On tracks with Elastic Audio enabled, pitch changes can be applied to whole clips. When you need to affect only a portion of a clip—for example, a single word in a vocal track—you can separate that portion into a clip of its own before applying an Elastic Pitch change.

Summary

This chapter provided a quick overview of many Pro Tools fundamentals. These concepts will become clearer as you work through practical examples in the rest of this book. It's essential to

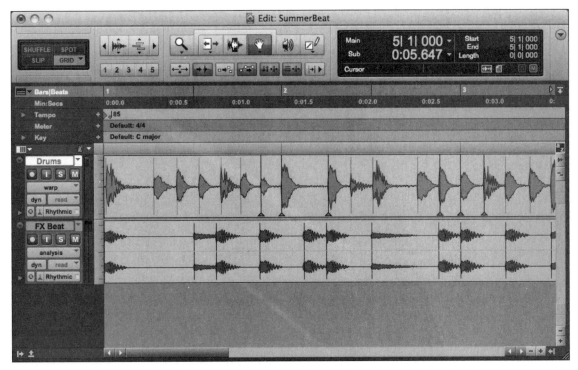

Figure 2.12 Elastic Audio allows events within audio clips to be adjusted to the session tempo or quantized via the same grid and groove options that are available for aligning MIDI events.

have a good handle on basic concepts and to be familiar with the proper Pro Tools terminology in order to organize your thoughts, solve problems, and use this software effectively. The *Pro Tools Reference Guide* also provides an excellent overview of these concepts and is a recommended resource for all users. A PDF version of the *Reference Guide* is installed with Pro Tools and is available from within the software by choosing Help > Pro Tools Reference Guide. The *Reference Guide*, combined with the *Pro Tools Shortcuts Guide* and *Audio Plug-ins Guide*, provides comprehensive and detailed reference information for Pro Tools. This book, by contrast, seeks to distill this wealth of information into the strategic essentials, with real-world examples and recommendations, and to explore how Pro Tools interacts with other studio gear. The practical tips in this book are aimed at both new and experienced users, addressing various specific applications (such as post-production, music, and interactive media), to get you up and running as quickly as possible. Appendix A of this book, "Further Study and Resources on the Web," guides you to other learning resources for Pro Tools and digital audio in general.

Chapter 3, "Your System Configuration," covers guidelines for setting up a working computer and audio hardware configuration for Pro Tools. Chapter 4, "Creating Your First Pro Tools Session," dives right into creating a session in Pro Tools. If you're already a Pro Tools user, you may want to skip ahead to Chapter 5, "The Transport Window," Chapter 6, "The Edit Window," and Chapter 7, "The Mix Window," which break down the elements in the main Pro Tools windows. Although some of this information may be review for experienced users, even long-time Pro Tools heavyweights may find some useful tidbits in these chapters.

3 Your System Configuration

I t can be hard to separate marketing hype from reality when dealing with computer systems in general and pro audio gear in particular. Just as computers evolve from year to year, so does Pro Tools software and hardware. These constant improvements and upgrades can also increase the system requirements for running Pro Tools. Some fundamental concepts apply for the computer system, as well as some particular requirements for multichannel digital audio and hard-disk recording. In addition to reviewing these topics, this chapter covers the basic peripheral devices required to successfully interconnect Pro Tools with other devices in your studio.

Basic Components

To get your Pro Tools system up and running, you will need certain basic hardware components—computer and peripheral gear—depending on your Pro Tools version and the requirements of your recording projects.

Computer

Exact system requirements vary widely according to your Pro Tools configuration—audio interfaces, Pro Tools software version, and optional hardware and software (including virtual instruments and other processing-intensive plug-ins). Currently shipping versions of Pro Tools require an Intel-based Macintosh computer running Snow Leopard or Lion or a Windows system running Windows 7.

The system requirements for Pro Tools evolve over time as newer versions of the program are released and as available hardware changes. For this reason, before purchasing *any* computer for Pro Tools use, be sure to check the Compatibility section of the Avid website (http://www. avid.com) for current system requirements and detailed compatibility documents. You may also wish to consult with companies that provide audio-optimized Windows systems for Pro Tools, such as Terra Digital Audio, Sweetwater, Guitar Center, PC Audio Labs, Rain Recording, and others.

Although the Avid website is always your best source for up-to-date information, you might also take a look at the Avid Audio Forums on the DUC (Digi User Conference) site at http://duc.avid.com for test results, advice, and recommendations from other Pro Tools users. Windows users in particular will want to note the ongoing "sticky" threads in the forums (which always stay at the top of the list), where users share their experiences with different CPUs and system components.

Given the unusual demands that digital audio makes on the computer, only very specific operating system versions are supported for a given release of Pro Tools software. Use caution when upgrading your operating system; be sure to confirm that it works properly with the version of Pro Tools you're using before upgrading.

OS Requirements for Older Versions of Pro Tools   Older versions of Pro Tools require the following:

- **Macintosh.** Pro Tools 9.0 and later require OS 10.6 (Snow Leopard) and (by extension) an Intel-based Mac system. Pro Tools 8.x required OS 10.5.5 (Leopard) or higher. For Pro Tools 7.x, OS 10.4.x (Tiger) was required. Mac OS 10.3 or higher was generally required for Pro Tools 6.x versions. Mac OS 8.6 was the minimum for most 5.x versions of Pro Tools, with Mac OS 9 highly recommended. None of the legacy Pro Tools software versions 5.31 and lower are supported under Mac OS X (even in Classic mode).

- **Windows.** Pro Tools 9.0 and later require Windows 7. Pro Tools 8.x required Windows XP with Service Pack 2 (minimum) or Windows Vista (32-bit). Pro Tools 7.4 was the first version to run on Windows Vista. Pro Tools 7.x ran under Windows XP with Service Pack 2, while 6.x versions of Pro Tools ran under Windows XP with Service Pack 1. Legacy Pro Tools software versions 5.3 and lower are not supported under Windows XP, and work with Windows 98 only.

As with most other software, you may find both minimum and recommended amounts of memory (RAM) listed among the system requirements on Avid's website. With Pro Tools HD 10 (or Pro Tools 10 with Complete Production Toolkit), more than ever, increasing your RAM will significantly impact the speed and flexibility of your system. The renewed importance of memory in this version is a direct result of the Disk Cache enhancements that enable Pro Tools to load a session into RAM for cached playback.

To maximize Pro Tools performance, you will also need to run a lean machine. As you might imagine, multitrack digital audio is fairly taxing on the computer's resources. Avoid cluttering up your operating system with unnecessary background processes that may interfere with performance (screensavers, file and printer sharing, disk indexers, MP3 and Internet time servers, and so on).

Caution: If It Ain't Broke...   Users of processing-intensive, real-time applications such as Pro Tools should avoid downloading operating system updates before confirming that the updates are compatible with their current software version. Avid is very thorough in their testing and, as a result, may be slow to qualify a given OS update. After seeing multiple users report no problems on the Digi User Conference, you may decide to assume the risk of installing a not-yet-qualified update. (For Macintosh Pro Tools users, it is always preferable to download the Combo Update from the Apple website, rather than allowing the Software Update utility to install any upgrade of the Mac OS itself.) If you do so, make *sure* you have thought out an exit strategy (including a full system restore from backup) before potentially debilitating your production system with an incompatible update.

Monitor Screen(s)

For all versions of Pro Tools, the monitor screen should be set at 1024 × 768 resolution or higher. Although a 15-inch monitor is definitely workable, you will be much more comfortable with a 17-inch or larger model. Most high-end Pro Tools users prefer to use *two* large monitors—for example, opening the Pro Tools Mix window on one and the Edit window on the other. Musicians using Pro Tools in a project studio should opt for an LCD flat-panel display to avoid the buzz caused by traditional CRT monitors through magnetic instrument pickups. Most users also find that LCD monitors cause less eyestrain. LCD monitors also produce less heat, which is almost always a consideration in small project studios.

Hard Drive(s)

You will need a very large, fast hard drive for recording and playing back multiple tracks of digital audio. Look for a 500 gigabyte (GB) drive or larger. Larger hard drives also routinely offer better performance. As a general rule, count on using a 7,200-RPM or faster hard drive for recording audio. Pro Tools users recording at high sample rates may want to consider 10,000-RPM drives. As with the basic computer model itself, performance requirements for drives used on digital audio workstations are much greater than for most traditional computer applications, even high-performance applications and games. For best results, investigate disk-drive offerings from companies that specialize in products for audio recording, such as Glyph. Be sure to consult with your Avid dealer or experienced Pro Tools users before making any sizable investment in disks for audio recording. Although it is possible to use USB drives for some systems, they do not offer optimal performance for recording audio.

Currently, the most common disk configuration among Pro Tools users consists of one or more Avid-certified hard drives connected to the computer's FireWire (IEEE 1394) port. This is very cost-effective on a Mac especially, as most recent models include built-in FireWire ports. The drive mechanism *must* be based on the Oxford 911, 912, 924, or 934 chipset to work properly with Pro Tools, however.

In the past, larger Pro Tools configurations used multiple drives on a SCSI connection (which would require an add-in SCSI card in virtually all current computer models). For example, expanded Pro Tools|HD (or 24 MIX) configurations can use SCSI drives attached to one of several ATTO SCSI accelerator cards. It's been many years since Mac and Windows computers have incorporated factory SCSI drives. Instead, they have an internal SATA drive for the operating system and programs. Although these systems can also use FireWire drives, other options may be desirable—especially if this helps lighten the load on the CPU itself.

SATA drives are an excellent option for Windows users, offering very high performance to support large track counts of high-resolution audio. One example is the Raptor 10,000-RPM drive by Western Digital, which, when combined with the Intel ICH-5 controller chipset on the computer's motherboard, can deliver levels of performance comparable to Ultra SCSI disks.

Current Mac Pro systems also allow you to add up three additional internal SATA drives (for a total of four). These additional drives can be used as audio and video drives for a Pro Tools configuration.

In all cases, it is preferable to dedicate one or more separate hard drives for audio data to maximize the available tracks of simultaneous playback. (A dedicated hard drive is obligatory for Pro Tools|HD and HDX systems.) If a dedicated drive isn't possible, you should at least format your large internal drive into two or more partitions, dedicating the larger one exclusively to Pro Tools and reserving the other for the operating system and programs. Along with the performance benefits, using separate drives or partitions makes maintenance and disk reorganization much easier and allows for disk optimization of the audio volume(s) while still booted off the system volume. If you're working at 44.1-kHz sample rates, and your Audio track counts typically don't exceed a dozen or so, you may find that this setup provides acceptable performance for your Pro Tools system.

Figure 3.1 shows the Workspace browser window in Pro Tools, where you can view all the hard disks on your system, their capacity, and available free space. You can also specify which are eligible for audio recording and search for audio files by name anywhere on the system. Once you locate the audio or MIDI files you want on your system's hard disk, you can drag them from the Workspace browser into the Edit window's Clip List or track display area. To provide some perspective on just how much space digital audio requires on your hard drive, Table 3.1 shows the effects of sample rate and bit depth on audio file size.

Tech Support Folder   The Avid website (http://www.avid.com) offers a downloadable set of utilities and test sessions called the Tech Support Folder. A few useful examples: The PC Wizard program generates a complete listing of what components are installed on your Windows system. The Generate Version List feature creates a text file with the version number of the Pro Tools program, all installed plug-ins, and other optional programs from Avid. Lastly, the Delete Preferences and Databases feature lets you eliminate all these in a single step for troubleshooting purposes. (On Windows, these files are moved into the Local Settings/Temp folder for your user name; on a Mac, they are moved directly into the Trash folder.)

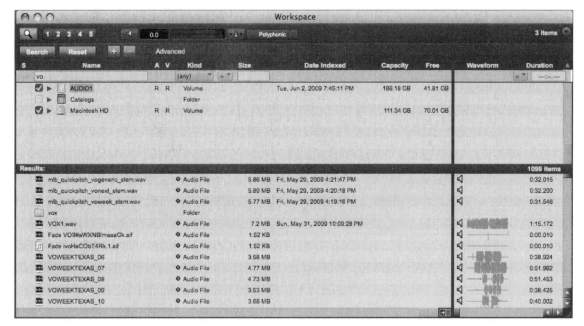

Figure 3.1 The Workspace browser in Pro Tools provides an overview of hard disks, available capacity, and status for recording or playback (transfer) only. You can also search for files here and drag them into the tracks or Clip List of your current session.

Table 3.1 Big and Bigger: The Effects of Sample Rate and Bit Depth on Audio File Size

Sample Rate	Bit Depth	1 Minute (Mono)	1 Minute (Stereo)
44.1 kHz	16 bits/sample	5 MB	10 MB
44.1 kHz	24 bits/sample	7.9 MB	15.8 MB
48 kHz	16 bits/sample	5.7 MB	11.4 MB
48 kHz	24 bits/sample	8.6 MB	17.2 MB
96 kHz	24 bits/sample	17.2 MB	34.4 MB
192 kHz	24 bits/sample	34.4 MB	68.8 MB

Peripheral Equipment

Pro Tools expansion options and additional hardware peripherals are covered in detail in Chapter 18, "Pro Tools Power: The Next Step." In the meantime, this section takes a look at some of the basic equipment that will complement your Pro Tools configuration in a studio setting.

MIDI Interface

At times, you may want to use external MIDI controllers or modules with Pro Tools (for example, to record MIDI performances, to play back MIDI data from Pro Tools through an external sound module or synthesizer, or to control Pro Tools with a MIDI control surface). In such cases, you may need some sort of MIDI interface (unless the devices you use can connect to the computer directly via USB). MIDI is a serial communications protocol that uses 5-pin DIN connectors. A MIDI interface acts as an adapter to convert the MIDI protocol to a format usable within the software environment. Various MIDI interfaces can be purchased, depending on your requirements and the connection methods your computer supports for this optional piece of gear. Figure 3.2 shows one example.

Figure 3.2 A multiport MIDI interface. (Shown: The MOTU MIDI Express XT, which connects to the computer via USB.)

Many Avid audio interfaces (such as the Pro Tools Mbox and Mbox Pro) offer built-in MIDI In and MIDI Out connectors. So do some of the Pro Tools–compatible audio interfaces from M-Audio and third-party manufacturers. If your audio interface does not include MIDI ports, your options include the following:

- **Windows.** Many standard PC soundcards have a small, built-in port for MIDI. (Be aware, however, that some of these consumer soundcards may present conflicts for Pro Tools applications.) Usually, you must separately purchase a small Y adapter cable, which splits out from a 15-pin D-shaped connector on the card into two 5-pin DIN connectors for MIDI in/out. For more serious applications, you can opt for a more professional, dedicated MIDI interface. For multiple MIDI ports or SMPTE synchronization, an external MIDI interface is generally required, connected via a card installed in the computer's PCI slot, a parallel port, or the computer's USB port.

- **Macintosh.** Any external MIDI interface that attaches to the USB port will work.

It's easy to upgrade your MIDI interface as requirements change. The Mac version of Pro Tools uses the configuration defined in the operating system's Audio MIDI Setup utility, an intermediate software layer that facilitates naming and connecting MIDI peripherals and negotiates between programs such as Pro Tools, the MIDI interface, and any external MIDI devices that are connected to it. After changing to another model of MIDI interface and setting it up in this system utility, the new port configuration will appear the next time you access MIDI output assignments from the MIDI tracks within Pro Tools.

In Windows, the MIDI Studio Setup window (discussed in Chapter 10, "MIDI," and shown there in Figure 10.4) provides very similar functionality. After configuring an external MIDI instrument on the appropriate port of your MIDI interface, you can select the enabled send/receive channels for MIDI from MIDI tracks within Pro Tools.

The now-discontinued MIDI I/O (introduced by Digidesign) is still in use in many studios and is supported in Pro Tools 10. This MIDI interface connects to Windows or Macintosh computers via USB, providing 10 MIDI input ports and 10 MIDI output ports. The MIDI I/O also supports MIDI timestamping in Pro Tools, a feature that uses a data buffer within the interface itself to maintain proper timing for very dense streams of MIDI data from multiple tracks. Chapter 10 includes a section about the MIDI I/O, providing more details and a look at the front and back panels of this unit.

Direct USB Connections for MIDI Controllers Many controller keyboards (and sound modules) can connect directly to the computer via a USB port. These range from very simple models to full-featured controllers. For such devices, you may not require a MIDI interface at all, especially if you use virtual instruments for all your MIDI and Instrument tracks.

SMPTE Interface

SMPTE time code is used in the video and film industry to synchronize audio devices to a master video deck and to synchronize MIDI and audio software to multitrack audiotape machines. SMPTE is an abbreviation for Society of Motion Picture and Television Engineers.

A SMPTE time code is a series of numbers representing hours, minutes, seconds, frames, and subframes that is encoded either into an audio signal (longitudinal time code, or LTC) or within the upper lines of the video frame (vertical interval time code, or VITC). A SMPTE interface for digital audio workstations translates these encoded signals into MIDI time code (MTC), which carries the same information, encoded in the MIDI protocol. With SMPTE synchronization, when the Pro Tools transport is in Online mode, Pro Tools will sync to the time location currently playing on the video and will play back from the corresponding SMPTE location in the session.

In many cases, multiport MIDI interfaces from manufacturers such as Mark of the Unicorn, M-Audio, and others additionally incorporate audio inputs/outputs for synchronizing to time code in LTC format. Because LTC is a way of encoding SMPTE time code as an audio signal, this is also the most common method for synchronizing Pro Tools with multitrack tape decks (both analog and digital). There are also synchronization peripherals for VITC (time code embedded into each frame of a video signal). More sophisticated units, such as the Sync I/O (now discontinued); its successor, the Avid Sync HD (shown in Figure 3.3); or Mark of the Unicorn's MIDI Timepiece AV also allow the internal sample clock of your Pro Tools audio hardware to be resolved or slaved to incoming time code or video sync to keep things perfectly locked together over long periods of time. For more information, see Chapter 11, "Synchronization."

(Photo courtesy of Avid.)

Figure 3.3 Sync HD, a SMPTE synchronizer from Avid.

MIDI Instruments/Controllers

Your keyboards, drum modules, MIDI modules, MIDI effects, and other MIDI controllers (guitar, wind, or percussion, for example) usually feature MIDI in/out—and sometimes thru—connectors. Multiple MIDI devices can be daisy-chained to a single MIDI port, if needed for a device with a single in/out port (such as the Pro Tools Mbox). (A single MIDI cable or port carries 16 separate channels of MIDI data.)

However, routing tracks from Pro Tools out to several multitimbral modules (which can respond with different sounds to incoming events on multiple MIDI channels) can be a little tricky in this setup because you've only got 16 MIDI channels to work with, and each module may be listening to all of them. If you have a large number of independently addressable MIDI ports (such as on the MIDI I/O), you can connect each external module to a separate port. With each port providing 16 channels of data, the MIDI I/O's 10 MIDI inputs and 10 MIDI outputs provide for a potential total of 160 MIDI channels each direction.

The important thing to remember is that MIDI events going between Pro Tools and your MIDI devices are data, and the MIDI interface connections described here have nothing to do with how all the audio outputs of your MIDI modules get back into the Pro Tools mix (for bouncing to disk with your Audio tracks and software instruments). If you have sufficient inputs on your external audio interface, audio from MIDI modules can enter the Pro Tools mix via various Aux Input tracks (or Instrument tracks). The input sources for such tracks would be set to monitor the physical inputs where those devices are attached to your audio interface.

Another option, particularly if you're using an audio interface that provides only two analog audio inputs, would be to use a small external mixing board. This would allow you to pre-mix all the MIDI modules to stereo before the signals enter the Pro Tools mix—via a single stereo Aux Input track set to monitor the mixer's outputs. Figure 3.4 shows a typical MIDI configuration for a project studio.

Software Instruments Software-based virtual synthesizers and samplers represent an increasingly popular class of MIDI instrument. Their audio outputs are routed within audio/MIDI programs such as Pro Tools. Benefits of virtual instruments over external physical sound sources for MIDI parts include the elimination of noise (there are no analog connections in the signal path) and the fact that you can use many MIDI sound sources without stacking up a lot of bulky modules in your studio! If you're just starting to build

Basic Audio/MIDI Configuration

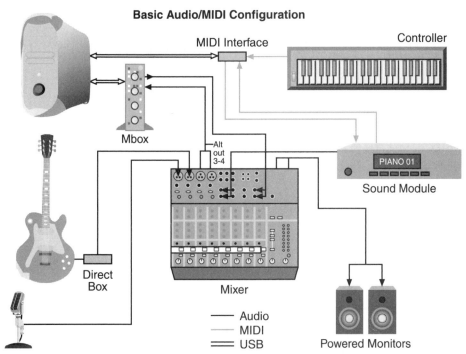

Figure 3.4 In this example, a separate MIDI interface handles transmission of MIDI data between Pro Tools, an external MIDI controller, and an external MIDI module. For the sound from external MIDI instruments to be incorporated when you bounce a mix file from Pro Tools, their audio is typically routed to Pro Tools inputs and monitored via an Aux Input or Instrument track.

up your Pro Tools/MIDI studio, this is a great way to go. Virtual instruments are much simpler than hardware devices, they offer total recall and greater control, and they take up less space.

Among the industry-standard software architectures that have emerged in recent years, here are the methods Pro Tools currently supports for using virtual (software-based) instruments:

- RTAS (Native) plug-ins: These can be used in both standard and HD versions of the Pro Tools software. Examples include the virtual instruments in the Pro Tools Creative Collection (Xpand!^{2}, Structure Free, Boom, Vacuum, DB-33, and Mini Grand; included with Pro Tools); the plug-ins in the Pro Tools Instrument Expansion Pack (Structure, Strike, Velvet, Transfuser, and Hybrid); and scores of third-party virtual instruments from IK Multimedia, Ultimate Sound Bank, MOTU, Applied Acoustics, FXpansion, Spectrasonics, Tascam, Native Instruments, and others.

- TDM (DSP) plug-ins (require Pro Tools HD hardware): These include McDSP's Synthesizer One (also available as RTAS), Access Music's Virus Indigo, Avid's SoundFuel SOLID, and Duy's SynthSpider.

- AAX plug-ins: This is a new format introduced in Pro Tools 10 that supports both Native and HDX DSP systems.

■ ReWire: This is a software protocol that allows audio programs to communicate with one another, routing audio and MIDI data between them. Audio from separate ReWire-compatible virtual instruments can thus be added to a Pro Tools mix. Examples of ReWire instruments include Propellerhead Reason, Celemony Melodyne Studio, and Ableton Live. The audio signals from these programs can be routed into Pro Tools via the ReWire plug-in.

Virtual instrument offerings continue to grow, and exciting new developments are regularly unveiled. For more information about software-based instruments, see the section "Virtual Instruments" in Chapter 10.

CD/DVD Recording Drive

A CD- or DVD-recording drive is not a system requirement for Pro Tools, but in all likelihood you will find yourself needing one. You will almost certainly want to burn an occasional audio CD from the mixes you bounce out of Pro Tools. And if you're creating audio files for interactive media, you may well need to throw all those AIF, MP3, or WAV files onto a CD-ROM or DVD-ROM for delivery to developers. In the field of video production, it can sometimes be simpler and more economical to burn CDs when delivering OMF or AAF files for Media Composer, FinalCut Pro, or Media 100 video editors (assuming you don't share a network server for media files) than to use some other removable media.

More importantly, however, when your Pro Tools session folders (including the Audio Files folders within them) run into hundreds of megabytes, you will need a way to back them up for data security or archive purposes. CD recorders and media have become very inexpensive, and this technology may be sufficient for many home-studio users. That said, the 700-MB capacity of a CD is somewhat limited when you consider the typical size of audio projects. The situation gets worse with high-resolution audio at 96-kHz to 192-kHz sampling rates. The availability of affordable recordable DVD drives for computer data has been a real boon for digital audio/video users. Several gigabytes fit onto a single recordable DVD, allowing entire projects to be backed up in a single operation. And the easier it is, the more often you'll do it. Even if the size of a Pro Tools project exceeds the space available on a single write-once DVD, burning programs such as Roxio's Toast will automatically spread the project's data among multiple blank DVDs, creating a cost-effective long-term backup. In short, you will be well served to purchase a DVD-recording drive for your computer (which can also record data and audio onto CDs, of course). *Whatever your method, you need to back up your data often!*

Audio Mixer or Mic Preamp

For many users, the goal is to use Pro Tools as a complete studio in a box. Various hardware options are available that combine audio inputs/outputs, MIDI in/out, and microphone preamps into a single audio interface. The Pro Tools Mbox (a compact USB audio interface) incorporates MIDI in/out and two mic preamps with 48-volt phantom power for studio condenser microphones. It also supports Hi-Z (high-impedance) input from musical-instrument pickups, which can produce impressive results with a guitar amplifier simulation plug-in such as Eleven or AmpliTube.

Most HD Series audio interfaces feature only line-level audio inputs (the exception being HD OMNI, which includes built-in mic preamps on two channels). This means that signals from microphone sources must be stepped up to this level in order to record their signal. A good mixer with multiple high-quality microphone preamps can be excellent for this purpose, and very cost effective. You might even use the mixer's insert points to patch in a compressor on a microphone source prior to recording it at the Pro Tools input if you happen to like the coloration that a particular compressor adds to your sound or if you have concerns about unexpected peaks in a live situation. The audio mixer can also be handy for other purposes, such as for monitoring different sources in your studio (for example, a CD player, DAT, or turntables) or for pre-mixing audio from multiple MIDI devices on their way into Pro Tools. Lastly, for certain users, it can be expedient to use the mixer itself to combine all the audio outputs from Pro Tools tracks, external effects such as reverb, and multiple MIDI modules in the studio when mixing in real time to a stereo recorder—especially if the audio interface on the Pro Tools system doesn't have enough simultaneous inputs for all external devices.

Some users might opt for one of the high-end microphone preamps available on the market. This can be a very effective choice for project studios in particular. Because single users don't typically require a large number of simultaneous mic inputs (unless a drum set needs to be recorded, for example), a single high-quality microphone preamp can deliver pristine sound on each microphone source it records. A given microphone preamp may have specific desirable sonic characteristics or offer its own onboard signal processing.

Another option is to use a rack-mounted preamp; several eight-channel mic preamps on the market are very good quality and cost effective. Many even offer digital outputs, meaning that after the mic preamp stage itself, the signal need not pass through any additional analog stages before entering Pro Tools. Such multiple-channel, rack-mountable microphone preamps are also very popular for Pro Tools users who do location recording, because a computer and a single small rack represent the entire recording system, making it easy to transport. All you have to do is set up the microphones, and you're ready to go. Avid manufactures its own high-end, eight-channel rack-mounted mic preamp. The Avid PRE (shown in Figure 3.5) offers the notable advantage of being completely configurable (via MIDI) from inside the Pro Tools software, which means that its settings will be recalled the next time you open a session.

Figure 3.5 PRE, Avid's eight-channel microphone preamp.

Speakers, Amplification

Of course, you also need to hear the audio while you work! If you're just setting up your project studio, you should consider some of the small, powered studio monitors that are available. These can be directly connected to the audio outputs you're using for your main stereo mix (on your computer, card, or external audio interface). Note that, although multimedia computer systems often include speakers that are sufficient to get started working in Pro Tools, such sound systems are typically not adequate for precision audio mixing and editing tasks. All kinds of audio garbage—especially background noise, hiss, and hum—can easily sneak into your final mixes if you are not listening carefully through a decent set of speakers. If you have to place the speakers near a CRT computer monitor, make sure the speakers you buy are magnetically shielded so that the magnetic field they produce doesn't interfere with your monitor, distorting the colors of the display or creating interference patterns. A good set of headphones can also be very useful to check the stereo localization (panning) and reverb, and to help you discern minor edit noises, clicks, and pops that may not be obvious when listening in a room (especially if you have other noisy gear—or occupants—in your studio).

Turn Down Your Speakers before Rebooting If you have your Macintosh built-in audio outputs connected to your main speakers at nice, loud monitoring levels, don't forget to turn down the audio output before you shut down or restart the system. That Macintosh startup sound is loud! This also applies to Windows users who have connected their computer's main audio output to studio monitors. Pops from system startup or launching/closing of certain audio programs can be annoying and even potentially damaging to your speakers. A good rule of thumb for your speakers when it comes to booting up or shutting down your system is *last on, first off*.

Pro Tools Hardware Configurations

This section reviews the primary Pro Tools configurations that are currently available. (Note that Chapter 18 breaks down hardware configurations and expansions in more detail.) The variety of possible Pro Tools setups means there is a configuration that's right for just about every purpose and budget.

Pro Tools Mbox Family

The Pro Tools Mbox family—the Mbox Mini, Mbox, and Mbox Pro—represents Avid's third-generation Mbox design. The product line consists of lightweight, portable audio interfaces for Pro Tools and third-party DAW software. The current Mbox lineup supports audio recording at 16- or 24-bit resolution, with sample rates up to 48 kHz (Mbox Mini), 96 kHz (Mbox), or 192 kHz (Mbox Pro).

The third-generation Mbox interfaces are each housed in a professional-grade, rugged metal chassis encasing a secondary inner metal chassis, ensuring precise alignment of all internal components. A molded plastic faceplate and soft-touch knobs enhance the design.

Mbox Mini (USB)

The Pro Tools Mbox Mini (shown in Figure 3.6) is an ultra-portable USB audio interface that provides 2 × 2 simultaneous channels of I/O and up to 24-bit/48-kHz audio resolution. Input options include one XLR mic/line combo input with a mic preamp and 48V phantom power and two 1/4-inch instrument inputs (one DI, one line-level/DI). Outputs include two balanced 1/4-inch monitor outputs and a 1/4-inch stereo headphone output.

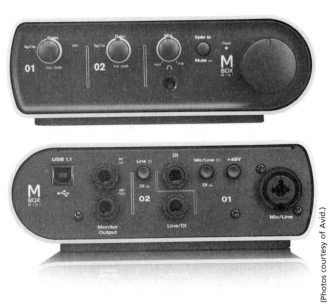

(Photos courtesy of Avid.)

Figure 3.6 Pro Tools Mbox Mini USB audio interface.

There are no digital audio inputs or MIDI ports on this interface. The Mini is powered through the USB bus, so it does not require any additional AC power. The unit provides a single 1/4-inch headphone output on its front panel. A single output level knob affects both the monitor output and headphone levels.

The Mbox Mini is a solid choice for personal recording in a portable package with a computer or appropriately configured laptop.

Mbox (USB)

The Pro Tools Mbox (shown in Figure 3.7) is a professional-grade audio interface, providing 4 × 4 simultaneous channels of I/O and up to 24-bit/96-kHz audio resolution with bus-powered USB 2.0 connectivity. Analog input options include two XLR mic/line combo inputs with mic preamps and 48V phantom power and two 1/4-inch DI inputs on the front panel. Analog outputs include two balanced 1/4-inch monitor outputs and a 1/4-inch stereo headphone output.

The Mbox also provides stereo S/PDIF digital I/O, as well as both MIDI input and MIDI output ports. The unit includes separate volume controls for the 1/4-inch headphone output on its front panel and the monitor output. The monitor section also includes Mono and Dim controls. Additionally, the Mbox provides access to a variety of hardware-based, low-latency effects.

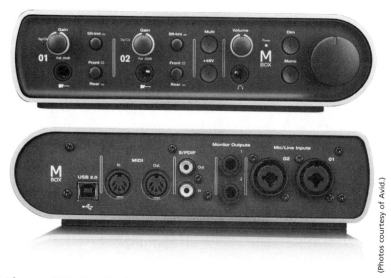

(Photos courtesy of Avid.)

Figure 3.7 Pro Tools Mbox USB interface.

The Mbox is an excellent choice for location recording with your computer or an appropriately configured laptop. It is also ideal for any home or project studio configuration. If you generally record only one or two channels at a time (as is common in a home studio), this interface will work nicely. The availability of digital I/O allows you to transfer DAT recordings into Pro Tools for subsequent editing and mastering. You can also consider a guitar preamp or high-end microphone preamp with a digital output as your front end for recording via the S/PDIF digital input. The Mbox can also be appropriate for video post-production (using a digital video file as the master, for instance), voiceover and broadcast audio, multimedia, spoken word, and many other applications.

Mbox Pro (FireWire)

The Mbox Pro (shown in Figure 3.8) is a high-resolution, high-performance 8 × 8 audio interface providing up to 24-bit, 192-kHz audio resolution via FireWire connectivity. Analog inputs include four mic inputs (two XLR mic/DI combo, two XLR) with mic preamps, 48V phantom

(Photos courtesy of Avid.)

Figure 3.8 Pro Tools Mbox Pro FireWire interface.

power, and high-pass filters; four 1/4-inch TRS line-level inputs; and two unbalanced Alt line-level inputs (two RCA, one stereo mini 1/8-inch). Analog outputs include six balanced 1/4-inch TRS line-level outputs and two 1/4-inch stereo headphone outputs with discrete volume controls.

The Mbox Pro also provides stereo S/PDIF digital I/O, as well as both MIDI input and MIDI output ports and word clock I/O. The monitor section has a dedicated output level knob and includes Mono, Mute, Dim, Alt Source, and Speaker A/B/C switching controls. Like the Mbox, the Mbox Pro provides access to a variety of hardware-based, low-latency effects via onboard DSP.

The Mbox Pro includes a back panel 1/4-inch TS connector for attaching a footswitch to control either playback start/stop or recording punch in/out. Additionally, the unit features critically acclaimed JetPLL technology to provide extremely accurate synchronization and eliminate jitter that can degrade audio quality.

Eleven Rack (USB)

The Eleven Rack (shown in Figure 3.9) is a guitar recording and effects processing system designed for Pro Tools and live performance. Eleven Rack provides a high-resolution, dual DSP-powered audio interface to eliminate latency when recording with its built-in amp/effects tones. Using Eleven Rack with Pro Tools lets you to record both dry and processed guitar signals simultaneously, allowing you to re-amplify later without patching a single cable.

Figure 3.9 Eleven Rack USB interface.

Eleven Rack features a high-speed USB 2.0 connection to Pro Tools, supporting up to eight simultaneous channels of recording at up to 24-bit/96-kHz. The unit provides a single XLR mic input with 48V phantom power and pad switch, two 1/4-inch line-level inputs, as well as AES/EBU and S/PDIF digital I/O. The stereo balanced XLR outputs provide main outputs from Pro Tools, while the dedicated 1/4-inch outputs provide outputs to amplifiers for live performance.

The included stereo 1/4-inch headphone jack can also be used to monitor the main output. Additionally, Eleven Rack includes MIDI input and output ports.

When used as a standalone amp tone and effects signal processor, Eleven Rack provides a selection of classic effects—from stompboxes to rackmount studio processors—that you can integrate into your existing rig. When used for recording, the settings for the Eleven Rack amp and effects are embedded into the recorded audio files, enabling you to automatically recall those settings on any Pro Tools system with a connected Eleven Rack.

Eleven Rack offers powerful control options using affordable MIDI controllers and expression pedals, providing full foot control over vintage wah effects, tempo-driven delays, and more.

Eleven Rack also features a variable-impedance circuit called True-Z, which automatically changes the input impedance of the Eleven Rack guitar input depending on the amp or effects model placed first in its signal chain. True-Z alters the frequency response of the incoming guitar signal by loading the pickups in the same manner as plugging into a real amp or effect. The True-Z input impedance can also be controlled manually and set to a value that best suits your playing style.

M-Audio Interfaces

Various audio hardware options from M-Audio (a subsidiary of Avid Technology since 2004) can be used with Pro Tools 9 and later. These interfaces were previously supported only with Pro Tools M-Powered software. Like the Pro Tools Mbox family, you can also use M-Audio hardware with many third-party audio-MIDI programs.

The sections that follow provide functional descriptions of many of the M-Audio hardware offerings that are currently available for use with Pro Tools.

FireWire-Based Systems

The following M-Audio hardware systems are all external audio interfaces that connect to the host computer via its FireWire port. They are all capable of either 24- or 16-bit resolution for digital audio. While FireWire has been standard on Macintosh computers for a number of years, some Windows computers may require an optional FireWire card. Also, Mac OS X or Windows XP with Service Pack 2 is the minimum requirement for using *any* of M-Audio's FireWire-based audio interfaces with Pro Tools. Users should check the Avid website for compatibility between OS versions, M-Audio interfaces, and Pro Tools software, especially for older hardware products.

Note   Beginning with version 9, Pro Tools requires OS X version 10.6 (Snow Leopard) or later on a Mac and Windows 7 on a PC.

FireWire Solo

The FireWire Solo (shown in Figure 3.10) features two inputs with gain controls on the front panel: one dedicated to microphone sources (and providing 48-volt phantom power) and the other to guitar or bass (also known as Hi-Z, high-impedance) sources. There is also a headphone output on the front panel. The rear panel offers two additional channels of analog input with TS (1/4-inch phone, tip-sleeve, unbalanced) jacks, analog output with TRS (1/4-inch phone, tip-ring-sleeve, balanced) jacks, as well as stereo coaxial S/PDIF digital I/O with RCA jacks. A switch on the front panel of the unit allows you to select between front (mic/instrument) and rear (line-level) inputs. If you simultaneously use both analog and S/PDIF digital I/O, you can use up to four input channels and four output channels on the FireWire Solo at the same time. The FireWire Solo supports 24-bit audio at sample rates up to 96 kHz and can be powered either directly from the FireWire bus or from the included 12-volt DC power supply.

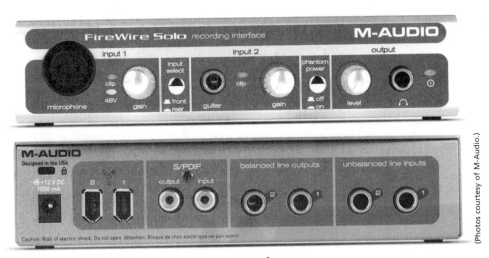

(Photos courtesy of M-Audio.)

Figure 3.10 M-Audio's FireWire Solo interface.

ProFire 2626

The ProFire 2626, shown in Figure 3.11, features 26 × 26 simultaneous analog/digital I/O, including eight preamps made with M-Audio's Octane technology. A user-assignable master volume control knob allows you to choose any or all of the eight analog output pairs for control, effectively creating the possibility for a user to configure a 7.1 surround output uniformly attenuated by one volume control. The interface can work with sample rates up to 192 kHz, with compatible software. In setups with multiple pieces of gear that would need a single clock source, the ProFire 2626 can act either as the clock master or a slave. A flexible onboard DSP mixer offers the option to send any of the 52 audio streams to any of the hardware outputs and lets the user create internally up to eight stereo mixes. Inputs include eight 1/4-inch TRS balanced line inputs, eight XLR mic inputs with phantom power, and two 1/4-inch TS instrument inputs. Digital connections include 2 × 2 optical S/PDIF or 16 × 16 ADAT I/O, as well as a 2 × 2 coaxial S/PDIF connection. Outputs include eight 1/4-inch TRS balanced line outputs and two 1/4-inch TRS headphone outputs. A 1 × 1 MIDI I/O and word clock I/O are also featured.

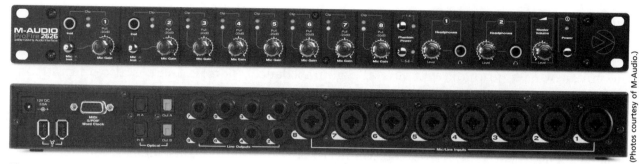

(Photos courtesy of M-Audio.)

Figure 3.11 The M-Audio ProFire 2626 features eight preamps, an onboard digital mixer, and the ability to create eight stereo mixes.

ProFire 610

A travel-friendly interface, the ProFire 610, shown in Figure 3.12, features 6 × 10 simultaneous analog/digital I/O including two preamps, again with M-Audio's Octane technology. Like the 2626, it features a user-assignable master volume knob that can be configured to control any or all of the four analog output pairs. Also echoing the 2626 is a DSP mixer coupled with a software control panel that enables the user to configure several stereo mixes, perfect for sending cue feeds of audio to the talent being recorded. Like the 2626, the ProFire 610 supports audio at 196 kHz with compatible software. Inputs on the 610 include two XLR/TS combo jacks for instrument-level or mic-level inputs, two 1/4-inch TRS balanced line inputs, and a stereo S/PDIF in. Outputs include eight 1/4-inch TRS balanced line outputs and a stereo S/PDIF out. Also included are a 1 × 1 MIDI interface, two 1/4-inch TRS headphone outputs, and two FireWire ports.

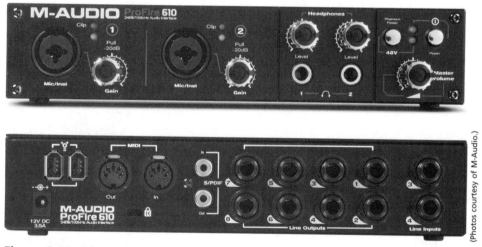

(Photos courtesy of M-Audio.)

Figure 3.12 The M-Audio ProFire 610, a portable interface featuring 6 × 10 analog/digital I/O.

ProjectMix I/O

The ProjectMix I/O (shown in Figure 3.13) combines a FireWire-based 18 × 14 audio interface with a control surface. As an audio interface, it is directly supported by Pro Tools (as well as several other audio programs). It offers eight analog inputs, each with an input gain knob and a mic/line switch for selecting between its separate XLR (with phantom power) and TRS jacks (plus a

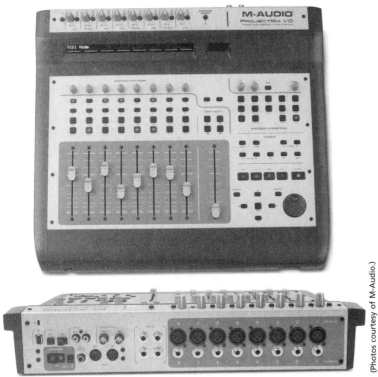

(Photos courtesy of M-Audio.)

Figure 3.13   M-Audio's ProjectMix I/O combines a FireWire audio interface and control surface.

selectable instrument-level input on the front panel, for Channel 1). Four TRS analog outputs are also provided. Additionally, the ProjectMix I/O has digital input/output in S/PDIF and ADAT Lightpipe formats, two headphone outputs on the front of the unit with independent level controls, MIDI input/output, and word clock input/output with BNC connectors. As a control surface, it offers transport buttons and a jog wheel, plus motorized faders for eight channel strips (each with an assignable rotary encoder plus dedicated record-enable, channel select, solo, and mute buttons) and the master level. A flip button allows you to use the 100mm faders for writing more precise automation moves instead of the rotary encoders. The ProjectMix I/O features a two-line LCD display across the top of the control surface. Various other dedicated buttons are provided for functions such as nudging, looping, and so on; a footswitch input is also available. The ProjectMix I/O supports Mackie Control, HUI, and Logic Control emulation modes.

ProFire Lightbridge

The ProFire Lightbridge interface (shown in Figure 3.14) offers up to 34 digital input and 34 digital output channels: four ADAT Lightpipe inputs/outputs that support eight digital audio channels on each of the TOSLINK connectors, plus stereo S/PDIF digital I/O with RCA coaxial connectors. (Pro Tools 10 software supports a maximum of 32 channels of I/O without Pro Tools|HD, HD Native, or HDX hardware.) The unit also provides two additional analog output channels with 1/4-inch TRS line-level jacks and a headphone output that all carry the same signal but with independent volume control. In addition to normal Lightpipe mode at up to 48 kHz, the

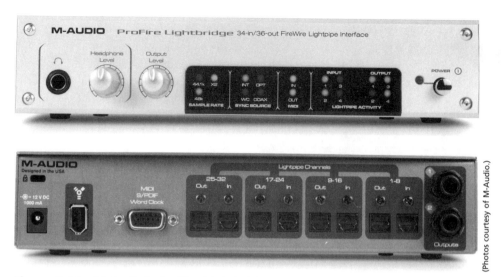

(Photos courtesy of M-Audio.)

Figure 3.14 M-Audio's ProFire Lightbridge.

ProFire Lightbridge also supports 16-channel Lightpipe operation at 88.2- and 96-kHz sample rates via the S/MUX protocol (which requires two TOSLINK connections for each eight-channel group in order to support higher sample rates). The ProFire Lightbridge is configured via the included control panel software.

NRV10

The NRV10 (shown in Figure 3.15) combines an 8 × 2 analog mixer with an audio interface that connects to the host computer via FireWire. Mixer channels 1–4 can be switched between separate XLR microphone (with globally switchable phantom power) and line-level inputs with TRS jacks, and provide analog inserts. The next mixer channel is switchable between a mono microphone Input 5 or balanced stereo line Inputs 5–6, while balanced Inputs 7–8 are on a single stereo mixer channel. All channels have 45mm faders. Three-band EQ is provided on each channel, along with a pre-fader Aux 1 mono send and a post-fader Aux 2 mono send that feeds both the mixer's Aux 2 analog output and the mixer's DFX internal effects unit (which can be used to feed reverb to the headphone mix while recording, for example). Channel source buttons above each of the NRV10's six faders can switch their signal sources between their analog inputs (Channel) and up to 10 digital-audio streams (FW) coming from Pro Tools during playback and recording. The master section of the mixer provides separate volume controls for the headphone and control-room outputs as well as two stereo returns. The main mix level fader affects the main stereo analog outputs on the rear of the interface, which offer both XLR and balanced 1/4-inch TRS jacks. (There are also analog insert connections on the main output bus.) Next to this in the master section is a control room fader, which affects a separate set of outputs, also with balanced TRS jacks. The FW 9/10 to Phones button allows you to route audio streams 9–10 from Pro Tools to the mixer's headphone output. Another button in the master section, Pre-EQ/Post-EQ, affects all the analog mixer's input channels and determines whether the signal source entering Pro Tools comes from a point before or after their three-band EQ section (after

(Photos courtesy of M-Audio.)

Figure 3.15 M-Audio's NRV10 combines an analog mixer and a FireWire interface.

their gain stage and analog insert points). The included control-panel software displays input/output levels on the device's 10 FireWire audio busses. The NRV10 supports 24-bit audio at sample rates up to 96 kHz. As a FireWire audio interface for Pro Tools, its inputs support recording up to 10 channels simultaneously.

Good Audio Cables Are a Sound Investment   Be sure to always use proper 75-ohm "digital" coaxial cable with all S/PDIF digital connections, especially at cable lengths over three feet.

USB-Based Systems

The following M-Audio interfaces connect to the host computer via USB. With the exception of the Ozone, most are also powered via this connection; no AC adapter is required.

MobilePre

The MobilePre (shown in Figure 3.16) is a stereo audio interface that exclusively supports 24-bit audio at a 48-kHz sample rate. This interface has two TS (1/4-inch unbalanced) outputs on the rear panel and a 1/4-inch stereo headphone output on the front panel. Gain knobs are provided on the top panel for Channels 1 and 2, as well as knobs for headphone and line output levels. Two XLR/TS combo jacks support microphone- and/or instrument-level sources. Alternatively, the rear panel of the interface offers line-level inputs for keyboards, drum machines, synthesizers, and so on. The MobilePre USB does not feature any digital I/O.

(Photos courtesy of M-Audio.)

Figure 3.16 M-Audio's MobilePre interface.

FastTrack

The FastTrack (shown in Figure 3.17) is a compact two-input, two-output audio interface that supports 24-bit audio at 48 kHz. The stereo outputs use RCA (unbalanced) jacks. The unit includes a 1/4-inch instrument input as well as an XLR input for microphone sources, both with associated top-panel gain controls. A back-panel switch provides phantom power for the microphone input. No digital I/O is available on this interface. The FastTrack features a top-panel output knob as well as a Direct Monitor switch for zero-latency monitoring, letting you hear your instruments directly through the interface before they go into the computer.

(Photo courtesy of M-Audio.)

Figure 3.17 M-Audio's FastTrack interface.

FastTrack Pro

The FastTrack Pro (shown in Figure 3.18) is another USB audio interface that supports up to 24-bit audio at 96 kHz. It features two front-panel analog audio inputs with combo XLR/TRS connectors (for microphone or balanced line-level sources), S/PDIF digital I/O with RCA jacks, four unbalanced analog outputs with RCA jacks, and two balanced outputs with 1/4-inch TRS jacks. Front-panel buttons provide for switching the 1/4-inch TS input between line and instrument levels, as well as enabling a –20dB pad on the input signal. A headphone output is provided on the front panel, which mirrors the audio signal at the main Outputs 1–2 with independent volume control. A front-panel mix knob allows for the adjustment of the balance between the input signal and audio being passed back from Pro Tools to address monitoring latency while recording. The FastTrack Pro also incorporates one MIDI input and one MIDI output, and can be powered via either USB or optional AC power adapter.

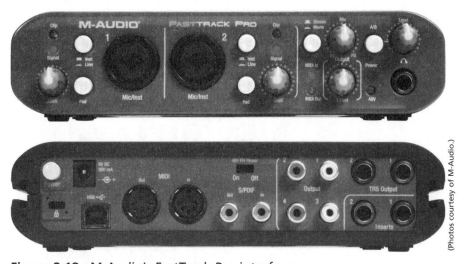

(Photos courtesy of M-Audio.)

Figure 3.18 M-Audio's FastTrack Pro interface.

FastTrack Ultra and Ultra 8R

The FastTrack Ultra (see Figure 3.19) is a USB 2.0-connecting audio/MIDI interface that features the ability to mix eight hardware inputs and eight software returns to eight hardware outputs,

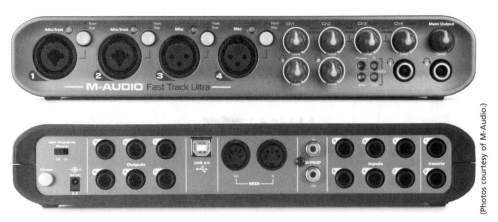

(Photos courtesy of M-Audio.)

Figure 3.19 The M-Audio FastTrack Ultra, featuring eight hardware inputs and outputs and the ability to record on eight tracks simultaneously.

allowing the user to record on eight channels simultaneously. With built-in effects processing for the headphone outputs, the unit can save some DSP processing that the computer host would otherwise handle. The FastTrack Ultra also allows the user to connect outboard gear and synthesizers to the hardware inputs, mixing those sources with a possible eight audio sources from the computer host to create a 16-input/8-output configuration. Inputs offered include six channels of 1/4-inch-jack analog ins and two-channel RCA-jack S/PDIF input. There are also four preamps with 48-volt phantom power included for use with the XLR microphone inputs. Outputs include six analog 1/4-inch jack outs and two-channel RCA-jack S/PDIF digital output. Also included are two analog 1/4-inch jack inserts, allowing the user to send the first two channels to outboard gear and return those channels' audio signals before the unit's analog-to-digital conversion stage. In addition, the unit provides two separate headphone mixes for cue feeds, corresponding to its two physical headphone outputs.

M-Audio also offers the FastTrack Ultra 8R (see Figure 3.20), a rackmount unit that adds an additional four preamps to the four included on the original Ultra.

(Photos courtesy of M-Audio.)

Figure 3.20 The M-Audio FastTrack Ultra 8R, featuring eight XLR/TRS combo jacks for mic or line-level inputs with preamps.

Transit

The Transit (shown in Figure 3.21) is another compact stereo audio interface. It has a stereo mini 1/8-inch connector that doubles as line/headphone output, a TOSLINK connector for S/PDIF optical output, plus a single input that doubles as a 1/8-inch stereo mini line/mic input or optical input (via a provided adapter). Ostensibly, 16- or 24-bit audio is supported at sample rates up to 96 kHz; however, due to the limitations of the USB 1.1 connection used by these units, high definition is possible when using the inputs or outputs *only*—not a practical option with Pro Tools.

(Photo courtesy of M-Audio.)

Figure 3.21   M-Audio's Transit interface.

PCI Card–Based Systems

The following M-Audio hardware systems use a PCI card installed in the host computer. In some cases, a breakout cable provides some or all of the actual audio connections, while in others an external box is connected directly to the PCI card. All of these PCI-based systems include M-Audio's Delta Control Panel software, which allows for level adjustments and signal routing between inputs and outputs on the hardware itself (for direct monitoring, for example). All of these interfaces are capable of either 24- or 16-bit operation.

> **Note**   All of the following units use PCI cards and are incompatible with the PCIe slots found on many modern computers, including all current Mac Pro models. As a result, these are not viable options for use with Pro Tools 9 or later on a Mac.

Audiophile 2496

The Audiophile 2496 audio card (shown in Figure 3.22) features two analog audio inputs and outputs with RCA jacks on the rear of the PCI card itself. Alternatively, stereo coaxial S/PDIF digital I/O with RCA jacks is available via a breakout cable that attaches to a 15-pin connector on the rear of the card, which also provides one MIDI input and output. As the name implies, the card supports 24-bit audio at sampling rates up to 96 kHz. The coaxial digital outputs are Dolby Digital 5.1 surround-sound capable (for sending out to an external decoder).

(Photo courtesy of M-Audio.)

Figure 3.22 M-Audio's Audiophile 2496 card has RCA jacks for analog I/O on the card, plus S/PDIF and MIDI I/O via a breakout cable.

Audiophile 192

The Audiophile 192 audio card (shown in Figure 3.23) features stereo coaxial S/PDIF digital I/O with RCA jacks on the rear of the PCI card itself. A breakout cable attaches to a 25-pin connector on the rear of the card. This cable provides TRS (1/4-inch phone, tip-ring-sleeve) jacks for analog audio I/O: two analog audio inputs, two main outputs, plus two dedicated monitor outputs. The monitor outputs can mirror the main output from Pro Tools (or another DAW program) and/or pass through signals from the inputs on the Audiophile 192 itself, whose levels are controlled by a software mixer in the included Delta Control Panel software. One MIDI input and output is also provided on the breakout cable. The Audiophile 192 supports 24-bit audio at sampling rates up to 192 kHz. The coaxial digital outputs are Dolby Digital 5.1 surround-sound capable (for sending out an external decoder) and offer a "professional" setting for running the AES/EBU protocol over the S/PDIF connection.

(Photo courtesy of M-Audio.)

Figure 3.23 M-Audio's Audiophile 192 card supports 4 × 4 operation when all analog and digital I/O is used.

Delta 44

The Delta 44 PCI card (shown in Figure 3.24) connects to an external audio interface called the Delta series breakout box, which provides all its audio and MIDI connections, via a cable with

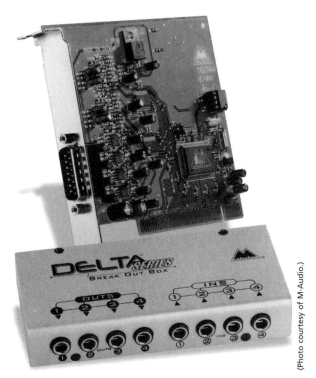

(Photo courtesy of M-Audio.)

Figure 3.24 M-Audio's Delta 44 card.

15-pin connectors. Four analog inputs and outputs use TRS (1/4-inch phone, tip-ring-sleeve) jacks and can be switched between –10 dBV and +4 dBu nominal levels via the included Delta Control Panel software. As with the other M-Audio interfaces listed here, the software allows for the routing of input audio signals directly to outputs on the interface as a workaround for latency issues when monitoring audio sources being recorded through the host program. No digital I/O is included with the Delta 44. It supports 24-bit audio at sampling rates up to 96 kHz.

Delta 66
The Delta 66 (shown in Figure 3.25) uses the same external breakout box and cable as the Delta 44 but expands I/O capability to six channels (four channels of analog I/O plus stereo coaxial jacks on the rear of the card for S/PDIF digital I/O). Other characteristics are similar to the Delta 44.

Delta 1010
The Delta 1010 (shown in Figure 3.26) consists of a PCI card that connects to an external, rack-mountable audio interface. This external rackmount converter unit provides all the analog audio, MIDI, and word-clock connections, while stereo coaxial S/PDIF digital I/O is available via coaxial jacks on the rear of the PCI card itself. The external audio interface provides eight channels of audio input via TRS (1/4-inch phone, tip-ring-sleeve) jacks, with individual switches for choosing –10 dBV or +4 dBu nominal levels independently on each input and output channel. Word-clock input and output on the rear of the interface provide for synchronizing the sample rate of the

(Photo courtesy of M-Audio.)

Figure 3.25 M-Audio's Delta 66 card adds S/PDIF digital I/O to the capabilities of the Delta 44.

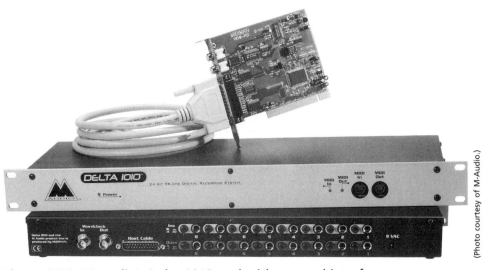

(Photo courtesy of M-Audio.)

Figure 3.26 M-Audio's Delta 1010 card with external interface.

Delta 1010 with external systems using 75-ohm coaxial cables with BNC connectors. One MIDI input and one MIDI output are provided on the front panel of the external audio interface. The Delta 1010 supports 24-bit audio at sampling rates up to 96 kHz.

Delta 1010LT
The Delta 1010LT (shown in Figure 3.27) consists of a PCI card with two breakout cables. The "analog" breakout cable attaches to a 25-pin connector and provides eight analog outputs with RCA jacks plus eight analog inputs. Six of the inputs have RCA jacks, while female XLR jacks

(Photo courtesy of M-Audio.)

Figure 3.27   M-Audio's Delta 1010LT card with breakout cables.

on Channels 1 and 2 can be switched between microphone or line levels via a jumper on the PCI card itself (not accessible from outside the computer). The "digital" breakout cable attaches to a 15-pin connector and provides stereo coaxial S/PDIF digital I/O with RCA jacks, one MIDI input and output, plus a word clock input and output (for synchronizing sample rates between the Delta 1010LT and external systems, using 75-ohm coaxial cables with BNC connectors). Using the eight analog and two digital channels simultaneously, a maximum of 10 channels of I/O is available on the Delta 1010LT.

Keyboard and Synthesizer-Based Systems

M-Audio also offers several keyboard controller and synthesizer models that function as audio/ MIDI interfaces for Pro Tools. Following are a few examples.

KeyStudio 49i

The KeyStudio 49i (shown in Figure 3.28) is a USB keyboard controller with a built-in audio interface and premium onboard piano sound. The unit provides a 2-in, 2-out audio interface featuring 16-bit, 44.1-kHz audio; an XLR microphone input, 1/4-instrument input, and RCA inputs; 1/4-inch jacks for stereo line output; dual front-mounted headphone jacks; and hardware direct monitoring for zero-latency recording.

(Photo courtesy of M-Audio.)

Figure 3.28   M-Audio's KeyStudio 49i.

ProKeys Sono 61

The ProKeys Sono 61 (shown in Figure 3.29) is a 61-key digital piano with a built-in audio interface. Featuring semi-weighted, velocity-sensitive keys, advanced scanning technology, and a stereo-sampled Steinway grand sound, the unit also provides instant access to high-quality electric piano, organ, and clav instruments. The USB audio interface lets you record your keyboard performance, plus vocals and instruments, directly to Pro Tools. The 2-in/2-out audio interface provides 16-bit/44.1-kHz audio. Like the KeyStudio 49i, it includes an XLR microphone input, a 1/4-inch instrument input, and RCA inputs; 1/4-inch jacks for stereo line output; dual front-mounted headphone jacks; and hardware direct monitoring for zero-latency recording.

(Photo courtesy of M-Audio.)

Figure 3.29 M-Audio's ProKeys Sono 61.

ProKeys Sono 88

The ProKeys Sono 88 (shown in Figure 3.30) is a larger version of the Sono 61, featuring an 88-note semi-weighted, velocity-sensitive keyboard with built-in audio interface. Onboard sounds include a stereo-sampled Steinway premium piano and high-quality electric piano, organ, clav, strings, and choir instruments. The USB audio interface has the same features as on the ProKeys Sono 61.

(Photo courtesy of M-Audio.)

Figure 3.30 M-Audio's ProKeys Sono 88.

Venom

The M-Audio Venom (shown in Figure 3.31) is a 49-key synthesizer that combines the character of classic analog synths with modern digital processing and a built-in Pro Tools-compatible USB audio/MIDI interface. Microphone, line, and stereo line inputs let you record vocals, guitar, and other instruments directly into Pro Tools.

Venom provides a 2-in/2-out audio interface supporting 24-bit, 44.1-kHz audio. The unit includes mic, instrument, and stereo line-level inputs; 1/4-inch stereo main audio outputs; a 1/4-inch stereo headphone output; a master volume knob; and instrument and mic gain knobs. It also provides MIDI In and MIDI Out ports.

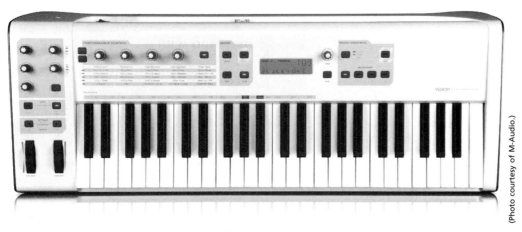

(Photo courtesy of M-Audio.)

Figure 3.31 M-Audio's Venom synthesizer.

A Comparison of M-Audio Interfaces for Pro Tools

With so many interface choices from M-Audio, you can see why it is worth the time to investigate all their technical characteristics on the Avid website. Table 3.2 summarizes how these interfaces connect to the host computer, and the number and type of audio inputs/outputs each of them provides.

Pro Tools|HD Hardware

Pro Tools 10 systems with Pro Tools|HD hardware support recording of up to 32-bit floating-point audio at sample rates up to 192 kHz. Pro Tools|HD 1, the basic Pro Tools|HD system, consists of a Core card in the host computer (either an HD Core card for computers with PCI slots or an Accel Core card for computers with PCIe slots), cabled to up to two external HD-series audio interfaces (see Figure 3.32). This configuration supports up to 32 channels of I/O (with the appropriate audio interfaces). Pro Tools|HD 2 systems add the HD Accel card (available in both PCIe and PCI versions) for increased mixing and processing power. Adding this second card allows the system to support up to 64 channels of I/O with up to four audio interfaces. (Each HD Accel card supports 32 channels of I/O.) Pro Tools|HD 3 systems have two HD Accel cards, in addition to the Core card (providing up to 96 channels of I/O). You can expand the processing power and I/O capacity of a Pro Tools|HD system by adding more HD Accel cards. A system with five or more cards, which requires an expansion chassis attached to the host computer, would support the maximum Pro Tools|HD capacity of 160 audio I/O channels.

Pro Tools HD Software   Prior to version 7, the Pro Tools software that supported TDM hardware and plug-ins was known as Pro Tools TDM. This term was used for the first Pro Tools|HD systems with Pro Tools 6.*xx* software, as well as 24 MIX and various other predecessors that supported the TDM plug-in architecture. Since version 7, the software itself has been called Pro Tools HD (while hardware configurations include Pro Tools|HD Native, Pro Tools|HD, and Pro Tools|HDX). The plug-in architecture supported by Pro

ToolslHD hardware is still commonly called TDM, however. Currently shipping versions of TDM plug-ins operate on Pro ToolslHD systems only. (Pro Tools HD software also supports RTAS plug-ins and Native AAX plug-ins, as does standard Pro Tools software.) Native plug-ins (including RTAS) rely on the CPU's processing power rather than on the DSP chips available on HD or HDX cards.

When running on Pro ToolslHD Native hardware, Pro Tools HD 10 runs as host-based software and cannot utilize any DSP plug-ins, either in TDM or AAX format. When running on Pro ToolslHDX hardware, Pro Tools does support DSP plug-ins, but only in the AAX format.

Table 3.2 M-Audio Interfaces: I/O Channels

Model	Connection	Input Channels Analog/S/PDIF/ADAT	Output Channels Analog/S/PDIF/ADAT
FireWire Solo	FireWire	4/2/–	2/2/–
ProFire 2626	FireWire	8/2/16	8/2/16
ProFire610	FireWire	4/2/–	8/2/–
ProjectMix I/O	FireWire	8/2/8	4/2/8
ProFire Lightbridge	FireWire	–/2/32	2/2/32
NRV10	FireWire	8/–/–	2/–/–
MobilePre USB	USB	2/–/–	2/–/–
FastTrack USB	USB	2/–/–	2/–/–
FastTrack Pro	USB	2/2/–	4/2/–
FastTrack Ultra 8R	USB	8/2/–	8/2/–
Transit	USB	2/2/–	2/2/–
Audiophile 2496	PCI*	2/2/–	2/2/–
Audiophile 192	PCI*	2/2/–	4/2/–
Delta 44	PCI*	4/–/–	4/–/–
Delta 66	PCI*	4/2/–	4/2/–
Delta 1010	PCI*	8/2/–	8/2/–
Delta 1010LT	PCI*	8/2/–	8/2/–
KeyStudio 49i	USB	2/–/–	2/–/–
ProKeys Sono 61	USB	2/–/–	2/–/–
ProKeys Sono 88	USB	2/–/–	2/–/–
Venom	USB	2/–/–	2/–/–

* Not compatible with current Mac Pro models or other computers featuring PCIe slots.

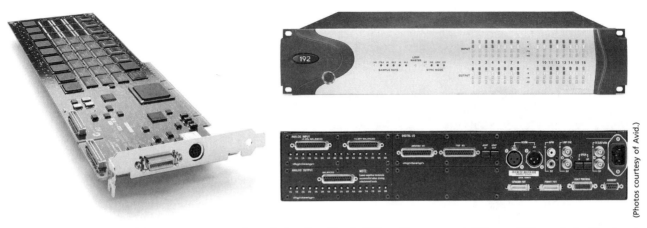

(Photos courtesy of Avid.)

Figure 3.32   Pro Tools|HD systems consist of the Pro Tools HD software and PCIe or PCI cards in the host computer, plus separately purchased multichannel audio interfaces attached to those cards.

PCIe Cards for Pro Tools|HD Systems   Avid offers PCIe card configurations for Pro Tools|HD on current computers with PCIe slots—the Macintosh G5 Quad and all Intel-based Mac Pro models, for example. PCI/PCI-X cards for Pro Tools|HD are not directly compatible with this newer slot format. However, PCI/PCI-X cards can be used in an expansion chassis, which connects to the host computer via a single PCIe card.

Pro Tools|HD Native Hardware

Pro Tools 10 systems with Pro Tools|HD Native hardware support recording of up to 32-bit floating-point audio at sample rates up to 192 kHz. Pro Tools|HD Native systems consist of an HD Native PCIe card in the host computer (see Figure 3.33) cabled to up to four external HD-series audio interfaces. This configuration supports up to 64 channels of I/O (with the appropriate audio interfaces). Pro Tools|HD Native systems are not expandable beyond the single card and connected interfaces.

Pro Tools|HD Native supports Pro Tools HD 10 software. The high-speed PCIe core card significantly improves monitoring while recording, virtually eliminating latency.

Pro Tools|HDX Hardware

Pro Tools HD 10 systems with Pro Tools|HDX hardware support recording of up to 32-bit floating-point audio at sample rates up to 192 kHz. Pro Tools HD systems with HDX acceleration consist of one or more HDX PCIe cards installed in the host computer (see Figure 3.34) cabled to up to four external HD-series audio interfaces each. This configuration supports up to 192 channels of I/O (with the appropriate audio interfaces).

(Photo courtesy of Avid.)

Figure 3.33   Pro Tools|HD Native card.

(Photo courtesy of Avid.)

Figure 3.34   Pro Tools|HDX card.

Pro Tools|HDX hardware supports Pro Tools HD 10 software as well as Core Audio (Mac) or ASIO (Windows) compatible third-party software (such as Logic, Live, or Cubase).

HD-Series Interfaces

Various audio interfaces can be added to expand Pro Tools|HD and HD Native systems, including the HD OMNI, HD I/O, and HD MADI, and the discontinued 192 I/O, 192 Digital I/O, 96i

I/O, and 96 I/O. Older systems often include interfaces from the 24 MIX hardware family, connected to the legacy ports on a 192 I/O or 96 I/O audio interface.

Pro Tools|HD and HD Native systems use DigiLink cabling, allowing audio interfaces to be connected to cards in the host computer at a distance as great as 100 feet. (Fifty-foot cable lengths are the limit for operation at sample rates higher than 96 kHz.)

HD OMNI

HD OMNI (shown in Figure 3.35) is a digital audio interface that features four channels of analog input, eight channels of analog output, 24-bit converters, and sample rates up to 192 kHz. HD OMNI provides a compact preamp, monitoring, and I/O solution for music production and post-production studios.

Only one HD OMNI can be connected to a Pro Tools system at any time.

(Photo courtesy of Avid.)

Figure 3.35 Avid HD OMNI audio interface.

HD I/O

HD I/O (shown in Figure 3.36) is a multichannel digital audio interface, available in one of three standard configurations:

- 8 × 8 × 8 (8 analog in, 8 analog out, and 8 digital in and out)
- 16 × 16 analog in and out
- 16 × 16 digital in and out

HD I/O features 24-bit converters and supports sample rates of up to 192 kHz.

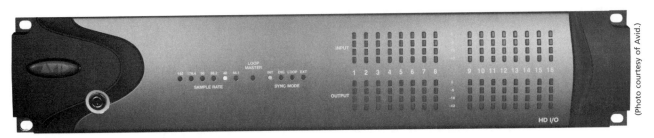

(Photo courtesy of Avid.)

Figure 3.36 Avid HD I/O audio interface.

HD MADI

HD MADI (shown in Figure 3.37) is a 64-channel digital audio interface that supports the Multichannel Audio Digital Interface (MADI) format and sample rates of up to 192 kHz.

(Photo courtesy of Avid.)

Figure 3.37 Avid HD MADI audio interface

HD MADI provides simplified connectivity between a Pro Tools|HD or HD Native system and MADI-compatible audio equipment, such as routers, digital mixing consoles, VENUE systems (with the MADI option), and converters.

Pro Tools|HD Cards vs. Pro Tools|HDX Cards   Pro Tools configurations with HD-series cards require a minimum of a single Core card (Pro Tools|HD 1). Expanded systems include one or more HD Accel cards, in addition to the Core card. Each card (Core or HD Accel) provides up to 96 tracks of simultaneous audio recording or playback (up to a maximum of 192 tracks with two or more cards), as well as 32 channels of I/O to the system (up to a maximum of 160 channels with five or more cards).

Pro Tools configurations with Pro Tools|HDX hardware acceleration represent a quantum leap forward for top-tier Pro Tools systems. These configurations require one or more HDX PCIe cards. Each HDX card provides up to 256 tracks of simultaneous audio recording or playback (up to a maximum of 768 tracks with three cards), as well as 64 channels of I/O to the system (up to a maximum of 192 channels with three cards).

Older PT Configurations

The 003 and Mbox 2 family interfaces (both now discontinued) remain compatible with current versions of Pro Tools. However, before upgrading beyond Pro Tools 10, be sure to check compatibility on www.avid.com, as technology changes have been known to break compatibility. The same goes for upgrading to a new operating system—confirm that your software, hardware, and essential plug-ins will still work before you upgrade!

Some previous incarnations of Pro Tools hardware continue to be viable options for many users, even though they don't support current versions of the Pro Tools software. Some of these legacy hardware configurations offer excellent audio specs and remain quite functional today. Repurposing this legacy hardware may be an excellent way to make use of an older Macintosh model that would otherwise be considered out of date. For recording voice-overs, beat mixing in your project studio, and other simple tasks, this can be an extremely cost-effective way to get into the game or have a second workstation in your facility. Be aware, however, that third-party plug-ins for older generations of Pro Tools software may no longer be available or supported by the manufacturer.

Mbox 2 Family

The Mbox 2 family—the Mbox 2, Mbox 2 Mini, Mbox 2 Micro, and Mbox 2 Pro—represents the previous generation of today's Pro Tools Mbox family (described earlier in this chapter). These interfaces support audio recording at 16- or 24-bit resolution (except for the Mbox 2 Micro, which has no audio inputs). Sample rates of 44.1 or 48 kHz are supported by all interfaces within the Mbox 2 family, while the Mbox 2 Pro supports additional sample rates up to 96 kHz. Bandwidth limitations of the USB connection itself—version 1.1, in the case of the Mbox 2—preclude 96 kHz and other higher sample rates on USB interfaces for Pro Tools.

Mbox 2

The Mbox 2 (shown in Figure 3.38) is an external USB audio/MIDI interface with two simultaneous channels of analog I/O, plus two more channels of digital input (S/PDIF jacks) that can be used simultaneously for 4 × 2 operation. It also incorporates one MIDI input and output. The analog inputs incorporate microphone preamps with 48-volt phantom power that is enabled/disabled via a button on the front of the unit. Except for the 1/4-inch headphone output, all audio connections are on the rear panel. Separate XLR, TRS (1/4-inch) balanced, and TS instrument-level jacks are provided for each of the two analog input channels. Buttons for each input channel toggle between the mic, line, and direct inputs. The main studio monitor outputs on the rear panel are also balanced 1/4-inch TRS. S/PDIF digital in/out is provided via coaxial RCA jacks. Front-panel gain knobs are provided for the headphone output and main monitor output. The mix knob on the Mbox 2 adjusts the relative levels between the interface's input and playback from Pro Tools (a workaround for low-latency monitoring during recording). The unit is exclusively powered by the USB connection itself; no AC power is required.

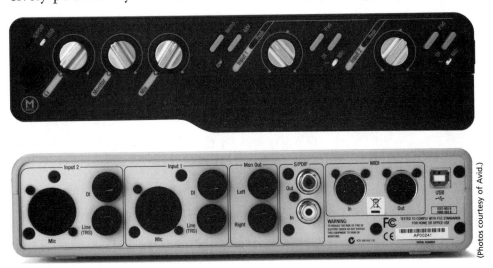

(Photos courtesy of Avid.)

Figure 3.38   Mbox 2 external USB audio/MIDI interface.

Mbox 2 Mini (USB)

The Mbox 2 Mini (shown in Figure 3.39) is a simpler external USB audio interface, offering only two channels of analog I/O. Input 1 offers both XLR (microphone) and 1/4-inch phone jacks, while Input 2 offers 1/4-inch phone only. The stereo monitor analog outputs also use 1/4-inch

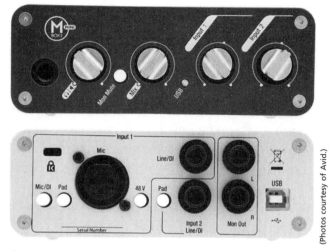

(Photos courtesy of Avid.)

Figure 3.39 Mbox 2 Mini USB audio interface.

jacks. Except for the XLR microphone input, all the audio jacks use unbalanced 1/4-inch phone (TS) connections. There are no inputs for digital audio or MIDI on this interface. Like the Mbox 2, the Mini is powered via the USB connection to the computer and provides a single 1/4-inch headphone output on its front panel. A single output level knob affects both the monitor output and headphone levels. (The Mbox 2 has dedicated level knobs for each of these.)

Mbox 2 Micro

The Mbox 2 Micro (shown in Figure 3.40) is a very small audio interface (small enough to fit on a key ring), offering only a single stereo output with an 1/8-inch TRS jack. There are no audio inputs on the Mbox 2 Micro. It is powered via the USB connection to the computer; an LED on the unit indicates when this power is active. A volume dial is provided for the analog stereo output jack, which can be used for either headphone or line-out connections. Sample rates of 44.1 and 48 kHz are supported at 16- or 24-bit depths. This interface was designed as an option for users who like to edit or mix on the go with a laptop. With the release of Pro Tools 9, however, this interface became all but irrelevant, since the software will now run without an audio interface, using the Aggregate I/O option on the Mac (or the ASIO4ALL option on compatible Windows systems; see asio4all.com for details).

(Photo courtesy of Avid.)

Figure 3.40 The Mbox 2 Micro interface (output only).

Mbox 2 Pro

The Mbox 2 Pro (shown in Figure 3.41) is an external audio/MIDI interface connected to the host computer via a FireWire cable. It can be powered directly via the FireWire connection to the computer or by an AC power cable. The Mbox 2 Pro supports sample rates up to 96 kHz. Four analog inputs are provided on the rear panel: mic/line inputs 1–2 use combo jacks (compatible with both XLR and 1/4-inch phone), while Aux In line inputs 3–4 use balanced TRS (1/4-inch phone, TRS) jacks. As a nice bonus, the Mbox 2 Pro includes a built-in phono preamp with RCA jacks for connecting a turntable. In addition to these inputs, two front-panel DI inputs for Channels 1–2 with 1/4-inch phone jacks (TS) are included for direct connection of electric guitars, basses, and similar instruments. Another bonus feature on the Mbox 2 Pro are the included BNC connectors for word clock input/output to facilitate hardware-level synchronization with other audio and video equipment. The Mbox 2 Pro features two front-panel headphone outputs, each with a dedicated volume control. Two dedicated monitor outputs on the rear panel correspond to outputs 1–2 from Pro Tools, and use unbalanced 1/4-inch TS jacks. In addition to this, line outputs 1–4 provide balanced 1/4-inch TRS jacks, and line outputs 5–6 share a single (unbalanced) stereo TRS jack. S/PDIF digital I/O is provided via coaxial RCA jacks.

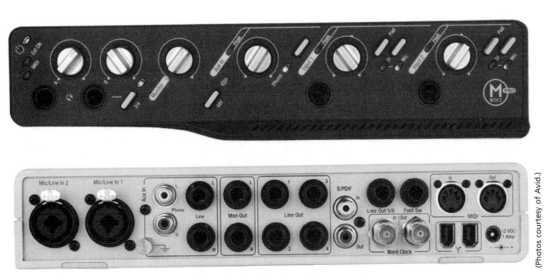

(Photos courtesy of Avid.)

Figure 3.41 The Mbox 2 Pro FireWire audio interface.

First-Generation Mbox (for Pro Tools LE)

This predecessor to the Mbox 2 was discontinued in the fall of 2005 and is no longer compatible with Pro Tools, as of version 9. The original Mbox (shown in Figure 3.42) was an external USB audio interface manufactured by Digidesign with up to two simultaneous channels of analog or digital I/O. The interface featured 24-bit analog/digital converters, Focusrite microphone preamps with 48-volt phantom power, and balanced I/O using combo connectors (compatible with both XLR and 1/4-inch phone) from Neutrik. Unlike the subsequent Mbox 2 model, 1/4-inch TRS analog insert jacks were provided for patching in a processor, such as compressor/limiter, prior

Figure 3.42 The Digidesign Mbox (discontinued).

to the Pro Tools recording input. S/PDIF digital in/out was supported via coaxial RCA jacks. Buttons on the front panel toggled either channel among mic, line, and instrument level (Hi-Z, high impedance, for direct connection from electric guitar or bass). The Mbox included front and rear headphone jacks, plus a mono switch. Front-panel knobs allowed adjustment of input gain, adjustment of the balance between input and playback to ameliorate monitoring latency while recording, and control of the output level for the headphone jacks. Mbox users running Pro Tools LE 8 or earlier can record at 16- or 24-bit resolution, and at 44.1- or 48-kHz sample rates.

Caution: Use the USB Cable That Came with Your Mbox!   The USB cable supplied with the Mbox incorporates a cylindrical ferrite *choke* to eliminate RF interference. If you substitute some other USB cable (regardless of whether it has a choke or is advertised as very high quality, shielded, and so on), you will probably hear a high-pitched whining from the Mbox's outputs (not unlike the sound of SMPTE time code, but higher pitched). The same thing will occur if you try to use a USB extender cable to increase the distance between the Mbox and the host computer. Although this noise is strictly on the outputs and doesn't end up in any mix files you bounce to disk, it can be quite annoying, especially in headphones.

---

003 Family

Although discontinued, the 003 family (the 003, the 003 Rack, and the 003 Rack+) is still supported in Pro Tools 10. As successors to the Digi 002 product line, this product line continued the tradition of providing more robust I/O options for Pro Tools LE users.

003

The 003 (shown in Figure 3.43) is an external audio interface for Pro Tools that connects to the computer via a FireWire connection. It incorporates a control surface, offering motorized faders, Transport controls, and many other dedicated functions for Pro Tools software.

(Photos courtesy of Avid.)

Figure 3.43   The 003 interface for Pro Tools.

The 003 offers eight analog inputs. Individual mic/DI switches on the front panel select the source for inputs 1–4 as either the balanced 1/4-inch TRS jacks for line levels or XLR connectors for built-in microphone preamps. (The microphone preamps also have switchable 48-volt phantom power, as well as a 75-Hz high-pass filter switch for reducing low-frequency noise.) Inputs

5–8 offer balanced 1/4-inch TRS jacks for line-level sources with enough gain to accommodate instrument-level sources. There are also eight analog outputs, each with balanced, 1/4-inch TRS jacks. Additionally, the main and alternate monitor outputs are controlled by a single level control and mirror outputs 1–2 from Pro Tools. These output pairs also provide balanced, 1/4-inch TRS jacks for each channel.

TOSLINK connectors are provided for ADAT Lightpipe digital I/O (up to eight channels of digital audio, alternatively configurable as stereo optical S/PDIF). RCA jacks support stereo coaxial S/PDIF digital I/O. BNC connectors are provided for word-clock connections in order to synchronize the unit's internal sample clock with other digital devices in your studio configuration.

Like its predecessor, the Digi 002, the 003 provides one MIDI input, two MIDI outputs, and a footswitch connector for controlling playback or record punch in and out. Two stereo headphone outputs are included on the front panel with separate level controls. Headphone 1 mirrors the output of main outputs 1–2, while a front-panel switch allows monitor outputs 3–4 to be selected as the signal source for the Headphone 2 output.

The control surface offers a two-row LCD display strip across the top for displaying track information or edit parameters during operation. Each main mixer strip offers a 100mm motorized touch-sensitive fader, a rotary encoder, dedicated solo and mute buttons, plus a Channel Select button. A global flip switch allows you to swap the functions of the faders and rotary encoders on all mixer strips. Dedicated buttons are included for automation modes and modifier keys (Shift/Command/Option/Control on Mac or Shift/Ctrl/Alt/Start on Windows). There are also various dedicated buttons for frequently accessed functions such as Save, Undo, and Enter, as well as for toggling between the Mix, Edit, and Plug-In windows. A Transport section offers dedicated buttons, plus dual-concentric jog/shuttle wheels.

003 Rack and 003 Rack+

The 003 Rack (shown in Figure 3.44) offers all the same connections and audio specifications as the 003, but without the control surface. The 003 Rack+ provides essentially the same functionality, enhanced with four additional XLR connectors with microphone preamps on the analog inputs, for a total of eight (all with 48-volt phantom power) and one MIDI I/O.

Digi 002 Family

The Digi 002 (shown in Figure 3.45) was the first audio interface/control surface combo unit available for Pro Tools LE. It connected to the host computer via its FireWire port. Though discontinued in 2006, it remains compatible with Pro Tools software through version 10. The Digi 002 hardware features eight analog inputs and outputs, ADAT Lightpipe digital I/O (also configurable as stereo optical S/PDIF), plus stereo coaxial S/PDIF digital I/O with RCA jacks. XLR jacks and microphone preamps with individual gain controls, 75-Hz high-pass filters, and 48-volt phantom power are provided for the first four input channels, as well as balanced TRS jacks for line/instrument-level inputs. Front-panel switches for these channels allow you to select between the inputs. The TRS inputs for Channels 5–8 can be switched between –10dBV and

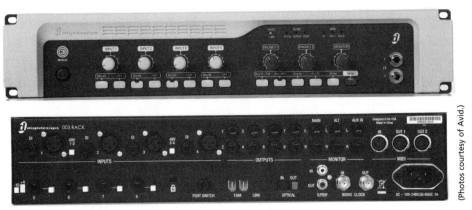

Figure 3.44 The 003 Rack interface for Pro Tools.

Figure 3.45 The Digi 002 interface for Pro Tools (discontinued).

+4dBu level. The Digi 002 offers one MIDI input and two MIDI output ports. There is a front-panel headphone jack, a dedicated monitor output with TRS jacks, and a dedicated volume control, plus a fixed-level output (with RCA jacks at –10dBV level). The interface supports 16-bit or 24-bit recording at sample rates up to 96 kHz.

The Digi 002 control surface includes eight channel strips with motorized 100mm faders and solo/mute buttons; eight soft rotary encoders (for controlling panning, sends, and plug-in parameters, among other things); LED-based display strips; Transport controls for Pro Tools; and trim controls for the four microphone preamps. There are also a number of other dedicated buttons for Pro Tools functions.

Digi 002 can be used without a computer (or Pro Tools) as a standalone 8 × 4 × 2 digital mixer complete with EQ, dynamics, delay, and reverb effects, plus the ability to store and recall mix snapshots from its built-in memory.

The Digi 002 Rack (shown in Figure 3.46) offers the same features as the Digi 002, but without the control surface in a rack-mountable chassis. It's useful for mobile recording racks or for users who generally prefer to create mix automation graphically or by moving onscreen controls in Pro Tools with the mouse.

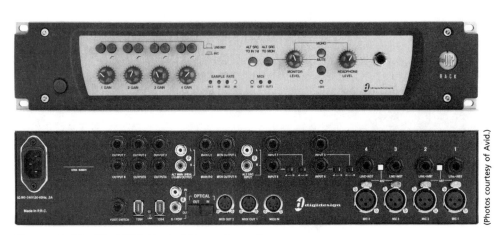

(Photos courtesy of Avid.)

Figure 3.46   Digi 002 Rack (discontinued).

Digi 001 (Pro Tools LE and Digi 001 Card, External Audio Interface)

The long-discontinued Pro Tools Digi 001 configuration (see Figure 3.47) included the Pro Tools LE software, the Digi 001 PCI card and cable, plus the Digi 001 I/O, a rack-mountable external audio interface. This hardware is no longer compatible with Pro Tools (on any version higher than Pro Tools 6.4.1) and cannot be installed in any G5 or Intel-based Macintosh computer. The Digi 001 I/O featured eight analog inputs and outputs, ADAT Lightpipe digital I/O (up to eight more channels and also configurable as stereo optical S/PDIF), stereo S/PDIF coaxial digital I/O (with RCA jacks), two microphone preamps with 48-volt phantom power, one MIDI input and one MIDI output, plus a headphone output. All inputs/outputs could be used simultaneously, for 18 channels of I/O.

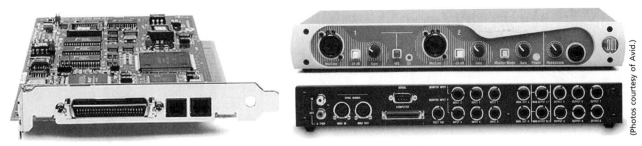

(Photos courtesy of Avid.)

Figure 3.47   Pro Tools Digi 001 interface and PCI card (discontinued).

Digi 001 was a revolutionary product, offering good specs at a very economical price. For recording a band or for multiple microphones in live theatre, Digi 001 provided a reasonable number of simultaneous recording channels (especially when using the ADAT Lightpipe and S/PDIF digital inputs). As an excellent all-in-one solution, the Digi 001 broke important ground in the evolution of digital audio workstations, combining the audio I/O, MIDI interface, and two moderate-quality microphone preamplifiers into a single rack-mounted interface. Combined with a high-quality mic preamp, the Digi 001 could produce very good-sounding results!

Previous-Generation HD Interfaces

Though discontinued, the original HD-series interfaces remain compatible with Pro Tools HD 10 software. The most popular of the original HD-series interfaces were the 192 I/O and 96 I/O; variations on each of these were also available, in the form of the 192 Digital I/O and 96i I/O.

192 I/O and 192 Digital I/O

The 192 I/O (shown in Figure 3.48) offers 16 discrete channels of input and output at sample rates up to 192 kHz. The I/O can be configured in the Hardware Setup dialog box to include 16 channels from the following I/O options:

- Eight channels of analog I/O from the analog card

- Eight channels of ADAT Optical I/O from the enclosure

- Two channels of AES/EBU, S/PDIF, or Optical (S/PDIF) from the enclosure

- One of the following formats from the digital card:
  - Eight channels of AES/EBU digital I/O
  - Eight channels of TDIF digital I/O
  - Eight channels of ADAT Optical I/O

The 192 Digital I/O offers up to 16 channels of AES/EBU digital I/O.

The ADAT and TDIF options on the 192 I/O and 192 Digital I/O support a maximum sample rate 48 kHz, whereas the AES/EBU options support sample rates up to 96 kHz at their maximum I/O capacities and up to 192 kHz with reduced I/O capacities.

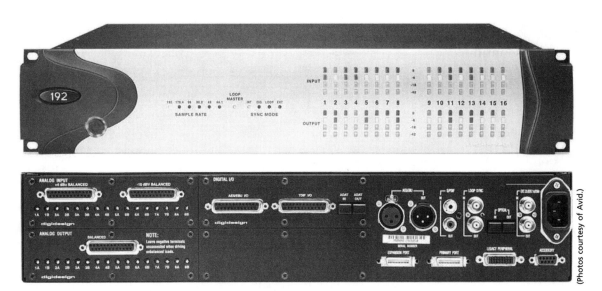

Figure 3.48   192 I/O audio interface (discontinued).

96 I/O and 96i I/O

The 96 I/O (shown in Figure 3.49) offers 16 discrete channels of input and output at sample rates up to 96 kHz. The I/O can be configured in the Hardware Setup dialog box to include 16 channels from the following I/O options:

- Eight channels of analog I/O from 1/4-inch TRS jacks
- Eight channels of ADAT Optical I/O from the enclosure
- Two channels of AES/EBU, S/PDIF, or Optical (S/PDIF) from the enclosure

The 96i I/O offers 16 discrete channels of input and 2 channels of output for use with MIDI sound modules, samplers, synthesizers, and other sound sources. The I/O can be configured from the 16 channels of analog I/O (1/4-inch TRS jacks) and 2 channels of S/PDIF I/O (coaxial RCA jacks).

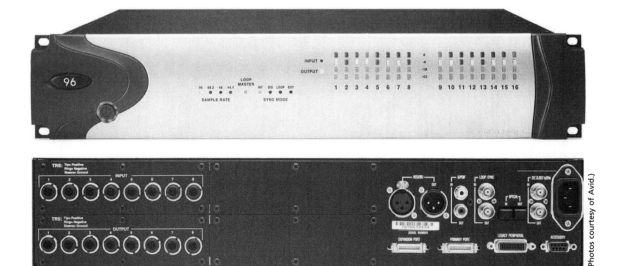

Figure 3.49   96 I/O audio interface (discontinued).

Pro Tools\24 MIX, Pro Tools\24 MIXplus, Pro Tools\24 MIX³ (TDM)

Digidesign's legacy (discontinued) high-end systems for professional applications use MIX hardware, which is no longer supported by Pro Tools software (since version 6.4.1). As shown in Figure 3.50, the basic Pro Tools\24 MIX system consisted of Pro Tools TDM software, a Mix Core PCI card, and one or more compatible external audio interfaces. MIX systems supported multiple audio interfaces (up to 16 channels of I/O per Mix Core or Mix Farm card). A MIXplus configuration added a second Mix Farm card with additional DSP chips for more powerful signal routing and processing within the Pro Tools TDM architecture. The MIX³ system bundled two additional Mix Farm cards with the Mix Core card. Each additional Mix Farm card allowed additional audio interfaces to be connected, providing up to 16 channels of additional I/O as well as increased voice count. The TDM version of the Pro Tools software (5.*xx* through 6.*xx* versions), supported AudioSuite, RTAS, and TDM plug-in architectures, as well as HTDM plug-ins. The older HTDM plug-in format is no longer supported in Pro Tools; where possible, these plug-ins are converted to RTAS plug-ins when an older TDM session is opened.

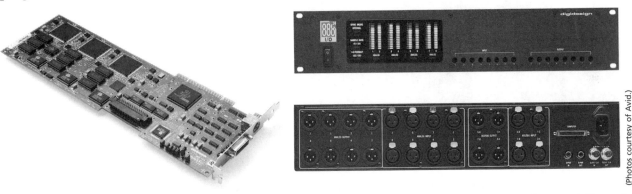

(Photos courtesy of Avid.)

Figure 3.50 Pro Tools\24 MIX systems (discontinued) consisted of the Pro Tools TDM software, PCI cards in the host computer, plus separately purchased external multichannel audio interfaces.

Although no longer manufactured, the Pro Tools\24 MIX product line can still be found in music and post-production facilities. Note, however, that the PCI audio cards used in MIX systems are incompatible with subsequent G5 and Intel-based Macintosh models.

Automatic Delay Compensation for plug-in processing and routing latency is not supported by 24 MIX systems, nor are the D-Control and D-Command control surfaces. Also, availability and support for third-party plug-ins that are compatible with this older generation of the Pro Tools software and hardware is extremely limited.

G5 Compatibility (Macintosh Versions)   Due to changes in how card voltages are supported by the PCI bus in these models, many of the discontinued Pro Tools hardware systems—including 24 MIX (the Mix I/O, Mix Farm, and DSP Farm cards), Digi 001, ToolBox (Audiomedia III card), and d24 card used by Pro Tools\24 systems—are incompatible with Macintosh G5 computers and their Intel-based successors. None of these older hardware options is compatible with Pro Tools 7 or later.

---

iLok USB Smart Key

The original iLok USB Smart Key and the newer, second-generation iLok key (see Figure 3.51) are USB hardware devices used for authorizing various programs and plug-ins on both Windows and Macintosh computers. An iLok key is required to authorize current Pro Tools software as well as many of the plug-ins used with Pro Tools. The keys are manufactured by PACE Anti-Piracy, which also developed the authorization diskette copy-protection mechanism used by many previous versions of Pro Tools and other audio/MIDI programs. An iLok key is also included with new Pro Tools purchases and must be attached to the host computer in order for the program to run. The iLok's important innovation is its ability to store authorizations for multiple programs and plug-ins, even from different developers.

Figure 3.51 A single iLok USB Smart Key stores authorizations for multiple programs and plug-ins.

iLok owners need to register for a free account at www.ilok.com to download any new licenses. With an active iLok account, you can purchase plug-ins online, and if the iLok is attached, it can be authorized for the plug-in as part of the purchase process. Typically, the plug-in vendor will deposit the license to your iLok account; from there, you download it into your iLok. Authorizations can be obtained by connecting the iLok to any computer that has access to the Internet and has the iLok Client Software installed, whether it has Pro Tools hardware attached or not.

Some older authorizations required a license card (included with certain plug-in software purchases). These used a small GSM plastic chip—a cutout that you would remove from the larger protective card. During the authorization process, you would insert the license card into a slot in the end of the iLok USB Smart Key.

The drivers that iLok requires may automatically be installed with your Pro Tools software. However, you may need to download new drivers from ilok.com before you are able to copy your authorizations to your iLok key, as the drivers are updated periodically. Whenever plug-ins are found that haven't been authorized yet, upon launch, a Pro Tools dialog box will prompt you to click the Authorization button to begin the process.

The advantage of the iLok system is the portability of your software authorizations. Consider how authorizations were performed prior to the iLok key. First, you would install the software (from a CD or, in the early days, from multiple diskettes). Upon launching the software, you would be prompted to insert a separate authorization diskette. The authorization routine would install invisible key files somewhere on your hard disk that enabled the program to run, and the authorization diskette would be disabled for further authorizations. Later, if you needed to install the software on a new disk or machine, you would need to de-authorize the program on the original machine, which removed the invisible key files and re-enabled the original key diskette. If your hard disk crashed—or you reformatted without remembering to de-authorize all the necessary programs and/or plug-ins—you would lose that authorization forever. Rewriting authorizations to the diskette also increased the probability that it would eventually fail. Add to that the potential for spending hours on the authorization process, depending on how much software you were dealing with. Clearly, this was not an ideal solution.

Conventional dongles—hardware authorization devices that are specific to a single program—also work pretty well. Like the iLok, they let you reformat and restore the contents of your hard disk without worrying about invisible key files or authorizations, move up to a new machine by simply transferring the dongle to the new software installation, and so on. Obviously, losing or breaking your dongle could be a real crisis—but this is equally a concern with the iLok system. The Zero Downtime coverage offered on iLok.com for a moderate yearly charge provides immediate, time-limited replacement authorizations of your licenses should your iLok get damaged, lost, or stolen. (Full authorizations require returning the iLok to Pace for inspection.) This coverage option is highly recommended for all professional applications.

Traditionally, one of the problems with dongles has been that dongles from certain programs can be incompatible with others—this was especially true back in the days of SCSI and parallel port dongles. But with the iLok, the same shared programmable device can store licenses for hundreds of different programs and plug-ins. You can back up your software and do a low-level reformat on your system disks, reload the programs, and then simply reattach the iLok key to get back to work with your previously authorized plug-ins. That's the attraction of the iLok system, and it has been overwhelmingly accepted by plug-in developers in the Pro Tools arena.

Control Surfaces for Pro Tools

Many users find that a mouse or trackball and keyboard are all they need to work with Pro Tools. Nevertheless, a physical control surface has its advantages. Among other things, having dedicated faders and switches that you can actually feel under your fingers can be a productivity enhancement when you're interacting with musicians in the studio or mixing long sequences for film and video. Also, being able to move multiple faders simultaneously is a must for intuitive, seat-of-your-pants mixing. It all comes down to your personal preference and the kind of work you do. Appendix B, "Add-Ons, Extensions, and Cool Stuff for Your Rig," addresses the subject of external control surfaces, including those from Avid and other manufacturers, such as Mackie, CM Labs, and other third parties. Following is a brief summary of the current offerings from Avid.

Command|8 (Discontinued)

Command|8 connects to the host computer via USB. Transport controls, eight motorized faders, and eight rotary encoders with LED rings around them indicate current parameter values or metering. These can be assigned to Pro Tools channels in groups of eight. A backlit LCD display (two rows of 55 characters) shows track information and parameter values. Command|8 incorporates a 1-in, 2-out MIDI interface and a footswitch jack for hands-free punching in/out of recording. Its monitoring section, designed by Focusrite, includes a main Pro Tools audio input, an external source input (for CD players and other audio devices around your studio), and dedicated control room/headphones outputs.

The Command|8 (shown in Figure 3.52) can be used with all current versions of Pro Tools, as well as with Avid Media Composer. It can be used as a fader expander for other legacy tactile control surfaces, such as the Pro Control, Control|24, or the Digi 002 or 003. The Command|8 offers a standalone MIDI controller mode for use with other MIDI applications.

(Photo courtesy of Avid.)

Figure 3.52 The Command|8 control surface.

Control|24 (Discontinued)

This control surface, shown in Figure 3.53, connects to the host computer via Ethernet (10BaseT, RJ-45 connectors). It features Transport controls with a scrub/shuttle wheel; a built-in talkback microphone; an 8 × 2 analog line submixer; 24 motorized faders with dedicated level meters; mute, solo, record-enable, channel select, automation mode, EQ, and dynamics buttons on each channel; as well as 16 class A mic/line preamps by Focusrite, with 48-volt phantom power. The Control|24 also includes an LED display for Transport locations, plus 26 illuminated display strips for names and parameter values. Dedicated modifier keys include Command, Option, and Control (equivalent to Ctrl, Alt, and Start on Windows). Control|24 is compatible with all current versions of Pro Tools.

(Photo courtesy of Avid.)

Figure 3.53 The Control|24 control surface.

C|24

This control surface (shown in Figure 3.54) was introduced in fall of 2007 as the successor to the original Control|24. The C|24 is compatible with all current versions of Pro Tools. It includes many of the same features as the Control|24 (and also connects to the computer via Ethernet), in a redesigned format. The faders are arranged in three banks of eight each, and the LED display strips have two lines of six characters each. The mic input section uses mic preamps based on the 003 design, with high-pass filters and –20dB pads on each channel. The 8 × 2 mixer section can be routed directly to the monitoring section. The C|24 also includes an updated 5.1 analog monitoring section whose outputs can be individually trimmed in 0.5dB increments for calibration. Soft keys are also provided for controlling certain functions, and a Window Configuration button directly accesses the Window Configuration feature available in Pro Tools versions 7.3 and higher.

(Photo courtesy of Avid.)

Figure 3.54 The C|24 control surface.

ProControl (Discontinued)

Although not officially supported since Pro Tools 8.1, the ProControl control surface continues to work with current versions of the software. (Note, however, that a few reported bugs will not be addressed, as Avid is no longer devoting resources to ProControl compatibility.) Like C|24, this control surface also connects to the host computer via Ethernet (10BaseT, RJ-45 connectors). It features Transport controls with a weighted scrub/shuttle wheel, eight motorized 100mm faders, and eight rotary encoders with LED rings around them to indicate current parameter values or metering. An analog monitoring section supports analog I/O via DB-25 connectors. The control surface also features a built-in talkback microphone and input for a listenback microphone; a dedicated control-room section with its own level controls, source selectors, and mute/dim, stereo/surround, and mono switches; a numeric keypad; and Edit/Assign scribble strips that show five insert slots on the selected channel or parameters for the effect currently being edited. A dedicated Send section is usable on any currently selected channel. The base ProControl unit (shown in Figure 3.55) is expandable via the Edit Pack option (featuring a machine control section; eight 40-segment level meters; Start, End, and Length LED displays; two joystick panners; a trackball; and a built-in color-coded keyboard with Pro Tools function labels), or additional fader expansion packs (eight faders each, up to a maximum of 48 channels). ProControl units continue to operate at many professional studios with current Pro Tools|HD systems and previous-generation Mix|24 hardware.

(Photo courtesy of Avid.)

Figure 3.55 The ProControl control surface.

D-Control

The ICON family of hardware was designed around the D-Control, D-Control ES, D-Command, and D-Command ES work surfaces, the rack-mounted XMON monitoring and communications module, and a Pro Tools|HD system. The D-Control (shown in Figure 3.56) is the most sophisticated external control surface for use with Pro Tools HD software in a studio environment. The D-Control ES, introduced in fall of 2007, features a darker color scheme; updated, higher-contrast text and graphics; and a new LED color layout for switches. D-Control tactile worksurfaces consist of a Main Module plus a single 16-channel Fader Module, which can be mounted to either side. Additional Fader Modules can be added, up to 80 channels/faders total.

(Photo courtesy of Avid.)

Figure 3.56 A D-Control Main Unit consists of a Main Module plus a 16-channel Fader Module.

Each D-Control channel strip has six rotary encoders, with LED rings around them to indicate current parameter values or metering. LED metering is provided for each channel, plus eight channels of metering for the master section. Twenty-nine illuminated switches per channel strip are provided for selecting channel modes and attributes. LED displays indicate channel names or the currently selected editing parameter for each, and dedicated LED displays provide the main/sub time indicators and Start, End, and Length readouts. A Focus channel strip in the center master module can be used for editing any selected channel without leaving the center of the console. In addition, D-Control has dedicated EQ and Dynamics sections, usable on any selected channel. Its Transport section includes separate Pro Tools Transport and Machine Transport switches, a scrub/shuttle wheel, a master record enable switch, dedicated buttons for selecting the various Pro Tools recording modes, pre/post-roll, and zoom/navigation controls.

The Main Module includes a built-in alphanumeric keyboard, a two-button trackball, and a swinging arm for mounting a flat-panel display of the user's choosing. D-Control connects to the core Pro Tools system via Ethernet.

An optional surround panner is also available for installation in the D-Control. In addition to hardware and software buttons, it incorporates a color LCD touchscreen as well as two touch-sensitive joysticks and two rotary encoders with LED rings, any of which can be used for surround panning in the X-Y axis or for controlling plug-in parameters and other mix features that are unrelated to panning.

Completing any ICON system (D-Control or D-Command) is a rack-mounted XMON monitor system. In addition to supporting surround mixing, it provides dedicated outputs for three separate stereo cue mixes, talkback, listenback, studio monitors, and headphones.

The D-Control is compatible with Pro Tools HD 10 software and Pro Tools 10 software with Complete Production Toolkit.

D-Command

The D-Command worksurface offers a more compact alternative to the D-Control. In its basic eight-fader configuration, D-Command is about 32 inches (82cm) wide by 29 inches (74cm) deep, compared to 55 inches (166cm) wide and 42 inches (107cm) deep for a basic 16-fader D-Control console. The D-Command main unit features a central control section with monitoring and communications controls and eight touch-sensitive motorized channel faders. It communicates with the host Pro Tools computer system via Ethernet.

Each D-Command channel strip has two rotary encoders, with LED rings to show either the current parameter setting or metering. D-Command (shown in Figure 3.57) is expandable up to 40 faders via two 16-channel fader modules. On each channel, a six-character LCD display shows channel information while two additional displays show information about the current parameter selected for each rotary encoder. Each channel can function independently, in a different mode from the others. Illuminated switches and meters on each channel and in the center section provide visual feedback. The center section has dedicated control panels for EQ (with 12 rotary controls) and dynamics plug-ins (with six rotary controls). D-Command includes the same XMON remote, rack-mounted analog I/O audio monitoring and communications module as D-Control, to which it is connected via a proprietary 15-pin cable. The monitoring section on D-Command provides control for up to two 5.1 surround inputs, three stereo inputs, and two cue sends.

Like the D-Control, the D-Command is compatible with Pro Tools HD 10 software and Pro Tools 10 software with Complete Production Toolkit. The ES version features a darker color aesthetic and better lighting than the original powder-blue model.

(Photo courtesy of Avid.)

Figure 3.57 An eight-channel D-Command Main Module expanded with a 16-channel Fader Module.

Artist-Series Control Surfaces

The Artist-Series control surfaces for Pro Tools include the Artist Control, Artist Mix, and Artist Transport, all of which came into the Avid family by way of the 2010 Euphonix acquisition. All Artist-Series control surfaces feature EUCON (Extended User Control), a high-speed open control protocol that has been adopted by many leading software developers for numerous applications. The EUCON protocol provides full integration of the Pro Tools 10 command set with the Soft Keys and other controls on Artist-Series controllers, including advanced automation functions formerly available exclusively on ICON worksurfaces.

Artist Control

The Artist Control (shown in Figure 3.58) is a compact, four-fader control surface with touch-screen. The customizable backlit LED touchscreen lets you view and access track information, activate track-based controls (select, record-arm, solo, mute), access programmable Soft Keys, perform surround panning, and more. The touchscreen Soft Keys, along with 12 physical Soft Keys, let you trigger keyboard shortcuts, macros (strings of commands assigned to trigger in succession), and application functions. The data entry wheel and Transport controls allow you to easily zoom, scroll, scrub, and otherwise navigate your session. Smooth mixing control is provided through the motorized, touch-sensitive 100mm faders on the control surface. Dedicated keys allow you to bank or nudge through all the tracks in your session.

Additional Artist-Series controllers can be added to grow your control surface, up to a total of four Artist Mixes and one Artist Transport in addition to the Artist Control.

(Photo courtesy of Avid.)

Figure 3.58 Artist Control control surface.

Artist Mix

The Artist Mix (shown in Figure 3.59) is a compact eight-fader control surface that can be used standalone or combined with the Artist Control and/or Artist Transport control surfaces. The Artist Mix features motorized, touch-sensitive 100mm faders; touch-sensitive rotary encoders and Knob Select/On Keys; high-resolution OLED displays; and channel Record, Automation, Select, and Assign keys. Dedicated keys allow you to bank or nudge through the tracks in your session, and a channel flip switch allows you to flip encoder assignments down to the long-throw faders.

(Photo courtesy of Avid.)

Figure 3.59 Artist Mix control surface.

Artist Transport

The Artist Transport (shown in Figure 3.60) is a high-performance jog/shuttle/transport control that can be used standalone or combined with the Artist Control and/or Artist Mix control surfaces. The Artist Transport features a weighted data wheel, spring-loaded shuttle ring, and ergonomic Transport controls with a numeric keypad. The six programmable Soft Keys can be used to reassign data wheel functions on the fly, allowing you to easily switch from navigation and editing to writing automation or adjusting plug-in parameters. As on the Artist Control, the Soft Keys on the Artist Transport can be used to trigger keyboard shortcuts, macros commands, and application functions.

(Photo courtesy of Avid.)

Figure 3.60 Artist Transport control surface.

VENUE

VENUE is Avid's live digital mixing console environment. The VENUE D-Show system consists of the D-Show mixing console shown in Figure 3.61 (the main unit plus one sidecar fader module) combined with an FOH Rack (which contains the computer to run VENUE's mix engine and D-Show software) and an expandable Stage Rack for system I/O with remote-controlled preamps and recallable settings. The I/O from the Stage Rack is connected to the system mix engine (FOH Rack) via multichannel digital snakes with BNC connectors that each support up to 48 bidirectional signals over distances of up to 500 feet. A fully expanded VENUE D-Show system (including two additional sidecar modules with 16 faders each and two Stage Racks) supports up to 96 microphone inputs and routing to 27 audio busses. Smaller systems include the VENUE Profile system, consisting of the smaller format Profile console combined with a Stage Rack and FOH Rack; the VENUE Mix Rack system, consisting of the Profile console combined with the all-in-one Mix Rack (computer and mix engine combined with I/O in a single rack enclosure); and

(Photo courtesy of Avid.)

Figure 3.61 The VENUE live sound solution also offers options for direct recording to Pro Tools. Shown here: the D-Show console.

the more compact, fully integrated SC48 console, which combines all I/O, digital signal processing, and tactile control in a single piece of hardware.

VENUE systems include many features we don't cover here—D-Show software, built-in effects processing (dynamics and EQ on every channel), TDM plug-ins, Matrix and PQ Mixers, the Personal Q option for artist-driven monitor mixes, virtual sound check, and more—these subjects are enough to fill another book! VENUE is mentioned here because, in addition to its capabilities as a live mixer, it can simultaneously act as the front-end for Pro Tools recording in live situations. With the optional FWx card—for recording and playback with standard Pro Tools systems—or HDx card—for recording and playback via Pro Tools|HD hardware—VENUE becomes the audio interface for Pro Tools. After recording a live event, the Pro Tools session can subsequently be edited and mixed on any Pro Tools system. The HDx card supports direct connection via DigiLink cables to an HD Core or HD Accel card (on a Pro Tools|HD system), a Pro Tools|HD Native card, or a Pro Tools|HDX card—without any external audio interfaces required. Various plug-in manufacturers, including Drawmer, Waves, and others, have introduced plug-ins that are specifically designed for live applications with VENUE systems. For more details on VENUE, visit www.avid.com.

Summary

As stated at the beginning of Chapter 1, Pro Tools consists of a program that runs on a computer plus specialized audio cards and/or interfaces. So for Pro Tools users, aside from needing to understand audio, it is important to be on top of the computer game. It certainly helps to understand the hardware options and peripheral devices that are available for—and compatible with—your system. It is also important to back up and archive your sessions on a regular basis to prevent data loss. Additionally, using discretion when installing other programs on the same computer can save you from downtime due to incompatibility (especially when installing background-operation utilities and operating-system upgrades).

Pro Tools makes your hard disks work very hard, so they need to offer good performance levels and be properly maintained. Additionally, Pro Tools needs much more RAM than, say, your typical spreadsheet program. If you need to connect external MIDI devices or synchronize to SMPTE time code or video, additional hardware is generally required. (Various interfaces in the Mbox, 003, and Digi 002 families have built-in MIDI inputs/outputs, as do many M-Audio interfaces and the Command|8 control surface.) In short, you're probably going to need a more robust computer setup for Pro Tools than for most other consumer applications (exceptions include other DAWs, video editors, 3D design applications, and high-performance games).

A final reminder: When you are excitedly preparing to load Pro Tools or connect a new interface to your computer, take the time to read the documentation that is bundled with your product. Avid recommends various tweaks for both Macintosh and Windows-based systems for better performance. Following the correct startup sequence for connected drives, interfaces, and consoles will also save you from headaches and possible equipment damage. In addition, consult the Avid website for specific products before purchasing to ensure compatibility with your system. Closely read the documentation associated with your product concerning the computer platform you are using, paying special attention to Avid-approved boards, chips, and hard drives. For troubleshooting, check for approved versions of common software like QuickTime. Also, it doesn't hurt to peruse the DUC support forum to see whether other users are reporting issues. The available online resources can be quite useful if used judiciously, possibly preventing hours of hair-pulling frustration when starting the loading and setup process with a new system.

4 Creating Your First Pro Tools Session

O nce you've installed the Pro Tools program, completed the appropriate installations and configurations for your hardware, and gotten the program running, you're ready to rock. Let's walk through a new session, look at some of the most important features, and get a feel for how to start on a Pro Tools project.

This chapter provides a quick tour of the basic Pro Tools working style for the new user who is eager to get started. If you're somewhat familiar with Pro Tools already, you may wish to skip ahead to Chapters 5, "The Transport Window," 6, "The Edit Window," and 7, "The Mix Window," to explore those subjects in much more detail. Note that this chapter assumes that all default preferences for a new installation of the Pro Tools program have been left unchanged.

For the sake of simplicity, in this chapter we're going to work only with audio, not MIDI or video. The chapter provides step-by-step instructions that you can follow to get practice recording and editing in Pro Tools; this will require that you have *some* audio source that can be recorded from the Channel 1 input of your audio hardware—a microphone, a guitar preamp, your kid brother's portable CD player, or whatever. We also review the Import Audio command, which requires that you have some 16-bit, 44-kHz audio files somewhere on your audio disks that you can import—for example, in AIF or WAV format. You can also import audio from a CD with this command.

You May See Things Differently! As explained in previous chapters, not only are different Pro Tools software and hardware options available, but the program also changes with each release. The examples in this chapter are equally applicable for all current versions of the software (Pro Tools 8, 9, and 10); however, the user interface has changed with the Pro Tools 10 release. Most of the screenshots throughout this book represent Pro Tools HD 10 software running on a Mac; readers may experience slight variations on other systems.

Your First Session

To get started, you'll want to open Pro Tools by selecting it from the Dock (Mac) or the Start menu (Windows), or by double-clicking its icon on the desktop. You will then set up a new Pro

Tools session document. Notice that you must select the session parameters (including audio file format, sample rate, and bit depth) *before* recording any audio or even creating a blank session! Once you've created the session, you have two choices for getting audio into Pro Tools: recording an audio source to a track and importing existing audio files from other disk locations.

Setting Up a New Session

As explained in Chapter 2, "Pro Tools Terms and Concepts," when you create a new session document, the file is placed within a folder of the same name, which Pro Tools automatically creates on your hard disk. An Audio Files subfolder is automatically created within this folder to store any audio files created by recording or processing in this session. As of Pro Tools 8, users have the choice of using a template as the basis of a new session or using the traditional blank session to start fresh. These choices are presented, along with Open Session and Open Recent Session options, in the Quick Start dialog box that appears when Pro Tools is opened. (Note that you can choose to *not* have the Quick Start dialog box appear when you start the program if you desire; simply uncheck Show Quick Start in the lower-left corner of the dialog box. This choice can be reversed later in the Display page of the Pro Tools Preferences dialog box.)

The templates that come with Pro Tools are designed to allow you to get working quickly and to provide some creative elements to jumpstart music making. For instance, the Ballad Guitar template comes with a pre-programmed MIDI drum track with the Xpand![2] plug-in as a sound source. It also has tracks with pre-assigned plug-ins and routings for bass, synth pad, rhythm guitar, lead guitar, and any sound source such as a microphone for vocals. For newer Pro Tools users, these templates can save time as well as provide good examples of signal routing within the program. Other users, however, might prefer to use a blank template to custom-design their signal routings and plug-in assignments. Regardless of whether you are interested in exploring the templates, it's a good idea to get familiar with the program's basic signal-routing functions first; otherwise, looking at a pre-configured template may just confuse you more than it helps.

As an alternative to using the Quick Start dialog box, you can choose to start a new session in Pro Tools the reliable old-school way, from the File menu:

1. After opening Pro Tools, choose File > New Session. In the New Session dialog box (shown in Figure 4.1), name the new session document anything you like, but be sure to create it on the disk drive you've designated for audio recording. The name you specify applies not only to the Pro Tools session document, but also to the session folder containing this document. For this session, select BWF (.WAV) as the file format, 44.1 kHz as the sample rate, and 24-bit as the bit depth.

Note   Unless you have specific reason *not* to do so (such as disk-space concerns), select 24-bit or 32-bit float (floating-point) resolution for all Pro Tools sessions where you plan to record new audio. Working at a higher bit depth allows you to record at lower input levels and still capture full-resolution audio. This can be important when source levels are unpredictable and/or when you aren't applying any dynamics processing prior to the inputs of your audio interface. You will have less quantization noise in very low-level signals or reverb decays on recorded tracks. At recording levels, you also leave more margin for unexpected volume peaks in the source signal you're recording.

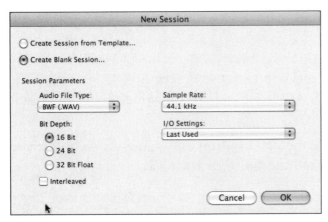

Figure 4.1 The New Session dialog box; some options in this dialog box vary depending on which version of Pro Tools you're using.

2. For the purpose of this quick tour, you will want the Edit window to be visible. If it isn't currently displayed, choose Window > Edit.

Tip You can toggle between the Mix and Edit windows by pressing Command+= (Mac) or Ctrl+= (Windows). That is, hold down the Command key or Ctrl key while pressing the equal-sign key. This key command is well worth memorizing.

Note The three main windows in Pro Tools are the Edit window (which displays the contents of individual tracks along a horizontal time scale), the Mix window (which displays Pro Tools tracks in a similar fashion to traditional audio mixers), and the Transport window (which floats on top of the other two windows). Your newly created session will have no tracks to display yet (you will create tracks as needed). A toolbar with various indicators and buttons will be visible at the top of the Edit window, while the Mix window will be completely blank until you create tracks to work in.

---

3. Next, you will need to create some tracks. Choose Track > New. The New Tracks dialog box will display on screen.

4. In the New Tracks dialog box (shown in Figure 4.2), type **4** in the Audio field to create four new Audio tracks and then click the Create button. Four new Audio tracks will appear in the Edit window, named Audio 1, Audio 2, Audio 3, and Audio 4.

Figure 4.2   The New Track dialog box lets you create new Audio, Aux Input, Master Fader, MIDI, or Instrument tracks in Pro Tools.

5. Next, you will want to rename the tracks to be more descriptive. Double-click the track nameplate of the first track (Audio 1, at the left side of the window). In the resulting dialog box, rename the track to MyStuff.

6. Without leaving the dialog box, click the Next button and name the second track Drums; repeat to name the third track FX1 and the fourth track FX2.

Tip   You can use the keyboard shortcut for the Next button to move from one track to another within the track naming dialog box. Press Command+Right Arrow (Mac) or Ctrl+Right Arrow (Windows).

---

7. When finished, click OK or simply press Return (Enter in Windows) on the alphanumeric keyboard.

8. Choose File > Save. (Be sure to also check out Chapter 8, "Menu Selections: Highlights," for information about the Auto Backup function in Pro Tools.) As with any software application, it is important to save regularly with Pro Tools; get to know the keyboard shortcut (Command+S for Mac, Ctrl+S for Windows) and use it often to prevent the heartbreak of losing your work.

9. Next, choose Track > New a second time. (Note the keyboard shortcut indicated in the menu selection.) In the New Track dialog box, change the middle pop-up selector from Audio Track to Aux Input and click Create. A new Aux Input track will be added to your session.

10. Double-click the track nameplate for the Aux Input and rename it from Aux 1 to Delay.

11. Press Command+Shift+N (Ctrl+Shift+N in Windows) to open the New Track dialog box a third time. Use the pop-up selectors to create a stereo Master Fader track and keep the default name, Master 1. (Note: You could have used the New Track dialog box to create all these tracks in a single operation, by adding rows as needed with the plus buttons at the end of each row.)

12. Next, select Window > Mix to display the Mix window (or press Command+= [Mac] or Ctrl+= [Windows]). The Mix window will become the topmost window in Pro Tools, although the Edit window will remain open behind it. These windows present two different views of the tracks you've created. You can choose to maximize each window to maximize the amount of screen space available for each.

Renaming Tracks in Pro Tools 7.3 and Later   Pro Tools provides several ways to rename a track. You can double-click a track nameplate in the Mix or Edit window as described in the preceding steps. Alternatively, in versions 7.3 and higher, you can right-click any track name (even inside the Track List if it's displayed at the left side of the windows) to access a pop-up menu that includes a Rename command. Along with renaming, this menu also lets you duplicate or delete tracks, hide tracks, make tracks inactive, export MIDI data, and perform several other common operations.

Your First Recording

Each time you record audio in a Pro Tools session, new digital audio files are created. Pro Tools automatically creates an Audio Files subfolder within the session's main folder on your hard disk to store these files. For our purposes, it's not terribly important exactly *what* you record—even 30 or 60 seconds worth of material will be sufficient. Our goal is simply to get familiar with how to enable individual tracks for recording in Pro Tools.

To record, do the following:

1. Click the R (Record Enable) button on the MyStuff track to arm this track for recording. If your sound source is properly connected, you should see some activity on the track's level meter. The Mix window provides an Audio Input Path selector for each Audio track (under the I/O label), from which you can select the physical input on your audio hardware that you are using for recording. (This section assumes that Analog Input 1 appears as the default selection for your first Audio track, and that your audio source is connected to Input 1 on your audio interface.)

2. Before continuing, test your levels; if the red clipping indicator on the track lights, click it once to reset it, reduce the volume of your input source (or the source gain control of the audio input, if your audio interface offers one), and test again.

Audio Record Levels Are Adjusted at the Source (Not Via the Track's Fader)   Pro Tools volume faders on Audio tracks have *no effect* on the level being recorded to disk. You can adjust the faders to a comfortable monitoring level without affecting your record levels. If you see a track's clip indicator light up when the track is record-enabled, you must reduce the level either at the source or on the audio interface itself, if this feature is available. (Gain controls are included on the Mbox and 003 family mic inputs and on some M-Audio interfaces.)

3. In the Transport window, click the Record button to place the session in record-ready mode and then click Play. If the Transport window isn't visible, you can open it by choosing Window > Transport or by pressing Command+1 (Mac) or Ctrl+1 (Windows) on your computer's numeric keypad.

4. Make some sound through your microphone, guitar/bass preamp, or other connected device. If the Edit window is still visible, you'll notice a red block that appears within the track, growing as you record, reflecting the duration of the audio clip being created (shown in Figure 4.3).

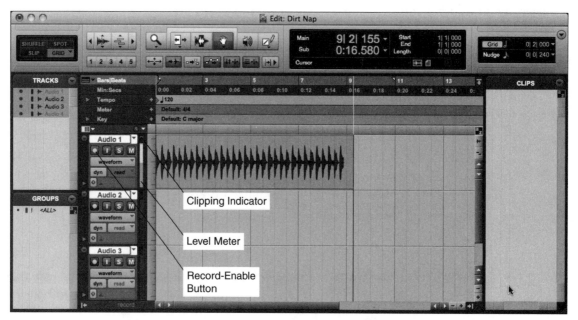

Figure 4.3 An Audio track during recording in the Edit window. The top of the level meter provides a clip indicator that lights red if levels are too high.

5. Click Stop in the Transport window. If you wish, you can now arm other tracks for recording and repeat these steps in order to create additional parts.

Importing Audio into Pro Tools

From time to time, you will want to use existing audio files in your sessions. These may be standard elements used in many projects (station identifications, tones, recurring sound effects, and so on), elements from other Pro Tools sessions being used to create a remix or submix, or musical phrases or beats that you want to loop to create repeating patterns. The File > Import > Audio command can be used to bring these files into your session. When using this command, the Import Audio dialog box will appear. In this dialog box, you can add audio files that are compatible with your session (referencing them in their current location), copy audio files that do not require conversion (creating a copy in the Audio Files folder for your current session), or convert audio files that are not directly supported—for example, if their audio file format, sample rate, or bit depth is incompatible with your session. If you use the Convert or Copy option, new copies of the imported files are created within the session's Audio Files folder.

Chapter 6 provides more detailed information about importing existing audio files into Pro Tools. For now, you can use this basic procedure:

1. If necessary, press Command+= (Mac) (or Ctrl+= in Windows) to switch back to the Edit window.

2. Select the File > Import Audio command. (You'll notice that the Clip List at the right side of the Edit window contains only the single audio clip you've recorded so far.)

3. In the Import Audio dialog box (shown in Figure 4.4), navigate through your disks and folders to the audio file you've chosen to import. (If you do not have any audio files available, you can select a track from a CD to import.)

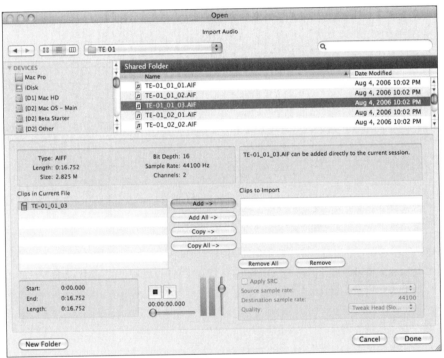

Figure 4.4 You can use the Import Audio dialog box to add existing audio files (or specific clips within them) to the current Pro Tools session. If no conversion is necessary, Pro Tools references these files in their original disk locations unless you click the Copy button.

4. Double-click the file to copy it into the list of clips to be imported (and converted, if necessary) and then click the Done button. The Audio Import Options dialog box will appear, as shown in Figure 4.5.

5. Select the Clip List button in the dialog box to import the new audio clip without placing it on a track. (See the sidebar in this section for information about the New Track option.)

The audio files you imported now appear in the Clip List for your session (right side column in the Edit window). Note that imported stereo files may be split into two new mono files with the

Figure 4.5 In the Audio Import Options dialog box, you can choose to create new Audio tracks for each audio file (or stereo pair) that you're importing.

suffixes .L and .R (depending on your session setup and the version of Pro Tools you are running). However, the files will appear and behave as a single stereo audio clip.

Creating New Tracks While Importing Audio   When you use the File menu's Import > Audio command, a dialog box lets you choose whether to simply import the audio to the Clip List or to place the files directly into one or more new tracks. If you select the New Track option, for each mono file or stereo pair that you import, Pro Tools automatically creates a new Audio track and places the corresponding clip on the track, at the location specified in the dialog box (Session Start, Song Start, at the start of the current selection or cursor location, or at the position specified in the Spot dialog box). The newly created track inherits the name of the source file. This can be a real time-saver.

An alternative method is to drag an audio file from either the Workspace browser window or the Macintosh Finder or Windows Explorer directly into the Track List (left side column of the Edit window); in a similar fashion, a new Audio track will be automatically created and named after the source file. The imported clip is placed on the corresponding track and located at the Session Start.

Editing and Effects

In this section, you'll perform some basic edit operations on the audio you recorded and imported, and then apply some plug-in effects to alter the sound.

Editing

Once you start editing your audio, the real fun and creativity begins! Unlike tape-based audio systems, where you have to physically cut up your original recording (a risky, destructive process), Pro Tools enables you to freely move segments of audio around non-destructively, adjusting their length, editing out sections, and rearranging their order—all without altering the original recordings in any way. This gives you freedom to experiment without fear of destroying a crucial record pass (or *take*).

To get some basic editing experience, we will experiment with selecting and moving clips, trimming clips, and deleting selections within a clip. To get started, do the following:

1. Click the Grabber tool to select it. The Grabber is represented by a hand icon in the toolbar at the top of the Edit window, as shown in Figure 4.6.

Figure 4.6 Use the Grabber tool to select and move clips within tracks.

Tip   Shift-click with the Grabber to select multiple clips. If you hold down the Option key (Alt key in Windows) as you drag a selected clip with the Grabber, the clip will be copied rather than moved.

Note   The Grabber tool can also be used to move MIDI notes or to edit automation data.

---

2. Locate the audio clip you imported to the Clip List earlier and drag it out into the Track Display area, releasing the mouse button to drop it anywhere near the beginning of the Drums track. Notice that as soon as you drag this clip over the Track Display area, an outline of the clip appears, reflecting its duration.

3. Again using the Grabber, click and drag the clip, pulling it down into the FX1 track. Audio clips can reside in any Pro Tools Audio track with a matching number of channels (mono, stereo, or multichannel), regardless of where they originated.

4. Select the Trim tool in the toolbar at the top of the Edit window; the icon looks like a partial rectangle with left/right arrows, as shown in Figure 4.7.

Figure 4.7 Use the Trim tool to alter the length of existing clips within a track.

Note   The Trim tool can also be used to change the duration of fades, lengthen/shorten MIDI notes, scale automation or MIDI controller data, and change the length of looped clips.

---

5. Click and drag with the Trim tool at a point near the end of the clip you recorded in the MyStuff track. (You must click inside the clip for the tool to be active.) Drag back and forth without releasing the mouse button to adjust the clip length, up to its original

length. Using the audio waveform as a guide, trim the clip to a shorter duration to make it end right at the point where the useful program material stops, trimming off any excess noise or silence at the tail end of the recording.

6. Release the mouse button to create a new clip definition, with –01 added to the end of the original clip name. Both this new clip (created as the result of an edit) and the original whole-file clip it came from now appear in the Clip List.

7. Repeat the above process near the start of the clip to trim off any unnecessary noise or silence at the beginning of the recording. The resulting clip should consist of only the usable program material (or some segment of recognizable audio that you recorded).

8. Click the Selector tool in the Edit window toolbar; this tool is located between the Trim tool and the Grabber tool and looks like an audio waveform with a selection in the middle, as shown in Figure 4.8.

Figure 4.8   Use the Selector tool to make selections within a clip or to make larger selections encompassing multiple clips or tracks.

Tip   To adjust the boundaries of a currently highlighted selection, hold down the Shift key as you click or drag. Shift-clicking in additional tracks adds them to the current Timeline selection. Pressing Shift+Tab extends the selection to the end of the current clip. Pressing Option+Shift+Tab (Alt+Shift+Tab in Windows) extends the selection to the beginning of the current clip.

---

9. Click and drag the Selector tool's I-beam cursor to highlight a portion in the *center* of the clip now residing in the FX1 track (the file you imported from disk).

10. Remove the selection either by pressing the Delete/Backspace key or by using the Edit > Clear command. Notice that new clip names are created for the two remaining pieces at the beginning and end, with edit numbers appended to the original clip name. When you delete, cut, or resize audio clips with tools in the Edit window, the process is always nondestructive—the original audio clips and files remain intact in the Clip List, and the complete audio file on disk is unaffected.

The Clip List   The Clip List is a sort of "bin" where all the audio, MIDI, and video referenced by the current Pro Tools session appears. You can drag audio clips directly from here onto an Audio track. You can also drag MIDI clips onto MIDI or Instrument tracks and video clips onto Video tracks. As you've seen, some clip definitions are automatically created by Pro Tools as a result of editing operations. (An option in the Clip List pop-up menu allows you to suppress display of these auto-created clips, if preferred.) In other instances, you can create your own new clip definitions—for example, via commands in the Edit and AudioSuite menus. Whole-file audio clips (as opposed to clips that represent only smaller portions within the parent audio files) appear in bold type in the Clip List.

11.   Select the Zoomer tool in the Edit window toolbar; this tool features a magnifying glass for its icon, as shown in Figure 4.9. The Zoomer is used for changing the magnification on your horizontal (time) view of Pro Tools tracks. Zooming in enables you to be extremely precise when cutting/copying audio data or trimming clips. Click and drag to highlight a small area of the waveform within any visible audio clip. The screen display will zoom in to show the selected area.

Figure 4.9 With the Zoomer tool, click anywhere in a track to zoom in, or Option-click (Alt-click in Windows) to zoom out. Click and drag to magnify a specific horizontal area within a track.

12.   To zoom back out, double-click the Zoomer tool icon in the Edit window toolbar. The display will zoom out to fit the entire session duration in the Edit window.

13.   Using the Grabber tool, select your trimmed audio clip on the MyStuff track. (The clip should not include any silence or unwanted noise at the beginning or end.)

14.   Choose Options > Loop Playback to enable the Loop Playback feature and then press the space bar to start playback. Pro Tools will play back your current selection in a continuous loop rather than the session's entire Timeline.

> **Note**   To loop playback of a selected clip, make sure that Options > Link Timeline and Edit Selection is enabled. Also, be sure to deselect the Timeline Insertion Follows Playback button (under the Pencil tool in the Edit window) to avoid losing your selection when playback stops.

15.   When finished, press the space bar again to stop playback. For the moment, leave the current clip selected.

Inserting Plug-In Effects

Digital signal processing (DSP) allows you to shape the sound of your recorded audio in Pro Tools. On conventional mixing boards, effects-processing elements are generally of fixed types and at fixed locations. For instance, each source audio channel may have several equalization stages, while submasters or groups have none, and any external effects (for example, reverbs, delays, and so on) must be connected to the mixer's auxiliary sends and returns or to the insert point of individual channels. Worse, if each song in a project requires a different effects-processing setup, you not only have to change parameters on every external effects unit, but you may also need to reconfigure your whole cabling setup. Patchbays help by providing flexible access to all the inputs and outputs of these devices (external effects processors and the mixing board itself), but even still, repatching is a laborious process.

In contrast, within Pro Tools we have virtual signal processors–modular software constructs called *plug-ins*. These can be inserted into the signal chain of *any* audio-related track type, including Audio, Aux Input, Instrument, or Master Fader tracks (but not MIDI tracks). The entire processing and signal-routing setup within each Pro Tools session document is recalled when it is reopened. As an added benefit, no additional noise is introduced by the routing or the signal processor (unlike when using external effects units). The complexity of any effects treatments that you create is limited only by the available processing power of your system and your imagination!

In this next series of steps, you'll have a chance to work with plug-in effects processors in Pro Tools, first as inserts in the signal chain of an individual Audio track and then as an insert on an Aux Input track that will function as a send destination. (Aux Input tracks are frequently used as an "effect return" destination for signals sent from multiple tracks.)

1. If necessary, press Command+= (or Ctrl+= in Windows) to switch from the Edit window to the Mix window. Press the space bar to start looped playback again.

2. Experiment with the controls on the mixer strip for the MyStuff track (volume fader, Pan knob, and Solo/Mute buttons), as desired. Stop playback when finished.

3. Locate the five Insert selectors at the top section of the track's mixer strip (small rectangles with dark round dots on their left sides). Click on the top Insert selector (insert position A) to open its pop-up menu and then choose Plug-In > EQ > EQ 3 7-Band (mono), as shown in Figure 4.10. The EQIII 7-band equalizer plug-in window will open.

4. Press the space bar to start looped playback again, and experiment with the EQ settings. Drag the Gain and Frequency sliders around to make adjustments, or click and drag on the colored nodes in the graphical display. When finished, press the space bar to stop playback.

Tip Option-click (Mac) or Alt-click (Windows) on any slider to reset it to default values. (*Many* other controls in Pro Tools work the same way.)

---

5. Now instantiate a compressor plug-in (under the Dynamics submenu of the Insert selector pop-up menu) on insert position B.

6. Press Return (or Enter in Windows) to return to the beginning of the song; start playback and experiment with the compressor's Threshold slider. (This control determines the level at which gain reduction starts to be applied.)

7. Next, locate the Delay Aux Input track you created earlier and instantiate a Medium Delay plug-in effect on its top insert position, similar to what you did on the Audio track. (Choose Plug-in > Delay > Medium Delay II.)

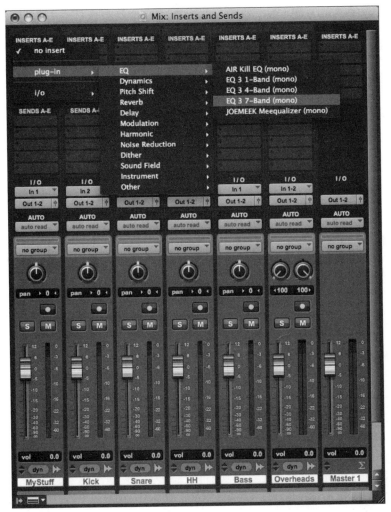

Figure 4.10   The Insert selector pop-up menu allows you to assign (or *instantiate*) a plug-in.

At this point, the Delay track has an effects processor assigned, but it doesn't contribute to the mix because the track has no audio assigned to it. If you were to click Play, you wouldn't hear anything passing through the Medium Delay II because you haven't yet routed anything into the Aux Input track. To remedy this, you will use an internal mix bus to route a split of the signal from the MyStuff track as a send to the audio input on the Delay track.

1. Locate the five Send selectors near the top of the MyStuff track (small rectangles with dark arrow icons on their left sides). Click on the top Send selector (send position A) to open its pop-up menu, and select Bus > Bus 1–2 (Stereo). An Output window will open for the send.

2. Option-click (Alt-click in Windows) on the send volume fader to set it directly to 0dB (instead of –∞).

3. Next, click and hold on the Audio Input Path selector for the Delay Aux Input track (under the I/O label) and select Bus > Bus 1–2 (Stereo) as its input source, as shown in Figure 4.11.

Figure 4.11 Selecting the bus pair 1–2 as the input source for the Delay Aux Input track.

4. Option-click (Alt-click in Windows) on the Aux Input track's main volume fader to set it to 0dB.

Note A volume setting of 0dB is also known as *unity gain*, because no gain change is being applied between the fader's input and output.

---

5. Start playback. You should now hear the audio from the MyStuff track with a delay applied from the Delay track. Adjust the send level (in the floating window) to suit your taste.

6. Adjust the settings in the Medium Delay plug-in window as desired. Experiment with the feedback parameter to produce multiple repeats.

Mixdown

At this point, we're ready to consider the basics of mixing audio to a stereo output and saving it. You will continue to work with the session you've been building, for demonstration purposes.

Mixing

As discussed elsewhere, *mixdown* is the process by which a number of source Audio tracks are combined into a standard playback format, such as a stereo MP3 file. For each track, you can set the volume, adjust apparent spatial placement and ambience, modify frequency content, and so on to create the desired audio perspective. In a Pro Tools mix, most parameters can change dynamically over time; you can automate the movement of faders, sliders, plug-in parameters, and so on to create an ideal mix or to create special effects.

In the following steps, you'll explore the two ways you can create mix automation in Pro Tools: by recording changes you make to mixing controls in real time and by using the mouse to edit breakpoints in the automation graphs within each track.

1. If desired, take some time in the Edit window to duplicate your clips (choose Edit > Duplicate) so that you have a longer mix to deal with.

2. Click the Return to Zero button in the Transport window (to the left of the Rewind button) to make sure the playback cursor is at the beginning of the session's Timeline.

3. Locate the Automation Mode selector for the MyStuff Audio track, currently set to Auto Read. Using the pop-up selector, change it to Touch so that any mix changes you make to this track during playback—on any controls that you actually touch—will be recorded as automation.

Note   The Pro Tools Automation Enable window (Window > Automation) allows you to globally enable/disable different types of automation. For this part of the chapter, all automation types should be enabled (the program's default).

---

4. Switch to the Mix window; then start playback and move the volume fader and Pan control for the MyStuff track a few times. Stop playback when finished.

5. Start playback again; Pro Tools will repeat the volume and pan moves you just performed.

6. Switch back to the Edit window and locate the Track View selector for the MyStuff track (shown in Figure 4.12), currently set to Waveform view.

Note   The Track View selector is easier to recognize at track heights of Medium or larger. To change the track height, click on the amplitude scale area at the head of the track (the area with vertical markings like a ruler) and select the desired height from the pop-up menu.

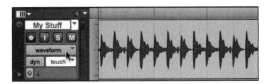

Figure 4.12 The Track View selector on the MyStuff track.

7. Click on the Track View selector and switch the display to Volume. The Volume automation graph will display, showing the volume changes you recorded on a line graph with breakpoints.

8. Use the Grabber tool to click and drag existing breakpoints to modify their placement. This is a common way to edit automation data. You can also click anywhere on the automation graph to create new breakpoints.

9. Next, change the Track View selector from Volume to Pan. The vertical ruler at the head of the track will now show L and R.

10. With the Grabber, click along the line (near the beginning of the track) to create new breakpoints and drag them to several extreme left/right positions.

11. Now switch back to the Mix window. Click the Return to Zero button in the Transport window again and then click Play. You will see the Pan knob moving back and forth, following the automation contours you created.

Automation Breakpoints   The automation for volume, pan, and many other mix or plug-in parameters can be displayed and edited graphically within Pro Tools tracks. When viewing a track in volume, pan, or any other mix-automation format, lines represent the changing values for that automation parameter (superimposed over a dimmed version of the audio waveform on Audio tracks). The breakpoints on these lines (sometimes referred to as *envelope points* or *automation event points* in other audio programs) are the handles you use to create automation shapes. Breakpoints are created automatically when you create automation by moving an onscreen control. They can also be drawn in using one of the Pencil tool's drawing modes (such as the Line or Free Hand mode, for example). Whether they've been created in one of these ways or with the Grabber tool, as you did above, you can always drag breakpoints with the Grabber, select a range of them with the Selector, and copy, delete, or scale their values up or down with the Trim tool.

- To delete a breakpoint, Option-click it (Alt-click in Windows) with the Grabber.

- For finer control, hold down the Command key (Ctrl key in Windows) while adjusting (or trimming) breakpoint values.

- To restrict movement of breakpoints to the vertical direction while dragging (so that their horizontal position in the Timeline is unaffected), hold down the Shift key.

■ To nudge a selected range of automation breakpoints right or left in the Timeline (without affecting any audio underneath them in Audio tracks), use the + and – (plus/minus) keys on the numeric keypad. (The Nudge function is described in more detail in Chapter 6.)

Bounce to Disk

In traditional audio studios, the mixdown would be performed in real time, and the mix output would be recorded to another audio device (for example, a two-track master recorder). In fact, this is sometimes done with Pro Tools, especially when laying off a mix to a DAT or videotape. More commonly, though, you will bounce the results of your Pro Tools mix into a brand-new file, which can then be used to create an audio CD or can be given to a computer-based video editor, interactive or DVD author, and so on. In Pro Tools, this is a real-time process, so you also have the option of incorporating external audio sources, such as MIDI modules, multitrack tape recorders, or effects processors, into the resultant file.

To bounce your mix to a new audio file, do the following:

1. Select File > Bounce to > Disk. In the Bounce dialog box (shown in Figure 4.13), configure the Format setting to Interleaved and set the other options as desired. For CD-compatible files, set the Bit Depth to 16-bit and the Sample Rate to 44.1 kHz.

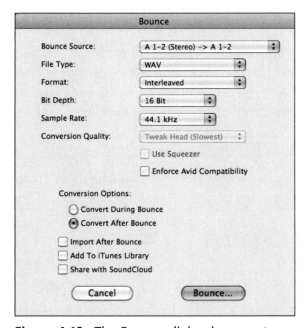

Figure 4.13 The Bounce dialog box creates new audio files based on your current mix.

Note   In Pro Tools 10, you have the options to add the bounced file to your iTunes library and/or to upload it to your SoundCloud account from within the Bounce dialog box.

2. Click the Bounce button. In the dialog box that appears, type a name for the bounced mix and choose the disk location where the resulting file will be saved; then click OK. You will hear your session play back in real time, and a small window will appear displaying the time remaining until the bounce is complete.

What's Included in Your Bounced Mixdown File   When nothing is selected in the Edit window, the entire session—from the beginning of the Timeline to the end of the last clip or breakpoint in any track—is included in the resultant file. If you make an Edit selection in any track (with Options > Link Timeline and Edit Selection enabled) or a Timeline selection in any Timebase Ruler, only the selected range will be included in your bounced file. Beware: Reverbs, echoes, and other time-based effects might need extra time for tail decays beyond the end of the last clip. When bouncing to disk, be sure to extend your selection enough for your effects to decay completely to silence before the bounce ends!

Summary

On a real-world project, you would almost certainly carry the recording, editing, and automation processes to greater extremes than what's been described in this chapter. However, the rudimentary exercises in this chapter should have provided you with a basic idea of what Pro Tools is about. By recording and/or importing audio to tracks; editing the resulting clips to clean them up or rearrange them in creative ways; adding plug-ins for EQ, dynamics, and effects processing; recording fader moves and other dynamic changes to automate your mix; and completing a final bounce to disk, you can take a project from concept to completion within the Pro Tools environment. In the remainder of the book, we'll get into further details on many of these topics (you'll especially want to check out the next three chapters on the Transport, Edit, and Mix windows), but you're already well on your way to understanding the creative possibilities that Pro Tools affords. Read on and rock on!

5 The Transport Window

This chapter and the next two provide specifics about many elements of the Transport, Edit, and Mix windows in Pro Tools. These key windows are where you will spend most of your time. Once you get a handle on them, you'll be ready to tackle serious Pro Tools projects. This chapter highlights the essential features and techniques you must know in order to be an all-around competent Pro Tools user. However, it doesn't address every selection in every menu—that's what the Pro Tools documentation is for. The *Pro Tools Reference Guide* and the *Menu Guide*, provided in PDF format with Pro Tools, are excellent sources for more detailed information.

Other chapters in this book provide additional practical examples for many of the features described here. Although we clarify some concepts and point out many useful tips and shortcuts along the way, much of the material in this chapter, as well as in Chapters 6, "The Edit Window," and 7, "The Mix Window," may be review for readers with significant Pro Tools experience. If that's your case, feel free to just browse or skip ahead.

The Transport window (shown in Figure 5.1) includes basic tape-type controls for controlling playback and recording, with numeric displays for the current selection, pre-/post-roll settings, and MIDI controls. This chapter reviews each of the elements in the Transport window.

Note   All four options under the View > Transport submenu should be enabled for this chapter—Counters, MIDI Controls, Synchronization, and Expanded.

Pro Tools Documentation   Be sure to check out the PDF documents that Avid provides in the Documentation folder (Avid > Documentation > Pro Tools). These documents (along with the book currently in your hands, of course) will be a great help in getting you up to speed. Even more convenient, you can open these documents directly from the Help menu inside Pro Tools.

Transport Buttons

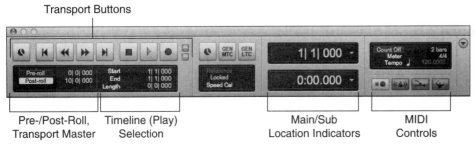

Pre-/Post-Roll,   Timeline (Play)   Main/Sub   MIDI
Transport Master   Selection   Location Indicators   Controls

Figure 5.1 The Transport window.

Keyboard Shortcuts   Like any complex program, Pro Tools offers many keyboard shortcuts, especially for frequently used features. This book always starts from the visible menu command or onscreen control, but it also emphasizes keyboard shortcuts that are important for basic operations (that is to say, worth the effort to memorize). That being said, you should absolutely print out and study the *Keyboard Shortcuts* PDF document included with Pro Tools. In particular, because Transport operations are so essential to using Pro Tools, you'll be well served to learn all the associated keyboard equivalents—this will definitely save you time!

For the purposes of this chapter, we'll be using the numeric keypad in Transport mode (the default) so that keys on the numeric keypad can be used to control various Transport functions. (You can switch the numeric keypad between Classic and Transport modes in the Operation page of the Preferences dialog box [Setup > Preferences]).

Lastly, note that in Pro Tools, the Return key on the alphanumeric keyboard (or the Enter key in Windows) is *not* the equivalent of the Enter key on the numeric keypad! The Enter key on the numeric keypad often performs different functions in Pro Tools—such as creating Memory locations.

Transport Buttons

Many of the Transport window buttons (shown in Figure 5.2) behave like their equivalent controls on a video, CD, DVD, or tape deck. They are used to control playback and recording. As indicated in the descriptions provided here, keyboard shortcuts are available for all the button functions, as summarized in Table 5.1 at the end of this chapter. If you're just starting with Pro Tools, these should be among the very first keyboard shortcuts you memorize.

             Return   Fast
             to Zero   Forward   Stop   Record

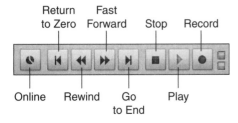

Online   Rewind   Go   Play
                       to End

Figure 5.2 The Transport window buttons resemble a CD or DVD player's controls.

Play/Stop

When you click the Play button in the Transport window, playback starts at the current position noted by the Main and Sub Location Indicators in this window. (The Transport window indicators always show Timeline positions; when Options > Link Timeline and Edit Selection is enabled, the Location Indicators in the Edit window will mirror these positions; more about this in Chapter 6.) When the Transport's start and end values are identical (and the length is therefore zero), playback continues indefinitely until you click Stop. Otherwise, playback begins at the start location and stops when the end value is reached (or loops back to the start, when Loop Playback is enabled). If you prefer using your computer keyboard to issue commands, press the space bar (or the 0 key on the numeric keypad) to start and stop playback. Later in this chapter, we discuss Dynamic Transport mode, introduced with Pro Tools 7.3, which allows you much more flexible control over the portion of the Timeline that will play back when you activate the Play function.

Half-Speed Play/Record in Pro Tools   Using Pro Tools, you can record or play audio at half speed—great for recording a chipmunk-style vocal or deciphering a shredding guitar solo! To record at half speed, hold down the Shift and Command keys (Shift and Ctrl keys in Windows) as you press the space bar. For half-speed playback, hold down the Shift key as you press the space bar.

Rewind/Fast Forward

Like the Play/Stop buttons, the Rewind/Fast Forward buttons are similar to the equivalent controls on a tape deck. You can also repeatedly click either of these to jump forward or backward through the session Timeline in set increments. (The increment size is determined by the currently active Main Timescale—Min:Secs or Bars|Beats, for example.) In the Edit window, it is often easy to click with the Selector tool to set the current play position, but the keypad shortcuts for Rewind and Fast Forward can be much faster when your hand is not on the mouse. You can also hold down the Transport buttons or their keypad equivalents to shuttle through the Pro Tools Timeline.

The keyboard equivalents for the Rewind/Fast Forward buttons are 1 and 2 on the numeric keypad, respectively.

Audio during Rewind/Fast Forward   To hear the audio you are passing over while using the Rewind and Fast Forward functions (either via the Transport buttons or the keypad equivalents), enable the Audio During Fast Forward/Rewind option in the Operation tab of the Preferences dialog box. While you hold down either of these buttons, playback skips forward or backward through the Timeline in a similar fashion to the scan buttons on a CD player. This makes it easy to locate or replay a range within your audio material and can be a useful option for most users.

During rewind/fast forward in Pro Tools, audio doesn't play back at fast speed or in reverse as on analog tape, and MIDI tracks don't play at all. However, some HD users opt to change their Numeric Keypad Preference setting to Shuttle, as opposed to the more conventional Transport mode generally used throughout this book. In Shuttle mode, audio will play back at accelerated speed while shuttling forward or backward through the Timeline.

Return to Zero/Go to End

Clicking the Return to Zero button sets the playback position (and the Timeline selection) to the beginning of the Pro Tools Timeline. Return to Zero sets the current playback position to the left edge of the Timeline, regardless of what Timeline units are in use or what actual bar number or session start time this corresponds to. Clicking the Go to End button resets the current playback position to the end of the last clip in the session (or to the last automation breakpoint). If you have anything selected in the Edit window (for example, a clip you've been looping), clicking Return to Zero or Go to End also drops the selection. The keyboard equivalent for Return to Zero is Return (Enter in Windows) on the alphanumeric keyboard; the equivalent for Go to End is Option+Return (Ctrl+Enter in Windows) on the alphanumeric keyboard.

Online

Clicking the Online button puts the Transport in Online mode, where playback/recording starts and stops according to SMPTE time code received. (SMPTE time code is explained in Chapter 11, "Synchronization.") In the Session Setup window (Setup > Session), you can set the start time for the current session. This determines the incoming SMPTE time-code value that corresponds to the left edge of the Edit window (the beginning of your session's Timeline).

If the incoming SMPTE time-code values (from a multitrack audio recorder or a video master, for example) are *earlier* than the session start time, Pro Tools will wait until the start time position is reached and then start playback. (Playback will stop when you press Stop on the master device sending time code and the flow of SMPTE time-code values into Pro Tools ends.) If the incoming SMPTE time-code values correspond to a location *later* than the session start time, Pro Tools will jump to the corresponding position and commence playback (even if this position is beyond the last clip of audio in your session).

The Command+J keyboard shortcut (Ctrl+J in Windows) toggles Online mode on/off.

Synchronizing Pro Tools to Video and Multitrack Recorders   As mentioned, in Online mode, Pro Tools' playback is triggered at a position determined by incoming time-code values (and the Start Time value specified in the Session Setup window). An external SMPTE synchronizer can be used to convert the incoming SMPTE (encoded into an audio or video signal) to MIDI Time Code (MTC). This, in turn, can be communicated to Pro Tools via an optional MIDI/SMPTE interface in your configuration. For more details about SMPTE time code, MTC, and synchronization in general, see Chapter 11.

Record

Clicking the Record button arms Pro Tools for recording mode. (At least one audio or MIDI track must be record-enabled for Pro Tools to be able to record.) After you click the Record button, it flashes; recording will commence when you click the Play button. If the Pre-Roll option is enabled (discussed later in this chapter, under "Transport Window Fields"), playback will begin ahead of the record position, by the indicated Pre-Roll amount. If the Post-Roll option is enabled, playback will continue beyond the record selection, by the indicated Post-Roll amount. If Timeline and Edit window selections are linked, selections made in the Edit window (or by entering Start, End, or Length values in the Transport window) can be used to specify where recording will punch in and punch out. Remember that, unless you've deliberately enabled Destructive Record mode (in the Options menu), every record pass is saved. A new file/clip is created for each take and automatically assigned a name derived from the track name where it is recorded. (By the way, it's good practice to assign meaningful names to your tracks *before* recording, so that your recorded clips have meaningful names as well.)

Pro Tools offers various recording modes: Normal, Destructive, Loop Record, and QuickPunch (as well as TrackPunch and DestructivePunch in Pro Tools HD and Pro Tools with Complete Production Toolkit). The mode that you have selected affects the appearance of the Record button itself, as shown in Figure 5.3. You can select recording modes by right-clicking the Record button—or toggle through the modes by Control-clicking (Mac) or Start-clicking (Windows) on the button. The recording modes are discussed in further detail in the "Options Menu" section of Chapter 8, "Menu Selections: Highlights."

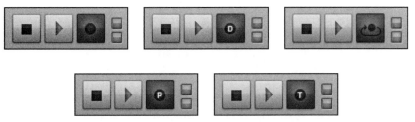

Figure 5.3 The appearance of the Record button indicates the current recording mode: Normal (non-destructive), Destructive, Loop, QuickPunch, and TrackPunch (Pro Tools HD) shown here.

Several keyboard shortcuts are available to start recording: Command+space bar (Ctrl+space bar in Windows), the 3 key on the numeric keypad, or the F12 key. (Mac users: See the upcoming sidebar about reassigning the shortcut key for Dashboard.)

Macintosh, Pro Tools, and Using Function Keys F9–F12   In Pro Tools, the function keys F5 through F10 are used to select each of the Edit tools (Zoomer tool through Pencil tool, left to right), and (if enabled in Preferences) F11 is used to toggle the Wait for Note function on and off. Similarly, the F12 key is commonly used to initiate recording. Current versions of Mac OS X, however, use many of these function-key shortcuts for operating system-level commands

(Dashboard and Exposé [Snow Leopard] or Mission Control [Lion]), making them unavailable for Pro Tools functions. Additional shortcut conflicts include the Control+Up/Down Arrow keys used to open Mission Control and Application Windows (Lion) and the Control+Left/Right Arrow keys used to move left and right through spaces.

Fortunately, each of these conflicts is easy to fix, though the process varies depending on your operating system:

1. Open the Apple menu and choose System Preferences.

2. Click Exposé & Spaces in the Personal section (Snow Leopard) or click Keyboard in the Hardware section (Lion).

3. Do one of the following, as appropriate for your system:
   - (Snow Leopard) Use the pop-up menus under the Exposé tab in the Exposé & Spaces System Preferences to reassign the keys used for Exposé and Dashboard; then switch to the Spaces tab and disable or reassign all of the Spaces shortcuts. Try adding the Shift key and/or other modifiers to the default shortcuts. (Hold the desired modifier key(s) while clicking the pop-up menu to make a new assignment.)

   - (Lion) Activate the Keyboard Shortcuts tab in the Keyboard System Preferences, click on Mission Control in the left column, and disable or reassign the shortcuts for Mission Control, Application Windows, Show Desktop, Show Dashboard, Move Left a Space, Move Right a Space, and Switch to Desktop 1.

About Numeric Keypad Modes (Preferences)   In the Preferences dialog box, you can switch the mode of numeric-keypad operation in Pro Tools. In Transport mode, the numeric-keypad equivalents shown in Table 5.1 are enabled. Most users consider Transport to be the most generally useful mode; throughout this book, we always refer to numeric-keypad shortcuts based on this mode, but you should experiment with the other modes to see what works best for you. Classic mode emulates how the numeric keypad worked in Pro Tools versions prior to 5.0. On Pro Tools HD and Pro Tools with Complete Production Toolkit, a third mode called Shuttle allows these keys to control Pro Tools playback at extra-slow or extra-fast speeds, stopping once you release the key; many users also find this handy.

Transport Window Fields

This section discusses additional fields that are displayed in the Transport window when the View > Transport > Expanded option is enabled. Not only can you directly enter numeric values into these fields (shown in Figure 5.4), but several of them are directly affected by your actions in the Transport and Edit windows, serving as data displays for your current Timeline selection, play position, and so on.

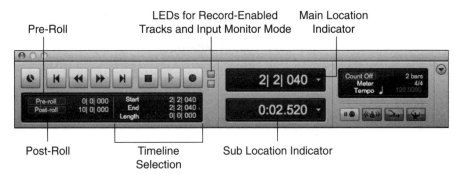

Figure 5.4 Various Transport window fields provide information about your current selection, playback position, pre-/post-roll times, and more.

Main/Sub Indicators for Current Location

The Main and Sub Location Indicators are counters that display the current play position. They are static while the Transport is stopped, are continually changing during play/record, and can be set to different time units at any time. When Options > Link Timeline and Edit Selection is enabled, making a selection in the Edit window also resets the Transport's Timeline selection—the current play position corresponds to the beginning of that selection. (The Main and Sub Counters at the top of the Edit window represent the Edit selection, which can be unlinked from the Timeline selection that will play back when you press the space bar.) A pop-up menu to the right of each counter lets you change the time units of each indicator. For example, you might choose to display musical bars and beats in the Main Counter and minutes and seconds in the Sub Counter.

You can change the location value in the Main Counter in any of the following ways:

- Using the Transport buttons—Rewind/Fast Forward, Return to Zero/Go to End, and so on

- Making a new selection or clicking anywhere in the Edit window's main Time Ruler—assuming Options > Link Timeline and Edit Selection is enabled

- Recalling a user-defined Memory location (more about these in Chapter 6)

- Clicking in the field and typing a new value (see the upcoming sidebar)

Quick Entry of New Locations in the Main Location Indicator   Pro Tools provides various shortcuts for quickly entering values in the Main Counter fields: Pressing the asterisk (*) key on the numeric keypad selects the Main Location Indicator for data entry, pressing the period (.) key switches between columns, pressing the Up/Down Arrow keys let you increment/decrement the selected value, and pressing the Return key on the alphanumeric keyboard (Enter in Windows) confirms an entry in a field. For example, with Minutes: Seconds selected as the timebase unit for the Main Counter, you could move the playback cursor to 1 minute, 30 seconds by pressing * 1.30 (Return/Enter) on the numeric keypad. In the Bars|Beats timebase, to set the playback cursor directly to Bar 15, Beat 3, you could press * 15.3 (Return/Enter).

As another example when working in Bars|Beats, you could move the play position ahead by four bars by pressing *, Up Arrow (four times), and Return/Enter on the alphanumeric keyboard.

Play Selection: Start/End/Length Fields

With the Link Timeline and Edit Selection option enabled, simply clicking somewhere in the Edit window with the Selector tool will set the values in the Start and End fields of the Transport window to be identical. (This is also the case if you use the Rewind, Fast Forward, Go to Zero, or Go to End buttons to change the playback location or if you recall a Marker Memory location. These are discussed in Chapter 8.) The Start value is the position where playback will begin when you click Play.

On the other hand, if you make a selection, either by clicking and dragging with the Selector or highlighting an existing clip with the Grabber, the beginning, end, and duration of the current selection will be indicated in the Start, End, and Length fields. You can also click in any of these three fields to manually enter new values. Time units displayed in the Transport's Start, End, and Length fields always match those of the Main location indicator.

The Start and End fields determine where recording stops and starts in Record mode. In both recording and playback, these start and end points may be preceded or followed by the specified pre-roll and post-roll intervals, if enabled—see the following section in this chapter for more details. When loop playback (or recording) is enabled, Pro Tools will continuously cycle the material between the start and end values until you stop playback.

Quick Entry in the Transport Window's Start/End/Length Fields   Like the Timeline location fields, the Play Selection Start, End, and Length fields respond to various keyboard commands: Hold down the Option key (Alt key in Windows) and press the forward slash key (/) on the numeric keypad to directly select the Start field in the Transport window. Each subsequent press of the / key cycles through the Start, End, and Length fields for numeric entry, as well as the Pre-Roll and Post-Roll fields. As with other time-value fields in Pro Tools, you can use the period key (.) or Left/Right Arrow keys to switch columns as you enter values, type numeric values (or use the Up/Down Arrow keys), and then hit Return or Enter to confirm your entry or the Esc key to exit without changing the field.

Pre-Roll/Post-Roll

If the Pre-Roll button is enabled, when you click Play, playback will start before the current Play selection in the Edit window by the time interval shown in the Pre-Roll field. Time units in this field always match the Main Time Scale (Bars|Beats, Minutes:Seconds, Samples, SMPTE time code, and so on). The Post-Roll button and field work in a similar fashion; playback continues past the end of the Play selection by the specified amount. In Record mode, however, recording (on record-enabled tracks) will always punch in and punch out exactly at the locations shown in the Start and End fields. Having Pre-Roll enabled facilitates making inserts or drop-ins on previously recorded takes because you can monitor the surrounding audio material as you record the new segment.

Besides double-clicking to manually enter new time values into the Pre-/Post-Roll fields, you can use the Pre-Roll and Post-Roll flags in the Edit window's Main Timebase Ruler, as shown in Figure 5.5. (Pre-/Post-Roll flags are white when Pre- and Post-Roll are disabled, yellow when enabled.) To change Pre-/Post-Roll intervals, simply drag the corresponding flag to the left or right outside of the Timeline Selection In and Out points. The Command+K keyboard shortcut (Ctrl+K in Windows) toggles both the Pre- and Post-Roll buttons on and off.

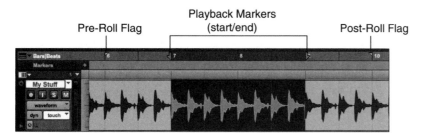

Figure 5.5   The Edit window's Main Timebase Ruler, shown here in Bars|Beats format, displays the Timeline Selection In and Out points (currently at Bars 7 and 9) with Pre-Roll and Post-Roll flags.

Dynamic Transport Mode (Versions 7.3 and Higher)   The first time you enable Dynamic Transport mode (Options > Dynamic Transport) Pre- and Post-Roll are automatically disabled, the Link Timeline and Edit Selection option is disabled, and Loop Playback is automatically enabled. In Dynamic Transport mode, an additional Play Marker strip appears below the Main Timebase Ruler. The position of the Play Start marker (seen in Figure 5.6) determines where playback will start, and you can click or drag in the strip to reposition this marker to new time locations—even during playback. You also can make different Timeline and/or Edit selections without affecting the position of the Play Start marker. (If you *want* the Play Start marker to follow the current Timeline selection, you can enable Play Start Marker Follows Timeline Selection in the Operation tab of the Preferences dialog box.) While Loop Playback is enabled, playback will start from the current position of the Play Start marker; afterward, the current play selection (as shown in the Transport window) will loop.

Another option to consider is the Timeline Insertion/Play Start Marker Follows Playback option in the Operation tab of the Preferences dialog box. (You can also toggle this option on/off by clicking the Insertion Follows Playback button under the Pencil tool in the Edit window.) Although not generally useful for loop-based workflows (it causes you to lose your selection when stopping the Transport), this option can be useful in Dynamic Transport mode. With Insertion Follows Playback enabled, the Play Start marker will continually advance to the point where you stop playback. This can be especially useful for long spoken-word projects or for auditioning Beat Trigger locations when using Beat Detective, for example.

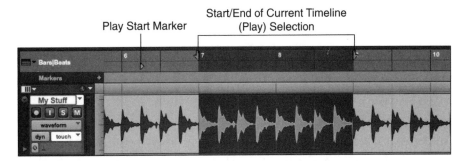

Figure 5.6 With Dynamic Transport mode enabled, the Play Start marker can be repositioned independent of the Timeline selection.

Tip Pro Tools includes several essential keyboard shortcuts for working in Dynamic Transport mode:

- To move the Play Start marker to the start of the current Edit selection (indicated by the Start field in the Edit window), press the period (.) on the numeric keypad and then the Down Arrow.

- To move the Play Start marker to the start or end of the current Timeline (Play) selection shown in the Transport window, press the period (.) on the numeric keypad and then the Left or Right Arrow key.

- To rewind or fast-forward the current position of the Play Start marker, press 1 or 2 on the numeric keypad, respectively.

Transport Master

Most users will leave the Transport Master set to control Pro Tools, the default option. However, if you want some other machine to directly control Transport functions in Pro Tools (which requires appropriate hardware/software, such as the synchronization peripherals discussed in Chapter 11, and optional MachineControl software), you would make that selection in the Transport Master field, selecting MachineControl, MMC (MIDI MachineControl), or ADAT. When MMC is selected, the playback position of Pro Tools is controlled by the position values transmitted from an external device via MIDI.

Record Enable Status/Input Status

These small indicators to the right of the Record button simulate LEDs. The top red indicator is lit whenever any track is record-enabled (that is, the R button in its track controls is red). The lower green indicator is lit when you enable Track > Input Only Monitoring so that all tracks monitor their selected input (regardless of whether any clips already reside on the track).

External Control Surfaces and the Pro Tools Transport Transport functions can be remote-controlled from external control surfaces. Options include Avid's D-Control, D-Command,

ProControl, Commandl8, Cl24 and older Controll24, and Artist Series and Pro Series controllers; the Mackie HUI; the J.L. Cooper CS-102; and others. (See Appendix B, "Add-Ons, Extensions, and Cool Stuff for Your Rig," for more information.)

MIDI Transport Controls

The Transport controls discussed in this section are related to tempo, time signature (meter), metronome settings, countoff settings, recording modes, and other features that are useful for music production, and especially for using MIDI and Instrument tracks in Pro Tools. They are also useful for working with loops and other beat-based material, especially in conjunction with Elastic Audio.

However, if you don't have any MIDI devices in your studio setup and don't use meter/tempo changes (with the Event > Identify Beat command or Elastic Audio, for example), you can save screen space by choosing not to view the MIDI Transport controls. By default, these controls appear at the right end of the Transport window (see Figure 5.7). To hide the MIDI Transport controls, deselect the option under View > Transport > MIDI Controls or deselect MIDI Controls from the pop-up menu in the upper-right corner of the Transport window.

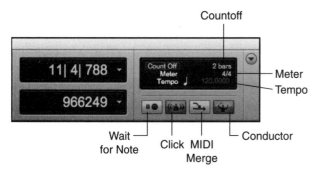

Figure 5.7   The MIDI controls portion of the Transport window.

Wait for Note

When the Wait for Note button is enabled during Record mode, recording on any record-enabled tracks (Audio, MIDI, and/or Instrument tracks) will not commence until a MIDI event is received from a connected controller. This option is really handy if you need time to get across the room to your keyboard, as the record pass won't start until you begin playing. This feature can also be useful for recording audio—a drummer I know uses a MIDI controller near his drum set to trigger recording remotely with Wait for Note, giving him time to climb behind his set after placing Pro Tools into Record mode.

Naturally, if the Pre-Roll option is enabled, Pro Tools will begin playback from an earlier point, punching into recording when the Start location is reached. The keyboard shortcut for enabling/disabling the Wait for Note option is F11. (Mac users: See the sidebar at the beginning of this chapter about changing the default Function key shortcuts in System Preferences.)

Metronome

The Metronome button, located to the right of the Wait for Note button, turns the metronome on and off. The metronome is typically used to drive the Click or TL Metro plug-in, but it can also be used to drive a click from a software instrument or an external sound module or synthesizer using MIDI.

Double-click the Metronome button to open the Click/Countoff Options dialog box (discussed in the next section), where you can specify whether the metronome sound should occur only while in Record mode, in Record and Play modes, or only during the countoff bars.

The Click plug-in (shown in Figure 5.8) is used as an insert on an Aux Input track. The Click plug-in automatically responds to the Pro Tools tempo when the Transport's Metronome button is enabled; no routing is necessary from the Click/Countoff Options dialog box. (Volume levels for accented and unaccented beats are set directly within the plug-in itself.)

To toggle the Metronome button on and off, you can also press the 7 key on the computer's numeric keypad.

Figure 5.8 The Click plug-in produces a variety of metronome sounds according to the current Pro Tools tempo.

Creating a Click Track (Versions 7.3 and Higher)   In the MIDI tab of the Preferences dialog box, you can elect to have Pro Tools automatically create a click track—an Aux Input track with the Click plug-in instantiated—in each new Pro Tools session you create. Alternatively, you can use the Track > Create Click Track command to add an Aux Input track with an active Click plug-in to an open session at any time.

Count Off

When Count Off is enabled (the Count Off display highlighted in the Transport window), Pro Tools plays the metronome click sound through the associated device (Click plug-in or other). The countoff will play for the specified number of measures, according to the current tempo and time signature, before playback or recording begins. When active, the Count Off click sound will play even if the Click button is turned off, in which case the click sound will stop once a Play or Record pass begins.

Clicking on the Count Off display in the Transport window toggles its status on/off. Double-clicking the bars display next to Count Off opens the Click/Countoff Options dialog box (shown in Figure 5.9), where you can modify the number or bars of countoff you want. (Notice that if you wish, countoff can occur only when you're in Record mode.) If you choose to use an external MIDI device (or software-based instrument) to produce the click sound, you can configure the MIDI notes, velocities, and output destination in this dialog box. (These settings have no effect when using the Click plug-in.)

Figure 5.9 Open the Click/Countoff Options dialog box by double-clicking the Click button or Count Off display in the Transport window.

To toggle the countoff on and off, you can also press the 8 key on your computer's numeric keypad.

MIDI Merge

With the MIDI Merge button enabled, when recording MIDI into a track already containing MIDI clips, the newly recorded MIDI data is combined into the existing material instead of replacing it as a new MIDI clip. For example, to build up a drum track while looping a couple bars, make your Timeline selection, ensure that Pro Tools is not in Destructive Recording mode, and enable Options > Loop Playback. Then enable the MIDI Merge button. The notes you play in each pass of the looped selection are *added* to the previous MIDI data instead of replacing it. (In Loop Recording mode, the MIDI Merge button is dimmed because it has no effect. Instead, for every cycle of loop recording where you input new MIDI data, a new separate take/MIDI clip is always created.)

To toggle MIDI Merge on and off, press the 9 key on the computer's numeric keypad.

Conductor Track (Tempo Ruler)

The Conductor Track button (which has a "conductor" icon) enables/disables the tempo map, as defined in the Tempo Ruler. If the Tempo Ruler in the Edit window contains tempo-change events, enabling this button makes these tempo events active. (To display the Tempo Ruler, choose View > Rulers > Tempo.) When the Conductor Track (or Tempo Ruler Enable) button is *not* active, the session will follow the tempo setting in the Transport window's Tempo field; this value, representing beats per minute (bpm), can be manually edited or modified while the Conductor Track button is disabled. Conversely, Pro Tools will *not* allow you to make manual changes to the Tempo field while the Conductor Track button is enabled.

Meter

The Meter display shows the time signature (such as 4/4, 3/4, 6/8, and so on) at the current play position, as defined in the Pro Tools Meter Ruler. (Different bars can have different meter settings in Pro Tools.) You can use the Time Operations/Meter Change window, shown in Figure 5.10, to create time signature events in Pro Tools.

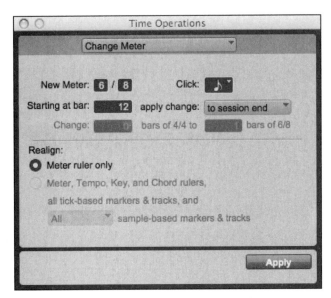

Figure 5.10 You can create changes of time signature (meter) in the Time Operations window.

Alternatively, double-clicking the Transport window's Current Meter indicator (or clicking the plus sign [+] in the Edit window's Meter Ruler) opens the Meter Change window, shown in Figure 5.11. The initial location for meter changes can be edited but defaults to the current Edit cursor position. Be sure to specify the beginning of Bar 1 (and select To Session End, if using the Time Operations window) if you want this new time signature to apply to the entire session.

Tempo

In this field, tempo settings appear in beats per minute. When the Conductor Track button is not enabled, the reference note value for the tempo (1/4 note, 1/8 note, and so on) appears in the pop-up Tempo Resolution selector at the left of the Tempo field. With the Conductor Track

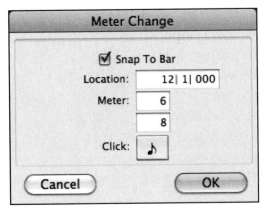

Figure 5.11 You can open the Meter Change window by double-clicking the Meter Indicator in the Transport window.

button off (i.e., Tempo Ruler disabled), the tempo setting can be manually changed in the Transport window in any of several ways:

- Click in the Tempo field and type a tempo value directly.

- Click and drag with the mouse to scroll the tempo value upward or downward.

- Select the Tempo field and tap in the tempo in real time using the T key on your computer keyboard.

- Select the Tempo field and tap in the tempo in real time from a connected MIDI controller (requires the Use MIDI to Tap Tempo option to be enabled in the MIDI tab of the Preferences dialog box).

When you enter a tempo using a Tap Tempo option, Pro Tools computes the average tempo based on your last eight (or fewer) taps. As discussed in Chapter 13, "A Multitrack Music Session," this can be a great method for setting up a click-track tempo when working with live performers. Just have them play through the song naturally while you tap along to set the tempo *before* feeding the click track into their cue mix.

Pro Tools also provides several options for setting the tempo and making tempo changes using the Tempo Ruler. One method is to set the tempo using the Identify Beat command. This command creates a tempo setting based on an audio selection. In this case, you will be using the tempo of an existing recording and setting the Pro Tools tempo to match. To use this feature, you must first enable the Conductor Track button (disabling the Tempo field in the Transport window).

You can also use the Tempo Operations window (shown in Figure 5.12) to create tempo-change events. (Select Bar 1, Beat 1 (1|1|000) and To Session End if you want these to apply to the entire session.)

Another method for creating tempo-change events is to click the plus sign (+) at the head of the Tempo Ruler in the Edit window. You can also *graphically* edit tempo changes in the Edit

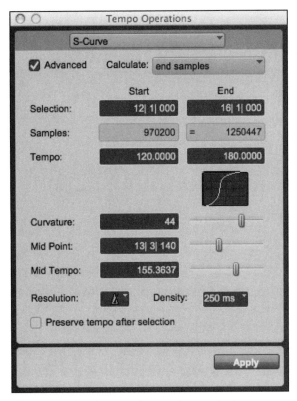

Figure 5.12 Tempo Operations window.

window using an editing pane that opens from the Tempo Ruler. To learn more sophisticated techniques for managing tempo settings in Pro Tools, see Chapter 8.

Tempo changes only affect material on tick-based tracks in Pro Tools. Typically, this includes MIDI notes and events on MIDI and Instrument tracks, which are tick-based by default (meaning their event positions are anchored to Bar|Beat locations). However, MIDI and Instrument tracks can be changed to sample-based so that the positions of the MIDI notes and events are not affected by subsequent tempo or meter changes. This is especially useful for MIDI-based sound effects for soundtrack work.

Similarly, Audio tracks, Aux Input tracks, and Master Fader tracks, which are sample-based by default, can be changed to tick-based. Material on tick-based tracks will move with tempo changes, meaning that audio clips and automation breakpoints will maintain their Bar|Beat locations as the tempo speeds up or slows down. This is especially useful for Elastic Audio–enabled Audio tracks.

Punching Recordings In/Out within Previously Recorded Material   Do you need to automate the replacement of one line of lyrics or dialog within an existing recording or one portion of an instrumental part? Here's a quick how-to. First, in the Edit window, use the Selector tool to precisely highlight the section of the track you want to replace. (Make sure that Options

> Link Timeline and Edit Selection is enabled.) Then enable the Pre-/Post-Roll buttons and set appropriate times in the Pre-/Post-Roll fields so that the performer can match the levels and sound of the material before and after the selection. Click on the track's Record button to record-enable it, click the Record button in the Transport, and then click Play. If the first take isn't perfect, you can repeat the recording as often as necessary.

This technique is useful for re-recording selections of audio. Alternatively, you can use the QuickPunch and TrackPunch recording modes. These modes allow you to punch in and out of recording on the fly. For more details, see the descriptions of these functions—which can be controlled via a footswitch with the 003 and Mbox Pro interfaces—in Chapter 8.

Table 5.1 lists just a few of the Transport-related keyboard shortcuts in Pro Tools. However, there are many more. Among the PDF documents included with the program is one entitled *Keyboard Shortcuts*, as mentioned previously. Print it out and keep it handy. In fact, consider using cardstock or even having it laminated. Learning keyboard shortcuts early in the process is one of the most important things you can do to increase your productivity with Pro Tools.

Table 5.1 Essential Keyboard Shortcuts for Transport Functions

Function	Macintosh	Windows
Play start/stop	Space bar 0 on numeric keypad	Space bar 0 on numeric keypad
Loop Playback On/Off	4 on numeric keypad Right-click Play button Control-click Play button	4 on numeric keypad Right-click Play button Start-click Play button
Rewind/Fast Forward	1 and 2 on numeric keypad	1 and 2 on numeric keypad
Return to Zero	Return on alpha keyboard	Enter on alpha keyboard
Go to End	Option+Return on alpha keyboard	Alt+Enter on alpha keyboard
Record start	Command+spacebar F12 3 on numeric keypad	Ctrl+spacebar F12 3 on numeric keypad
Record stop	Space bar	Space bar
Record stop and discard take	Command+. (period)	Ctrl+. (period) Esc key
Loop Record On/Off	5 on numeric keypad	5 on numeric keypad

(Continues)

Table 5.1 Essential Keyboard Shortcuts for Transport Functions (*Continued*)

Function	Macintosh	Windows
Select or Toggle through Record modes	Right-click on Record button Control-click on Record button	Right-click on Record button Start-click on Record button
Pre-/Post-Roll On/Off	Command+K	Ctrl+K
Show/Hide Transport	Command+1 on numeric keypad	Ctrl+1 on numeric keypad
Online mode On/Off	Command+J Option+spacebar	Ctrl+J Alt+spacebar
Online Record On/Off	Command+Option+spacebar	Ctrl+Alt+spacebar
Wait for Note (MIDI)	F11	F11
Click On/Off (MIDI)	7 on numeric keypad	7 on numeric keypad
Countoff On/Off (MIDI)	8 on numeric keypad	8 on numeric keypad
MIDI Merge On/Off (MIDI)	9 on numeric keypad	9 on numeric keypad
Select & cycle through time fields for numerical entry	Option+/ on numeric keypad	Alt+/ on numeric keypad
Select Main Counter for numerical entry	* (asterisk) on numeric keypad	* (asterisk) on numeric keypad
Move between columns during numeric entry in time fields	Period or Arrow keys	Period or Arrow keys

Summary

The Transport functions are the most frequently used features in Pro Tools; it is worth the effort to learn these keyboard shortcuts early. The keyboard shortcuts work regardless of whether the Transport window itself is currently visible. In this chapter and throughout this book, key commands are based on the default Transport mode for the numeric keypad; if desired, you can change the Transport mode in the Preferences dialog box.

The next chapter explores the most important elements in the Edit window.

6 The Edit Window

The Edit window (see Figure 6.1) is the heart of Pro Tools. This is where you can view the contents of your tracks, edit audio and MIDI clips, edit MIDI notes, create fades and crossfades, and draw automation changes for volume, panning, and plug-in parameters. In many respects, however, the Edit and Mix windows present two views of the same thing. Some items appear in both windows, including track names and the Mute, Solo, and Record Enable buttons. Furthermore, you can choose to have sends, inserts, I/O columns, and more display in the Edit window (displays that are typically associated with the Mix window). In any case, the Edit window is where you will spend much of your time in Pro Tools. The length of this chapter should give you an indication of how essential the features in the Edit window are for mastering Pro Tools.

The basic idea of the Edit window is a simple one. Underneath the toolbar and numerical display area at the top of the screen are the tracks in your session, stretching along a Timeline from left to right. Pro Tools provides seven types of tracks: Audio, Aux Input, Master Fader, Instrument, MIDI, and Video, plus VCA Master tracks in Pro Tools HD and Pro Tools with Complete Production Toolkit only. The Clip List is a "bin" that can be displayed or hidden at the right side of the Edit window. Clips (segments) of audio or MIDI you've recorded or imported into Pro Tools appear here. Pro Tools assigns clip names automatically as a result of recording, editing, or processing—regardless of whether the clips are currently placed into a track. You can drag clips directly from the Clip List onto tracks (Audio, MIDI, or Instrument, as appropriate). You can also preview audio clips inside the Clip List, and rename, export, or delete clips using either the pop-up menu at the top of the Clip List or the local menu that appears when you right-click one or more selected clips.

You can change the track view (display) of each track in the Edit window. For example, you can display automation graphs for each track's volume or panning. On Audio, MIDI, and Instrument tracks, the automation graph is superimposed over a dimmed-out version of the audio waveforms (or MIDI notes) within the clips that the track contains.

The four basic Edit modes in the Edit window are Shuffle, Slip, Spot, and Grid. These Edit modes determine how selections are made and how clips, automation, and MIDI data behave as they are moved within tracks. The Edit modes also affect how the Edit tools behave. Briefly, the Slip mode allows you to freely make selections and move clips; Shuffle mode causes clips to snap to each other like magnets; Grid mode constrains selections and clip movement to grid increments,

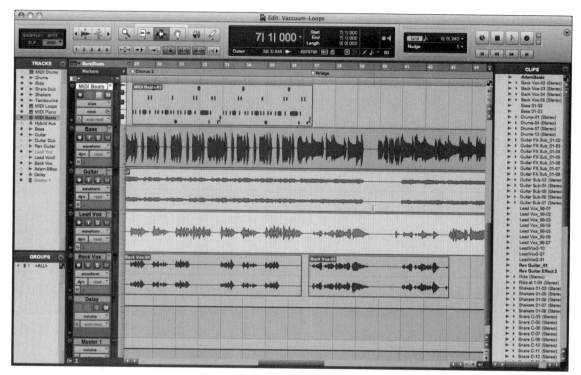

Figure 6.1 The Edit window, showing various track types and display formats.

causing clips to snap to the nearest Grid line when moved; while Spot mode allows new locations to be entered numerically in a dialog box.

Tip   Pressing the ~ (tilde) key will toggle between the four Edit modes. You can also select Shuffle, Slip, Spot, or Grid mode using the F1, F2, F3, or F4 key, respectively.

The first several sections in this chapter elaborate on the Edit tools, Edit modes, and Edit window controls available in Pro Tools. Following those sections, we discuss the Clip List, Track List, and Group List; track views and controls; rulers, ruler events, and markers; working with multiple takes; and displaying MIDI Real-Time Properties. We finish with a review of automation, automation controls, and the Tempo Editor.

Edit Tools: The Zoomer, Trim, Selector, Grabber, Smart Tool, Scrubber, and Pencil

The editing tools, shown in Figure 6.2, provide a multitude of ways to manipulate clips, automation, and MIDI events within Pro Tools tracks. (You can also use many of these in the graphic Tempo Editor.)

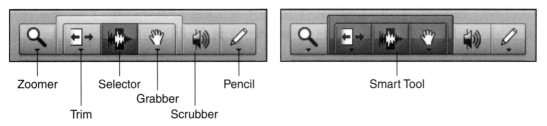

Figure 6.2   Editing tools: Zoomer, Trim, Selector, Grabber, Scrubber, and Pencil (left); Smart Tool (right).

Zoomer

When you select the Zoomer tool, the cursor will turn into a miniature magnifying glass, as shown in Figure 6.3. Click anywhere in a track to zoom in. Holding down the Option key (Alt key in Windows) will switch from zooming *in* to zooming *out*. (The plus sign in the zoom cursor will change to a minus sign.)

Figure 6.3   The Zoomer's magnifying glass cursor.

Clicking and dragging over a specific area of a track with the Zoomer will magnify it horizontally to fill the current width of the Edit window's track display area.

> **Tip**   Hold down the Command key (Mac) or Ctrl key (Windows) while clicking and dragging to zoom in vertically and horizontally on the selected area.

The Zoomer tool has a drop-down selector for its two modes: Normal Zoom and Single Zoom. Single Zoom deselects the Zoomer tool after one zoom, returning to whatever editing tool was previously selected—a handy timesaver! Use the F5 keyboard shortcut to select this tool and to toggle between the two Zoomer modes.

Later in this chapter, we'll discuss more handy zoom functions: zoom controls and preset buttons, keyboard shortcuts, and the Zoom Toggle icon.

Trim Tool

The Trim tool can be used to shorten or lengthen clips and MIDI notes and to scale automation shapes up or down. The current cursor location within the note or clip determines whether the tool will trim the beginning or end—the cursor changes from a left trim to a right trim as you move across a clip's midpoint, as shown in Figure 6.4. To force the Trim tool to flip to the opposite direction, press and hold the Option key (Alt key in Windows). In Grid Edit mode, the Trim tool snaps to each time increment on the editing grid as you drag. This lets you adjust a clip's end or beginning based on grid subdivisions (based on the current Grid value).

Figure 6.4 The Trim cursor is a left or right bracket at the beginning/end of clips and MIDI notes, or a horizontal bracket when scaling automation or MIDI controller data up or down.

Think of a clip as a window into an audio or MIDI recording, which you can make wider or narrower with the Trim tool. (You can't lengthen a clip beyond the actual beginning or end of its parent audio file, however.)

The Trim tool can also be used to scale automation shapes (such as volume, pan, send parameters, and some MIDI controller types) up or down within a track—for example, if you're satisfied with the overall volume changes you've created but want to trim them downward a few decibels.

Note   The *decibel*, abbreviated dB, is a measurement unit for power levels (volume).

To trim your volume automation, for example, you would use the Track View selector to display the Volume playlist (see the discussion of the Track View selector later in this chapter), make a selection of any portion of the automation, and then use the Trim tool to adjust the entire volume shape upward or downward. As you drag with the Trim tool, the *delta*, or amount of change, is indicated in dB.

The Trim tool has a drop-down selector for its different modes: Standard, Scrub, Time Compression/Expansion (or TCE), and Loop Trim. In Scrub Trim mode, the Trim tool functions like the Scrubber when you click and drag, allowing you to audition the track to locate an edit point by ear. Releasing the Scrub Trim tool trims the clip at the current location.

In TCE mode, the audio within the current selection is stretched or compressed to match the time range you've trimmed to. You can also use the TCE Trim tool on MIDI clips, scaling the MIDI data they contain. While the Tempo Operations window offers more practical ways to adjust tempos to specific durations or start/end points, users who compose or arrange music in Pro Tools may appreciate this function's usefulness for creating half-time or double-time versions of selected clips. For example, in Grid mode, you could select a four-bar clip and then use the TCE Trim tool to compress it to a two-bar duration.

In Loop Trim mode, the Trim tool allows you to loop audio clips or adjust of the length of a clip loop. Placing the Loop Trim cursor over the upper half of a looped audio or MIDI clip will trim either its beginning or end.

Use the F6 keyboard shortcut to select the Trim tool and to switch between its modes.

Selector

When you use this tool, the mouse cursor changes to an I-beam, as shown in Figure 6.5. Clicking and dragging within a track selects a horizontal range in the Timeline within a track. (The selection may or may not include or overlap clips.) With an existing selection, you can hold down the Shift key and click or drag to adjust the selection's duration. You can also Shift-click on additional tracks to select the same range in multiple tracks.

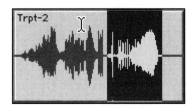

Figure 6.5 Use the Selector tool to select a horizontal range in the Timeline within a track.

The selected range is reflected in the Start, End, and Length indicators of the Transport window, and you'll hear it when you press Play (provided the Link Timeline and Edit Selection option is enabled). Be aware that the currently selected Edit mode also affects the behavior of the Selector as you click and drag. For example, in Grid mode, the beginning and end of your selections will snap to the nearest time increment. (See the next section in this chapter for more detail on Edit modes.)

The keyboard shortcut for the Selector is F7.

Fine-Tuning Your Selections Let's say you want to select four bars within a drum or rhythm track that was not recorded to a click (that is, not correlated with the Pro Tools tempo) and then loop the phrase to start building up a groove. It's extremely important that the selection be precise and that it's able to loop smoothly back onto itself. Here's a selection method you can use that is also handy for many other situations:

1. Select Slip Edit mode.

2. Click with the Selector tool to place the playback cursor exactly at the beginning of the four-bar phrase. (Zoom in to the sample level and place your cursor *precisely* at the zero crossing where the downbeat begins; then zoom back out.)

3. Hold down Control+Shift (Start+Shift in Windows) to *temporarily* select the Scrubber tool. Click and drag the Scrubber to the right until you locate the downbeat of

the bar following the end of your four-bar phrase; then release the mouse button (and the modifier keys). Your selection should now *roughly* correspond to the four bars, and the Selector tool should still be active.

4. Enable Options > Loop Playback and press the spacebar to play the selection. If you notice a hiccup in your looping phrase, you will need to refine your selection. Let's start by adjusting the end point of the selection to create a smooth loop.

5. Locate the numerical field labeled "Nudge" to the right of the Main Counter and Sub Counter in the Edit window. This sets the increments by which nudging is applied. Click to the right of the Nudge field to open the pop-up menu, select Min:Secs as the reference time units, and then select 1 millisecond as your initial nudge amount.

6. Hold down Command+Shift (Ctrl+Shift in Windows) and press the + and − (plus and minus) keys on the numeric keypad; the end point of the current selection will move forward or backward by the 1-millisecond nudge increment. Restart playback after making each adjustment to audition the change.

7. If needed, adjust the start point by holding down Option+Shift (Alt+Shift in Windows) and pressing the + and − (plus and minus) keys on the numeric keypad.

8. If you find that one millisecond is too large an increment to get a precise loop, you can select Samples as the Nudge value and work in 10-, 2-, or 1-sample nudge increments as necessary until the loop is completely smooth.

9. If desired, separate this selection as a new clip (Edit > Separate Clip > At Selection) and rename it.

10. Use the Clip menu's Loop command (Option+Command+L on Mac, Ctrl+Alt+L in Windows) to create any number of loop iterations. Have fun!

For more on beat-mixing techniques, see Chapter 12, "The Pro Tools Groove."

Grabber

When the Grabber tool is selected, the mouse cursor turns into a hand shape, as shown in Figure 6.6. The Grabber can be used to click and drag clips within tracks, adjust breakpoints in a track's automation, and drag notes within MIDI and Instrument tracks, among other things. The currently selected Edit mode (see the section "Edit Modes: Slip, Shuffle, Grid, and Spot" later in this chapter) determines how clips will behave when you use the Grabber to move them

Figure 6.6 Use the Grabber's hand cursor to drag clips, MIDI notes, and automation breakpoints.

around within tracks. For example, in Shuffle mode, a clip will always snap to the beginning or end of another existing clip (or to the beginning of the track). When you are in Grid mode, clips will snap to the nearest time increment when moved, according to the current Grid value.

Several important modifier keys alter how the Grabber tool operates:

- When viewing automation, clicking with the Grabber creates a new breakpoint. Option-click (Alt-click in Windows) on existing automation breakpoints with the Grabber cursor to delete them. For finer adjustment of breakpoint levels (for example, volume increments), hold down the Command (Mac) or Ctrl (Windows) key as you drag the breakpoint with the Grabber.

Note   The Command (Mac) or Ctrl (Windows) modifier provides fine adjustment of *many* fader and slider values in Pro Tools.

- Option-drag (Alt-drag in Windows) audio/MIDI clips or MIDI notes with the Grabber tool to *copy* instead of move them.
- When dragging or copying a clip from one track to another, hold down the Control key (Start key in Windows) to constrain its movement to the vertical direction—the clip will maintain its original Timeline location regardless of the current Edit mode.

The Grabber tool has three modes:

- **Time Grabber.** The Time Grabber is the standard mode for the Grabber tool. You can use the Time Grabber to drag entire clips within tracks.
- **Separation Grabber.** The Separation Grabber automatically splits an existing selection into a new clip as you drag (to move) or Option/Alt-drag (to copy). If the initial selection covers multiple tracks and clips, new clips will be created in each track.
- **Object Grabber.** The Object Grabber allows you to select non-contiguous clips, even on different tracks. This means that as you Shift-click to select additional clips within a track, for example, the range in the Timeline between them is not also selected, as is the case with the Time Grabber.

The F8 keyboard shortcut selects the Grabber and switches between the various Grabber tool modes.

Enhanced Features for Moving Clips   Right-clicking on a clip with any Edit tool produces a pop-up menu. For clips that are not bordered by an adjacent clip in the same track, the pop-up menu will enable the Snap to Next and Snap to Previous commands. These commands move the affected clip to the boundary of the next or previous clip, respectively, without requiring you to switch to Shuffle mode to accomplish the same thing.

Smart Tool

By clicking the bar above the Trim, Selector, and Grabber tools, you can activate the Smart Tool. This tool enables you to alternate between Trim, Selector, and Grabber tools without having to click individual tool buttons to select them. The Smart Tool activates each tool based on the position of the cursor over clips or MIDI notes (see Figure 6.7). To switch to the Smart Tool with a keyboard shortcut, press any two keys F6 through F8 simultaneously on both Mac and Windows setups.

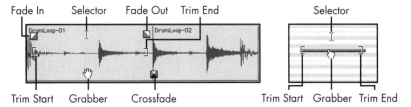

Figure 6.7 The Smart Tool changes function according to the cursor's position within a track or clip; the cursor shape changes accordingly. Shown here are cursors and edit operations within an Audio track (Waveform view) and a MIDI track (Notes view).

Here's how the Smart Tool features are triggered:

■ When the cursor is over the middle of any clip—in Waveform (audio), Clips (MIDI), or Blocks track view—and in the lower half of the clip graphic, the Grabber tool becomes active. In the upper half, the Selector tool becomes active.

■ When the cursor is near the beginning or end of any clip in these same views and in the clip's lower half, the Trim tool becomes active.

■ When the cursor is near the beginning or end of an audio clip and in the clip's upper half, the fade in/out function becomes active. (Fades are not applicable to MIDI clips.) When the cursor is near the boundary between two adjacent audio clips and in the lower half of either, the crossfade function becomes active.

■ On MIDI tracks in Notes view, the Selector tool is active whenever you are not directly over any MIDI notes and switches to the Grabber tool when directly over the middle of a MIDI note. The Trim tool becomes active when the cursor nears the beginning or ending of a MIDI note.

■ With automation displayed on a track (and certain MIDI controller parameters, such as Volume, Pan, Pitch Bend, Mod Wheel, Mute, Aftertouch, Velocity, and so on), the Smart Tool changes from the Selector to the Trim tool when positioned in the upper portion of the track. When the velocity stalks are displayed for MIDI note events, the tool changes to the Grabber when directly over the head of each stalk.

Using Modifier Keys with the Smart Tool   Pro Tools provides several options for temporarily switching to other editing tools while the Smart Tool is still selected:

- On Audio tracks, switch to scrubbing mode while using the Smart Tool in Waveform view (for example, to locate an audio event by ear) by holding down the Control key (Start key in Windows) and dragging.

- On MIDI and Instrument tracks, switch to the Pencil while using the Smart Tool in Notes view (for example, to insert a note event) by holding down the Control key (Start key in Windows).

- When displaying automation, switch to the Grabber while using the Smart Tool (for example, to insert or drag breakpoints) by holding down the Command key (Ctrl key in Windows). For finer control, keep this modifier key pressed down as you drag the breakpoint; otherwise, release the key for standard adjustments.

Note that when you select the Smart Tool, the current Trim tool mode (TCE, Scrub, and so on) will be in effect. This also applies to the current Grabber tool mode, with the exception of the Object Grabber, which will revert to standard mode (Time Grabber) when the Smart Tool is selected.

Scrubber

When you click and drag on a clip with the Scrubber tool (see Figure 6.8), the clip's audio will play back in the direction that you drag. This is handy for locating audio events. The farther and faster you drag from the initial click point, the faster the playback.

Figure 6.8 The Scrubber tool's speaker cursor.

The Scrubber tool takes its name from a feature on professional analog tape decks that allows you to engage the playback head and rock the tape back and forth (or *scrub*) across the head to audition the audio. This was the standard method for locating audio events on magnetic tape prior to physically cutting the tape to make edits.

Note that the Trim tool has an additional Scrub Trim mode, which scrubs audio in a similar fashion as you click and drag to lengthen or shorten audio clips.

To select the Scrubber tool from the keyboard, press F9.

Scrubber Operation Modes: Using Modifier Keys   Holding down the Shift key as you scrub audio playback selects a range within the track up to the point where you release the Scrubber tool. This makes it easy to locate the start or end of a specific sound as you're making a selection.

For finer control and slower playback while using the Scrubber, hold down the Command+ Control keys as you click and drag (Ctrl+Start in Windows). You can also combine these modifier keys with the Shift-scrubbing technique described in the preceding paragraph. Hold down the Option (Mac) or Alt (Windows) key as you scrub for extra-fast scrubbing (Shuttle mode).

You can also temporarily switch from the Selector tool (or Smart Tool) to the Scrubber by holding down the Control key (Start key in Windows) as you click and drag.

Pencil

When you are zoomed in far enough on the Waveform view of Audio tracks, you can actually *destructively* draw changes to the waveform with the Pencil tool (see Figure 6.9)—for example, to eliminate clicks. Note that this causes an immediate, permanent change to the audio file.

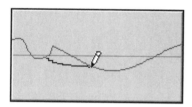

Figure 6.9 Use the Pencil tool to draw MIDI controller events or to correct small clicks in audio waveforms (when zoomed in to sample level).

On MIDI and Instrument tracks, you can draw in note events with the Pencil (and then reposition them with the Grabber, of course). If you draw a series of notes with the Pencil tool using the Line shape, their spacing reflects the current Grid value. However, you can also set a custom duration if you wish (for instance, to draw notes with 1/8-note duration and 1/2-note spacing between them).

You can also use the Pencil tool's Line shape to draw new velocity contours for existing MIDI notes (in Velocity view). When displaying automation on a track (such as volume, pan, send levels, or other parameters), you can also draw new shapes with the Pencil. The Pencil tool has a drop-down selector for its various drawing shapes: Free Hand, Line, Triangle, Square, Random, Parabolic, and S-Curve.

Use the F10 keyboard shortcut to select the Pencil and toggle through its modes.

Table 6.1 lists the keyboard shortcuts for the various editing tools.

For the Zoomer, Trim, Grabber, and Pencil tools, you can also repeat their function key shortcuts to toggle through their operation modes. (Mac users should see the sidebar in Chapter 5 about reassigning function keys F9, F10, F11, and F12.)

To cycle through the editing tools, press the Esc key or click the center mouse button (Windows only).

Table 6.1 Keyboard Shortcuts for Editing Tools

Keyboard Shortcut	Tool
F5	Zoomer
F6	Trim
F7	Selector
F8	Grabber
F6+F7 or F7+F8	Smart Tool
F9	Scrubber
F10	Pencil

Oops!   If you make a mistake, don't panic! Pro Tools supports up to 32 levels of undo. (The number can be changed in the Editing tab of the Preferences dialog box; users with slower computers can improve system performance by choosing a smaller number.) As a general rule, Pro Tools clearly warns you when a critical action cannot be undone. The Undo History window displays a list of undoable actions (optionally including their creation times), allowing you to return to a previous state—even if you've saved the session to disk since then.

Edit Modes: Slip, Shuffle, Grid, and Spot

The four Edit mode buttons in the upper-left area of the Edit window (see Figure 6.10) affect the behavior of the editing tools: how clips and MIDI notes respond when moved or placed within tracks (or lengthened/shorted by the Trim tool), how selections can be made, and how markers and breakpoints (for automation and tempo events) can be placed or moved around in the Timeline. During the course of a project, you will often find yourself switching between Edit modes for specific tasks; you can save significant time by learning to using function keys F1–F4 for this.

Figure 6.10 Edit modes affect selection, movement, and trimming of automation, audio, and MIDI clips/ notes.

Slip

In Slip edit mode, no restrictions are applied. You can freely drag clips and MIDI notes to any position within tracks, and the exact ranges you highlight with the Selector and Scrubber tools are not affected in any way. When using the Grabber, you can even place clips so that they overlap existing clips in the track. (In the View menu, you can choose to display an overlap icon; these are added to indicate wherever a clip boundary overlaps another underlying clip.) Slip mode allows extremely accurate selection, positioning, and trimming, all the way down to the level of individual audio samples, with no restrictions.

The keyboard shortcut for Slip mode is F3.

Shuffle

In Shuffle mode, clips move more or less like magnets. If you use the Grabber to drag a clip from the Clip List onto an empty track, it snaps to the beginning of the track. If you drag it into a track already containing a clip, the clip you're dragging snaps to the beginning or end point of the nearest clip already on the track, depending on where you release the mouse. All clips (and empty spaces between them) following a newly inserted clip in the track are pushed later in time (or *shuffled* to the right) by the duration of the new clip. When using the Trim tool in Shuffle mode, as you lengthen or shorten clips in a track, adjacent clips are moved as necessary so that they remain adjacent. When you have clips lined up in a track (for example, sections of a musical arrangement or drum variations) and use the Grabber to change their order in Shuffle mode, they remain stuck together, with no gaps between them, as you move them around.

The keyboard shortcut for Shuffle mode is F1.

> **Shuffle Lock Mode and Individual Clip Locking Commands**   To avoid accidentally enabling Shuffle mode, in which the positions of later events will change if you cut, paste, or trim earlier events, Command-click the Shuffle button (Ctrl-click in Windows). Also, you can Edit lock or Time lock clips while in Shuffle mode. The Clip > Edit Lock command prevents any editing or Timeline movement from occurring to the selected clip(s). The Clip > Time Lock command locks the selected clip(s) to their current location in the Timeline but allows certain editing functions to be applied.

Grid

Grid mode works like the snap-to-grid function in many drawing programs. All selections, trimming, and dragging of clips (as well as drawing of breakpoint automation) is constrained to the nearest time increment on the grid. You can use the Grid Value indicator and its pop-up menu in the Edit window toolbar to adjust the time units and spacing of the grid.

The keyboard shortcut for Grid mode is F4.

Pro Tools supports Bars|Beats, Min:Secs, Timecode, Feet+Frames, and Samples formats for grid increments. As shown in the "Grid Value Display" section later in this chapter, time units in the Grid Value selector can either follow the Time Scale of the Main Counter or be set independently.

Following are some key points for understanding how the Edit tools interact with Grid mode:

- When enabling the Tempo Ruler (also known as the Conductor track), you can set the Edit window's Main Counter to Bars|Beats and the Grid value to 1/4 or 1/8 notes to constrain your selections within audio and MIDI clips to these musical values. If you'd like to drop a snare sample on the second and fourth beats of each bar, for example, adjust the Grid value to 1/4 notes for precise placement.

- Grid mode can be very handy when you're dragging (Grabber) or drawing (Pencil) MIDI notes, as it force-quantizes their placement. As you drag an existing clip on a track to a new location, its left boundary is adjusted to the nearest grid increment, snapping from one to another as you drag left or right. Likewise, as you click (or click and drag) with the Pencil tool to create MIDI notes, the note beginnings and endings snap to the nearest grid increment. To temporarily suspend Grid mode so that you can freely reposition any event, hold down the Command key (Ctrl key in Windows).

- Grid mode is convenient for snapping automation breakpoints for volume or panning to exact beats and bar lines.

- Clips and MIDI notes resized with the Trim tool are snapped to the nearest grid increment while in Grid mode.

- Pro Tools users working on video and film projects will appreciate Grid mode for precisely adjusting the boundaries of audio events to whole seconds or frames. For sound designers creating button sounds or backgrounds that must be exactly 2 seconds, 500 milliseconds, or some other exact duration, trimming clips or selecting time ranges to bounce to disk in Grid mode can save time.

- Activating the Clips/Markers option in the Grid Value pop-up menu (shown in the "Grid Value Display" section later in this chapter) allows your selections, resizing, and movement of clips and MIDI notes to snap not only to the nearest grid increment, but also to marker locations and the boundaries of any clip in any track. Be sure to explore this commonly overlooked feature.

An extension of the Edit modes, called Snap To Grid, provides Grid mode functionality for selections while in any of the other Edit modes. This blends some aspects of Grid mode with features of the other primary mode. For instance, enabling Snap To Grid while in Shuffle mode enables you to make a precise grid-based selection of clips, delete or move the selection, and have the clips that follow the edit(s) in the track shuffle to the left or right.

Spot

Spot mode is convenient for placing clips at precise numerical locations—for example, when placing (spotting) sound effects during a film or video project. In this Edit mode, the Spot dialog box (shown in Figure 6.11) appears as soon as you click a clip with the Grabber, drag it onto a track from the Clip List, or click it with the Trim tool. In the Spot dialog box, you specify time values *numerically* for the start and/or end, duration, or sync point (Grabber only) of the selected clip.

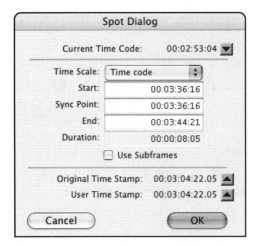

Figure 6.11 Use the Spot dialog box to specify positions (and selections) numerically. This can be especially powerful when Pro Tools is slaved to an external device via SMPTE timecode.

Spot mode is especially handy for audio editors in video facilities. Using a video master tape with a time-code window burned into the video image, you can jog the video tape exactly to the frame where an audio hit needs to be placed, click an audio clip or drag it onto a track, and then simply type the correct time into the Spot dialog box. Even easier, as timecode is received into Pro Tools, if the Spot dialog box is open—and the master video transport is in Play mode using LTC (longitudinal time code) or paused or stopped using VITC (vertical interval time code)—you can press the = (equals sign) key on your computer keyboard to automatically enter the current SMPTE position into its numeric fields.

For more information about using SMPTE timecode in post-production, see Chapter 14, "Post-Production and Soundtracks." The keyboard shortcut for Spot edit mode is F2.

Quick Entry in the Spot Dialog Box with the Plus/Minus Keys   Here's a quick way to add or subtract a given number of video frames to/from any of the time value fields in the Spot dialog box when using SMPTE time code as your Time Scale:

1. Make sure the pop-up Time Scale selector in the dialog box is set to Timecode.

2. Click in the last segment of the number to select the frames column.

3. Press + or − (plus or minus) on the numeric keypad.

4. Enter the number of frames to add or subtract.

5. Press Return (Enter in Windows) on the alphanumeric keyboard.

You can use the same function with the Time Scale set to Min:Secs, Bars|Beats, or Samples in the Spot dialog box.

As with other time value fields in Pro Tools, you can also use the up- and down-arrow keys on your computer keyboard to nudge numerical values in the Spot dialog box. Pressing the period or Right and Left Arrow keys lets you move from one column to another. You can also press Tab or Shift+Tab to toggle forward or backward from one field to another and use the Esc and Enter keys as shortcuts for the Cancel and OK buttons, as in many dialog boxes.

Zoom Controls and Zoom Preset Buttons

The zoom controls and zoom preset buttons, shown in Figure 6.12, change your view magnification for the contents of tracks in the Edit window either horizontally for the time scale or vertically for audio amplitude or MIDI pitches. You can store and recall your own zoom presets, which can be a significant time saver.

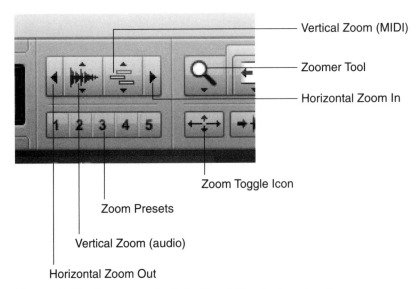

Figure 6.12   Zoom controls in the Edit window toolbar.

If you don't see the zoom controls in the Edit window toolbar, click on the triangle icon in the upper-right corner to access the menu for displaying features in the toolbar. Simply select the Zoom Controls option, and they will appear to the right of the Edit Mode selectors.

The zoom controls include the following:

■ **Horizontal Zoom In/Out.** Clicking the Horizontal Zoom In button expands your current view along the (horizontal) Time Scale of the Edit window, while clicking the Horizontal Zoom Out contracts your current view. Zoom in to display more detail with a shorter duration; zoom out to display a longer duration with less detail.

■ **Vertical Zoom In/Out (Audio).** These buttons affect the displayed range on the amplitude (vertical) axis of audio waveforms within Audio tracks only. They have no effect on the view of other track types or on the actual amplitude of the clips.

- **Vertical Zoom In/Out (MIDI).** These buttons zoom the vertical axis (pitch, or note number) on all MIDI and Instrument tracks only. They have no effect on your view of MIDI *controller* data in these tracks, and they don't affect other track types.

- **Zoom Presets.** These buttons (1–5) are used to store horizontal (Time Scale) zoom presets for the current session. Click any Zoom Preset button to recall its stored zoom settings; Command-click (Ctrl-click in Windows) on any Zoom Preset button to store the current horizontal zoom settings under that preset.

As additional zoom methods, Pro Tools provides track height buttons and horizontal zoom buttons in the lower-right corner of the Edit window (see Figure 6.13). The + and − buttons beneath the vertical scroll bar increase or decrease the track heights of all visible tracks in the session. The + and − buttons along the bottom, to the right of the horizontal scroll bar, zoom the Timeline in or out, similar to the Horizontal Zoom In/Out buttons in the toolbar.

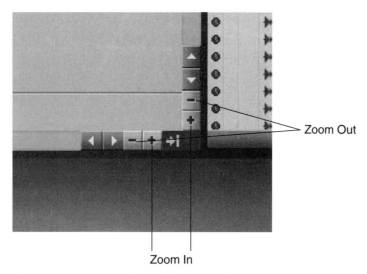

Figure 6.13 Vertical and horizontal zoom buttons in the Edit window.

In addition, Pro Tools provides audio and MIDI zoom buttons in the upper-right corner of the Edit window (see Figure 6.14). As with the Vertical Zoom In/Out controls in the toolbar for audio and MIDI, clicking the top of the button will zoom in and clicking the bottom of the button will zoom out.

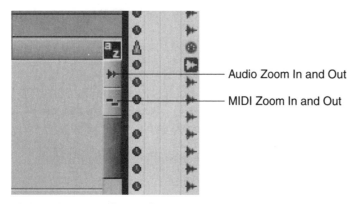

Figure 6.14 Audio and MIDI zoom buttons in the Edit window.

You will commonly need to zoom in and out as you edit data in your tracks. Be sure to check out the sidebar that follows about keyboard shortcuts for zooming. Along with the basic Transport functions, zooming shortcuts should be among the first ones you memorize in Pro Tools!

Zoom! Faster!—Zooming Shortcuts   Getting around quickly in your project is essential, not only for building up creative momentum but also to satisfy impatient clients. Here are some shortcuts to make navigation a bit easier:

- Hold down the Command key (Ctrl key in Windows) and press the bracket keys ([and]) to zoom in and out horizontally in the Edit window.

- Hold down the Command+Option keys (Ctrl+Alt in Windows) and press the bracket keys ([and]) to zoom in and out vertically on all Audio tracks.

- Hold down the Command+Shift keys (Ctrl+Shift in Windows) and press the bracket keys ([and]) to zoom in and out vertically on all MIDI tracks.

- Hold down the Command key (Ctrl key in Windows) while highlighting an area of an audio waveform with the Zoomer tool to simultaneously zoom in horizontally and vertically.

- Double-click the Zoomer to zoom completely out so that the entire session fits into the Edit window.

- Option-click (Alt-click in Windows) the Zoomer tool to horizontally zoom your current track selection to fill the current width of the Edit window.

- Option-click (Alt-click in Windows) the zoom arrow buttons (or the Vertical Zoom buttons) to recall the *previous* horizontal zoom setting. Let's say, for example, that you're viewing tracks at a comfortable horizontal zoom level, but just to confirm where you are within the entire session, you double-click the Zoomer tool so that the entire session's duration fits into the Edit window. Option/Alt-clicking on either of the Zoom In/Out buttons will return you to the previous zoom level.

- Learn to use the Single Zoom mode (which reverts to the previous Edit tool after zooming once). This is a real time-saver and is all too easy to overlook.

- Store zoom settings as an attribute of any marker or selection Memory location. (See the "Timeline Display: Timebase Rulers and Marker Memory Locations" section later in this chapter.)

Zoom Toggle Icon

This icon appears beneath the Zoomer tool. It allows you to store certain parameters of an Edit window view and toggle them on/off at any time. The parameters affected by the Zoom Toggle settings are track height, display mode, horizontal and vertical (audio/MIDI) zoom, and Grid value.

To use Zoom Toggle, make a selection and click the Zoom Toggle button to enable it. The selection display will change, based on your current Zoom Toggle preferences. Click the Zoom Toggle button again to disable it and return to your previous zoom display.

The Zoom Toggle preference settings have a significant impact on the results of activating Zoom Toggle and can often produce unexpected results. Many of the options are useful for advanced workflows but can be disorienting for general use. The following settings are convenient for general use without being overly confusing for users who are less familiar with this function (choose Setup > Preferences and select the Editing tab):

- Set both Vertical MIDI Zoom and Horizontal Zoom to Selection.
- Uncheck Remove Range Selection After Zooming In.
- Set Track Height to Jumbo or Extreme.
- Set Track View to Waveform/Notes.
- Uncheck both Separate Grid Settings When Zoomed In and Zoom Toggle Follows Edit Selection.

Once you are familiar with basic Zoom Toggle functionality using the above preference settings, you can experiment with other settings to determine what fits best for your working style. No matter what settings you use, keep in mind that Zoom Toggle works best as a temporary mode: get in the habit of enabling it only when needed, always toggling back to the disabled state when the zoom settings are no longer needed. This will help prevent issues the next time you need to use Zoom Toggle, especially if any of the preference settings are configured to Last Used.

Track Resizing Shortcuts   Pro Tools offers several handy shortcuts for changing the track heights in your session:

- To resize one or more tracks in relation to others in the same session, hold down the Control key (Start key in Windows) as you press the Up and Down Arrow keys on the computer keyboard. All tracks containing the Edit cursor or an Edit selection will resize.
- To resize all tracks simultaneously, add the Option key (Alt key in Windows) to the previous combination.
- To fit all tracks in the session into the Edit window, hold Control+Option+Command (Ctrl+Start+Alt in Windows) as you press the Up or Down Arrow key.

Event Edit Area (Counters and Edit Selection Fields)

How can you edit your audio if you don't know where you *are*? The indicators in the Event Edit area, shown in Figure 6.15, let you know where you are in the session's Timeline, the time values for your current selection, and where your cursor is as you move it around within Pro Tools tracks. You will find these very useful when making edit selections, when selecting audio material for bouncing out mix files to disk, and for controlling playback in Pro Tools.

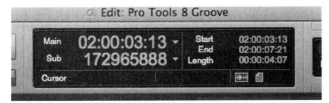

Figure 6.15 The Event Edit area provides information about the current selection and playback location.

Edit Selection Fields (Start/End/Length)

The Start, End, and Length numerical fields display information about the current Edit window selection in the Main Counter's current time units. As you use the Selector and Grabber tools to make selections within tracks, the selection details will be indicated in the Start, End, and Length fields. When using the Trim tool to lengthen or shorten clips, the values here also change in real time as you drag the cursor.

You can enter values directly into these fields to modify or create a selection and/or change the current playback cursor location if Options > Link Timeline and Edit Selection is enabled. Here are a few shortcuts for quick entry into these fields:

- Use the / (forward slash) key to toggle between the Start, End, and Length indicators.

- Use the . (period) key or Right and Left Arrow keys to switch from one column to another within these fields.

- Use the Up and Down Arrow keys to incrementally increase or decrease the selected value.

- Press the + or – (plus or minus) key followed by a number and the Return or Enter key to increase or decrease a value by a specific amount.

Main/Sub Counters

During playback or recording, the Main and Sub Counters display the current play position. If the Sub Counter is not displayed, click the triangle drop-down menu next to the Main Counter and choose Show Sub Counter. If Options > Link Timeline and Edit Selections is enabled, the Start and End fields in the Transport window will match your current Timeline selection in the Edit window. If not, the Transport's Timeline (play) selection and Main Location Indicator (the playback cursor position) will not change when you make a new edit selection. This can be useful while editing; for example, you can have the same four-bar selection always play when you press the spacebar, even as you edit and move clips within that range.

A pop-up menu to the right of the Main Counter and Sub Counter allows you to select different timebase units. The timebase units you select for the Main Counter will affect the timebase units displayed in the Edit window's main ruler (and vice versa). The units currently selected for the Main Counter are also reflected in the Cursor Location Indicator and in the Start, End, and Length indicators for edit selections.

Main Counter   To directly highlight the Edit window's Main Counter, press the = (equals sign) key on the numeric keypad. As in other time value fields in Pro Tools, there are several methods for directly entering values here: direct numerical entry, Up and Down Arrows, or plus and minus keys, for example. Press Return or Enter to confirm your entry, moving the playback cursor to the new position. Remember that you can use the period key or Right and Left Arrow keys to navigate between columns in any timebase that has multiple segments (for example, minutes, seconds, or milliseconds). Lastly, if you open the Big Counter (Window > Big Counter), the Main Counter's values are displayed large enough for you to see them from across the room while recording takes; you can also type values directly into this oversized view.

MIDI Note Attributes

When a single MIDI note is selected in a MIDI or Instrument track in Notes or Velocity view, the editable value fields shown in Figure 6.16 display the note's pitch, attack velocity, and release velocity. The keyboard techniques described for the Main Counter and Sub Counter also work in these fields, once you click within them to enable them for editing. Additionally, you can enter new values for each of these MIDI note attributes by striking keys on a connected MIDI keyboard or other controller. This can save time, especially if you record-enable the track—you'll hear the result of the new values in real time as you repeatedly strike the key.

Figure 6.16 Additional fields appear in the Event Edit area when MIDI notes are selected.

When *multiple* MIDI notes are selected, each of these fields initially appears with a zero value and a delta symbol (for the amount of change). As you drag the group of selected notes to a new pitch, the corresponding amount of transposition (in semitones) is displayed in the Pitch field. Alternatively, you can select the Pitch field and enter a desired transposition for the selected notes—for example, +7 semitones to raise them by a perfect fifth or +12 for an octave. Typing numbers or clicking and dragging also works for altering Attack and Release Velocity values of multiple notes; the amount of change (the delta) is displayed (compared to the original velocity values for each note in the selection). As always with MIDI, there are upper and lower limits for both pitch and velocity; values can't exceed these, no matter how much change you apply.

Edit Window Transport Buttons

The Transport buttons in the Edit window (see Figure 6.17) duplicate the buttons in the Transport window for convenience while working in the Edit window. Even when the Transport window isn't visible, all the same keyboard shortcuts apply; for example, you can press the spacebar to start and stop playback, press Return (Enter in Windows) on the alphanumeric keyboard to return to the beginning of the session Timeline, press Command+spacebar (Ctrl+spacebar in Windows) to start recording, and so on.

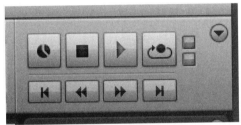

Figure 6.17   For convenience, the Transport buttons are duplicated at the upper-right corner of the Edit window.

Using a Scroll-Wheel Mouse   Like most Internet browsers, word processors, and other programs, Pro Tools supports use of the scroll wheel. Productivity in Pro Tools is greatly improved by using a mouse or trackball with two-button functionality and a scroll wheel. Pro Tools scroll-wheel techniques include the following:

■ You can roll the mouse wheel to scroll vertically in any active window or area in which a scroll bar is currently visible—for example, the Mix and Edit windows, Memory Locations window, Clip List, or MIDI Event List.

■ To scroll your view horizontally in the Edit or Mix window, you can hold down the Shift key as you use the mouse's scroll wheel.

■ To zoom in/out horizontally in the Edit window, hold down the Option key (Alt key in Windows) as you roll the wheel up or down.

■ To zoom the audio waveform display in/out vertically in the Edit window, hold down the Option+Shift keys (Alt+Shift keys in Windows) as you scroll.

■ To zoom MIDI notes display in/out vertically in the Edit window, hold down the Control+Option keys (Alt+Start keys in Windows) as you scroll up or down.

■ To scroll the Notes display of a specific MIDI or Instrument track up or down, hold down Command+Control+Option keys (Alt+Start+Ctrl in Windows) as you scroll up or down.

Edit Window Option Buttons and Functions

Additional buttons/indicators appear in the Edit window toolbar, providing a convenient way to toggle certain options and preferences on/off. These are shown in Figure 6.18.

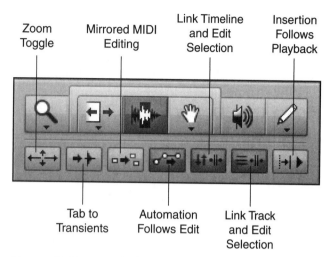

Figure 6.18 Toggle buttons in the Edit window toolbar (Pro Tools 10 shown).

Tab to Transients

When this button is enabled, pressing the Tab key within an Audio track automatically moves the cursor to a location immediately before the next transient peak in the track or to the next clip boundary (beginning or end). This can be an important time saver when editing a long recording such as a voice-over. Within a vocal or guitar overdub, you can select from the current location or selection to the beginning of the next phrase by holding down the Shift key as you tab. (As when selecting clips within tracks, pressing Option+Tab moves backward, and you can combine it with the Shift key to make selections.) Tab to Transients also works when multiple tracks are selected, moving the playback location (or extending the selection, if you're holding down the Shift key) to the next transient found in *any* of these tracks. This is especially convenient when editing multiple drum or backing vocal tracks. Using Tab to Transients within MIDI tracks lets you tab to the start of subsequent or previous MIDI notes in the same manner as you do transients in Audio tracks.

Link Timeline and Edit Selection

When the Link Timeline and Edit Selection button is enabled, the selections you make within tracks or on rulers will not only set the values of the Start and End indicators at the top of the Edit window (the edit selection), but also in the Transport window (the play selection, which determines where playback starts and stops). In the event you wish to unlink the two, simply deselect this button (refer to Figure 6.18). For example, you might want to select and edit individual notes and clips while a longer four-bar selection loops or edit a different part of the session without losing your current timeline selection for playback. Toggling this button on and off is the same as choosing Options > Link Timeline and Edit Selection.

Note   Activating Dynamic Transport mode, via the Options > Dynamic Transport command, automatically enables loop playback and disables Link Timeline and Edit Selection.

Link Track and Edit Selection

When this option is enabled, via the Edit window button or the corresponding command in the Options menu, selecting any material for editing within the track also automatically selects the track itself, highlighting its track name. This is a convenient way to select one or more tracks for track-level operations—for example, grouping them, making them inactive, or dragging them to a new position in the Track List. If you hold down Option+Shift (Alt+Shift in Windows) as you change a track parameter, this change is applied to all currently *selected* tracks. In contrast, if you hold down the Option key (Alt key in Windows) without the additional Shift key modifier, the change applies to *all* tracks, whether selected or not. Used in conjunction with the Link Track and Edit Selection feature, this Option+Shift (Alt+Shift) technique is a convenient way to change the track height, view format, Record/Solo/Mute button states, automation mode, time-base format, and other track attributes based on your current selections within multiple tracks.

Mirrored MIDI Editing

When you use this feature, any changes you make to a MIDI clip are also applied to all other MIDI clips with the same name. For instance, suppose you start with a very simple four-bar drum pattern—say, a MIDI clip called Drum4—to build your arrangement and you want to edit velocities or otherwise embellish this basic pattern after adding a few more instrumental parts. With Mirrored MIDI Editing enabled, as you make each edit in a single instance of this MIDI clip, the same change is applied to all other instances of the MIDI clip.

Insertion Follows Playback

When selected, this feature relocates the edit cursor to the point on the Timeline where playback stops. If you play back from the session start for two bars, the edit cursor and playback cursor will relocate to the end of the second bar after playback. This feature is useful for certain Pro Tools workflows, but it is not typically the desired behavior. When not active, the playback cursor returns to the point on the Timeline where playback started, which is standard Transport behavior for Pro Tools.

If you have made a selection in the Timeline you want to keep while starting and stopping playback, make sure to de-select Insertion Follows Playback to prevent your selection from being dropped when you stop playback.

Automation Follows Edit

The Automation Follows Edit button is new to Pro Tools 10. This button toggles the Automation Follows Edit option on/off. Enabling the button has the same effect as selecting Options > Automation Follows Edit. When enabled, any automation present within the boundaries of an audio or MIDI clip or selection will be affected by edits to that clip or selection. For example, moving an audio clip that has volume automation associated with it will move the corresponding section of volume automation. When disabled, automation is not affected by edits to audio or MIDI clips or notes. This option should typically be enabled for general-purpose editing.

Other Edit Window Controls and Functions

Various additional selectors and buttons appear in the Edit window toolbar, Rulers, and the display area just above the tracks display. These are discussed in the following sections.

Grid Display and Grid Value Display

The Grid Display button controls whether the grid lines are displayed in the Edit window. When the button is green, the grid is displayed. The Grid Value setting reflects the current time increments that govern the selection and movement of clips, trimming, and automation when Grid edit mode is enabled. As shown in Figure 6.19, the pop-up Grid Value selector menu to the right of this indicator lets you change the grid size. The Grid timebase defaults to match the Main Time Scale, but you can set the timebase for the Grid Value field separately. When Grid mode is selected, moving and trimming (resizing) clips and MIDI notes is constrained (quantized) to grid increments. When you drag with the Selector tool, the beginning and end values of the selected time range also snap to the nearest grid increment. (Refer to the "Grid" section under "Edit Modes: Slip, Shuffle, Grid, and Spot," earlier in this chapter.)

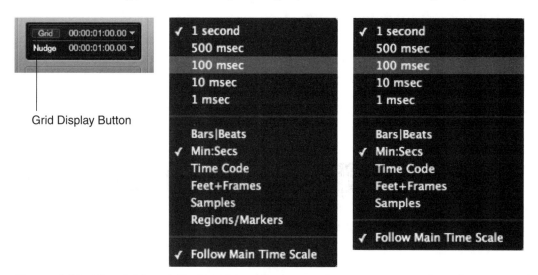

Figure 6.19 The Grid and Nudge Value displays and pop-up menus for selecting Grid/Nudge increments.

Nudge Value Display

This field's pop-up selector (also shown in Figure 6.19) sets the time increment to be used when you nudge clips, selections, and events with the + and – (plus and minus) keys on the numeric keypad (as discussed previously). As with the Grid value, the units for nudging can reflect those of the Main Time Scale, or you can set them separately. For example, if you select an audio or MIDI clip and use the pop-up display to the right of the Nudge Value indicator to select a

1-millisecond nudge increment (or one SMPTE frame, or one 1/8 note), each time you press the + or – key, the clip will move forward or backward from its present position by that amount of time. This lets you make fine adjustments to timing without zooming all the way in to drag clips around. Nudging also works on MIDI note selections within MIDI tracks as well as selected breakpoints for automation and MIDI controller data, such as mod wheel, pitch bend, after-touch, and others. Besides the preset Nudge values, you can also type in any other amount. This can be useful if, for example, you are nudging sound effects and you find that 100 milliseconds is too large while 10 milliseconds is too small.

Here are some other useful techniques for nudging:

- To nudge a selection forward or backward by the current Nudge value without altering the selected audio or MIDI data, hold Shift while pressing the + and – (plus and minus) keys on the numeric keypad.

- To nudge only the end of a selection, hold down the Command key (Ctrl key in Windows) as you nudge with the + and – (plus and minus) keys on the numeric keypad.

- To nudge only the beginning of the selection, hold down the Option key (Alt key in Windows) as you nudge with the + and – (plus and minus) keys on the numeric keypad.

- To nudge the waveform contents of an audio clip without affecting the clip's current start and end points in the track, hold down the Control key (Start key in Windows) as you nudge with the + and – (plus and minus) keys on the numeric keypad. (Additional audio must be available within the clip's parent audio file for this to work.) This can be handy, for example, to trim excess silence at the beginning of a clip without changing the clip start time (such as a cymbal crash that you've already placed exactly on the 1/4 note).

- With Commands Keyboard Focus mode enabled (the a...z button in the upper-right corner of the Edit window's tracks area), you can nudge by the current Nudge value using the . (period) and , (comma) keys or by the next-larger Nudge value using the / (forward slash) and M keys.

Tip As with many other Commands Keyboard Focus shortcuts, you can hold down the Control key (Start key in Windows) to use the keyboard shortcuts for nudging when Commands Keyboard Focus mode is not active.

Cursor Location/Cursor Value

The Cursor Location display reflects the (horizontal) time location as you move the cursor within the Edit window (in whatever units the Main Counter is using). The Cursor Value display reflects the current vertical position of the cursor within a track. For example, while moving your cursor vertically over a MIDI track in Notes view, the Cursor Value display shows note numbers to indicate its current position. When the track view display is set to Volume, the value shown for the current cursor position is decibels (dB) for audio or 0–127 for MIDI track volumes. Both of these fields are shown in Figure 6.20. They're not editable fields, but instead provide feedback about the current position as you move the cursor—for example, while dragging automation breakpoints up and down or resizing notes and clips.

Figure 6.20 These fields indicate that the cursor is currently within a MIDI track, at SMPTE time code 1 hour, 59 minutes, 20 seconds, and 8 frames, with a vertical position corresponding to MIDI volume 82.

Ruler View Selector

This pop-up selector, shown in Figure 6.21, enables/disables the different ruler types in the Edit window and duplicates options in the View > Rulers submenu.

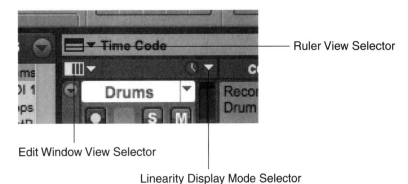

Figure 6.21 The Ruler View selector, the Edit Window View selector, and the Linearity Display Mode selector.

Edit Window View Selector

Use this pop-up selector, also shown in Figure 6.21, to display the Comments, I/O, Inserts, Sends, Instrument, Real-Time Properties, and Track Color columns at the left side of the Edit window's tracks. This selector duplicates options available in the View > Edit Window submenu.

Linearity Display Mode Selector

You can use this selector, also shown in Figure 6.21, to switch the horizontal scale for displaying all track events in the Edit window between Linear Sample Display (absolute time) and Linear Ticks Display (relative to the current tempo settings). In Linear Sample Display format, the display corresponds to actual audio samples at the current sample rate, so if you increase the musical tempo, each bar (in the Bars|Beats Ruler, for example) occupies less space. Conversely, in Linear Ticks Display format, all bars of 4/4 occupy the same amount of horizontal space in the Edit window, even if tempo changes actually mean that each bar corresponds to a different amount of absolute time (as measured in samples).

Commands Focus

In Pro Tools, a...z Keyboard Focus buttons are available in the upper-right corner of the Clip List, the Group List, and the Edit window tracks area, providing key-focus shortcuts for commands associated with the active area (see Figure 6.22). When one of these buttons is highlighted, its keyboard-focus commands (single-key shortcuts from the alphanumeric keyboard) are active. For example, when the Keyboard Focus button for the Clip List is active, you can select clips by typing the first few letters of the clip name. When Keyboard Focus is active for the Group List, you can toggle Edit and Mix groups on and off by typing the group ID letter. When Commands Keyboard Focus is active, you can access many editing and play commands via single keystrokes on the alphanumeric keyboard.

Figure 6.22   The Keyboard Focus button, available for the Clip List, the Group List, and the Edit window tracks area.

Clip List

This "bin" at the right edge of the Edit window, shown in Figure 6.23, lists all the MIDI and audio clip names referenced within the session—regardless of whether they have been placed into tracks—as well as clip group names.

Figure 6.23   The Clip List shows audio clips, MIDI clips, and clip groups.

When you create a new session, the Clip List is empty. As soon as you record into any audio, MIDI, or Instrument track, a new clip is created based on the name of the track in which it was recorded. You can also import external audio files directly into the Clip List (or directly into a track) by dragging from the Workspace browser window or Finder (or Explorer in Windows) or by using the File > Import > Audio command. Imported audio files and clips appear with their original names in the Clip List; to change a clip's name, double-click it and type the new name in the Name dialog box that appears.

Renaming Clips   As mentioned, you can double-click to rename any clip in the Clip List. In addition to this, you can use the Grabber to double-click audio clips directly within tracks; this opens the renaming dialog box. Alternatively, you can right-click any clip—either in the Clip List or within a track—to display a pop-up menu that enables you to rename that clip. Remember that as you record into audio and MIDI tracks, clip names are created based on the track name in which they were recorded. Take a moment to name your tracks as you prepare to record; it will save time and confusion later!

Note   Many clip names represent portions within longer "parent" audio files. Other clip names represent entire audio files, in which case their names appear in bold type inside the Clip List. When you rename any of these whole-file audio clips, an additional option appears in the dialog box, enabling you to specify whether you want to also rename the source disk file or only the clip name as it appears within the current Pro Tools session.

Many of your edits in Pro Tools will cause additional clips to be created. For example, if you cut the middle out of an existing audio clip, you will end up with three clip definitions, all referring to different selections with the same parent audio file: the original clip, plus two additional clip definitions for the portions before and after the cut. An option in the local menu of the Clip List allows you to choose whether these auto-created clips should be shown.

As elsewhere, you can Shift-click to select multiple adjacent items in the Clip List and/or Command-click (Ctrl-click in Windows) to make non-contiguous selections. If you wish, you can also choose to display the source file names, full directory paths, and/or disk locations in the Clip List, although doing so will make the displayed clip names much longer.

Previewing Audio and MIDI Clips in the Clip List   Option-click (Alt-click in Windows) and hold on any audio or MIDI clip in the Clip List to listen to it without having to drag it out onto a track. MIDI clips will be previewed via the default Thru instrument defined in the MIDI tab of the Preferences dialog box; this can be configured to always follow the MIDI output assignment of the first selected MIDI/Instrument track. Of course, you can also preview audio and MIDI clips in the Project and Workspace browser windows, even before importing them into the current Pro Tools session.

How Pro Tools Creates Clip Names as You Record and Edit   As mentioned previously, when you record the first audio (or MIDI) clip into a track, a new clip is created based on that track's name. For example, if you record onto a track named "Cornet," here's what happens:

1. The first recorded clip will appear on the track and in the Clip List with the name "Cornet_01," and a similarly named file will be created inside your session's Audio Files folder.

2. The second recorded clip will appear with the name "Cornet_02." The numerical suffix is used to identify successive recordings.

If you delete a section in the middle of the second clip, Pro Tools automatically assigns two new clip names to the segments remaining before and after the cut, appending -01 and -02 to the original clip's name—in this case, Cornet_02-01 and Cornet_02-02. Pro Tools will often create new clip definitions as a result of editing operations, using these numerical suffixes to identify them.

To identify what clips are used where, you can select any clip within the Clip List, and it will also be selected every place it occurs within a track (and vice versa). This behavior is based on the default options in Preferences > Editing; some users prefer to have Clip List and Edit selections function independent of each other.

Using the Clip List Pop-Up Menu

Audio files are very large. No matter what your system's disk capacity is, it is still important to limit your audio projects to a reasonable amount of disk space. For one thing, this will make the backing up and archiving of your project data more efficient.

Many of the commands in the Clip List pop-up menu (shown in Figure 6.24) are self-explanatory. This section lists a few commands that are especially useful for making sure your projects don't needlessly occupy disk space for unused audio data. As stated before, it is extremely important to assign meaningful names to clips as you work in Pro Tools. Imagine sorting through hundreds of clips from dozens of tracks (and takes) to delete unused files and reduce the amount of disk space consumed by your session, and consider how much easier this would be if the clips all had meaningful names (if the tenor sax solo is actually named TenorSax_12 rather than, say, Audio 17_12)!

Select Unused Clips, Unused Clips Except Whole Files, Offline

The Select Unused Clips and Select Unused Clips Except Whole Files commands select all clips in the list that are not currently placed on any Audio tracks in this session. Audio clips that represent entire audio files appear in bold type within the Clip List. (These may have been created by new recordings, by importing audio files into the session, as a result of menu commands such as Consolidate Selection, or by applying any function in the AudioSuite menu with the Create

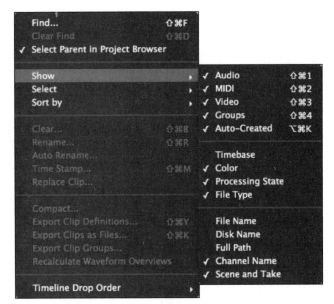

Figure 6.24 The Clip List pop-up menu helps manage clips (and clip groups) as well as MIDI and audio files in Pro Tools projects.

Continuous File or Create Individual Files option enabled.) It's common to exclude whole-file clips (via the Select > Unused Regions Except Whole Files option) if you're going to use the Clear Selected command. That way, the whole-file clips that represent the parent audio files for other smaller clips that actually reside in your tracks will remain in the Clip List. This makes it easier to compact these later to recover disk space; see the section "Compact Selected" in this chapter for more information. The Select Offline Clips command selects clips (for removal or other operations) that correspond to audio files that Pro Tools could not locate when the project session was launched. The names of offline files are italicized and dimmed in the Clip List.

Clear Selected

When the selected audio clips represent portions within larger parent audio files, the Clear Selected command simply removes this reference from the current Pro Tools session document. For whole-file clips that correspond to entire sound files (and therefore appear in bold type within the Clip List), you have the option either to remove the clip from the session (leaving it intact on your disk) or to delete the file from the disk entirely. Obviously, the second option is potentially dangerous, especially if you might also use this audio file in a different session. After using the Select Unused Clips command, you can always Command-click (Ctrl-click in Windows) to deselect any of them before executing the Clear Selected command.

Compact Selected

Applying the Compact Selected command to selected clips in the Clip List eliminates any portions within the selected audio file that are not actually being used in any clip definitions in the current session document. Suppose you record some backing vocal harmonies for a song. Out of the four minutes you record, the vocalists only sing two lines at the bridge, plus another few lines at the closing refrain. No problem; use the Edit window tools to cut and trim, leaving clips in the track only where vocal lines are actually sung. At this point, however, your original four-minute recording is still taking up many megabytes of disk space. After eliminating the unused clips created as a result of your editing, select the whole-file clip that corresponds to that complete four-minute file for the backing vocals and then execute the Compact Selected command.

The Padding setting in the Compact dialog box provides space outside of the boundaries of currently used clips before eliminating the excess audio. This provides a buffer in case you inadvertently trimmed the attack or release of a clip too much and later need to lengthen it some; it also provides room for future crossfades between clips.

By compacting your audio files, your overall project size is reduced, and it becomes quicker to back up and archive your audio data. One drawback is that compacting often creates many small edits on many files, which can increase disk fragmentation over time.

As with the Delete option in the Clear Selected dialog box, keep in mind that the Compact Selected command only addresses usage of the audio files in the current session. If you are also using the same audio files in other sessions, applying the Compact Selected command could eliminate portions of audio that you actually still need in other sessions.

Right-Click Menu in the Clip List   Among other right-click functionalities available in Pro Tools, you can right-click directly on a selected clip to access a pop-up menu with common operations such as clearing and renaming. For audio clips, you can also compact, edit their time stamp, export, recalculate waveform overviews, select the clip in the Edit window, or select the parent audio file in the Workspace browser or, in Pro Tools 10, in the Finder (Mac) or Explorer (Windows).

Export Clip Definitions

The Export Clip Definitions command incorporates the selected clip definitions into their parent audio files. This is necessary if you want to be able to view and import the non-whole-file clips in a different Pro Tools session. For example, you might find this option useful after chopping up a drum loop into useful segments or after taking the time to define clips for specific events within a much longer sound-effects file. (The Bias Peak Pro program and several others also recognize clip definitions exported into their parent AIF audio files from Pro Tools. There is also a very useful Windows utility, Region Synch from Rail Jon Rogut, that converts Pro Tools clip definitions exported into parent audio files to Sound Forge regions, which are recognized by CD Architect, WaveLab, Vegas, Adobe Audition, and other audio programs.)

Export Clips as Files

The Export Clips as Files command batch-exports the currently selected audio clips to external files. (Shift-click to select multiple clips in the list.) In the Export Selected dialog box, you can select the destination directory, file formats, number of channels, sample rate, bit depth, and other attributes. However, the results of this operation will not reflect any automation or plug-in effects processing applied on the Pro Tools track in which these clips reside. For that, you might consider soloing the track (and any send destinations to which it may be routed) and bouncing to disk in real time instead.

Importing Audio Files and Clips   Besides recording audio directly into Pro Tools, you may often import existing audio files into a Pro Tools session—for example, sound effects (or drum grooves) that you've created yourself or copied from a CD library to your hard disk. Or you might want to use an audio file that resides within another Pro Tools session's Audio Files folder. Current versions of Pro Tools can directly import the following audio file formats:

- AIFF (.AIF)

- WAV, including Broadcast WAV

- ACID WAV files

- REX (ReCycle)

- Sound Designer I and II (.SD2)

- QuickTime (audio only)

- Sound Resource (Mac versions only)

- WMA, Windows Media (Windows versions only)

- CD-DA (Audio tracks on standard Red Book audio CDs)

- MP3

- AAC (a variant of MPEG-4)

- MXF (Material eXchange Format)

If you need to import a file into a session with a different sample rate, the Import Audio dialog box will alert you that conversion is required and will enable the Convert/Convert All buttons instead of Add/Add All. The same will apply in all versions prior to Pro Tools 10 if the bit depth doesn't match that of the current session. (Pro Tools 10 supports mixed bit-depth files in the same session.) By default, Pro Tools saves any converted files in the current session's Audio Files folder, although you can choose to save them elsewhere.

If no conversion is required, imported files (or clips within them, which can also be imported) can remain in their original disk locations. If you want to ensure that a duplicate copy of the file is added to your session's Audio Files folder (even if conversion is not required), click the Copy or Copy All button in the Import Audio dialog box instead of Add or Add All.

Pro Tools versions prior to Pro Tools 10 must convert any imported stereo files into two new, separate mono files (also known as split stereo files) in your session's Audio Files folder. (Pro Tools 10 directly supports multichannel interleaved files.) After import, Pro Tools not only displays a stereo clip in the Clip List, but also two mono clips underneath it with the suffixes .L and .R added to their file names.

You can batch-import multiple files from your hard disk by selecting the files from the desktop or the Workspace browser window and then dragging them into the Clip List, onto an existing track, or directly into the Track List so that the appropriate number of new tracks will be created. Pro Tools will automatically handle any necessary conversions for the session's audio format.

Lastly, when the Automatically Copy Files on Import option is enabled in the Processing tab of the Preferences dialog box, new copies are made in your session's Audio Files folder for *all* imported audio files, regardless of whether conversion is required. This is one way of ensuring that all audio files a session requires reside within its own folder. This also reduces the possibility of accidentally deleting or altering source files if they happen to also be used in a different session.

Importing Audio from CDs   Various utilities exist for extracting tracks from audio CDs into different hard-disk file formats. These are especially useful when you only want a specific portion within a given CD track. For Macintosh, you can open the CD icon on your desktop and drag entire tracks to any disk location, or use iTunes or the QuickTime Player itself (if you upgrade to QuickTime Pro). For Windows, programs include Roxio's CD Spin Doctor, the MusicMatch Jukebox, and the Windows freeware program CDex, each of which can extract CD tracks onto the hard disk as WAV files. (Be aware that MP3 or AAC formats are not good choices for importing into Pro Tools because they compress the audio data in a lossy manner.) Many audio-editing programs, such as Bias' Peak (Mac), Audacity (Mac/Windows/Linux), Steinberg's WaveLab (Windows), and Sony/Sonic Foundry's Sound Forge (Windows) can also extract audio directly from CDs.

You can also use the File menu's Import > Audio command in Pro Tools to import from audio CDs—keeping in mind any applicable copyrights, of course—using the same preview and selection options as with audio files residing on your computer's hard disks. Or you can simply place the audio CD in your computer's drive, open it either in the Workspace browser window or in the operating system itself, select the desired track, and drag it into the Edit window—into the Clip List or directly onto an existing stereo Audio track. You can also drop CD tracks into the Track List at the left side of the Edit window to create a new Audio track in the process. The CD track's audio data will be converted to the current session's audio file format, bit depth, and sample rate.

Edit Group List

Chapter 2 discussed groups. You can use the pop-up menu in the Edit Group List (shown in Figure 6.25) to choose the type of groups to display in the list area, to delete or create new groups, or to suspend all groups. (See Chapter 7, "The Mix Window," for further details about the Mix Groups selector.) By default, Edit and Mix groups are linked, but you can change this in Preferences > Mixing with the Link Mix/Edit Group Enables option.

Figure 6.25 Pop-up menu for the Edit Group List.

You can also use the Color Palette window to assign colors to selected Edit and Mix groups. An option in the Display tab of the Preferences dialog box also allows you to automatically reassign the colors of audio and MIDI clips in the Edit window according to the group assignments of the tracks where they currently reside.

The features for grouping tracks are quite powerful. In the Group List pop-up menu, the Modify Groups command allows you to quickly add or remove tracks from existing groups. When creating new groups (either via the Group List pop-up menu, the Track menu, or the Command+G shortcut [Ctrl+G in Windows]), the Create Groups dialog box lets you choose whether the new group should be for the Edit window, Mix window, or both. In addition to linking the main volume faders of the grouped tracks (which maintain the same relative levels between group member tracks), you can also choose whether Mute buttons, Solo buttons, send mutes, or send levels should be linked within the group. Figure 6.26 shows the Create Groups dialog box. You can also right-click a group name in the Group List to access a pop-up menu that lets you select all tracks within that group, hide or display only those tracks, or show *all* tracks. Lastly, current versions of Pro Tools provide four banks of 26 group IDs each (assigned group IDs from a–z), for a total of 104 possible groups in each session.

Track List

The Track List panel can be displayed at the left edge of the Edit and Mix windows. To conserve screen space, you can enable/disable display of individual tracks by clicking the show/hide icons (black dots) next to them in the Track List. Hidden tracks will still play (unless they're muted, of course). The pop-up menu at the top of the Track List offers other options for controlling the display of tracks. The Show Only Selected Tracks command in this menu is especially handy to temporarily focus on only a small number of tracks (perhaps increasing their height for detailed editing) or when you're running out of room to display all tracks at their current sizes. Another especially useful feature here is the ability to hide or show all Audio tracks, MIDI tracks, Aux Input tracks, Instrument tracks, or Master Faders.

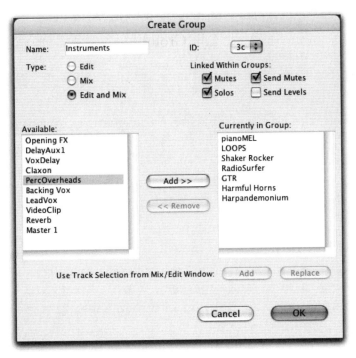

Figure 6.26 In the Create Group dialog box, in addition to linking the main Track Faders, you can also link additional controls.

Track View Selector for Track Data

The Track View selector for each track enables you to change how its contents appear in the Edit window. This selector opens a pop-up menu, as shown in Figure 6.27. Available display format options for the data contained in a track depend on its type (Audio, Aux Input, Master Fader, Instrument, or MIDI).

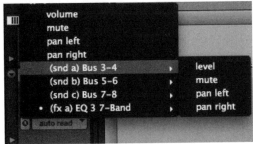

Figure 6.27 Display options for an Audio track (with three active sends and one plug-in insert).

Audio

The Track View pop-up menu for Audio tracks offers the following options:

- **Blocks.** This is similar to the default Waveform track view, but the waveform is not displayed inside the clip rectangles. This option is mainly useful for working on underpowered systems where screen redraws for audio waveforms are slowing the operation of Pro Tools.

- **Playlists.** In Playlist view, any track with alternate playlists will display all alternate playlists simultaneously. The primary playlist appears as the main track display, and the alternate playlists appear in playlist lanes underneath the track display. Playlist view creates a convenient, easy way to move or copy parts from the track's alternate playlists onto the main playlist, an action called *compositing*.

- **Analysis.** This view is used in conjunction with the Pro Tools Elastic Audio features. When any Elastic Audio mode is enabled on an Audio track, Pro Tools analyzes the audio on the track. This analysis identifies audio events and places Event markers according to the transients detected by the Elastic Audio algorithm used for that track. In Analysis view, you can add, delete, or move Event markers within the audio waveform as needed.

- **Warp.** Warp view is also related to Elastic Audio and displays up to three types of Elastic Audio markers. Event markers appear as vertical gray lines and indicate where audio events have been detected. Moving Event markers in this view will stretch or compress the surrounding audio in the affected clips, converting them to Warp markers. Warp markers are used to anchor a point in the audio waveform to a specific position in the timeline. Tempo Event–Generated Warp markers are not editable, but appear on tick-based tracks to show where Elastic Audio processing has conformed the audio to a tempo change at that location.

- **Waveform.** This is the default view for Audio tracks. Audio clips appear as rectangles (containing the clip name, if View > Clip > Name is enabled), with a graphic representation of the audio waveforms they contain. If a Sync Point has been defined within any clip, this also appears as a small inverted triangle at the bottom of the rectangular clip graphic.

Clip Layers   You can layer clips to overlap within a track (although only the top-most visible clip plays at any given point) and then change their order via the Clip > Send to Back/Bring to Front commands. A dog-ear graphic on the corner of a clip rectangle indicates that its boundary overlaps another clip in the same track (if the View > Clip > Overlap option is enabled).

- **Volume.** This track view format is a graphical representation of volume automation. A black line with moveable *breakpoints* represents how values for the volume parameter on the track (corresponding to its main volume fader) change over time. You can draw volume changes directly with the editing tools or record volume automation in real time using onscreen faders or an external control surface. Volume automation can be edited graphically at any time. For example, you can use the Grabber tool to insert, delete, or move existing breakpoints, while you can use different modes of the Pencil tool to draw automation. You can highlight automation events with the Selector tool and cut, paste, and so on without affecting the audio waveforms shown underneath. You can also use the Trim tool to scale existing automation events up or down.

- **Volume Trim (Pro Tools HD and Pro Tools with Complete Production Toolkit only).** When you record volume automation on HD systems in Trim automation mode (automation that applies a *relative* change to existing volume and send automation levels), breakpoints for the Trim automation can be displayed within the track.

- **Mute.** This view shows the mute automation playlist for a track. This playlist can toggle between Not Muted and Muted as its only possible values.

- **Pan.** Pan view also shows the automation playlist for the pan parameter, which affects the Audio track's position in the sound field. A single Pan control is provided for mono tracks; both Left Pan and Right Pan controls are provided for stereo tracks. (Note that even if your source audio clip is mono, inserting a stereo plug-in on a track makes its output and panning controls stereo.) On multichannel surround channels, the number of pan options available for display and editing corresponds to the surround format in use. For example, on a 5.1 track, separately editable pan automation includes Front Position, Rear Position, Front/Rear Position, Front Divergence, Rear Divergence, Front/Rear Divergence, and Center.

- **Sends (Level/Mute/Pan).** For each of the sends currently enabled on an Audio, Aux Input, or Instrument track, you can record and graphically edit automation for the send's Level, Mute, and Pan parameters in a similar fashion to the Volume, Mute, and Pan parameters for the track's main output (described above). For each of the track's active sends, a submenu lets you select which send parameter to display.

- **Plug-in parameters.** Many parameters can be automated. The Plug-in window for each plug-in has an Auto button, which opens a dialog box where you can individually enable its parameters for automation. Each enabled plug-in automation parameter then appears as a Track View option in the pop-up selector for the track where you enabled that plug-in. For example, if you instantiate the 7-band EQ 3 plug-in on Insert A and then enable the gain parameter of its high-band filter for automation, an option labeled "(fx a) 7-Band EQ 3 > Hi Band Gain" appears among that track's view options.

Aux Input

The Track View pop-up menu for Aux Input tracks features the same options as the pop-up for Audio tracks, minus the Blocks, Playlists, Analysis, Warp, and Waveform options (because Aux Input tracks contain no clips).

VCA Master (Pro Tools HD or Pro Tools with Complete Production Toolkit Only)

Only three view options are available for VCA Master tracks, which pass no audio but can be used to "slave" the controls of multiple tracks in a mix group: Volume, Volume Trim, and Mute.

Master Fader

By default, the only view for a Master Fader track is Volume (plus Volume Trim on Pro Tools HD or Pro Tools with Complete Production Toolkit systems). If any of the plug-ins inserted on a Master Fader track has parameters currently enabled for automation, however, those parameters appear as additional view options, as with audio plug-ins on Audio, Aux Input, and Instrument tracks. There are no pan controls or sends on Master Faders.

MIDI and Instrument Tracks

MIDI tracks and the clips within them contain MIDI *events* (note events, data for pedals, modulation, pitch bend, and other types of MIDI controllers) rather than audio data. This is also true of Instrument tracks (although they behave more like Aux Input tracks in the Mix window; see Chapter 7 for more information). Accordingly, the Track View options shown in Figure 6.28 for MIDI and Instrument tracks are rather different from those offered for Audio, Aux Input, and Master Fader tracks. In fact, on MIDI tracks, the only data type that *is* the same as on these other track types is Mute/Unmute. The volume and pan shapes you view and edit as breakpoint automation on MIDI tracks actually represent a type of MIDI controller data that is stored as part of the MIDI clips themselves. In contrast, while Instrument tracks offer all the same Track View options as MIDI tracks, you can additionally view and edit audio volume and panning automation on their output as well as plug-in parameters for instrument or other audio plug-ins that you have instantiated on the track and enabled for automation. You can think of an Instrument track as an Aux Input track with a MIDI track on the front end. Both MIDI and Instrument tracks offer the following Track View options:

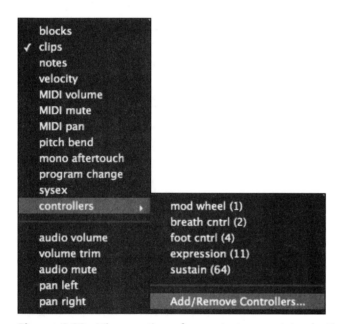

Figure 6.28 View options for an Instrument track. Except for the audio-related options in the lower panel, the options for MIDI tracks are identical.

■ **Clips.** In this view, MIDI clips appear as rectangles, with bars representing MIDI note events within each clip. The Grabber and Trim tools work on the clip boundaries, but when viewing a track's contents as MIDI clips, you cannot edit individual MIDI notes.

- **Notes.** Notes view enables you to edit MIDI notes with the Grabber (to move or copy a note) and Trim tools (to change a note's length). You will often find it useful to switch your main time ruler to Bars|Beats format and enable the Grid Edit mode when working with MIDI notes. You can draw notes with the Pencil tool while in Notes view; click once to create notes whose duration corresponds to the current Grid value (regardless of whether Grid mode is currently active), or click and drag to draw a note with a different duration when using the Freehand Pencil mode.

- **Blocks.** Blocks view is the same as Clips view, but without MIDI note events shown within each rectangular clip graphic.

- **Velocity.** If you use MIDI and Instrument tracks in Pro Tools, you will find yourself using Velocity view often (as well as the Notes view). Velocity stalks appear for each MIDI note event. You can scale them with the Trim tool or drag up and down with the Grabber. When you click any MIDI note, its velocity stalk will also be selected. You can modify velocities using the Pencil tool—for example, using the Pencil in Line drawing mode to create a decrescendo at the end of a phrase.

- **MIDI Volume, Mute, Pan.** These views of mix parameters work pretty much the same way as Volume, Mute, and Pan for audio clips, but with one important difference: MIDI Volume and pan data are MIDI *controller* messages that get sent to the connected external MIDI device or virtual instrument plug-in rather than being audio mixing events. MIDI volume and pan data are part of the contents of each MIDI clip rather than pertaining to the MIDI or Instrument track itself. On MIDI tracks, Mute/Unmute are the only automation events that are actually part of the track itself, as opposed to MIDI controller messages contained within the clips. (By contrast, Instrument tracks include both MIDI (clip-based) and Audio (track-based) parameters for Volume, Mute, and Pan.) Note that some MIDI devices (or patches) don't respond to incoming volume and pan messages. For example, most drum patches don't respond to MIDI panning because the elements of a drum set are already spread across the stereo field as part of the patch's design.

- **Other (Pitch Bend, Aftertouch, Mod Wheel, and so on).** You can view additional MIDI controllers as breakpoint automation in the Edit window and edit them with the same tools. Pro Tools automatically detects when any MIDI controller type is recorded that doesn't appear in the default pop-up list and adds it accordingly.

About Instrument Tracks   As mentioned in the previous section, all MIDI-related options in the Track View selector for Instrument tracks are identical to MIDI tracks. However, an Instrument track combines the functionality of an Aux Input with a MIDI track. Accordingly, in addition to MIDI parameters, it offers the same display options as an Aux Input track for volume (and volume trim on systems with Pro Tools HD or Pro Tools with Complete Production Toolkit), pan, and any plug-in parameters that you enable for automation.

Track Height Selector

The Track Height selector is fairly self-explanatory: It's a pop-up menu that allows you to change the height of each track (see Figure 6.29). The basic options are Micro, Mini, Small, Medium, Large, Jumbo, Extreme, and Fit to Window. You can also continuously resize any track vertically by dragging its lower border. As your sessions get larger, you will tend to minimize the size of the tracks you're not currently editing to save screen space. (Options in the Track List are also useful when you start running out of space in the Edit window.) On MIDI tracks, you have the additional option of displaying only a single note (the MIDI note value D1 for all snare hits, for example). Hold down the Option key (Alt key in Windows) as you change any track's height to simultaneously change the height of *all* tracks.

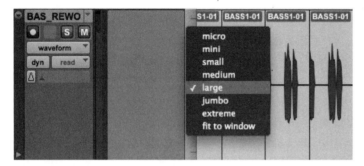

Figure 6.29   Click an Audio track's Track Height Selector button or anywhere in its Amplitude Ruler to open this pop-up menu.

Using the Do-to-All Modifier to Affect All Tracks   With many track parameters in Pro Tools, if you hold down the Option key (Alt key in Windows) as you make a change on one track, the same change is applied to *all* tracks in your session. For example, to set the display view for all tracks to Volume, hold down the Option/Alt key as you set the view for any individual track. This modifier also works with the Mute and Solo buttons, Input and Output selectors, track heights, and many other functions.

Playlist Selector (Audio and MIDI Tracks)

As explained in Chapter 2, an *Edit Playlist* is a list of the clips to be played back by each Audio or MIDI track. The Playlist selector, immediately to the right of the track name (see Figure 6.30), enables you to create and duplicate any Edit Playlists for the track and to quickly change from one playlist to another. Playlists are handy if you want to experiment with different arrangements, edits, and so on, but still be able to quickly change back to the original version. The automation (for example, volume, panning, or send levels) on Audio tracks is global for the track, so a single automation playlist applies no matter which Edit Playlist is currently active. MIDI volume and panning events actually comprise part of the data within MIDI clips, so these can be

Figure 6.30 The Playlist selector opens a pop-up menu, where you can select between alternate playlists for each Audio or MIDI track, create new playlists, and duplicate or rename existing ones.

different in each Edit Playlist on a MIDI or Instrument track. Playlists give you freedom to experiment; they are non-destructive and don't occupy significant disk space. In fact, if you change the notes and other events within a MIDI clip that Pro Tools uses in another playlist, it automatically creates a new MIDI clip name for the altered version.

Lastly, the Note Chasing parameter affects what happens when you initiate playback at any point between the Note On and Note Off messages for MIDI note events on a given track. For example, if a chord played with a string sound is supposed to sustain from Bars 9 through 16, you will probably want to hear those notes sound even if you happen to start playback at Bar 13. The only exception to this would be when MIDI note events are triggering rhythm loops that play on a sampling instrument (either external or a similar instrument plug-in). If Note Chasing were enabled on that track, playback of the loop would get triggered at whatever point you start playback—and not necessarily in time with the music!

Pitched MIDI and Instrument Tracks   When the Pitched option is enabled in the pop-up selector for MIDI and Instrument tracks (default), the MIDI note events on that track will be affected by key change events in the session Timeline. The notes will be transposed and/or diatonically constrained to the new scale, as specified in the Key Change dialog box. You can deselect the Pitched option for MIDI and Instrument tracks that are not pitch-based—performances that trigger sound effects, rhythmic loops, drum patterns or individual drum hits, and so on—to prevent these tracks from being effected by key change events.

Samples/Ticks Timebase Selector

The Timebase selector, shown in Figure 6.31, enables you to choose whether the locations of events on a track are treated as *absolute* locations (samples timebase) or *relative* locations (ticks timebase). On sample-based tracks, changing the Pro Tools tempo, whether via events in the Tempo Ruler or manual settings in the Transport window's Tempo field, has no effect on the

Figure 6.31 The timebase for event locations in Audio, MIDI, and Instrument tracks can be absolute (samples) or relative (ticks).

location of events on the track. On tick-based tracks, making tempo adjustments causes events to move to a new position to maintain their bar|beat locations relative to the new tempo.

Tip   Ticks are subdivisions of the musical beat, with 960 ticks comprising a quarter note.

Audio, Aux Input, and Master Fader tracks are sample-based by default; however, they can be switched to tick-based as needed. When Ticks timebase is chosen for an Audio track, the clips it contains will shift whenever you apply a tempo change. Any crossfades between audio clips on the affected tracks will be re-rendered if their positions are altered as a result of tempo changes, but durations of fade-ins and fade-outs will be unaffected.

Existing automation data on tick-based tracks will also be remapped to reflect subsequent tempo changes. With this capability, for example, any shots from a send to a reverb or delay effect, or the Master Fader's volume fade at the end of a song, will automatically adjust for the new tempo so that they still occur at the same bar and beat relative to the new tempo.

MIDI and Instrument tracks are tick-based by default; however, they can also be set to sample-based as needed. This is useful not only for sound-effects design with external or software MIDI instruments but also when recording freeform MIDI performances that do not correlate to the session tempo.

Track Color Indicators

The color strip to the left of all tracks in the Edit window (also visible in Figure 6.31) can be toggled on/off using the View > Edit Window Views > Track Color option. You can use the Color Palette window (Window > Color Palette) to reassign colors for selected tracks to conveniently flag groups of tracks that are related, or you can let tracks follow the color coding settings specified in the Preferences dialog box (Setup > Preferences, Display tab).

For example, using the Color Palette you might assign one color to all percussion tracks, whether MIDI or audio, or use different colors for basic tracks versus instrumental overdubs—whatever helps you keep track of things in a complex session. Additionally, you can display Track Color indicators at the top and bottom of the Mix window, as discussed in Chapter 7. Some users may prefer *not* to display Track Color indicators in order to conserve screen space.

Timeline Display: Timebase Rulers and Marker Memory Locations

You can display various Timebase Rulers (Min:Secs, Bars|Beats, Samples, Timecode, and Feet+Frames) and Conductor Rulers (Tempo, Meter, Key Signature, Chord Symbols, and Markers) along the top of the Edit window. Enable these rulers using either the View > Rulers submenu or the Ruler View selector on the Main Timbase Ruler in the Edit window. The available rulers are shown in Figure 6.32. The display units for the Main Timebase Ruler reflect those of the Main Counter at the top of the Edit window. You can also click the title area at the left end of any Timebase Ruler to switch the Main Counter to that ruler's time units. The Main Timebase Ruler is always indicated by a highlight across the length of the ruler. Click and drag rulers by their titles to change their vertical order in the Edit window.

Figure 6.32   You can display multiple Timebase Rulers at once: Bars|Beats, Min:Secs, Samples, Timecode, and Feet+Frames. Additional rulers display markers, tempo events, meter events, and more.

No matter which editing tool is currently selected, the cursor changes to the Selector tool's I-beam shape when positioned over any of the rulers in the Edit window (except when Dynamic Transport is enabled, in which case the cursor becomes the Grabber tool). Click and drag on any Timebase Ruler to select a Timeline range in all tracks.

Note   When Options > Dynamic Transport is enabled, an additional lane for the moveable Play Start maker appears underneath the Main Timebase Ruler.

Markers Ruler

The Markers Ruler displays all marker Memory locations (but not selection Memory locations) created in your session. Markers identify single points in time. Among other things, you can use markers to identify parts of a song, scenes, punch in/out points that you expect to use again, or any other location that you might want to quickly find later. Click the plus-sign button at the left end of the Markers Ruler or simply press the Enter key on the numeric keypad to create a new Memory location (marker or selection) based on the current playback cursor position or selection. (Incidentally, you can do this even while in Play or Record mode! Many users drop markers into the Pro Tools Timeline while recording a performer to identify song sections or spots where punch-ins may be necessary.)

A marker Memory location specifies a single time value (and appears in the Markers Ruler with the name you've defined), while a selection Memory location represents a *range* of time. Typical selections might include the verse of a song, a portion within a longer session that you may bounce to disk more than once, or a section that you will repeat numerous times (perhaps in Loop Recording mode) while overdubbing a solo. Selection Memory locations recall not only the Timeline range but also *which* tracks were highlighted. Both markers and selections can be displayed and recalled in the Memory Locations window (see Figure 6.33). Because the stored attributes of any Memory location can optionally include zoom settings, pre- or post-roll times, group enables, track show/hide, and other track-display options, some users create Memory locations with no time reference at all for the specific purpose of storing and recalling customized views.

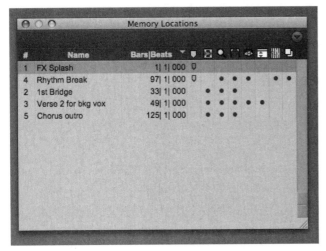

Figure 6.33 The Memory Locations window displays markers and selections, including their absolute or relative position. The icons indicate additional view properties stored with each Memory location.

Markers and selections can reference either an absolute position in the session's Timeline or a relative position in Bars:Beats:Ticks whose absolute time position is affected by tempo changes in the session. In the New Memory Location dialog box, the default reference type reflects the time units currently displayed in the Main Counter.

When the Always Display Marker Colors option in the Display tab of the Preferences dialog box is enabled, the Markers Ruler will display colors between existing marker locations. Colors are automatically assigned to each marker and can be changed using the Color Palette window. Marker colors are useful for keeping track of what section of a song or soundtrack is displayed, even while editing track data at a very high zoom level.

You can drag markers to new positions within the Markers Ruler; their movement will be affected by Grid mode (if enabled). You can also use markers to make Timeline selections in the Edit window. Shift-clicking a marker highlights the range between the current Main Counter location and that marker. To delete a marker, Option-click (Alt-click in Windows) on the marker in the Markers Ruler or the Memory Locations window. Double-click any marker to edit its properties—for example, to change its time reference or to set the pre- and post-roll times. To redefine an existing selection Memory location, highlight a different range, open the Memory Locations window, and Control-click (Mac) or right-click on that selection's name. This technique also works on marker Memory locations; the current Start value replaces the marker's original time reference.

Memory locations are explained in more detail in the "Memory Locations" section of Chapter 8, "Menu Selections: Highlights." Memory locations are an underused feature of Pro Tools; it's worth taking some time to learn how to use them.

Recalling Memory Locations from the Keyboard   When the numeric keypad is in Transport mode, you can recall Memory locations (both marker and selection) from your computer's numeric keypad. Press the period key on the numeric keypad, then the desired Memory location number, followed by another period.

Pro Tools Gives You Ticks!   Memory locations can be absolute (fixed time) or relative (Bar| Beat). An *absolute* time reference is located at a specific number of samples from the session's start and is unaffected by tempo settings. In contrast, the actual time location of a *relative* reference depends on musical tempo. If the tempo is set to 60 beats per minute (BPM), each beat lasts one second; therefore, the ninth beat (the downbeat of the third bar in 4/4 time) occurs precisely eight seconds into the session's absolute Timeline. But if you double the tempo setting to 120 BPM, the downbeat of that third bar is now only four seconds into the session Timeline.

In the Bars|Beats Time Scale, Pro Tools subdivides each 1/4 note into 960 pulses, or *ticks*. The actual time represented by each tick depends on the tempo. So a full 1/4-note has a duration of 960 ticks (one second at 60 BPM, but only 500 milliseconds at 120 BPM). An 1/8 note represents 480 ticks, a 1/16 note 240 ticks, and so on.

If you need to tie the markers or selections that you create to musical events and the Pro Tools tempo, use the pop-up selector in the New Memory Location dialog box to make their positions relative (Bar|Beat). When you change the tempo settings, the

Memory location's absolute time position will also be altered such that it stays in the proper musical location.

Tempo and Meter Rulers

In Pro Tools, changes of tempo and meter (how fast the beat is and how many beats per bar) are represented by tempo and meter events. Clicking the plus-sign buttons next to the Tempo and Meter Rulers creates a new tempo/meter event at the current position. Another triangle button to the left of the Tempo Ruler opens the Tempo Editor, where you can use the editing tools to graphically edit a series of tempo events, as discussed in the "Using the Tempo Editor" section later in this chapter. Click and drag to change the position of any event in these rulers or double-click to alter its properties. To delete any event in the Tempo or Meter Ruler, Option-click the event (Alt-click in Windows) or simply drag it up or down to remove it from the ruler.

Song Start Marker

By default, in new sessions, the Song Start marker appears at the beginning of the Timeline within the Tempo Ruler. Double-click this marker to enter a new bar number or time signature in the Edit Bar|Beat Marker dialog box. If you want Bar 1 of the song to begin at some other point in the Timeline (for example, at exactly seven seconds), drag the Song Start marker to that location within the Tempo Ruler. Its movement will be affected by Grid mode, if enabled. By default, the location of events (clips, automation, and so on) within any tick-based tracks will also be displaced to maintain their previous positions relative to the Song Start marker's new location. However, you can hold down Control+Shift while dragging (Start+Shift in Windows) if you don't want the position of events in tick-based tracks to be affected by moving the Song Start marker. (MIDI and Instrument tracks can optionally be set to sample-based, in which case the locations of MIDI events within them are unaffected by changes to the tempo and location of the Song Start marker.)

The Move Song Start page of the Time Operations window provides a more precise method for changing the location of the Song Start marker in the Tempo Ruler. For example, you can specify its new position numerically using any Timeline units available in your version of Pro Tools regardless of which main ruler is currently active in the Edit window. At the same time, you can assign a new bar number to the Song Start marker's new location. The Time Operations and Tempo Operations windows are discussed further in Chapter 8.

Key Signature Ruler

The Key Signature Ruler displays key-signature events added either via the Event > Add Key Change command or by clicking the plus sign at the left end of ruler. As shown in Figure 6.34, all the standard major and minor key signatures can be selected in the Key Change dialog box. These are useful when MIDI data will be exported from Pro Tools to the Sibelius music notation program. However, the most important use of key signatures within Pro Tools is for diatonic

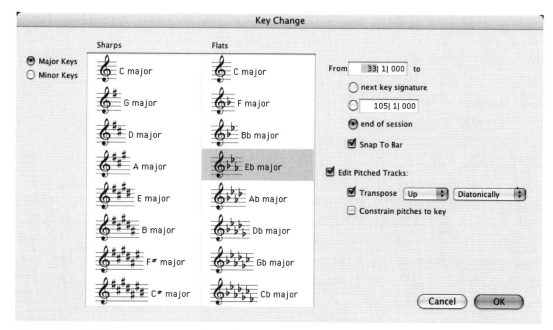

Figure 6.34 When you create key-signature events in Pro Tools, the Key Change dialog box appears. Existing MIDI notes in pitched tracks can be transposed and/or have their accidentals (sharps/flats) adjusted to match the new key signature.

transposition. The Transpose page of the Event Operations window offers a Transpose in Key option for shifting MIDI pitches by a specified number of scale steps (rather than semitones, as with conventional transposition). So, if the key signature in effect for the currently selected MIDI events is F major (one flat), shifting the note sequence F-G-A-B♭ upward diatonically by one scale step would transpose this to G-A-B♭-C, whereas a simple transposition upward by two semitones would produce the sequence G-A-B-C. (The Real-Time Properties windows for tracks and clips also offer an In Key option for diatonic transposition.)

A related feature introduced along with key-signature events is the Pitched option for MIDI and Instrument tracks (enabled via the pop-up Playlist selector menu for each track). When this option is enabled, the pitches of MIDI notes will be adjusted automatically if you introduce key-signature events in the ruler that affect the portion of the Timeline where those MIDI note events reside. Appendix D, "Power Tips and Loopy Ideas," includes an example of using this feature to create a repeating ostinato figure on a pitched MIDI track whose notes shift diatonically (according to key-signature events in the Timeline) to match a chord progression.

Managing Multiple Takes

When you've recorded multiple takes with the same start and end time within a track—perhaps by using Loop Record mode, or because you've used a Timeline selection and pre-/post-roll fields to automatically punch in a series of recordings at the exact same place—Pro Tools offers several features to help you keep track. As mentioned elsewhere, new clip names are automatically created for each take (Trackname_01, Trackname_02, and so on), and these all appear in the Clip List. Additionally, though, there's a really quick way to review and select among these alternate takes: Using the Selector tool, Command-click (Ctrl-click in Windows) within the clip currently displayed on the track. A pop-up Takes List will appear (see Figure 6.35), allowing you select criteria to apply in choosing alternate takes via the Match Criteria menu. The Alternates List, which is also available by right-clicking a clip, includes options to expand alternates to either new playlists or new tracks and shows the list of alternate takes. The Matching Criteria options for refining the Alternates List include Track ID for all audio files recorded on a specific track, Track Name for all audio files sharing the same root name, and Clip Rating (see the next section, "Assembling a Comp Track"). In addition, you can choose to narrow down the alternates to those that share the clip start, that share the clip start and end, or that are entirely within the edit selection. Upon choosing your Matching Criteria settings, Command-click (Ctrl-click in Windows) on the clip to select from the alternate audio files that are listed. As you do this, take some time to edit the clip names (for example, "Gtr fill OK," "Gtr fill bad," "Gtr fill best") or use Clip Ratings (discussed below) to organize your thoughts.

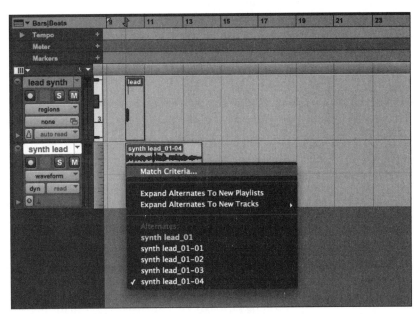

Figure 6.35 Command/Ctrl-clicking with the Selector tool displays the Takes List pop-up menu for selecting between multiple takes recorded with Loop Record mode.

Assembling a Comp Track

Comping multiple takes together (that is, assembling a composite take using segments of each) is very easy to do in Pro Tools. Using the example of a session containing a loop record of several passes, choose the Selector tool and Command-click (Ctrl-click in Windows) the record track's currently displayed audio clip, which is the last take recorded. Choose the Expand Alternates to

New Playlists option to display all the takes created from the loop record below the main track display (see Figure 6.36). (The alternates may include a playlist representing all takes from the looped recording as one long audio clip, depending on the current Match Criteria settings.) Using the Solo buttons on the various playlist lanes, play the individual takes back and choose the best take. Alternatively, with the Selector tool, choose segments of takes that you want to use in the "master" playlist. Then, click the Copy Selection to Main Playlist button on the playlist lane or choose Edit > Copy Selection To > Main Playlist. Do this until your master playlist is complete, with all your selections included.

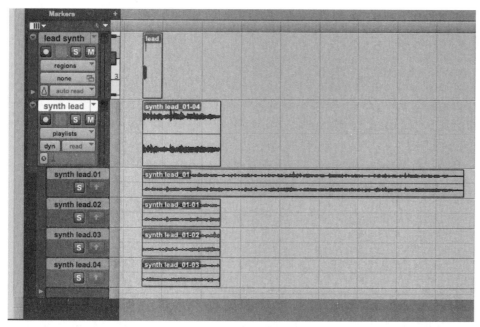

Figure 6.36 After a loop record on the synth lead Audio track, the Expand Alternates to New Playlists command creates playlists of all the takes. Notice that the main playlist displays the last take recorded.

A feature added to aid with comping is Clip Rating. This enables you to assign numbers from 1 to 5 to identify a clip's worth in creating a comp for better organization when choosing from several playlists. To assign a number to a clip, choose Clip > Rating or right-click on the clip to display the pop-up menu and choose Rate. Then choose a number from 1 (worst) to 5 (best). Make sure that View > Clip > Rating is selected in order to see the rating number in the clip.

Real-Time Properties on MIDI/Instrument Tracks

The Real-Time Properties feature is immensely useful for anyone who composes and edits MIDI performances. Real-time MIDI properties are non-destructive, real-time versions of key MIDI processes, all of which are also available in non-real-time form under the Event menu. Without altering the original contents of the MIDI clips on the track, Real-Time Properties let you apply quantization (including swing and groove quantize), duration and velocity changes, delay offsets, and transposition (including diatonic transposition within the current key signature). You also have the option of permanently incorporating the results of the Real-Time Properties into the affected clip or track using the Write to Region/Write to Track button in the Real-Time Properties window. You can display the Real-Time Properties column in the Edit window (see Figure 6.37) via the View > Edit Window > Real-Time Properties command. Using Real-Time Properties on MIDI and Instrument tracks is discussed further in Chapter 10, "MIDI." That chapter also discusses how you can apply Real-Time Properties to individual clips on MIDI and Instrument tracks, as well as to the track itself, affecting all MIDI data played back through the track.

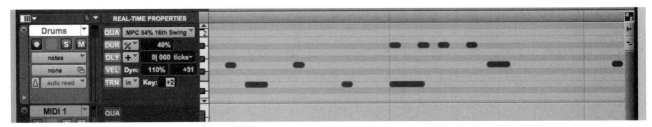

Figure 6.37   The Real-Time Properties column for MIDI and Instrument tracks in the Edit window.

More about Automation in Pro Tools

As mentioned previously, there are two ways to create mix automation in Pro Tools:

- Record your automation moves in real time using either the onscreen controls in the Pro Tools software or an external control surface.

- Draw breakpoint automation directly in the Edit window using the Grabber or Pencil tool.

Of course, you can use any combination of these two techniques during a project. Many new Pro Tools users with a background in old-school mixing consoles and tape tend to place a lot of priority on the real-time automation recording capabilities, but with time, they find that in many cases it's faster to draw in volume, panning, and other automatable parameters by hand using the Grabber, Pencil, and Trim tools. Nevertheless, there will always be times when you prefer to record (or revise) automation by ear, in real time—with the mouse or, even better, with an external control surface.

Automation Modes

Mix automation is so essential to Pro Tools that, by default, the Automation Mode selector for each track appears in both the Edit and Mix windows. The Automation Mode selector provides a pop-up menu with these options:

- **Off.** This mode disables all automation in the track; no automation is written and existing automation is ignored.

- **Read.** This mode plays all existing automation in the track.

- **Touch.** This mode records automation only while any of the faders or other controls for the track are touched, clicked or moved with the mouse, or moved via a touch-sensitive fader or control on an external control surface. When you release the control, it returns to its position according to the previous automation values for this track (per the current AutoMatch Time in Preferences > Mixing). Touch mode is handy for punching in a section within a track's existing automation data.

- **Latch.** Like Touch mode, automation recording in Latch mode doesn't start until a fader is moved or touched/clicked. However, when you release the fader in Latch mode, it *stays* at its current level, recording new automation data until playback is stopped. This mode is especially handy for automating plug-in parameters, for example, or other situations where you want to overwrite existing automation data from a certain point forward.

- **Write.** This mode records automation for every enabled parameter on a track from the moment playback is started until it's stopped, regardless of whether you touch or move any faders or other controls. In the Preferences, you can choose whether tracks automatically switch to Touch or Latch mode when you stop playback after an automation pass in Write mode. This reduces the danger of accidentally overwriting the data you just recorded when you press Play again!

- **Trim (HD systems and Pro Tools with Complete Production Toolkit only).** This mode applies to volume and send-level automation only. Trim mode works in conjunction with other automation modes—but the fader changes you make in Trim mode apply *relative* changes rather than *absolute* values to the existing automation data in the track. While recording automation in Trim mode, onscreen faders show the delta value (the amount of increase or decrease to their level) rather than the usual absolute value.

Trimming Automation Data   You can use the Trim tool to scale existing automation data up or down within Pro Tools tracks, as shown in Figure 6.38. For example, to reduce the overall level of a send from an Audio track that you've routed to an Aux Input where a delay effect has been inserted, first change the view of the track to show the level for the send you want to edit. Next, use the Selector tool to highlight the portion of this send's level automation you want to alter. Then, drag it upward or downward with the Trim tool; as you do so, the amount of change being applied (the *delta*) is indicated in decibels (dB). The contour of your send-level changes will be retained, but the overall level will be louder or softer.

Figure 6.38 You can use the Trim tool to scale selected automation data up or down.

Automation Window

The Automation window (Window > Automation), shown in Figure 6.39, enables you to suspend playback of *all* animation in a Pro Tools session or to individually enable or disable automation parameters for recording (volume, pan, and mute for track outputs; any enabled plug-in parameters; or level, pan, and mute for sends).

Figure 6.39 The Automation window globally affects how automation is recorded/played back in the session. (Standard Pro Tools version shown here; Pro Tools HD and Pro Tools with Complete Production Toolkit offer additional options.)

Tip If recording or playback of automation on your tracks doesn't seem to be working, check the Automation window to make sure the target automation parameters are enabled (for recording) and that automation isn't suspended (for playback and recording).

Basic Rules for Cutting and Pasting Automation Data Editing automation is somewhat different from editing audio/MIDI clips. Understanding the relationship between clip editing and automation data will help you unlock the power of editing tracks to further shape your projects. Here are some of the most basic rules to keep in mind:

- If Options > Automation Follows Edit is enabled, when you cut, copy, paste, or drag audio waveform selections/clips (in Waveform or Blocks view) or MIDI data (in Clips, Blocks, Notes, or Velocity views), the associated automation data will accompany the material to the new location. You can disable this whenever you don't want these clip-editing operations to affect the concurrent automation data in your tracks.

- Trimming audio clips to change their length does *not* affect any overlapping automation data.

- When an Audio track's view is set to any of the automation types, you can select, cut, copy, and paste automation data without affecting the audio clips visible underneath it.

- You can't paste automation from an Audio track into a MIDI track or vice versa.

Automatically Enabling Automation on New Plug-ins   Pro Tools includes a setting in the Mixing tab of the Preferences dialog box that lets you choose to automatically enable all available parameters of each plug-in as it is instantiated in your Pro Tools session.

Automation and Controller Lanes

Pro Tools 8 and later include Automation and Controller lanes, which enable you to look at multiple displays of automation and controller data for a track at the same time. As shown in Figure 6.40, the lower corner of the color strip of each track in the Edit window features a triangle button; clicking the triangle reveals a lane of automation or controller data. You can change the type of automation or controller data displayed using the Automation Type selector. You can also add lanes to display data by clicking the plus button in the previous lane's color strip. Similarly, you can hide (not delete) an automation/controller lane by clicking that lane's minus button. The size of the lanes can also be changed by the same method as the primary tracks: by clicking the left edge of the track's waveform display area to access a pop-up menu.

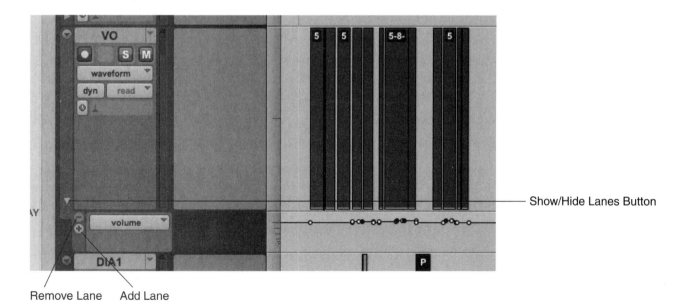

Figure 6.40   Clicking the Show/Hide Lanes triangle button on the lower end of a track's color strip reveals an Automation/Controller lane, which includes buttons to choose the type of data displayed and to display or remove additional lanes of data.

Working with Clip-Based Gain

A new feature in Pro Tools 10, clip-based gain can be used to apply quick and easy gain changes to clips and selections or to apply dynamic gain changes to a waveform over time. Clip-based gain is applied pre-mixer (pre-fader and pre-plug-in processing). This can be especially useful when working with field recordings and sample libraries in post-production sessions.

Clip gain settings stay with the clip, allowing you to move, copy, and paste clips with their corresponding clip gain settings intact. Clip gain settings can also be rendered (written in) to their associated clips by right-clicking on a clip and choosing Render Clip Gain from the pop-up menu. Similarly, unrendered clip gain can be removed from a clip by choosing Clear Clip Gain from the right-click pop-up menu.

Two new clip views are available in Pro Tools 10 associated with clip-based gain: Clip Gain Info and Clip Gain Line (see Figure 6.41). The Clip Gain Info view (View > Clip > Clip Gain Info) displays a Clip Gain Fader icon at the beginning of the clip, in the lower left corner. This fader can be used to adjust the gain across the entire clip, increasing or decreasing the gain by a static amount. (Click on the fader icon and drag up or down to boost or attenuate the clip gain.)

Figure 6.41 Clip showing the Clip Gain Info view (fader icon) and Clip Gain Line with dynamic changes applied.

The Clip Gain Line view (View > Clip > Clip Gain Line) can be used to edit the clip gain settings for a clip using breakpoint editing, much like volume automation. Using the Grabber tool, you can add, adjust, and delete individual clip gain breakpoints. (Click at any point on the Clip Gain Line to add a breakpoint; Option-click [Mac] or Alt-click [Windows] on an existing breakpoint to delete the breakpoint.)

As with Automation graphs, clip gain lines can be edited with other Edit tools. The different modes of the Pencil tool allow you to draw clip gain settings with various shapes; the Trim tool modes let you adjust all selected breakpoints up or down by dragging within a selection. Clip gain can also be nudged up or down by an amount specified in the Pro Tools Editing Preferences. (Press Control+Shift+Up Arrow/Down Arrow [Mac] or Start+Shift+Up Arrow/Down Arrow [Windows] to nudge the clip gain for a selected range up or down).

Using the Tempo Editor

Clicking the button to the left of the Tempo Ruler opens a resizable, horizontal pane beneath the ruler called the Tempo Editor. In a manner similar to automation, you can use the edit tools to graphically draw changes (Pencil), select a range (Grabber and Selector), or scale the tempo

(Trim tool). As you can see in Figure 6.42, each tempo change in Pro Tools is a discrete event that stays in effect until another tempo-change event is encountered. Even when drawn with the Pencil tool, the end result of graphically editing tempos is a series of individual tempo events, which are visible in the Tempo Ruler even after the Graphic Editor is closed.

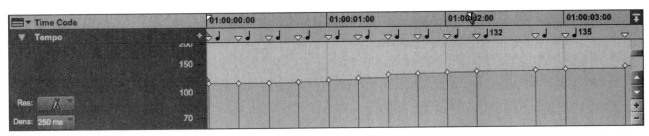

Figure 6.42 The Tempo Editor allows you to graphically edit the tempo track.

Use the Grabber tool to drag a tempo event vertically to a new tempo setting or horizontally to a new position in the Timeline. If enabled, Grid mode snaps the horizontal movement of tempo events to the nearest grid increment as you drag them. As with automation breakpoints within tracks, you can delete existing tempo events in this editor by Option-clicking (Alt-clicking in Windows) with the Grabber. While dragging or trimming tempo events in the Tempo Editor, you will notice that the units in the Cursor Location Display switch to BPM.

You can use the Trim tool to scale multiple tempo events up or down—either within a previously selected range or across the entire session Timeline when no range is selected.

You can use the Pencil tool to create a series of tempo events in the Graphic Editor using the Freehand, Line, or Curve drawing modes. (You cannot use the Triangle, Square, or Random drawing modes in the Tempo Editor.) The pop-up Density menu gives you control over the spacing of these newly created tempo events, specified in either note-value or millisecond time units. The pop-up Resolution menu determines the note value that will be the basis for all beats-per-minute settings created when you draw tempo curves with the Pencil tool.

Immediately after creating a tempo curve using the Pencil tool, blue adjustment handles appear; these allow you to adjust the beginning and end points (and also the midpoint, when using the S-curve drawing mode). You can only make adjustments immediately after creating the curve, however; as soon as you apply any other editing command, select a different Edit tool, or switch the drawing mode of the Pencil tool, the adjustment handles will no longer be available.

If you move the Song Start marker (either by dragging in the Tempo Ruler or by using the Time Operations window), the locations of existing tempo events may shift accordingly. (This is not obligatory, though; in the "Time Operations" section of Chapter 10, you will find more techniques and applications for moving the Song Start marker, renumbering bars, and so on.) To extend the currently selected range in the Tempo Editor to the next tempo event in the Timeline, press Shift+Tab. To instead extend the current tempo selection to the previous tempo event, press Option+Shift+Tab (Ctrl+Shift+Tab in Windows).

You can use the Tempo Editor instead of, or in conjunction with, the Tempo Operations window (discussed in Chapter 10). However, in some situations, using the Tempo Operations window may allow you finer control—especially when adjusting tempos to match musical events with absolute time references in minutes, seconds, and frames while scoring video or film, for example.

Switching the main timebase for the Edit window between Linear Samples (absolute) and Linear Ticks (relative) will affect how tempo events are displayed in the Tempo Editor. For example, in Linear Sample format, tempo events at Bars 3 and 5 would appear more closely spaced after increasing tempo settings because the absolute time difference between their positions has been reduced.

As discussed above, you can set the timebase that controls the positions of clips and/or automation events in each track to Samples or Ticks. Here's a brief summary of how tempo changes affect Pro Tools operation with different settings:

■ With your session set to Linear Sample Display (absolute), as you trim or otherwise alter tempos, you will see bar numbers shifting in the Bars|Beats Ruler. Events inside any tracks whose Timebase selector is set to Ticks will shift in relation to this absolute (samples) Timeline. If you use individual audio samples in conjunction with tick-based MIDI or Instrument tracks (for example, individual drum hits or cymbal crashes), you can use the Ticks timebase so that individual clip locations will automatically adjust to follow the Pro Tools tempo.

■ If your session is set to Linear Tick Display (relative), you will instead see the unit increments in rulers for absolute time formats (such as Min:Secs, Samples, Timecode, or Feet+Frames) shifting as you alter tempo events, while the horizontal display of each MIDI and Instrument track stays fixed throughout all tempo variations.

■ In Linear Tick Display, events on tracks set to the Ticks timebase won't slide around onscreen as you alter tempos, but material on tracks set to Samples timebase *will*.

■ Even though they cannot contain clips, you can set Aux Input and Master Fader tracks to either Ticks or Sample timebase. As with other track types, when using Ticks timebase, any existing automation breakpoints will be automatically adjusted to the same relative musical location as you alter tempos.

Summary

Because the Edit window is where you will probably spend much of your time, this chapter has covered a lot of ground. It is only an introduction, however. You will find many other Edit window operations covered in other chapters. Be sure to consult your *Pro Tools Reference Guide* (a PDF document included with the program) for further details. There are many more timesaving shortcuts and tips to find there. Also, print out *Keyboard Shortcuts*, another PDF document provided with the program, and keep it handy!

7 The Mix Window

To a certain extent, the Mix window is an alternative view of the same material found in the Edit window. In fact, you can view many track parameters in both the Mix window and the Edit window, including comments, track I/O, inserts, sends, and more. The optional views are available from the View > Edit/Mix Window submenus. However, it's usually more convenient to deal with audio and MIDI mixing via the familiar metaphor of a conventional mixing board. Therefore, in the Mix window, the same tracks whose contents appear as horizontal strips in the Edit window are shown as vertical mixer strips, with the familiar volume faders, level meters, pan controls, effects sections, and sends.

This "virtual mixer" metaphor is especially relevant for those who prefer to use a physical control surface, such as the Artist Series controllers, C|24, D-Control, D-Command, and so on. Other users find that using a mouse or trackball—combined with Edit window automation—is sufficient for their needs. But most users alternate between real-time and graphical control of their mixes, frequently switching back and forth between the Mix and Edit windows.

Tip Having two monitors on the computer you use for Pro Tools can be a huge productivity boost; you can leave the Mix window open on the second monitor (and perhaps an output window or two, as discussed later in this chapter) as you work in the Edit window.

Chapter 9, "Plug-ins, Inserts, and Sends," goes into more detail about the use of inserts, sends, signal routing, and plug-in architectures; this chapter mainly focuses on the elements of the Mix window's user interface. If any of the Pro Tools terminology you see here is unfamiliar, refer to Chapter 2, "Pro Tools Terms and Concepts."

Mixer Strip Elements

The tracks you create in Pro Tools appear in the Mix window as a vertical mixer strips, also commonly referred to as *channel strips*. Each mixer strip in the Mix window corresponds to a horizontal track in the Edit window—they're two different views of the same thing. The controls available for each track in the Mix window depend on the track type: Audio, MIDI, Aux Input, Instrument, VCA Master, or Master Fader. Let's start by reviewing the track classes in Pro Tools and the elements that can appear in the mixer strip for each track type.

Audio Tracks

Audio tracks contain Edit Playlists that designate which audio clips are played when. Like Aux Inputs, Instrument tracks, VCA Masters, and Master Faders, Audio tracks also contain automation data. Mixer strips for Audio tracks in the Mix window are shown in Figure 7.1. The main output from an Audio track can be routed either to any physical audio output path on the system or to one of Pro Tools' internal mixing busses. Audio tracks can be mono, stereo, or multichannel. An Audio track can record from any physical audio input path (that is, mono, stereo, or multiple channels on your audio interface, according to the track's channel format) or from any one of Pro Tools' internal mixing busses. In Pro Tools, only Audio tracks can record audio and contain audio clips.

Track Name and Comments

Double-click the Track Name field to enter a meaningful name for your Audio tracks. This is useful for keeping tracks in your session properly labeled; however, it is also important because new clips and audio files created by recording into each track are automatically assigned names derived from the track name. The same is true of clips created as a result of the Edit > Consolidate command, as well as clips resulting from certain AudioSuite processes. Some users take advantage of track renaming so that each set of new recordings into the same track creates a group of similarly named clips in the Clip List. For instance, if you record scratch lead vocals during basic tracking, before recording keeper versions in the same track, you might change the track name from "ScratchVox" to "VoxGood." Clip and file names created by subsequent recordings will begin with the text "VoxGood" and can appear grouped together in alphabetical order within the Edit window's Clip List.

The Comments area (beneath each Track Name field) is for keeping your own reminders, recording notes, and so on, and has no effect on audio recording or playback. Use this text entry area however you like, similar to the strip of tape commonly used for writing on conventional mixing boards. For example, you might make note of the microphones you used for a given track and how they were positioned; settings or patches on a source guitar amplifier, MIDI device, or effects unit; settings and other information about additional programs being used with Pro Tools via ReWire; or items on that track that need to be fixed before mixdown. It's also helpful to list the names of the performers you're recording in the Comments area for each track. This provides some historical data in the archived session document. (If you want to contact that talent again, for example, having a phone number or email address here can be handy.) More importantly, anyone who has ever recorded bands can relate to that awkward moment when you need to address the bass player, for example, and can't remember his name! Besides the technical information, it can be convenient to include the names/nicknames in the Comments area when introductions are made during setup.

Right-Click Options for Track Management   Right-clicking any track name in the Mix or Edit window opens a local menu for common operations, such as renaming, deleting, and duplicating the track, as well as hiding it or making it inactive.

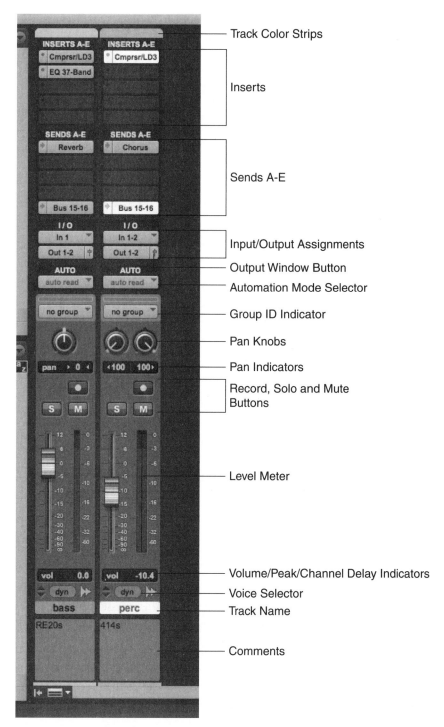

Track Color Strips

Inserts

Sends A-E

Input/Output Assignments

Output Window Button

Automation Mode Selector

Group ID Indicator

Pan Knobs

Pan Indicators

Record, Solo and Mute Buttons

Level Meter

Volume/Peak/Channel Delay Indicators

Voice Selector

Track Name

Comments

Figure 7.1 Mixer strips for mono and stereo Audio tracks in the Mix window, showing the Inserts, Sends, I/O, Track Controls, Comments, and Color Strip sections.

Track and Channel Color Strips

You can toggle display of the color strips above and below all tracks in the Mix window using the View > Mix Window > Track Color option. If desired, you can use the Color Palette window to assign colors to selected tracks so that you can immediately identify groups of related tracks.

For example, to help keep track of a complex session, you might assign distinct colors to all vocal tracks, guitar tracks, drum and percussion tracks, or sound effects. To reassign a track's color, double-click its color strip to open the Color Palette window. You can also apply a shade of the chosen track color to the channel strip with the Apply to Channel Strip button (next to the Saturation slider) and adjust the intensity with the Saturation slider.

Volume Fader and Level Meter

The volume fader adjusts the output level of a track on any output path(s) you've assigned. The output selection can be a path to one or more physical audio outputs (as configured in the I/O Setup dialog box) or to any internal Pro Tools mixing bus. The track's level meter appears to the right of its volume fader. If the top-most red segment (the clip indicator) lights up while you record, your input level to this track is too high, and you need to adjust it to avoid distortion. The clip indicator may also light up during playback due to gain changes applied in one of the track's inserts or its main volume fader setting (assuming that the Options > Pre-Fader Metering option is not enabled). Click to clear a track's clip indicator or Option-click it (Alt-click in Windows) to clear the clip indicator on *all* tracks.

Tip To clear all clip indicators from the keyboard, press Option+C (Mac) or Alt+C (Windows).

Volume faders can boost the track's level by as much as +12 dB. For finer adjustment of any volume fader (as with many other onscreen controls), hold down the Command key (Ctrl key in Windows) as you drag the control. To return a track's volume fader to its default setting of 0 dB (Unity), Option-click (Alt-click in Windows) the fader. If the sends on a track are set to post-fader, their level will also be affected by the track's main volume fader level. (See "Sends A–E, F–J," later in this section, for more information.)

In the Mix window, each track's type is indicated by a distinctive icon (Audio, MIDI, Aux Input, Instrument, or Master Fader) just below its main level meter. You can hold down Command+ Control (or Ctrl+Start in Windows) as you click on this icon to make a track inactive, which conserves CPU power. (This duplicates a function in the Track menu and is not available for MIDI tracks.) Repeat the same action to make a track active again. The Group ID indicator, which is above the Pan knob, opens a pop-up menu for track-group management. You can use this pop-up menu to delete or duplicate groups; modify their attributes (such as group control over mute, solo, and send controls); select, show, or hide all tracks that belong to the same group; and perform other useful functions.

Setting Input Recording Levels Volume faders on Audio tracks affect only the track's output, *not* the input recording level. If you want to change the input signal level to a Pro Tools audio channel, either to avoid clipping or to boost a low-level signal, you must do this *prior* to the track's software input—for example, by boosting the source signal, increasing the preamp gain on your audio interface, routing through an external mixer prior to input to your audio interface, and so on. The Mbox family and many M-Audio and third-party interfaces provide input gain knobs for their analog inputs, especially for microphone inputs.

While recording on an Audio track, feel free to adjust the volume fader to whatever level is convenient for your listening requirements. This has no effect on the actual audio level being recorded to disk. It's highly recommended, however, to always enable the Options > Pre-Fader Metering option (default) while recording into Audio tracks. That way, you see what the levels are at the selected input for each track, regardless of the current fader setting or any insert processing that may affect the final output level.

Pan

In a stereo mix, a *panner* determines the left-right position of each track's audio output. Mono tracks have a single left-right pan knob. Stereo tracks and mono tracks with a stereo plug-in—for example, a mono-to-stereo delay—will have two separate Pan knobs for the track's left and right channels. In surround mixing, on tracks whose outputs are assigned to multichannel paths (more about this in Chapter 14, "Post-Production and Soundtracks"), you can use an XY panner to move the track left/right and front/rear in the surround field.

Option-click a Pan control (Alt-click in Windows) to reset the pan to center.

Setting Each Audio Track to a Separate Output   Sometimes it's convenient to set the output from each Audio track in Pro Tools to a separate mono path—for example, the individual physical outputs on your audio interface. This is useful when you're outputting all your individual Pro Tools tracks to the inputs of a multitrack tape recorder or an analog mixing console. Rather than setting the output assignments one by one, here's a quicker way: After using the I/O Setup dialog box to create individual mono paths for each output on your audio interface, hold down Command+Option (Ctrl+Alt in Windows) as you set the Output selector of the first track (leftmost in the Mix window) to Output #1. The remainder of the Audio tracks will cascade, automatically assigning to consecutive output paths.

Track Controls: Solo, Mute, Record Enable, Voice Selector, Track Input Enable

While the basic functionality of the Solo, Mute, and Record Enable buttons is familiar to anyone who has used a multitrack tape recorder, Pro Tools offers a few enhancements. The Track Input Enable button is similar to the selector on traditional recording consoles that switches a channel strip to its mic/line inputs instead of the tape input, while the Voice selector represents a digital audio workstation–only concept.

- **Solo button.** Enables playback for the soloed track(s) only, muting all others. Command-click (Ctrl-click in Windows) any track's Solo button to put it in Solo Safe mode; its Solo button will be dimmed. Tracks in Solo Safe mode will not be muted when other tracks are soloed.

■ **Mute button.** Disables the main audio output from the muted track(s) as well as any *post*-fader sends (the default). Any *pre*-fader sends will not be affected by muting the track, however. Option-click (Alt-click in Windows) any track's Mute button to mute/unmute all tracks at once.

■ **Record Enable (Rec) button.** Enables the track for recording and, when an Audio track is in the default Track > Auto Input Monitor mode, switches the track to monitor audio signals at its selected input source—either a physical input path or a bus that you are using to route audio from other tracks within Pro Tools. When you press the Record and Play buttons in the Transport window, all record-enabled tracks start recording their selected sources. Only Audio, MIDI, Instrument, and VCA Master tracks have Record Enable buttons.

■ **Voice selector.** Determines which of Pro Tools' pool of voices this Audio track will use to play back its audio clips. Ordinarily, you can leave this set to dynamic (Dyn) so that Pro Tools will automatically make a voice assignment according to your system configuration. (On Pro Tools systems without HD hardware, that and "off" are the *only* available voice assignment modes.) Dynamic voice allocation is usually the most convenient choice, even if you have an HD system providing a relatively large number of voices. The exception would be when you are deliberately using *voice stealing* so that clips in one track interrupt playback in another track set to the same voice (when bleeping dialog, for example). With Pro Tools HD software running on a DSP-based system, you can manually assign voice numbers to each track. At any particular point where two tracks are using the same voice for playback, the track with higher priority (leftmost in the Mix window or highest in the Edit window) always gets the voice—even if this means cutting off the previously playing audio in the other track. Where applicable, the Voice Selector pop-up menu displays voices that are already in use by other tracks in bold type.

■ **Track Input Enable (Pro Tools systems with Complete Production Toolkit and Pro Tools HD systems only).** Switches an individual Audio track to monitoring its input, whether record enabled or not, and regardless of whether the Track > Input Only Monitor setting is enabled.

Record-Safe Your Tracks   Record Safe mode disables recording on an Audio, MIDI, or Instrument track. Especially when working with large sessions and/or viewing tracks at small sizes, this simple technique can help you avoid mistakes as you record new takes into additional tracks. When you are finished recording on a track, Command-click (Ctrl-click in Windows) its Rec button to put it in Record-Safe mode. (The button will be dimmed; see Figure 7.2.) Repeat to re-enable recording on the track.

Don't... Stop...   Many aspects of the mixer configuration can be changed during playback (although not during recording). You can create, delete, or move tracks, inserts, sends, and track I/O assignments on the fly.

Figure 7.2   Dimmed Rec buttons indicate Record Safe mode. The dimmed Solo button in the Aux 1 track indicates Solo Safe mode. (It won't be muted when other tracks are soloed.)

Automation Mode Selector

A track's Automation Mode selector is used to determine how its mix automation will be recorded and played back. Options are Off, Read, Touch, Latch, and Write, plus Touch/Latch and Trim mode (systems with Pro Tools HD software or Pro Tools with Complete Production Toolkit only). For more details about automation modes, refer to Chapter 6. Remember that you can also use the Automation window (also discussed in Chapter 6) to globally enable or disable automation parameters for recording and globally suspend all recording and playback of automation for the session.

Input/Output Section: Output Selector, Input Selector, Pan Indicator, Volume/Peak/Channel Delay Indicators

As you might expect, the I/O section of each track's mixer strip provides selectors that determine where its audio is coming from and where it's going. The numerical value displays in this section are also essential for keeping an eye on the level and position (for example, left-right panning in a stereo perspective) of each track in your mix.

- **Input Path selector.** Determines what physical input or internal bus will be monitored/recorded when a track is record enabled or monitored when the Track > Input Only Monitor option (or Track Input monitoring) is enabled. Software instrument plug-ins can have extra, auxiliary outputs enabled, if available. If this is the case, these will appear among the options in the Input selector for Audio and Aux Input tracks.

■ **Output Path selector.** Determines the main destination where a track's audio will be routed within the Pro Tools mix environment. You can choose any of the available output bus paths on your system or any of Pro Tools' internal mixing busses. The output paths available in this pop-up selector—and especially the grouping of their mono subpaths—depend on the track's channel format (mono, stereo, or multichannel) and the currently active configuration in the I/O Setup dialog box (which determines the naming and grouping for output busses, physical audio outputs on your audio hardware, and the internal mixing busses within Pro Tools).

Routing a Track's Output to Multiple Destinations   In addition to using sends for routing a track's audio to another destination, as discussed in the next section of this chapter, the main output from each Pro Tools track (except VCA Masters and Master Faders) can be assigned to *multiple* destinations. After you've made the main output assignment, hold down the Control key (Start key in Windows) as you open the track's Output selector again to choose additional paths. When you assign a track to multiple output destinations, a plus sign appears in front of the main output assignment displayed within the Output selector.

■ **Pan indicators.** These numerical displays for the current positions of the Pan knobs change in real time as you make adjustments and, during playback, continuously reflect the changing values for any pan automation on this track.

■ **Volume/Peak/Channel Delay indicators.** These fields are located at the bottom of the mixer strip, just above the Track Name field. They display current values for the track's volume fader, peak level, or channel delay. (See the following sidebar for more information.)

Volume/Peak/Channel Delay Indicator Modes   The Volume/Peak/Channel Delay indicator for any Pro Tools track (other than a MIDI track) has three modes. Click on the indicator while holding down the Command key (Ctrl key in Windows) to toggle between these modes.

■ **Volume (default).** Reflects the current level of the track's main volume fader. Displayed values change in real time as you move the fader manually or via volume automation.

■ **Peak.** Displays the most recent peak playback or input level in the track. In other words, if the audio on a track reaches a maximum level of –3 dB during playback, that value is displayed. Click it to reset it. This setting is useful for managing your session's gain structure. It lets you know exactly how much headroom is left on the track— especially since its output level may be affected by level changes made in its plug-ins or hardware inserts. For both the Peak/Hold and Clipping Indicator functions, you can choose to have Pro Tools hold values infinitely (for instance, the most recent peak level during playback, even after you hit Stop), to hold for three seconds, or to not hold at all (configured in the Display tab of the Preferences dialog box). You can clear the red clip indicators on *all* tracks simultaneously by Option-clicking any one of them (Alt-click in Windows) or via the Option+C keyboard shortcut (Alt+C in Windows). Experienced mixers will also find the metering options in the included Signal Tools plug-in extremely useful.

- **Channel Delay.** This setting indicates the processing delay introduced on a track as a result of the plug-ins you've added, in samples. The absolute amount of delay time this represents is proportionate to your session's sample rate; a given number of samples is a progressively smaller amount of time at higher rates. For most Native DigiRack plug-ins supplied with Pro Tools systems, the effective latency added by these plug-ins is very small and correctly displays as almost, but not quite, zero. The Time Adjuster plug-in is very useful for fine adjustment of time alignment on tracks. Alternatively, you can use the Automatic Delay Compensation feature to eliminate delays caused by processing latency in the plug-ins on your tracks.

In addition to their default appearance in the Mix window, you can also display the Volume/Peak/Channel Delay indicators for each track in the Edit window, where an additional button in the I/O panel can be used to directly open an output window for the track. You can also expand these indicators to additionally display the current amount of automatic delay compensation (if any) being applied to each track, using the Delay Compensation view. This view also provides an editable field where you can manually enter a negative or positive offset value for each track, if necessary. To show this expanded view, choose View > Mix Window > Delay Compensation View.

Sends A–E, F–J

As explained in Chapter 2, *sends* are access points in a track's signal chain from which you can route its audio signal to other destinations, independent from the track's main output assignment. In a traditional mixing console, this is how you route part of a vocal track's signal to an external reverb—for instance, using a knob on each channel strip that feeds an audio output labeled Aux Send or similar. In Pro Tools, you can enable up to 10 sends. In the Mix window, these are grouped into two sections (labeled A–E and F–J) on each Audio, Aux Input, or Instrument track. Like the Insert views, discussed below, the two Send section views can be toggled on and off to conserve screen space. Sends are not available on MIDI, VCA Master, or Master Fader tracks.

Each send can be mono or stereo (or multichannel, where available), as shown in Figure 7.3. You can assign the destination of each send to any of the physical outputs available on your system—to connect to an external effects device or a performer's headphone mix out in the studio, for example. More commonly, Pro Tools sends are used to route signals to an internal mixing bus.

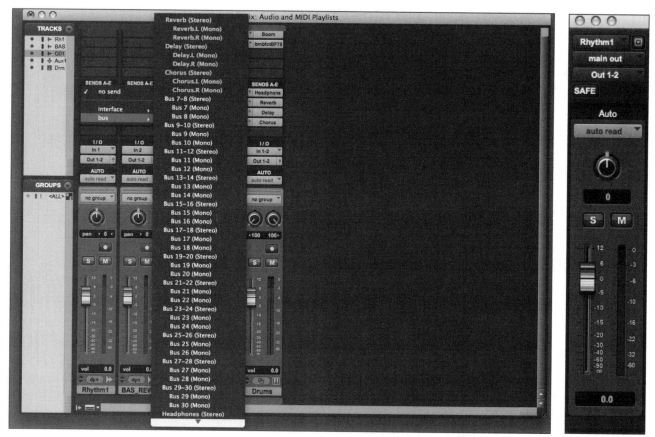

Figure 7.3 Selecting an internal bus send (left); the Send window (right).

Sends default to post-fader, but you can switch them to pre-fader, if required, using the Send window. Controls in the Send window include Output Assignment, Pre/Post selector, Level, Pan (stereo and multichannel surround sends only), Mute, and FMP (Follow Main Pan, which links the Pan setting of the send to the main Pan control of the track itself).

When deciding between the pre- or post-fader position for each send, consider how the send will be used. This varies a lot from one session (and Pro Tools user) to another. Here are examples of typical uses for pre- and post-fader sends:

- *Post-fader sends* are commonly used to feed effects for parallel processing. In addition to any adjustment by the send volume fader, the amount of signal entering the send (and consequently arriving to its assigned destination) is affected by the track's main volume fader. When you mute a track, all of its post-fader sends are also muted.

- In contrast, *pre-fader sends* are commonly used for creating an independent headphone mix for performers out in the studio. Pre-fader sends route audio from the track to the specified destination, strictly according to the send volume fader setting. The send level is unaffected by the track's main volume fader and Mute buttons. This allows you to change volumes or mute tracks while monitoring the recording in the control room without affecting what the talent hears in the headphone mix.

Send Compatibility with Older Pro Tools Versions   Versions prior to Pro Tools 7 support only five sends per track. If compatibility with older versions is a concern (for example, when using the File > Save Copy In command to create a 6.*xx* version of your session), be aware that sends F–J and their associated automation data will be dropped in the process of converting to the older PTS session format.

Example: Creating an Aux Send to a Reverb Effect

If you'd like to send audio from multiple tracks to a stereo reverb, do the following:

1. Create a stereo, post-fader send on each track, assigned to bus pair 1–2.

2. Create a stereo Aux Input track whose input is set to bus pair 1–2.

3. Insert the D-Verb plug-in (or other reverb plug-in) on this stereo Aux Input (checking to make sure the Mix parameter is set to 100 percent wet so that that no direct, unprocessed signal passes through it).

Now you can use the send levels on each source Audio track (which can also be automated) to determine how much of a track's signal will be sent to the reverb.

Tip   Pro Tools 9 and later provide a convenient shortcut for setting up send and return configurations. When clicking a send selector, in addition to the Output and Bus options, you will see the Track and New Track options. To create a send to an existing track, choose the Track option and select the desired destination track. To create a send to a new track, select the New Track option. Pro Tools will create a new destination track and automatically route a bus from the selected send position to the input on the new track.

Don't Be Afraid to Name Names!   The I/O Setup dialog box, which you can open via the Setup > I/O command, allows you to assign names to your inputs, outputs, inserts, and busses. Although you *can* set default name assignments for all subsequent sessions, it's also useful to create specific name assignments each session. For instance, in the preceding example, a stereo Pro Tools bus is used to send signals on Bus 1–2 to an Aux Input that contains a reverb plug-in. You can use I/O Setup to change the name of bus pair 1–2 to Reverb Bus or something similar. This allows you to see at a glance where sends are going instead of having to remember a lot of bus numbers. Also, when you open any send or output assignment pop-up to select a bus, they appear by name instead of number.

The I/O Setup dialog box is also where multichannel paths for inputs, outputs, busses, and sends are managed. This enables surround mixing, of course; Pro Tools HD includes I/O settings files specifically for surround mixing formats. As you get more adept at using the I/O Setup dialog box, be sure to learn how to import and export its settings so that you can reuse them in other sessions. (The default I/O Settings folder is a good place to store your collection.) In the long run, your life will be *much* simpler if you use a consistent set of configurations for the I/O Setup dialog box in all your sessions, especially if, for example, you use distinct names and path groupings during record and mix phases of your projects.

Tip   Another timesaver in current Pro Tools systems is the ability to right-click on a send nameplate after assigning a bus to rename the bus path. This is identical to renaming the bus path in the I/O setup dialog box. Input paths, Output busses, and Insert I/O paths can be renamed in the same way.

Inserts

As explained in Chapter 2, a track's entire audio signal passes through each of the track's insert points in series. Using Insert Selectors A through J that Pro Tools provides, you can patch in a plug-in (a software-based effects processor) at any insert point. Alternatively, you can loop the track's signal through external outputs and inputs on your Pro Tools hardware via a hardware I/O insert before it continues through the channel to the main output assignment for the track. For example, you might use such a hardware insert to route the signal through some favorite high-end compressor or signal-processing device in your studio.

The 10 insert points are always *pre*-fader on Audio tracks, Aux Inputs, and Instrument tracks; however, inserts are always *post*-fader on Master Faders. Because a track's audio passes through each insert in series, from A through J, the order in which you place effects in these inserts makes a difference in the resultant sound. For example, placing the EQ (equalization) after the compressor (a dynamics processor) will generally sound different from configuring them the other way around. To move the insert effects on a track into a different order, drag the insert nameplates in the Mix window; any existing automation for these inserts is adjusted accordingly. Alternatively, Option-drag (Alt-drag in Windows) the nameplates to copy them instead of moving them to a new location—either on the same track or any other track that has a matching number of audio channels.

Right-Click Tricks for Managing Sends and Inserts   In addition to allowing you to rename I/O paths, the right-click menu on any send or insert nameplate in the Mix (or Edit) window provides access to mute (send)/bypass (insert), make inactive, and automation-safe (plug-ins) functions. Right-clicking on plug-ins also provides access to a dialog box for enabling automation parameters.

A new feature of Pro Tools 10 is the bus-interrogation right-click function. This lets you select or show tracks based upon input or output assignment, send assignment, or hardware insert assignment. Bus interrogation can be useful for quickly identifying all tracks that use a specific input, internal bus, output bus, or hardware insert.

The bus interrogation options include the following:

- **Select Assignments To.** This option selects all tracks that use a specific input, internal bus, output bus, or hardware insert.

- **Show Assignments To.** This option displays all tracks, including hidden tracks, that use a specific input, internal bus, output bus, or hardware insert.

- **Show Only Assignments To.** This option shows *only* those tracks that use a specific input, internal bus, output bus, or hardware insert. All other tracks are automatically hidden.

An additional option, Restore Previously Shown Tracks, appears after choosing one of the bus interrogation options to show tracks. This option restores the previous state of shown and hidden tracks.

Using Native Plug-Ins in Pro Tools|HD and Pro Tools|HDX

Pro Tools|HD and Pro Tools|HDX allow you to place both Native and DSP plug-ins on any track type (except MIDI tracks and VCA Master tracks). However, here are some points to keep in mind about voice count:

- The first instance of a Native plug-in on an Aux Input or Master Fader track takes up two additional voices per channel (in other words, two voices for a mono track or four voices for a stereo track).

- On *any* track type, wherever a Native plug-in follows a DSP plug-in in the track's signal chain, the Native plug-in requires two additional voices per channel.

- When Native plug-ins are used on any track, any use of sidechaining (on a dynamics plug-in, for example) or multiple output assignments for the track also uses additional voices.

- Given these limitations, especially on systems with limited voices, try to use DSP equivalents on Aux Inputs and Master Faders, when available. As a general rule, place Native plug-ins *prior* to DSP plug-ins on all track types, if practical.

- However, note that when an Audio track is record-enabled (or switched to Input Monitor mode), any Native plug-ins that precede DSP plug-ins will be bypassed. If you need to hear a Native plug-in as you record on a track, you can place it *after* a DSP plug-in, despite the voice-usage consideration.

Selecting Favorite Plug-Ins   The Insert Selector menu groups the available plug-ins within hierarchical submenus by default. Users with large collections of plug-ins might change settings in the Display tab of the Preferences dialog box so that the plug-ins are grouped by manufacturer. In either case, you can also select plug-ins favorites, which always appear at the top of the plug-in submenus, *before* any additional categorized submenus. Just click on any Insert selector for any track and, while holding down the Command key

(Ctrl key in Windows), select the plug-in you want to add as a favorite. Repeat this procedure to add more or to remove existing favorites. (Stereo favorites won't appear on mono tracks, and vice versa.) Additionally, the Mixing tab of the Preferences dialog box lets you designate default plug-ins for EQ and dynamics. These will appear at the topmost level of the Insert Selector menu, *prior* to either the plug-in or I/O insert submenus for insert selection. Most users will find it very convenient to enable this preference.

Aux Inputs

Aux Inputs behave much like Audio tracks, although they cannot record or contain audio clips. Aux Inputs act in real time upon incoming audio in their selected audio input(s)—either a physical input path on your system or one of Pro Tools' internal mixing busses. You can automate the controls on Aux Inputs and place hardware and software inserts into their signal paths. You can also route a portion of their signals to one of the sends they provide. Like Audio tracks and Master Faders, Aux Inputs can be mono, stereo, or multichannel, and you can assign the output of each Aux Input track to any physical audio output path or internal mixing bus. Figure 7.4 shows how Aux Input tracks appear in the Mix window.

Typical uses of Aux Inputs include the following:

- **Global send effects.** An effects plug-in, such as a reverb or delay, is placed as an insert on the Aux Input. The selected input for the Aux Input is a bus (mono, stereo, or multichannel), which is used for sends from various source Audio tracks.

- **Subgroups/submasters.** The main outputs from multiple source Audio tracks are assigned to a common bus, which is selected as the input source for an Aux Input. The volume fader on the Aux Input thereby controls the entire submix—for example, multiple drum tracks, a wind section, multiple backing vocals, or a complex sound-effects background. Also, you can conveniently apply plug-ins to the entire submix by placing them on this Aux Input. This makes more efficient use of available processing resources and may also produce more appropriate-sounding results—for example, applying a single stereo compressor plug-in to a submix of backing vocals instead of many individual compressors on their mono source tracks. Some people route the same source audio simultaneously through multiple subgroups (generally called *mults* or *double-bussing* when used in this fashion) to apply radically different effects treatments to each. During mixdown, you can blend the submixes together or drop them in and out at strategic points in the arrangement. (Make sure to apply delay compensation to maintain proper time alignment between tracks.) This is a popular technique for processed drum loops, for example.

- **Monitoring external sources.** You can use Aux Inputs to monitor the input from external MIDI instruments, tracks from a multitrack audio recorder, and so on. You can even use Aux Inputs to premix multiple external input sources during the recording process (assigning the outputs from multiple Aux Inputs to a single bus, which then feeds the input on an Audio track used for recording).

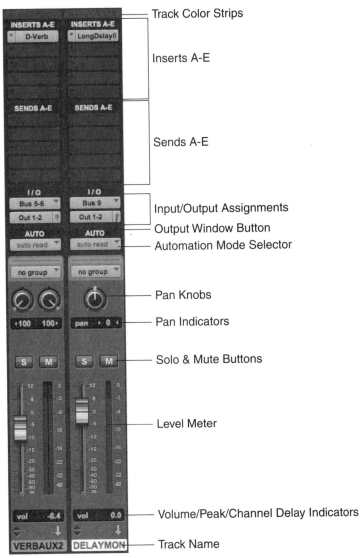

Track Color Strips

Inserts A-E

Sends A-E

Input/Output Assignments

Output Window Button

Automation Mode Selector

Pan Knobs

Pan Indicators

Solo & Mute Buttons

Level Meter

Volume/Peak/Channel Delay Indicators

Track Name

Figure 7.4 Aux Inputs (mono and stereo) in the Mix window (in a stereo mix).

- **Virtual instruments.** You can instantiate software virtual instruments, such as Xpand!^{2}, Boom, or MiniGrand, using plug-ins on Aux Input tracks (as well as on Instrument and Audio tracks).

- **Monitoring audio from ReWire sources.** If you're running a ReWire application concurrently with Pro Tools, you can instantiate a plug-in that allows you to monitor that program's output through an Aux Input (or Instrument track).

Subsequent sections review the available controls and indicators for Aux Inputs. Some elements behave exactly as already described for Audio tracks, so the descriptions are not repeated here.

Don't Overload the Bus   When you route sends or main output assignments from multiple tracks to the same bus and Aux Input destination, beware of exceeding the maximum input level of that bus! If the clipping indicator lights up on an Aux Input track (assuming that Options > Pre-Fader Metering is enabled), you may need to reduce levels being sent to it from the source tracks to avoid unpleasant digital distortion. One strategy is to display a Master Fader for that bus by creating a mono or stereo Master Fader track, as appropriate. This allows you to display and adjust the bus levels. Master Faders have virtually no impact on system resources, so don't hesitate to create them for such purposes!

Pan

Pan controls on Aux Inputs behave the same as on Audio tracks. Bear in mind that when individual sends or main outputs from other tracks are routed to a stereo or multichannel Aux Input, their original pan positions also impact the panning on the Aux Input itself.

Aux Input Track Controls: Solo, Mute

These buttons on Aux Inputs behave the same as on Audio tracks. Remember, however, that when you *solo* an Aux Input—containing your delay effect, for example—other tracks will be muted. This might include sends or outputs from tracks that are feeding your soloed Aux Input!

Solo-Safe Your Aux Input Tracks   In Solo Safe mode, a track will not mute when other tracks are soloed. Command-click (Ctrl-click in Windows) any track's Solo button to put it in Solo Safe mode. (The Solo button will be dimmed.) This is *especially* useful for Aux Inputs. Whether you're using the Aux Input as a send destination with an effect plug-in or as a stereo subgroup to which various Audio tracks' output assignments have been routed, you probably *won't* want the Aux Input to be muted just because you momentarily solo some other track.

Input/Output Section: Volume/Peak/Channel Delay and Pan Indicators, Output Assignment, Input Selector

You can set the Input Path selector on an Aux Input to any appropriate physical audio input path or internal mixing bus available on your configuration. Aux Inputs can be mono, stereo, or multichannel; the Input Path selector menu will only display input paths that match the format of the Aux Input itself. For mono Aux Inputs, you select single audio inputs or mixing busses; for stereo Aux Inputs, you select stereo pairs of physical inputs or busses; and for multichannel Aux Inputs, you select matching multichannel inputs or bus paths. The input and bus paths are all configured within the I/O Setup dialog box, which is discussed in more detail in Chapter 8, "Menu Selections: Highlights." If any software instrument plug-ins have auxiliary outputs enabled, these will also appear among the input options for an Aux Input track.

You can also assign the output of an Aux Input track to any physical audio output path (often the main mix output or an output pair feeding a cue mix to the performers' headphones) or any internal mixing bus. Again, the available selections depend on your system configuration; whether the Aux Input is mono, stereo, or multichannel; and how you have set up your output paths in the I/O Setup dialog box.

Sends

Sends on Aux Inputs behave the same as on Audio tracks. As with Audio tracks, sends from Aux Inputs can be either *post*-fader or *pre*-fader.

Inserts

Inserts on Aux Inputs behave the same as on Audio tracks. As with Audio tracks, the Inserts section on Aux Inputs is always *pre*-fader.

Pro Tools, the Ultimate Digital Mixer You can use Pro Tools configurations with multichannel audio hardware as an automated digital mixer, even if you don't record any tracks to hard disk. For example, many audio interfaces feature not only analog audio inputs but also an eight-channel Lightpipe connector compatible with ADAT multitrack digital recorders. (Lightpipe is an eight-channel digital audio connection standard, using optical cables that terminate in a TOSLINK connector.)

To use Pro Tools as a digital mixer, connect the Lightpipe output from an ADAT (or compatible device) to the Lightpipe input on your audio interface. Create eight mono Aux Inputs in your Pro Tools session and set each of their inputs to a separate ADAT Lightpipe channel. Alternatively, you can group some of these as pairs on stereo tracks if appropriate. Option-click the volume fader for each Aux Input to set its level to 0 dB (also known as *unity gain*, because no gain change is being applied). Play back the tracks recorded on the ADAT (or compatible device) to mix them in the Pro Tools mixing environment.

You can insert plug-in effects on the Aux Inputs to apply signal processing to the incoming audio and use sends to route the signals to other effects (such as reverb and delay) within the Pro Tools mixer. Then, either bounce it all to a disk file or mix it in real time to a DAT recorder to create your stereo master. (The simple method described here doesn't address synchronizing Pro Tools to the tape source, so you wouldn't be able create accurate real-time automation; however, you can purchase one of several synchronization peripherals that are available for this purpose.)

Master Faders

Like Aux Inputs, Master Fader tracks cannot contain clips. Master Faders can be mono, stereo, or multichannel. Figure 7.5 shows mono and stereo Master Faders as they appear in the Mix window. They can act as a master gain stage and control for the audio signal going through an output bus for a physical output path on your audio hardware (mono, stereo, or multichannel) *or* through any of Pro Tools' internal mixing busses. Master Faders are commonly used as a final level control over the main stereo (or surround) output bus (for monitoring and bouncing to disk). Not only does this provide a volume fader, but more importantly, the Master Fader's level meter facilitates final adjustment of your session's gain structure, to ensure that the output does not clip. Using a Master Fader for your main mix output also provides post-fader insert points, where you can apply compression, limiting, EQ, or other effects to an entire mix—especially dithering, which is useful when bouncing down to a lower resolution or recording digitally to a lower-resolution device. You should never bounce a mix to disk (or record to an external device, for that matter) without first creating a Master Fader where you can monitor and optimize the levels on your main mix output!

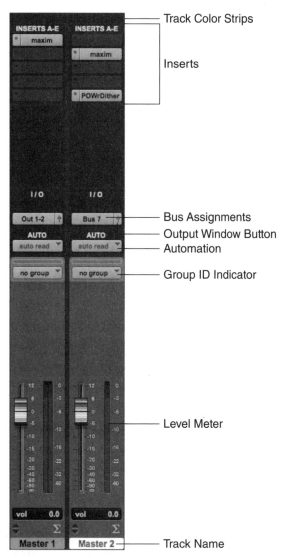

Figure 7.5 Master Faders (mono and stereo) in the Mix window. Master Faders have no sends or pan controls, and their inserts are post-fader.

Although you can place inserts (both hardware inserts and software plug-ins) on a Master Fader, sends are *not* available from Master Faders. Also keep in mind that, unlike Audio tracks and Aux Inputs, the inserts on Master Fader tracks are always *post*-fader. You can automate volume as well as plug-in parameters on Master Fader tracks.

Input/Output Section: Volume/Peak/Channel Delay Indicator, Output Selector

Unlike Audio tracks and Aux Inputs, Master Faders have no Input Path selector—only a selector for choosing the output path (or internal mixing bus) whose signal path you want to control with the Master Fader track. Master Fader tracks also have no Pan controls.

Sends

Master Faders do *not* have sends!

Inserts

Inserts behave the same way on Master Faders as they do on Audio tracks, except that as mentioned earlier, the inserts on Master Faders are always *post*-fader. In other words, the input level to the Inserts section *is* affected by the Master Fader track's main volume fader—unlike Audio tracks, Aux Inputs, and Instrument tracks, where inserts are always *pre*-fader.

Wide Meters View   A hidden Pro Tools command lets you increase the width of all the track level meters. This can help you keep a better eye on what's going on in your mix. To switch to Wide Meters view, hold down the Command, Option, and Control keys (Start, Alt, and Ctrl in Windows) as you click on the level meter for any track. Repeat this operation to switch back to the normal meter width.

MIDI Tracks

MIDI tracks contain MIDI clips (see Figure 7.6). The output assignment for each MIDI track determines where the MIDI data contained in its clips will be transmitted. MIDI tracks can route to an external MIDI destination available on your system (as determined by your current MIDI setup) or to a virtual instrument that is active in the current session. MIDI routing can be done through any available MIDI port and/or a specific MIDI channel. Remember that MIDI is data, not audio! If you want to route the *audio* outputs of your external MIDI devices into Pro Tools, you must connect them to physical audio inputs on your Pro Tools audio hardware and monitor their audio via Audio tracks (or Aux Inputs). Prior to bouncing your final mix, and especially before archiving the finished project, you may want to record the output of your external MIDI devices to Audio tracks. Years down to the road, even if the same source instruments are available, it may be difficult to re-create patch settings or output levels. If the sound sources used by your MIDI tracks are synthesizer and sampler plug-ins or external programs via ReWire, these are generally also instantiated on and/or monitored through Aux Inputs (or Instrument tracks).

MIDI Input/Output & Device/Channel Selectors

Automation Mode Selectors

Group ID Indicator

MIDI Pan Control

MIDI Pan Indicators

Record, Solo and Mute Buttons

MIDI Velocity Meter

MIDI Program Selector

Track Name

Comments

Color Strip

Figure 7.6 MIDI tracks contain MIDI data. Each track is assigned to a MIDI channel, program number, and output (either a physical port on the MIDI interface, a direct USB connection, or a virtual instrument).

Track Name and Comments

As on Audio tracks, the MIDI clips created as a result of recording into MIDI tracks inherit the current track name. So again, it's much better to assign meaningful track names as you record (for example, "bass," "drums," or "strings"); it will prevent confusion later. On *all* track types, take advantage of the Comments field to make notes to yourself—for instance, any manual settings that must be restored on one of your external MIDI devices the next time you open this session.

MIDI Volume and Velocity Level Meters

The volume fader on MIDI tracks send out values for MIDI Controller #7, Main Volume, which range from 0 to 127, on the MIDI channel selected for each track. The level meter on MIDI tracks display Note On velocities of the MIDI note events being played back—*not* the output audio volume of whatever instrument (physical or software-based) is playing back the MIDI events being sent from this track!

MIDI Volume and Panning Are Controller Data   Volume and panning (and other MIDI controller events) work differently in MIDI tracks and the MIDI component of Instrument tracks than in other Pro Tools track types—especially in relation to automation and alternate playlists on the same track. On MIDI tracks, both volume and pan are numerical MIDI values, with a range from 0 to 127. These values are transmitted like any other MIDI controller type. The connected MIDI device or software instrument responds, changing the volume on whatever part or patch is configured to receive the MIDI signal.

When you record fader automation or draw volume changes on a MIDI track, these become part of the data actually contained in each affected MIDI clip. If you record or draw automation outside of the track's existing clips, the clip boundaries will be extended to include the new automation/controller data events.

On Audio tracks, there's only one automation playlist for the track. Therefore, when you choose between alternate Edit Playlists (the list of audio clips and fades to play), the same automation data applies to each. Also, cutting and pasting audio clips in one playlist on an Audio track causes underlying automation events to be moved (when Automation Follows Edit is enabled); this automation change affects *all* of the track's playlists. On MIDI tracks, by contrast, because controller data for volume, pan, and other types of MIDI controller data are part of the MIDI clips themselves, the automation data can be completely different for each playlist. If you alter the MIDI data within MIDI clips after switching to an alternate Track Playlist for a MIDI track, a new MIDI clip is automatically created, and the existing MIDI clips in the other playlists are unaffected.

MIDI Pan

The Pan knob on MIDI tracks sends out values for MIDI Controller #10, Pan, on the track's selected MIDI output channel(s). Values range from 0 to 127, with 0 equaling hard left, 127 equaling hard right, and 64 representing the center position.

Who's the (MIDI) Boss?   If you assign two MIDI or Instrument tracks to the same MIDI output and MIDI channel, the associated external MIDI device or software instrument will respond to MIDI volume, pan, and other controller messages arriving from either track. This can get confusing, especially if you're using automation for MIDI controllers! If you ever *do* need to assign multiple MIDI tracks to an identical output and channel (for example, to create and edit left- and right-hand keyboard parts separately or to use separate tracks for the individual elements of a drum kit in your software instrument), it's better to choose a single track to use for controlling volume and pan—and for all MIDI controller automation—and stick to it. Otherwise, things can get very confusing, as MIDI control messages may overlap each other.

MIDI Track Controls: Solo, Mute, Record Enable, MIDI Program Selector

On MIDI tracks, the Solo, Mute, and Record Enable buttons work in a comparable way to Audio tracks. The MIDI Patch selector (below the track's main volume fader in the Mix window) opens a dialog box displaying patch numbers from 1–127. The patch number you choose (for example, an electric piano sound, program #005 on your synthesizer) is sent as a MIDI program change message on the MIDI output currently selected for the track. If you have the patch name file for your synthesizer properly configured with the Audio MIDI Setup utility (Mac) or MIDI Studio Setup (Windows), you can use the Change button shown in Figure 7.7 to load a MID-NAM file. This is a list of program names and numbers that, when active, allows you to select sounds on your particular synth (as previously defined, attached to a specific port on your computer's MIDI interface) *by name* rather than by program number. Once you import a patch name file for an instrument that's available in your MIDI setup, it is also available in any other Pro Tools session.

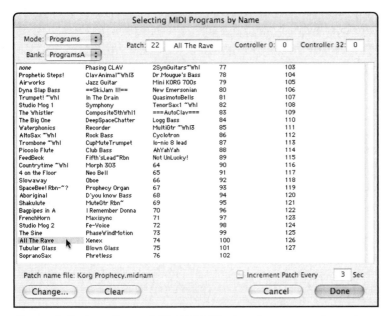

Figure 7.7 Loading a MIDNAM file for the external synth used by this track allows selection of sounds by name rather than by MIDI program numbers.

Automation Mode Selector

The Automation Mode selector for MIDI tracks behaves more or less like the one for Audio tracks, as described earlier in this chapter; you select between Off, Read, Touch, Latch, and Write modes (and Trim mode with Pro Tools HD or the Complete Production Toolkit). However, automation on MIDI tracks—with the exception of mute/unmute events—is recorded into the current MIDI clips as MIDI controller events instead of track automation for the Pro Tools mixer. The destination MIDI module or software instrument then responds to incoming data for volume, pan, or other MIDI controller types on the relevant MIDI channel.

Input/Output Section: MIDI Volume/Pan Indicators, Device/Channel Selectors for MIDI Input/Output

Again, remember that changes in MIDI volume and pan are actually MIDI *controller* messages, sent on a track's currently assigned MIDI channel. These messages also get stored as contents of the MIDI clips on a track. Pan values in Pro Tools range from <64 (100 percent left) to 63> (100 percent right). MIDI Volume values range from 0 to 127.

You can change the MIDI device and channel for each MIDI track's input and output via a pop-up selector. Available choices depend on your configuration, based on the Audio MIDI Setup utility for Mac users or the MIDI Studio Setup window for Windows—and, of course, the active software instruments, MIDI interface, and devices on your system. For editing convenience, you may occasionally assign more than one track to the same MIDI destination (device and MIDI channel, or software instrument). Bear in mind, however, that volume, pan, and program changes arriving at the same destination from multiple MIDI tracks can cause confusion.

You can also assign a single source MIDI track to *multiple* devices/channels or software instrument destinations. Once you've made the main assignment, hold down the Control key (Start key in Windows) and click to open the track's MIDI Device/Channel selector again to choose additional destinations. This can be used as a way to double the current part you've created within a MIDI track, using some completely different MIDI device or channel with a distinct timbre. However, you could also simply duplicate the current MIDI track using the Track > Duplicate command and assign the duplicate track to its own output destination. Duplicating the track also provides separate control for real-time properties—for example, volume and panning.

The Automatic Delay Compensation feature also extends to MIDI tracks that are routed to software instrument plug-ins. This helps time-align the output from duplicated tracks that are passed through different signal paths and processing chains.

Instrument Tracks

Instrument tracks are like Aux Inputs with a MIDI track on the front end. When you create a new Instrument track in the Mix window, except for the distinctive keyboard icon at the bottom of the mixer strip, for all intents and purposes it *is* an Aux Input (with the addition of a Record button for MIDI events and a MIDI patch selector). However, when you view the same Instrument track in the Edit window, it generally looks and acts like a MIDI track.

Unlike Aux Inputs, Instrument tracks can contain MIDI clips and can be used to record MIDI. Once you instantiate a software instrument on an insert of an Instrument track, it is automatically selected as the MIDI output destination that will respond to MIDI events recorded or placed on this Instrument track. Like software instruments residing on an Aux Input, however, you can select software plug-ins on Instrument tracks as the output assignment from any other MIDI or Instrument track. (As with MIDI tracks, you could also route the MIDI output of an Instrument track to some other destination, for that matter.) Instrument tracks save screen space—especially when using monotimbral instrument plug-ins, which can only respond to events on one incoming MIDI channel at a time.

In the Mix window, if you enable display of the topmost Instrument panel (shown in Figure 7.8), it shows MIDI input/output selections for each Instrument track, plus MIDI Volume, Pan, and Mute controls. (The main I/O selection by the volume fader is identical to that of an Aux Input or Audio track and affects the track's *audio* signal path.) In the Edit window, the Track View selector for an Instrument track shows the usual options for MIDI tracks (including MIDI volume and pan and other controllers, which are contained in the MIDI clips on that track), plus volume, pan, and mute automation data (identical to the ones on Aux Input and Audio tracks), which affect the audio output of the Instrument track itself. If you enable any audio plug-in parameters for automation in a track—for example, one of the sound parameters on the Structure software instrument—these will also appear in the Track View selector.

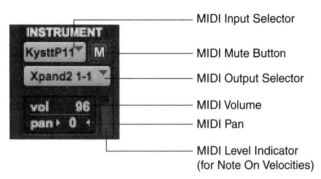

Figure 7.8   On Instrument tracks, the Instrument panel in the upper portion of the Mix window offers controls for MIDI input/output, volume, pan, and mute.

Volume Fader and Level Meter

These elements behave the same way on Instrument tracks as they do on Audio tracks and Aux Inputs, described earlier in the chapter. Bear in mind, though, that volume settings and levels here are related to the *audio* output of the Instrument track (following the output of its software instrument plug-in, if applicable), not to the MIDI data being sent from that track to its own instrument plug-in or other destination.

Pan

Pan behaves the same way on Instrument tracks as it does on Audio tracks and Aux Inputs, but again, this affects the *audio* output of the track (and doesn't send MIDI pan data like the Pan control on MIDI tracks does).

Instrument Track Controls: Solo, Mute, Record Enable

The Solo and Mute buttons on Instrument tracks work as on Aux Input tracks, affecting their audio output only. These buttons don't affect playback of any MIDI data that the Instrument track contains. In fact, if the MIDI output of the track is assigned to a MIDI destination other than an instrument plug-in on the track, the MIDI destination will still sound even when the main Mute button for the Instrument track is engaged. The Record Enable button on an Instrument track (which is *not* available on Aux Inputs) arms the track for MIDI recording, just as on MIDI tracks.

Input/Output Section: Input Selector, Output Selector, Pan Indicators, Volume/Peak/Channel Delay

These elements behave the same way on Instrument tracks as they do on Audio tracks and Aux Inputs. Note that certain software instrument plug-ins may require that *something* be selected as the audio input for track—even if they don't use that incoming signal in any way! Unlike MIDI tracks, there are no MIDI input and output selectors in this section for Instrument tracks. Instead, these selectors are available in the Instrument section at the top of the Mix window. You can toggle display of the Instrument panel in the Mix window either via the View > Mix Window submenu or, more conveniently, by using the Mix Window View selector in the bottom-left corner of the Mix window itself.

Inserts

Inserts behave the same way on Instrument tracks as on Audio tracks and Aux Inputs, described earlier in this chapter. Remember, however, that most software instrument plug-ins don't use the track's input signal. As such, it doesn't make sense to place plug-ins in insert slots prior to the instrument plug-in itself. Only effects plug-ins that you place *after* the instrument plug-in in the track's signal chain will affect the track's audio output.

Instrument Section

This area at the top of the Mixer window is blank on every track type except Instrument tracks. When virtual instruments have been instantiated on an Instrument track, parameters including MIDI volume, MIDI pan, and MIDI Input and Output assignments are displayed in the Instrument view. This is discussed further in Chapter 10, "MIDI."

Mix Window View Selector

This pop-up selector, in the lower-left corner of the Mix window (see Figure 7.9), provides the same options as the View > Mix Window submenu, allowing you to enable/disable display of the following sections for each channel strip: Instrument, Inserts, Sends A–E, Sends F–J (sends not applicable on MIDI tracks and Master Faders), Track Color Strips, and Comments.

Reconfiguring the Pro Tools Mixer during Playback/Recording   In current versions of Pro Tools, you can change which sections of the Mix and Edit windows are visible during either playback or recording. Tracks, sends, and inserts can be created or moved during playback, but not during recording.

Output Windows

On the right side of the Audio Output Path selector for each track (not applicable on MIDI tracks) is an icon that opens the track's output window (see Figure 7.10). This floating window stays open and in place even as you switch between the Mix, Edit, and other windows. An

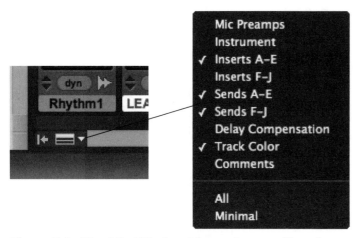

Figure 7.9 The Mix Window View selector offers the same options as the View > Mix Window submenu.

output window provides a secondary set of controls for the track's volume fader, Pan controls (including surround panners, if appropriate), and Mute, Solo, and Automation Mode selectors. Output windows also feature an automation Safe button, which prevents writing of automation data on the track in question. Additionally, for stereo Audio tracks, Aux Inputs, and Instrument tracks, Link and Inverse buttons are provided (discussed later in this section).

Clicking on any send button in the Sends section of the Mix window (or Edit window, if displayed there) also opens an output window. Output windows for sends have an additional Pre button for selecting whether the send is pre- or post-fader. Sends also have an FMP (Follow Main Pan) button, which links the Pan control for the send control to that of the main Pan control for the track itself.

The Path Meter View button in the upper bar of the output window, next to its Close button, is of particular interest when viewing sends. It opens a side panel showing a level meter for the send's destination (a bus used to route audio to a reverb or delay effect, for example). This expanded view is shown in the right half of Figure 7.10.

Without leaving the output window, you can switch between displaying the track's main output section and displaying any of its 10 sends using the pop-up Output selector in the upper panel of the output window.

You can leave output windows open to provide quick access—regardless of whether the Mix window or even the track itself is currently visible. By default, the target icon is lit in an output window, which means that clicking the Output icon for a different Audio track (or send) in the Mix window replaces the contents of the current output window. However, you can click on the current output window's target icon to disable (dim) it. Untargeted windows stay open so that clicking other sends or the Output icon for another track opens an *additional* output window. (The new window might appear right over the previous one, giving the impression that the first output window has been replaced. Drag the new window to a location to see both.)

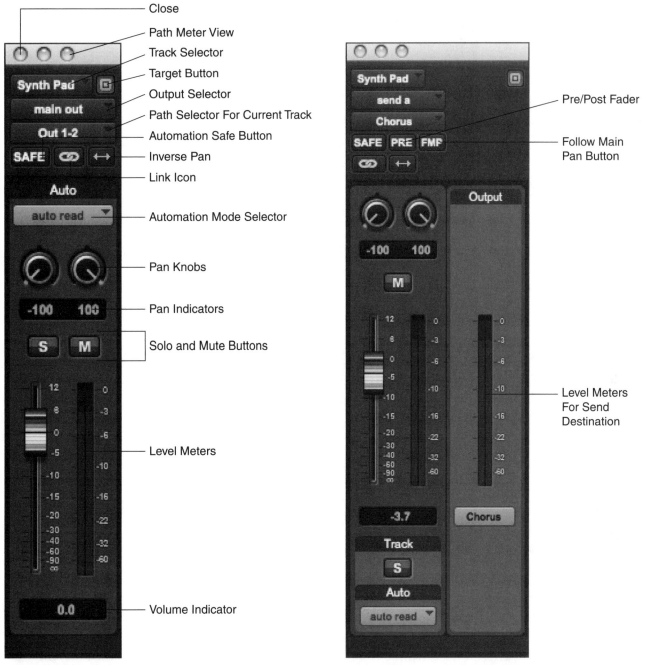

Close
Path Meter View
Track Selector
Target Button
Output Selector
Path Selector For Current Track
Automation Safe Button
Inverse Pan
Link Icon
Automation Mode Selector
Pan Knobs
Pan Indicators
Solo and Mute Buttons
Level Meters
Volume Indicator

Pre/Post Fader
Follow Main Pan Button
Level Meters For Send Destination

Figure 7.10 Output windows for a track (left) and a send (right). In the send output window, the Path Meter view has been opened (using the button in the upper bar) to simultaneously display the send output from the track and the current levels on the destination bus.

Using Output Windows By default, the target icon in the first output window you open is enabled. As you click on other sends or track output window buttons, their contents are swapped into the output window that is already open. As mentioned, clicking the target icon to disable it lets the current output window stay open, even as you open others.

Especially for large sessions, keeping several output windows open can make your life *much* simpler, with frequently accessed controls always immediately available even as you scroll through massive sessions in the Mix or Edit windows. Here are a few applications where you might want to keep an output window open:

- Reverb sends from key vocal and soloist tracks. (Don't forget to open the Path Meter view so that you can also avoid overloading by monitoring levels on the send bus.)

- Aux Inputs used as mixer subgroups for multiple source tracks—for instance, the entire rhythm section, a drum set, a bed of backing vocals or guitars, a set of choir microphones within a larger ensemble, or submixes of dialog, effects, or music for post-production.

- The Master Fader for the main mix output. Having this visible in an output window makes it easier to keep an eye on your levels, as the Master Fader track might not always be visible as you navigate in the Mix window on a large session.

Safe Button for Automation

When enabled, the automation Safe button prevents writing of automation data on the track currently displayed in an output window. This can save a lot of hassle. If you might record subsequent real-time automation passes on other tracks, get in the habit of using the automation Safe button to avoid accidentally overwriting your mix automation.

Linked Panners (Multichannel and Stereo Tracks Only)

When the Link icon is enabled in an output window, both Pan knobs in the output window move left and right in sync, with identical values. If you additionally activate the Inverse button, the two Pan knobs are linked but move in opposite directions. This is useful for adjusting the width of a stereo track, for example.

Inverse Pan (Multichannel and Stereo Tracks Only)

The Inverse Pan button is used on stereo or multichannel tracks in conjunction with the Link icon. In Inverse mode, the panners mirror each other in opposite directions. As you move the one Pan control toward the middle (using either the knobs in the output window or the Pan knobs in the Mix window itself), the other one automatically moves inward by a corresponding amount. For a stereo track, for instance, enabling Panner Linking and Inverse mode provides a convenient way to reduce the stereo width.

As counterintuitive as it may seem, sometimes it's desirable to *narrow* the stereo image of a track—for example, reducing clutter by having a stereo drum loop not extend as far out to the edges of the mix as other loops and percussion tracks that are layered over it. In surround mixing, inverse linking of panners takes on a whole new dimension—literally—allowing you to link the two front channels, the two rear channels, or front and back.

Track List

The Track List (shown in Figure 7.11) is a side column that can be displayed at the left edge of both the Mix and Edit windows for selecting and moving tracks as well as controlling what tracks are visible in the Edit and/or Mix window. Each track is represented by a small black Show/Hide icon that controls whether it is visible for editing, a mini strip to show the track's color coding, an icon denoting what type of track it is, and the track name. Track listings that are highlighted gray are currently selected. The pop-up menu at the top-right of the Track List offers commands for showing, hiding, and sorting tracks in various configurations.

Figure 7.11   The Track List and its pop-up menu.

Here's a typical scenario for hiding tracks: You're posting a video project and have assembled a fairly complex mix for the background ambience and sound effects in a scene, requiring many tracks. You're ready to work on several tracks of dialog, but your Mix and Edit windows now contain a huge number of tracks, making your work cumbersome. The solution: Change the output assignment of each sound-effects track to one of Pro Tools' internal bus pairs and create a stereo Aux Input that monitors that same bus as its input. Now you can hide all these sound-effects tracks (by using their Track Show/Hide icon in the Track List pane) and use the Aux Input track's fader to control their overall level.

Slimming Down Your Mix Window   When the number of tracks in your Mix window exceeds what will fit in the current screen, you have several options:

■ Scroll back and forth to view the desired tracks.

■ Use the Track List to display only certain tracks or track types.

■ Enable the View > Narrow Mix option, which squeezes each vertical mixer strip into a smaller space.

■ Purchase a larger monitor with higher resolution.

Lastly, in the Track List, you can also drag tracks up or down to change their order. This has the same effect as dragging tracks by their nameplates, either horizontally in the Mix window or vertically in the Edit window.

Mix Group List

This area displays any mix groups you've created with the Track > Group command and the All group, which is always present. When a group's name is selected in the Mix Group List, it becomes active. Volume changes on any track belonging to the group will be mirrored in the other member tracks (maintaining their original *relative* levels). As discussed in Chapter 6, in the Create Groups and Modify Groups dialog boxes, you can choose whether Mute and Solo buttons, send levels, and send mutes of tracks in the group are linked (as well as various other track attributes in Pro Tools HD or Pro Tools with Complete Production Toolkit). In standard Pro Tools software, settings for record-enable, panning, and output assignments remain independent for grouped tracks.

When you deselect a group name, it becomes inactive; you can make changes on any of its tracks without affecting the others in the group. By default, Pro Tools creates groups that are active in both the Mix and Edit windows. In that case, enabling a group in either window affects the same group in the other window. To deal with Mix and Edit functions separately, click either the Edit or Mix button (instead of the Edit and Mix button) in the dialog box as you create or modify each group or deselect the Preferences > Mixing > Link Mix/Edit Group Enables option.

Color-Coding Mix Groups   You can use the Color Palette window to assign colors to selected Mix or Edit groups (independent of color assignments for the tracks that pertain to them and/or the audio and MIDI clips *within* those tracks). Not only will these colors appear in the Mix Group List, they will also display in the pop-up Mix Groups button for each track in the Mix window.

Double-click in the color bar or group select column to the left of any group in this list to modify the group (for example, to convert a Mix and Edit group into a Mix-only group). Single-click in either column to select all tracks belonging to the group. The pop-up menu at the top of the Mix Groups List (see Figure 7.12) also allows you to delete any group or *suspend* all groups.

Figure 7.12 Mix groups allow you to select or mute/solo multiple tracks with a single operation and change their volumes simultaneously.

Underneath each track's level meter, a pop-up menu allows you to confirm the active Mix group (s) to which that track is assigned and to see what other tracks share that same group assignment (as well as to duplicate, delete, and modify existing groups).

Adjusting Individual Volumes on Grouped Tracks   When tracks are grouped in the Mix window, moving any one of their volume faders changes the levels of the other tracks in the group by a corresponding amount. Their *relative* levels are maintained, however, from when they were first grouped. In this way, for example, you could move the faders for all drum tracks up and down together without altering the relative balances. However, you may also need to make independent volume adjustments on individual tracks within a Mix group. It's not strictly necessary to suspend the group to adjust a single track. Just hold down the Control key (Start key in Windows) as you drag the fader for any grouped track; other tracks in the same Mix group won't be affected. Alternatively, you can independently adjust a grouped track's volume by holding down the right mouse button as you drag its fader. As always, if you hold down the Command key (Ctrl key in Windows) as you drag *any* onscreen control, its value changes in smaller increments, allowing for fine adjustments. You can use both of these modifier keys simultaneously.

Summary

Whether you control (and automate) your mixes in Pro Tools mainly through graphic break-points in the Edit window or using the controls in the Mix window depends on the nature of your work and on personal preference. This chapter focused on the onscreen elements of the Mix window and how they behave; the issue of signal routing within Pro Tools is explored in more detail in Chapter 9. For a schematic view of Pro Tools signal-routing architecture, see the illustrations in Appendix E, "Signal Flow in Pro Tools."

8 Menu Selections: Highlights

The goal of this chapter is *not* to review every selection in every menu. Most of the functions are well documented in the *Pro Tools Reference Guide*, and especially in the *Pro Tools Menus Guide* (PDF files provided with Pro Tools, available under the Help menu). Instead, the intent of this chapter is to highlight those menu items that are key to Pro Tools operation, that have specific characteristics in the Pro Tools environment, that are new to Pro Tools 10, or that are simply ignored by too many Pro Tools users.

File Menu

Some commands in the File menu concern creating new session files, opening existing sessions, or saving the current session under a different name. Others enable you to import audio or MIDI files *into* your Pro Tools session (although this can also be accomplished via the Workspace browser window) or to bounce mixes out to disk as new audio files. You can also import data from other Pro Tools session documents, send items via DigiDelivery (if you have an account on a DigiDelivery server), and export MIDI data for the Sibelius music-notation program. Pro Tools 10 also provides the option to export selected tracks as an OMF or AAF sequence or as a new session.

Remember that by nature, most Pro Tools projects consist of multiple files; the audio files that you use and create are not actually part of the Pro Tools session document itself. The following subsections provide details on some of the items under the File menu.

Save, Save As, Save Copy In, Revert to Saved

These commands concern saving the currently open session document to disk, either under the present name or with a different name and location.

Save

The File > Save command writes the current session document to disk—including all edits, settings, and MIDI recordings up this point—under the existing file name. Remember: You must save *often* as you work; get used to using the Command+S (Mac) or Ctrl+S (Windows) keyboard shortcut!

Oh No! My Computer Crashed before I Saved My Session! If the unthinkable should happen as you record audio—that is, your computer hangs before you can save the session—don't despair! All MIDI recording, automation, parameter changes, and clip edits you've performed since the last save may be lost, but you won't necessarily lose all the recorded audio takes. And although the recording that was in progress when the computer crashed may not be retrievable, other completed audio recordings will probably be usable. That's because in Pro Tools, each time you click the Stop button on the Transport after recording, the resultant audio files are stored within your session's Audio Files folder—*regardless of whether you save the session file.*

So even though you may have to start over from the last saved version of the session (or the last backup, if available), you can do the following to recover any recordings that did not get saved on Audio tracks:

1. Re-create the Audio tracks if necessary, and then use the File > Import > Audio command to import the missing audio files from the session's Audio Files folder into the Clip List. (If you were smart and gave your tracks meaningful names, you should be able to easily identify the files, clips, and takes for each track by their file names.)

2. Drag the clips onto the appropriate tracks. For example, drop the whole-file clip named GtrSolo_03, the third take of the guitar solo overdub, into the track named GtrSolo. Don't worry about the exact position for now—you'll fix that next.

3. Switch to Spot Edit mode and click one of the clips you just placed on a track. The Spot dialog box will open. In the lower half of this dialog box, click the button next to the Original Time Stamp value. That value will be entered into the Start field. Click OK. Your clip will be spotted to the exact time location where it was originally recorded! This is possible because Pro Tools automatically timestamps clips as they are recorded.

Even so, you still may have lost a good amount of work done since the last time you saved the session—because automation, MIDI recordings, clip edits, plug-in or software instrument settings, assignment of sends, enabling of hardware or plug-in inserts, and so on are all stored within the session document itself. That's why you must be sure to save your session often (Command+S on Mac, Ctrl+S in Windows) as you work!

Save As

This command saves the current session document under a new file name. From that point on, you're working on (and saving to) the newly created session. The new session references the same audio files as the original session. All additional audio recordings you create in the new session will continue to be stored inside the same Audio Files folder.

The File > Save As command is useful for saving different versions of a session—for example, if you want to try some extended experimentation but maintain the possibility of returning to a previously saved session document.

Saving Iterations of Your Pro Tools Session In addition to using the Auto Backup feature (discussed in the "Preferences" section later in this chapter), many experienced operators use the Save As command as a backup strategy in case the current session document should become corrupted for any reason. Common practice includes appending the date, time, or version number to successive versions of the same session (for example, MySession_01, MySession_02, or MySession_Sept20, MySession_Sept21). This not only protects you against file damage (although you should be saving incremental backups of your important work files anyway) but also gives you a specific "go back" state for your project, in case you make any mistakes or bad decisions…or clients change their minds!

For users with extremely limited tracks or DSP power on their systems, it can be practical to bounce out submixes from a session, create a new copy using Save Session As, import the submix, eliminate source tracks bounced to disk in the submix (or merely disable them using the Track > Make Inactive command), and then start recording more overdubs. Because you created the session using the Save Session As command, both the previously existing and the new audio files reside together in a single Audio Files folder.

Save Copy In

This command can be used to save a snapshot of the current session document—including all audio files—without leaving the session document that's currently open or changing its name. If you close the current session and then open this other copy, any subsequent audio recordings will be stored within the session copy's Audio Files folder. (When using Save Copy In, always be sure to create a new folder for that session copy to reside in, to keep things orderly.) You could also use the Save Copy In command simply as a method for saving snapshots of the work in progress without changing the main session file name you're still using (as would be the case with the Save As command). This is also the command you will use for saving Pro Tools 10 sessions (which use the new .ptx extension and file format) to earlier formats, such as Pro Tools 7–9 (with the .ptf extension), Pro Tools 6 (with the .pts extension), or Pro Tools 5 (with the .pt5 extension).

The Save Session Copy dialog box (shown in Figure 8.1), which opens when you choose the Save Copy In command, provides several other important options. For example, you can choose to save audio files for the session copy in 16-bit, 24-bit, or 32-bit float format, choose to save multi-channel audio in interleaved format, and/or choose a different sample rate for your audio files. When saving back to Pro Tools format 5.1–6.9, enabling the Enforce Mac/PC Compatibility option facilitates opening the session from either Mac or Windows, especially in versions prior to 6.7. You can choose whether the maximum gain boost permitted by track volume faders in the new session copy is +12 dB or +6 dB. (This is necessary only if session compatibility with versions prior to 6.4 is a concern. However, be aware that any existing fader settings over +12 dB will automatically be reduced to +6 dB.)

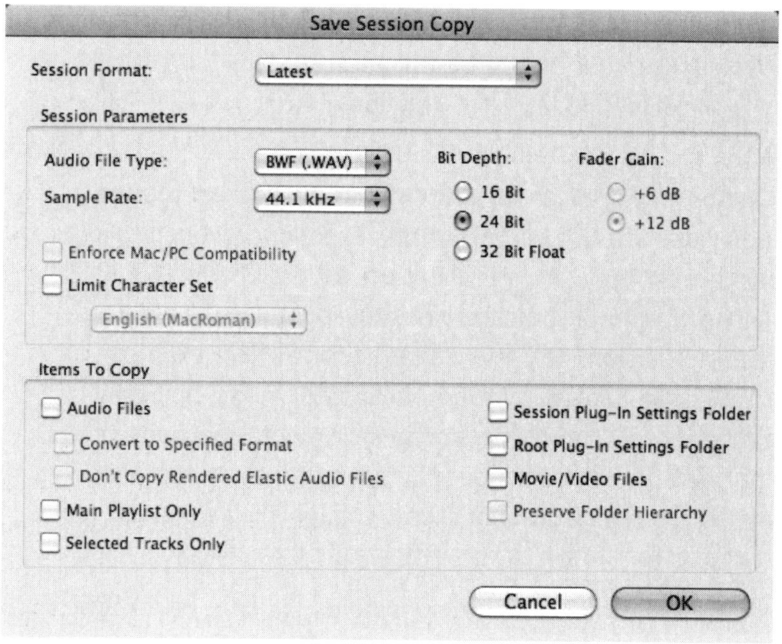

Figure 8.1 The Save Session Copy dialog box.

The Items to Copy section at the bottom of this dialog box provides further options:

- **Audio Files.** Select this option to duplicate the Audio Files folder *and its entire contents* to the folder where you save the session copy. If you choose a different sample rate from the current session (or a different bit depth for Pro Tools 9 or earlier), this option is automatically enabled because the new session copy will require all of the audio files to be converted. The new session file copy will reference a new Audio Files folder created by this operation—all audio clips in the new session's Audio tracks and Clip List will refer to the converted file copies rather than to the originals. Regardless of whether you enable this option to copy the audio files, if the new session created by the Save Copy In command is saved in a new location, all subsequently created audio files will be stored into their own Audio Files folder. (In Pro Tools 9 or earlier, new fades will also be saved in their own Fade Files folder.)

Tip   When copying all audio files from a source session, it can save time and disk space if you take a moment beforehand to identify unused files/clips and apply the Clear Selected command in the local menu of the Clip List, as well as apply its Compact command on some of the remaining whole-file clips.

- **Session Plug-In Settings Folder.** Select this option to copy plug-in settings from the current session to a new folder, which will be referenced in the new copy. This ensures that the plug-in presets for the session continue to appear by name (and are available for assignment to additional instances of those plug-ins) when you open the session on another system supporting the same plug-in architecture.

- **Root Plug-In Settings Folder.** Select this option to copy the main Plug-In Settings folder into a subfolder of the disk/folder location where you create your session copy, named Plug-in Settings Folder. This is also useful when moving sessions from one Pro Tools system to another because all saved plug-in settings (for example, a favorite compressor or EQ setting that you generally use for the same voice) can then be recalled by name on the new system, regardless of whether they are used in the current session. (The same plug-in and plug-in architecture must be available on the destination system. DSP-only plug-ins, for example, are omitted when an HD session is opened on a host-based system.)

- **Movie/Video Files.** Select this option to copy digital video files used in your Pro Tools session into the new session's Video Files folder. (The new session will point to this new copy of the video.) If you don't select this option, the new session will reference any video files it uses from their original locations.

- **Limit Character Set.** This option (in the Session Parameters section) is automatically enabled when saving to older session formats; it is especially relevant when saving sessions to or from Japanese, Chinese, or Korean character sets.

It should be noted that when saving a Pro Tools 10 session copy in an older format, the features introduced in newer versions will not be available. Some Pro Tools 10 features that will be dropped or unsupported include Clip Gain, the Maximum Delay Compensation setting, real-time fades, the 24-hour Timeline, and AAX plug-ins.

Saving Pro Tools Sessions to Older Formats   Pro Tools versions 7 through 9 share the same file format, although various features are not available as you work back through earlier versions. Key features of each version that get dropped in earlier versions include support for third-party hardware, Automatic Delay Compensation for host-based systems, and support for Pro Tools|HD Native hardware (Pro Tools 9); Elastic Pitch, Clip (Region) Ratings, MIDI and Score Editor windows, Playlists view, and Inserts F–J (Pro Tools 8); and Elastic Audio and the Key Signature Ruler (Pro Tools 7.4).

When you use the Save Copy In command to save a session back to 5.1–6.9 formats, the following occurs:

- File names are shortened to 31 characters, including the file-name extension. This affects the session file and any source audio files. Audio files that exceed this limit have their names truncated and are placed into a new folder called Converted Audio Files.

- Sends F–J are dropped, along with any associated automation for them (versions 6.9 and earlier only support five sends per track).

- On host-based systems, busses 17–32 are omitted, since only 16 busses are supported in previous versions (versus 128 in Pro Tools HD).

- Clip groups (region groups) are omitted, as are clip loop (region loop) aliases.

- Markers/Memory locations 201–999 are dropped. (Only 200 are supported in 6.9 and earlier.)

- Sample-based MIDI clips (regions) and tracks are dropped. Both the sample-based MIDI track and the clips (regions) it contains are completely deleted from the session.

- Instrument tracks are split into separate Aux Input and MIDI tracks.

- VCA Master tracks are deleted after their results are automatically coalesced into the affected tracks.

- Clips (regions) on Audio tracks that have been warped using Elastic Audio revert to their original timings, playing back unwarped.

Revert to Saved

This command reverts the session to its previous state as saved on disk, undoing all changes since the last time you saved it. However, as Pro Tools will warn you, you cannot undo some operations. For example, if, while using the Clip List menu's Clear Selection command, you opt to delete a selected audio file completely from disk, you can't use the Revert to Saved command to get it back!

The Open Recent Command   Command+O (Alt+O in Windows) accesses the Open file dialog box, where you can choose any Pro Tools session. However, if you add Shift to this keyboard shortcut, the most recent session in the Open Recent submenu is opened directly. This shortcut is worth learning!

Bounce to Disk

The most typical use of this command is to create a single new audio mix file (or multiple mono files) of the entire Pro Tools session (or the current Timeline selection, as shown in the Transport window's Start and End fields) in real time—including all plug-in processing, automation, auxiliary inputs, and other factors that affect the mix you're currently hearing through the main mix output. You can choose the desired audio output path to use as the source for your bounced mix, and you can specify a variety of file formats and resolutions for the resultant audio file. (See Chapter 16, "Bouncing to Disk, Other File Formats," for more detailed information.) You will often use Bounce to Disk to save out stereo files for CD mastering, stereo or mono mix files for video editors, interactive authors, and so on. Pro Tools 10 also allows you to add your bounce to your iTunes library and/or to share it on SoundCloud.

If you've chosen a multichannel audio output path as the source for your bounce (for example, a surround mix), in addition to stereo and mono, the pop-up Format selector in the Bounce dialog box has a multiple mono option. With this option, one audio file is created for each mono subpath in your surround mix. When you select a stereo bus or output pair as the source for the bounce, you can also create split stereo files (pairs of mono files, with .L or .R inserted into their file names) using the multiple mono option. This is the best choice if you're planning to import the bounce files in older systems (for instance, using the Import After Bounce check box when submixing tracks to free up voices or DSP resources). Interleaved stereo files must be split into separate left and right mono file copies to be usable from within a Pro Tools 9 or earlier session.

You can also use the Bounce to Disk function to "print" tracks to disk (after soloing them, or muting other unwanted tracks), incorporating all their current effects processing and automation. In very large or complex sessions, you might max out the digital signal processing (DSP) capacity that your CPU and/or Pro Tools HD hardware provides. Bouncing one or more tracks to disk (or submixing multiple tracks) and then re-importing the bounced files into your session is one way to free up DSP resources for additional tasks on a slower system and is a convenient method for loop creation.

Yet another option is to choose any active bus (mono, stereo, or multichannel) in your Pro Tools session as the source for your bounce. If you enable display of the Master Fader for that bus, its (post-fader) effects will be included in the bounced mix.

Loud Is Good, Louder Is Better?   Careful use of gain-optimization plug-ins—such as Avid's Maxim; iZotope Ozone; the Massey L2007; and L1, L2, or L3 from Waves—can ensure that your mixes are peaking at the maximum possible output level without digital *clipping* (signal overload, which distorts the audio waveforms by cutting off their peaks). Nevertheless, for burning one-off CDs or turning mix files over to a video editor (as well as preparing a final music mix for mastering), it *can* sometimes be convenient and prudent to normalize bounced mixes.

Peak-mode normalization (as opposed to RMS mode) is very straightforward: It finds the peak level within the audio file and adjusts that to whatever level you designate. (If 100% is "full code," or 0 dBFS, then 94.4% is equivalent to –0.5 dBFS. For bouncing out music mixes, it's recommended to normalize somewhere between this and a more conservative –2 dBFS, which is just under 71% on an absolute scale, in order to prevent clipping during sample-rate conversion. This also avoids potential distortion on some older CD players!) As a result of the normalization process, the level in the audio file changes proportionally… including any previously inaudible background noise if the normalization parameters you specify dramatically increase the file's level (beware!). Still, if you're trying to get gigs, local airplay, or 30 seconds of attention from an agent or record-company rep, you don't want your CDs to be dramatically softer than everyone else's.

Contrary to what you might hear, however, normalizing does *not* "decrease your dynamic range" or make everything slam up against maximum level all the time (which *can* be the case when gain optimization, maximizer plug-ins, or even conventional limiters are abused). As a matter of fact, as pointed out in Chapter 15, "Sound Design for Interactive Media," normalization is frequently used to make the peak levels of entire batches of files more consistent, often effectively *reducing* their original level—for example, when creating large collections of button sounds or background effects that should be uniformly lower in volume than accompanying voiceovers in a multimedia project. Again, Chapter 16 goes into much more detail about bouncing files to disk in other formats and the use of normalization.

It is always best to optimize your mix output by adjusting track and Master Fader levels prior to bouncing to disk (as opposed to normalizing a mix file that has already been reduced to 16 bits). However, if someone else will be doing the final mastering on your mix, do not normalize or apply your own aggressive dynamics processing to the supplied mixes (including plug-ins on the Master Fader for the mix output), as this severely limits the options for the mastering engineers.

Here's a process you can use to normalize a bounced mix without leaving Pro Tools:

1. In the Bounce dialog box, select Multiple Mono as the file format (optional in Pro Tools 10) and enable the Import After Bounce check box. (The audio file type must be WAV or AIFF, and the sample rate must match that of the source session for this option to be enabled; in Pro Tools 9 and earlier, the sample rate must also match the session sample rate.)

2. After the bounce completes and the bounced mix is imported, select the imported stereo file pair in the Clip List. Select AudioSuite > Other > Normalize.

3. In the Normalize dialog box, select Clip List for the Selection Reference (instead of Playlist), and select the Overwrite Files option for the Processing Output Mode (instead of Create Individual Files). Choose a peak level of 94.4% (−0.5 dB) or less to leave a little bit of headroom and avoid possible distortion on older CD players.

4. Click the Render (Process) button in the Normalize plug-in window.

5. With the .L and .R split audio files for your normalized stereo mix still selected in the Clip List, select Export Clips as Files from the Clip List pop-up menu. Choose the AIFF or WAV file type, stereo format, 44,100 (44.1 kHz) sample rate, and 16-bit resolution.

For those who prefer to use a separate program to normalize or perform final trimming on stereo or mono bounced mixes, here are some common options (which also offer many other processing and conversion features):

■ **Mac:** Peak Pro (Bias), Soundbooth CS5 (Adobe), Audition 5.5 (Adobe), Cleaner (Autodesk), Audacity (open source freeware), and Cacophony (shareware, by Richard F. Bannister)

■ **Windows:** Sound Forge (Sony; formerly Sonic Foundry), WaveLab (Steinberg), Nero Ultra (Nero AG), Soundbooth CS5 (Adobe), Audition 5.5 (Adobe), Cleaner XL (Autodesk), and Audacity (freeware originally developed by Dominic Mazzoni, with subsequent contributions from many others)

Bounce to QuickTime Movie

In a similar fashion to the Bounce to Disk command, this command bounces the session's audio mix (or currently selected range) directly into a new copy of the QuickTime video file currently in use in this session. The most common sample rate for professional video applications is 48 kHz. For multimedia applications, some interactive authors may request a lower sample rate for the audio in their QuickTime movies (such as 22,050 Hz or even 11,025 Hz) in order to keep file size and throughput requirements to a minimum. See Chapter 15 for more information.

Import Submenu

This menu offers options for importing audio files and clips, MIDI files, video files (and audio soundtracks from within them), as well as clip groups. You can also import track data from other Pro Tools sessions.

Import Session Data

Use this command, which opens the Import Session Data dialog box (see Figure 8.2), for importing tracks and other data from other Pro Tools sessions into the current one. You can reference the source audio and video files for tracks you're importing from another session in their original locations (via the Refer to Source Media selection in the pop-up selectors for Audio and Video

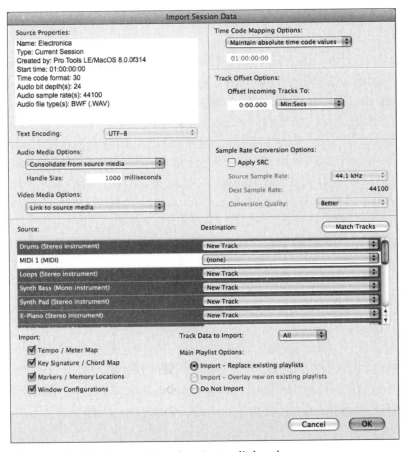

Figure 8.2 The Import Session Data dialog box.

Media Options) or copy those files into the current session's Audio Files folder (via the Copy from Source Media option). The Consolidate from Source Media selection, seen in the figure, has an effect similar to the Compact command in the Clip List pop-up menu. It copies only the utilized portions of the imported track's audio files, with the "handle" size providing a padding factor in case you need to slightly lengthen any of the clips afterward. If necessary, you can convert the file type, sample rate, and bit depth of source audio files to those of the current session.

The location of clips and events in the newly imported tracks can be identical to the absolute time references in their original session, adjusted relative to those of the current session, or offset by a given amount. For music and soundtrack work, you can even import the tempo/meter map and markers from the source session, as well as key-signature events and window configurations. Tempo events, markers, and key-signature events could be handy, for example, when you bring various work sessions for musical segments into the final master session for a film or video soundtrack.

Saving Session Templates   In Appendix D, "Power Tips and Loopy Ideas," you will find instructions for saving session templates. Both this and importing session data from other "boilerplate" Pro Tools sessions are important timesaving techniques that you will want to incorporate into your working style.

Import Audio and Import MIDI

These File menu commands are used for importing audio files and standard MIDI files. After you select one or more source audio files or clips and then click the Done button in the dialog box shown in Figure 8.3 (and after specifying the destination audio files folder, if applicable), a second dialog box will appear. A similar dialog box appears when importing MIDI files. In this Import Options dialog box, if you choose the Clip List option, new clips simply appear there without being placed onto any track. The new clip names will be based on the source file name and, in the case of a standard MIDI file, the MIDI track names within it. If you choose New Track instead, a new Audio track is created for each imported audio file, or a new MIDI track for each MIDI channel within the Standard MIDI File (SMF) file you import. The audio or MIDI clips are automatically placed into these new tracks; likewise, the new track names reflect the names of the source files.

Audio Import Options

The Location pop-up selector in the Audio Import Options dialog box (shown in Figure 8.4) determines where the new audio clips appear within your newly created tracks:

- Choose Session Start to place the imported file(s) at the earliest existing point in the Timeline.

- Choose Song Start to place the imported file(s) at the Song Start marker (which typically might indicate where Bar 1 occurs after some pickup bars or some other sort of intro).

- Choose Selection to place the newly imported file(s) at the current location of the edit cursor or the beginning of the current selection.

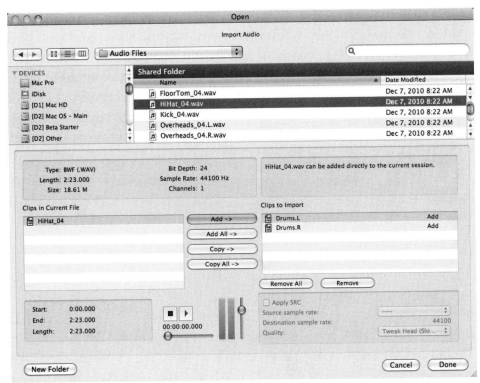

Figure 8.3 The Import Audio dialog box enables you to import entire audio files or clips within them. You can also preview audio files here.

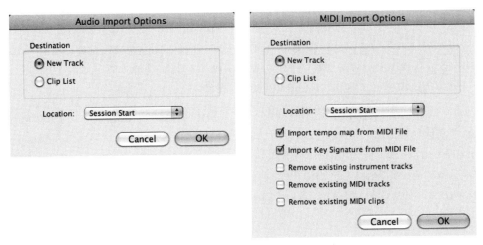

Figure 8.4 The Audio and MIDI Import Options dialog boxes offer flexibility when importing audio or standard MIDI files into the current session.

■ Choose Spot to open the Spot dialog box, where you can specify the new location numerically or capture it from incoming time code.

For importing and previewing larger numbers of files, be sure to learn how to use the Workspace browser window; it enables you to browse the contents of disks on your system, dragging audio and MIDI files directly into the Clip List or Track List.

MIDI *Import Options*

The MIDI Import Options dialog box offers some additional flexibility for bringing Standard MIDI File (SMF) files into the current Pro Tools session. When the Clip List button is selected, a separate clip will be added to the Clip List for each MIDI channel that actually contains data. However, additional MIDI import options (shown in Figure 8.4) give you more control. If you import the tempo map from the incoming MIDI file, any tempo and meter events already existing in your session will be overwritten. The same applies if you choose to import key-signature information (if any exists) in the MIDI file. Other check boxes allow for deletion of existing Instrument tracks, MIDI tracks, or clips, when appropriate.

Import Video

Use this command to import digital video files in QuickTime, AVI, MPEG, and other formats into your Pro Tools session. The Video window displays this video during Pro Tools' playback and freezes the movie's current frame wherever you stop the Transport. A Video track is also created in the Edit window, where the movie can be displayed in Blocks view or Frames view. (Be aware that the system overhead in Frames view for redrawing the thumbnails—called *picons*, or picture icons—as you zoom in and out can slow your pace in the Edit window. You can improve the speed of screen operations by setting the Video track to Blocks view whenever you don't need to use these thumbnails for spotting events.) Many professionals prefer to dedicate a separate video card/monitor and hard drive for video playback.

The imported digital video files will play back in the Video window, in sync with the Pro Tools Transport functions. Users who create video soundtracks and interactive sound designers who create audio for video files will definitely appreciate the nonlinear video-playback features. You can jump around in the session's Timeline, with the Video window and Video track serving as a frame-accurate reference for *spotting* audio events to specific locations.

As you can guess, using an onscreen digital video file as your master can be extremely useful when collaborating with video editors (for example, users of Avid Media Composer, Media 100, Adobe Premiere, or FinalCut Pro). This is all discussed in more detail in Chapter 14, "Post-Production and Soundtracks," and in Chapter 15. Here's a brief overview of a typical work process (when *not* using one of the Avid hardware options for video with Pro Tools):

1. The editor exports a low-resolution video for you to use in Pro Tools. This should be full frame rate, but with the image compressed to a much smaller size and data rate. This is so that video playback doesn't negatively impact Pro Tools' performance. However, you do want the video editor to provide full-resolution, uncompressed *audio* inside this video file. If you're a newcomer to audio for video, don't overlook the fact that audio soundtracks in video-editing systems (and PCM Audio tracks in professional video-tape formats) typically use a 48 kHz sample rate! Generally, your Pro Tools session also should be set to this rate.

2. Bring this digital video file into your session via the File > Import > Video command. In the Video Import Options dialog box, you can choose to import the audio soundtrack of that video file, if it contains one. A Video track will be created automatically, and the Video window will open.

3. You can complete your audio post-production on the project—arranging music, sound effects, and dialog or voiceover—without requiring a video deck in your setup at all. Furthermore, because of the frame-accurate display in the Video track, extremely precise placement of sound effects and other audio events is easy.

4. After you finish the soundtrack, you have several options for returning this finished mix to the video editor. You could simply use the File > Bounce To > Disk command to give the video editor stereo, 48-kHz files for the entire soundtrack (in AIFF or Broadcast WAV audio file format, for example). In Pro Tools 9 and later, you can instead export an OMF file if the video-editing system supports this interchange format. (Earlier versions require the DigiTranslator 2 option.) A third option is to bounce your audio mix to a new copy of the original video file using the File > Bounce To > QuickTime Movie command, also discussed in this section.

Import Clip Groups

Creating a clip group from currently selected clips (via the Clip > Group command) allows you to treat it as a single object while editing. Clip groups can span multiple tracks, even if they are not in contiguous order in the Edit window. Other commands in the Clip menu allow ungrouping and regrouping of clips. As soon as you create any clip group, a Clip Groups subfolder is created for the current session. You can use a command in the Clip List pop-up menu to export clip groups as separate files, which you can then import into other sessions via the Import > Clip Groups command.

Edit Menu

As you might expect, the Edit menu is where you'll find the Cut, Copy, Paste, and Clear commands. Here you will also find the Select All command and the beloved Undo command! The Edit menu also includes many key functions you will use for editing clips. The following sections discuss some of the more advanced and most essential commands.

Cut/Copy/Paste/Clear Special

The "special" versions of these basic editing commands enable you to apply actions to automation or clip gain in the Edit window. The Repeat to Fill Selection command enables you to automatically paste the required number of repetitions of the audio or MIDI data currently in the clipboard to fill the current track selection. When MIDI data is in the clipboard, another Paste > Special command enables you to merge it into the existing MIDI data at the destination (instead of replacing it as with the normal Edit > Paste command).

Selection Submenu

The commands under the Edit > Selection submenu are useful if you occasionally unlink the Timeline and Edit selections while editing your Pro Tools tracks. You may also want to learn the keyboard shortcuts for these commands, especially the play commands:

- **Change Timeline to Match Edit.** This command copies the Edit selection to the Timeline selection. The keyboard shortcut for this command is Control+O (Mac) or Start+O (Windows) (or just press O with Commands Keyboard Focus mode enabled).

- **Change Edit to Match Timeline.** This command copies the Timeline selection to the Edit selection. The keyboard shortcut for this command is Control+0 (Mac) or Start+0 (Windows) (or just press 0 with Commands Keyboard Focus mode enabled).

- **Play Edit.** This command plays back the current Edit selection. Its keyboard shortcut is Option+[(left bracket) (Mac) or Alt+[(Windows).

- **Play Timeline.** This command plays back the current Timeline selection. Its keyboard shortcut is Opton+] (right bracket) (Mac) or Alt+] (Windows).

Duplicate, Repeat

Many users overlook these commands. Duplicate makes one copy of the current selection immediately following its current position, even if the selection is on multiple tracks. Repeat does the same thing but lets you specify how many copies you want—for example, to add 15 more copies of a four-bar drum loop you've just dropped into the track. If the current selection in any track is only a portion within a longer clip, a new clip definition is created in the process. In contrast, if an entire clip is selected, these commands simply create additional instances of the same clip within their tracks. Naturally, if you're in Shuffle mode, any material that follows the current selection within the track(s) will be pushed back later in the track by a corresponding amount.

That said, for repeating ambient or musical loops, the Clip > Loop command (discussed later in this chapter) offers a much more effective method.

Shift

Shift is another underused command. It opens a dialog box for moving the current selection (even on multiple tracks) earlier or later in the track. You can specify the amount of displacement for the selection in Bars|Beats, Min:Secs, Samples, Timecode, or Feet+Frames time-scale format. If your selection is within an existing clip or if its new location will overlap existing clips in the track, new clip definitions are created as necessary.

> **Tip** Although you *can* use the Shift function on all the tracks in your session simultaneously, the Insert Time tab of the Time Operations dialog box offers a much more effective and flexible way of achieving the same thing.

Trim Clip Submenu

The Trim to Selection command (whose keyboard shortcut is Command+T, or Ctrl+T in Windows) trims the current clip, creating a new clip definition based on the current Edit selection. This is another overlooked command in Pro Tools. Rather than using the Trim tool to drag both the beginning and end of a clip inward, you can use the Selector tool to select the portion you wish to keep and then use the Trim to Selection command. On MIDI tracks in Notes view, you can also use Trim to Selection to crop beginnings or ends of MIDI notes to the boundaries of the current selection.

The Trim Start/End to Insertion commands are also fairly simple: The left or right boundaries of one or more clips are trimmed (cropped) to the current location of insertion cursor. You can use the Trim Start/End to Fill Selection commands when multiple clips are selected in the same track(s). Each clip's start/end is extended to adjoin the boundary of the previous/next clip in the track. Alternatively, highlight an additional range of time before or after a single clip, and the Trim Start/End to Fill Selection command extends the boundary of the clip up to that point.

Separate Clip Submenu/Heal Separation

After making a selection within an existing audio or MIDI clip, you can separate the selection as a new clip (create a new clip definition) using the Separate Clip > At Selection command. A new clip appears on the track and in the Clip List. (As required, additional clips are created for portions of the original clip before and after the selection.) This command is handy when you're planning to move the selection elsewhere. You will also find two variations on the basic Separate Clip command in this submenu: On Grid splits the selection into clips at each grid increment, while At Transients creates the splits at each transient peak in the audio within the selection.

Note The Capture Clip command in the Clip menu serves a similar function to Separate Clip > At Selection. The difference is that while the Separate Clip command creates the new clip definition on the track, Capture Region merely adds it to the Clip List without creating a separation on the track.

Another Way to Create Clip Definitions from a Selection Copying a selection within an existing clip also automatically creates a new clip definition in the Clip List, even if you *don't* paste the selection afterward. This can be a very quick way to create a series of new clip definitions, using the Command+C shortcut, or Ctrl+C in Windows.

Heal Separation restores an audio selection that was split using the Separate Clip command (or the Delete key)—as long as its segments are still in their original, adjacent locations and haven't been moved. Separate Clip operations are non-destructive; the original clip names still exist, and the clips remain in the Clip List. Clip definitions are merely pointers (references) to sections of audio within the parent sound files.

Strip Silence

The basic Strip Silence mode breaks up currently selected audio clips into smaller ones, omitting sections where the audio level falls below the specified Strip Threshold value. (This threshold is typically *not* set to complete silence; there may be low-level background noise, bleed from other microphones, and so on.) In the Strip Silence window (shown in Figure 8.5), the Min Strip Duration setting establishes the minimum size, in milliseconds, for the clips that will be created when the Strip Silence function is applied to the selection. (An excessive number of extremely short clips can be cumbersome.) Clip Start Pad and Clip End Pad leave the specified amount of "silence" appended to the boundaries of the resultant clips, providing a cushion to ensure that you don't cut off soft attacks, breath intakes, finger noise, decays, or other low-level sounds that might otherwise get cut off at the specified threshold audio level for the Strip Silence function. As you adjust all these parameters, you'll see a preview of the results in the Edit window. Because Strip Silence is a non-destructive process (it merely creates new clip definitions—the original, longer clip remains intact in the Clip List), you can always make adjustments afterward by trimming or editing the new clips it has created on the track.

Figure 8.5 The Strip Silence window. The basic function breaks longer clips into a number of smaller ones by eliminating sections where the audio level falls beneath the specified threshold.

The buttons in the Strip Silence window include Strip, Separate, Extract, and Rename. As the main button, Strip executes the standard Strip Silence function. The Separate button performs the same action, without removing the areas that fall below the Strip Threshold—it creates separations at the threshold boundaries but doesn't remove the "silent" parts. Extract is the inverse of the ordinary Strip Silence mode: Only those portions of audio that *are below* the threshold are retained in the track. As the *Pro Tools Reference Guide* points out, this can be useful for extracting room tone, amp buzz, or background noise for some other use. The Rename option can be used after performing a Strip Silence function to batch rename the resulting clips. (This option is also useful for renaming collections of clips resulting from general recording and editing operations, without executing the Strip Silence function.)

Consolidate

The Consolidate Clip command is very useful: It creates a new clip (and a new audio file, on Audio tracks) based on the current track selection and substitutes it for the original selection. The entire contents of the selection—one or more partial or whole clips, fade-ins, fade-outs, and crossfades—are rendered as a new whole-file clip. If multiple tracks are selected, the Consolidate command creates new clips in each. Because the new clips also contain any silence that existed between or around clips, Consolidate also can be handy for creating new clip definitions that begin and end right on a bar or beat, even if they contain silence on either side. This simplifies moving clips in Grid mode, for example, or using the Duplicate, Repeat, or Clip > Loop commands. (Another method to achieve the same thing is to use the Clip > Group command to create clip groups that start and end on the grid. Clip groups are discussed later in this chapter.)

In addition to fades, any clip gain adjustments you've made on the selected clips (but not automation) will be permanently incorporated into new clips created by the Consolidate command.

Mute/Unmute

Muting and unmuting individual clips within a track (rather than the entire track) enables you to experiment without making the commitment of removing the clips from their original track locations. In the Edit window, muted clips appear dimmed (grayed out). You can use the keyboard shortcut Command+M (Ctrl+M in Windows) to mute/unmute selected clips.

Fades

Creating fade-ins, fade-outs, and crossfades on audio clips is discussed in many places in this book. New Pro Tools users very quickly learn to select the first or last portion of audio clips and then use the Command+F (Mac) or Ctrl+F (Windows) keyboard shortcut to create fades using the dialog box shown in Figure 8.6. Pro Tools 10 utilizes real-time fades, meaning the fades are generated on the fly during playback. In earlier versions, fades are separate audio files stored in the session's Fade Files folder. Fades can be lengthened or shortened with the Trim tool, selected and moved/repositioned with the Grabber tool, and double-clicked with the Grabber tool to edit their fade curves.

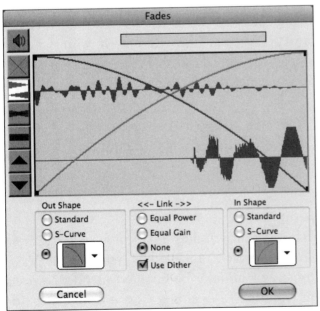

Figure 8.6 The Fades dialog box. Shown here, a crossfade between two adjacent audio clips.

Creating fade-ins, fade-outs, and crossfades for audio clips is a fundamental technique for working in Pro Tools. However, even many experienced users overlook the other commands in the Edit > Fades submenu—especially their keyboard equivalents. Although the submenu itself is a good place to start, you will save a lot of time by assimilating the following shortcuts:

- When a portion of an audio clip that includes its beginning or end is selected, Command+F (Ctrl+F in Windows) opens the Fades dialog box with a single fade-in or fade-out shape.

- When the selection crosses the boundary between two contiguous (adjoining) clips in the same track, the same keyboard shortcut opens the Fades dialog box for creating crossfades between the clips.

- With the insertion cursor anywhere in an audio clip, the Edit > Fades > Fade to Start command creates a fade from the clip's beginning border up to that point, using the default fade-in shape. (You can edit the shape afterward by double-clicking with the Grabber tool.) The keyboard shortcut for Fade to Start is Option+D (Alt+D in Windows).

- The Fade to End command does the opposite, creating a fade from the insertion point to the *end* of the clip using the default fade-out shape. The keyboard shortcut for Fade to End is Option+G (Alt+G in Windows).

Default in, out, and crossfade shapes can be changed in the Editing tab of the Preferences dialog box. Be sure to alter these preferences if the default shapes aren't what you use most frequently!

View Menu

Options in the View menu enable you to optimize your screen display during each phase of a project. You can select items to display in the Mix, Edit, and Transport windows; set how sends are displayed; determine which Timebase Rulers are visible; and set the time units for the Main Counter and main Timebase Ruler. You can also choose whether to have names, ratings, clip gain, and other attributes displayed within the clips on your Pro Tools tracks. All this serves to help you work more comfortably and efficiently and to manage the content of your sessions with ease. Some of the options are fairly self-explanatory or only need to be tried once for their purpose to be clear. The following subsections discuss some of the key items in this menu.

Narrow Mix Window

This option makes all the mixer strips in the Mix window narrower, allowing more tracks to fit on the screen.

Mix Window Views and Edit Window Views

These options affect what items are visible in the Mix and Edit windows. You may change these settings often, during different phases of your work on a project. Like other items in the View and Options menus, the most recently selected settings will initially be enabled in new sessions you create with the File > New Session command (as opposed to opening a session template, for example). For instance, if the last saved session displayed the MIDI Controls section of the

Transport window, Transport controls in the Edit window, and the Comments view in the Mix window, the next new session you create will also have these view settings enabled.

By default, the Instrument section, located in the upper part of the Mix window, is not displayed. When using Instrument tracks, the View > Mix Window Views > Instruments setting enables display of these track controls (which include MIDI volume, pan, solo, and mute on the Instrument track).

In addition to (or instead of) their default location in the Mix window, some items can optionally be displayed in the Edit window: the Instrument, Inserts, Sends, Comments, I/O, and Real-Time Properties views for each track. Displaying these track elements in the Edit window may enable you to spend almost all your time there—as long as your monitor is large enough to work comfortably with the added space this requires. Otherwise, use the options in these submenus to optimize your use of screen real estate during each phase of a project.

You can also toggle display of track color strips (in the Mix and/or Edit window) from these submenus. Additionally, you can enable Delay Compensation View for the Mix window to display—and adjust for—the total amount of plug-in delay on each track.

Rulers Submenu

You use this submenu to select which Timebase and Conductor Rulers are visible in the Edit window. The available Timebase Rulers include Bars|Beats, Minutes:Seconds, Timecode, Timecode 2, Feet+Frames, and Samples. The main Timebase Ruler is always visible and displays with a highlight across the length of the ruler. The main Timebase Ruler always corresponds to the Main Counter—changing the main Timebase Ruler affects the units in the Main Counter, and vice versa. (Timescale units for the Sub Counter can always be set separately, however.) When multiple rulers are displayed, clicking on any one of their nameplates will make it the main Timebase Ruler. This also changes the default units for the Grid value and Nudge value, among other things. Alternatively, you can use the Main Time Scale pop-up selector to the right of the Main Counter.

The available Conductor Rulers include Markers, Tempo, Meter, Key Signature, and Chords. The Tempo Editor (a pane underneath the Tempo Ruler, where you can graphically edit tempo events) can be opened from the View > Rulers submenu, although it's quicker to just click the triangular Expand/Collapse button at the left side of the Tempo Ruler's nameplate. The Key Signature Staff can be opened beneath the main Key Signature Ruler in a similar fashion.

Other Displays

The views available under the Other Displays submenu include the Universe view, the Track List and Clip List side columns for the Edit window, and the docked MIDI Editor view. The Universe view displays at the top of the Edit window, showing a miniature view of your entire session. The highlighted area in the Universe view represents the currently displayed area in the Edit window. Clicking and dragging in the Universe view scrolls the Edit window display to the selected location.

The docked MIDI Editor view is a smaller version of the MIDI Editor window that displays docked at the bottom of the Edit window. This view provides quick access to the advanced MIDI editing functions available through the MIDI Editor.

Clip Submenu

In the View > Clip submenu you can select information to display within the clips in your Pro Tools tracks: the Sync Point symbol, the processing state (Warp indicator), the clip name, clip ratings (from the Rating submenu in the Clip menu), the "dog-ear" overlap icon, clip gain line and info (fader), current time, and original/user time stamp. Display of metadata from field recorders, such as Channel Name and Scene and Take, can also be enabled here.

Sync Point

When this option is enabled, a small triangle indicates the location of Sync Points within clips in the Edit window. If a clip has a Sync Point at a location other than at its beginning, this is the "hook" that will be adjusted to the nearest time increment in Grid Edit mode (or to a specified time location in Spot mode) rather than the default location at the left boundary of the clip itself.

Warp Indicator

When the Processing State view is enabled, the Warp icon appears for audio clips that have been warped using Elastic Audio processing. For example, this icon appears for clips where Warp markers have been moved by dragging them in Warp view or by applying quantization, or on clips that have been automatically warped to conform to the session tempo map. (Display of the Warp icon can also be toggled on/off for audio clips in the Clip List.)

Overlap

Enabling this option displays a "dog-ear" edge on each clip that overlaps a single boundary of another clip. Even though the edges of clips can overlap each other in the same track, only one clip can sound at a time. Two Clip menu commands, Send to Back and Send to Front, are used in conjunction with this feature. The topmost clip at any point is the one that is heard; when it ends, any underlying clip that extends beyond that point will again be audible. (It is worth noting here, however, that this applies only to cases where one edge of a clip overlaps another. In contrast, when a longer clip is placed so that it completely covers a short one already in the track, the previous clip is removed from the track. Likewise, placing a shorter clip completely within the boundaries of a longer clip splits that long clip into two new clips; it will remain that way even after you remove that shorter clip from within its boundaries.)

Track Number

Pro Tools assigns numbers to tracks in ascending order from the top of the Edit window (or left of the Mix window). If you drag tracks into a different order in either window, numbers are reassigned automatically. Enabling View > Track Number displays the track number in the track nameplates in the Mix and Edit windows and in the display strips on Avid control surfaces. Making track numbers visible is convenient when using the Track > Scroll to Track command.

Transport Submenu

The View > Transport submenu toggles the display of additional views in the Transport window aside from the basic Transport buttons: counters (displays the Main and Sub Location Indicators), MIDI controls (displays the Metronome, Wait for Note, Countoff, Tempo, Meter, and other controls), Synchronization, and Expanded view (displays the lower section, with Pre/Post-Roll, Start, End, and Length fields, and so on). The range of time between the Transport window's Start and End fields determines the playback range when you click Play or press the spacebar, as well as the range for the File > Bounce to Disk command.

Main Counter Submenu

These last selections in the View menu change the format of the main Timebase Ruler for the session: Bars|Beats, Minutes:Seconds, Timecode, Feet+Frames, or Samples. If the desired ruler for one of these time formats is already visible in the Edit window, you can make it the main Timebase Ruler by clicking it; the ruler that represents the main Time Scale is highlighted in gray.

Track Menu

Options under the Track menu have to do with creating, duplicating, and grouping tracks, as well as deleting tracks or making them inactive. This menu also provides options for splitting stereo tracks into mono, changing their input monitoring mode, and so on.

New (Tracks)

The Track > New command (Shift+Command+N, or Shift+Ctrl+N in Windows) opens the New Tracks dialog box (shown in Figure 8.7). The timebase for any track can be either *absolute* (Samples) or *relative* to musical bars and beats (Ticks). On tick-based tracks, events will be shifted to maintain their relative musical position if you alter the tempo of the Pro Tools session. You can change the timebase of tracks in the Edit window at any time, as well as the timebase for display of events for the session in general. However, a selector in the New Tracks dialog box assigns an initial timebase for each track as it's created.

Figure 8.7 The New Tracks dialog box enables you to create multiple tracks and track types simultaneously.

The New Tracks dialog box enables you create many different types of tracks *simultaneously*—for example, multiple mono/stereo Audio tracks, Aux Input tracks, Instrument tracks, Master Faders, and MIDI tracks. Click the button with the plus sign (+) to add a new row of fields for creating additional tracks of a different type. Some very useful keyboard shortcuts within this dialog box are explained in the "Editing Tips" section of Appendix D.

Note also that the tracks you create in your session are initially in the same order that you configure them in the New Tracks dialog box. Within the dialog box, you can use the button on the right end of each row to drag the rows into your preferred order before clicking the Create button. Keep this in mind; it may save you some time rearranging your track order afterward.

Group (Tracks)

When you group two or more selected tracks, their faders move together in the Mix window (for Mix groups). Changes in track view and track selections in one track of the group can also be made in the others (for Edit groups). Other group attributes can include solo, mute, and other track controls, depending on which of these you enable for the group; eligible track controls for grouped operation differ between standard Pro Tools software and Pro Tools with Complete Production Toolkit or Pro Tools HD software. Any group-enabled automation type that you draw within a grouped track is also reflected in the others. Groups can be active in the Mix window, the Edit window, or both (the default) and are managed in the Group List at the left edge of the Mix and Edit windows. (The Track > Group command, whose keyboard shortcut is Command+G, or Ctrl+G in Windows, also appears in the Group List pop-up menu.) Be sure to give your Mix and Edit groups meaningful names!

Split into Mono

Sometimes you may need to separate a stereo track into two separate mono tracks. For example, even though you may have recorded a source into a single track with a stereo pair of microphones (a piano or acoustic guitar, for instance), there may be occasions when you would like to apply different plug-in processing or automation to each side. The Track > Split Into Mono command creates the two new mono tracks but leaves the original stereo track intact until you disable or delete it.

Make Inactive/Active

When you mute a track in Pro Tools, its audio, automation data, sends, and insert plug-ins still consume your system's processing capacity for audio. In other words, a muted track still requires the same amount of processing power from your CPU and/or DSP cards. By contrast, the Track > Make Inactive command will effectively turn off the track, freeing the processing power for the track's plug-ins, sends, and audio playback for use by other Pro Tools tracks.

On an underpowered system, you might find the Make Inactive command very useful. For example, say you're near the end of a complex project and have decided you'd like to layer 10–12 additional backing vocal parts. However, with all the existing tracks and effects already active in the session, after laying down just a few vocal parts, you start to hear audio glitching and choppy playback because your system can't keep up with the demand. After checking the Hardware Buffer Size (Setup > Playback Engine), you find that the buffer is already at maximum (or that increasing it induces a delay for input monitoring that is unacceptable for the singers). In such a case, you can take a look at which of your tracks is using the most processing-intensive plug-ins. Reverbs are obvious candidates, especially some of those gorgeous-sounding, CPU-hungry ones from third parties. Virtual instruments are also likely suspects. Or perhaps you have a complex chain on some instrumental part, such as an amp simulator, compressor, EQ, and then flanger on a lead guitar part. If you can do without hearing any of these tracks while tracking the vocals, you can deactivate the track(s) (Track > Make Inactive) to free up DSP capacity while completing the recording tasks.

After you finish recording, you can bounce your backing vocals to disk (checking the Import After Bounce option to bring the mix file right back into the session on its own stereo track). Then select all the source backing vocal tracks and apply the Track > Make Inactive command, and select the CPU-hungry track(s) you deactivated earlier and choose Track > Make Active. If you ever change your mind about the balance in the vocal submix, you can simply use the Make Active command on the inactive vocal tracks again and repeat the process.

Shortcuts for Making Tracks Inactive/Active   At the bottom of each mixer strip in the Mix window, each track type has a distinctive color icon just above the track nameplate on the right. Click this icon to toggle any track to its active/inactive state using the pop-up menu. In the Edit window, the pop-up menu that appears when you Control-click (Start-click in Windows) or right-click on the track name also lets you make the track (and any other selected tracks) active/inactive.

Delete

The Track > Delete command deletes the currently selected track(s) and any playlists (audio, MIDI, or automation) that they contain. However, after using the Delete (track) command, any audio or MIDI clips residing on the affected tracks will remain in the Clip List.

Write MIDI Real-Time Properties

This command permanently alters the MIDI data within clips on the selected track, applying the net results of the track's current real-time property settings to the MIDI events themselves. On MIDI and Instrument tracks, *track*-based real-time properties apply non-destructive changes to all MIDI played back through the track—for example, quantization, transposition, changes to velocity and duration, and so on.

Note   There are also *clip*-based real-time properties, which are applied prior to any real-time properties assigned to the MIDI or Instrument track itself. When you open the Real-Time Properties window for a selected MIDI clip via the Event menu, a Write to Clip button enables you to permanently alter the contents of any currently selected clips, incorporating the results of their current real-time properties settings. The Apply To selector in this window lets you toggle back and forth between clip- and track-based properties. The window's Write to Clip button changes to Write to Track if that's what you have selected in the Apply To field. Write to Track has the same effect as the Track > Write MIDI Real-Time Properties menu command.

Input Only/Auto Input Monitoring

As the name implies, when Input Only monitoring is enabled, *only* input signal will be heard on any record-enabled tracks—regardless of whether a punch-in point exists and whether Record mode is engaged. In the "normal" Auto Input monitoring mode, when playback is *stopped*, you hear the input signal on any record-enabled Audio tracks. Likewise, if you simply start recording without making any selection for punch in/out, you hear the record-enabled track's audio input. However, when recording a punch-in in Auto Input monitoring mode, you hear the pre-existing audio in the track before and after the punch-in point (which helps you match its level and timbre), and you hear the input source during the punched-in segment. Note that in Pro Tools HD software (and Pro Tools with Complete Production Toolkit), each Audio track has a Track Input button, which toggles the individual track between Input Only (with the button enabled) and Auto Input (button disabled) modes. In Pro Tools HD (and Pro Tools with Complete Production Toolkit), the Track Input button is not affected by the mode selected in the Track menu.

Scroll to Track

As mentioned earlier, each Pro Tools track is assigned a number reflecting its current position: ascending from left to right in the Mix window or top to bottom in the Edit window. To display these numbers, enable that option in the View menu. The Scroll to Track command lets you scroll the Edit or Mix window as necessary so that a specified track number is visible. This helps you get around in large sessions. Of course, you can drag tracks into any order, at any time, which changes their track numbers. The keyboard shortcut for the Scroll to Track command is Command+Option+F (Ctrl+Alt+F in Windows).

Clear All Clip Indicators

As mentioned in Chapter 7, "The Mix Window," and elsewhere, the red clipping indicator lights up in the level meter for a track or plug-in window when an excess signal level may have overloaded and distorted the audio passing through it, clipping off the top of its waveform. You can click on clip indicators to clear them and Option-click (Alt-click in Windows) any clip indicator to clear *all* of them simultaneously. The Track > Clear All Clip Indicators menu command can also be used. Even more convenient is its keyboard equivalent: Option+C (Alt+C in Windows).

Don't forget that, aside from the track output level as set by the main volume fader itself, the settings for each active plug-in on a track affect the level entering the next plug-in in the track's signal-processing chain. Additionally, the audio signal entering all sends (both pre- and post-fader) is subsequent to the entire Inserts section in a track's signal chain. Also, be sure to watch for clipping at your send destinations if your insert effects end up applying a significant amount of gain increase—for example, if you radically boost some frequency range with an EQ plug-in. To do this, either enable the Path Meter View panel in the send's Output window or, even better, create a Master Fader track for the bus path you're using for sends from multiple tracks.

Create Click Track

The Track > Create Click Track command automatically creates a mono Aux Input track with the Click plug-in enabled. If almost all of your sessions are music-related, you might want to select the option in the MIDI tab of the Preferences dialog box that allows automatic creation of a click track in each new session.

Clip Menu

Clip menu options affect both audio and MIDI clips currently placed in Edit window tracks. Learn their keyboard shortcuts early; you will probably be using some of these commands quite often.

Edit Lock/Unlock

When a clip is locked, a small padlock graphic appears in its lower-left corner. You can't drag, trim, or delete edit-locked clips. Also, edit-locked clips can't be pushed aside or repositioned as a result of moving other clips in Shuffle mode. You can still edit the automation that overlaps a locked clip, though, or record over it (so always be especially careful when recording in Destructive Recording mode). As you can imagine, edit locking a clip protects you from yourself and is definitely a feature you want to be familiar with. You can use the keyboard shortcut Command+L (Ctrl+L in Windows) to edit lock/unlock selected clips.

Time Lock/Unlock

The Time Lock command is similar to the Edit Lock command in that a clip cannot be moved from its location. Time lock differs from edit lock in that it allows a clip to be edited in any way that does not shift the clip to another time, such as by trimming and separating. In addition, unlike edit lock, a time-locked clip can be deleted. Time-locked clips will not be displaced in Shuffle mode by any activity. The time lock shortcut is Control+Option+L (Start+Alt+L in Windows).

Send to Back/Bring to Front

Pro Tools allows clips to be layered within a track (although only one audio clip can play at a given time within a single track). With the View > Clip > Overlap option enabled, a dog-ear icon on the upper corner of clips indicates where their boundaries overlap a single boundary of some other clip underneath them in the same track. The topmost clip always has priority and will play back where the two clips overlap. However, you can swap the order of layered clips to change which clip gets priority using the Clip > Send to Back and Clip > Bring to Front commands on a selected clip. The keyboard shortcuts for sending clips to the back/front are Option+Shift+B and Option+Shift+F (Alt+Shift+B and Alt+Shift+F in Windows), respectively.

Group/Ungroup/Ungroup All/Regroup

When you group multiple clips together, a new clip group is created, with a waveform representation of the clips it contains. This enables you to move a more complex group of audio events around as a single unit. By the way, it isn't necessary for grouped clips to reside on the same track or even on adjacent tracks. As shown in Figure 8.8, a rectangular clip group graphic appears in the lower-left corner of each clip group to help distinguish it from individual clips on a track. When creating clip groups, you can rename them like ordinary clips so that their names are meaningful for your project. Clip groups appear in the Clip List; from there, they can be dragged onto tracks and exported to disk for use in other sessions.

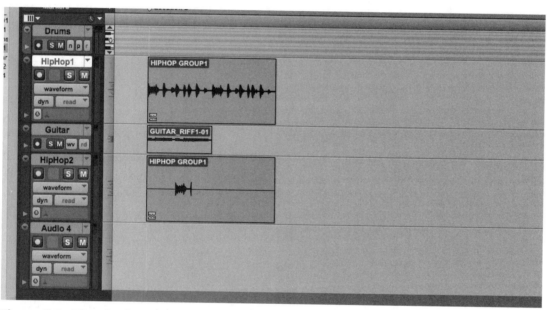

Figure 8.8 The "broken" clip group icons indicate that the members of the HipHop clip group are on non-adjacent tracks.

Loop/Unloop

You can use this command on audio clips, MIDI clips, and clip groups. A specified number of loop *aliases* are created, which mirror the original source clip. In the Clip Looping dialog box (see Figure 8.9), you can specify a duration and shape for crossfades between loop iterations; this is especially useful for ambient, sustained, and background loops. Note that unlike the Duplicate and Repeat commands (when the Options > Automation Follows Edit option is enabled), the automation coinciding with the source loop is *not* copied along with the loop aliases.

Selecting the Unloop command presents you with a dialog box in which you can choose to simply revert to a single instance of the source loop (Remove) or to flatten the loop (Flatten), which creates individual clips for each loop alias.

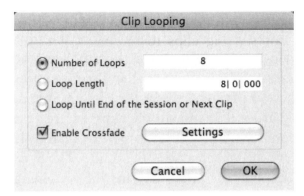

Figure 8.9 Options in the Clip Looping dialog box enable you to control how many times the clip or clip group will repeat.

Capture

This command creates a new clip definition based on the current track selection. Unlike the Edit > Separate Clip command, however, the new clip(s) created by the Clip > Capture command don't take the place of the current selection and split existing clips. Like Separate Clip, you can use this command on mono, stereo, or multichannel tracks, as well as on multiple tracks simultaneously.

Identify Sync Point/Remove Sync Point

A *Sync Point* is a precise location within a clip that is used as the positional reference whenever the clip is snapped to the nearest time increment in Grid mode (rather than the beginning of the clip, which is the standard behavior). Likewise, in Spot mode, the Sync Point can be aligned to a specified position (a SMPTE timecode location, for example), with the rest of the clip surrounding it.

You can think of the Sync Point as the hook used for positioning a clip at specific Timeline positions in Grid or Spot mode. Identifying a Sync Point within a clip positions this hook at a particular location within the clip.

In the Edit window, Sync Points within clips appear as small inverted triangles at the bottom of each rectangular clip graphic. You can drag Sync Points with the Grabber tool to alter their locations within the clip. You can also use the Scrubber tool to drag a Sync Point, providing audible feedback as you drag it within the audio waveform.

Sync Points are relevant for both music and post-production work. Say you've got a nice backward-reverb snare sound you'd like to drop on the occasional backbeat. The clip will need to actually begin *before* the backbeat and fade up to it. To prepare the clip, you can position the Selector tool precisely at the peak of the backward sound (probably near the end of the clip) and then select the Clip > Identify Sync Point command. You will now see a small triangle at the bottom of the clip, indicating the location of the Sync Point. You can now switch to Grid mode and select 1/4 notes as the Grid value. When you drag the clip to a specific 1/4 note, the Sync Point (rather than the beginning of the clip) is snapped into position. The backward snare ramps up to peak right on the 1/4 note, regardless of where the sound actually begins.

With regard to post-production, a classic Sync Point example is a vehicle (train, plane, or automobile) passing through the video frame. You should hear the vehicle coming *before* the time code location where it actually enters the frame. However, as you position this sound effect, the point inside the audio clip that interests you is that loudest moment, where the Doppler effect changes pitch. You need *that* point to coincide with where the vehicle enters the picture. Again, you can use the Selector to position the cursor right at that loudest spot in the clip and create a Sync Point. Based on your video master's time code location (visible in its Transport or time code window), use Spot mode to enter the exact reference where the vehicle enters the frame. The Sync Point itself will be spotted to that time code position, although the audio clip for the oncoming vehicle sound actually begins sooner.

Sync Points in the Edit Window   The View > Clip > Sync Point option enables you to choose whether Sync Points are visible within clips in the Edit window. You can drag Sync Points with the Grabber or the Scrubber tool. Their movement will be affected by Grid mode, if enabled.

Quantize to Grid

The Clip > Quantize to Grid command moves the beginning of all currently selected clips (audio or MIDI) to the nearest grid increment, according to the current grid value. However, for any clip that contains a Sync Point, the Sync Point itself is moved to the nearest grid increment instead of the clip's beginning boundary. The Quantize to Grid command does not alter clip durations; it simply moves the clips. When used on MIDI clips, the command does not apply any quantization to notes contained within the MIDI clips; they just get repositioned along with the clip itself, maintaining their relative locations within its boundaries. (The Event Operations > Quantize command can be used to adjust individual note positions within MIDI clips and tracks.)

Clip Gain

The commands under the Clip > Clip Gain submenu allow you to toggle Bypass on/off for any clip gain on the selected clip(s) or to render the effects of clip gain changes into the selected clip(s). Rendering clip gain creates a new clip and parent audio file for the entire underlying whole-file clip.

Elastic Properties

The Clip > Elastic Properties command opens the Elastic Properties window for one or more selected audio clips (see Figure 8.10). You can also open this window via a pop-up menu, accessible by right-clicking a clip. Generally, you will only alter the Source Length and Source Tempo fields if you find that they have been calculated incorrectly by the Elastic Audio analysis when the audio file was imported. However, this analysis always assumes that all files are in 4/4 meter, so you will definitely want to change this if you know that a loop is in 3/4, 5/4, 7/8, or what have you. The Time Compression/Expansion field is for display only when viewing properties of clips on tick-based tracks but can be changed manually on sample-based tracks. By reducing the Event Sensitivity value, you can reduce the number of false transients detected by the Elastic Audio analysis. Lastly, especially if levels in your source clips are close to full-code (0 dB), time compression can sometimes produce clipping; in that case, reducing the Input Gain value will resolve the problem.

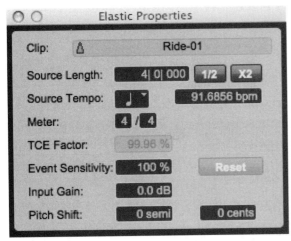

Figure 8.10 The Elastic Properties window for an audio clip.

Conform to Tempo

The Conform to Tempo command relates to Elastic Audio features and can also be executed via the right-click pop-up menu for any audio clip on a track with one of the Elastic Audio analysis modes enabled. For audio clips that have not been conformed to the session tempo (for instance, if no Elastic Audio algorithm was enabled during import), this command performs the Elastic Audio analysis and stretches or compresses the file to match the session tempo. The Elastic Audio icon will appear afterward for the clip, both within tracks and in the Clip List.

Remove Warp/Remove Pitch Shift

The last two commands under the Clip menu also relate to Elastic Audio. The Clip > Remove Warp command removes any Elastic Audio warping that has been applied to the selected clip(s)—by manually applying Warp markers, by applying TCE processing, or by conforming a clip to the session tempo. Remove Warp removes all Warp markers and resets the clip to its original, unwarped state. This command does not affect the Elastic Pitch properties of the clip.

The Clip > Remove Pitch Shift command removes any Elastic Pitch changes that have been applied to the clip—either from within the Elastic Properties window or from the Event > Event Operations > Transpose function. Remove Pitch resets the clip to its original, unmodified pitch.

Event Menu

The Event menu is where you will find the commands related to time and tempo operations, setting tempos according to track selections, creating time slices and groove templates for quantization, plus most of the MIDI-related operations in Pro Tools.

Time Operations Submenu: Change Meter, Insert Time, Cut Time, Move Song Start

All four of these operations open the Time Operations window, within which you can switch directly from one page to another. These features may be useful when the song you're going to record has multiple time signatures, you need more room in the Timeline for an intro, or you need to move a music cue to a different time location while scoring a video or film. Because these are explained in more detail in Chapter 10, "MIDI," the following descriptions are relatively brief.

Change Meter

Use this command to insert a meter change into the Meter Ruler. You can choose to have meter settings stay in effect through the end of the session, during the current selected range in the Pro Tools Timeline only, or only until the next bar. The Change Meter page of the Time Operations window also provides a pop-up selector to change the note value for the metronome click in the new meter. For example, the click could change from 1/4 notes in a 4/4 time signature to 1/8 notes during a section in 6/8 time, and then revert back to 1/4 notes for the remainder of the song. If a range of time is selected when you open the Change Meter page of the Time Operations window, you can also use this dialog box to change a given number of bars at one time signature to a different number of bars at another. Depending on what combination of bar numbers and time signatures you enter in these fields, some bars in the Timeline may be added or deleted as a result. See the "Time Operations" section in Chapter 10 for more information.

Another Way to Insert Meter Changes in Pro Tools   You can also insert meter changes using the Meter Change dialog box, which you can open by clicking the plus sign (+) in the Meter Ruler, double-clicking the Meter field in the Transport window, or Control-clicking (Mac) or Start-clicking (Windows) directly on the Meter Ruler. As in the Change Meter page of the Time Operations window, you can either accept the current Start value as the location for the new meter change event or type some other location, and also change the note value for the metronome click.

Insert Time, Cut Time

The units for inserting or cutting time in these two pages of the Time Operations window always reflect those of the main Timebase Ruler. You can choose whether the time shift is applied to tick-based (relative) and/or sample-based (absolute) tracks.

Move Song Start

This feature is especially handy for film and video scoring. For instance, suppose you've created an entire musical arrangement starting at the left edge of the Pro Tools Timeline. In this window, you can quickly move the song beginning to a specific location—perhaps the Minutes:Seconds or SMPTE timecode reference where the musical cue needs to begin in relation to the picture. Events in the Meter and Tempo Rulers will shift accordingly. The Move Song Start page of the Time Operations window (shown in Figure 8.11) also enables you to specify a bar number to assign to the new location of the Song Start marker. This is useful if you worked out a musical arrangement but later decide you need to insert some pickup bars (or a full intro) before the beginning of the song proper, which should be identified as Bar 1, Beat 1.

Figure 8.11 The Move Song Start page of the Time Operations window.

If the timebase is set to Bars|Beats, you additionally have the option to move the Song Start marker without affecting the positions of any events in your tracks. Also, note the pop-up selector that lets you choose whether the positions of sample-based (absolute) markers and events in sample-based tracks should also be affected by the Move Song Start operation.

The Move Song Start function is described in more detail in the "Time Operations" section of Chapter 10. As described there, you can alternatively drag the Song Start marker to a new location in the Tempo Ruler. Its movement will be affected by Grid mode, if enabled. When you change the Song Start setting by dragging this marker, any events in all MIDI, Audio, Aux Input, Instrument, or Master Fader tracks whose timebase is set to Ticks will be adjusted to new positions in the Timeline to maintain their previous relative position to the Song Start marker. Any markers whose reference is set to Bars|Beats (relative) rather than absolute will also change positions accordingly.

Tip Hold Control+Shift (Mac) or Start+Shift (Windows) while dragging the Song Start marker to reposition it without affecting tick-based events.

Additional Information about Time and Tempo Operations More details about changing meter and tempos, renumbering bars, and other music-related options are provided in Chapter 10.

Tempo Operations Submenu

The options in the Event > Tempo Operations submenu all open the Tempo Operations window. (We discuss it only briefly here; more details are provided in the "Tempo Operations" section of Chapter 10.) You can use the Tempo Operations window to create a single tempo event or to apply a constant tempo over the currently selected range in the Edit window's Timeline. Alternatively, you can apply a variety of curve shapes (line, parabola, S-curve, and so on) for increasing or decreasing the tempo over a range of time, in which case the result is a series of tempo events at the density specified in this window (see Figure 8.12). You can use the Scale page of the Tempo Operations window to increase or decrease an existing series of tempo events by percentage. The end point is automatically calculated in minutes and seconds (or other timebase units available on your system). As you can imagine, this can be very useful for soundtrack or jingle work, as it helps you set a specific duration for your music cue.

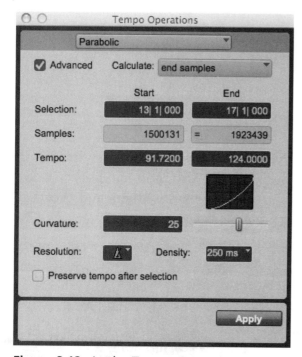

Figure 8.12 In the Tempo Operations window, you can create a variety of shapes to increase or decrease musical tempo over time.

The Stretch page of the Tempo Operations window can also affect an entire tempo map (a series of tempo events) within the currently selected portion of the session's Timeline, adjusting all these relative tempos so that the selection's start or end point coincides with a desired time location. This is how you might adjust a complex underscore, with multiple tempo and time signature changes, so that it ends at precisely the close of a scene, minutes later. Remember that the location of events (including automation) in all MIDI, Audio, Aux Input, Instrument, or Master Fader tracks whose timebase is set to Ticks is affected by tempo changes, as are any Memory locations whose Reference attribute for Time Properties is set to Bars|Beats (rather than Absolute).

Event Operations Submenu

Many of the functions in the Event > Event Operations submenu, along with several other commands in the Event menu, are of most interest to people who use MIDI instruments (either external or software-based) with their Pro Tools configuration. All the selections under this submenu open the Event Operations window. A pop-up field enables you to switch directly from one function's page to another. This window doesn't close after you apply each function—or successive iterations of the same function, like some percentage of quantization, for instance. Except for Quantize (which is equally applicable to audio clips and the events that have been detected within them by Elastic Audio analysis) and Transpose (which can be applied to audio clips on Elastic Audio–enabled tracks), the other commands act only upon MIDI data, within MIDI clips. Because there is an entire section dedicated to these MIDI functions in Chapter 10, we include just a few brief descriptions here.

Quantize

The Quantize command affects all MIDI notes within a selection (on MIDI or Instrument tracks) and either all audio clips within the selection (on Audio tracks) or all Event markers within the selection (on Audio tracks with Elastic Audio enabled). The affected events/clips snap to a specified rhythmic value, as set by the Quantize Grid selector in the Event Operations (Quantize) window (see Figure 8.13).

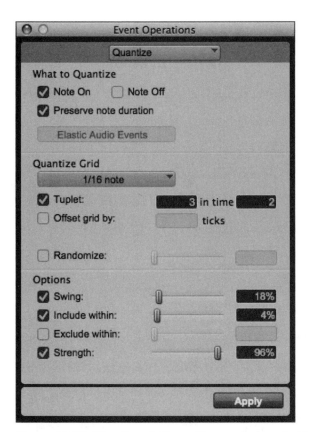

Figure 8.13 The Event Operations window in Quantize mode.

Note When applying the Quantize command to audio clips (such as a drum pattern that has been sliced into short rhythmic clips), the start of each clip will be aligned to the specified Quantize Grid without affecting the absolute duration of each clip. By contrast, when quantizing Elastic Audio events, the transients in the audio waveform (as identified by Event markers) will be aligned to the Quantize Grid. This *can* affect the absolute duration of the selected clips.

Make special note of the Strength parameter in the Quantize window; if you set it to less than 100%, events/clips are not moved all the way to the specified quantization grid increment. This preserves some of the natural feel of your performance (assuming that's a good thing). The Swing parameter is also very useful for making your performances sound in time but not completely mechanical. For a subtle effect, start at about 10% and work from there.

Being able to add a swing factor to a straight quantization is great (1/16 notes, for instance), but for some music, you really need a more complex sort of grid for adjusting timing in order to accomplish specific feels. Various preset groove templates are included in the pop-up Quantize Grid selector, along with the more conventional straight, dotted, and triplet note values. With Beat Detective, you can extract the groove from an audio selection, saving it either to the Groove Clipboard or as a groove template. Groove information can also be extracted from MIDI selections and applied to audio material (and vice versa).

To Learn More about Quantization and MIDI... More details about the Quantize feature and other options in the Event Operations menu that affect MIDI events are provided in Chapter 10.

Change Velocity and Change Duration

These transformations under the Event > Event Operations submenu affect MIDI notes only and are frequently used to add to, subtract from, or scale velocity values or to lengthen or shorten MIDI notes for a more legato or staccato feel.

Transpose

MIDI composers will use this feature often. For example, you might select a group of notes or an entire clip and select Transpose to transpose it up or down an octave (plus or minus 12 semitones) either because you're doubling another part at the octave or because you've changed to another sound on the MIDI module or software instrument plug-in for the part and it's pitched in a different octave. For applying transposition to entire tracks or clips, however, the Real-Time Properties feature will usually be the better choice. When used in conjunction with Mirrored MIDI editing mode, if you change note events or controllers within the original MIDI clip, the changes will be reflected immediately in other copies of the same clip, each with its own clip-level transposition (and/or other real-time properties). In conjunction with key-signature events, you can also apply diatonic transposition—by a certain number of scale degrees within the current key signature.

Select/Split Notes

The Select Notes and Split Notes functions are combined into a single dialog box, shown in Figure 8.14. Select Notes enables you to select only notes within a given pitch range or the top/bottom notes of each chord. After making this selection, you can move the selected notes, copy them, apply velocity or duration changes, and so on. You might be able to accomplish the same thing by drawing a rectangle around many different notes with the Grabber tool (holding down the Shift key to select/deselect additional notes), but this can get cumbersome very quickly.

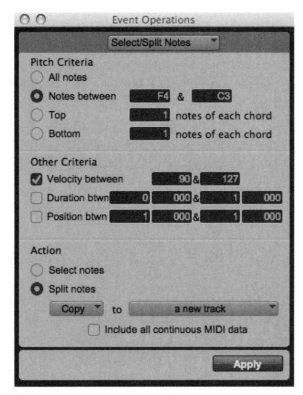

Figure 8.14 The Select/Split Notes page of the Event Operations window applies only to MIDI note events.

The Split Notes feature is useful for composing and arranging. The options for Split Notes are identical to Select Notes, except for the additional options in the lower half for cutting or copying notes that meet the pitch criterion. This places the selected note events onto the clipboard so you can paste them elsewhere, directly into a new track, or onto multiple new tracks by pitch (useful for splitting drum parts onto separate drum tracks, for example).

Input Quantize

This feature, also known as Auto Quantize on many MIDI sequencers, applies quantization upon input. The options in the Input Quantize page of the MIDI Operations window are identical to those in the Quantize page, except for an additional check box that enables or disables this feature. In truth, however, you may never use this, because it's just as easy—and a *lot* more flexible—to experiment with quantization after the fact (especially through the non-destructive method of using real-time properties on a clip or track) instead of discarding the original timing in your performance during the recording process. (That said, Input Quantize can be undone with the Restore Performance command.)

Step Input

The Step Input feature will be familiar to users of other popular MIDI sequencers. In this step-entry mode, you can enter MIDI notes or chords one by one, with the input cursor advancing by the specified increment each time you enter something. Not only can this non–real-time entry of note events be convenient for creating "impossible" rapid-fire arpeggios and so on, it can also be useful for entering certain types of drum parts.

The "Step Input" section of Chapter 10 goes into the details of Step Input mode for MIDI notes. The basic idea is as follows: First, choose Event > Event Operations > Step Input to open the Step Input page of the Event Operations window (shown in Figure 8.15). Next, select the MIDI or Instrument track in your current Pro Tools session to use as the destination for the note events. You can then choose the step increment (the rhythmic spacing between the notes that will be created), set a duration percentage for notes created in each step, and set the velocity to use the performed input velocity (how you actually strike the keys during step input) or a fixed value. The

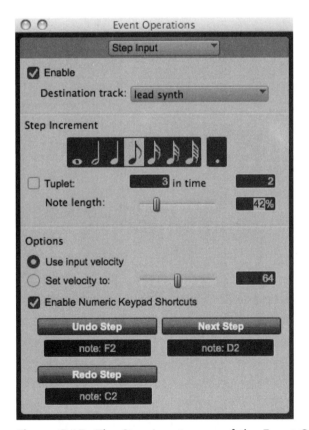

Figure 8.15 The Step Input page of the Event Operations window, for non–real-time creation of MIDI events.

Undo Step and Next Step buttons (which can be assigned to keys on your MIDI keyboard) enable you to back up and redo a step or skip forward a step to create rests for syncopated rhythms. You can change all of these parameters while you continue to create notes, and you can even switch from one target track to another within this window.

Restore Performance

The Event > Event Operations > Restore Performance command restores the selected MIDI clip to its original recorded form (or to the most recent flattened version; see the next paragraph), undoing any Event Operation changes affecting timing, duration, velocity, and/or pitch. This command can even be used to undo the effects of the Input Quantize feature.

The Restore Performance command can be used at any time to revert a MIDI clip to its original or most recent flattened state, even hours, days, or months after applying an Event Operation change.

Note that this command cannot undo any manual changes made to MIDI data, such as by editing the clips, adding or adjusting individual MIDI notes, or modifying controller data graphs.

Flatten Performance

Flattening a selected MIDI clip freezes it at its current state. This is the state to which the clip will return the next time you apply the Restore Performance command. You can select timing, duration, velocity, and/or or pitch parameters for flattening. In Chapter 10, you will find a practical example of the Flatten and Restore Performance commands.

MIDI Track Offsets

Some MIDI devices (especially older ones) have an appreciable latency time before they respond to incoming MIDI events, but this is not the most common reason for using MIDI track offsets. A more typical scenario is when you are using Aux Input tracks (and audio inputs on your hardware) to monitor audio coming from your external MIDI devices; these must be digitized and brought into the Pro Tools mixing environment. On a standard Pro Tools system, this can introduce a noticeable latency factor—a processing delay due to the analog-to-digital conversion process, the current setting of the Hardware Buffer Size, and the overhead of the operating system itself—in addition to the amount of time it takes the external MIDI modules to respond to incoming MIDI note events. The MIDI Track Offsets window enables you to individually specify a negative offset, in samples or milliseconds, for each MIDI track in your Pro Tools session. You can also set a global MIDI offset (also accessible via the MIDI tab of the Preferences dialog box), which may be all you need if there is only one external MIDI synth in your configuration. Bear in mind that the offset for each MIDI track is a playback parameter only; it doesn't affect where MIDI events are located or displayed within Pro Tools tracks. The following sidebar provides a fairly simple technique that will get you in the ballpark for calculating your system's overall MIDI-to-audio latency factor. When using the Automatic Delay Compensation feature, and when using software instrument plug-ins as the sound source for MIDI tracks, this sort of manual adjustment may not be required.

Calculating Monitoring Latency for MIDI Track Offsets   To calculate the latency caused by MIDI transmission and the response times of your external MIDI modules, do the following:

1. Create a MIDI track with MIDI 1/4 notes triggering a cowbell or wood block sound on your external MIDI device (synthesizer or sound module).

2. Record the output of the external synthesizer or sound module into an Audio track.

3. Switch your main Time Scale to samples (activating that Timebase Ruler) and select one of the MIDI notes used to trigger the external device.

4. Take note of the precise sample number shown in the Edit window's Start field.

5. Zoom in on the corresponding attack in the Audio track you just recorded.

6. Click the Selector tool precisely at the initial attack of the audio waveform and note the (higher) sample number now shown.

The difference between the sample numbers approximates the total amount of monitoring latency (between MIDI transmission of the note event from Pro Tools, the MIDI device's response time, and the audio-to-digital conversion back into Pro Tools). This gives you the negative offset amount to use (in samples) for MIDI tracks played through this particular device.

Here's a typical situation in which a negative MIDI track offset is definitely required: Say you're doubling a MIDI snare sound with a snare sample in a Pro Tools Audio track whose attack is *precisely* on the 1/4 notes. If you hear a flam effect (closely spaced double attacks), you could empirically adjust the MIDI snare part's negative offset until you hear the two attacks converge.

MIDI Real-Time Properties

Real-time properties apply non-destructive changes to the contents of MIDI clips or tracks—for example, quantization, transposition, changes to velocity and duration, and so on. Real-time properties can be track-based (affecting all MIDI events on the track) and/or clip-based (affecting only the currently selected instance of that clip). The Real-Time Properties window has a pop-up Apply To selector that defaults to clip-based if one or more MIDI clips are selected or to track-based if a MIDI or Instrument track is selected. However, you can use the Apply To selector to switch between these two modes without leaving this window. A Real-Time Properties column can also be displayed in the Edit window, for track-based properties only. Real-time properties assigned to a selected clip take priority over any real-time properties that may be assigned to the track on which it resides.

It is common to use both types of real-time properties, in various combinations. In the Real-Time Properties window, you can also permanently incorporate the effect of these parameters into the actual MIDI data that a clip or track contains. (For example, note locations would be changed according to the quantization settings, velocities and durations would be altered, and transposition applied.)

Figure 8.16 shows the Real-Time Properties window for a selected MIDI clip.

Figure 8.16   Real-time MIDI properties are applied to selected MIDI clips or to selected MIDI or Instrument tracks.

Remove Duplicate Notes

When working with MIDI, especially when loop recording a MIDI part, it is all too easy to create duplicate notes at a given location. This can also occur as a result of quantization. The Event > Remove Duplicate Notes command will take care of the problem, removing duplicates in the selected clip(s) or range.

Add Key Change

The Key Change dialog box is discussed in Chapter 6, "The Edit Window," in the section about the Key Signature Ruler. The Event > Add Key Change command enables you to create a key-signature event at the current location. Key-signature events affect pitched MIDI and Instrument tracks and are also used by the diatonic transposition options in the Event Operations and Real-Time Properties windows and the Real-Time Properties view in the Edit window.

> **Note**   You can also insert key changes by clicking the plus sign (+) in the Key Signature Ruler or by Control-clicking (Mac) or Start-clicking (Windows) directly on the Key Signature Ruler.

Beat Detective

Beat Detective is commonly used to conform an audio clip to the session's tempo by breaking it up into multiple clips and aligning these to the beats. Alternatively, Beat Detective can be used to generate a tempo map based on transients contained within selected audio (using *Beat Triggers*). You can also use Beat Detective to extract a groove template from an audio or MIDI selection. You can use these templates with the Groove Quantize function for MIDI parts, for example, effectively applying the feel extracted from an audio selection in the Beat Detective window to a MIDI performance. The Analysis button in the Beat Detective window enables you to specify whether low or high frequencies should have more weight for the beat-detection process in the source audio selection—for example, whether the kick drum or the hi-hat may be a more reliable tempo indicator. Collection mode can be used for analyzing multiple tracks simultaneously.

The Beat Detective window (shown in Figure 8.17) provides five operational modes. Many of its functions are quite complex; Chapter 12, "The Pro Tools Groove," provides more discussion of the basic Beat Detective modes.

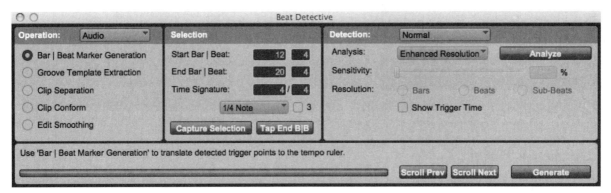

Figure 8.17 The Beat Detective window is immensely useful for beat mixing and dance production, allowing you to utilize source audio with differing tempos to deconstruct beats and build entirely new arrangements.

Identify Beat

Use the Event > Identify Beat command to indicate the Bar|Beat location that should correspond to the current Edit cursor location or Edit selection. The Identify Beat command creates a Beat Marker in the Tempo Ruler based on the tick-based location you specify (in Bars|Beats|Ticks). For dance mixing (or something similar), the Identify Beat function can be very important—be sure to check out Chapter 12 for more information! (The Pro Tools Tempo Ruler must be active for the Identify Beat command to be available; if needed, click to enable the Conductor button in the MIDI Controls section of the Transport window.) You can also use Identify Beat to (rather painstakingly) create a tempo/meter map for music that was not recorded to a click, or even at a strict tempo.

Let's say you've imported an interesting drum figure or a musical phrase under which you will build a rhythm groove in Pro Tools. Select *exactly* four bars of the phrase. If necessary, enable Options > Loop Playback and then press Play. If the four bars don't loop smoothly, zoom in and adjust the selection length. Alternatively, you could nudge the end of the selection by holding down the Command key (Ctrl in Windows) while pressing the + and – (plus/minus) keys on the numeric keypad. Refine the current selection until you get a sample-accurate, smooth loop. (On older Pro Tools systems you may need to click Stop and then Play again to reset the Timeline selection for looped playback after making an adjustment.)

After you've created an *accurate* four-bar selection that loops in correct rhythm (take the time to get this right!), select Event > Identify Beat. In the Add Bar|Beat Markers dialog box (shown in Figure 8.18), enter the correct meter (4/4, for example) and bar numbers for the beginning and end of the selection. For example, if the beginning of a four-bar phrase is at 1|1|00, the end would be at 5|1|00 (four bars later). Make sure your main Time Ruler is set to Bars|Beats, set the Grid value to 1/4 notes or 1/8 notes, and activate Grid mode.

Figure 8.18 You can use Identify Beat to create Pro Tools tempos based on Timeline selections corresponding to a precise number of bars and beats (such as audio files containing drum loops or phrases within musical arrangements).

Now you can start chopping up the longer musical piece (assuming it was recorded at a steady tempo in the first place). Because you're in Grid mode, when you make or adjust selections within clips, they will snap to the nearest note value. As you start dropping drum sounds or recording and quantizing additional MIDI or Instrument tracks, everything can be snapped to the tempo grid created from that first phrase. (This is why it is important to be precise when using the Identify Beat command.) See Chapter 12 for more examples and tips about how Elastic Audio features fit into this process.

Renumber Bars

The Event > Renumber Bars command assigns a new number to the first bar of your session; all subsequent bars are renumbered accordingly. Negative numbers are supported in case you prefer Bar 1 to be somewhere farther into the session's Timeline to better reflect the song structure.

All MIDI Notes Off: The Panic Button!

Use the All MIDI Notes Off command in the Event menu if you ever need to turn off stuck MIDI notes on your MIDI instruments. The keyboard shortcut for the All MIDI Notes Off command is Command+Shift+period (Ctrl+Shift+period in Windows). If you're a MIDI user, memorizing this keyboard shortcut can come in handy.

AudioSuite Menu

AudioSuite plug-ins appear in this menu, grouped into categories (although you can change your preferences to group them first by manufacturer and then by category). By default, the following plug-in categories appear: EQ, Dynamics, Pitch Shift, Reverb, Delay, Modulation, Harmonic, and Other. Additional categories may also appear if other optional plug-ins are installed on your system. AudioSuite effects are strictly file-based. In other words, they create new audio files and don't operate in real time. (Some AudioSuite effects can also *destructively* overwrite the current selection, depending on the plug-in settings.)

In addition to the AudioSuite plug-ins supplied with Pro Tools, you can purchase third-party plug-ins in the RTAS, AAX, or TDM format separately. (TDM plug-ins run on Pro Tools|HD hardware only.) Some RTAS and AAX plug-ins also function as AudioSuite plug-ins, while others, such as software instruments and the Click plug-in, can only be used as real-time effects on tracks—these won't appear among these AudioSuite menu selections.

Favorite Plug-ins   If you designate a plug-in as a favorite, it will always appear at the top of the plug-in submenu. To designate a favorite, hold down the Command key (Ctrl key in Windows) while selecting a plug-in from the AudioSuite menu (or from an insert on a track). Repeat this procedure to remove a plug-in from your favorites. This is a very useful feature; creating your own half-dozen plug-in favorites will save you a lot of time!

The precise contents of the plug-in window differ for each AudioSuite effect, but a Render (or Process) button is always available. Clicking that button creates a new clip, which replaces the current selection on the track (unless you select Overwrite Files, in which case the data in the source file itself is destructively overwritten). AudioSuite plug-in windows frequently also include a Preview button and a Bypass button so that you can toggle the preview between the processed and unprocessed version. The Use in Playlist button, if enabled, substitutes the processed result for the selected original in the track. Most importantly, a pop-up menu enables you to copy and save settings for each plug-in—or import them from another session's plug-in settings folder. Additionally, if any part of the current selection includes multiple audio clips within a single track, you can choose whether the result of the AudioSuite processing creates a single new clip for the selection or individual clips/files corresponding to each original clip in the track.

Pro Tools 10 provides several new features for AudioSuite plug-ins, including the addition of a numeric field at the bottom of the AudioSuite window to specify handles for AudioSuite processing and a Whole File button for applying the AudioSuite processing to the entire underlying parent file referenced by the clip. AudioSuite handles can range from 0 to 60 seconds in length, allowing you to trim out the processed clip to the specified handle length. Enabling the Whole File option disregards the handle setting, resulting in a new parent file equal in length to the original parent file for the clip.

Free Up Your DSP Resources For users with limited DSP capacity, a point may come in a project where Pro Tools tells you that you are low on DSP resources and won't, for example, enable you to add any more plug-ins, Aux Input tracks, Instrument tracks, or sends. At that point, it may be practical to commit some of your real-time effects to new clips to free up signal-processing power for the rest of your mix. Fortunately, most Native real-time insert effects are also available as process-based functions in the AudioSuite menu. You can copy settings from the real-time plug-in insert (via a pop-up menu in the plug-in window), disable or remove the plug-in from the Audio track, select all audio in the Audio track, and then paste these settings into the corresponding file-based (non–real-time) AudioSuite effect before clicking the Render (Process) button. To print (record) multiple real-time effects to a new file in a single operation (also useful if your Pro Tools sessions will be shared with someone who doesn't have the same plug-ins), you can alternatively use the Bounce To > Disk command, muting all tracks except the one(s) you want incorporated into the bounced file. (The Bounce dialog box's Import into Session after Bounce option is also very useful in these cases.) Alternatively, you can bus the source track's output to the input of a new record track to print the track within Pro Tools.

Options Menu

The selections in the Options menu affect the operating modes of Pro Tools: recording modes, monitoring modes, synchronization status, pre-/post-roll, and looped playback—how edit selections affect play selections, for example. Here, we concentrate on the options in this menu that we consider essential for *any* Pro Tools user. For information about other commands not discussed here, see the *Pro Tools Menus Guide*, provided in PDF format with the program; it describes every selection in every menu of Pro Tools, including those in the Options menu.

Tip Every command under the Options menu enables a single feature or toggles the feature on/off. Keep this in mind when trying to remember what menu to look under for a given operation; if it toggles on or off, check under the Options menu.

Destructive Record

In Destructive Recording mode, any new audio recorded into an existing clip *replaces* and *erases* the previously recorded audio data in the same location. Ordinarily, recording in Pro Tools is *non-destructive*. In standard record mode, even if you record right over a clip already in a track (thus replacing it with a new clip), the previous clip is still intact and can be accessed in the Clip

List. Saving every take of audio can consume unnecessary disk space, so users who wish to conserve disk space will occasionally use Destructive Record mode. Recording narration for books on tape is a situation where using Destructive Recording mode can be useful, especially if your disk capacity is relatively limited. Otherwise, using the Clip List's pop-up menu to eliminate unused clips and compact existing audio files is the customary and effective way to keep the disk space used by your sessions under control.

Loop Record

The Loop Record feature under the Options menu is of special interest to musicians. When this recording option is enabled, you can keep looping the same Timeline selection (between the Start and End locations, as indicated in the Transport window) as you record multiple takes. Every take you record for a track is saved within a single audio file, containing all the takes. While still in Loop Recording mode, you can discard all takes since you last began loop-recording by pressing Command+period (Ctrl+period in Windows). Each take recorded in Loop Recording mode appears in the Clip List when you stop recording and is numbered sequentially. You can also choose to have Pro Tools place each looped recording onto a new playlist by selecting Automatically Create New Playlists When Loop Recording within Setup > Preferences, under the Operations tab.

After recording multiple takes, you may want to listen to each one to decide which is the keeper. Click with the Grabber to select the most recent take currently appearing within the track, and then switch to the Selector tool and Command-click (Ctrl-click in Windows) on the clip. A pop-up Takes List will appear, where you can toggle between all the takes (alternate clips) matching the Edit selection. (Note that several selections in Preferences > Editing affect behavior of the Takes List.)

Another method for selecting among alternate takes is to right-click the clip; a pop-up menu will appear, providing a Matches submenu, where you can also select among alternate takes. (If you want clip definitions corresponding to the multiple takes within a loop-recorded audio file to be visible in other Pro Tools sessions, you can apply the Clip List's Export Clip Definitions command.)

Lastly, if you enabled the Automatically Create New Playlists When Loop Recording preference before recording, you can display the looped record takes as individual playlists and use the solo buttons in each lane while playing back to audition each take. (Choose Playlist view using the track's Track View selector.) Incidentally, the Options > Loop Record option only affects how audio plays while in Record mode; the Options > Loop Playback option is used to enable looping during normal playback.

QuickPunch

This Options menu command toggles on and off the QuickPunch recording mode for audio. When QuickPunch mode is enabled, you can manually click the Record button during playback to punch recording in and out on any record-enabled Audio tracks. Mbox Pro users can connect a footswitch for this function in QuickPunch mode (also available on the 003 and Digi002 interfaces, no longer in production).

Using QuickPunch What do you do when the performer hasn't provided adequate information about when to punch in recording? The QuickPunch feature enables you to avoid recording a lot of empty space on the Timeline before you get the high sign, letting you turn the Record button on and off during playback to activate recording into any record-enabled tracks. Here's how you do it:

1. Choose Options > QuickPunch (also available via a pop-up menu that appears when you right-click the Record button). Notice that the Record button in the Transport (and in the Edit window) now has a P in it.

2. Record-enable any tracks on which you want to record to by clicking their Record button. Start playback; the Record button in the Transport will begin flashing.

3. When your performer gives you the signal that he or she is ready for punch-in, click the Record button. Pro Tools starts recording in all record-enabled tracks.

4. Once the take is over, click Record again to exit Record mode. Pro Tools continues playback; you can click the Record button again to punch in at a different section (the same section in the second verse, for example). Alternatively, click Stop or press the spacebar when the performer has finished.

The Command+spacebar (Ctrl+spacebar in Windows) keyboard shortcut also works for dropping in and out of QuickPunch mode, as does the F12 key—although Mac users must be careful that this shortcut key is not assigned to something else. Only those portions of the track(s) where the Transport's Record button was enabled will have new audio clips on them.

One benefit and potential drawback of using QuickPunch mode is that, as long as a track is armed, Pro Tools will record audio to disk whenever playback begins (regardless of whether you are punched in); all audio will be kept so long as you punch in at some point during the pass. The benefit here is that if you miss the punch-in point, you merely need to trim the recorded clip back to the intended punch location. The downside is that this can result in sizeable audio files. If you plan to use QuickPunch, make sure you have a good amount of open space on the audio drive or drives.

Note that QuickPunch is *not* required on MIDI and Instrument tracks. Any record-enabled MIDI or Instrument tracks drop in and out of Record mode when you toggle the Record button in the Transport during playback, even during *normal* Play mode. QuickPunch is only required for Audio tracks.

Note You should disable Options > Delay Compensation while recording in either QuickPunch or TrackPunch mode.

TrackPunch (Systems with Pro Tools HD or Complete Production Toolkit Only)

This menu command toggles the TrackPunch recording mode for audio on/off. TrackPunch lets you independently use Record Enable buttons in multiple tracks, punching each one in and out of Record mode in real time during playback. As with QuickPunch mode, crossfades are automatically generated at the punch-in/punch-out points; the crossfade duration is determined in the Editing tab of the Preferences dialog box.

Using TrackPunch   Imagine for a moment that you're recording a jazz session in which multiple soloists will each take a few choruses, but it's not clear exactly when. You have individual microphones on each solo instrument, and you want to avoid recording multiple takes of the entire song on six tracks simultaneously. With TrackPunch recording mode, you have the option to drop in and out of Record Enable mode on the fly on individual tracks—enabling microphones for each player at the opportune moment. (You might also use this technique for a Foley artist, for expansive percussion setups with numerous microphones, for conference recordings, and so on.)

1. Activate TrackPunch mode by selecting Options > TrackPunch. (TrackPunch mode can also be enabled via a pop-up menu that appears when you right-click the Record button.) The Record button in the Transport window will display a T, for TrackPunch.

2. Control-click (Start-click in Windows) on the Record Enable buttons for each individual track that may be required, making them active for recording in TrackPunch mode. Up to 16 tracks can be in TrackPunch mode simultaneously. Record Enable buttons turn blue on TrackPunch-enabled tracks, as does the Record button in the Transport window.

3. Press the spacebar to start playback.

4. When you're ready to punch in recording on any TrackPunch-enabled track, click its Record Enable button. The Transport button turns solid red while recording is in progress.

5. Click the track's Record Enable button again to punch out of Record mode. The Transport button turns blue again.

6. Repeat as many times (and on as many tracks) as necessary.

To punch in simultaneously on *all* TrackPunch-enabled tracks, hold down the Option key (Alt key in Windows) as you click any of their Record Enable buttons, or click the Record button in the Transport window.

Video Track Online

When this option is enabled under the Options menu, contents of the movie window scroll according to cursor position and selections (and as you drag clips back and forth in the Timeline, to spot them to video events). When disabled, playback of the video is frozen at its current point. If you find that playback in the Movie window is significantly affecting performance on your system configuration, you might occasionally take the movie offline to free up system overhead for metering and other display tasks or while editing a sequence that doesn't require the video as a reference.

Video Out FireWire (Mac Only)

If you have a DV-compatible video deck, camera, or monitor with a FireWire input (officially known as IEEE 1394 and also called i.Link by Sony), you can enable this command to send playback of the current video file in your Pro Tools session out the FireWire port on your computer. This allows the video to be transcoded and displayed outside of your system, reducing the processing load on your computer.

Scrub in Video Window

When the Video Out FireWire option is enabled, the Scrub in Video Window option brings the video back to the Pro Tools Video window whenever the Scrubber tool is active. This avoids transcode latency so that scrubbing is much more accurate.

Loop Playback

The Options > Loop Playback setting enables the current Timeline selection (displayed in the Start/End/Length fields of the Transport window) to loop continuously during playback until you press Stop or the spacebar. This is really handy for repeating a section while you make mix and effects adjustments. You can also loop playback while refining the selection on a musical phrase so that it loops exactly at a precise number of bars or beats, either to capture/separate a new clip definition or to establish a precise selection as the basis for the Identify Beat command. The keyboard shortcut to enable looped playback is Command+Shift+L (or Ctrl+Shift+L in Windows). Loop Playback can also be enabled via the pop-up menu that appears when you right-click the Play button.

Link Timeline and Edit Selection

When this option is enabled (the default), selections you make in the Edit window affect not only the values in the Edit window's Start, End, and Length indicators (the Edit selection), but also those of the Transport window (the Timeline selection). The Timeline Selection in the Transport window (whether or not it's currently visible) determines the playback range (or loop selection in Loop Playback mode) as well as punch-in/out points for recording. In other words, when Options > Link Timeline and Edit Selection is enabled, the Transport range is always slaved to the current Edit selection and will change as you select clips and MIDI notes or highlight any area of the Timeline within the tracks or Timebase Rulers.

Sometimes, however, you won't want track selections in the Edit window to alter the Transport range. For example, you might want a portion of the Timeline to continue looping, even as you select, drag, or trim clips and notes within the Edit window. In this case, you would temporarily disable the Link Timeline and Edit Selections mode. In addition using the Options menu, you can toggle this function using the Link Timeline and Edit Selection button located below and to the right of the Grabber tool in the Edit window or the keyboard shortcut Shift+/ (forward slash).

Playing the Edit Selection versus the Timeline Selection   The Edit > Selection > Play Edit command plays back the Edit selection only, with no pre-roll, even when the Timeline and Edit selections are linked. The keyboard shortcut for Play Edit Selection is Option+[(left bracket) (Alt+[in Windows).

Link Track and Edit Selection

When enabled, this option automatically selects a track whenever you make an Edit selection within the track, highlighting its nameplate in the Edit/Mix windows. This feature facilitates applying track-based commands as you edit. For example, with this option enabled, you might group the tracks that get selected as a result. Also, if you hold down the Option+Shift key combination (Alt+Shift in Windows) when changing a track parameter (track view, automation mode, or track timebase, for instance), the same change will be applied to all currently selected tracks. Even better, when Commands Keyboard Focus mode is enabled (via the a...z button, in the upper-right corner of the Tracks display in the Edit window), pressing the minus (–) key on your alphanumeric keyboard (the main QWERTY keyboard, *not* the numeric keypad) toggles any currently selected tracks between two predefined track views: Waveform (Clips) and Volume on Audio tracks or Clips and Notes on MIDI and Instrument tracks.

Another useful technique enabled by this option is the ability to easily move Edit selections between different tracks by selecting them. Let's say, for example, that you need to make a four-bar selection on several backing vocal tracks to use as the basis for a looping pattern. If the recording was not done to a click, and therefore not on the grid, making an exact selection on these tracks could prove difficult. However, using Tab to Transients on a more rhythmic track, such as the kick drum track, you can easily define an appropriate selection. Now with Link Track and Edit Selection enabled, you can simply click on the nameplate of one of the backing vocal tracks to move the selection to that track. Hold the Shift key while selecting additional tracks to extend the selection to those tracks as well.

This function can also be toggled on/off using the Link Track and Edit Selection button located below the Scrubber tool in the Edit window.

Changing Track Heights for the Current Selection   To change track heights on tracks with Edit selections (or containing the Edit cursor), press Control+Up/Down Arrow key (or Start+Up/Down Arrow key in Windows).

Mirror MIDI Editing

When Mirrored MIDI Editing is enabled, edits you perform on a MIDI clip (changing notes or drawing new MIDI controller automation, for example) are automatically applied to all other copies of the MIDI clip, in any track. Say you've created a very basic four-bar drum pattern named Groove, which you've copied to various places in a MIDI or Instrument track in order to start laying down parts. Once you have a couple more instrumental parts working, with Mirror MIDI Editing enabled you can tweak any instance of this Groove MIDI clip (altering the hi-hat, for instance, or adding a kick drum accent), and that change is immediately reflected in its other instances. Being able to mirror MIDI clips is important not only in this linear sense, but also for simultaneously doubling parts in separate tracks (where different output assignments and real-time MIDI properties could be applied to each).

You can toggle this function on/off under the Options menu or using the Mirrored MIDI Editing button located below and to the left of the Selector tool in the Edit window.

Automation Follows Edit

When this option is enabled, edit operations performed on Pro Tools data also affect the underlying automation playlist: Dragging or pasting clips to a new location also moves or copies all their underlying automation data; deleting clips removes any underlying automation. For example, suppose you have created automation for the send level to the delay effect from a track, so that a single note in a lead vocal or guitar line spikes the delay. In the default Automation Follows Edit mode, if you copy or drag this clip to a new location, it will still have that automation event associated with it, at the same relative location within the clip. However, for certain editing tasks, such as replacing a sound effect without affecting the existing mix, you may choose to disable Automation Follows Edit. In that case, the automation on a track stays in place, even as you drag, cut, copy, and paste clips to different locations within it.

In addition to the Options > Automation Follows Edit command, you can toggle this function using the new Automation Follows Edit button located below and to the right of the Selector tool in the Edit window (Pro Tools 10 and later).

Click/Countoff

This menu command simply turns the metronome click on or off—which can also be done by clicking the Metronome Click button in the Transport window. To set up the kind of click sound you want and how it will behave, open the Click/Countoff Options dialog box (shown later, in Figure 8.25) by double-clicking the Metronome Click button or the Countoff display in the MIDI controls section of the Transport window, or by selecting Setup > Click/Countoff.

MIDI Thru

Generally, the MIDI Thru option should be enabled. Here's a typical setup: You turn local mode *off* on the external keyboard, MIDI guitar, wind or percussion controller, or what have you—whatever instrument you're using for the MIDI performance. This cuts the internal connection between the keyboard and its own internal sounds. Otherwise, every note you play would be doubled, because your synth would not only play a note in response to its *own* keyboard, but also in response to that same note event coming back from the record-enabled track in Pro Tools (perhaps on a different channel, and with a different sound). On record-enabled MIDI tracks, the MIDI data received from your keyboard (via one of the MIDI inputs on your MIDI interface or a direct USB connection) is echoed back out through the MIDI interface or USB connection—redirected to the MIDI port, channel, and MIDI program number assigned to the track.

So why use MIDI Thru? Without changing anything on your keyboard, you can quickly switch between its own MIDI channels and program settings and those of a software instrument (either a Pro Tools plug-in or some other ReWired application) or some completely different external MIDI module connected to another port on your MIDI interface as shown in Figure 8.19. Changes to volume, pan, and other parameters are done on the Pro Tools track rather than on the controller itself.

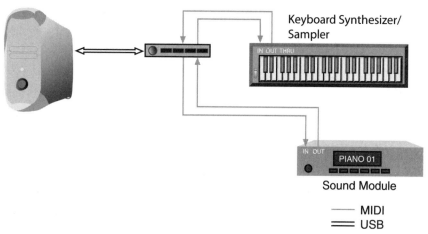

Figure 8.19 A simple MIDI setup for a Pro Tools system: one keyboard synth/sampler, one multitimbral MIDI module, and a multiport external MIDI interface connected to the computer's USB port. Many MIDI keyboard controllers and sound modules can also be connected directly to the computer's USB port.

Auto-Spot Clips

This feature is especially useful when using VITC or the MachineControl option (or with LTC while the transport of the master device is in Play mode). When Options > Auto-Spot Clips is enabled, clicking any clip with the Grabber *spots* its beginning (or its Sync Point, if available) to the current time code location. With MachineControl or VITC synchronization, you can jog or shuttle the master video transport to spot a selected clip to the desired location.

Pre-Fader Metering

When the Pre-Fader Metering option is enabled, level meters for each track in the Edit or Mix window display the level prior to being modified by its main volume fader (which of course can apply gain changes of its own). Pre-fader levels are unaffected by the volume fader's current position, and more accurately reflect the levels for the audio source feeding the track (disk-based audio data, a hardware input path, an internal mix bus, or the output from a software instrument). However, because pre-fader metering derives from a point in the track's signal chain immediately after the Inserts section, the pre-fader levels *do* reflect gain changes caused by any plug-ins on the track.

This is actually quite useful. For example, when track meters are displaying *post*-fader levels (in other words, when Options > Pre-Fader Metering is disabled), a low main volume setting on a track's output makes it all too easy to overlook the fact that makeup gain on the compressor and boosted EQ settings are producing clipping (overload) prior to its main output. This book will remind you many times that digital clipping is not pretty; you need to manage the gain structure of your session (that is, the amount of boost or cut at the various stages in the signal chain from track inputs and outputs to the Master Fader track for your final mix output) so that it doesn't occur anywhere. Experienced users will switch between pre- and post-fader metering many times at different stages of the work process (generally using pre-fader metering while recording to tracks, for example).

Delay Compensation

This Options menu item toggles Delay Compensation on/off (when the Delay Compensation Engine is enabled in the Playback Engine dialog box). Delay Compensation adjusts for the differences in processing latency (delay) between tracks due to plug-in inserts and any audio routing (for example, internal bussing). This consequently improves your mix by maintaining better time alignment between various tracks. For most DigiRack plug-ins, the delay is only on the order of four samples or so. This can accumulate to a noticeable amount, however, when several plug-ins are used in series and also when a given track's audio passes through its own plug-ins, those of an Aux Input, plus a couple more in the Master Fader prior to the main output, for example. Third-party plug-ins and processing-intensive plug-in types, such as reverb or noise reduction, can have much greater amounts of inherent latency. Expert operators often compensate for accumulated latency manually, using the Delay indicators at the bottom of tracks in the Mix window and the Time Adjuster plug-in, for example; however, the Pro Tools Automatic Delay Compensation feature can simplify this process.

Maintaining proper time alignment between all the tracks in your mix keeps it more phase-coherent. This is especially important when the same signal is present in several tracks with different routing or processing setups (due to bleed into different microphones in a drum set or double-bussing, for example). Small time-alignment discrepancies can create phase cancellation in high frequencies, and even very tiny amounts can affect the overall coherency of your mix. You can set the parameters for delay compensation in the Setup > Playback Engine dialog box. You can also use the I/O Setup dialog box to manually compute and adjust latency compensation for external hardware connected via hardware I/O inserts.

If you're just getting started with audio recording, be aware that when recording from multiple simultaneous microphone sources, your first time-alignment concern should be with microphone placement and acoustical isolation of each sound source. To cite a common example, if you have a snare or cymbal bleeding into a vocal microphone 11 feet away, you've already got time-alignment discrepancies (in the neighborhood of 10 milliseconds in typical studio conditions) and phase-cancellation issues on your tracks—before even using any plug-ins!

Low-Latency Monitoring

The Options > Low Latency Monitoring feature is available for host-based Pro Tools systems with certain hardware configurations (HD Native, 003 family, Digi 002 family, Mbox Pro, Mbox 2 Pro, and Core Audio and ASIO interfaces with built-in mixers). This feature can be very useful while laying down tracks. Instead of the relatively long monitoring delay (latency) between the input signal and when it is heard back through the Pro Tools mixer (especially noticeable with larger hardware buffer sizes), this feature reduces latency to a minimum—on tracks whose output is assigned to Outputs 1–2 only (or to the Low Latency Monitoring Path configured in I/O Setup for HD Native systems).

When Options > Low-Latency Monitoring is enabled, however, all plug-ins and sends are automatically bypassed on all record-enabled tracks assigned to Outputs 1–2 (or to the Low Latency Monitoring Path for HD Native systems). (Other audio interfaces for Pro Tools offer alternative workarounds for monitoring latency. For example, the Mbox and Mbox Pro include a stereo mix section in their Driver Control Panel for setting up near-zero latency cue mixes; Mbox Mini includes a front-panel mix knob to adjust the balance between incoming analog signals and audio playback from Pro Tools. Various M-Audio interfaces also feature internal mixing capabilities, controlled by their included control panel software, that allow routing incoming signals directly through to their line and headphone outputs.)

Bouncing to Disk   Do not forget to disable the Options > Low-Latency Monitoring option before bouncing to disk! Although this feature is very handy while tracking, if you forget to turn it off, only the output from *Audio track*s will be included in your audio mixdown file and none of the Instrument or Aux Input tracks (where you might have instantiated plug-ins for reverbs, delays, or software instruments, for example).

"Zero-Latency" Monitoring   Product documentation and marketing materials often use this term for a useful feature included on the Mbox Mini and the older Mbox 2 and Mbox 2 Mini audio interfaces. A Mix knob on the front panel adjusts the balance between the input signal entering the interface's analog inputs and playback of the main stereo output from Pro Tools. Because the interface's analog input is heard via a direct signal path to the analog outputs, there's no latency. When recording a mono source using this Mix-knob monitoring feature, don't forget to press the Mono button on the front panel of these units so that the signal comes out both sides of your headphones or speakers.

Setup Menu

Selections in the Setup menu not only pertain to the hardware on your system, but also enable you to control how available disks on your system are used for recording on each Audio track in the current session. It is also here that you establish your preferences and your MIDI setup, as well as inform Pro Tools what sort of external hardware peripherals are attached to your computer (for example, synchronization peripherals, external control surfaces, and devices linked via the MachineControl protocol). Another extremely important feature accessed via the Setup menu is the I/O Setup dialog box, where you can define and select audio paths for use within Pro Tools, representing inputs, outputs, inserts, and busses, from simple mono and stereo paths to multichannel configurations for surround mixing.

Tip Every item under the Setup menu opens a dialog box for configuring options, features, settings, and other aspects of Pro Tools operation. Keep this in mind when trying to remember what menu to look under for a given operation; if it's in a dialog box, check under the Setup menu.

Hardware (Setup)

The contents of the Hardware Setup dialog box (shown in Figure 8.20) depend on your Pro Tools hardware configuration. Configurable options can include setting your audio hardware's sample rate and input gain, selecting between analog or digital input, selecting the clock source and optical format, selecting the operation for a footswitch control, and more.

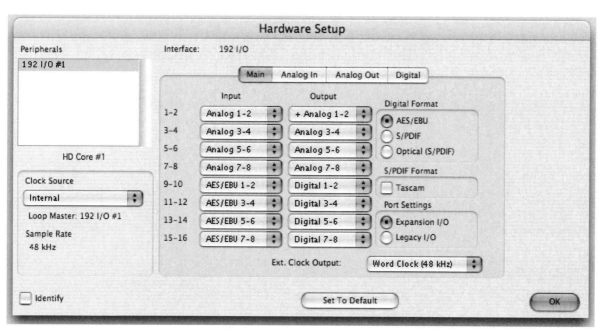

Figure 8.20 The contents of the Hardware Setup dialog box depend on your Pro Tools hardware. Shown here are the options for a Pro Tools|HD system, with a 192 I/O audio interface.

You can also configure the hardware settings for any M-Audio or third-party Core Audio (Mac) or ASIO (Windows) audio interfaces connected to your Pro Tools system (including Pro Tools Aggregate I/O for the built-in sound on Mac) from the Hardware Setup dialog box using the Launch Setup App button.

Additional options for HD systems may include the following:

- Selecting digital or analog connectors for various input channels on the audio interface

- Setting reference levels for analog connectors (+4 dBu or –10 dBV) associated with pro and consumer equipment

- Setting the clock source for sample rate and external clock output

- Setting the level sensitivity and peak hold characteristics on the audio interface's front-panel display (if applicable)

- Selecting digital input and output formats

- Applying limiter options to input channels

Pro Tools|HD systems offer auto-configuration features, so you don't have to manually select the interface when installing or expanding the hardware configuration. Users of the HD OMNI can also use the Hardware Setup dialog box to configure physical outputs to use for the Main and Alt monitoring paths and to mix the signals from the unit's physical inputs to the currently active Monitor paths for direct monitoring—this lets you listen to connected devices without having to route the signal through a Pro Tools session.

Playback Engine

As with the Hardware Setup dialog box, the contents of the Playback Engine dialog box (shown in Figure 8.21) depend on your system configuration. The settings at the top of the Playback

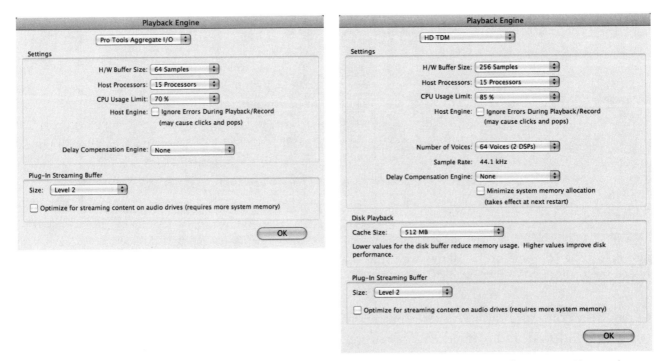

Figure 8.21 Contents of the Playback Engine dialog box depend on your Pro Tools system. Shown here are the options for standard Pro Tools 10 and Pro Tools HD 10 software.

Engine (discussed below) let you adjust the system resources available for Native processing. The Delay Compensation Engine setting lets you specify how much of your DSP resources to allocate to Automatic Delay Compensation. Options include None, Short, and Long; with Pro Tools 10, a Maximum setting is also included (not available on systems with Pro Tools|HD hardware).

With Pro Tools HD 10 software (or Pro Tools 10 with the Complete Production Toolkit), the Cache Size setting in the Playback Engine dialog box lets you specify how much of your available RAM should be made available to the Disk Cache for cached playback. This lets you load the audio files used in your Pro Tools session into RAM so that when you press Play, the files are already cached for playback. This can be especially useful when working with shared media storage on a network. You can use meters in the System Usage window (Window > System Usage) to monitor the Disk Cache usage and determine the percentage of the Timeline that is currently cached.

The three all-important settings at the top of the Playback Engine dialog box affect Native processing on all systems and are especially relevant for host-based Pro Tools systems:

- The rule of thumb for the Hardware Buffer Size is to set it low during tracking (to reduce monitoring latency) and to set it higher during mixing (to increase processing power for Native plug-ins). Larger buffer sizes increase latency (processing delay) when monitoring input signals through the Pro Tools mixer during recording (unless you're able to use the Low-Latency Monitoring option, the Mix knob on your audio interface, or another direct input monitoring option as a suitable workaround). However, larger hardware buffer sizes may be required to record a large number of tracks simultaneously on host-based systems. So you'll need to find a good balance for your tracking and monitoring needs. After tracking is complete, if you hear artifacts or choppiness during playback, especially due to intensive use of plug-ins or virtual instruments, try increasing the H/W Buffer Size. The larger this setting, the more plug-ins are supported; this can be especially beneficial when using processing-intensive plug-in types, such as reverbs and software instruments.

- The Host Processors setting determines the number of processors in your computer that are allocated to Native plug-in processing. This setting lets you enable multi-processor support for Native processes. Used in combination with the CPU Usage Limit setting, the Host Processors setting lets you control the way Native plug-in processing and other Pro Tools tasks are carried out by the system. Selecting more processors allocates more CPU processing capacity for plug-ins; selecting fewer processors reserves more CPU processing capacity for automation, screen redraws, and video playback in Pro Tools, or for other applications running alongside Pro Tools at the same time (such as Reason, Live, BFD, and so on). Multi-core systems are commonly set to one less than the maximum number of available processors for best performance.

- The CPU Usage Limit setting controls how much of the CPU's processing power is devoted to audio-processing tasks for Pro Tools. Larger settings allow smooth playback of sessions with more numerous or processing-intensive Native plug-ins. However, higher CPU Usage Limit settings take away processing power from screen redraws (including moving faders, real-time displays in track level meters, and waveform rendering), video playback, and any other programs running concurrently with Pro Tools. A good initial setting for the CPU Usage Limit option on multi-processor systems is between 70 and 80%. Single-processor systems may need to be set higher (85% or higher, depending on the system). The System Usage window (Window > System Usage) provides a graphic display of the combined load on *all* the currently enabled processors. In sessions with many processing-intensive Native plug-ins (reverbs and software instruments, for example), you will see a notable difference when you switch from one to multiple processors.

Tip   On Pro Tools 9 and earlier systems, the DAE Playback Buffer setting affects how much of your computer's RAM is used to manage disk buffers for audio playback. If your hard disk can't keep up with playback and recording in complex sessions (with lots of tracks, clips, and automation), you can increase this setting. The tradeoff is that with larger DAE Playback Buffer sizes, Pro Tools takes longer to start playback or record after you click Play.

Pro Tools 10 uses a new disk engine that improves performance for audio recording and playback. As a consequence, the DAE Playback Buffer Size setting is no longer necessary and has been removed. The Cache Size setting has been removed for standard Pro Tools software as well.

Disk Allocation

If you have multiple hard drives available for audio recording on your system, you can use the Disk Allocation dialog box to specify which drives and folders are used to record new audio for each individual track. This helps to spread out the load on your disks (although it could make manual backup of a session's audio data more confusing). Alternatively, in some sessions you may choose to record all tracks onto a single drive while using a different drive for other sessions, clients, or users. (For convenience, you can highlight multiple tracks in this dialog box and simultaneously assign them to the same destination.) The Disk Allocation dialog box offers a pop-up Disk Destination selector for each Audio track, where you can even choose specific *folders* for new recordings from each track. Another available option is round-robin allocation: For each new track you create, a different audio-recording drive on your system is selected in rotation. Use this option with caution, as it may be difficult to determine where your various audio files end up.

Make Your System Volume/Partition Transfer-Only   If you can avoid it, try not to include your startup system volume (the drive with the operating system and programs such as Pro Tools) among the eligible disks for audio recording. If you must use a single drive in your computer for both the operating system and audio recording, at the very least create two separate logical partitions. (However, you may need to reload your operating system and programs after doing this!) Using separate partitions permits running disk optimization or simple defragmentation on the audio volume (partition) while still booting from the system volume. It also makes your disk-management routines a little simpler in general. In

Pro Tools' Workspace browser (discussed later in this chapter), you can designate each drive (or partition) on your system as Playback and/or Record, or Transfer Only. Volumes set to Transfer Only won't appear in the Disk Allocation window at all and will never be used during round-robin allocation for new tracks.

Peripherals

The Peripherals dialog box (shown in Figure 8.22) includes choices for SMPTE timecode source (port and device type, such as the Avid Sync HD), MIDI MachineControl (MMC) settings, and MachineControl. (The MachineControl software option is required for use of 9-pin controller connections with video decks, DATs, and other compatible devices.) External MIDI controllers for Pro Tools are also configured here under the MIDI Controllers tab. This tab lets you configure up to four different MIDI controllers for Pro Tools. Available options include the Mackie Control Universal or its predecessor, the HUI (emulated by several other controllers including the wireless TranzPort); the CM Labs MotorMix; one of the J.L. Cooper controllers; and various M-Audio keyboards. Also configured here are the Command|8 USB controller for Pro Tools; the

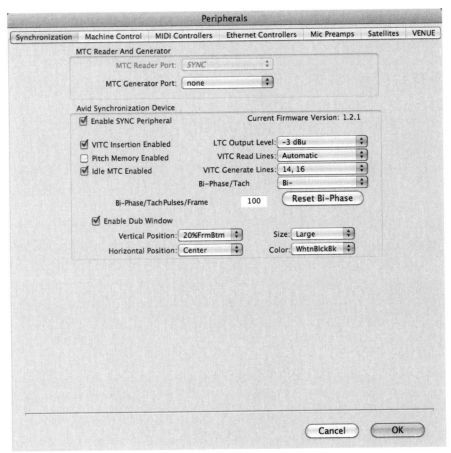

Figure 8.22 The Peripherals dialog box, where you identify external sources for SMPTE time code, MIDI MachineControl, and external controllers for Pro Tools functions. (Options for an HD system with a Sync I/O are shown here.)

D-Control, D-Command, Cl24, and Controll24 Ethernet-based controllers; and any EUCON controllers, such as the Artist Series controllers. The Peripherals dialog box also includes a Satellites tab (which displays selections for software options), Video Satellite, Video Satellite for LE, and Satellite Link; a Mic Preamps tab, for use in configuring remote control of the Avid PRE; and a VENUE tab, which lets you configure Pro Tools for use with a VENUE system over Ethernet using VENUE Link. The Pro Tools VENUE Link option lets you import VENUE Settings into Pro Tools, create Pro Tools markers from VENUE Snapshots, and locate to Pro Tools markers from VENUE Snapshots.

I/O

The I/O Setup dialog box (shown in Figure 8.23) is where you manage signal paths (also known as *paths*) for inputs, outputs, inserts, and busses (plus inputs on the optional Avid PRE microphone preamplifier, as well as delay-compensation adjustments for external devices on hardware I/O inserts). In this dialog box you can assign meaningful names to your signal paths to match how you're actually using them. On larger system configurations and for surround mixing, this can be a fairly complex subject—in the *Pro Tools Reference Guide* (included with the program as a PDF file), an entire chapter is dedicated to I/O setup—so only a brief overview and some general recommendations are provided here.

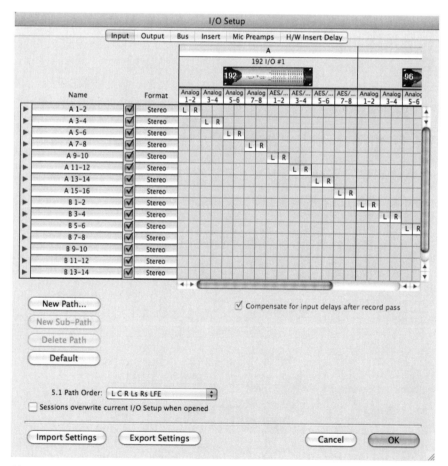

Figure 8.23 The I/O Setup dialog box lets you define named paths for inputs, outputs, inserts, and internal mixing busses.

The I/O Setup dialog box is organized into various tabs (Inputs, Outputs, Busses, Inserts, Mic Preamps, and Hardware Insert Delay), most of which contain a channel grid that varies according to the audio interface(s) available in your configuration. A *path* is essentially a label for one of these audio pathways, which can be either mono, stereo pairs, or multichannel. The available choices for Input and Output selectors on Audio, Aux Input, or Instrument tracks, Output selectors on Master Fader tracks, send assignments, and Hardware I/O inserts are all determined by the paths that have been defined in the I/O Setup dialog box. Stereo and multichannel *main paths* are logical groupings of multiple mono *subpaths*; use the dialog box's Channel grid to specify exactly which physical inputs and outputs correspond to each of these mono subpaths. (I/O settings files are provided for the common surround formats, and of course, you can create your own configurations. Chapter 14 provides more information about surround mixing in Pro Tools.) Note that you can use the check box in front of each main path in the Channel grid to toggle its active/inactive status. This can reduce clutter in pop-up menus, when selecting inputs, outputs, and send destinations.

If your audio hardware has multiple inputs and outputs, it's a good idea to assign meaningful names to the inputs, outputs, hardware I/O inserts. For example, you might have your Focusrite microphone preamp more or less permanently connected to Inputs 1–2 of the audio interface and a Korg Triton synth connected to Inputs 7–8. You could create two stereo input paths named Focusrite and Triton, each consisting of two mono subpaths for the corresponding physical inputs, so that these names always appear in the Input selector on Audio tracks or Auxiliary Inputs. Likewise, if you have an external reverb more or less permanently looped into Outputs 5–6 so that it can be used as a stereo hardware I/O insert from Pro Tools tracks, you can assign this insert path a default name. You can also manually set a latency amount for each hardware I/O insert. This delay time (representing how long it takes for audio to get out through that external device and back into the Pro Tools mixing environment) is compensated for when the Automation Delay Compensation engine is enabled. If Outputs 3–4 on the audio interface are always connected to an audio tie line or studio feed, go ahead and set a default name for this stereo output path that will always be obvious.

Alternatively, you may use the I/O Setup dialog box to assign names that are pertinent only to the *current* session simply to make a complex routing scenario easier to manage. When you use internal mixing busses to route multiple sends to a stereo Aux Input with an effect, it can make life simpler, for example, if you name that bus pair Delay Send. The bus pair will appear by name in the Send selectors for the source tracks and the Input selector for the Aux Input track used for the delay plug-in—this can be a heck of a lot easier to identify than, say, Bus 7–8.

Using descriptive names for your internal mix busses makes it much easier to see at a glance what's going on in your session. Using consistent naming conventions and regular habits save you time later and become *extremely* important when more than one operator has a hand in the same session! (By the way, you can change the names of input/output paths and internal mixing busses at any time by right-clicking on an audio input, output, or send selector and selecting Rename from the pop-up menu. The contents of the I/O Setup dialog box will be updated accordingly.)

Click the Default button in the I/O Setup dialog box to reset the display for the path type in the current tab (Input, Output, Insert, Bus, Mic Preamps, or HW Insert Delays) to a factory-defined default configuration. In this default configuration, all possible main stereo paths are created for your audio hardware, plus two mono subpaths for each.

Use as Many (Or as Few) Paths as You Require   If you're using an M-Audio audio interface with ADAT Lightpipe I/O, you may be surprised to discover that, by default, these inputs and outputs don't appear in the I/O Setup dialog box. If you don't have Lightpipe devices in your studio configuration, that's appropriate. Otherwise, these unnecessary selections would appear every time you select track inputs and outputs. If you *do* want to use this type of I/O on your interface, however, two steps are usually required. First, in the device's own setup application, be sure to activate the ADAT input/output. Then, in Pro Tools' I/O Setup dialog box, click the Default button in both the Input and Output tabs to automatically create all possible stereo paths (with mono subpaths) for ADAT input/output on the interface.

After configuring I/O Setup to your taste, click the Export Settings button so that you can recall this setup at any time. Experienced users will have many different I/O configurations stored this way as presets for various tasks. It is also a great idea to periodically back up the contents of the IO Settings subfolder of the main Pro Tools program folder, especially before installing any new version of the Pro Tools software.

Session

The sample rate parameter displayed in the Session Setup window (see Figure 8.24) is fixed when you first create the current Pro Tools session. Other parameters, including audio file format, bit depth, and the Interleaved option, can be changed at any time (new to Pro Tools 10). The Session Start Time setting is important when synchronizing to incoming SMPTE time code (converted to MIDI time code by your SMPTE synchronization peripheral) because this is how Pro Tools knows what time-code position corresponds to the beginning of the session's Timeline. The frame rate (number of frames per second) you specify for your Pro Tools session must match that of the incoming time code for Pro Tools to synchronize properly to the video (or audio) master. Pro

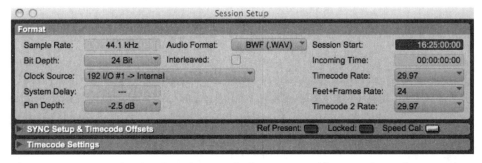

Figure 8.24   Use the Session Setup window to specify a session's frame rate and other options for SMPTE time code.

Tools can also *generate* time code with certain peripherals, as well as MIDI time code. (See Chapter 11, "Synchronization," for more detailed information about synchronization.) In Pro Tools HD, you can select the Sync HD or a digital audio input here as the external clock source that controls the sample rate of your audio hardware, as opposed to its internal clock. Clock-source changes here are reflected in the Hardware Setup dialog box and vice versa.

Reminder: When you record from a digital input (S/PDIF coaxial or optical, AES/EBU, TDIF, or ADAT Lightpipe, according to the audio interface you're using), it's common to switch the clock source from internal to the source digital input from the external device. (This will be the case unless you're using a central, high-quality clock source as the master for both Pro Tools and the external device.) This slaves the sample clock of your Pro Tools hardware to that of the specified incoming digital audio signal. If the clock source is still set to the digital input when you are no longer using the device (after powering it off, for example), your audio hardware will try to synchronize to a nonexistent external timing reference, and your playback speed may be very slow and peculiar—or more likely, you will get errors. Just switch the clock source back from the digital input to internal clock, and you'll be back to normal.

In larger studios with multiple digital audio devices, however, it's common to use a highly stable, centralized clock source to which the sample rates of all the devices are slaved in a sort of star configuration. Not only does this improve synchronization as these devices play back together, but the better units can noticeably improve audio quality by reducing jitter and other irregularities in the clock. The "Word Clock and Sync Generators" section of Appendix B, "Add-Ons, Extensions, and Cool Stuff for Your Rig," provides a few examples of these master clock devices.

Time Code Formats around the World   We discuss SMPTE time code in greater detail in Chapter 11, but if you're configuring the Session Setup window, here's a quick reference for where the various frame rates are commonly used:

- For audio-only applications, 30 frames per second (fps) non-drop is very common throughout the world (although theoretically, you could use any frame rate for syncing two MIDI or audio-only devices).

- For video in North America, parts of Latin America, most of the Caribbean, as well as South Korea, Taiwan, and Japan, 29.97 fps drop or non-drop is the norm for video work. (It makes a difference whether the frame rate is drop or non-drop; be sure to ask!) This frame rate is associated with the NTSC color television format used in these parts of the world.

- 25 fps is used for video projects in Europe, Africa, Brazil, Argentina, Paraguay, Uruguay, Australia, parts of the Middle East, and most of Asia. The 25 fps frame rate corresponds to that the PAL and SECAM television formats common in these regions.

- 24 fps is used for film everywhere.

Setup > MIDI Submenu

These options affect how MIDI data is sent and received from Pro Tools in general.

MIDI Studio Setup (Mac)

Audio MIDI Setup (sometimes referred to as AMS) is a utility included in Mac OS X that manages your MIDI configuration—in other words, what kind of MIDI interface you're using and how many ports/channels it has, which MIDI controllers and modules are available on your system, where they are attached to the interface, and so on. In Mac versions, the Setup > MIDI > MIDI Studio menu selection in Pro Tools launches the operating system's Audio MIDI Setup utility. You indicate where your MIDI keyboards and modules are connected by dragging cables between symbols for input/output ports to those of your MIDI interface. You specify whether each is a controller, whether it's multitimbral, what channel it transmits/receives, and other attributes. You can also assign logical names to each MIDI device, which then appear as you select MIDI destinations for tracks within Pro Tools (and any other MIDI-compatible program under Mac OS X). Lastly, you can subscribe to a patchname document in Pro Tools for your MIDI device so that you can use the MIDI Program Selector button for each MIDI track in the Mix window to select programs for MIDI tracks on the destination device by *name* rather than by program number. Note that if your MIDI device doesn't appear in the pre-configured list included with Audio MIDI Setup or Pro Tools itself, there are user-supported websites where you may be able to download patchname documents.

MIDI Studio Setup (Windows)

The MIDI Studio Setup window in Windows versions of Pro Tools serves a similar function to the Audio MIDI Setup utility for Mac and is discussed further in Chapter 10. Briefly, you can define instruments for each of the external MIDI controllers or modules, also indicating where each is connected to the available ports of your system's MIDI interface. (You can also daisy-chain multiple devices on a single port of the interface, of course, via their In/Out/Thru ports.) You can assign a descriptive name to each port on your MIDI interface.

You can click the MIDI Program Selector button on each MIDI track in the Mix window and assign a MIDI patchname file (.MIDNAM) so that you can select sounds on its destination device by *name* instead of by program number. As with the patchname files on Mac, these are simple text files containing data in the XML language. You can very easily edit these files' contents in Notepad, WordPad, or any word processor capable of saving back to TXT format. This is highly recommended if you've altered the contents of the user banks on the device, for example.

MIDI Beat Clock

Some external drum machines, sequencers inside keyboard workstations, and arpeggiators can synchronize to Pro Tools using MIDI Beat Clock. Part of the original MIDI data specification, MIDI Beat Clock doesn't transmit location information (bar number or time code). Instead, it represents the current tempo—at 24 pulses per 1/4 note (PPQN). In the MIDI Beat Clock dialog box, you simply indicate the MIDI device/output where you want MIDI Clock data to be transmitted. Appendix D contains information about transferring sequences from external MIDI workstations (or drum machines) into Pro Tools.

Input Filter

In this dialog box, you select what types of MIDI data Pro Tools will record and/or pass through. For example, you may choose to disable polyphonic aftertouch received from your MIDI controller if you know that none of the MIDI modules or plug-ins you're using respond to this type of data (especially since polyphonic aftertouch dramatically increases the number of MIDI events recorded on the track). Or, in a scenario where you're recording keyboardists via MIDI during a live performance, you might choose not to record their changes to the master volume control (MIDI controller 7) made for the purpose of onstage monitoring levels.

Input Devices

In larger MIDI configurations, there may be many MIDI devices that you could potentially use as controllers. To minimize the number of selections that appear each time you select the MIDI input source for MIDI and Instrument tracks, you can use this dialog box to disable display of certain devices.

Connect to SoundCloud

Pro Tools 10 lets you share your mix using the Share with SoundCloud option in the Bounce to Disk dialog box. When this option is selected, the bounced file is automatically uploaded to your SoundCloud account. The Setup > Connect to SoundCloud command lets you log in to your existing account, or create a new account, to enable this functionality.

Click/Countoff

To set up the click sound you want and how it will behave, open the Click/Countoff Options dialog box (shown in Figure 8.25). When you instantiate the Click plug-in on a mono Aux Input track (or use the Track > Create Click Track command), the Click plug-in produces a metronome click sound following the tempo map or manual tempo setting in Pro Tools. The Click plug-in itself enables you to choose what sound to use for the metronome click and the relative levels of accented and unaccented beats. If you instead prefer to use some external MIDI device as the source for your click sound, you'd select its MIDI output and channel, as well as the MIDI note numbers, velocities, and durations to use for accented and unaccented beats, in the Click/Countoff Options dialog box. You can enable the click to always sound, to sound only during record, or to sound only during countoff bars. You can also set the desired number of countoff bars in this dialog box.

Preferences

Many of the items in the Preferences dialog box are self-explanatory, so this section mentions only a few of the most important or poorly understood settings.

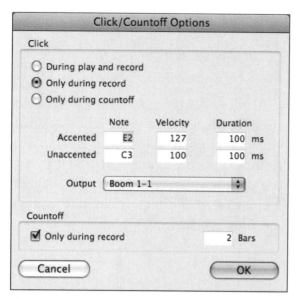

Figure 8.25 You can open the Click/Countoff Options dialog box by choosing Setup > Click/Countoff (or by double-clicking the Metronome Click button or Countoff display in the Transport window).

Display Preferences

Options in this tab of the Preferences dialog box affect how track data is displayed and how peak levels and clipping indicators are handled in Pro Tools.

- **Color Coding > Always Display Marker Colors.** This is a useful feature for most users. In the Markers Ruler, the color assigned (automatically or manually) to each marker will fill the ruler until the next marker is reached in the Timeline. If you're using markers to identify sections of a song or scenes in a video, the colors help you see at a glance where you are in the session. If, however, the colors bother you, or you're using a large number of markers for a different purpose, you may prefer to keep this option disabled.

- **Color Coding > Default Track/Clip Color.** These two options determine how colors are assigned to tracks and clips. Color-coding for tracks and especially the clips within them helps you keep track of what's going on in a large session. Tracks and MIDI Channels is perhaps the best initial setting; then, as you experiment with the use of colors to keep track of your session material (such as Mix and Edit groups, MIDI devices, or location of clips between markers in the Timeline), you will discover other useful settings for specific editing tasks or project types.

- **Meters > Peak Hold.** A small, horizontal yellow line in the level meters on tracks indicates the highest peak level reached during playback. Three modes can be selected for this feature: 3 Second, Infinite, and None. For most uses, the 3 Second setting is practical, although you can also set this to Infinite. The Peak Hold feature helps you monitor how close your levels are getting to maximum, for example. Another approach to monitoring peak levels on Audio, Aux Input, Instrument, or Master Fader tracks is to Command-click (Ctrl-click in Windows) the Volume/Peak/Delay indicator at the bottom of each track in the Mix window to display peak levels. This peak indicator holds the maximum level attained during playback infinitely until you Option-click (Alt-click in Windows) to clear it. Because it provides an actual numerical value, the peak indicator field is usually a more practical tool than the level meter display when you are interested in monitoring peak levels.

■ **Meters > Clip Indication.** Level meters on Audio, Aux Input, Instrument, and Master Fader tracks feature a top red segment that indicates when 100% is exceeded (which causes clipping, distorting the original audio waveform passing through that track). Some people prefer the 3 Second setting. When set to Infinite, however, the clipping indicator remains lit until you reset it (by clicking it). But remember: You *never* want to see the red clipping indicator light up—on any track (or in any plug-in window). Be especially sure to check for this before bouncing out any mixes. Any digital distortion is undesirable, and you should adjust your gain structure (the audio levels going in and out of each component in the mixing environment) to avoid it.

PhaseScope Plug-In   For more detailed information about signal level and phase (either on the Master Fader for your main mix output or any other audio-related track type), you should use the PhaseScope metering plug-in, provided with Pro Tools. Metering views include Peak, RMS, Peak+RMS, VU, BBC, DIN, Nordic, and VENUE.

Operation Preferences

As you become more adept with Pro Tools, you will find it convenient to change some of the options in the Operation tab of the Preferences dialog box for specific projects, or even for different phases of the same project.

■ **Transport > Timeline Insertion/Play Start Marker Follows Playback.** Ordinarily, when you click Stop after recording or playback, the Transport's Start value (and therefore the position in the Timeline where playback will next commence) remains the same. When you enable Timeline Insertion/Play Start Marker Follows Playback, the Start value (where playback or the next recording will start) and the location of the Play Start marker (used in Dynamic Transport mode) always update to wherever you last clicked Stop. This is very useful, for example, when recording spoken-word projects such as long narrations or books on tape (but can be disastrous when working with loops). When recording live speakers and theatrical presentations, you could stop during pauses and then simply click Record again to pick up recording at the exact point in the session's Timeline where you left off. Also note the button in the Edit window below the Pencil tool that can be used to toggle this preference.

■ **Transport > Edit Insertion Follows Scrub/Shuttle.** If you frequently use the Scrub tool or a scrub wheel on an external controller to scan through audio clips, you may find it helpful to enable this item. With this option enabled, the time value for the Edit insertion point (indicated by the Main/Sub Location Indicators of the Edit window) is updated to wherever you stop scrubbing. When you hold down the Rewind or Fast Forward button (or the 1 or 2 key on the numeric keypad—a very good shortcut to know!), Pro Tools shuttles quickly through the Timeline. In a similar manner, when you enable Edit Insertion Follows Scrub/Shuttle in Preferences, the Edit insertion point ends up at whatever point you stop shuttling.

■ **Numeric Keypad Mode.** Although a few users prefer the Classic or Shuttle modes for controlling Transport functions with the numeric keypad, most prefer to leave this set to Transport. Transport mode is required for the numeric keypad shortcuts identified for Transport functions in this book.

■ **Record > Link Record and Play Faders.** When enabled, any volume changes you make on a track during recording (remember that these do not affect the actual levels recorded to disk!) are retained in Playback mode. Many users prefer to leave this disabled. That way, you can adjust volumes while recording (for example, to hear a part better or to *reduce* its level if you're otherwise hearing some of the direct signal during recording anyway) without having to worry about this affecting this fader's level in the mix during playback.

■ **Enable Session File Auto Backup.** When this option is enabled, backup copies of your session files are automatically saved while you work. Here, you specify how often backups happen and how many backup copies should be saved. The backup sessions are stored inside your session folder in the Session File Backups subfolder, which is created automatically. Backup copies are numbered, and .bak is added to your session's file name. If your main session file ever becomes corrupted—or if you completely mess it up yourself—this feature could save a lot of frustration. You can open any auto-saved backup copy of your session with the File > Open Session command. (Pro Tools will add "recovered" to the title bar for this session document to prevent you from confusing it with the original file when/if you save this backup version of the session to disk.) This is a very important feature of Pro Tools that can save you from disaster—and save your reputation. Unless you have overpowering reasons not to (such as marginal system performance), it is strongly recommended that you enable Auto Backup!

Editing Preferences

You will change some of the settings in the Editing tab of the Preferences dialog box to suit your working style. As with other tabs in Preferences, only some of the most critical options are mentioned here; more details for the other selections are available in the *Menu Guide* PDF document supplied with Pro Tools.

■ **Auto-Name Memory Locations While Playing.** Ordinarily, when you use the numeric keyboard's Enter key to create markers during play or record, a dialog box appears. You enter a marker name, specify its properties (absolute or relative, zoom settings, track heights, and other attributes, including comments), and then click OK. If you don't want to go through these steps (for example, because you're creating frequent markers while recording or listening back to a performance and don't want to be distracted), you can enable this option. Pro Tools automatically assigns new marker names each time you hit the Enter key—Marker 1, Marker 2, and so on—*without* the dialog box appearing each time. You can always change marker names, properties, and locations afterward.

- **Default Fade Settings.** This is fairly self-explanatory: Change the default fade shape display format for the fade-in, fade-out, and crossfade types to match the settings you use the most. It's mentioned here only because many users never seem to get around to changing this preference!

- **Zoom Toggle.** The Edit window's Zoom Toggle button (beneath the Zoomer tool) is used to switch between the current zoom level and some other defined zoom level for the current selection. Here are just a few examples, although as you get adept at Pro Tools editing you will definitely want to explore these functions more. If you set your preference to Selection for vertical and/or horizontal zoom, the current selection will be zoomed in to fill available space when you click the Zoom toggle button. Click it again, and the track selection reverts to the previous zoom level. You can also define a track view (for example, waveform) and a track height that will always be enabled when you click the Zoom Toggle button.

Note The Zoom Toggle preference settings are a common source of unexpected behavior in Pro Tools. For example, when Track Height is set to Last Used, Pro Tools operators who forget to turn Zoom Toggle off after using it will frequently reset the zoomed track back to a small size manually (usually Micro, to save space). The next time they need to use Zoom Toggle to zoom in on a selection, it will toggle the track to Micro size, making the selection smaller rather than larger! (Consider setting the Track Height preference to Jumbo or Extreme instead to avoid this issue.)

Another source of puzzlement is the Zoom Toggle Follows Edit Selection check box. With this preference enabled, making a selection on a different track while Zoom Toggle is active will cause the previous track to return to its original track height and the new track to switch to the track height associated with Zoom Toggle. Although this can be handy if done intentionally, more often than not it catches users by surprise to see their tracks changing height unexpectedly. (Again, most prevalent when users forget that Zoom Toggle is active.) Things get really bizarre when this option *and* the Last Used Track Height preference are both selected with the above scenario unfolding—now every time you click on a different track, it shrinks to Micro size!

- **Levels of Undo.** The default setting for Levels of Undo is 32 (the maximum), and this is fine for most users. The Undo History window also greatly facilitates the process of stepping back through many editing operations to a previous state of the session. The number of steps available in the Undo History window is also determined by this Preference setting.

Mixing Preferences

The options in the Mixing tab of the Preferences dialog box are mostly self-explanatory. Among other things, they affect automation behavior and how external control surfaces interact with the Pro Tools Mix and Edit windows. This is also where you specify whether the newly created sends should default to −∞ (minus infinity).

- **Set Pans Default to Follow Main Pan.** This is a good option to enable to simplify working with sends. On new tracks, this option causes the FMP (Follow Main Pan) button to be enabled by default. Therefore, the send's position in the stereo or surround-sound field will be slaved to that of the track's main panner for its output. When required (for example, when you want panning for a delay or reverb send to be on the opposite side from its main output), you can always disable this button on any track.

- **Default EQ, Default Dynamics.** The EQ and Dynamics plug-ins you choose in these two fields will automatically appear at the top of the Insert selector menu in your tracks, making it much quicker to access these frequently used effects.

Processing Preferences

Processing preferences affect the operation of AudioSuite plug-ins, time compression and expansion, audio-file import options, and the defaults for Elastic Audio processing.

- **Automatically Copy Files on Import.** If the audio files you import into a session are directly compatible with the session, they won't necessarily be copied into its Audio Files subfolder (unless you deliberately click the Copy button instead of the Add button in the Import Audio dialog box, for example). If you generally *do* want to copy files rather than referencing them in their original locations (especially if they're on a CD-ROM or some other removable media, for example, or to avoid potential risk when the same source files are used in multiple sessions), you can enable this option.

- **Drag and Drop from Desktop Conforms to Session Tempo.** This preference relates to Elastic Audio features. The default is for only Rex and ACID files (with their inherent support of timeslices) to automatically conform to the session tempo when dragged in from the operating system's desktop. If most of your work involves conforming loops to existing tempos in the Pro Tools session, or if you're merely experimenting with a large number of alternatives for this purpose, you might want to enable this automatic conforming option for all audio files.

- **Elastic Audio > Enable Elastic Audio on New Tracks.** When enabled, the default Elastic Audio mode (selectable in this same section of the preferences) will be enabled on all new Audio tracks.

- **TC/E Plug-in.** The default plug in for using the Time Compression/Expansion mode of the Trim tool is Time Shift. However, if available, you should choose Avid's X-Form for higher quality TCE results. You can also select any other third-party time-compression/expansion plug-in available on your system, if you prefer.

MIDI Preferences

Most users will find the default settings here to be a good starting point—although you may eventually set your own default Note On velocity for when you create notes with the Pencil tool, for instance, or enable Use MIDI to Tap Tempo. The following are several essential options in the MIDI tab of the Preferences dialog box.

- **Use F11 Key for Wait for Note.** As mentioned in Chapter 5, when the Wait for MIDI Note function is enabled, after you click Record in the Transport, recording doesn't begin until the first MIDI event is received (even if you are recording on an Audio track). This option enables the F11 key as a shortcut for turning the Wait for Note function on and off. Note that Macintosh users should see the sidebar in Chapter 5 entitled "Macintosh, Pro Tools, and Using Function Keys F9–F12" about reassigning the default function keys for Exposé, which otherwise interfere with the Wait for Note feature in Pro Tools.

- **Default Thru Instrument.** This is where you select the destination that is used when you preview MIDI clips. Just as you can Option-click (Alt-click in Windows) on an audio clip to preview it in the Clip List, doing this on a MIDI clip will play it through the destination chosen for the Default Thru Instrument setting. Generally speaking, the most useful option in this pop-up menu is Follows First Selected MIDI Track. When this is enabled, you can select a MIDI or Instrument track whose assigned output has an appropriate-sounding patch so that its sound will be used for previewing MIDI clips in the Clip List.

- **Global MIDI Playback Offset.** When using external MIDI instruments, you may find that there is a more or less fixed amount of delay with respect to the actual start point of the note events on your MIDI and Instrument tracks. It does take some small interval of time for MIDI events to be transmitted from your MIDI interface, plus some degree of analog-to-digital conversion delay that is added when you monitor these external sources through inputs on your audio interface. Much more significant, however, is that, after receiving a Note On event, many MIDI keyboards and modules can take several milliseconds to trigger an actual sound in response. Setting a negative playback offset globally for MIDI tracks in this Preferences page can be the easiest way to compensate for the delay. Nevertheless, remember that the MIDI Track Offsets dialog box (discussed in this chapter, under the Event menu) always enables you to set offsets for each MIDI or Instrument track individually.

- **Automatically Create Click Track in New Sessions.** If the majority of your projects are music sessions, you may want to enable this setting. That way, in each new Pro Tools session, a mono Aux Input track is automatically created with the Click plug-in already instantiated.

Window Menu

The selections in this menu are primarily for showing/hiding the various windows in Pro Tools. Many are discussed elsewhere in this book and won't be covered here, but several commands are worth special mention.

Window Configurations

Window Configurations enable you to store view sets in Pro Tools. These include the size and location of most Pro Tools windows (including Mix, Edit, and Transport), plug-ins and panners, Memory locations, Workspace/Project browsers, time/tempo/event operations, the Video window, and various others. When you create a new Window Configuration, a check box in the New Window Configuration dialog box enables you to choose whether current display settings in the Mix, Edit, and Transport windows should also be stored as part of the window layout. Alternatively, you can store display settings for the Mix, Edit, and Transport windows separately, without including size or location settings that affect any other windows. From the Window > Configurations submenu, you can open the Window Configurations List, shown in Figure 8.26. The keyboard shortcut for this window is Command+Option+J (Ctrl+Alt+J in Windows). In this figure, you can see Window Configurations that are specific to the Mix, Edit, and Transport windows, plus others that are more general for use during specific phases of a project.

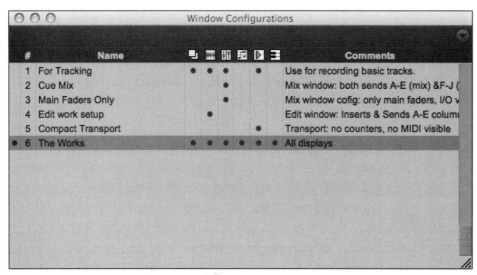

Figure 8.26 Use the Window Configurations List to store your own presets for the sizes and locations of the numerous windows in Pro Tools or display settings within the Mix, Edit, and Transport windows.

MIDI Editor

The Window > MIDI Editor command opens a MIDI Editor window in your session. MIDI Editor windows let you view and edit MIDI notes and controller data from multiple tracks in a single, large Notes pane display. MIDI Editor windows show Instrument and MIDI track data superimposed in Notes view (or on separate tracks in Notation view). You can also view and edit MIDI controller data (such as velocity, pitch bend, and mod wheel) in controller lanes under the Notes pane.

The keyboard shortcut for toggling the MIDI Editor window is Control+= (Mac) or Start+= (Windows).

Score Editor

The Window > Score Editor command opens the Score Editor window in your session. The Score Editor window lets you view and edit Instrument and MIDI tracks as music notation. Upon opening, the Score Editor automatically transcribes MIDI performances into notation. From this window, you can print a score of your session or selectively show/hide tracks from the Track List to view or print parts from individual tracks.

The keyboard shortcut for toggling the Score Editor window is Control+Option+= (Mac) or Alt+Start+= (Windows).

MIDI Event List

The MIDI Event List window (shown in Figure 8.27) displays MIDI events in a track as numerical data in a table format, as opposed to the standard graphical representation within MIDI tracks in the Edit window. Some MIDI editing operations are easier to perform in this list view. In a sense, this is the most accurate view of what is recorded and played back in your MIDI performances—even though it may not be especially intuitive, musically speaking! The MIDI Event List window is also the only place where you can view and edit polyphonic key pressure data (also called *polyphonic aftertouch*—MIDI data for the pressure applied to each individual key, as opposed to the more common *monophonic* aftertouch data sent from most keyboards, more properly known as *channel pressure*). When you enable real-time MIDI properties on the clips or tracks containing the selected MIDI data, the display in the MIDI Event List window will reflect this. An R indicates events that are affected by clip-based properties, while a T indicates those affected by track-based properties.

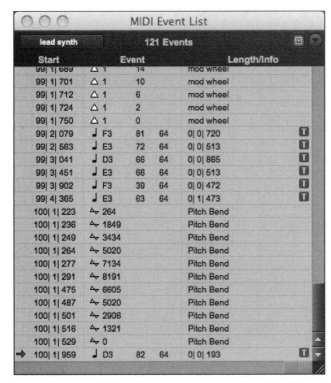

Figure 8.27 The MIDI Event List window displays the actual data that selected MIDI parts contain and transmit out to their selected destination.

Task Manager Window

Many tasks in Pro Tools occur in the background—for example, fade creation, relinking to files that are missing or were moved since the last time a Pro Tools session was saved, copying source files as you import track data from other Pro Tools session documents, redrawing audio waveforms, and so on. All of these have some effect on your system's performance at any given moment, so it's handy to be able to check what's going on. Be sure to check out the options in the pop-up menu in the upper-left corner of the Task Manager window. Among other things, you can cancel, pause, or resume individual tasks.

If a complex project is heavily taxing the capabilities of your system as you edit and play audio, pausing or canceling these background tasks may be a short-term solution. In particular, though, notice the last item in this pop-up menu, Pause During Playback. This global preference prevents background tasks from diverting resources while Pro Tools is in Record or Playback mode. If your system is already underpowered for the kind of projects you work on, be sure to enable this option.

Status Indicators in the Edit Window   Two indicators, called Timeline and Session, appear below the Edit Selection display in the Edit window. When the Timeline indicator is green, it means that all files used by clips within Audio tracks are properly linked and available for playback. Otherwise, this indicator is red, meaning that some files need to be located and relinked. (Check in the Task Manager window; this may already be in progress.) When the Session indicator is green, it means that all source files referenced by the session (both audio and video) are properly linked and available for playback, regardless of whether they are currently being used within a track.

Pro Tools 10 adds two additional status indicators: the Track Solo indicator and the Track Mute indicator. The Track Solo indicator lights yellow when any track in the session is soloed. When lit, you can click it to clear all soloed tracks in the session. The Track Mute indicator lights orange when any track in the session is muted; this indicator does not function to clear all mutes.

Workspace Browser Window

The Window > Workspace command provides direct access to the DigiBase Workspace browser. DigiBase is an audio (and video) file database engine that is an integral part of the Pro Tools platform. Other DigiBase browsers include the Project, Volume, and Catalog browsers.

At the simplest level, the Workspace browser window provides a bird's-eye view of all eligible disk volumes for audio playback and recording on your system, their capacity, and how much space is currently available. You can also specify whether each of your disk volumes should be used for playback, for recording (and playback), or for transfer only—meaning that you can view and copy files from the disk but not play back audio files from it in real time. In addition, you can unmount disk volumes directly from the Workspace browser by highlighting the drive and choosing Unmount from the pull-down menu in the upper-right corner of the browser. Within this window, you can browse the entire folder/file hierarchy on each disk without leaving Pro Tools, as well as view audio file attributes and audition audio files. You can rename, duplicate, and delete folders and files in the Workspace browser window. You can even add comments about these audio files that will be visible in this window, within this or other Pro Tools sessions.

From the Workspace browser window, you can drag the audio files (seen in their original disk locations) directly to the Clip List or onto an Audio track with a matching number of channels (for example, mono or stereo). You can import audio files into Pro Tools from audio CDs by dragging tracks directly from the Workspace browser window to the Clip List or onto a stereo Audio track in the Edit window. The Preview button enables you to listen to audio and MIDI files before deciding to import them into your session. A pop-up selector, which you access by right-clicking the Preview button, enables you to use two additional preview mode options: Loop Preview, which loops playback of the selected file while the button is active, and Auto-Play, which initiates preview playback as soon as you select each source audio or MIDI file while in this browser. The preview volume can be adjusted by a pop-up fader when the volume display next to the Preview button is clicked and held.

The audio output path for previewing is determined by your Audition Path settings in the I/O Setup dialog box (while preview playback of MIDI files is determined by the Default Thru Instrument setting in the MIDI tab of the Preferences dialog box). Clicking the Metronome button at the top of this browser window enables the Audio Files Conform to Session Tempo button. In this mode, audio preview of audio files that are successfully analyzed for Elastic Audio will be conformed to the current session tempo (using the algorithm currently chosen in the Elastic Audio plug-in selector, immediately to the right of this button in the browser window). This is very useful for loop selection, for example. If you want to automatically create a new track, either drag the file from the Workspace browser window into the Track List at the left edge of the Edit window or hold down the Shift key as you drag it directly into the Edit window's track display area.

You can also preview standard MIDI files in the Workspace browser window and import them by dragging them into the Clip List. If you instead drag the MIDI file into the Track List (when visible at the left edge of the Edit window), an appropriate number of new MIDI tracks is created. An Import MIDI Settings dialog box enables you to choose whether to import the existing tempo map in the file and whether to delete existing MIDI/Instrument tracks and/or MIDI clips.

The Find button (magnifying glass) in the Workspace and Project browser windows lets you search for files by name on multiple volumes (including searches with wildcard characters and the Boolean operators OR/AND), by kind (folder, audio, video, session, OMF, AAF, MIDI, or clip group), and by modification date. You can constrain searches to certain volumes and folders, or you can scan the entire system simultaneously. You can additionally search by attributes in the other columns of these windows, such as file format, sample rate, bit depth, creation date, and comments.

Don't Use Your System Volume for Audio Recording In the Workspace browser window, you can designate each of the disk volumes on your system (whether entire disks or logical partitions on a single physical disk) for audio playback and/or recording (P or R), or transfer only (T). Be sure that your system volume (the disk or partition containing the operating system used to boot up the computer, and usually most of the program files as well) is set to Transfer to prevent session audio files from getting stored there as the result of recording or editing operations.

Project Browser Window

This window (shown in Figure 8.28) provides powerful features for organizing complex projects and for working in collaboration with other people on large Pro Tools sessions. It also helps you keep track of which files are used in the current session, including their disk locations and other attributes. For example, for each source audio file, columns in the Project browser window can display its name, a waveform graphic with an Audition button, its absolute duration, a user-editable file and database comments, creation and modification dates, the number of channels, file size, format, sample rate, bit depth, and the original and user timestamp information. Very importantly, the full file name and path location for the file on your computer system are shown in the Project browser window, with a unique file ID assigned by Pro Tools. When you encounter missing audio files upon reopening a Pro Tools session (perhaps because you changed their disk or folder locations or moved the project from one Pro Tools system to another), the Project browser window provides tools for relinking references from clips used in that session to the correct source files, in the form of the Relink window. The unique file IDs that Pro Tools assigns to each audio file you import make it much easier to locate them afterward in the Project browser window, even if there are other files on the same disks with similar or identical names.

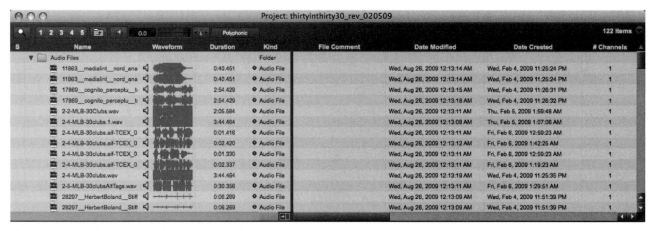

Figure 8.28 The Project browser window.

Find and Import Files Directly from Workspace, Project Browser Windows   After you locate an audio or MIDI file you want to use, you can drag it from either one of these DigiBase browser windows directly into the Clip List or a Pro Tools track with a matching number of channels to import it into your current session. To create a brand-new Audio track at the same time, either drag the audio files into the Track List or hold down the Shift key as you drag the clip to a specific Timeline location in the track display area. You can also preview and import source tracks on audio CDs from these windows in the same manner.

Catalog Browser Window

Catalog browsers function like a list of favorite shortcuts or aliases; items in a catalog represent references to files that reside in many different disk/folder locations. You can store and recall many different catalogs when locating files in your Pro Tools sessions. To add files or entire folders to the currently displayed catalog, drag them directly into the Catalog browser window from any other browser window. Alternatively, you can create a new catalog by selecting a group of files in a browser window and using the Create Catalog from Selection command in the browser window's pop-up menu. To copy all the files referenced in a catalog to a new disk location, drag the catalog in the Workspace browser window onto another disk volume. And as with the other browser windows, you can drag and drop catalog items directly into the Clip List or Track List or onto Audio, MIDI, or Instrument tracks in the Edit window.

Big Counter

The Window > Big Counter menu item opens a large display of the current playback location, visible from across the room as you perform. Time units in the Big Counter window reflect those of the main Time Scale (the active ruler, whose time units are also reflected in the Main Location Indicator). You can type new values into the Big Counter window fields to change the play location or click and drag to scroll numerical values in any of its columns up or down. Many users seem to overlook the Big Counter; however, it can be *very* convenient.

Automation Enable

The buttons in this window (shown in Figure 8.29) enable you to suspend *all* automation in a Pro Tools session or to individually enable or disable recording for each type of automation data (volume, pan, mute, and plug-in parameters; level, pan, and mute for sends). In Pro Tools HD and Pro Tools with Complete Production Toolkit, the Automation Enable window includes additional controls. For instance, the AutoMatch button enables you to return controls to their previously existing levels while writing a new automation pass at a rate determined by the Auto-Match Time setting in the Mixing tab of the Preferences dialog box. (When using the D-Control or D-Command control surface, you can AutoMatch individual controls, such as sends, inserts, and plug-ins, without affecting other types of controls.) Another useful automation feature in HD systems is AutoJoin, which enables you to automatically pick up automation recording at the point in time where a previous automation pass in Latch mode ended.

Figure 8.29 The Automation Enable window with all automation parameters disabled (standard Pro Tools software shown).

Disabling Automation on Individual Tracks   You can set the Automation Mode selector for any individual track to Auto Off, disabling *all* automation on that track. You can also suspend any *specific* automation parameter on an individual track. Use the Track View selector to display the type of automation you wish to suspend on the track (for example, the level of Send A, which you may have routed through a bus to an Aux Input track where a delay effect is inserted). Next, Command-click (Ctrl-click in Windows) on the Track View selector (showing the name of the currently displayed automation parameter— Send A in this case). The name will be dimmed, indicating that this type of automation data no longer plays back. Command-click (Ctrl-click in Windows) the Track View selector again to re-enable playback of the automation type. Reminder: In the Output window for any track, a Safe button for automation helps prevent accidental writing of automation into a track.

Memory Locations

The Window > Memory Locations command opens the Memory Locations window. Memory locations are commonly used for Timeline positions; they can be *marker* Memory locations (Timeline locations) or *selection* Memory locations (Edit selections). Both types of Memory locations can store any of the following properties: current zoom settings, pre-/post-roll times, track show/hide state, track heights, window configurations, and active groups. (You can even create Memory locations with their time properties set to None that won't alter the current Timeline selection.) Both markers and selections can refer to absolute time locations or Bar|Beat values (whose location in absolute time varies according to the current tempo). Memory locations support adding comments up to 255 characters long, which you can optionally display in the Memory Locations window.

Markers

Markers are Memory locations that identify single points in time. They appear on the Markers Ruler (in the Timeline at the top of the Edit window)—yellow diamonds for absolute time references and yellow chevrons for relative time references (Bars|Beats). You might use markers to flag the verses and choruses of a song or a scene transition in a video or film project. Click the plus (+) button at the left end of the Markers Ruler to create a new marker (or selection) at the current position or simply press the Enter key on the numeric keypad. This can even be done during recording and playback. Clicking any marker symbol in the Markers Ruler moves the playback cursor to that position and recalls view properties stored with that marker, if any. You can also click one marker and then Shift-click another to select the entire range between them on all tracks. You can also drag markers to new positions within the Markers Ruler. (Their movement is affected by Grid mode.) To reposition markers numerically, click them while in Spot edit mode. You can change the properties of a marker by double-clicking it either in the Markers Ruler itself or in the Memory Locations window (look ahead to Figure 8.30).

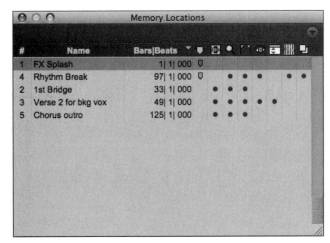

Figure 8.30 You can use Memory locations to create markers or to recall selections (along with their zoom settings, track heights, and other attributes, if desired).

Creating Markers on the Fly In either Play or Record mode, you can create Memory locations by pressing Enter on the numeric keypad. This is handy, for example, to mark sections of a song or narration even as it's being recorded. (Remember, you can always drag markers around in the Markers Ruler to fine-tune their locations afterward or use Spot Edit mode to change marker locations numerically.) While recording a performer, you may notice mistakes, noises, or other items that you'll need to fix afterward. When this happens, create markers on the fly so that you can easily find those locations later. If you don't want to deal with the New Memory Location dialog box as you do this, enable the Auto-Name Memory Locations When Playing option in the Editing tab of the Preferences dialog box.

Selections

A selection Memory location stores the currently highlighted range in the Edit window's Timeline as either an absolute time reference or as Bars|Beats relative to the current Tempo setting. If you need to bounce a section of the Timeline to disk more than once (perhaps an entire song, with enough extra time at the end to allow for reverbs and delays to decay completely to silence), create a Selection Memory location for it and call it Bounce. Or if you find yourself repeatedly highlighting a section of music for editing, perhaps the bridge of a song, and like to view it at a specific zoom level (for detailed vocal editing perhaps, or so that eight bars fit into the Edit window), create a selection Memory location that also recalls the current zoom setting. While recording punch-ins by selecting the range within the track where recording should occur, it is also a good idea to create a selection Memory location for the punch-in range. If you accidentally deselect the punch-in range while listening back to takes, you can simply recall the Memory location. Unlike markers, selection Memory locations do not appear in the Markers Ruler. The Memory Locations window (shown in Figure 8.30) lets you view all markers and selections in your session, change their properties, rename them, or double-click to move the Pro Tools playback cursor directly to that location.

Video Universe

The Video Universe window displays the center frame of each video clip in the main Video track and gives the user options to select and zoom in to/out of active video clips in the session. The zoom function can be activated by moving the cursor over the top half of the video frames within the Video Universe window. Actions you can perform with the zoom function include filling the Edit window with a video clip by double-clicking on the clip's frame with the zoom cursor and selecting a range of video clips to fill the Edit window by dragging on the desired video frames. Moving the cursor along the bottom of the video frames causes the cursor to act like the Selector tool; you can then perform actions such as double-clicking a clip's frame to select an entire video clip and dragging the cursor over clips' frames to select a number of video clips.

Color Palette

You open the Color Palette window (shown in Figure 8.31) via this command in the Windows menu. You can also open this floating window by double-clicking a color strip. (The Track Color view must be active in the Mix window to display the color strips.) You can assign colors to currently selected tracks and to clips and clip groups either within tracks or in the Clip List. You can also assign colors to Mix and Edit groups; these color assignments will appear in the pop-up group indicator for each track in the Mix window.

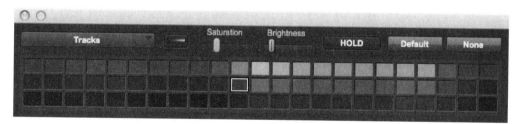

Figure 8.31 Use the Color Palette window to assign colors to tracks, individual clips, groups, or markers.

Color-coding options in the Display tab of the Preferences dialog box enable you to automatically assign colors to tracks according to track type, group assignments, MIDI device, and channel assignments. For clips, you can also automatically assign colors per all of the above plus track color, Clip List color, and marker locations.

If you assign colors to markers, these colors are shown in the Markers Ruler of the Edit window (when Always Show Marker Colors is enabled in the Display tab of the Preferences dialog box). The range from one marker until the next (or until the end of the session Timeline, if it's the last marker) is highlighted in the preceding marker's color, and Pro Tools automatically assigns different colors (which you can change afterward using the Color Palette window) as adjacent markers are created in the Timeline. This is especially useful when editing large sessions; even when you're at a high zoom level for editing events, you'll know you're within a specific scene or song section because you can see the color you assigned to that marker in the Markers Ruler.

Most useful, perhaps, is that in the Edit window, you can use the Color Palette to manually assign colors to selected clips within tracks. This is a huge productivity booster, as anyone who has managed sessions with scores of individual loops, sound effects, vocal segments, or guitar segments within a single track can tell you. For example, by assigning colors before moving clips around, it's much easier to identify at a glance all the occurrences of a repeated item or the smaller clips created by cutting up a much longer one. Color-coding your source clips is also very helpful when *comping* (compositing) a vocal track from multiple source takes.

Pro Tools also gives you the ability to assign colors to channel strips in the Mix and Edit windows, making desired groupings of tracks considerably easier to quickly identify. Look for the Apply to Channel Strip button next to the Saturation slider, and click the button to toggle the function on and off and adjust the slider to increase/decrease the amount of colorization.

Undo History

Another very useful feature, the Undo History window enables you to step back through various operations (edits, menu commands, and so on—anything that is immediately reversible via the Edit > Undo command). Pro Tools supports up to 32 levels of undo. The columnar display in the Undo History window lets you display the hours and minutes for each editing and recording action you've carried out (the Creation Time), as shown in Figure 8.32. Backing up to a previous state can be as easy as clicking the appropriate position in the Undo History window's list of actions. Note that the Undo History pop-up menu enables you to manually clear the Undo Queue; however, certain editing actions also clear it automatically, such as deleting or importing tracks or using one of the Select Unused Clips commands in the Clip List pop-up menu.

Figure 8.32 The Undo History window lets you undo or redo multiple editing operations at once.

Disk Space and System Usage

The System Usage window shows how much of your system's processing capacity the current session is using: the CPU, disk usage, and the computer's PCI bus (which is relevant if your system includes Pro Tools audio cards). On HD systems, the System Usage window (shown in Figure 8.33) can also show how DSP resources on any HD audio cards are currently allocated to mixing and plug-in processing tasks.

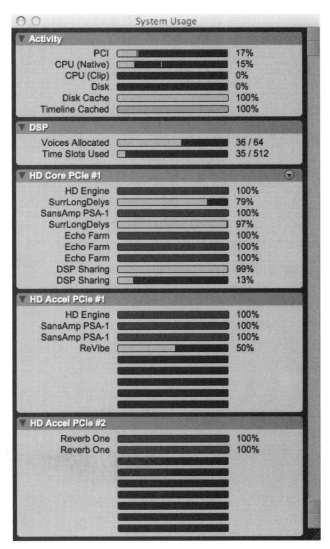

Figure 8.33 The System Usage window. Shown here, a Pro Tools|HD 3 system with three HD Accel cards.

Marketplace

New in Pro Tools 10 is the Marketplace menu, providing easy access to your Avid account and the online Avid Store with a new in-application web browser. The options under this menu—Your Account, Plug-Ins, Support and Training, and Upgrades—take you directly to pages within the browser for online commerce.

Summary

As stated way back at the beginning of this chapter, only the more essential menu selections are highlighted here. Further information about these menu selections (and others not included here) is available in PDF documents provided with Pro Tools, including *Pro Tools Reference Guide*, *Pro Tools Shortcuts Guide*, and especially the *Pro Tools Menu Guide*. It is well worth your time to explore these.

The next chapter explores plug-ins, inserts, and sends in more detail; digital signal processing (DSP); RTAS, TDM, and AAX audio plug-in architectures and ReWire; plus some tips for getting the most power out of the audio resources that your Pro Tools system provides. Read on!

9 Plug-Ins, Inserts, and Sends

This chapter looks a little more closely at how audio can be processed and routed within Pro Tools' software-based mixing environment. Plug-ins, inserts, and sends are discussed in Chapter 2 and especially in Chapter 7, but this chapter will help deepen your understanding of how audio moves around in Pro Tools' virtual signal-routing environment. If you are completely new to Pro Tools, be sure to read Chapter 7 first, which introduces you to the elements in the Mix window; this chapter expands on the concepts presented there.

Signal Routing in Pro Tools

Appendix E, "Signal Flow in Pro Tools," provides basic diagrams of audio signal flow within Pro Tools. While recording audio onto a track in Pro Tools, the signal flow is often as simple as this: An input source is connected to one of the analog or digital input channels on your audio hardware and is then recorded straight to hard disk by a record-enabled Audio track assigned to that channel.

Note that unless your Pro Tools audio hardware has physical controls for input gain, you must adjust your levels *at the source*. Audio interfaces in the Mbox family have front-panel gain knobs for their analog inputs with microphone preamps. Similarly, the 003 and Digi 002 have individual gain knobs on their four mic/line inputs, while their line inputs 5–8 can be switched as a group between fixed +4 dBu and –10 dBV levels. Among the M-Audio audio interfaces, many FireWire models (and others that have microphone-level inputs) provide front-panel knobs for preamp gain adjustment on one or more channels. Make sure to consult the documentation for your particular interface.

As far as what you *hear* on an Audio track, the signal path is pretty much the same whether the signal source is the track's input in record-enable or input-only monitoring mode, an audio file from disk, or one of the internal audio busses in the Pro Tools mixing environment. It goes like this: Input audio (which goes directly to hard disk from the selected input path, if a recording is in progress) goes through the Inserts section (after which it can optionally be directed to *pre*-fader send destinations), then through the track's main volume fader (a *gain stage*), and then optionally to any *post*-fader send destinations, through the pan control, and finally to the track's current output assignment (either physical outputs or an internal mixing bus within Pro Tools).

Figure 9.1 shows typical signal flow for an Audio track in Record versus Playback mode. (As you will see later in this chapter, the signal path for Aux Inputs is similar, while Master Faders differ because they have no sends and their inserts are always post-fader.) Audio tracks can also be set to monitor their selected input in several ways, even when *not* in Record mode. For example, enabling Track > Input Only Monitoring affects all Audio tracks; on HD systems and Pro Tools with Complete Production Toolkit, a Track Input button on each Audio track switches the individual track to Input Monitor mode during normal playback, even if it already contains audio clips.

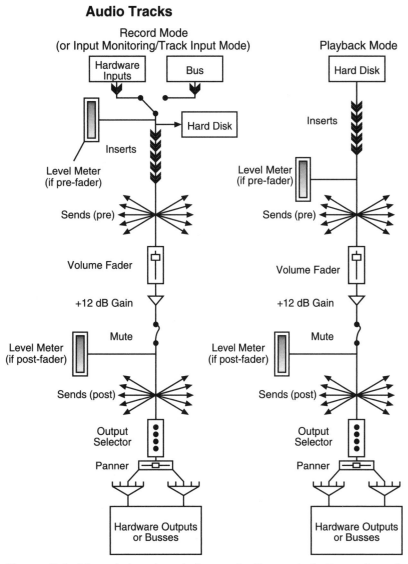

Figure 9.1 Virtual signal path for an Audio track, in Record mode versus Playback mode.

Track Volume Faders Do Not Affect Record Level   While recording on an Audio track, its volume fader and mute button have *no effect* on the input level to the audio hardware. This gives you the freedom to adjust monitoring levels while recording, either for your control-room mix or for the comfort of the performer(s). Unless Preferences > Operation >

Link Record and Play Faders is enabled, when the track is no longer record-enabled, its volume fader returns to its previous playback level. The volume fader on Audio tracks (as well as Aux Input, Instrument, and Master Fader tracks) can either decrease the track's level or apply as much as +12 dB of gain boost.

About the Level Meters in Pro Tools   When Options > Pre Fader Metering is enabled, during *playback*, level meters on Audio tracks, Aux Inputs, Instrument tracks, and Master Faders always reflect *post*-insert, *pre*-fader levels. In Pre-Fader Metering mode, the displayed levels on tracks *do* reflect any gain changes resulting from their inserts or plug-in effects, but are unaffected by current volume-fader settings (or the track's Mute button).

When the Pre-Fader Metering setting is *not* enabled, meters are post-fader. If you reduce a track's main volume fader, this is reflected in its level meter.

Whenever tracks are record enabled (or when Track > Input Only Monitoring is enabled), the track level meters display *pre*-insert levels at the track's input. On MIDI tracks the level meters display MIDI note-on velocities.

Input Channels

As explained in Chapter 2, to avoid confusion, this book distinguishes between *channels* for input/output of audio on the audio interface and *tracks* within the software itself—even though in the Mix window, tracks look like channel strips on a conventional mixing board. (Although they are often referred to as *channel strips*, this book uses the term *mixer strips* for the track displays in the Mix window to indicate that the displays represent virtual signal paths and not necessarily input/output paths to or from the outside world.) Every Pro Tools system has some finite number of actual audio input channels on the hardware (either digital or analog). Some audio interfaces offer only one or two input/output channels. Others provide a larger but still predetermined (non-expandable) maximum number of inputs. Regardless of the interface, standard Pro Tools software is limited to a maximum of 32 channels of I/O.

Expandable I/O configurations are possible with Pro Tools|HD Native, Pro Tools|HD, and Pro Tools|HDX hardware. Whatever system configuration you're using, the number of independent channels on your audio hardware determines the maximum number of discrete audio sources you can record simultaneously. By way of example, the HD OMNI interface provides four channels of analog input, eight channels of analog output, and various digital I/O options, allowing for up to eight channels of simultaneous I/O. The HD I/O is available in one of three configurations: 8 × 8 × 8 (8 analog in, 8 analog out, and 8 digital in/out); 16 × 16 analog in/out; and 16 × 16 digital in/out. HD MADI is a purely digital audio interface, providing up to 64 channels of I/O in the Multichannel Audio Digital Interface (MADI) format. Expanding a system with multiple HD-series interfaces provides additional I/O for the system. (Note that, though only one HD OMNI can be used at a time, the HD OMNI can be combined with other HD-series interfaces on a system.)

The Pro Tools|HD Native card supports up to four HD-series interfaces, for a maximum of 64 channels of I/O. Each Pro Tools|HD card supports up to two HD-series interfaces, for a maximum configuration of 160 channels of I/O on a multi-card system. Each Pro Tools|HDX card supports up to four HD-series interfaces, for a maximum configuration of up to 192 channels of I/O on a multi-card system.

Some audio interfaces—such as the HD OMNI and those in the 003 family, as well as the M-Audio FireWire 1814—offer ADAT Lightpipe connectors for input/output of digital audio. Each Lightpipe connector supports up to eight channels of audio via a TOSLINK optical cable. Often some or all of these input channels can be used *simultaneously* with the analog inputs on the interface. For example, on the 003 or FireWire 1814 interface, you can record up to 18 separate source channels by using all eight analog inputs, the eight Lightpipe channels, plus the included stereo S/PDIF digital input. But of course, digital inputs require a digital source. Unless the external source you're recording or monitoring is already equipped with a Lightpipe digital output (like some keyboards, effects, and multi-channel mic preamps), an additional device is required to convert the signal to Lightpipe prior to your Pro Tools interface to take advantage of the optical digital inputs.

Remember that the input of each Audio track or Aux Input can be assigned to any available audio input path from your hardware; the I/O Setup dialog box allows you to define these input paths (mono, stereo, or multichannel, according to which system you're using) and assign them convenient names.

Audio and Aux Input Tracks

Tracks are discrete audio pathways in the Pro Tools virtual signal-routing environment. Obviously, in ordinary Play mode, an Audio track's source signal derives from the playback of audio data (within files on one of your system's disks), which is referenced by the audio clips within the track. With Track > Auto Input Monitoring active, whenever an Audio track's Record Enable button is lit in Stop (or during punch-in recording), the selected input source is monitored through it.

For Audio and Aux Input tracks, the input source can be either a physical audio input path on your hardware or one of Pro Tools' internal mix busses. (A *bus* is a utility pathway for routing audio signals around within Pro Tools; for more information, see the "Busses" section later in this chapter, and also Chapter 2 for a basic definition.) Figure 9.2 shows the signal path for an Aux Input.

Input Sources for Audio Tracks In addition to hardware inputs (or audio clips from hard disk during normal playback), a Pro Tools mixing bus can also be the selected input for any Audio track or Aux Input track. On Audio tracks, a bus could be used as a front end during recording, combining a larger number of inputs from external sources (assuming you have a multichannel audio interface, as opposed to a stereo-only alternative like the Mbox Mini). Here's an example: You might create a stereo Aux Input for each pair of physical audio inputs on your audio interface where audio signals from external MIDI modules are connected. If you like, you can instantiate compression, EQ, or any other insert effect on each Aux Input. Assign the main outputs from each of these Aux Inputs to a bus pair and select that bus pair as the input source for a stereo Audio track. You can then record this submix to disk. Creating this stereo audio submix from your MIDI instruments could have several advantages. First, your session will be usable on other Pro Tools systems without the MIDI gear attached. Second, you won't have to worry about reestablishing audio connections, gain structure, and so on if you ever reopen the session in the distant future. Lastly, using this submix instead of monitoring the outputs from these external MIDI devices (either temporarily or permanently) will free up all those inputs on your audio interface for recording other sources.

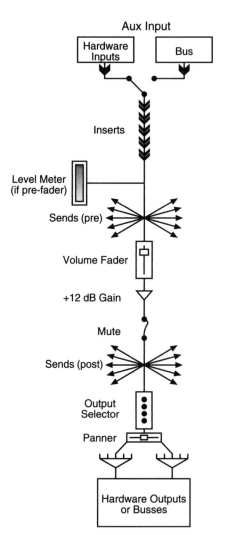

Figure 9.2 Virtual signal path for an Aux Input track. If any enabled auxiliary outputs are available from virtual instrument plug-ins in the session, they are also available as an input source.

Whatever the source of the audio, the controls on Audio and Aux Input tracks are otherwise very similar. The source might be audio data being read from disk, an audio input or bus being recorded and/or monitored on an Audio track, the selected audio input or bus being monitored on an Aux Input, or a software instrument operating via a Native or ReWire plug-in placed on the track's Inserts section. An Aux Input track has no Record button, of course, because it cannot contain audio clips. Either track type can be mono (one audio channel), stereo, or multichannel. If you insert a mono-to-stereo plug-in at any point on a mono Audio track or Aux Input, however, the remainder of its audio path becomes stereo, including both the subsequent insert slots and its main output stage. The main output from each Audio track or Aux Input can be assigned to one or more physical output paths or, again, to any of Pro Tools' internal mix busses. If you hold down the Control key (Start key in Windows) while choosing another destination from the pop-up selector, you can assign *additional* output destinations from the same track.

Instrument Tracks

Instrument tracks combine aspects of an Aux Input and a MIDI track. As seen in the Mix window, Instrument tracks look similar to Aux Inputs—with a keyboard icon that indicates their track type. However, like MIDI tracks, they have a Patch Select button and a Record Enable button for MIDI instead of audio. Instrument tracks also have an Audio Input Path selector. Many instrument plug-ins don't actually use this input audio signal, in which case this audio input path is simply cut off at the point where the instrument plug-in is instantiated in the track's signal chain. In the Edit window, however, Instrument tracks are treated much like MIDI tracks. (However, they offer audio-related view options in the Edit window, such as inserts, sends, and so on, that aren't available on a MIDI track. Also, in addition to MIDI controllers, audio parameters such as pan and volume can be graphically edited on an Instrument track, just as on an Aux Input.)

One of the main reasons the Instrument track feature was created was so that, for single-timbre instrument plug-ins, a single track can provide MIDI event display in the Edit window and a channel-strip view of its audio signal path in the Mix window. For multi-timbral plug-ins, however, it's common to route the MIDI outputs from multiple conventional MIDI tracks to the plug-in—whether it resides on an Instrument, Aux Input, or Audio track. (Even when instantiated on an Audio track, if you decide to render the output of the instrument plug-in to audio form—for instance, so that it's resultant signal would be available on any Pro Tools system—you would need to record it to a separate Audio track.)

The Instrument view can be enabled at the top of the Mix window for Instrument tracks. This view can also be displayed as a column at the left of the track display area in the Edit window. Controls in the Instrument view affect the active software instrument plug-in on an individual Instrument track. This view provides selectors for the track's MIDI input and output (allowing the Instrument track's MIDI data to be additionally routed to another destination), volume, pan, and mute, plus a small LED and velocity meter for MIDI data on the track. On an Instrument track, inserts and sends (which are covered in the next two sections) work identically to those on Aux Inputs and Audio tracks. (However, aside from the occasional instrument plug-in that actually uses the audio signal at the track's input, it doesn't make any sense to place any insert effects prior to the software instrument in the track's signal chain.)

Enable Audio Inputs on Your Instrument Tracks Some instrument plug-ins, such as DB-33, actually have the option to use the selected audio input for the Instrument track as part of their processing (although most won't). Nevertheless, you may find that even if you know the selected instrument plug-in doesn't use that source audio in any way, if you *don't* select some physical input on your interface—instead of None—the instrument plug-in won't sound.

Inserts

After each track's selected input (or disk-playback source, in the case of Audio tracks), the signal passes through 10 insert points. Effects can be placed on these inserts in the form of software modules (plug-ins). Alternatively, hardware I/O inserts can be spliced into these access points in the track's signal path, using physical inputs and outputs on the audio hardware to route the track's audio to and from external devices. (This is, of course, more practical on a multichannel audio interface that has plenty of available I/O.) On Audio tracks, Aux Inputs, and Instrument tracks, inserts are always *pre*-fader. This means that the level of the signal passing through the Inserts section is entirely unaffected by the track's main volume fader or volume automation. In contrast (as mentioned in Chapter 7), inserts on Master Faders are always *post*-fader.

A track's entire signal passes through each of the inserts, and each insert on the track affects the signal going to the next one in series. Pro Tools displays inserts in two groups of five—labeled "a" through "e" and "f" through "j"—for a total of 10 inserts per track. It is entirely possible to overload any one of these inserts and produce clipping if the output of an earlier insert is too hot.

Sends

As explained in Chapter 2, a *send* is an access point from which a track's audio can be routed to a secondary audio pathway, independent of the main output assignment for the track. In Pro Tools, 10 sends are available for each Audio, Aux Input, and Instrument track. Like inserts, the sends are organized into two groups of five: "a" through "e" and "f" through "j." Separate sections in the Mix and Edit windows allow you to enable display of these two send views separately. Mono or stereo sends are supported in all versions of Pro Tools (even from a mono source track); stereo sends incorporate a Pan slider. On HD systems and Pro Tools systems with Complete Production Toolkit, sends can also be created to multichannel paths. If the Follow Main Pan (FMP) button is enabled, the pan position of the send will follow that of the track's main Pan control.

The destination of each send might be a single physical audio output on your hardware (or a multiple output, if the send is to a stereo or multichannel path). Even more typical is to select a mono or stereo (or multichannel) bus within Pro Tools as the destination for a send. If the send is set to *pre*-fader (that is, its Pre button is enabled), the signal split is taken directly after the output of the Inserts section in the track's audio pathway. The level of a pre-fader send is therefore not affected by the main volume setting or Mute button on the track. In contrast, the level of a post-fader send (the default send type) is also reduced whenever the track's main volume fader is lowered, because it follows the fader in the track's signal path.

Typically, when you enable a new send in Pro Tools, its level is automatically set to the absolute minimum, –∞; no level is sent at all (although you can change this default in Preferences). In the Send window (which automatically opens when you create a send), you can drag the fader upward to increase the level being sent to its destination. At any time, you can Option-click (Alt-click in Windows) a send's level fader to set it directly to 0 dB. You can also Option-drag (or Alt-drag in Windows) to copy sends from one track to another.

The FMP button in the Send window links the pan setting of the send to the track's main panner. This is useful for setting up panning in cue mixes to reflect that of your main mix, for example. It's also handy when you want the send's position in the stereo bus that feeds a delay or reverb effect to match its position in the main stereo mix. Also, users with Pro Tools HD or the Complete Production Toolkit have access to the Copy to Send function, which copies either the current settings of the selected automation controls or their entire automation playlists to the specified sends. You can select from volume, pan, mute, and LFE automation to copy, which is especially useful when a send is used for a cue headphone mix. You can access the Copy to Send dialog function via the Edit > Automation menu command.

Again, a send's audio source can be either directly after the Inserts section of the source track on pre-fader sends (and therefore after any software instrument or ReWire channels in that track's signal path) or after the main track volume fader (and Mute button) on post-fader sends. Each option has its uses, as you will see elsewhere in this book. When you click any send to edit its parameters, its Send window opens (see Figure 9.3 for mono and stereo versions).

Busses

In Pro Tools, an *internal mix bus* is an audio pathway for moving audio around within the program's mixing environment. Among other things, you can use a bus as a sort of pipeline for routing audio signals from multiple inputs, track outputs, or sends to a common destination. Pro Tools 10 provides up to 256 busses. You can use busses individually in mono or as stereo pairs: 1–2, 3–4, 5–6, and so on. On systems with Pro Tools HD or the Complete Production Toolkit, you can also create multichannel bus paths—for surround mixing, among other things. Common uses of busses are reviewed in Chapter 7.

One use for busses is to create subgroups (known as "submasters" on a physical mixing console). For example, you might reassign the outputs from multiple drum tracks to bus pair 3–4 and then select that bus as the input for a stereo Aux Input. This lets you use a single fader to control the overall volume of the drums and provides stereo insert points where a single EQ or compressor plug-in could be applied across the entire stereo drum mix. This construct would be equally useful for stacks of backing vocals, for walls of backing guitars, or, in audio for video, for an entire foundation of sound effects and ambience.

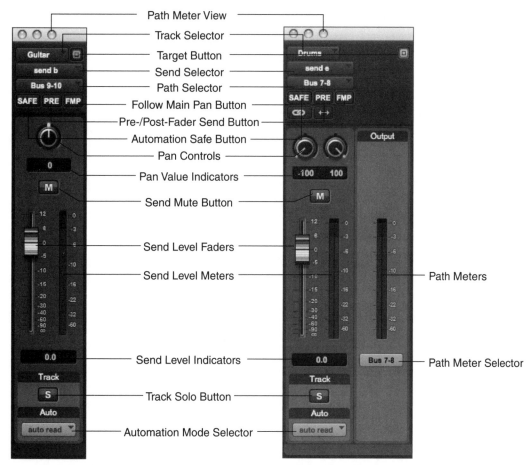

Figure 9.3 Send output windows mono (left) and stereo (right): Track selector (switches to other tracks, without leaving the window), Send selector (switches among 10 sends on the current track), and Path selector (the send's destination—busses or physical outputs). Solo and Automation Mode selector buttons for the source tracks are duplicated here. The Path Meter view is enabled in the stereo Send window (right).

Another possibility is to use busses like aux sends on a hardware mixing console: Sends from multiple tracks route a portion of their signals to a common audio pathway that in turn feeds either some effect like a delay or reverb or perhaps a cue mix. To do this in Pro Tools, you could select an internal bus path (previously defined in the I/O Setup dialog box) as the input for an Aux Input track where the delay or reverb effect has been inserted. Alternatively, the main audio output path of the Aux Input monitoring that bus could be the source of a performer's headphone mix out in the studio.

You can also use busses to route the output from an Aux Input to the input of an Audio track used for recording. A sidebar earlier in this chapter entitled "Input Sources for Audio Tracks" alludes to this possibility—using multiple Aux Input tracks to combine audio from several external MIDI modules before recording them to a stereo Audio track. (You might also do this with a single audio source to print it to disk with effects already incorporated.) Here's how to set up a record track to print the output of one or more Aux Input tracks:

1. Create one or more Aux Input tracks with the appropriate input sources selected.

2. Instantiate whatever plug-in effects are required.

3. Assign the main output from the Aux Input track(s) to a bus (either mono or a stereo pair, as appropriate).

4. Create a new mono/stereo Audio track, select this mono/stereo bus as its input, and click its Record Enable button.

5. To adjust the input recording level to the Audio track—perhaps because some of the plug-in effects you're using are altering the gain of the original input signal—simply use the main level fader on the Aux Input track or tracks that are feeding the Audio track.

The possibilities are immense, but keep in mind that essentially, a bus is nothing more than a convenient pathway for you to pass audio around inside Pro Tools. You can assign the output from any Audio, Aux Input, or Instrument track, or the destination of any send, to any bus, bus *pair* (if it's a stereo track output or send), or multichannel bus path (in Pro Tools HD) that has been defined in the I/O Setup dialog box. Of course, if no Aux Input (or Audio record track) is listening to the bus (because the bus hasn't yet been selected as the *input* to be monitored by anything), you won't hear it!

Clipping, Overload, and Distortion   *Clipping* is a form of distortion caused when the top of the audio waveform is cut off (clipped) because it reaches amplitude levels that exceed the capacity of the channel or device it is passing through. On some gear, like tube guitar amplifiers and magnetic tape recorders, a controlled amount of this kind of distortion can be desirable and warm sounding. But digital clipping is nasty, rude, and ugly—it should be avoided.

Audio tracks, Aux Input tracks, Instrument tracks, and Master Faders each have clipping indicators—the topmost red segment on their level meters. As a general rule, if you see any of these red indicators light up during playback, you should adjust your gain structure so that they don't. (Remember, if necessary you can use the Trim tool to scale any existing volume automation up or down.) Click a level meter to reset its clip indicator; Option-click (Alt-click in Windows) to reset the clip indicators on *all* tracks simultaneously. (Note: The behavior of the clip indicator can be changed in Preferences—for example, if you only want it to stay lit for three seconds after a peak is detected.)

Obviously, clipping is a critical issue while recording Audio tracks (many people advise keeping peak levels during recording to Pro Tools at −6 dB or below), but also be careful when using plug-in effects during mixdown that can increase gain—such as EQ and compression—and especially when routing multiple sends or track outputs to the same destination. Many of the DigiRack plug-ins (for dynamics and reverb, for example) include volume meters with clipping indicators within the plug-in window itself. Keep an eye on these!

So what can you do about an audio file that was recorded just below maximum level, when you need to use an EQ to brighten it—which will raise the audio file's level enough to clip? You have several possible solutions: Some EQ plug-ins, such as the DigiRack EQ III, provide

Input and Output level controls; if available, you can use these controls to attenuate the signal and avoid clipping, both within the plug-in and further down the signal chain. Alternatively, in Pro Tools 10 you can use clip gain to adjust the audio levels in the clip for pre-insert attenuation: Press Control+Shift+= (Mac) or Start+Shift+= (Windows) to display the Clip Gain Info view; then click on the Clip Gain Fader shown in the lower-left corner of the clip and drag downward to apply an appropriate gain reduction. The waveform will update in real time to reflect the change.

If neither of these options is available, you can use the Trim plug-in (found in the "Other" section of the Insert selector menu). Insert this plug-in before the EQ plug-in and adjust the Gain slider to apply an appropriate gain reduction.

Lastly, you might encounter an audio file that was recorded too hot and has clipping distortion inherent in the sound. There is rarely (if ever) a way to completely remove the effects of clipping distortion, but many plug-in offerings have functions to lessen the sonic effect of clipping. One very effective plug-in is part of the NoNOISE Audio Restoration suite by Sonic.

Master Faders

A Master Fader track controls the signal passing through either an output bus for a physical output path (mono, stereo, or multichannel) or one of the mono, stereo, or multichannel internal mix busses within the Pro Tools mixing environment. Master Faders have no sends and no Pan controls. Like Audio and Aux Input tracks, Master Fader tracks have 10 inserts, in two groups of five each. However, Master Fader inserts are *post-fader only*; the input level to these inserts will always be affected by the Master Fader's main volume fader. Master Faders are also convenient for placing post-fader plug-in effects or hardware inserts on the entire mix output, such as limiting, compression, EQ, and others, or *especially* dithering plug-ins (discussed in Chapter 16, "Bouncing to Disk, Other File Formats").

Because you can use a Master Fader as a final gain stage for the audio output path used for your mix output, it is a very convenient place to manage your final levels. For example, you will often create a stereo master fader for Outputs 1–2 on your audio interface (functioning as your main output pair). If you see levels clipping on this Master Fader—or conversely, if you see that they're too low—your solution might be as simple as adjusting the volume fader on that Master Fader track. Of course, another possible approach to taming the dynamics in your mix is to place a compressor, limiter, or some more sophisticated gain optimization plug-in on the Master Fader to affect the entire mix (such Maxim [included with Pro Tools], the multiband compressor in IK Multimedia's T-RackS, or one of the well-known maximizer plug-ins from Waves). As always, the best choice depends on the sound you're after. If you include a dithering plug-in on the Master Fader for your mix output (because you're bouncing or recording digitally to a lower bit depth), always make sure it's the *last* plug-in on the Master Fader.

About Master Faders on Bus or Output Paths   The Master Fader stage always exists in any bus or output path, regardless of whether the Master Fader control is currently visible as a track in Pro Tools. This is why creating additional Master Fader tracks has no effect on the DSP usage and almost no effect on the performance of your system. For audio routed to external destinations (for example, cue mixes and broadcast feeds), Master Faders can sometimes be more useful than Aux Inputs. Their exclusively post-fader inserts are also handy. More importantly, although the Path Metering view in the Send window is handy for internal mix busses, you will find that a good metering plug-in, such as the PhaseScope plug-in included in Pro Tools, is much more informative about the levels going through the bus when used as an insert on an associated Master Fader.

Output Channels

As with inputs, the potential number and type of output channels available to you (selectable as send destinations or track or mix outputs) depends on the audio interface used in your Pro Tools configuration. For many users, a stereo output pair is the source for mixes bounced to disk or recorded to DAT. When bouncing your final mix to disk, you use the Bounce dialog box to choose the stereo output (either a pair of physical outputs or a stereo bus pair) to use as the source for the bounced mix. For stereo mixing, you would generally use the same pair of physical audio outputs you've been monitoring during the edit process (that is, a stereo output *path*, configured in the I/O Setup dialog box). Some users record their mix in real time to another device instead of bouncing mix files to disk. For example, they might record their Pro Tools output digitally to a DAT. (Be sure to read about dithering plug-ins in Chapter 16.) In typical video post-production scenarios, real-time output from Pro Tools is used when performing a layback of mixed audio to master video tape—although with computer-based video-editing systems such as Avid Media Composer, Media 100, and FinalCut Pro, it's more common to bounce out a mix-down file or use the OMF interchange format for audio data.

For some situations, *direct-out routing* from individual tracks to output channels can also be handy. Each output channel on a multichannel audio interface can be assigned as the mono output path from individual tracks instead of routing all tracks to a common stereo output pair. A sidebar in Chapter 7 describes how to set these track assignments quickly. This setup can be useful when transferring an entire session to a multitrack tape recorder, for instance, or when you use an external mixing board for mixing and processing while Pro Tools essentially acts as a multitrack playback machine. Some post-production operators will assign many individual outputs from the Pro Tools audio interface to physical inputs on hardware-based digital surround mixers with dedicated joystick controllers. However, with the availability of surround encoding/decoding plug-ins for Pro Tools systems, such as Neyrinck's SoundCode, Dolby's Surround Tools, and SRS's Circle Tools (not to mention the joystick controllers on several Avid control surfaces), it is increasingly popular to create surround mixes completely within Pro Tools (in LCR, Quad, LCRS, 5.1, 6.1, and 7.1; for Dolby Surround/Pro Logic, Dolby Digital, DTS, and SDDS formats).

You can configure multichannel routing in Pro Tools using the I/O Setup dialog box. Multichannel tracks (for example, six channels for Dolby Digital 5.1) allow you to edit clips in their native multichannel format. Multichannel sends, Aux Input tracks, Instrument tracks, and Master Faders can also be created for any multichannel bus or output path. In the I/O Setup dialog box, you define main *paths*—logical groupings of input or output channels, inserts, or busses. This may be as simple as the main stereo output pair you use to monitor a mix, or six physical outputs on your audio interface that are your 5.1 path (the five surround speakers plus the LFE subwoofer channel). Each mono signal path that comprises a stereo or multichannel main path is known as a *subpath*. For example, even in stereo, the main output used for your mix consists of two mono subpaths—commonly Outputs 1 and 2—on your audio interface. After creating a new stereo or multichannel path, if you also want the option of individually addressing the subpaths within it, you would use the I/O Setup dialog box's New Subpath button to enable these. This might be handy, for instance, if you wanted the low-frequency effects (LFE) channel in a surround path to also be available as a send destination.

Plug-In Architectures

As explained in Chapter 2, a *plug-in* is a software component that acts as an add-in module for processing audio within Pro Tools or other digital audio workstations. Many Avid plug-ins are included with Pro Tools, such as the AudioSuite and DigiRack (RTAS) plug-ins provided with all systems and a similar DigiRack collection of TDM plug-ins provided with HD systems. There are also many plug-ins available from Avid and numerous other manufacturers for the TDM and RTAS plug-in architectures directly supported by Pro Tools through version 10.

Pro Tools 10 also introduces a new plug-in architecture with the AAX plug-in format. The AAX specification strives to unify development so that the same algorithm can run natively (on all systems) or with DSP hardware acceleration on Pro Tools|HDX systems. The AAX format will essentially replace RTAS and TDM plug-ins for future Pro Tools systems. The downside to the AAX format is that AAX plug-ins cannot utilize the DSP processors on existing Pro Tools|HD cards, meaning that operators running Pro Tools|HD hardware will either need to settle for running their AAX plug-ins in Native mode or upgrade to Pro Tools|HDX hardware.

Unlike AudioSuite plug-ins (which are *offline*, or rendered effects and save the results of their processing to an audio file), real-time plug-ins (AAX, RTAS, and TDM) can be placed into the virtual signal path of Pro Tools using any one of the 10 inserts provided for Audio tracks, Aux Inputs, Instrument tracks, and Master Faders. A track's audio signal passes through each insert in turn (from "a" through "j"), and therefore through any real-time plug-in effect placed at any of these insert locations.

Why AAX? The RTAS and TDM plug-in architectures are well established and highly supported in the industry, so why has Avid introduced the new AAX format? The basic answer is to provide a platform for transitioning Pro Tools to a 64-bit application. Like the RTAS format, AAX uses 32-bit floating-point data streams to pass audio around, for both Native and DSP systems (although internal processing can be done at 32 bits, 64 bits, 80 bits, or more). This is in contrast to the 24-bit fixed-point stream used by the TDM architecture (with internal processing done at 24 bits, 48 bits, or 56 bits).

The TDM specification was written for Macintosh computers in the early 1990s, when computer processors had a fraction of the power they harness today, hard drives were measured in megabytes, and black-and-white monitors were commonplace. The RTAS architecture was an add-on to the original specification, as was Windows compatibility. The specification has evolved over the years and has held up remarkably well. But the evolution of OS X and the fundamental structural incompatibilities with operation in a 64-bit host application environment led Avid to rewrite the plug-in specification.

Pro Tools|HDX hardware uses a floating-point architecture. Although Avid initially sought to add HDX support to the original TDM specification, this approach could not support the feature requests coming in from plug-in developers. Eventually Avid settled on the more aggressive approach of creating a new plug-in format to meet the needs and capabilities of modern (and future) computer systems. The AAX format enables the possibility of writing a single implementation of the algorithm that compiles to both the native and hardware-accelerated (DSP) versions.

Virtual Instrument Plug-Ins   Because this chapter is mainly concerned with signal flow and effects processing in Pro Tools, we discuss plug-ins specifically in that context. However, most software-based instruments are also used within Pro Tools as plug-ins (although some standalone applications that also contain software instruments communicate with Pro Tools via ReWire, such as Reason, Live, and GigaStudio 3). Instrument plug-ins are discussed in Chapter 10, "MIDI."

AudioSuite

AudioSuite effects are not real-time processes; they are file-based. After adjusting the effects parameters of an AudioSuite plug-in and using the Preview button in its window (if available) to hear a sample of how the current settings will affect the final audio, you can click the Render (Process) button. Generally, a new file is then created, wherein the effect is applied to whatever audio was selected. (If you wish, the results of the processing can instead be destructively written over the data in the original file.) Many Avid plug-ins are available both as offline AudioSuite processes and AAX, RTAS, and/or TDM real-time effects. This can be useful if you need to conserve your real-time DSP resources by printing effect treatments to new disk files. Figure 9.4 shows the AudioSuite window and the parameters for the Normalize process (which includes an RMS mode, in addition to the traditional Peak mode for calculating target gain levels).

Figure 9.4   The AudioSuite window for the Normalize function.

RTAS (Real-Time AudioSuite) and AAX Native

The Real-Time AudioSuite (RTAS) plug-in architecture was developed by Digidesign for Pro Tools in the late '90s. More recently, Avid developed the AAX plug-in architecture for Pro Tools 10 and beyond, supporting both Native and DSP processing. RTAS and AAX Native plug-ins operate in real time as insert effects on Audio tracks, Aux Input tracks, Instrument tracks, or Master Faders. DigiRack plug-ins in RTAS/AAX format are provided with Pro Tools and Pro Tools HD software. (Some of these are also available as non–real-time effects that process audio files, under the AudioSuite menu.)

RTAS and AAX Native plug-ins are *host based*; that is, they rely on the computer's CPU for their effects-processing power rather than relying on specialized DSP chips on a card within the computer (as is the case with TDM plug-ins used in Pro Tools|HD systems). In addition to the DigiRack plug-ins for RTAS/AAX included with Pro Tools, many more RTAS/AAX plug-ins are available from Avid and third-party manufacturers. Like TDM plug-ins, you can enable many parameters of an RTAS/AAX Native plug-in for automation by clicking the Auto button within its plug-in window, allowing you to build up some very complex and interesting mixes. For example, you might automate the feedback parameter on a delay plug-in to change the number of repeats at different locations in a song. Lastly, many virtual instrument plug-ins are also offered in RTAS format. These can be used as the sound sources for data in MIDI and Instrument tracks in Pro Tools. The Click plug-in that provides a metronome sound (typically inserted on an Aux Input track) is also a sort of rudimentary RTAS instrument plug-in. Figure 9.5 shows a typical plug-in window.

Maximizing Native Plug-In Capacity   To maximize host-based processing power, you should disable or quit any other system tasks (background processes, energy savers or "sleep" functions, other open programs, and so on) that compete with Pro Tools for access to the computer's CPU. Here are a few more tips:

■ The capacity of your system to handle large numbers of simultaneous Native plug-ins (especially more intensive types such as reverbs and software instruments) is proportional to the size of the hardware buffer (set via Setup > Playback Engine). Because host-based systems exclusively support Native plug-ins, this is an important system-performance issue. This setting can also affect Pro Tools HD users who rely heavily on

Native plug-ins, such as software instruments. (Like some reverbs, software instruments tend to be processor-intensive.) If you start hearing choppy playback or get a "CPU is too busy" message, try increasing this setting. (The message "CPU usage is holding off USB audio" may also require an increase to the hardware buffer size.) On host-based systems, however, larger buffer sizes can increase monitoring latency during recording and the response time of software instruments to real-time MIDI input, which can negatively affect timing of performances.

- For host computers with two or more processors, the Host Processors selection in the Playback Engine dialog box allows you to assign more than one CPU to Native processing.

- The CPU Usage Limit selector in the Playback Engine dialog box can be set as high as 99% on some systems. However, on slower systems, the highest setting may affect video playback or screen response. Otherwise, the high settings are usually desirable when using a lot of Native plug-ins.

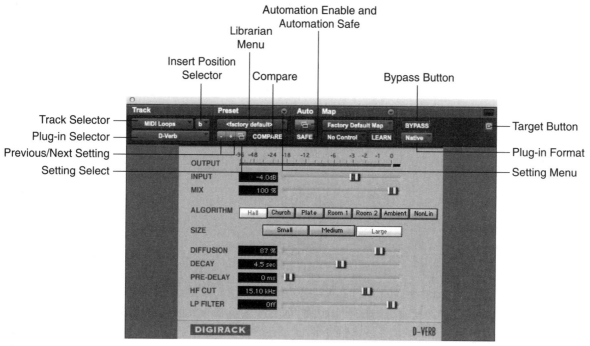

Figure 9.5 Plug-in windows have these common controls. Seen here: D-Verb, which Pro Tools provides in Native, DSP, and AudioSuite formats.

Using Native Plug-Ins in Pro Tools HD   Native plug-ins are compatible with standard and HD versions of Pro Tools. The basic set of DigiRack RTAS/AAX Native plug-ins is also included with Pro Tools HD software (in addition to their DSP versions).

On HD systems, for most DigiRack plug-ins, the Plug-In window will have a Convert Plug-In button that switches the current DSP plug-in to its Native counterpart (if available) or vice versa. Look for a small inverted triangle to the right of the DSP or Native text and the

Target icon (as seen in Figure 9.5). For DigiRack plug-ins, switching from DSP processing to host-based Native processing is a possible strategy if you ever max out the available DSP resources on your HD or HDX cards. As a general rule, to avoid excessive use of playback voices, you should avoid placing DSP plug-ins between two Native plug-ins in the same track. Also, be aware that sidechaining on a Native plug-in uses an extra voice.

TDM (Time-Division Multiplexing), TDM II

TDM is a high-performance effects-processing and signal-routing architecture, introduced by Digidesign for Pro Tools in the early 1990s. (A redesigned version, with much more robust capabilities, was introduced in 2002 with the high-resolution Pro Tools|HD hardware family. Although this technically is known as "TDM II," for the sake of simplicity we simply refer to TDM plug-ins and architecture.) Unlike AudioSuite and RTAS/AAX Native architectures (which can be used concurrently with the TDM option), TDM enables the use of specialized HD hardware, providing a more stable platform that is less dependent on the host CPU and provides better support for demanding signal-routing and processing capabilities in expanded, high-resolution systems. Specifically, the HD Core and Accel (or HD Process) cards in Pro Tools|HD systems all contain DSP (*digital signal processing*) chips, which are required to support TDM processing.

By using these hardware resources to support its audio-processing needs, TDM doesn't exclusively depend on the processing power of the computer's CPU (which also supports the operating system and other tasks, including the Pro Tools program itself) in order to process audio in real time. Plug-in developers can count on this hardware-based DSP capacity when creating more calculation-intensive effects-processing algorithms, often achieving sonically superior results. Also, the monitoring latency during recording (the delay between the selected source and when it is heard back out through the mixer) is less significant on TDM systems than on host-based systems. Most importantly, the processing latency induced by each TDM plug-in can be compensated for automatically by the Pro Tools software. (For the standard DigiRack TDM plug-ins, this is usually about 3–4 samples at the session's sample rate, but some other plug-ins have much greater amounts of latency.) Some plug-ins are available exclusively in TDM format—both effects plug-ins and software instruments such as Access Virus Indigo and others. TDM-based Pro Tools systems support a larger number of voices and I/O channels than non-TDM configurations, as well as audio hardware expansion through the addition of multiple audio interfaces. Figure 9.6 shows an example of a reverb TDM plug-in for HD systems, while Figure 9.7 shows a dynamics processing plug-in available in both TDM and RTAS formats.

About HTDM Plug-Ins (Discontinued) HTDM plug-ins were used on 24|Mix and HD systems with software versions prior to Pro Tools 7. They are *not* supported in any current versions. Like RTAS plug-ins, HTDM plug-ins relied on the processing power of the host computer's CPU to carry out their tasks, although they were instantiated and routed within the TDM environment. When you open an older session containing HTDM plug-ins, where possible these are automatically converted to their Native equivalents.

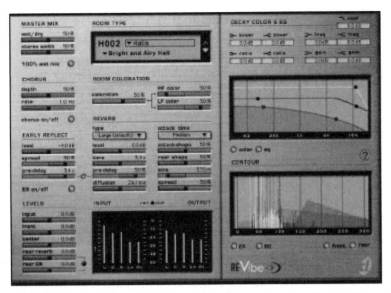

Figure 9.6   ReVibe, a TDM reverb plug-in for Pro Tools|HD systems only.

Figure 9.7   Smack!, a TDM/RTAS compressor/limiter plug-in, supports multichannel tracks and can emulate tube and analog tape saturation with second- and third-order harmonic distortion.

Duplicating Plug-Ins   You can Option-drag (Alt-drag in Windows) plug-ins (and inserts) to copy them from one track to another, along with their current settings, *if* the source and destination tracks have the same number of channels. Also, if you hold down the Option key (Alt key in Windows) as you assign a plug-in on an Audio track, it will simultaneously be created in the same insert slot on all other Audio tracks with the same number of channels. (You can also use this shortcut to simultaneously assign the same plug-in on multiple Aux Inputs.) Bear in mind, though, that the digital-signal-processing resources have a practical limit, even on more powerful Pro Tools systems. You will often *instantiate* (that is, create instances of) equalization or compression plug-ins, which typically make relatively small demands on your system's processing power, on numerous Audio tracks. However, it is usually more DSP-efficient (and simpler to manage) if you place delays and reverbs on Aux Inputs, using these as a common send destination from multiple source tracks.

AAX DSP Plug-Ins

Like TDM plug-ins, AAX DSP plug-ins rely on processing provided by DSP chips on cards added to the host computer. However, AAX DSP plug-ins are not supported on Pro Tools|HD hardware. Instead, they require Pro Tools|HDX hardware for their processing power.

AAX DSP plug-ins provide all the advantages of TDM plug-ins in the newer, HDX-compatible format.

Wrapped Plug-Ins

Wrapper programs allow for the use of plug-ins that were originally created for one architecture—for example, VST—within a different architecture, such as RTAS for Pro Tools (or Apple's Audio Units plug-in format). One excellent example is the VST-to-RTAS Adapter for Mac/Windows by FXpansion. This wrapper supports a great number of VST effects plug-ins, plus various VST virtual instrument plug-ins.

When available, wrapped plug-ins appear as a separate category when you open an Insert selector menu for Pro Tools (and the AudioSuite menu, if applicable for that particular plug-in). Although you may encounter occasional stability issues with wrapped plug-ins used as real-time effects in channels, having the ability to tap into the vast network of VST plug-ins being created by the worldwide music and programming community can be worth the potential inconvenience. One way to deal with instability issues is to insert a wrapped plug-in on the desired channel, tweak its settings to your liking, and then permanently apply the effect to the chosen audio files by using the Bounce function (File > Bounce To > Disk) or other printing/rendering technique.

Multiple Outputs from Software Instrument Plug-Ins   In addition to the main output from a software instrument plug-in that passes on through the signal chain in its host track, plug-ins with multiple output capabilities allow you to enable mono or stereo auxiliary outputs. Whenever any of these are active in a session, they appear as options in the Track Input selector for Audio and Aux Input tracks (mono or stereo, as appropriate). For example, you could route the drum parts from the Strike plug-in (available in the Pro Tools Instrument Expansion Pack) through a separate Aux Input track, where distinct reverb or compression treatments can be applied without affecting the other instrumental parts played by the plug-in through its main track output.

Plug-In Effects

In addition to the DigiRack plug-ins included with all versions of Pro Tools, many more are available from Avid and third parties. The Avid website provides updated information about the plug-ins available for the various Pro Tools versions. These range from familiar effects, such as reverb, delay, dynamics, processing, EQ, and so on, to much more exotic processes. To provide a little context, this section briefly reviews what digital signal processing is and groups audio-processing effects into a few very broad categories.

About Digital Signal Processing (DSP)

For the purposes of Pro Tools users, *digital signal processing* means the use of special computational algorithms to alter the data that represents audio waveforms. These algorithms can simulate classic analog audio-processing devices, such as equalizers (which change the frequency content of the original material); dynamics processors, such as compressors, expanders, and limiters (which alter the level of the audio over time in response to loudness changes in the original signal or some secondary source assigned as the key input); delay and modulated delay effects (which reproduce some or all of the original signal at some later point in time); and so on. Other plug-ins simulate actual devices, such as tube amplifiers and analog tape. Many others provide special effects that are hard to categorize.

Categories of Audio Effects

Many effect types can be grouped into several simple categories. Plug-ins appear within hierarchical submenus according to their category (as assigned by the plug-in manufacturer); they can also be subgrouped by manufacturer, if you enable that option in Preferences. The grouping used in this chapter is much more general, however, and does not correspond to the categories used in the Pro Tools menu. Although many variants exist within each effect category (and many plug-ins exist that combine aspects of various categories), this overview simply provides a conceptual framework. We are primarily concerned with effects plug-ins here, so we don't discuss noise-reduction, software instruments, tuners, metering, and other tools that are also implemented via plug-ins in Pro Tools. For experienced audio professionals, most of this will be review. However, some of the Pro Tools–specific aspects mentioned here are worth keeping in mind for all users.

Frequency-Based Effects

These processors affect the frequency content of the audio input, usually by increasing or decreasing the gain (level) in various frequency ranges. Equalization, or EQ, is the most common frequency-based effect; Figure 9.8 shows an example of an EQ plug-in. Two main types of equalizers are common:

- **Parametric EQ.** These are so named because the characteristics of one or several bands of boost/cut are adjusted based on various *parameters*, such as the amount of boost/cut (gain setting), the center frequency of the affected frequency band, and the curve with which the amount of boost/cut decreases at frequencies progressively farther from the band's center frequency. (Known as the slope, or Q, this describes the shape of the curve of boost/cut around that band's center frequency.)

- **Graphic EQ.** This type of EQ divides the frequency spectrum into a fixed number of bands and allows you to boost or cut each frequency band. When the individual bands correspond to octaves or subdivisions of an octave, as is common, the absolute frequency range of each band gets progressively larger because each higher octave is double the frequency of the previous one. Traditional graphic equalizers were essentially banks of band-pass filters at set frequencies and a fixed Q. The volume sliders for each frequency band provide a graphical view of how the frequency spectrum is being altered.

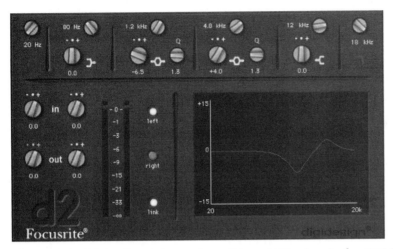

Figure 9.8 D2 by Focusrite, a 4- or 6-band EQ plug-in for TDM.

Gain-Based Effects

Dynamics processors apply gain changes (affecting the amplitude of the audio waveform) to the original audio signal over time. Examples include compressors, limiters, expanders, gates, and de-essers. You can use these processors in many ways to decrease or increase the dynamic range of the input audio. Figure 9.9 provides two examples of compression plug-ins:

- **Compressors.** Compressors (and limiters) are often used to reduce peak levels in an Audio track so that the entire track's level can be increased for a louder, in-your-face sound

Figure 9.9 Two compressor plug-ins from Avid: the DigiRack Dynamics III compressor included with all versions and the optional Impact mix-bus compressor for Pro Tools HD.

throughout the track (usually essential in contemporary music mixes for bass, guitars, and vocals, for example). A compressor reduces the signal level by a specified ratio whenever it exceeds the threshold setting. (A limiter completely prevents the audio from exceeding a specified threshold, like a compressor with an extremely high ratio.)

- **Expanders.** Expanders do the opposite: Audio levels *beneath* a specified threshold are further reduced, again by a specified ratio. Expanders can be useful for decreasing noise from guitar pickups or amplifiers between phrases or room noise between sentences during a voiceover. A *gate* is like an expander at an extremely high ratio—any audio levels under the threshold are completely closed off by the gate (which might be very handy for drums leaking into neighboring microphones, for example).

A *de-esser* is technically a specialized type of compressor. Instead of reacting to the entire frequency range of the input signal to determine how much gain reduction to apply, only a narrow frequency band—adjustable within a range roughly corresponding to "s" sounds in the human voice—is used as the key input for the compression effect, which then acts upon the full frequency range of the input signal. By using a de-esser to clamp down on a track's level where prominent "s" and "ch" sounds occur in a voice, for example, you can apply more high-frequency boost to the track in general without this sibilance becoming too noticeable. Like any other effect, however, de-essers also have other creative uses—for example, controlling sibilance on vocal sends before they enter a reverb or reducing finger squeaks on an acoustic guitar.

The amount of gain change applied by a dynamics processor is typically based on the level changes within the input audio itself. Alternatively, gain changes on a current track can be keyed by level variations within a completely different audio source. This technique is called *sidechaining*. To sidechain (or *key*) a dynamics plug-in in Pro Tools, activate its External Key mode (if it offers this feature) and designate some other Pro Tools bus (to which you have routed a send from another track) or input path as the key source. This could be handy with a compressor for slightly *ducking* (reducing) the level of background music (or rhythm guitars, in a rock mix) whenever the voice is present. You could also use a kick drum track to key an expander, using a slight amount of expansion to make the bass guitar bump a little harder with each beat of the kick drum.

Time-Based Effects

Delays store all or some of the input signal and then reproduce it at a later time. Sometimes, a portion of the delayed signal is re-routed back to the input to be delayed again. (This is called *regeneration* or *feedback* and can be used to create multiple repeats, or echoes.) For plug-ins, as a general rule, longer delays require more processing power than shorter ones to store and process a potentially longer amount of delayed audio in digital memory.

Modulated delays additionally apply a varying amount of change to the delay time, usually controlled by the values of a low-frequency oscillator, or *LFO* (or its software equivalent). You can adjust the frequency of the LFO as well as the degree of effect it has on the amount of delay. When such an oscillation is applied to very short delays, which are then mixed with the original audio, a characteristic sweeping, comb-filtered sound is produced, especially when the Feedback (regeneration) value is increased. This is the basis of so-called *chorus* and *flange* effects, whose base delay times may be 20–30 or 2–10 milliseconds, respectively, and may also incorporate multiple simultaneous delays and/or polarity inversion.

Figure 9.10 shows one example of such a processor. The effect can be even more dramatic if differing delay times and/or modulation speeds are applied in the left and right channels. Pro Tools includes Native Chorus and Flanger plug-ins among its real-time effects, under the Modulation category. Novice Pro Tools users should be wary of overusing chorus and flanging on rock and pop rhythm tracks, however. As many a rock guitarist or bassist will attest, these tend to soften or diffuse the visceral impact of the track to which they're applied—which may or may not be desirable, according to the musical style.

Figure 9.10   Instant Flanger, by Eventide, is part of the Anthology II bundle for TDM.

In current versions of Pro Tools, the Medium Delay II, Long Delay II, and Extra Long Delay II plug-ins (varieties of the DigiRack Mod Delay II) can be synced to the session tempo. This lets you easily set delay times to specific rhythmic intervals (musical note values) without making any calculations—sometimes a good idea for music projects, especially with multiple delay repeats. This tempo-syncing feature is enabled or disabled by a button in the plug-in window that looks like a metronome.

Note   The Mod Delay III plug-in, included with Pro Tools 10, provides the same functions as the DigiRack Mod Delay II plug-ins in a single, modern plug-in interface.

Reverb Effects

Reverberation is technically another type of time-based effect. In practice, though, it's complex enough to merit its own heading because it involves aspects of all the preceding categories. In technical terms, *reverb* is the persistence of a sound within an acoustical space—that is, multiple reflected sound waves that continue after the original sound has ceased.

Reverb processors simulate the reverberant characteristics of an acoustic space—the myriad reflections/delays and persistence of ambient sound following the original sound, early reflections, resonances, and other acoustical aspects of the environment. Various spaces can be modeled (halls, rooms, cathedrals, and so on), as well as classic electronic reverb units (plate, spring) and special-effect reverb types (non-linear, gated, reverse, and others). Most sophisticated reverb processors include elements similar to delays (for introducing pre-delay prior to the reverberation, or early reflections) and EQ (for high-frequency damping and tailoring the resonances of the modeled reverberant space). In fact, for many mixes, the reverb can often have more influence over the mix's overall character than any other single effect processor, especially as it is applied to the snare or lead vocal track in rock or dance mixes.

Compared to most compressor, EQ, and delay plug-ins, though, reverb is a much more intensive form of digital signal processing. It consequently makes greater demands on the processing power of your CPU (or the DSP chips on the cards of your Pro Tools|HD or Pro Tools|HDX system). D-Verb is included with all Pro Tools systems, but other more sophisticated or specialized reverbs are available from third parties (the ReVibe room-modeling reverb for Pro Tools|HD and VENUE systems, and Reverb One for TDM). One of these is shown in Figure 9.11.

Figure 9.11 Altiverb, by Audio Ease, is a convolution reverb plug-in for TDM, RTAS, and other plug-in formats.

Note   Avid plans to release both ReVibe and Reverb One as Native AAX plug-ins in the near future.

Pitch-Based Effects

Pitch plug-in processors apply real-time pitch changes to the input audio. Some pitch-based processors provide a fixed amount of pitch transposition (for example, an octave up or down, or just a few cents—1/100 of a semitone—in order to achieve more subtle doubling effects through detuning). Other more sophisticated pitch-based processors offer more intelligent correction within a specific musical scale, such as Antares Auto-Tune, shown in Figure 9.12.

Modeling Effects

Some effects emulate an existing physical device (or, sometimes, one that could never exist). Although these processes certainly involve frequency, dynamics, and time-based elements, the overall result is much more complex. Examples of physical modeling among digital plug-ins and processors include simulators for guitar effects and amplifiers (such as the Eleven plug-in, shown in Figure 9.13), speaker cabinets, rotary speakers, microphones, tube preamplifiers, tape saturation, classic mixing board channels, previously existing hardware effects, and so on.

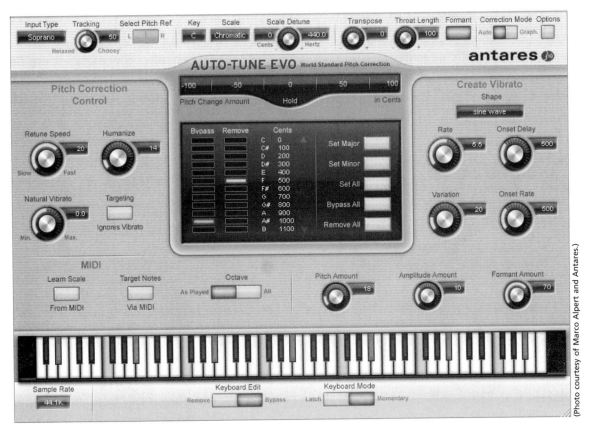

Figure 9.12 Auto-Tune EVO, by Antares: a pitch-processing plug-in for TDM or RTAS.

Figure 9.13 Eleven, by Avid: an amp-simulation plug-in.

Other: Special FX

Many special effects defy categorization. For example, phase shifters, vocoders, and exciters (such as the one that appears in Figure 9.14) incorporate aspects of several of the preceding categories, making them hard to pin down. Other effects are just too odd to classify (and that's why we love 'em!). For example, the D-Fi plug-in bundle from Avid includes Sci-Fi (various combinations of effects related to ring modulation and resonance), Lo-Fi (a sort of digital bit crusher and distorter), Recti-Fi (harmonic processing, additive synthesis effects, and rectification), and Vari-Fi (vari-speed effects, including changes over time). Vocoders are another type of effect that combine characteristics from many categories. Avid's Bruno and Reso for TDM offer cross-synthesis, with time-slicing and resonance effects. Various stereo imaging plug-ins are available, including the S1 and PS22 Stereomaker plug-ins from Waves.

Figure 9.14 MaxxBass, by Waves: a psycho-acoustic bass extension plug-in.

Plug-Ins Included with Pro Tools

With current versions of Pro Tools, Avid includes a vast collection of plug-ins. These include the DigiRack plug-ins, the Creative Collection plug-ins from Avid's Advanced Instrument Research (AIR) group, and various plug-ins acquired by Avid from third parties, such as Bombfactory and Trillium Lane Labs. The following list of plug-ins comes with standard Pro Tools and Pro Tools HD software.

- **Frequency-based effects:** AIR Kill EQ, EQ 3 1-Band, EQ 3 4-Band, EQ 3 7-Band, Channel Strip

- **Gain-based effects:** Bombfactory BF76, Compressor/Limiter Dyn 3, De-Esser Dyn 3, Expander/Gate Dyn 3, Maxim, Gain (AudioSuite only), Normalize (AudioSuite only), Trim, Channel Strip

- **Time-based effects:** AIR Dynamic Delay, AIR Multi-Delay, Extra Long Delay 2, Long Delay 2, Medium Delay 2, Short Delay 2, Slap Delay 2, Mod Delay 2 (AudioSuite only), Multi-Tap Delay (AudioSuite only), Ping-Pong Delay (AudioSuite only)

- **Reverb effects:** IR Non-Linear Reverb, AIR Reverb, AIR Spring Reverb, D-Verb.

- **Pitch-shift effects:** AIR Frequency Shifter, Pitch-Shift (AudioSuite only), Time-Shift (Audio-Suite only), Vari-Fi (AudioSuite only).

- **Modulation effects:** AIR Chorus, AIR Ensemble, AIR Filter Gate, AIR Flanger, AIR Fuzz-Wah, AIR Multi-Chorus, AIR Phaser, AIR Talkbox, AIR Vintage Filter, Sci-Fi, Chorus (AudioSuite only), Flanger (AudioSuite only).

- **Harmonic effects:** AIR Distortion, AIR Enhancer, AIR Fuzz-Wah, AIR Lo-Fi, Lo-FI, Recti_Fi, SansAmp PSA-1, Eleven Free.

- **Instrument effects:** BFD Lite, Boom, D8-33, MelodyneEssential, Mini Grand, Structure Free, Vacuum, Xpand![2].

- **Sound field effects:** AIR Stereo Width, PhaseScope (stereo only), TL AutoPan, BF Essential Meter Bridge, BF Essential Noise Meter, BF Essential Correlation (stereo only), TL MasterMeter

- **Additional effects:** Click, TL Metro, TimeAdjuster Long, TimeAdjuster Medium, TimeAdjuster Short, Dither, POWr Dither, Signal Generator, TL InTune, BNR (DINR Broadband Noise Reduction), BF Essential Clip Remover (AudioSuite only), DC Offset Removal (AudioSuite only), Duplicate (AudioSuite only), Invert (AudioSuite only), Reverse (AudioSuite only), Time Compression Expansion

Note that the Advanced Instrument Research (AIR) plug-ins currently bundled with Pro Tools are not available as AudioSuite plug-ins. For guidance in using the plug-ins, Avid offers various manuals, such as the *Audio Plug-ins Guide*, in the Support section of its website (also included in the documentation installed with Pro Tools).

Making a Plug-In Inactive   Every plug-in window has a Bypass button, which allows input audio to pass through without any processing applied. (Hardware I/O inserts cannot be bypassed from within Pro Tools.) To bypass any plug-in directly from the Mix window, Command-click (Ctrl-click in Windows) its plug-in button in the Inserts section. However, even in Bypass mode, the plug-in is still in the signal chain and utilizes the same proportion of your system's DSP resources. (On HD systems, the Show System Usage window provides an overview of how the DSP resources on your PCI cards are currently allocated to plug-ins, mixing, and other Pro Tools tasks.)

To make a plug-in *completely* inactive, thereby freeing up its demands on your system's resources, right-click its insert button and use the Make Inactive command in the pop-up menu. Alternatively, you can hold down the Command+Control keys (Ctrl+Start keys in Windows) as you click the plug-in's button. As opposed to simply removing the plug-in from the track, making it inactive retains its current settings for whenever you choose to reactivate it. Use the same key combination to make a plug-in active again.

Third-Party Plug-In Developers

Avid offers various additional plug-ins for purchase, including the Focusrite plug-ins that Avid distributes. Separate plug-in guides explain how to use each of these Avid-distributed plug-ins. These documents are available on the Avid website.

In addition to Avid, many other companies offer plug-ins that are compatible with TDM or RTAS architectures—for example, DUY, URS, Waves, Antares, TC|Works, Sonic Solutions, Native Instruments, Aphex, Serato, Arturia, Line 6, Trillium, Audio Ease, IK Multimedia, Synchro Arts, Sound Toys, Sonnox (formerly Sony), Serato, iZotope, Roger Nichols Digital, Massenburg Design Works, Drawmer, and McDSP, to name a few. The Products > Plug-Ins section of the Avid website will help you seek them out.

Tips for Using Sends (to External I/O, PT Busses, and Aux Inputs)

When it comes to effects processing and building a creative mix, you should of course feel free to break all the rules! However, to avoid some of the common pitfalls and to get a good start on designing a coherent soundscape, keep these basic rules in mind when using sends to route audio from Pro Tools tracks to a secondary destination:

- As a general rule, unless they're unique to a single track, delays and reverbs are better placed on Aux Inputs; it's typical to create sends from multiple Audio tracks to common delay or reverb destinations. This also simplifies controlling the mix of the wet signal (processed effects) to dry audio. Plus you get a more efficient use of your system's DSP resources by sending multiple tracks to one reverb, for example, rather than using multiple separate reverbs, one on each track. Even if running out of DSP power isn't a concern, using one or several common reverb destinations for multiple tracks can be the glue that helps a mix hang together. It contributes to the impression that the sounds all share a common space. When you're overdubbing multiple parts and need some help making them sound cohesive, keep this in mind—it can make a big difference.

- Be mindful of clipping when sending audio from multiple tracks to a common bus. If you find the clipping indicators on your Aux Inputs (used for effects plug-ins) lighting up, reduce the send levels from each track (and remember that you can use the Trim tool to scale down any existing send automation). Pro Tools offers two tools that are especially useful for monitoring the busses you're using for sends. First, by clicking the Path Meter View button in any send's Output window, a side level meter will display, giving you an idea of the levels in the destination bus. Second, you can create a Master Fader for any bus path in Pro Tools. This gives you a full-size track level meter in the Mix window and also allows you to instantiate PhaseScope or some other sophisticated metering plug-in on the Master Fader to determine exactly what your levels are.

- Sometimes sends are routed to physical outputs (for external effects processors, cue mixes for performers, and other uses). Watch your gain structure here as well. Creating a Master Fader for the physical output path is a good way to monitor its levels.

- If required, signals can pass through more than one bus path within Pro Tools. Here's one example: Say you create a send from a track that should eventually pass through some reverb or delay plug-in placed on an Aux Input (with a bus selected as its input). For the effect you want, however, you'd like one track's audio to be filtered before it hits the delay, while audio sent from other tracks to the same delay should *not* be filtered. To achieve this, you can set the source track's send destination to a separate bus, create a second Aux Input track that monitors that bus as its input, and place the EQ on that Aux Input. Then assign the output of that second Aux Input to the bus already selected as the input source for the Aux Input where the delay or reverb is inserted.

- Lastly, don't overlook the Follow Main Pan (FMP) button in the Send window. This links the send's panner to the main panner of the track itself.

ReWire

ReWire is a standard for real-time routing of digital audio between separate programs. The ReWire protocol was developed by Propellerhead Software (the manufacturers of Reason). Compatible ReWire programs, such as Reason (shown in Figure 9.15), can be slaved to Pro Tools so that they follow the Pro Tools tempo and Transport functions. After instantiating the ReWire plug-in in Pro Tools (on an Aux Input, Instrument track, *or* Audio track), you can select the virtual audio channels coming from the ReWire application that you want to stream into Pro Tools. From that point, those channels are subject to the same options for plug-in processing, mix automation, and send routing as any other input signal passing through a track. Many users will find it convenient to instantiate ReWire plug-ins on Instrument tracks (even though no instrument plug-in is enabled on the track). That way, not only is it immediately clear from the track's Mix window icon that this mixer strip represents an instrumental sound source, but you can also use

Figure 9.15 You can integrate Reason's audio outputs into the Pro Tools environment by instantiating the ReWire plug-in.

the Instrument track's MIDI functionality in the Edit window to record and edit a MIDI performance for the ReWire destination.

ReWire Programs and Voice Allocation in Pro Tools   On DSP-based systems, each ReWire channel you enable on an Audio track occupies one voice out of your system's total pool of voices for audio playback. This is *not* the case when the ReWire plug-in is enabled on Aux Input or Instrument tracks of host-based systems, however. Depending on how the slaved ReWire application is used—especially considering that several of them support not only virtual instruments but long samples and Audio tracks—this may allow you to get more out of host-based Pro Tools systems without compromising the available voices.

Additionally, many ReWire applications include their own virtual instruments (for example, Reason includes synthesizers, samplers, and programmable drum machines, and GigaStudio 3 [discontinued] provides a sampler instrument with many other features). When a slaved ReWire application is detected, you can choose any of its instruments as output destinations from your MIDI tracks within Pro Tools.

Any ReWire setup requires one program to act as the master and another as the slave—being controlled via the other program's transport and tempo and also relying on the other program for access to the audio hardware and mixing environment. Some programs—including the current version of Apple's GarageBand, many MIDI sequencers, and Pro Tools itself—must be the ReWire "master" (or "host") program and therefore can't be slaved via ReWire. Examples of ReWire applications that *can* work in slave mode with Pro Tools include the following:

■ **Reason.** Virtual instruments, effects, mixing, and sequencing, from Propellerhead Software. A limited-feature version, Reason Adapted, was formerly bundled with certain Pro Tools configurations.

■ **Live.** Sophisticated looping tools, recording, mixing, and effects, from Ableton; available for both Mac and Windows.

■ **Soundminer.** Catalog-management and auditioning tool for audio files, from Soundminer.

■ **GigaStudio 3 (discontinued).** A sampler program for Windows from Tascam that includes sample streaming from disk, sequencing, mixing, convolution effects, custom sample recording, and mapping.

Getting the Most Out of Available DSP

When you don't have an unlimited budget for upgrading your system, in complex Pro Tools sessions, you may eventually get one of those dreaded messages from Pro Tools, such as "CPU is too busy" or "CPU usage is holding off USB audio" when using a USB-based interface, meaning that you've reached the limit of your system's resources. At that point, you have several potential solutions. The first thing to look at is whether you're using the routing and plug-in processing of Pro Tools in the most efficient manner. Most of us add effects and sends on an ad-hoc basis during the editing process. Once a session becomes sufficiently large and complex, it can definitely be worth taking a moment to reexamine your signal routing and processing configuration. Making improvements might even make the final mix much easier.

Here are some strategies to try if you ever slam into this limit on your projects:

- Check your CPU Usage Limit setting (under Setup > Playback Engine). Though increasing this setting might slow down screen redraws on slower computers, the tradeoff might just be enough to get your project finished and bounced to disk!

- On multiprocessor systems using a lot of Native plug-ins, open the Playback Engine dialog box from the Setup menu and confirm that the Host Processors parameter is set to take maximum advantage of the available processors.

- Try increasing the value for the Hardware Buffer Size, under Setup > Playback Engine. Higher settings allow more intensive use of Native plug-ins. The tradeoff here is an increase in monitoring latency; however, if you are finished tracking, that may not present a concern.

- Pro Tools|HD systems have a selector for Number of Voices in the Setup > Playback Engine dialog box. Setting this to a lower number (although still high enough to support the voices required by your mono, stereo, and multichannel Audio tracks and signal routing, of course) also frees up some processing power for plug-ins.

- Where appropriate, try placing a single instance of a plug-in on an Aux Input used as submix destination for multiple tracks instead of placing similar plug-ins on each individual track. For example, if you have four or five backing vocal tracks, instead of putting a compressor on each one, route all their outputs to a single stereo bus and then place a compressor on the stereo Aux Input monitoring that bus. You might even find that this makes the parts sound tighter once a single dynamic shape is uniformly affecting them all.

- Bear in mind that every active bus, send, and hardware insert also uses some of the available DSP resources on your system. For this reason, try not to create an excessive number of these in your session, and be sure to eliminate them when they are no longer needed. For example, if you required a send, a bus, and an Aux Input for a headphone mix only during the recording process, consider eliminating these if your DSP resources are running short during the final mix.

- Examine how you're using your plug-ins and DSP resources. On Pro Tools|HD and Pro Tools|HDX systems, the first instance of a given plug-in type requires more of your DSP resources than subsequent instances of the same plug-in. Therefore, from an efficiency standpoint, it makes fewer demands on your available DSP to use the same compressor type in two different places (with different settings, of course) rather than using, say, a DigiRack compressor on one track and a Focusrite compressor on another—as long as the sound you want can still be achieved.

- With the DigiRack EQ III, the *total* number of bands of EQ used determines usage of your DSP resources on TDM systems. If you're only boosting or cutting one band in any of your 7-band EQ plug-ins, try replacing them with 1-band EQs instead. Likewise, on all Pro Tools systems, the longer the delay, the larger the demand on available DSP resources. It's inefficient to use the Long Delay plug-in if its current delay time setting is short enough for the Medium or Slap Delay instead. Fortunately, with DigiRack delays, as you change from one type to another, the settings are maintained—including the delay time, as long as it fits into the available duration of the new, shorter delay type.

■ Consider bouncing some of your tracks with effects to disk (or to another track) and then using the bounced audio in place of the tracks with effects. Use the Track > Make Inactive command to disable the original tracks and their plug-in effects so that they no longer consume your system's DSP resources. For some projects, you could also bounce out the entire mix and import it into a brand-new session with no plug-ins at all.

■ If you're happy with the current settings of a DigiRack plug-in, use the plug-in window's pop-up Settings menu to copy its settings, and then paste them into the AudioSuite version of the same effect. Duplicate the track's current playlist (using its pop-up Playlist selector in the Edit window) and then select the entire contents of the track and process it with the Audio-Suite plug-in. When you render the AudioSuite effect parameters, new clips can be created, leaving your original audio clips unchanged, should you decide at some later point to return to the original playlist. If the Use in Playlist button is enabled, the new, processed clips will take the place of the original clips in the track on the duplicate playlist. At this point, you can make the insert plug-in inactive to conserve processing power. If you ever need to revert to the original state of the track, just use the track's Playlist selector to restore the original playlist and reactivate the plug-in.

Where to Place Plug-Ins

Plug-ins can be placed on any track types except MIDI and Video tracks. The best option depends on what you're trying to achieve, but here are a few basic thoughts:

■ As mentioned already, it's often more efficient to assign the main outputs of multiple tracks to a mix bus and place a single plug-in on an Aux Input set to that bus than to insert redundant plug-ins into each individual Audio track. If you're layering up a dozen harmony tracks with the same vocalist, it's an inefficient use of DSP to instantiate identical EQ plug-ins on each track; this also makes adjusting your settings more laborious. In many cases—such as with multiple backing vocals or rhythm guitars, for example—having a single compressor apply dynamic shaping to an entire submix can also contribute to a tighter, more coherent sound.

■ As a general rule, get into the habit of putting delays and reverbs on Aux Inputs rather than in any single Audio track's signal chain. It gives you more control and flexibility later if you decide to send some additional track's signal to the same delay.

■ The amount of gain or boost you apply in an EQ plug-in affects not only audio levels on the track's main output (and any post-fader sends) but also the level entering any plug-ins that follow the track's signal chain. If EQ is followed by a compressor or limiter, for example, a dramatic boost in some frequency range can cause that dynamics-processing effect to clamp down harder—because the increased gain coming out of the EQ plug-in causes the track's peak audio levels to exceed the specified threshold more often. With high-frequency boosts, the net result may be to darken the sound. There are no set rules for effects processing, of course, but as a general guideline for a more transparent sound, start by placing the EQ *after* any dynamics-processing plug-ins on the track.

■ Speaking of EQ, remember that if you can't quite achieve the sound you're looking for with a delay or reverb plug-in, you always have the option of placing an EQ plug-in before and/or after it in the Aux Input track where it resides. For example, reducing the amount of high frequencies entering the effect can solve problems with vocal sibilance or other bright transients from the source tracks that might otherwise clutter up your mix after they hit the effect. (To avoid confusion, note that generally in reverb and delay plug-ins, Low-Pass Filter or High-Frequency Cut controls apply to the effect's output or delay regeneration, *not* its input signal.) Compressors or even de-essers can also be effective for taming the dynamics of a signal entering a delay or reverb. This allows you to increase the effect's overall level without worrying about whether occasional peaks in the source tracks will create splashes of reverb that are too prominent in the mix.

■ Reverb plug-ins don't usually have gated reverb presets (although "non-linear" reverb algorithms sound somewhat similar), and novice users may consider this an omission. If you're overcome by 1980s nostalgia (and long to see a return of monster snares), here's a quick tip: select your choice of reverb from among the plug-ins included with Pro Tools, then place a gate after it in the same signal chain. Viola!—gated reverb.

■ Remember that inserts on Master Fader tracks are always *post*-fader, while on Audio tracks, Aux Inputs, and Instrument tracks, inserts are *pre*-fader. On a Master Fader, the input level to the plug-ins is therefore affected by the track's main volume fader. If you're using a limiter or compressor plug-in on the Master Fader for your main mix output, you could use the track's main volume fader to adjust how hard you're driving the input of that plug-in, as with many traditional hardware compressors. When using dithering plug-ins for bouncing to disk or recording digitally to another device at a lower bit depth, the dithering step should always be the *last* plug-in on the Master Fader (or other track controlling a selected bus) for your mix output.

Copying/Moving Plug-Ins Option-drag (Alt-drag in Windows) any plug-in to copy it to a different track, along with all its current settings. (The source and destination track must have the same number of inputs and outputs.) You can also drag plug-ins among the different insert positions within the same track, which changes their signal-processing order and the resultant sound. You can even do this during playback! (Remember that on HD systems, Native plug-ins should generally be placed *before* any DSP plug-ins in the same Audio track to conserve voices.)

In addition to saving and recalling plug-in settings from disk (as shown in Figure 9.16), you can also copy and paste them directly. For example, to copy current settings from the 7-band EQ plug-in on one track to another, use the Copy Settings and Paste Settings commands in the pop-up plug-in settings menu within the plug-in window.

Figure 9.16 Settings for each plug-in type can be saved, recalled, cut, pasted, or imported from other Pro Tools sessions and systems.

AudioSuite Effects versus Real-Time Plug-Ins

AudioSuite processing is discussed in Chapter 8. As stated there, two basic classes of software effects are available in Pro Tools. First are the plug-ins that function in real time as inserts on Audio, Aux Input, Instrument, or Master Fader tracks. Depending on your system configuration, these may consist of RTAS, TDM, and/or AAX plug-ins. In contrast, the effects in the AudioSuite menu are file based—they must either destructively alter the data in the original file or, more typically, create a new file to store the result of the processing. As mentioned in the section "Getting the Most Out of Available DSP" earlier in this chapter, if your system's DSP resources are extremely limited, there may be times when you start off using one of the real-time plug-ins and eventually copy and paste its parameters into the corresponding AudioSuite plug-in. This is one way to free up DSP power for subsequent mixing tasks. Even on current Pro Tools systems and contemporary computers, you may find cases where you hit the limit for processing capacity on your system; it is good to know you still have some options for getting your project completed!

Bouncing Effects into Tracks and Submixes

We've already mentioned bouncing mixes to free up DSP resources. Here are a few more observations that may be helpful during this process.

Managing Multiple Session Documents

Remember that the Select > Unused Clips command in the Clip List menu only looks at the *current* session document! If you have bounced submix and created a new session (perhaps through the File > Save As command) to keep adding more tracks, be cognizant that this new session knows nothing about how any of the audio files and clips referenced by its Clip List may be used in *other* sessions. Also, remember that when Save As creates a new session document, that new copy still uses the same Audio Files folder as the previous session (not to mention the Session File Backups, Clip Groups, and Rendered Files folders, plus the WaveCache file for waveform overviews).

Session copies created by the File > Save Copy In command also continue to use the original audio files in the current session's folder—*unless* you specify in the Save Session Copy dialog box that source audio files should be copied to a new folder along with the session file itself. Regardless, any session created by the Save Copy In command will subsequently use its own subfolders for any new audio files created by recording or editing (if saved to a different location).

Keep in mind that audio clips and bounced files are automatically timestamped by Pro Tools with their original location information. This allows you to use the Spot dialog box to make sure that the bounced files you import into other session copies are placed exactly in their original location.

Turning Voice Assignment Off

If you turn a track's voice assignment to Off as opposed to leaving it set to Dynamic (or to a manually assigned voice number on a Pro Tools|HD system), the track is made inactive. It no longer competes with other tracks for voices and, of course, won't be heard. It's usually more effective to use the Track > Make Inactive command. You might do this on multiple source tracks after they have been bounced to disk as part of a submix and reimported into another track.

Track Muting, Voice Allocation within a Session (HD Only)

Generally, you will want the Options > Mute Frees Assigned Voice option enabled, especially if you are going through the process of bouncing tracks to which effects have been applied and then reimporting them into the session to free up DSP resources. That way, when you mute the original track, that voice is now available to play other tracks.

Summary

The possibilities for signal routing in Pro Tools are as varied as the working styles of each operator. You will see another example in Chapter 13, "A Multitrack Music Session," which describes setting up cue mixes for performers. Multichannel tracks and surround mixing are discussed in Chapter 14, "Post-Production and Soundtracks." Also, if you skipped Chapter 7, you may want to flip back to it now for more insight into the virtual mixing, signal routing, and processing environment that Pro Tools provides for your virtual studio.

10 MIDI

As explained earlier, *MIDI* stands for *Musical Instrument Digital Interface*. MIDI devices transmit and receive data about a performance—how you strike a key, press a pedal, apply pressure to the keyboard, turn a knob, push a slider, and so on. MIDI is a communications language; it transmits instructions rather than audio signals. To put it another way, although sound does not travel though MIDI cables, the data that MIDI cables carry can be used to *control* things that can make sound.

A Technical Overview of MIDI

The MIDI standard is maintained and expanded on an ongoing basis by the MIDI Manufacturer's Association, a consortium of hardware and software companies (www.midi.org). In technical terms, MIDI is a 31.25-kilobaud serial communications protocol that uses 5-pin DIN connectors to cable together MIDI-compatible devices. MIDI event messages and timing references are transmitted as binary code.

MIDI was introduced in 1983 to address incompatibility issues between electronic musical instruments from different manufacturers (synthesizers, samplers, and so on). The MIDI specification defines data events and timing references to be commonly recognized by all devices that support the standard. For example, a Note On event includes two additional parameters: the note number (from 0–127) and the velocity with which the key was struck (from 1–127). For common performance controllers such as the damper (sustain) pedal on a keyboard, the modulation wheel or lever, the pitch bend wheel or lever, or the main volume control and panner, standard controller numbers and their range of possible values are also standardized for the MIDI protocol. The result is that you can connect the MIDI Out of one keyboard to the MIDI In of another, and it will more or less respond with the same notes. The MIDI standard proved to be quite an improvement over the voltage-controlled synthesizers and early digital-connection protocols from different manufacturers, all of which were mutually incompatible!

Fortunately, the developers of the MIDI specification were much more ambitious than this. MIDI sequencers (data recorders that capture MIDI performance events in real time) needed a common timing reference, called MIDI Clock, so that events could be timestamped in order to play back in proper order and timing, as well as to synchronize one MIDI sequencer to another. Naturally, as personal computers became commonplace in the early 1980s, MIDI interfaces were developed so that MIDI cabling could be connected to personal computers, and software sequencers could receive and retransmit MIDI performance data. Later enhancements to the MIDI specification included the following:

- **MIDI Time Code (MTC).** This encodes the same time-location information as SMPTE time code (more about this in Chapter 11, "Synchronization").

- **MIDI Show Control.** These are event and controller message types relating to lighting, special effects, hydraulics, audio level controls, and so on.

- **MIDI MachineControl (MMC).** This protocol is used for remote control and interlocking of audio or video tape deck transport functions with other devices (including Pro Tools) via MIDI. This is the MIDI counterpart of an even more prevalent MachineControl method, based on serial connections between hardware devices. As discussed in Chapter 14, "Post-Production and Soundtracks," with the Avid MachineControl option, you can use DigiSerial ports on HD cards or 9-pin serial ports on the Sync HD to slave external devices such as video decks and DAT recorders together with Pro Tools if these don't support MIDI MachineControl.

For Pro Tools users, MIDI Time Code and MIDI MachineControl are especially relevant. Additionally, it's worth mentioning that all parameters of PRE, Avid's microphone preamplifier, are controllable via MIDI (and therefore can be restored when a session is reopened), as are many external effects processors.

MIDI Data

Chapter 1 touched on some basic MIDI concepts. We don't cover all the technical details here—that is, the communications protocol, interfacing, and the low-level structure (status bytes, data bytes, most- and least-significant bits, and so on) that actually comprise the messages transmitted from one MIDI device to another. Many excellent relevant resources cover these topics in both book and online form, including *MIDI Power!* (Course Technology PTR, 2005) by Robert Guerin.

Some MIDI messages represent actual performance events—the press of a key or pedal, the movement of a lever or slider, and so on. Other message types are more system level, perhaps telling the receiving device to switch to a different sound or operating mode, controlling its internal sequencer or even loading sound-parameter data that is specific to that device alone. Regardless, however MIDI data may appear onscreen (as horizontal bars for note events or as data curves for modulation, aftertouch, and other types of continuous controllers within Pro Tools), what is actually recorded and played from your MIDI tracks is a series of numerical MIDI messages. Figure 10.1 shows the MIDI Event List window in Pro Tools, which gives you a simplified view of what's actually going on.

Although many types of MIDI messages exist, they can all be classified into one of five basic categories:

- **Channel Voice messages.** These represent performance events such as Note On/Off, volume, pan, modulation, pitch bend, aftertouch, pedals or breath controllers, and so on. Each

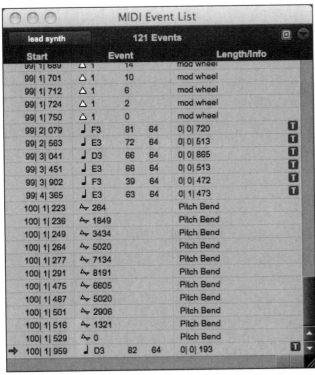

Figure 10.1 The MIDI Event List window displays MIDI events as numerical data. For the most part, you will deal with Channel Voice messages in Pro Tools (although other types of MIDI messages, such as System Exclusive messages, are also supported).

Channel Voice message is transmitted specifically on one of the 16 MIDI channels (a Note On message on channel 5, for example). Program Change messages are also in this category—usually causing the part or patch on that MIDI channel to switch to a different sound for responding to the MIDI note events it receives.

■ **Channel Mode messages.** These include messages for switching between operating modes on the receiving devices, which determine how the device will respond to incoming notes and other MIDI events. In Omni mode, the device responds to incoming note events on any channel; in Poly mode, it responds to incoming MIDI events on multiple channels, each with an independently selectable timbre; and Mono mode responds to a single channel only. All Notes Off is also a Channel Mode message, used for stuck notes. (Pro Tools provides a command for this in the MIDI menu.)

■ **System Common messages.** These include Song Position Pointer, Song Select, and Tune Request messages.

■ **System Real Time messages.** These are used for messages such as MIDI Clock, Start/Stop, Active Sensing, and so on.

■ **System Exclusive messages.** These messages contain manufacturers' proprietary control data. They are ignored by all units that don't respond to the unique manufacturer ID included at the beginning of each message. System Exclusive (or SysEx) messages are used for editing, loading, or archiving sound parameters specific to an instrument.

For the most part, when you're editing data in Pro Tools MIDI tracks, you will be dealing with Channel Voice events, although each of the other types can come into play in given situations.

Aftertouch: Can Pro Tools Handle the Pressure?   In addition to registering attack and release velocity (how rapidly you strike and release each key on your MIDI controller), the MIDI specification includes two types of aftertouch controller data: channel pressure and polyphonic pressure.

Channel pressure, often simply referred to as *aftertouch data*, generates a series of values as you vary the pressure applied to the entire keyboard. On many synthesizer patches, for example, pressing harder on the controller keyboard as you hold a note or chord may increase the filter cutoff frequency, amount or speed of low-frequency modulation, volume, and so on.

Polyphonic pressure data (sometimes called *polyphonic key pressure* or *polyphonic aftertouch*) reflects the pressure applied to each individual key. Only some MIDI controllers are capable of generating this type of data, and many sampler programs and synth patches may not respond to it at all. Polyphonic pressure events can also dramatically increase the density of your recorded MIDI data, since a continuous stream of pressure events is generated for each key instead of a single value for the entire keyboard as in the case of channel pressure data. If none of the MIDI modules or software synths you're using respond to this type of controller data, consider using the MIDI menu's Input Filter selection to disable recording of polyphonic pressure into Pro Tools.

Although channel pressure (mono aftertouch) is one of the standard Data Display options for MIDI tracks in the Edit window, the MIDI Event List window is the *only* place you can view/edit polyphonic pressure events in Pro Tools.

MIDI Interface Options

As mentioned in Chapter 3, a MIDI interface is a sort of adapter that translates the MIDI data communications protocol to a format that your computer can understand. MIDI interfaces can be external devices—typically connected to the computer via USB in current models (especially when interfaces with numerous MIDI connections are required). Many generic Windows soundcards have built-in connectors for MIDI, where for simple applications you can attach a breakout cable with one DIN-5 connector for MIDI In and another for MIDI Out (although some consumer-level cards may present conflicts with professional audio programs).

Pro Tools systems often have MIDI input/output connectors integrated into the audio interface itself, as is the case with the Mbox, Mbox Pro, and 003. Several M-Audio audio interfaces also incorporate MIDI inputs/outputs, which you can use with Pro Tools.

Whichever MIDI interface you're using in your Pro Tools configuration, the number of independently addressable MIDI inputs or outputs (ports) it provides will determine the total number of

MIDI channels available for communicating with external MIDI devices—16 MIDI channels per port. For example, if you have a one-in, two-out MIDI interface (as on the 003 and Digi 002 interfaces), that's 16 MIDI input channels and 32 output channels available for external MIDI communication to or from each Pro Tools MIDI (or Instrument) track. Of course, many different types of MIDI interfaces are available, with varying numbers of ports. More sophisticated units might include routing or filtering capabilities for the MIDI data passing through them, stored presets and operation in standalone mode without a computer, SMPTE time code synchronization, word clock features for slaving your audio hardware's sample rate to external sources, and the ability to slave multiple MIDI interfaces together to expand the number of independently addressable MIDI ports. Pro Tools supports most external MIDI interfaces currently available, including units from MOTU, M-Audio, Yamaha, E-MU Systems, and others.

MIDI via USB and FireWire Various MIDI controllers and sound modules can connect directly to the host computer via USB—from M-Audio, Fatar, Alesis, Roland/Edirol, E-MU, Korg, and others. M-Audio offers keyboard controllers that also act as audio interfaces, such as the KeyStudio 49i and the ProKeys Sono 61 and 88.

Digidesign MIDI I/O

The MIDI I/O (shown in Figure 10.2), no longer produced but still prevalent in the audio industry, is a MIDI interface manufactured under the former Digidesign name. It features 10 MIDI inputs (with two of these on the front panel) and 10 outputs, and it connects to the host computer via the USB port (which also powers the device). In addition to working with Pro Tools, the MIDI I/O also features a standalone hardware thru mode. You can daisy-chain up to four MIDI I/Os together, for up to 640 MIDI channels (16 channels per MIDI port).

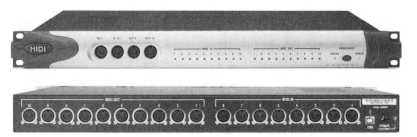

Figure 10.2 The MIDI I/O, a multiport MIDI interface that connects to the host computer via USB. Two of its 10 MIDI inputs/outputs are available on the front panel.

Although many options exist for multiport MIDI interfaces, a unique feature offered by the MIDI I/O is support for the MIDI Timestamping feature in Pro Tools. This addresses an inherent timing problem when you transmit many channels of dense MIDI data in real time over a single connection. Imagine you're sending or receiving 30–40 separate channels of MIDI data, each containing constant pitch bend and polyphonic pressure events or fader and knob movements recorded from an external control surface for Pro Tools that communicates with the computer via MIDI. The sheer volume of MIDI events could exceed the real-time capacity of a single USB connection. Even more likely, a conventional MIDI interface may not be able to receive, convert, and reroute all this information between multiple ports and the data connection to the computer itself without some kind of processing delay, or latency. The result will be random timing discrepancies that become an audible problem in your project. Via the MIDI Timestamping feature, each incoming MIDI event is automatically timestamped during recording. During MIDI playback, data sent from Pro Tools is *preloaded* into a buffer in the MIDI I/O in real time to ensure more accurate playback.

MIDI Setup

Pro Tools handles MIDI setup slightly differently in Macintosh than in Windows. In Mac OS X (operating system versions 10 and above), you use the Audio MIDI Setup utility to configure the MIDI interface and external MIDI devices (for example, keyboards, guitar, wind, and percussion controllers, drum machines, and sound modules). The available selections for MIDI input/output (I/O) on Pro Tools tracks reflect the currently active configuration in that utility. Once you've run the installer program for whatever drivers an external MIDI interface requires (if any), this interface automatically appears in Audio MIDI Setup.

In Windows versions of Pro Tools, the MIDI Studio Setup window automatically finds MIDI interface drivers and translates that information into XML-based documents. You can assign custom names for the MIDI ports on the interface and use XML-based patchname documents (which can be customized, as in Mac OS X) for selecting sounds on your external MIDI devices. You must always first run the installer program provided with the MIDI interface itself. Note that the proper procedures in Windows can be highly variable from one model to another—read the instructions before installing *anything*!

Again, the 003 and Digi 002 interfaces include one MIDI input and two MIDI outputs. Some of the current M-Audio interfaces also offer a single MIDI input and output, as do the Pro Tools Mbox and Mbox Pro. For other Pro Tools hardware configurations, the MIDI interface is a separate hardware peripheral (or possibly a port commonly found on generic Windows soundcards, if the modest performance offered by this option is sufficient for your needs).

Macintosh (Audio MIDI Setup)

The Audio MIDI Setup utility (shown in Figure 10.3) is part of Mac OS X. It can be launched directly from within Pro Tools using the Setup > MIDI Studio Setup command. You use it to configure the type of MIDI interface (if any) that is connected to your computer and to tell the computer how your external MIDI controllers and sound modules are connected to the interface. Many devices are already preconfigured so that you can select by manufacturer/model, but you can manually configure any other device. The most important issues are how many MIDI ports the device has, which MIDI channels it transmits/receives, whether it receives or transmits MIDI Beat Clock and MIDI Time Code, and whether it's General MIDI compatible. You then simply drag onscreen cables between the MIDI inputs/outputs on each MIDI device and the corresponding ports on the MIDI interface to mirror their actual physical connections.

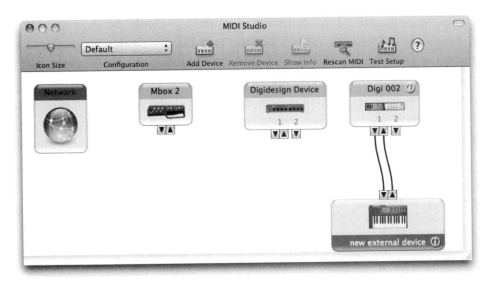

Figure 10.3 The Audio MIDI Setup utility on Mac provides a uniform method for configuring the communication between all MIDI-capable programs and any MIDI interfaces, external keyboards/controllers, and modules attached to your system.

Note In current versions of the Mac OS, Audio MIDI Setup (AMS) provides separate windows for Audio Devices and MIDI Studio. If the MIDI Studio window does not appear after opening AMS (Setup > MIDI > MIDI Studio in Pro Tools), choose Window > Show MIDI Window in the AMS menu bar.

Windows

Most MIDI interfaces come with their own driver installer disks. MIDI drivers are installed via INF files for Windows Device Manager (WDM), which instructs the operating system about how and when to use those driver files. For common (SoundBlaster-compatible) PC soundcards, an optional cable converts a DB-15 data connector on the card into MIDI In/Out 5-pin DIN connectors. However, for professional applications, USB is currently the most common connection for attaching external MIDI interfaces to Windows computers. Installation procedures can vary widely by manufacturer and model. Be sure to carefully read the manufacturer's instructions before installing software for a new MIDI interface on your system; doing so takes much less time than trying to undo an improper installation!

The Pro Tools for Windows MIDI Studio Setup window (shown in Figure 10.4) makes managing a complex MIDI configuration simple. Here you define *instruments* for each of your external MIDI devices by clicking the Create button. Properties appear in the right panel of this window for each selected instrument. A list of predefined instruments is provided in your Pro Tools installation; these MIDI device files are written in a language known as *XML* (*Extensible Markup Language*). If the MIDI device you're defining as a new instrument is included in that default list, you can select it in the Manufacturer and Model pop-up lists. Otherwise, you can leave these fields set to None and simply enter your own name for the instrument. You can also define where this instrument is connected for input and output to and from Pro Tools by indicating the port on your MIDI interface. Lastly, you indicate which MIDI channels the device is sending on and the specific output MIDI channels from Pro Tools to which this device responds. For example, your keyboard may be configured to transmit only on MIDI channel 1, while it can respond to all 16 MIDI channels. A MIDI module may not transmit on any channels at all, but may respond to all of them. A MIDI guitar controller may transmit on six MIDI channels simultaneously, while some MIDI percussion controllers transmit on an even greater number of simultaneous channels.

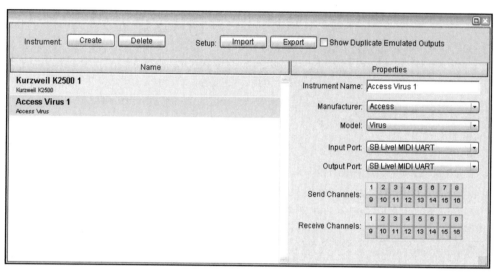

Figure 10.4   The MIDI Studio Setup window is used for Pro Tools on Windows systems.

The active instruments in your current MIDI Studio Setup configuration then appear in the MIDI Input and MIDI Output selectors on MIDI tracks. (To make an instrument not appear, without having to delete its definition from MIDI Studio Setup, change its input and output port assignments to None.)

Patchname files, which are also written in XML and use the .midnam file extension, also enhance management of multiple external MIDI devices. As with MIDI device files, a collection of predefined patchname files is included with the Pro Tools installation. MIDI tracks have a Program button in both the Mix window and the Edit window that opens the Patch Select dialog box. In this dialog box, you can select a patchname file for the current track (using the Change button) from among the MIDNAM files residing in that directory. If you choose a Korg Triton, for example, all the factory internal programs and banks for that device will appear *by name* rather than simply by program number each time you open the Patch Select dialog box. This is a huge boost to productivity, making it much quicker to select and experiment with different sounds for your MIDI parts.

Patchname files are ordinary text files—as are the patchname files used with the Mac Audio MIDI Setup utility. If you've edited program names or customized the contents of the user bank on your external synthesizer, you can edit the program names inside the corresponding patchname file on your computer using any text-editor program. Be sure to make a backup copy of the original first, however! Some third-party librarian or patch-editor programs also provide tools for creating your own patchname files from scratch. You can find many of these patchname files on the web if your particular device isn't included in the predefined list provided with Pro Tools.

External MIDI Devices

Many types of external MIDI devices exist, including standard synthesizers and samplers with keyboards, MIDI sound modules with no keyboards, and MIDI controllers that feature no internal sound-generation capabilities at all (keyboard controllers, guitar controllers, wind controllers, electronic percussion, and so on). Of course, many other devices also support MIDI. For example, you can control parameters of many effects processors via MIDI, as well as control automated mixers or, for that matter, some lighting gear and amplifiers.

Besides MIDI controllers used for performance (keyboard, guitar controller, wind controller, electronic drums, and so on), MIDI peripherals are also available that function as control surfaces for Pro Tools itself. The Mackie Control Series, the J.L. Cooper Media Command Station 3000 Series, the CM Labs MotorMix 2, and the Artist Series controllers are all examples of external devices that you can use to control Pro Tools faders, sliders, and/or the Pro Tools Transport via a MIDI connection.

Lastly, other alternatives exist for connecting musical peripherals to your computer: USB controller keyboards and/or USB modules are available from M-Audio, Roland/Edirol, Alesis, E-MU, Fatar, Korg, and others; these don't require a MIDI interface at all. These alternatives are especially attractive for laptop users. For users who rely exclusively on software instruments as MIDI sound sources—an increasingly common option—a full-featured keyboard controller with a direct USB connection and no internal sounds may be all that is required. Various units from M-Audio, including the Ozone (connected via USB) and Ozonic (connected via FireWire), also double as audio interfaces for Pro Tools.

The following sections discuss software-based virtual instruments. You can use these in conjunction with or instead of any external sound modules for MIDI. You also have the option of using third-party programs via the ReWire plug-in, which routes the external program's audio output into an Aux channel in Pro Tools. Figure 10.5 shows the AIR Xpand![2] plug-in on an Instrument track controlled by an M-Audio Oxygen 8. The audio output of this Instrument track is sent out the bus labeled MIDI Audio Bus, which is also chosen as the audio input of the Audio track Xpand![2] Record. This enables the user to record the output of the Instrument track, creating an audio file within the session.

Virtual Instruments

Software-based MIDI instruments are among the most exciting tools to have emerged for computer-based music production in the last 15 years. Virtual instrument plug-ins have been around for a while in RTAS and TDM formats (as well as VST, AU, DirectX, and additional formats used by

Figure 10.5 A Pro Tools session with the Xpand![2] virtual instrument on an Instrument track. Note that the MIDI Audio Bus routes to the Audio track xpand_rcrd to capture the output of the Instrument track as an audio file.

other audio programs). ReWire technology enables many more options for integrating software-based synthesizers and samplers into the Pro Tools environment. Virtual instruments for current Pro Tools versions can be broken down into four general classes:

- RTAS synthesizer/sampler plug-ins (for all Pro Tools systems).

- TDM synthesizer/sampler plug-ins (for Pro Tools|HD systems).

- Separate synthesizer/sampler programs such as Reason and Ableton Live, whose virtual audio outputs can be routed into Pro Tools via the ReWire plug-in (for all Pro Tools systems).

- Plug-ins in other formats that are not native to Pro Tools, used via so-called "wrapper" programs. One very useful example is the VST to RTAS Adapter program, by FXpansion, which allows you to use VST effects and instrument plug-ins within the Pro Tools RTAS plug-in environment on either Mac or Windows.

You might instantiate a virtual instrument plug-in in one of the insert slots of an Instrument or Aux Input track—although you could also place it on an Audio track. Alternatively, if the virtual instrument is within a separate program communicating with Pro Tools via ReWire (such as

Reason or Ableton Live), you can select that program as an insert via the ReWire plug-in. You can then use the ReWire plug-in window to select which of that program's output channels you want to stream into Pro Tools at the selected insert point on the track. From that point in the signal chain, treatment of the audio output from any virtual instrument is identical to other signal sources in Pro Tools, including mix automation and plug-in processing and creating sends and other routing assignments. Not only do software-based instruments greatly simplify your life when working with multiple projects and MIDI sound sources, but the virtual signal path from these synths and samplers into the Pro Tools mixing environment is as clean as it gets!

Why Use Virtual Instruments Instead of External MIDI Gear?

Software-based instruments have numerous benefits over physical MIDI devices. First, they can be less noisy because there are no physical inputs/outputs, cabling, digital converters, and so on, all of which are subject to potential degradation. Second, virtual instruments can be more cost effective because you don't have to pay for the RAM, disk storage, and other hardware components for each device, as you would for an external sampler or synthesizer, nor do you have to pay a premium for vintage or hard-to-come-by gear. The whole routing and reconnection scenario becomes immensely simple as well: There are no cables to reconnect (which also means less noise).

In the case of ReWire, you can launch the separate virtual instrument application, reloading its patch and entire routing configuration, the next time you open your Pro Tools session—without touching any cables or adjusting levels. Sampler virtual instruments use standard PC or Mac disk and file formats (as opposed to the proprietary formats used by many standalone samplers), which means that you can much more easily create or acquire new audio files for them. (The sound-generation method in samplers relies on playing back digital audio recordings from RAM, varying their playback speed or resynthesizing as required to produce different pitches and sometimes looping short audio segments to produce sustained tones.) You may even decide midway through a Pro Tools session that you'd like to use a particular audio clip for a sampler, triggering its playback at different speeds/pitches via MIDI note events. No problem; you can bounce the clip as a file (in the same standard AIF or WAV formats you're already using with Pro Tools) and load it into a sampler such as Structure, SampleTank 2.5, Kontakt 5, or MachFive 3 so that it can be played from the keyboard. Need to apply some editing to that sample so that it works better in the software sampler? Open it again in Pro Tools, make your changes, save again to disk, and reload.

To be fair, though, there are some advantages to using external synthesizers and samplers (not to mention more traditional instruments whose physical characteristics are an essential aspect of their sound and the playing experience itself). For one thing, virtual instruments make intensive processing demands on your system's resources, which can impact track counts and other DSP-intensive plug-ins. Also, especially on host-based systems and relatively underpowered host computers, audio and plug-in demands may make it impractical to reduce the size of the hardware buffer enough so that latency during the actual MIDI performance doesn't create perceptual or timing problems.

Virtual Instrument Programs (ReWire)

Most ReWire programs support both audio and MIDI processing, and many offer robust sequencing and composing tools of their own. In addition to streaming their audio output into Pro Tools tracks via the ReWire plug-in, you can use MIDI-capable software instruments within client ReWire programs as sound sources by assigning them as the output from your MIDI or Instrument tracks in Pro Tools. Several of these ReWire-capable applications offer VST plug-in support, chord, scale matrix, and arpeggio generators, and other powerful real-time MIDI processing tools (for example, the Follow Actions and Racks functions in Ableton Live). These can be a very interesting adjunct to Pro Tools' basic MIDI functionality. Third-party programs that are compatible with ReWire and can work in client mode (under the control of Pro Tools, which is always the ReWire master in this setup) include the following:

- Reason (Propellerhead Software)
- Live (Ableton)
- GigaStudio (Tascam; Windows only [discontinued])
- ACID by Sony Creative (originally developed by Sonic Foundry; Windows only)
- Bidule (Plogue)
- Sibelius (Avid)
- VST to ReWire Adapter (FXpansion) (hosts VST instruments in Mac or Windows so that they can be controlled by Pro Tools MIDI tracks with multiple outputs routed back into Pro Tools via ReWire)

Virtual Instrument Plug-Ins for Pro Tools

Software-based synthesis and sampling plug-ins have proliferated in recent years. Software-based samplers, synths, and drum modules must be in Native (RTAS or AAX) format to be used as plug-ins directly within host-based Pro Tools systems, while systems with Pro Tools|HD hardware support software instrument plug-ins in the TDM format in addition to Native plug-ins. (Pro Tools|HDX hardware supports both AAX [Native and DSP] and RTAS plug-ins, but not TDM.) The parameters of any software instrument plug-ins (and references to any external sample files on disk, if applicable) are stored and recalled along with the session document. This is a huge productivity advantage, as any veteran user of multiple external modules can attest. The sound-generation parameters of these software instrument plug-ins can also be enabled for Pro Tools automation (like most other plug-ins), even from an external control surface.

Other virtual instruments can be used via separate ReWire programs that communicate with Pro Tools. The audio output from the virtual instrument is incorporated into the Pro Tools mixing environment at the insert point where you place the ReWire plug-in. Audio plug-in or hardware I/O effects can be used on the insert slots following the instrument or ReWire plug-in to further process its output. You can also create sends from any track containing an instrument plug-in.

Because host-based Pro Tools systems use Native virtual instrument plug-ins (including wrapped VST plug-ins and any separate software-based instruments that stream into Pro Tools via ReWire), the performance of these virtual instruments depends on your system's resources—the CPU type and speed, available RAM, and so on. This is also true of the Pro Tools program in general. If your computer is already having a hard time with the number of tracks and plug-ins you're using in Pro Tools, this may set a practical limit on how many voices, channels, and effects you can use within any software instruments. Users with Pro Tools|HD or Pro Tools|HDX hardware will also experience this when using Native instrument plug-ins; however, they also have access to some DSP-only instrument plug-ins that rely on the DSP capacity of the cards themselves for their processing needs. Shown in Figure 10.6 is the AIR Xpand!^{2} virtual instrument workstation bundled with current Pro Tools systems.

Figure 10.6   The AIR Xpand!^{2} virtual instrument plug-in in RTAS format. Currently included with all versions of Pro Tools, Xpand!^{2} features more than 1,000 preset sounds along with volume envelope, portamento, and low-pass filter cutoff controls (among others).

Recording into MIDI and Instrument Tracks

Pro Tools MIDI and Instrument tracks can record from any active port on your MIDI interface, on whatever channel(s) your controller is transmitting. Ordinarily, you will have the MIDI Thru function enabled (via a selection in the Options menu). That way, regardless of which MIDI input you record *from*, the MIDI output (either within the software, a physical port on your external MIDI interface, or a direct USB connection), MIDI channel, and program number you've chosen for the currently record-enabled track will be echoed through to the correct instrument, channel, and program.

If, however, the selected output for the current track happens to be the same MIDI keyboard controller you're currently playing, the MIDI Thru function can present some issues. In this situation, the sound generation within your synth can end up not only responding directly to its own local keyboard, but also to the same note and controller events echoed back around through Pro Tools via the current track assignment. You will hear doubled notes, and the external keyboard might lock up due to the infinite loop you've set up between the output assignment on your MIDI/Instrument track and the global MIDI Thru feature in Pro Tools. As with other MIDI-capable programs, when using MIDI Thru, you can avoid this problem by simply turning Local mode off on your external keyboard. When a MIDI controller's Local mode is off, its internal sound-generation capability no longer responds to its own keyboard; instead, it responds only to incoming MIDI events at its MIDI input. (If you need to use this MIDI keyboard later in stand-alone mode, don't forget to turn Local mode back on!)

MIDI Recording Modes

In addition to the four standard recording modes in Pro Tools, a button in the Transport window enables MIDI Merge mode. (More about this in a moment.) Let's take a look at how these modes affect MIDI recording, because there are some differences compared to audio:

- **Normal mode.** Non-destructive. If you record anywhere into a MIDI or Instrument track where MIDI clips/data already exist, a new clip is created for the newly recorded MIDI data. The clip(s) replaced by the new MIDI recording in the track are still available and unchanged in the Clip List.

- **Destructive mode.** In MIDI and Instrument tracks, there is no difference between Normal and Destructive modes; they work in exactly the same way. In contrast, in Audio tracks, Destructive recording mode actually overwrites any existing audio data at that track location.

- **QuickPunch mode.** Not required for MIDI and Instrument tracks, because for all record-enabled MIDI tracks, you can *always* use the Transport's Record button to drop in and out of recording mode.

- **Loop Record mode.** Works similarly to loop recording on Audio tracks. A new MIDI clip is created and auto-numbered for every pass through the looped selection (although in MIDI tracks, if you don't play anything on a pass, Pro Tools waits until the next time you play something before creating additional clips). As with multiple audio takes recorded in Loop Record mode, you can Command-click with the Selector tool (Ctrl-click in Windows) within the clip currently in the track to view the Takes List pop-up menu. MIDI Merge mode (see the next bullet) cannot be used in Loop Record mode; its button in the Transport is dimmed whenever Loop Record mode is active.

- **MIDI Merge mode.** When this button in the Pro Tools Transport window is enabled, as you record over existing MIDI clips, the new MIDI data is *added* to the MIDI data already in the track instead of replacing it. However, if you enable Loop Playback mode before recording in

MIDI Merge mode, each subsequent pass that you record through the looping section of the Timeline will be merged into the previous one (drum-machine style) instead of replacing it.

Loop Recording   You can record MIDI and/or audio in Loop Record mode. Simply set pre- and post-roll parameters, make a Timeline selection, and enable Loop Record mode (in the Options menu or by right-clicking the Record button). As you record, the portion of the session's Timeline between the Transport window's Start and End indicators (the Timeline selection) is looped until you press the spacebar to stop. A new clip is created for each pass. To discard all takes recorded so far without exiting Loop Record mode, press Command+Period (Ctrl+Period in Windows).

Afterward, if you Command-click (Ctrl-click in Windows) with the Selector tool within the loop-recorded clip, the pop-up Takes List appears, allowing you to switch between multiple takes. You can also right-click the clip to select among alternate matching clips via a pop-up menu.

Editing MIDI and Instrument Tracks in the Edit Window

When MIDI and Instrument tracks are in Clips or Blocks view, you can drag MIDI clips with the Grabber tool. Use the Selector tool to select areas within clips for cut/copy/paste operations, more or less like audio clips. However, one important difference applies here: When the initial Note On message for any MIDI note event begins inside the clip's current boundaries, even after trimming the end of this MIDI clip, those notes can extend beyond the clip's right edge (and sound for their full lengths). Conversely, if you trim a MIDI clip's left edge so that it no longer includes a note's beginning, that note is no longer part of the clip (and won't play), even if it originally extended far beyond the trim location.

In addition to using the standard Trim mode to shorten/lengthen the boundaries of MIDI clips, you can also use the TCE Trim tool to compress or expand not only the clip's length, but the spacing of all the MIDI events within it as well. As always with the editing tools, the currently active Edit mode affects this time trimming. Spot mode opens the Spot dialog box, Slip mode allows free adjustment of the duration, Grid mode snaps the clip boundary from one grid increment to another as you drag, and Shuffle mode always leaves the beginning of the new compressed/expanded MIDI clip at the same start point as the original clip, whether you trim its beginning or end. In particular, using the TCE Trim tool in Grid mode may be handy for composers; compressing a four-bar clip to two bars creates a double-time version of the events it contains, while expanding it to eight bars creates a half-time version.

Things get more interesting in Notes or Velocity view. Here are some specific tricks you should know when using the different Edit window tools on MIDI tracks while in Notes view:

■ **Grabber.** You can drag individual notes or multiple selected notes with the Grabber in Notes view. Use the Shift key to select/deselect additional notes and Option-drag (Alt-drag in

Windows) to copy notes instead of moving them. When you click between notes in the track, the Grabber cursor turns into a selection rectangle so that you can select ranges of notes.

- **Trim tool.** This trims note lengths (end or beginning). Hold down the Option key (Alt key in Windows) to force the Trim tool to change direction (that is, to trim the note at its beginning or its end), regardless of which half of the note graphic you're in.

- **Pencil.** This tool inserts new note events. Hold down the Option key (Alt key in Windows) to change the Pencil to the Eraser so you can delete notes (or double-click on a note with the Pencil). The velocity of newly created notes is set in the Edit window, the MIDI Editor window, or the Score Editor window. When the Pencil is in Freehand mode, click and drag as you create new MIDI notes to stretch them out to a desired length. In the Line Pencil drawing mode (and other available modes), if you click and drag, a series of notes is created at a single pitch whose spacing corresponds to the current grid value. If you use the Line drawing mode, all these notes will have the default Note On Velocity value. In the Triangle, Square, and Random drawing modes, you still can only create notes of a single pitch. (Parabolic and S-curve shapes can be used for adjusting velocities and editing controllers, but *not* for creating new notes.) However, the *velocities* of these new notes will vary: every eight notes for a full cycle of the triangle shape, alternate notes for the square shape, and, well, *random* for the random shape! The Pencil drawing modes use a Custom Note Duration option. In sessions with MIDI or Instrument tracks, an additional pop-up selector for note durations (which looks like a musical note) appears to the right of the status indicators in the Edit window toolbar. This allows you to create various combinations of note spacing and durations as you draw with the Pencil tool. For example, a series of 1/8 notes (the Grid value), each with a duration of 1/32 note (the Custom Note Duration value), would produce a staccato effect.

Zooming Shortcuts for MIDI Tracks   You can use the Edit window's MIDI vertical zoom buttons to change how much of a MIDI track's pitch range fits into the track at its current height. You can also use the Command+Shift (Ctrl+Shift in Windows) keyboard shortcut and the left and right square bracket keys ([and]) to zoom in/out vertically on MIDI and Instrument tracks.

- **Selector.** This tool is used to select notes and note ranges, although you will notice that a MIDI note isn't selected unless the highlighted range includes its beginning (the Note On event). And no, you cannot select the tail end of a MIDI note and press the Delete key to shorten it; use the Trim tool instead.

- **Scrubber.** You can use the Scrubber tool to play through a MIDI or Instrument track's notes either backward or forward, but keep in mind that the Scrubber cannot act the same way it does when applied to audio files.

Edit with Your Ears   As a general rule, Pro Tools operators who use MIDI should enable the Play MIDI Notes When Editing option found in the Edit, MIDI Editor, and Score Editor windows (represented by an icon of a MIDI 5-pin connector with a speaker next to it— click the icon to toggle the function on/off). When enabled, as you drag or create notes, you will hear the notes played out to that track's MIDI destination.

Selecting MIDI Note Ranges with the Mini-Keyboard   Each MIDI/Instrument track in the Edit window has a mini-keyboard at the left edge of the display area. When Notes view is selected, you can click the appropriate key to select all instances of a given pitch on the track or click and drag (or simply Shift-click on an additional key) to select a range of pitches. To hear a pitch on this keyboard without selecting all those note events in the track, hold down the Option key (Alt key in Windows) as you click the key. Command-click (Ctrl-click in Windows) to remove or add keys from a previous selection or to select non-contiguous keys on this mini-keyboard.

In Velocity view (shown in Figure 10.7 and also discussed in Chapter 6), velocity stalks appear for each MIDI note. You can drag these stalks up and down with the Grabber, draw contours with the Pencil tool (especially in its Line drawing mode), and trim the attack velocities of selected note ranges. Bear in mind, of course, that each program (or *patch*) on a MIDI instrument may respond differently to variations in attack velocity. Whether the sound actually gets louder (or softer) at higher attack velocities, adds another sound layer, or switches to a completely different sound depends entirely on how the program is designed within the currently selected destination instrument. If you switch a MIDI track's output assignment to a different MIDI instrument or program number, you may have to occasionally adjust the velocities of MIDI notes.

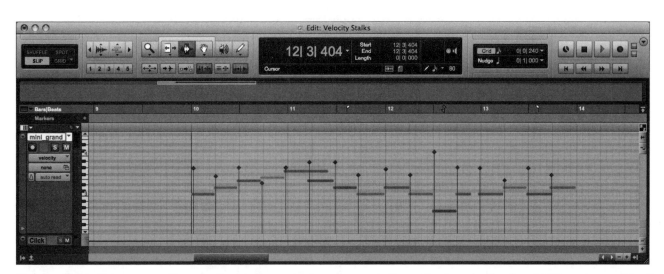

Figure 10.7 You can edit velocity stalks, which represent the attack velocity for MIDI notes, with the Grabber, Trim, and Pencil tools.

Editing MIDI Note Velocities Here's another easy way to edit individual note velocities that's especially handy when several notes coincide: Hold down the Command key (Ctrl key in Windows) as you click and hold directly on a note in the track (or several previously selected notes); dragging up and down with this modifier changes the selected notes' velocity values.

Editing MIDI Note Names, Attack/Release Velocities As shown in Figure 10.8, when a single MIDI note is selected in Notes view, the Start, End, and Length indicators reflect the values for that note. Three additional fields display the pitch (Note Name), attack velocity, and release velocity. Click any of these fields to enter a new value. (A fairly large proportion of MIDI controllers do not transmit release velocities, in which case all note events recorded into Pro Tools appear with the value you set in the Default Note On Velocity selector in the Edit window toolbar. Likewise, many sampler and synthesizer patches do not respond to variations in the Release Velocity values that are received.)

Figure 10.8 When MIDI notes are selected, Note Name, Attack Velocity, and Release Velocity fields appear to the right of the Start, End, and Length indicators.

Any time you press the forward slash (/) key on the numeric keypad while in the Edit window, the Start field is selected. Repeatedly pressing this key toggles through the Start, End, and Length fields.

You can also enter values in most MIDI note and velocity fields throughout Pro Tools from your MIDI controller. For example, you could select the MIDI Note field and play the correct note, again pressing Return (or Enter in Windows) to confirm your entry.

If multiple notes are selected, the amount of change (or *delta*) is displayed in these fields. For example, if you type 15 into the Attack Velocity field and press Return (or Enter in Windows) on the alphanumeric keyboard, the velocity values of all currently selected notes are increased by that amount.

The MIDI Editor Window

The MIDI Editor window is a separate window from the normal MIDI and Instrument track display in the Edit window that offers features to speed the MIDI editing process and provides options for how editing is performed. As shown in Figure 10.9, many of the displays included in the MIDI Editor window are the same as those featured in the Edit window. In fact, most of the tools, selectors, and options—such as the Grid selector and the Edit modes—function exactly how they do in the Edit window. Some features are unique to the MIDI Editor window, however, offering unique ways of tweaking one's MIDI, Instrument, and Auxiliary tracks.

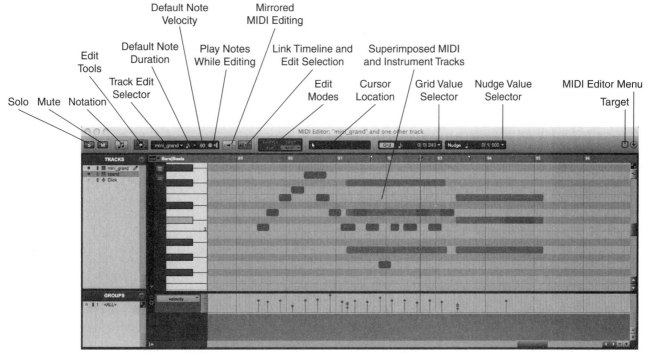

Figure 10.9 The MIDI Editor window.

One quick way to open the MIDI Editor window is to right-click a MIDI clip in a track and choose Open in MIDI Editor from the menu that appears. Unlike a MIDI or Instrument track display in the Edit window, which can show only that particular track's note and controller information, the MIDI Editor window can superimpose note and velocity information from several tracks into one display, even color-coding each track's information for quick recognition if desired.

Tip   Double-clicking on a MIDI clip in the Edit window will also open the MIDI Editor window by default. This behavior can be modified in the MIDI page of the Pro Tools Preferences dialog box.

Note that one or more tracks listed in the Track List (on the left side of the MIDI Editor window) can be displayed in the MIDI Editor window. You can toggle each MIDI, Instrument, and Aux Input track's Show/Hide buttons in the Track List. The tracks display using the familiar notes display, with velocity displayed in a lane below it, both representing all the tracks enabled in the Track List.

You can color-code items in the MIDI Editor window by track or by velocity (see Figure 10.10). When you select the Color Coding by Track option (located below the Ruler Menu selector in the MIDI Editor window), each source MIDI or Instrument track's note and velocity information will reflect the color of that track's color strip. When you select the Color Coding by Velocity option, located below the Color Coding by Track option, all the notes will turn red but will have varying degrees of saturation depending on the note's velocity. The darker the note's red, the higher the note's velocity.

Figure 10.10 The Color Coding by Track option (left of the keyboard) and, below it, the Color Coding by Velocity option.

Similar to the automation lanes for Audio tracks, the MIDI Editor window gives you the option to display controller and automation lanes for the selected tracks, as shown in Figure 10.11. Click the Add Lane button at the far left of the velocity lane, and a new lane appears. Notice that when multiple tracks' note and velocity data is displayed, when you create a new controller or automation lane, each track is represented by its own sub-lane. This is because unlike with velocity, all other automation or controller data is *not* merged in the display. Using the

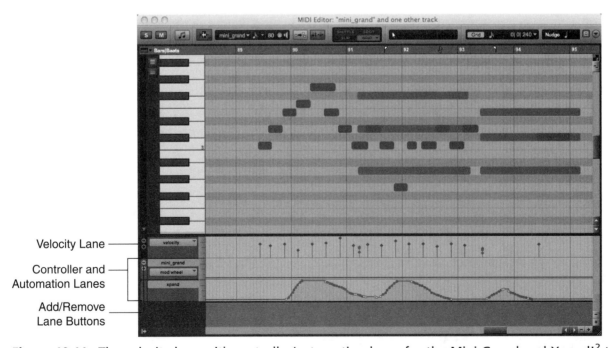

Figure 10.11 The velocity lane with controller/automation lanes for the Mini Grand and Xpand![2] tracks immediately below.

Controller/Automation pull-down selector, choose the type of data you want to view in the newly created lane/sub-lanes. Use the Remove Lane button, represented by the minus sign, on lanes you no longer need to display.

Note editing in the MIDI Editor window is the same as in the Edit window in terms of tool function, the basic Edit menu functions such as Cut and Copy, and the insertion of items such as key and meter changes. Right-clicking in the main Notes pane displays a convenient menu of functions, including those just mentioned. That said, because the MIDI Editor window can display multiple tracks' note data, you need a way to indicate which track (or tracks) you wish to affect when using the Pencil tool to manually insert notes. To address this, the MIDI Editor window allows you to pencil-enable a track. Simply click in the track's Pencil column in the Track List to display a small pencil icon. This enables you to use the Pencil tool to insert new notes the same way you would in a MIDI or Instrument track in the Edit window. You also have the option to insert notes on multiple tracks at the same time; to enable this, click in the Pencil column for the first track, hold down the Shift key, and click in the Pencil column for all other desired tracks. Any notes you create using the Pencil tool will be reflected in all the pencil-enabled tracks. To deselect the tracks, simply click in the Pencil column again to remove the pencil icon for the chosen tracks.

Also available in the MIDI Editor window is the option to view a track or tracks' note information in a standard music notation display. When you select the Notation Display Enable button to the right of the Mute button at the top of the MIDI Editor window, music notation is displayed in Grand Staff, Treble, Bass, Alto, and Tenor staves in a linear fashion similar to the Note pane. The velocity lane and any automation or controller lanes are shown below this Notation pane. On the left side of the Notation pane is a column with tracks' names showing what staves belong to the individual track note information. Editing in this Notation view is covered in Chapter 17, "The Score Editor Window," which delves into the notation options in Pro Tools.

The Event Menu

Chapter 8 provides an overview of the selections in the Event menu. If you are a composer, arranger, or performer who uses MIDI in Pro Tools, however, you will want to explore all these options in much more detail. We will start with a discussion of the Time Operations, Tempo Operations, and Event Operations submenus (see Figure 10.12).

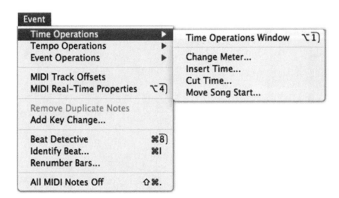

Figure 10.12 The Time Operations submenu.

Time Operations

All the functions listed in the Event > Time Operations submenu are also accessible as pages within the Time Operations window, which you can open by pressing Option+1 on the numeric keypad (Alt+1 in Windows).

Change Meter

Selecting the Change Meter command opens a window for inserting a meter change event into the Meter Ruler. A pop-up selector lets you choose whether this new time signature will remain in effect through the end of the session, for the current bar only, or for the selected range of bars. This Change Meter page of the Time Operations window also provides the option to change the meter of the click.

To better understand how this function works, imagine that the bridge of your song needs to change from 4/4 to 3/4 time signature for four bars beginning at Bar 33, followed by 32 more bars of 4/4, and then another 3/4 section at Bar 69 when the bridge is repeated. Before you start recording your audio and MIDI parts, take a moment to set up the song structure using the following steps:

1. Switch to Grid Edit mode. If you haven't already done so, switch your main ruler to Bars| Beats format (via the View > Main Counter submenu). Using the pop-up selector in the Edit menu, change the Grid Value setting to 1 bar.

2. Using the Selector tool, select Bars 33–37 either within an existing track or in the ruler itself if you haven't yet created any tracks in the session.

3. Select Event > Time Operations > Change Meter. The Time Operations window will open with the Change Meter page displayed, as shown in Figure 10.13.

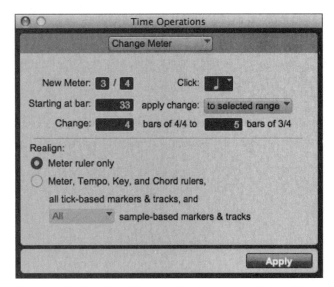

Figure 10.13 The Change Meter page of the Time Operations window.

4. Change the new meter to 3/4. For this example, leave the pop-up click selector at 1/4 notes. However, if your new meter were 3/8—or 5/8, 7/8, or 11/8—you would usually have the click change to 1/8 notes for the section.

5. Bar 33 is already selected as the starting bar for the meter change. Use the pop-up selector to the right of this field to choose To Selected Range (rather than To Session End or Until Next Bar).

6. Be sure to specify that you want these four bars of 4/4 changed to *four* bars of 3/4 (and not some other number) because in this case, you want the tempo to remain constant—that is, the 1/4 notes should be equivalent between the two sections.

7. In this case, the Realign option will be fine if left set to its default, Meter Ruler Only.

8. Click the Apply button.

9. If the Meter Ruler is currently visible (enabled either using the Ruler View selector in the Edit window or via the View > Ruler submenu), two new Meter Change events will now appear: one for the beginning of the 3/4 section and another where it returns to 4/4.

10. Highlight Bars 69–72 (the next occurrence of the 3/4 section) and repeat these steps.

Insert Time

The time units displayed in the Insert Time page of the Time Operations window always reflect those of the currently active main ruler. Even if you're not a MIDI user and don't edit music at all, the Insert Time and Cut Time functions will occasionally be useful. For example, when creating soundtracks for video or multimedia, somewhere along the line, you may need to add more time at the beginning of the session because the segment needs a longer intro. When creating music with MIDI, of course, this command is essential, allowing you to work in the Bars|Beats Time Scale, adding bars at the beginning of the song or at any point within its Timeline, as shown in Figure 10.14. Usually, you will choose to have this command affect locations of all the subsequent markers and tempo and meter events, which are then pushed later in the Timeline by a corresponding amount. (One exception might be when working on a video or film soundtrack, where you might add bars to the music without wanting to affect the positions of sample-based markers—absolute time locations—that reference dialog or sound effects.)

Cut Time

Options in the Cut Time page of the Time Operations window are similar to those for Insert Time. Time units here also reflect the currently active main ruler. If desired, you can adjust all subsequent markers, tempo events, and meter events to an earlier position in the session's Timeline after the specified range is cut.

Move Song Start

In the Move Song Start page of the Time Operations window, choosing musical bars as the Time Scale units (time base) for this function allows you to move the beginning of the session's

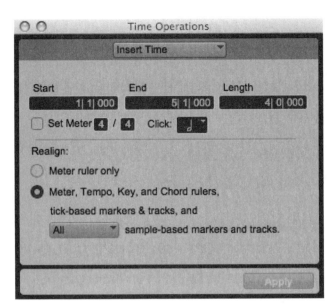

Figure 10.14 The Insert Time page of the Time Operations window.

Timeline to a specified bar location and at the same time assign a new bar number to that new location (if desired). Whether you choose to have this operation apply to marker locations and Audio tracks that are sample-based (that is, their positional references are based on absolute time rather than musical bars and beats) depends on the situation. As with the Insert Time function, when scoring a soundtrack, you might use Move Song Start to move a music cue to a later position. Using the Minutes:Seconds time units here, for example, allows you to specify that Bar 1 should now start at exactly five seconds into the Timeline while leaving sample-based markers and tracks unaffected. This is shown in Figure 10.15.

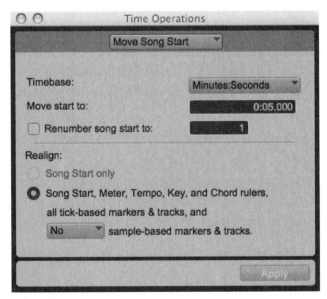

Figure 10.15 The Move Song Start page of the Time Operations window. Here, we're inserting five seconds at the beginning of the song without affecting bar numbering or the position of any markers or clips within tracks whose timebase is set to samples (absolute).

In the Tempo Ruler of the Edit window, a Song Start marker appears (a small red diamond-shaped icon, which appears at the beginning of the session's Timeline by default). The Song Start marker's position changes as a result of applying the Move Song Start function. However, you can also accomplish more or less the same thing by dragging this marker directly in the Tempo Ruler if you prefer. As with most events in the Edit window, if Grid Edit mode is active, the current grid value governs the movement of the markers you drag in the rulers; they will snap from one grid increment to another. (For example, seconds might be convenient in Minutes:Seconds format, or frames on system configurations supporting SMPTE time code format for Grid mode.) When moving the song start in this manner, it's important to note that, by default, the position of clips and other events in all tick-based tracks will also be affected. If instead you don't want tick-based events to be affected (including all MIDI track events and clips, or automation event locations in Audio tracks, Aux Input tracks, and Master Fader tracks whose timebase is set to Ticks), hold down Shift+Control (Shift+Start in Windows) as you drag the Song Start marker.

Tempo Operations

All selections in this submenu open the Tempo Operations window. Each of the functions in this window allows you to insert one or more tempo events into your session's Timeline. Tempo events can be viewed in the Tempo Ruler and graphically edited in the Graphic Tempo Editor window that can be displayed beneath the Tempo Ruler by clicking the Expand/Collapse triangle in the Tempo Ruler. You can also move existing tempo events in the Tempo Ruler itself (even when the Tempo Editor window is not visible). If Grid mode is enabled, adding or moving tempo events will affect the grid spacing.

When you adjust tempos in Pro Tools, the positions of all events in tick-based tracks are displaced by a corresponding amount. In contrast to the absolute time references in sample-based tracks, event positions in tick-based tracks are defined by musical time references—bars, beats, and ticks (subdivisions of a 1/4 note). Consequently, these events are always *relative* to the current tempo. If you're using audio clips for cymbal crashes, individual drum hits, or sound effects in conjunction with MIDI or Instrument tracks, for example, using the Ticks timebase in those Audio tracks will keep the audio clip locations in sync with the MIDI tracks even after a tempo change is applied. Likewise, events on tick-based tracks with active Elastic Audio plug-ins will be adjusted for the tempo-change operations you make in this window. In this case, Tempo Event–Generated Warp markers (vertical lines, similar to Warp markers but with diamonds at their tops) will appear within the affected audio clips to indicate where Elastic Audio processing has been applied to conform the audio to the changed tempos.

Following are brief descriptions of each tempo operation. Incidentally, if you control where the selection will end in real time (minutes, seconds, and milliseconds, for example), you will almost always want to enable the Advanced check box in the Tempo Operations window. Lastly, although not discussed here, several of these options can be useful for building tempo maps should you ever need to build a MIDI orchestration based on a recorded performance with constantly changing tempos.

- **Constant.** Applies a single tempo setting to the currently selected range. A single tempo event is created at the beginning of the range, and any previously existing tempo events within it are deleted. If the Preserve Tempo After Selection option is enabled, a second tempo event returns the tempo to its original setting at the end of the selection.

- **Linear.** Creates a series of tempo events to establish a ramp-shaped progression from one tempo setting to another. As with some of these other tempo operations, if you enable the Advanced option, you can specify the density and resolution of the resulting series of tempo events. A pop-up selector among the Advanced options (also available for the other tempo shapes) allows for the automatic calculation of the new real-time end point that will result from your tempo-change settings (in minutes and seconds, for example).

- **Parabolic.** Instead of a straight ramp up or down between the two tempo settings, you can adjust the curvature of this parabola shape with a slider or numerical field. A zero curvature is a straight ramp identical to the Linear tempo operation. Larger positive values push most of the tempo acceleration toward the end of the selection, while negative values push it toward the beginning.

- **S-curve.** With this shape, you can specify the exact time location for the midpoint (using the main timebase units, as with all other tempo operations). You also specify exactly what tempo (somewhere between the starting and ending tempo values for the range) should be in effect at that midpoint. The Curvature value determines how steeply the tempo increases or decreases between the midpoint and the start/end points of the range. Larger positive values push most of the tempo acceleration from the midpoint value toward the start/end points of the current selection, while negative values push the acceleration to/from the midpoint tempo near the midpoint itself.

- **Scale.** Unlike the other tempo operations here, scaling tempos doesn't overwrite existing tempo events. Instead, scaling is used to relatively increase or decrease the value of all tempos within the currently selected range. You can specify this either as a percentage or by altering the average tempo within the current selection (which is automatically calculated for you).

- **Stretch.** The Stretch function (shown in Figure 10.16) automatically adjusts the tempo of the current selection to match a specific duration.

Using the Tempo Ruler's Tempo Change Dialog Box

Bear in mind that the tempo operations described here must be used on a currently selected range in your session's Timeline (either within a track or in a ruler). You could also insert a single tempo event, either at the beginning of the Timeline or at some specific point in the Timeline. (Tempo events remain in effect until the end of the session or until another tempo event is reached.) After setting the Start value to the desired location—either by clicking on a clip with the Grabber tool or by clicking somewhere with the Selector tool—click the + (plus) sign at the left end of the Tempo Ruler. The Tempo Change dialog box (shown in Figure 10.17) will open.

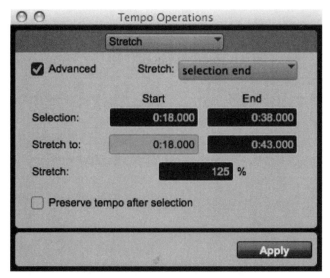

Figure 10.16 The Tempo Operations dialog box, used to adjust the tempo so that the selected musical segment will match a given length of time.

Figure 10.17 The Tempo Change dialog box.

Event Operations

All selections in the Event Operations submenu (shown in Figure 10.18) open the Event Operations window: Quantize, Change Velocity, Change Duration, Transpose, Select/Split Notes, Input Quantize, Step Input, Restore Performance, and Flatten Performance. A pop-up selector in this window switches between pages for these options that alter currently selected MIDI data (or quantize audio clips or events, when using the Elastic Audio). You can click the Apply button repeatedly to apply the current settings for each function without leaving this window. You can find brief descriptions of each of these operations in Chapter 8; the next section explores the Pro Tools quantization features for MIDI note events and Elastic Audio events in more detail, along with the use of Flatten/Restore Performance and the Step Input feature.

Figure 10.18 The Event Operations submenu.

Using the Event Operations Window on MIDI Events   After clicking the Apply button in the Event Operations window to hear the effect of your change on selected data, you can undo the operation by pressing Command+Z (Ctrl+Z in Windows). If you want the Event Operations window to stay open after applying each function, click the Apply button or press Enter on the numeric keypad. If you want the window to close after applying a function, press Return (Enter in Windows) on the alphanumeric keyboard instead.

Most of the functions in the Event Operations window (shown in Figure 10.19) are used exclusively for transforming currently selected MIDI data. Like many other windows in Pro Tools,

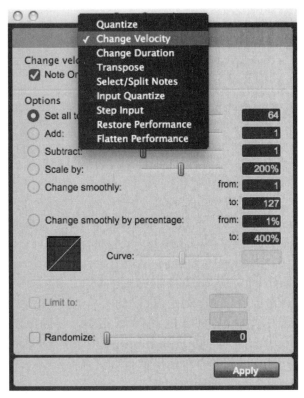
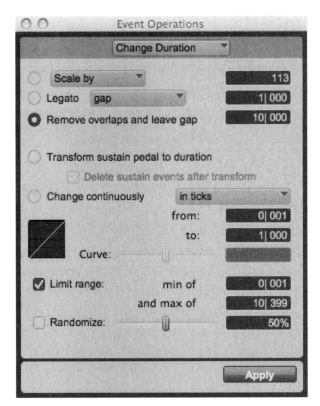

Figure 10.19 Without leaving the Event Operations window, you can use a pop-up selector to switch between Quantize, Change Velocity/Duration, Transpose, Flatten/Restore Performance, and other functions.

pressing the Tab key cycles through the fields (press Shift+Tab to move backward); pressing the Up and Down Arrow keys increases/decreases the value for the selected field. When any pitch or velocity field is selected, you can also enter new values by playing a note on your MIDI controller.

Quantize

As explained in Chapter 8, quantization snaps all MIDI notes and audio clips or Elastic Audio events within the current selection to a specified rhythmic value. The attacks and/or releases of MIDI notes (their beginnings or ends, as defined by Note On and Note Off events) are moved to the nearest increment on the horizontal time grid. The spacing of this quantization grid is determined by the selected note value in the Quantize window. Quantization doesn't affect the beginning and end positions of MIDI *clips*, however; although it does affect the beginning position of *audio* clips (when applied to audio clips rather than Elastic Audio events). Many of the options in this window (see Figure 10.20) are self-explanatory, so this section mentions just a few items of special interest. Note that the Option+0 (zero) keyboard shortcut (Alt+0 in Windows) opens the Quantize window directly.

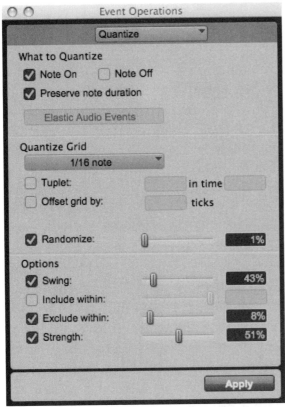

Figure 10.20 Use the Quantize window for adjusting time locations of MIDI notes, audio clips, or Elastic Audio events. It can be useful for cleaning up rhythmic timing or conforming multiple recordings by some percentage toward a common feel.

Quantize Grid

In this pop-up selector, you can choose among note values that will serve as the increments for the quantization grid (the basis for adjusting audio or MIDI note event positions, in conjunction with the other parameters in the Quantize window). Along with standard note values (whole/half notes, 1/4 notes, 1/8 notes, and so on), you can also choose dotted values and triplets.

You can also choose from among various Groove templates that are provided with the program or others that you create with Beat Detective. Groove templates are irregular grids that you can use to quantize MIDI or audio events. Sometimes, these can produce more human-sounding results than simply adding a swing factor to a straight (symmetrical) time grid for quantization. For example, try manually creating a straight MIDI drum part with a constant 1/16-note hi-hat pattern and applying various grooves to get a feel for the effects they produce. For recorded MIDI parts, one trick is to use the percentage sliders to reduce somewhat the effect of quantization on note position, relying more on velocity patterns from the Groove template to produce a more subtle transformation.

As discussed in Chapter 12, "The Pro Tools Groove," you can create your own Groove templates based on audio or MIDI selections and use these to quantize MIDI events and audio clips/ events. If you combine live MIDI performances (especially MIDI parts created with the Step Input feature), this is an essential technique for obtaining a tighter groove between multiple overdubbed parts.

Tuplet

A *tuplet* is a rhythmic grouping where some irregular number of notes fits into the normal duration of two (or four, and so on) notes (see Figure 10.21). For example, 1/8 note triplets are a 3:2 tuplet because three 1/8 notes fit into the duration of two normal 1/8 notes (three notes at 1|000, 1|320, and 1|640 instead of only two at 1|000 and 1|480). Those creating dance music may want to experiment with quantizing to 1/8-note quintuplets and septuplets for some funky grooves.

Randomize

Marketing types claim that *randomizing* is the way to humanize MIDI parts that have been over-quantized. However, while the timing of good musicians is indeed irregular, it's actually quite complex—not simply random. Nevertheless, if your quantized parts really do sound stiff, some *small* amount of randomization (usually less than 10%) can sometimes help. Experimentation is the key. On a drum part, for example, you may get better results applying randomness to only one element (say, the hi-hat or small percussion parts) rather than the entire groove. And even in these cases, a small amount of randomization applied on the *velocities* (using the Change Velocity command) may be all you need. Here's another recommendation: The stiffness of over-quantized parts often has more to do with the upbeats than the downbeats. For this reason, try using a small amount of swing—10% or less—to loosen up a drum groove rather than random-izing the timing in general.

Swing

Any swing factor greater than 0% delays every upbeat of the specified musical value. In other words, if you're swinging 1/8 notes, the ones that coincide with 1/4-note divisions are unaffected by the swing factor, but the ones between 1/4 notes are moved somewhat later. This can go from

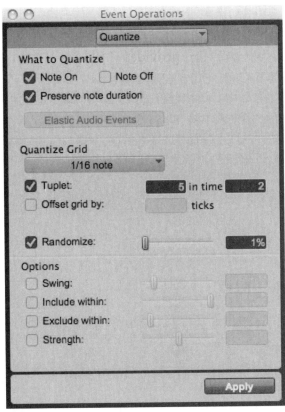

Figure 10.21 Tuplets allow you to create rhythmic groupings of the main beat that aren't multiples of two or three. For example, here 1/16-note quintuplets are selected as a basis for quantization (with a small degree of randomization).

a very subtle groove factor (<10%) through various degrees of shuffle to a full triplet feel (100%) or even more. Very small amounts of swing (for example, 2–5% on 1/8 notes or 1/16 notes in drum and/or bass parts) can make a huge feel improvement on quantized MIDI parts that sound a little stiff compared to the Audio tracks you've laid down.

Swing quantization is very musically useful, but many users find its parameters a bit confusing in Pro Tools. Here's how it works:

- **0% swing.** Applies no swing at all. If you're quantizing a series of 1/8 notes, each 1/4-note downbeat in a measure is at 1|000, 2|000, and so on, and each 1/8-note upbeat is at 1|480, 2|480, and so on. (Because there are 960 ticks, or subdivisions, for every 1/4 note in Pro Tools, each 1/8 note corresponds to exactly half that: 480 ticks.)

- **100% swing.** A full triplet (or 12/8) feel. Each 1/8 note upbeat is quantized to the third note of an 1/8-note triplet, 1|640, 2|640, and so on. 960 ticks per 1/4 note divided by 3 equals 320, so the three notes in an 1/8-note triplet are at 1|000, 1|320, and 1|640. The effect of 100% swing is the same as quantizing to a 3:2 tuplet (see Table 10.1). As always, the 1/4-note downbeats (the first note in each triplet group) stay at 1|000, 2|000, and so on, and are unaffected by any 1/8-note swing percentage.

- **150% swing.** Quantizes each 1/8-note upbeat to the fourth 1/16 note: 1|720, 2|720, and so on. (960 ticks divided by 4 equals 240, so the four 1/16 notes are at 1|000, 1|240, 1|480, and 1|720. It's the same thing as quantizing to dotted 1/8 notes, in this example.)

- **300% swing.** If 100% swing moves each 1/8 note upbeat one-third of the way (160 ticks) toward the following downbeat, 300% swing moves it *all* the way there. It's as if you quantized to 1/4 notes, except that notes are always moved to the *following* 1/4 note.

In Table 10.1, you can see how progressively greater amounts of swing gradually move the timing of offbeat notes toward a full triplet value (or even beyond it at swing factors greater than 100%). There are no hard and fast rules here; you will have to experiment with all the values to achieve the feel you want. However, you will find that this is one of your most important tools for achieving a more natural feel in heavily quantized MIDI parts.

Table 10.1 Quantizing with Swing (1/4 Note = 960 Ticks)

Note Value	0% Swing	25% Swing	50% Swing	75% Swing	100% Swing	150% Swing
1/8 note	1|480	1|520	1|560	1|600	1|640	1|720
1/16 note	1|240	1|260	1|280	1|300	1|320	1|360

Include Within

This quantization parameter is worth exploring; it only quantizes notes within a certain distance of the specified note value. For example, you might use this if you want to make sure the downbeats of the hi-hat part coincide exactly with kick and snare 1/4 notes (which are strictly quantized) without changing any of the looser upbeats between them. Select the hi-hat notes only and then set the Quantize grid to 1/4 notes, changing the Include Within parameter to 50% or less (which leaves anything further than a 1/16 note in either direction from the nearest 1/4 note unaffected). Your hi-hat downbeats are moved to exactly 1|000, 2|000, and so on (unless you set the Strength parameter to less than 100%, of course), while the upbeats remain at their original locations.

Strength

When this parameter is set to anything less than 100%, notes are moved only that percentage of the distance between their current location and the nearest quantization grid increment. This improves timing while preserving some of the natural feel of your performance.

Quantizing Clips   The Clip > Quantize to Grid command does *not* apply quantization to individual MIDI notes, even when MIDI clips are selected. A more accurate description of this function might be "snap clips to grid." It moves selected audio or MIDI clips and all their contents by snapping their left boundaries—or the Sync Point within them, if they contain one—to the nearest grid increment, based on the current grid value. The Quantize to Grid command predates the relatively sophisticated MIDI editing and Elastic Audio features in current versions of Pro Tools. However, many novice Pro Tools users (including veterans of other MIDI programs) might select this command, thinking it will allow them to quantize their MIDI drum part. Not so!

Restore Performance

Pro Tools "remembers" the original recorded MIDI performance in MIDI clips, even after you've made multiple edits (not including manual changes) and have saved and reopened the session any number of times. The Restore Performance command opens the page of the Event Operations window (shown in Figure 10.22), where you can restore selected MIDI clips to their original recorded form (or to the most recent flattened version; see the next section), choosing one or all of the following attributes for restoration: Timing, Duration, Velocity, and Pitch.

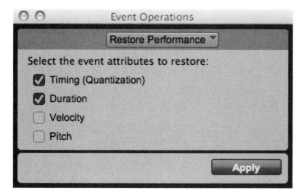

Figure 10.22 Restore Performance lets you return parameters of a MIDI recording to their original, "as recorded" state.

Flatten Performance

The Flatten Performance page of the Event Operations window, shown in Figure 10.23, enables you to freeze the current state of the selected MIDI clip. This flattened version will then be the state to which the clip returns the next time you execute the Restore Performance command. As before, you can choose Timing, Duration, Velocity, or Pitch as the parameters for flattening.

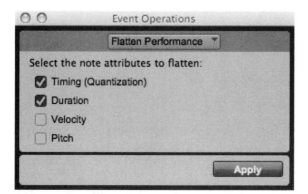

Figure 10.23 Flatten Performance establishes the current state of a MIDI recording as the condition to which it will revert if you later apply the Restore Performance command.

Here's a typical scenario for using the Flatten Performance command: Imagine you've applied some basic note corrections, global velocity changes, or other edits to a drum part you've previously recorded on a MIDI or Instrument track. Now you will apply some quantization before recording additional parts because the timing seems a little too loose. A common pitfall of quantization, however, is that you can "correct" all the humanity right out of a piece by applying too much of it. Once you've added a few more instrumental parts, you may discover that the original timing in the drums really wasn't as bad as it once seemed when heard all by itself or with only one or two other parts. The Restore Performance function is great because it lets you go all the way back the original performance. But what if you'd really rather not lose all those changes you made *before* starting to quantize? No problem: At any point in the process when you know that all changes made so far to the selected MIDI clip are keepers, apply the Flatten Performance command. This now becomes your new go-back state for that clip should you ever decide to retrace your steps and apply a different set of edits to it from that point forward.

Step Input

Even if you're not severely keyboard challenged, non–real-time entry of a sequence of MIDI notes or chords can sometimes be a useful technique. The important thing to understand about Step Input mode is that you can enter one or several notes simultaneously. Some people use Step Input when creating specific drum patterns, for example. Of course, you can also use this feature to create "impossible" *ostinatos* (rhythmic, persistently repeating musical figures) and arpeggios.

Following are some basic rules and techniques for using Step Input to create sequences of MIDI notes in Pro Tools:

- Step Input begins at the Edit window's current Start position, so you should set this to the correct time location before you begin entering notes.

- As you can see in Figure 10.24, options in the Step Input window allow you to either fix the note velocities at a specific value or use the velocity data created as you strike notes on your keyboard (or other MIDI controller).

- A destination MIDI or Instrument track must be selected as the target for Step Input. The notes will generally sound as you enter them, whether or not you record-enable the MIDI or Instrument track. (Tracks do not need to be record-enabled for Step Input recording.)

- Pro Tools allows you to change the destination track for the note events you're creating in Step Input mode on the fly, which opens up some interesting possibilities for *hocketing* (rapid alternation of notes or very short phrases between distinct instrumental timbres) or call-and-answer effects between two different tracks, for example.

- Setting the Note Length percentage to less than 100% provides a more *staccato* style (each note ends before the next one begins); setting the value closer to 100% creates a more *legato* style (the end of each note sustains to the beginning of the next note). You can also use length percentages greater than 100% if you want each note to overlap the beginning of the next note.

Figure 10.24 The Step Input window allows non–real-time entry of MIDI notes. In this example, keys on the MIDI controller have been mapped to the Undo Step, Next Step, and Redo Step functions.

- When the Step Input window's Numeric Keypad Shortcuts option is enabled, the Transport commands for these keys are temporarily suspended, and you can use them for Step Input functions. The shortcuts are as follows:

  - The numeric keypad's Enter key is the same as the Next Step button; it skips the insertion point forward to the next step. You can use this to create rests, for example.

  - The 0 key on the numeric keypad is the same as the Undo Step button; it undoes the previously entered step and moves the insertion point back to its previous position.

  - While holding down the key(s) on the MIDI controller during Step Input, you can also use the Next Step and Undo Step buttons—or their keyboard shortcuts—to lengthen or shorten the notes by the current step increment value.

  - The 1 key on the numeric keypad selects whole-note step increments.

  - The 2 key on the numeric keypad selects 1/2 notes.

  - The 3 key on the numeric keypad enables tuplets in relation to the selected step increment. (For example, 3:2 tuplets with an 1/8-note step increment creates 1/8-note triplets; 5:2 creates quintuplets; 7:2 creates septuplets; and so on.)

  - The 4 key on the numeric keypad selects 1/4 notes.

- The 5 key on the numeric keypad selects 1/8 notes.

- The 6 key on the numeric keypad selects 1/16 notes.

- The 7 key on the numeric keypad selects 1/32 notes.

- The 8 key on the numeric keypad selects 1/64 notes.

- The decimal point key on the numeric keypad enables dotted-note values (half again as long as the ordinary note value—so a dotted 1/8-note increment is 720 ticks instead of 480, for example).

MIDI Real-Time Properties

The MIDI Real-Time Properties window enables you to apply real-time, non-destructive changes to the events in MIDI tracks and clips. These include quantization of note positions, changes to the duration and velocity of MIDI notes, transposition of their pitches (in octaves and/or semitones), and delay (which can cause the MIDI events in the affected track or clip to play back either earlier or later than their original position).

In Figure 10.25, you can see the Real-Time Properties window for a selected MIDI clip. Note that unless you click the Write to Clip button, these changes are applied in real time and don't affect the actual contents of the selected clip. In fact, unless you specifically enable that option in the MIDI tab of the Preferences dialog box, Pro Tools always displays the original "source" location of MIDI events, not their position as modified by MIDI real-time properties applied to the clip or track where they reside.

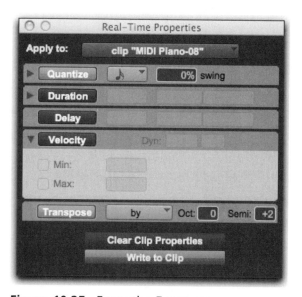

Figure 10.25 From the Event menu, you can open the Real-Time Properties window for a selected MIDI clip.

The Edit window also includes a Real-Time Properties view (column) that affects entire tracks. As you can see in Figure 10.26, many of the options in this column are similar to those in the

Real-Time Properties window. It's important to understand that clip-based properties always override track-based properties. Clip-based properties can provide a powerful compositional tool, especially when combined with Mirrored MIDI Editing mode (which you can enable via a button in the Edit window or via a selection in the Options menu). For example, if you want to double a part at the octave, one method is to copy the MIDI clip to another track (by Option-dragging, or Alt-dragging in Windows while in Grid mode) and then apply a transposition value of +12. If you enable Mirrored MIDI Editing, any note changes you make in the original copy of the clip are immediately reflected in all other identically named copies. You might apply additional real-time property changes to the transposed part, such as velocity or duration changes, according to the characteristics of the sound used on the MIDI destination for each track. Within a single track, you might use Mirrored MIDI Editing to apply clip-based properties to various copies of a single MIDI clip—perhaps repeating a bass line or melody shifted by an interval of a fifth or octave higher, for example.

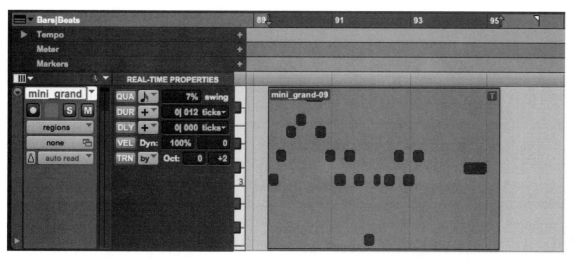

Figure 10.26 Parameters in the Real-Time Properties column of the Edit window affect the entire MIDI or Instrument track (which in turn may contain clips with their own real-time properties).

Figure 10.1 at the beginning of this chapter shows the MIDI Event List (which is also briefly described in Chapter 8). You will note that where MIDI events are affected by real-time properties, a T or R appears to indicate whether these are track-based or clip-based. (Note that clips were previously called *regions* in Pro Tools; the letter R represents the former "region-based" properties.)

Remove Duplicate Notes

When you are layering up parts in Loop Record mode (drum-machine style), it is all too easy to end up with duplicate notes. Especially after quantizing, these duplicate notes may not be easy to see, but they can cause phase-cancelled, flanger-like effects as notes are double triggered. While the MIDI Event List might also be handy for these instances, the Event > Remove Duplicate Notes command makes the process much easier.

Beat Detective

Beat Detective is discussed in more detail in Chapter 12. With Beat Detective, you can extract Groove templates from either audio or MIDI selections (to be used by the Grid/Groove Quantize command in the MIDI Operations window).

Identify Beat

This command is one of the ways you can tell Pro Tools what the starting and ending bar|beat positions should be for the current selection. One thing you can do with this command is use a precise audio selection (four or eight bars that you've precisely selected using Loop Playback mode, for example) to establish a Pro Tools tempo so you can effectively edit in Grid mode. (Steps for this technique are also described in Chapter 12.)

Renumber Bars

The Renumber Bars command is very straightforward; selecting it simply renumbers the bars in your song. A typical scenario for renumbering bars is when your song begins with a drum fill of some kind that begins before Bar 1, where the band enters. Similarly, for songs with a slow or *rubato* introduction (freely played, without a strict tempo), you may prefer to have the point where the groove kicks in numbered as Bar 1. In either of these cases, all the bars before Bar 1 will have negative numbers after renumbering.

All MIDI Notes Off

This command silences any stuck MIDI notes (caused by system malfunction or interruption of MIDI data transmission—a Note On message is transmitted, but a Note Off message is never received). The keyboard shortcut for this command is Command+Shift+period (Ctrl+Shift+period in Windows). If you are a MIDI user, this one is worth committing to memory!

Other Commands Relating to MIDI

These are also discussed in Chapters 5 and 8. Here is a brief summary:

- Options > Click turns the MIDI metronome click on and off. This command is also accessible from the Transport window.

- Setup > Click/Countoff opens the Click/Countoff Options dialog box. This command is also accessible by double-clicking the Metronome button in the Transport window.

- Options > MIDI Thru enables the performance being recorded to a MIDI or Instrument track in Pro Tools to be echoed back out of Pro Tools, according to the track's settings (MIDI port and channel, program number, volume, pan, and so on).

Summary

Pro Tools has some very powerful tools for editing MIDI events and for creating musical arrangements based on MIDI performances mixed with digital audio. Be sure to check out Chapter 12, "The Pro Tools Groove," and Chapter 13, "A Multitrack Music Session," for more musical applications of Pro Tools. Other audio-savvy programs also place a strong emphasis on MIDI and composition—Digital Performer, Logic Pro, Cubase, and SONAR, to name just a few. Whenever required, Pro Tools can import and export Standard MIDI Files (using the .smf file name extension) for sharing with other applications. However, many composers prefer to use nothing *but* Pro Tools for their projects, regardless of whether their emphasis is more on MIDI or audio. The dedicated MIDI editing features in Pro Tools make this a more compelling option today than it has been in years gone by.

11 Synchronization

If you need to synchronize playback and recording in Pro Tools to some external device (such as a video deck or a multitrack tape recorder), this chapter will be of special interest to you. It includes both basic concepts and some fairly technical information. You may not absorb it all at first reading, but it will provide some context for dealing with synchronization issues when they arise.

As you will see, various levels of synchronization are possible with Pro Tools. Your synchronization requirements may be no more complicated than simply triggering playback at the correct position in the session's Timeline, when the corresponding time code location is received from the master device (trigger sync). More sophisticated techniques lock the internal audio clock of Pro Tools to a very stable external reference (for example, video sync, a digital reference known as *word clock* or *word sync*, or a timing reference generated by an external synchronization peripheral, such as the Avid Sync HD). When Pro Tools and the master device share a common *reference sync*, they can stay perfectly locked together over longer periods of time. Sample-accurate sync is also extremely important when Pro Tools audio channels are combined with other audio playing simultaneously from another source, especially where there might be some shared information in these signals (such as microphone leakage!). Otherwise, phase cancellation can occur due to slight differences in playback speed on the two devices (for example, between Pro Tools and a multitrack tape recorder).

Synchronization Defined

Synchronization refers to the technology and procedures required to ensure that two (or more) devices record and play back information together in a consistent fashion over time. Synchronized devices must always start at the same position relative to one another—and, ideally, *stay* in the same relative position as the devices continue to operate so that they don't drift apart.

Synchronization Theory: The Basics Though the focus of this book is always on practical applications of the concepts in Pro Tools rather than pure theory, in the interest of being clear, here's just a bit of theoretical perspective. The following information is drawn from Vol. 3 (Desktop Audio) of this publisher's CSi (*Cool School Interactus*) and Course Clips CD-ROM series.

For synchronizing (audio and video) devices, three fundamental time attributes come into play:

■ A defined unit of measurement for the information storage method (for example, time units such as hours, minutes, seconds, frames, samples—or inches on a moving tape)

■ A nominal rate at which these measurements are taken (number of measurements taken per unit of time—for example, how many frames, samples, or inches per second)

■ A stable timing reference that ensures measurements are recorded and reproduced at a precise rate, maintaining their correct time relationship (for example, video sync, sample clock or word sync, capstan tachometer)

In short, synchronization requires a *measurement*, a *speed*, and a *reference* that keeps that speed consistent.

Time code adds a fourth element: timestamp, or location information. Like the address of your house, a *timestamp* is a precise, numerical reference. It's used for positioning devices for playback from specific time locations, or to indicate exactly where an event (a video edit, a sound effect, the beginning of a musical cue, and so on) should occur.

SMPTE timecode (and its equivalent in the MIDI protocol, MIDI time code) is a standard timestamping (addressing) method, used to get playback from multiple devices to start from the correct point in time. For digital audio, some sort of digital clock sync should also be used as a timing reference if these devices need to stay precisely locked together over longer durations. (Both continuous resync and reference sync methods use an external timing reference to control the playback sample rate of Pro Tools; these are discussed later in this chapter.)

In any synchronization setup, one device is designated as the *master*. The other devices in the setup, the *slaves*, get their location information from this master and start (trigger) playback at the appropriate location. Figure 11.1 shows a simple configuration, where Pro Tools is slaved to another device via an external SMPTE interface on the host computer. Pro Tools can begin near-instantaneous playback after analyzing the received timestamp information, whereas analog or digital tape machines first have to rewind or fast-forward the tape to reach the appropriate location. In certain situations, a master also provides a speed reference for the slaved devices (for example, two synced analog tape machines, or a digital audio device whose sample rate is continuously adjusted to that of an external source).

In audio-for-video production, the video Transport is typically the master (although Machine-Control users often reverse this relationship; see Chapter 14, "Post-Production and Soundtracks"). The master provides a location reference (in the form of SMPTE time code) that triggers where audio playback begins so that audio events can be correctly placed in relation to the picture. In most professional facilities, a speed reference is also provided in the form of a stable video signal called *black burst* or *house sync*. With the appropriate synchronization peripheral (like the Sync HD or MOTU Digital Timepiece), this external timing reference can be converted to control the audio sample rate of the external Pro Tools hardware interface itself.

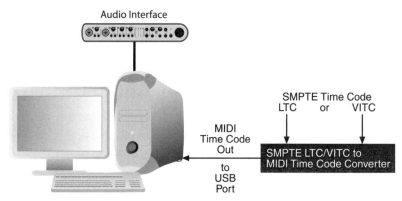

Figure 11.1 A typical SMPTE synchronization setup. An external SMPTE interface translates incoming SMPTE data from its audio or video encoded format to MIDI Time Code (MTC), which is then routed to Pro Tools via the computer's USB port.

SMPTE Time Code

Named for the Society of Motion Picture and Television Engineers, the organization that standardized the format, SMPTE time code is used throughout the video and film industries for cameras, switchers, editing systems, and audio post-production. Time-location data is encoded into a data "word" that consists of 80 bits, representing hours, minutes, seconds, frames, and subframes. The number of frames per minute depends on the application or geographical location. (See the "Frame Rates" section later in this chapter.) SMPTE time code provides a standard language for identifying time locations among various operators and devices in an audio, video, or film project. *Edit Decision Lists* (*EDLs*) are text documents that contain time-code locations for edits made from multiple source tapes; they can be automatically generated by some video-editing systems (and are comparable to *playlists* in Pro Tools tracks). Hit points for audio events (events in the video to which specific sounds or music cues are synchronized) are also sometimes listed in a similar format.

SMPTE time code allows events to be properly placed during edit and permits multiple devices to maintain a correct time relationship during recording and playback. When Pro Tools is in Online mode (that is, the playback location is controlled by incoming time code), it looks at the incoming SMPTE timestamp information (from a separate SMPTE peripheral attached to your computer) and then calculates the proper position to start playback within the session's Timeline. (The offset for the Timeline of your Pro Tools session, known as the Session Start time, appears in an editable field of the Session Setup window, which is opened via Setup > Session.)

If the incoming SMPTE location is *prior* to the start of the session, Pro Tools waits until the Session Start time is reached before starting playback. If the first time-code location received is *later* than the Session Start time (for example, if you press the Play button on the video deck that's serving as the master device when it's somewhere in the middle of the tape), Pro Tools will jump to the appropriate position in its Timeline and start playing back—regardless of whether the session actually contains any clips at that point. (So make sure you get your SMPTE references right!)

Synchronization Example with an External Video Deck

Let's say a video editor provides you a BetaCam SP master tape containing a 30-second spot for which you need to provide sound effects and music. The video editor tells you that the time-code location for the beginning of the program is one hour, zero minutes, zero seconds, zero frames (01:00:00:00), and most importantly, that the time-code format is 29.97 frames per second, non-drop. You pop the tape into your BetaCam deck and notice that prior to the actual beginning of the spot, there are color bars, audio tones, and so on. (The LTC time-code output of the BetaCam deck—a BNC connector for audio—is connected to the time-code audio input of your computer's SMPTE/MIDI interface, which you indicate as the synchronization source for Pro Tools.)

Here is the process you would follow for your work in Pro Tools:

1. Create a new Pro Tools session. Set the sample rate of this session to 48 kHz (standard for professional video).

2. Open Setup > Session. Set the Session Start time to 01:00:00:00. Use the pop-up Time Code Rate selector to choose 29.97 fps.

3. Create a stereo Audio track. You want to record the original sound from the video master into Pro Tools—not only because it will inevitably require your audio engineer's magic touch to correct inconsistent levels, background noise, and so on, but because the finished stereo mix you lay back onto the video tape must contain your music and sound effects as well as the original spoken dialog and ambient sound.

4. Arm your track(s) for recording and check your levels. If your video editors have been doing their jobs, you can trust that the reference tones prior to the spot truly represent 0 VU. (You should check this, just in case.) If you get no level at all, verify that the audio outputs of the Beta deck are properly connected to your audio hardware inputs.

5. Open Setup > Peripherals and select the Synchronization tab. Confirm that the configuration is correct for the synchronization hardware you're using, as shown in Figure 11.2.

6. Open the Preferences dialog box; under the Operation tab, confirm in the Record section that the Record Online at Time Code (or ADAT) Lock setting is enabled.

7. Now enable the Online button in the Pro Tools Transport window so that recording of Pro Tools will be engaged when time code is received, at the corresponding location in the session's Timeline, according to the Session Start time you've specified in the Session Setup window.

8. Click the Record button in the Pro Tools Transport window.

9. Roll the video master back perhaps 9–10 seconds prior to the top of the hour and press the Play button on the video deck. After a few seconds, you should see Pro Tools kick into Record mode at the beginning of the session's Timeline, 01:00:00:00.

10. Once the spot has finished playing, press Stop on the video deck.

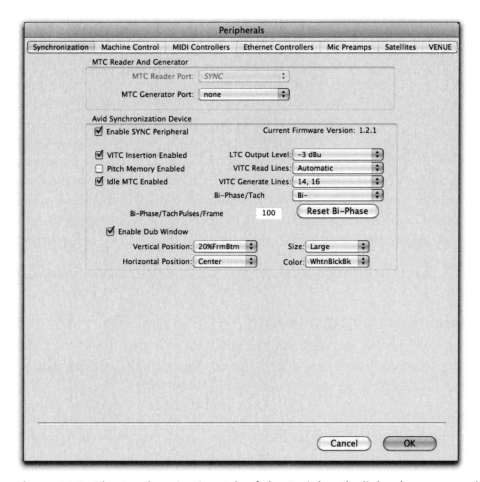

Figure 11.2 The Synchronization tab of the Peripherals dialog box, accessed from the Setup menu, enables you to specify what type of external synchronization device(s) you're using.

11. Click the Record button again in Pro Tools to disable recording mode. However, keep Pro Tools in Online mode so that time code arriving from the video continues to determine where Pro Tools starts playback as you place sound effects and music in your session.

12. At the end of the edit process, you can record the stereo mix from Pro Tools back onto the video deck, while still locked to time code (that is, with the Online button enabled), a procedure known as *layback*.

One final note: In many video facilities, when you lay your audio back to the master, you might actually be locking playback of Pro Tools to SMPTE time code arriving from a video deck in a completely separate room. In that case, you would route your audio through either analog or digital tie lines, to be recorded directly onto the first-generation master tape in the video-editing suite rather than the tape copy you've been using while editing. This layback procedure is typical in "online" video editing suites (that is, real-time and tape-based suites). However, when collaborating with Avid Media Composer or other computer-based video editing systems, it's much more common to either bounce out an audio mixdown file they can use directly or export a file in OMF or AAF interchange format. See Chapter 14 for more details.

Spotting Sound Effects and Music to Time-Code Locations   Remember to use Spot mode when Pro Tools is slaved to a master video transport! Use the video transport itself, rocking its jog/shuttle wheel to locate the precise frame location where an audio effect should be placed. Then, in Spot mode, click clips with the Grabber (or drag clips into the Edit window from the Clip List) and type their target time position directly into the Spot dialog box's Start time field. Or, once the Spot dialog box is open, roll the video tape and press the = key at the desired location or click the Current Time Code field in the dialog box. The time-code position will automatically be entered into the Start field of the Spot dialog box, and the beginning (or Sync Point) of the selected clip will move there when you click the OK button. If you're using VITC (SMPTE time code that is encoded into each video frame), you can capture the current time code even when the master video transport is stopped.

SMPTE Time Code Formats: LTC, VITC, and MTC

SMPTE time-code information can be encoded and transmitted in any of three ways. Pro Tools can work with any of these time-code formats, depending on the optional synchronization hardware you add to your Pro Tools rig.

- **LTC (Longitudinal Time Code).** This is the most common format. An audio signal encodes the time data through biphase modulation (encoding that rapidly alternates a carrier signal between two tones). The audio signal containing the time-code information might be recorded onto an Audio track of a video deck, or onto one track of a multitrack audio recorder. LTC may also be directly generated by either of these (possibly via some additional device) in real time, based on the device's own internal timing reference. Because an audio signal is conveying the SMPTE data, the master device's transport has to be in Play (or Record) mode for SMPTE information to be sent to Pro Tools as the slave device.

- **VITC (Vertical Interval Time Code).** This format incorporates time-code data into a video signal within the *overscan* area (that is, the first few lines at the top of each video frame, which are not usually visible on consumer televisions). Figure 11.3 shows a video frame where the VITC information is visible in line 22 of the video image. VITC is used in video post applications; it offers a great advantage in that time-code values are sent even when you are paused in a frame or jogging from one frame to another with the video transport paused. Synchronization peripherals that support VITC will include a video input.

- **MTC (MIDI Time Code).** This format conveys SMPTE information as MIDI data. MTC is in fact the SMPTE format that Pro Tools eventually receives, no matter what type of external SMPTE synchronization peripheral you're using (audio, video, or MIDI). Some digital multitracks and computer programs can transmit MTC directly through their MIDI Outs. In this scenario, the MTC could be received by Pro Tools even with a standard (that is, non-SMPTE) MIDI interface. MTC should not be confused with MIDI Clock, whose 24 pulse per quarter note (ppqn) subdivisions represent longer or shorter absolute time values depending on the current musical tempo, and which is sometimes transmitted by the onboard MIDI sequencers in MIDI keyboards. MTC is exactly the same absolute-time reference as SMPTE; it has no relation to the current musical tempo.

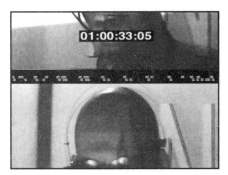

Figure 11.3 Here, the top fields of a video frame are pulled down so that the VITC in video field 22 is visible.

Frame Rates (30/29.97 Drop/Non-Drop, 25, 24 Frames per Second)

As stated before, various SMPTE frame rates are employed depending on the application or television standard in use in a particular geographical location. In the Pro Tools Session Setup window, you can select the SMPTE time-code rate. It is important for the time-code rate to be set correctly: if your setting doesn't match the actual time code being received, Pro Tools will start playback at the wrong place or drift out of correct synchronization.

■ **30 frames per second (fps).** This is the original SMPTE format developed for monochrome (black-and-white) television in North America. This frame rate is still the standard for audio-only applications in North America. It's also sometimes (though rarely) used for short-duration, industrial video; 29.97 non-drop is much more common and recommended even for these applications.

■ **30 fps drop frame.** This frame rate is used only for film sync pull-up applications—and even then, only infrequently—for correcting transfer errors between film and video.

■ **29.97 fps drop frame.** This frame rate is used in NTSC color video broadcast applications. (*NTSC* refers to the National Television Standards Committee standard, used in North America, most of Latin America and most of the Caribbean, South Korea, Japan, Taiwan, and so on.) The 29.97 drop frame format is especially indicated for longer-duration projects, where SMPTE time-code values need to exactly match absolute time. Also, as a general rule, 29.97 drop is mandatory for any video submitted to broadcast stations in countries using the NTSC standard. (As stated before, many industrial video production houses in North America use 29.97 fps *non-drop* SMPTE for short durations—corporate and marketing videos and the like—in spite of the gradual discrepancies, simply because it makes calculating event timings less complicated than when using drop frame format.)

How Drop-Frame Format Works Because the 29.97 frame rate used in NTSC color television doesn't evenly divide into minutes and seconds, certain frames are dropped in order for SMPTE to keep pace with actual time as measured by the clock. By skipping two frames at the beginning of every minute (except with minutes that are multiples of 10—00, 10, 20, 30, 40, 50, and so on) a total of 108 frames are dropped per hour. This compensates for the accumulated discrepancy between 30 fps and 29.97 fps, which amounts to 3.6 seconds per hour. (Two frames skipped times 60 minutes, less a total of 12 extra frames for the six minutes per hour that don't skip two frames, equals 108 skipped frames per hour.)

- **29.97 fps non-drop.** This frame rate is used in NTSC color video applications, especially for broadcast and shorter-duration pieces. This format makes no drop-frame adjustments in its frame-numbering scheme, and for each hour that passes, it accumulates an approximate 3.6-second timing discrepancy (108 frames, the equivalent of three seconds plus 18 frames) compared to actual time. For this reason, use of 29.97 fps non-drop is common in NTSC video projects of shorter duration, such as consumer and industrial videos, where precise durations with respect to the wall clock don't have to match exactly. In contrast, 29.97 drop frame is required when producing a 30-minute video program for broadcast.

- **25 fps.** This frame rate is used with the European PAL and SECAM video standards, which run at 25 frames per second. The PAL television format is also known as EBU (*European Broadcasting Union*). The 25 fps rate is used for video throughout Europe, Africa, Brazil, Paraguay, Uruguay, Argentina, the Middle East, Australia, and most of Asia. It is commonly used in Europe for many audio-only applications. Converting between video frames and real time is elegantly simple in this environment: One frame equals 40 milliseconds.

- **24 fps.** This frame rate is used for film applications. At 24 frames per second, each frame of time code corresponds exactly to one frame of film. There is also a 24 fps frame rate used for 24P high-definition video.

- **23.976 fps.** This is another frame rate used for high-definition video.

MIDI Time Code (MTC)

MIDI Time Code (MTC) is the MIDI equivalent of SMPTE time code. The MTC addendum to the MIDI specification became official in 1987. The timing formats are identical, but the time-stamp information is conveyed as MIDI data rather than carried in an audio or video signal. Like SMPTE, MTC is an absolute timing reference, independent of musical tempo. Generally, in order to synchronize to an external time-code master, Pro Tools requires an external interface (translator) that converts SMPTE (LTC or VITC) to MIDI Time Code, which is the format that Pro Tools directly understands. Often, a single device performs both of these functions; for example, some MIDI interfaces feature an audio or video input for receiving SMPTE time code from a master audio or video master device, which is then translated to MTC for the Pro Tools software. This information then enters the computer via the port where that peripheral is attached (typically USB in current configurations).

Digital Clock Sources for Pro Tools This chapter focuses on synchronization as a means of sharing location information between devices in a studio configuration. On a more basic level, however, it's also common to sync devices together on more of a hardware level. For example, video sync is used to ensure that the boundaries between frames in the video signals generated by two separate devices correspond exactly (even if their current locations within the material are unrelated). For digital audio devices, word clock (a.k.a. word sync) serves a similar function, ensuring that the devices' audio sample clocks, which control the *rate* of audio playback, are exactly in sync. (Again, because word clock alone transmits no *location* information, this doesn't ensure that the multiple devices will start playback at the appropriate point. That's what SMPTE time code is for!) Simply put, you might think of word clock as a way to keep digital audio playback from multiple devices in phase.

The Hardware Setup dialog box in Pro Tools allows you to select AES/EBU, S/PDIF, or ADAT Lightpipe digital inputs on your audio hardware (if available) as the clock source for your Pro Tools session (or word clock, if your audio interface supports this connection, usually via a BNC connector on the rear panel). The clock source defaults to internal, meaning the audio-playback rate is determined by the audio interface's internal sample clock. When you are digitally transferring Audio tracks from a DAT or ADAT into Pro Tools, it's often desirable to also designate that source audio device as the clock source. Just make sure that, in addition to slaving their clocks together, you specifically set the source and destination to the same nominal sample rate. Also, after completing a digital transfer into Pro Tools, if you later disconnect or power off the external device, be sure to set the Clock Source setting in Pro Tools back to Internal; failure to do so may adversely affect playback.

Conversely, when you are transferring audio *from* Pro Tools to another device, you would typically set the Clock Source setting in Pro Tools to Internal and configure the destination device to slave its sample clock to the incoming digital audio signal from Pro Tools. Again, after the transfer is completed, set that device back to its internal clock source—unless you are using a separate, external clock source for all these devices (such as the Sync HD, Big Ben, Aardsync, SSG192, Nanosyncs, TL-Sync, and so on). As discussed later in this chapter, a central clock source is highly recommended when using multiple sources and destinations and frequent two-way transfers in your studio configuration.

SMPTE Peripherals

Of course, Pro Tools understands SMPTE time-code values, which it receives via whatever SMPTE synchronization device you're using. The Pro Tools audio hardware doesn't feature any inputs for SMPTE sources, whether encoded in an audio or video signal; you'll need to purchase a SMPTE peripheral separately, according to your requirements. Most synchronization peripherals include other features; for example, many MIDI interfaces for computers also offer SMPTE-synchronization capabilities, especially LTC (SMPTE information encoded within an audio signal). Various degrees of precision are possible, according to your requirements and budget. To help you get a handle on the capabilities of the units out there, here's a theoretical breakdown of the three basic methods for synchronizing Pro Tools with external devices:

- SMPTE/MIDI interface (trigger sync)

- SMPTE/MIDI interface plus separate hardware clock

- Synchronizers that include reference sync

SMPTE/MIDI Interface (Trigger Sync)

This category includes many common MIDI interfaces that offer an audio input only for LTC (SMPTE information encoded into an audio signal). Along with the MIDI data that they transmit/receive from their MIDI ports, they also translate the audio time code into MTC and communicate this to Pro Tools via whatever connection the external device has with the computer. However, once playback starts from Pro Tools (after it figures out the appropriate location based on the time code received), the program no longer attempts to keep strict pace with the SMPTE location data being received (other than stopping once the SMPTE *stops* arriving). Therefore, a certain amount of drift could result. This sync relationship is represented in Figure 11.4. For MIDI-only projects, for example, this degree of precision may be sufficient. But for audio, especially where the audio from Pro Tools must maintain a sample-accurate level of precision with audio or video from some other device over an extended period of time, a more sophisticated synchronization method is called for. Trigger sync simply starts playback when the correct timestamp (location) value is received. Once playback starts, the slaved device doesn't again calibrate its position to the incoming time code, and the playback speed of the slave device is not governed by the incoming time-code information.

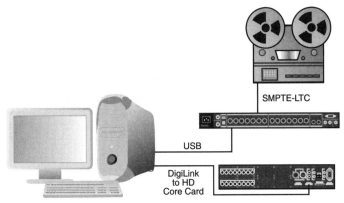

Figure 11.4 LTC (encoded as an audio signal) from a multitrack audio recorder is "translated" for Pro Tools by a MIDI interface that also has SMPTE synchronization capabilities.

SMPTE/MIDI Interface Plus Separate Hardware Clock

In these configurations, in addition to the timestamp information received as MTC from the SMPTE/MIDI interface, a separate connection links the internal clock that controls the sample rate for audio playback in the Pro Tools hardware (that is, its speed) to an external source. In some situations, both the timestamp and the clock information may come from the same master device, but often they do not. For example, in video-production houses, it is common to use a single, stable video signal known as *black burst* or *house sync* as the timing reference for all devices in the facility, providing speed information for all video decks, switchers, and Pro Tools systems equipped with the appropriate hardware. (Otherwise, it wouldn't be practical to use a video switcher to combine video signals from various sources, because their scan rates would be out of sync.) This signal contains no timestamp information, although it does help Pro Tools lock on to incoming time code somewhat more quickly. Because both the video master and the sample clock of your Pro Tools hardware are slaved to the same speed reference, they remain in frame-accurate synchronization over long durations. This is shown in Figure 11.5.

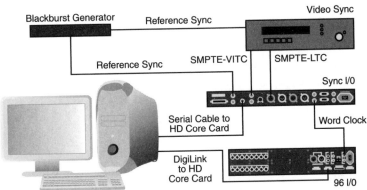

Figure 11.5 Often, as shown here, a single unit can perform both functions—SMPTE for location reference, plus various methods for resolving the sample clock of the audio hardware to an external source.

Certain devices, including Avid's Sync HD (and the discontinued Sync I/O), can translate this video-sync reference to various digital word clock input formats, including the higher-frequency Loop Sync and SuperClock used by Avid audio interfaces, so that the audio clock of the hardware itself is locked to the master video sync (the speed reference). Digital clock references in common use for audio hardware are called *word sync* or *word clock*. The advantage of using a common speed reference for both the video and audio hardware is that the beginning of each received SMPTE time-code frame and the beginning of each actual frame in the reference video signal correspond *exactly* (that is, they're *edge-aligned*). This helps Pro Tools determine the correct location and lock on to SMPTE time code more quickly and reliably and also maintains more precise sync with the video master over extended periods of time. In fact, many synchronization units combine both SMPTE synchronization (location) and hardware clock sync in the same unit (see the following section in this chapter).

That said, there are situations in which the sample clock of your Pro Tools hardware (which governs audio-playback speed) may be slaved to an external source. (Keep in mind that this doesn't necessarily have anything to do with whether the start location for audio playback and MIDI inside Pro Tools is coordinated to the location reference provided by SMPTE time code.) In the Hardware Setup dialog box, you can switch the Sync Mode setting from Internal (the internal sample clock of your audio hardware) to Digital (where your audio hardware's sample rate is slaved to that of a digital audio signal arriving on the specified input). For example, you would usually switch to Digital sync mode while transferring audio from a DAT machine via S/PDIF or AES/EBU digital inputs or while transferring from an ADAT via the Lightpipe input (or from one of Tascam's digital multitrack tape recorders via TDIF) on some audio interfaces. If you accidentally leave Digital sync mode on—if the DAT is missing or powered off the next time you open Pro Tools, for example—Pro Tools will try to sync playback speed to a nonexistent clock source.

More about Digital Audio Clock Sources   A single digital clock reference for multiple devices can be a very useful tool for audio-production facilities. Just as house sync provides a single reference for video gear, using a single device as the digital clock reference for all your audio devices can make it much easier to route audio among digital mixers, multitrack recorders, Pro Tools, DAT recorders, digital patchbays, digital effects, and so on. One example is Apogee's Big Ben Master Clock. It supports a variety of sample rates (including pull-up and pull-down; see Chapter 14) and generates a very stable, low-jitter clock reference usable by all devices. Lucid, Aardvark, HHB/Rosendahl, and Session Control also make some excellent master clock generators; see Appendix B, "Add-Ons, Extensions, and Cool Stuff for Your Rig," for more details.

Synchronizers That Include Reference Sync

These devices combine SMPTE and sample clock synchronization duties into a single unit. Examples from Avid include the Sync HD (shown in Figure 11.6), a high-end synchronization peripheral, and its predecessors, Sync I/O, Universal Slave Driver, and SMPTE Slave Driver. With these units, not only can you control Pro Tools playback according to the location references arriving via SMPTE time code, you can simultaneously synchronize the speed of the sample clock in your audio hardware to various external sources. These devices also feature *continuous resync* mode, where the audio hardware's playback rate is resolved to the incoming time code (rather than to some hardware-based speed reference), making continuous and minute adjustments to the playback rate so that it stays phase-locked to the incoming timestamp information. In other words, in continuous resync mode, these units generate a speed reference that is derived from (and continually adjusted to) the location references being received as SMPTE time code.

Figure 11.6 The Sync HD features SMPTE synchronization in LTC (audio), VITC (video), and MTC (MIDI) format; hardware-level synchronization through video sync (black burst); word clock (audio hardware sync); and two 9-pin serial ports (for interlocking Transport functions with video decks via the MachineControl option for Pro Tools). It can also add time-code window burns to passed-through video signals.

Types of Synchronization

Now that you've taken a brief look at the physical methods for synchronizing Pro Tools to external sources, let's review some general synchronization concepts from a more theoretical perspective. Remember, our objective in synchronization is simply to ensure that events on multiple devices happen consistently over time at the appropriate places. Relationships between the master and slave device(s) for dealing with location and speed references roughly break down into the following categories: trigger sync, continuous resync (also referred to as *jam sync*), and reference sync.

Trigger Sync

Trigger sync has a master/slave relationship for start, or trigger, information, but no resolving capabilities. Instead, trigger sync relies on each device's internal speed reference and stability for them to play in sync. Figure 11.7 is a simplified representation of this synchronization relationship. Once the slaved device receives time code, it calculates the correct place for playback to commence; then, after playback starts (possibly following some rewind/fast-forward action on a tape Transport), the slave's playback speed is not affected by time code that continues to be received.

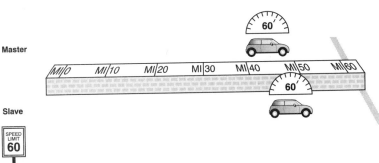

Figure 11.7 Trigger sync. Both devices start out at an agreed-upon speed of 60 miles an hour after the master provides the start command, or trigger, but the slave device can't monitor the master's speed to keep pace with it. Instead, it relies on its own speedometer—its internal speed reference. Therefore, some drift may occur over time.

Continuous Resync

Continuous resync also has a master/slave relationship for start, or trigger, information, plus resolving capabilities through the use of a device known as a *synchronizer*. The synchronizer compares the time-code location of the devices and adjusts the speed of the slave so that event playback continuously matches the location of the master. After the master machine provides a start command (trigger) and location information, the synchronizer compares the master and slave locations and tells the slave where to go to match the master. Once *lock* (matched locations) is reached, the synchronizer continues to compare the two locations. If the two drift apart, the synchronizer tells the slave(s) to speed up or slow down to match the master's location (hopefully rather smoothly). Figure 11.8 illustrates the basic idea of continuous resync. In this situation, the SMPTE location information received from the master provides a constant speed reference for the slave.

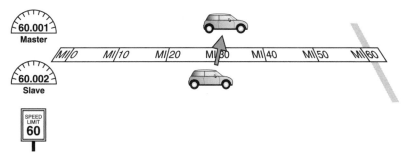

Figure 11.8 Continuous resync. After receiving the trigger to start, the slaved device continually adjusts its speed to keep pace with the master, matching the location information that the master continues to send to the slave. The slave can watch and compare its speed to the master and resolve its own speed to it so that they stay synchronized over extended periods.

Reference Sync

Reference sync (see Figure 11.9) has a master/slave relationship for start, or trigger, information and additionally utilizes a common clock or reference signal to resolve the speed of the two devices (sometimes from the master itself, or from an external source, as in the case with house sync). In larger studio configurations, it is often best to sync all digital audio devices to a single, highly stable clock source that will be the common timing reference for their sample rates. Appendix B mentions a few of the current options under "Word Clock and Sync Generators."

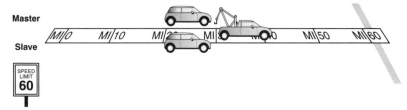

Figure 11.9 Reference sync. Trigger (location) information received from the master starts the slave into motion, while an external device controls the speed of both vehicles. They resolve to it instead of to each other.

Using QuickTime, Other Digital Video File Formats

For Pro Tools users who collaborate with nonlinear video editors, importing digital video files into a session can be very attractive. Using a digital video file as your "master" allows you to do audio post-production for video projects without having a video deck in your studio at all. (Working with video files in Pro Tools is discussed in more detail in Chapter 14. Pro Tools HD supports multiple video files in the same session, as does Pro Tools with the Complete Production Toolkit.) Video-editing systems such as Avid Xpress, Avid Media Composer, and other Avid video-editing systems; Media 100; Apple FinalCut Pro; and Adobe Premiere can export a video project for you as a QuickTime file (an industry-standard format for video files). The original video frame rate and audio sample rate (48 kHz in professional video) should be retained in the file provided for your use in Pro Tools. To minimize file size (especially important if you're not using a video accelerator card and/or you have an underpowered system), you will typically want the video editor to reduce the image size of the video frame—perhaps to DV25 720 × 480 pixels or smaller.

You import video file(s) into your Pro Tools session via the File > Import > Video command. This creates a Video track in the Edit window. (You can also import video files by dragging from the Finder/Desktop, a DigiBase browser window, or the Clip List.) You will usually also import the audio soundtrack inside the video file to your session. As when using VITC on an external video deck, using a digital video file inside Pro Tools as your video master allows frame-accurate positioning of audio events with respect to video frames (which you can zoom in to view individually as "picon" thumbnails in the Video track) even while video playback is stopped. Nonlinear access is another advantage; you can jump immediately to and from any point in the video program (that is, the session Timeline). Using digital video files eliminates the hassle and expense of shuttling a video transport back and forth as you edit your audio.

The Video window, where the video plays in real time, is also enabled after you import a video file into your session. Keep in mind that playing back video files makes additional demands on your computer's processing power. For large-scale post-production work, a video accelerator card with a separate monitor and/or a separate hard disk dedicated to video playback is highly recommended for optimum performance. However, changing the Video track to Blocks view (or even closing the Video window) also greatly reduces the overhead from video playback and can improve the speed of operation. The Edit Window offers a Video Online button for the Video track, and the Video window can be resized within Pro Tools by dragging one of its sides or corners.

Some audio facilities also have their own video-capture hardware so that outside clients can simply submit video tapes, even on VHS. The Avid Mojo SDI peripheral can capture video to the Pro Tools timeline and send out a standard video signal for your NTSC monitor or video projection system. For serious professional work, viewing the video master on large-format monitors makes the post-production process more comfortable. The Blackmagic Design Decklink Extreme PCIe card provides video playback from Pro Tools, allowing you to display the video on an external HD television monitor. In addition to a dedicated hardware option, you can also enable Options > Video Out FireWire. This routes video playback through your computer's FireWire port to any video peripheral with an IEEE 1394 port, including many common video cameras and digital video decks.

When you've finished assembling all the audio for the project, you have several options:

- Bounce out a stereo file (or multiple mono files for surround mixing), which the video editor can then import and place in the video-editing software.

- Use the File > Bounce To > QuickTime Movie command to bounce your mix directly into a QuickTime movie. You might do this, for example, when the final destination is a CD-ROM or the Internet, and your audio work is the last stage in the process (because the video data in the QuickTime file has already been compressed to the final size for playback). However, it is sometimes a good idea to use this option even when your audio is going to be used on a video-editing system. Most video-editing software can import just the Audio tracks from the QuickTime file you've provided. (Note that although they can be imported, AVI, MPG, and other digital video file formats cannot be bounced back out from Pro Tools.) That way, if there's ever any question about how you thought things were supposed to sync up between the audio and video, the video editor has the file you provided as a reference.

■ Export the session as an Open Media Framework Interchange (OMFI) file (sequence), supported by video-editing systems such as Avid Media Composer, Final Cut Pro, Media 100, and others (not to mention other digital-audio programs such as Digital Performer, Nuendo, Cubase, Logic Studio, and SONAR). Note that exporting your session as an OMFI file will *not* keep the effects of the real-time plug-ins used as inserts on your tracks.

■ Export your session as an Advanced Authoring Format (AAF) sequence to be used by Avid Media Composer and other video-editing systems. AAF sequences always refer to external media files (unlike OMFI files, which can optionally have media files embedded within them) and may in turn refer to OMF media files. While AAF is a newer and more versatile format than OMFI, for most situations you will simply provide whichever exchange format the video editor requests.

Summary

This chapter was designed to provide a bit of grounding for synchronizing Pro Tools with other devices. We revisit some of these concepts in Chapter 14 and discuss MIDI MachineControl technology and the Pro Tools MachineControl option. In Appendix B you'll find further information about synchronization peripherals.

12 The Pro Tools Groove

This chapter looks at a few specific techniques for basic beat mixing: combining samples from various sources with MIDI performances and additional audio recording to build up a groove, for example, using the dance, trance, or pop style. It also provides some details about the Elastic Audio features available in current Pro Tools systems.

If you talk with seasoned dance producers who use Pro Tools, you will discover that they usually supplement the program with numerous synthesizers and samplers (either the software or external hardware variety) and/or dedicated programs for manipulating beats and loops, such as ACID by Sony/Sonic Foundry (Windows), Live by Ableton, and so on—some of which can work in tandem on the same computer with Pro Tools via ReWire. If you're involved in this genre, you might want to investigate the sampling/synthesis plug-ins for Pro Tools mentioned later in this chapter. Having your entire complex synthesis and signal-routing setup tightly integrated into a single Pro Tools session is an enormous benefit and allows you to experiment, continually perfecting previous mixes. As you can imagine, every Pro Tools user has his or her own methods, and you can make things as simple or as complicated as you like. This is definitely a subject that, by itself, could fill an entire book! This chapter focuses on the basics, limiting its discussion to techniques available to *all* Pro Tools users, and lets you build from there.

Combining MIDI and Audio

As stated elsewhere, MIDI is a communications protocol. That is, it's a way to represent performance events (such as a key or pedal press on your MIDI controller, a strike to a drum pad, and so on) so that these can be transmitted from one device (or program) to another. With a MIDI interface connected to your computer, you attach MIDI cables (In to Out, Out to In) between the interface's ports and those of any external MIDI controllers and/or sound modules (or a MIDI-controllable effects processor, recorder, and so on). Alternatively, you can connect most current MIDI modules directly to the computer via USB cable. MIDI and Instrument tracks in Pro Tools record incoming MIDI data and provide you with editing tools to alter or create MIDI information. As mentioned in Chapter 10, software-based synthesizers and samplers provide powerful alternatives to hardware devices. These can be RTAS or AAX Native plug-ins (all systems), TDM plug-ins (HD systems), AAX DSP plug-ins (HDX systems), or separate programs whose audio output is streamed into the Pro Tools mixing environment via ReWire technology (all systems).

Let's assume for a moment that your setup consists of a single MIDI keyboard sitting beside your Pro Tools rig, and you're using that keyboard's internal sounds for some of your MIDI tracks. What are your options for combining the audio output of this external MIDI device with the Audio tracks playing back from hard disk within Pro Tools?

■ You could connect the audio outputs from the external MIDI keyboard to available inputs on your audio interface, and configure Aux Input or Instrument tracks to monitor those inputs within Pro Tools. If your audio interface has numerous inputs available, the audio outputs from *several* MIDI modules can stay more or less permanently connected, leaving the remaining inputs free for audio recordings (guitar or vocal tracks, for example). This is simple to set up. For example, you might create a stereo Aux Input track, selecting input pair 7–8 on your multichannel audio interface as its source (where you've connected the audio outputs from your MIDI keyboard). The signal from this Aux Input (with whatever plug-ins or additional audio routing you have created) will be included when you bounce a mixdown to disk in real time.

Instrument Tracks Can Also Be Used for External MIDI Devices   Many people immediately associate Instrument tracks with software instrument plug-ins. In this case, a single track serves as the audio channel (similar to an Aux Input) whose sound source is an instrument plug-in in its insert slot, and also as the Edit Playlist location for recording and editing MIDI performances. This saves screen space and makes your session easier to manage. You can also use Instrument tracks for external MIDI modules, however. Set the audio input for your Instrument track to the ports on your audio interface where the external MIDI device is connected. Then, with the Instrument controls section visible at the top of the Mix window (or the corresponding column in the Edit window), select the appropriate MIDI port and channel for the external device to use it as the MIDI destination for the track. Even if you end up using additional MIDI tracks for a multi-timbral external module, having separate Mute and Solo buttons for the Instrument controls section (MIDI) and the audio portion of the Instrument track itself makes it easy to manage this "hybrid" track.

■ You could use a small mixer to monitor your Pro Tools outputs along with the audio output from your MIDI keyboard(s), also routed to the mixer. In this scenario, you'd have to record the mixer's stereo output to some other device in real time—for example, a DAT, in order to capture the audio output. Mixing to an external recorder has some operational disadvantages (not to mention the additional expense), however. For one thing, once you've bounced out a series of mixes, you may have to record them right back onto hard disk if you're going to use Pro Tools or another program to sequence them and apply any other mastering processes. Some users may find themselves in this situation anyway—for instance, if the number of external, real-time audio sources entering their mix exceeds the available inputs on their Pro Tools audio hardware. This would be the case if, for example, you have stereo outputs coming from five different MIDI modules plus several external effects processors used as send destinations from Pro Tools outputs and only eight analog inputs available on your audio interface. Even so, a more practical alternative might be to use a small external mixer to *submix* audio from these devices, perhaps entering the Pro Tools mixing environment via a single stereo Aux Input. In this scenario, however, it's usually preferable to separately record the stereo audio output from each of your MIDI modules to its own Audio track before mixdown and definitely before disconnecting those modules and archiving the Pro Tools project. That way, you have mixable tracks and reproducible levels if those modules are no longer connected in the future.

- If a single external keyboard is your sound source for multiple MIDI tracks, you may opt to record each instrumental part onto a separate Audio track before mixdown. This enables you to apply separate plug-in processing to each part in Pro Tools, usually producing superior quality when compared to the shared, built-in effects on the MIDI keyboard or module itself. For example, you might use compression or a small-room reverb on the recorded Audio track for the MIDI drum part and a completely different effects treatment on the other instrumental parts recorded from this MIDI sound source. Again, having an audio version of your MIDI parts saved with the final mixdown session also guarantees that the project will sound the same in the future if that original MIDI sound source is no longer available.

Using "Assembled" Percussion Parts and Clip Groups

Assembling multitrack percussion arrangements can be a creative way to put together a groove. Besides the simplistic technique of assembling a pattern out of individual drum-hit samples, you could also use more exotic industrial and ambient sounds to put together interesting rhythmic patterns. Working in Grid mode is an essential part of this process. Another handy command is Clip > Quantize to Grid, which moves the beginning of audio clips to the nearest grid increment as specified in the Grid Value field. If a Sync Point exists within the clip (see Chapter 8 for a description of the Clip > Identify Sync Point command), the Sync Point itself is snapped to the nearest grid increment instead of to the clip's beginning. This is handy for a snare sample with backward reverb on the front end or turntable scratch and vocal effects, for example.

When using individual samples to build a percussive groove on a series of Audio tracks in Grid mode, be sure to set the Timebase selector for these tracks to Ticks. That way, if you subsequently alter the tempo, the clips in the tracks will automatically reposition to maintain their same relative Bar|Beat locations at the new tempo. Later, you can simplify your session in different ways after building your groove, such as by grouping all your "percussion" tracks together or by submixing them to a stereo Aux Input track and then hiding the original tracks to save screen space.

Clip groups can also come in handy for the editing and composing process. To create a clip group, simply select all the clips you want to include—in this case, perhaps your entire eight-bar groove that spans multiple Audio tracks. Then choose the Clip > Group command. The entire selection will now appear as a single clip group, with a clip group icon in the lower-left corner.

Clip groups can be looped, duplicated, trimmed, and so on. If you constructed your composite beat on tick-based tracks, when the Pro Tools tempo changes, the start point for each instance of the clip group *and each of the source clips within the group* will adjust accordingly to maintain its bar|beat location at the new tempo. (This capability is also essential to working with sliced audio from REX and ACID files, by the way.) Later in this chapter, Figure 12.2 shows a composite percussion track that has been combined into a single clip group and then looped.

You can use the Clip > Ungroup command to return the clips in a selected clip group to an ungrouped state for editing. You can use the Clip > Regroup command after making your edits to reassemble the clip group. If the clip group (such as your "assembled" percussion groove) is being used elsewhere in the current session, a dialog box will appear, providing you with two choices: modify the original clip group (affecting all other instances) or create a new copy (leaving other existing instances of the clip group unchanged). The first option provides a quick way to apply changes session-wide, if you have used the same groove in each verse or chorus, for example.

Looping Audio Clips

Certain styles of music involve repetition of rhythm loops, drum beats, and other sounds. For that matter, in post-production, it is not uncommon to loop certain background sounds—especially the source audio from an effects library, which may not be long enough to fill the required duration. The Edit menu's Duplicate and Repeat commands (for creating multiple duplicates of selected clips in a single operation) are useful for this, as is the Clip > Loop command and the Loop mode of the Trim tool. Here we take a look at some other aspects of looping audio in Pro Tools, starting with setting your Pro Tools tempo based on the current selection.

The Event > Identify Beat Command

As you may have read in previous chapters, you can loop any selection via the Options > Loop Playback menu command. Pro Tools will keep cycling between the start and end locations until you stop playback.

Let's say that, instead of importing an existing loop, you've imported a full-length stereo rhythm groove from CD (at a single, steady tempo), and you want to use bits and pieces to create a completely new rhythm track. You can use the Event > Identify Beat command to set the Pro Tools tempo based on your audio selection. Here's the traditional method (make sure Insertion Follows Playback is not selected):

1. Drag the original rhythm groove clip onto a stereo Audio track. Click the Selector tool anywhere in that track prior to the beginning of the section you want to loop and then press the spacebar to start playback in Pro Tools.

2. Press the Down Arrow key on your computer keyboard at the beginning of the phrase you want to loop (such as a four-bar section). Then press the Up Arrow key on the next downbeat *after* the end of the phrase.

3. Stop playback. A portion of the track's audio waveform will be selected, corresponding to exactly where you pressed the Down and Up Arrow keys.

4. Make sure Options > Loop Playback is enabled (it can also be enabled via the right-click menu on the Play button itself) and then press Play (or the spacebar) again. At this point your selection should roughly cover the phrase you are after; however, chances are your loop is not exactly smooth yet. For best results, you'll need to refine the selection to create a sample-accurate loop.

5. Use the Zoomer tool to click and drag immediately around the beginning of your current selection. Then switch to the Selector tool and, while holding down the Shift key, adjust the beginning of your selection until it exactly matches the downbeat of the phrase, with no excess audio selected before the attack but without omitting any of the attack. You may need to zoom in and out several levels to zero in on the proper position. (Remember: You can hold down the Command key, or Ctrl key in Windows, and use the left/right bracket keys to zoom in or out.) After each adjustment, click Play to confirm that your phrase starts *exactly* at the beginning of the selection.

6. Once you've precisely defined the beginning, press the Right Arrow key on your computer keyboard once. This moves the waveform display to the end of the current selection. Now, while holding down the Shift key, adjust the end of your selection so that it ends immediately *before* the downbeat of the following phrase. Press the spacebar to play your selection after making each adjustment; you'll know you have the end point exactly right when the selected phrase loops smoothly.

7. Choose Edit > Separate Clip > At Selection. Give this new clip a meaningful name (such as "4 Bars") and click OK to close the dialog box.

8. Eliminate the audio preceding your new clip in the track by selecting it with the Grabber and pressing the Delete or Backspace key. Then drag the clip all the way to the beginning of the track.

9. With the clip still selected, enable the Tempo Ruler (the conductor icon in the Transport window); then select Event > Identify Beat. In the Identify Beat dialog box, set the beginning of the current selection at Bar 1, Beat 1 and the end of the selection at the appropriate location based on the musical length of your phrase (for a four-bar phrase, set the end to Bar 5, Beat 1). This tells Pro Tools how long the phrase is at its native tempo so that Pro Tools can set the Bars|Beats Ruler to match.

10. If needed, set the Time Signature fields to match the time signature of your phrase. Then click OK.

11. Switch to Bars|Beats as your main timebase (View > Main Counter > Bars:Beats). Enable Grid mode and set the Grid value to 1/4 notes.

12. If you've made an accurate phrase selection for the Identify Beat command, you can now select anywhere within the track, and your selection will automatically snap to the nearest 1/4-note increment. You're ready to start carving up some phrases out of the groove and putting them back together into a different arrangement.

Other Ways to Adjust Selections   In Chapter 6, "The Edit Window," we describe another method for making precise phrase selections: using the Scrubber tool and then *nudging* the selection with the plus and minus (+/−) keys. You can also hold down the Option or Command modifier keys—Alt or Ctrl in Windows—to nudge only the beginning or end of a selection without affecting its other boundary. For drum loops, however, the Tab to Transients button is often the quickest way to define a loop selection. Click with the Selector tool somewhere close to the beginning of the audio you want to define as a clip to be looped and press the Tab key. The cursor jumps forward to the next detected transient peak in the audio material. Hold down the Shift key and click somewhere prior to the end of the selection you want to define. Then press Shift+Tab as needed to extend the selection of the transient following the end of the desired phrase.

The Clip > Loop/Unloop Commands

You can loop both individual clips and clip groups (whether on single or multiple tracks). Figure 12.1 shows the dialog box that appears when you select the Clip > Loop command. You can choose a specific number of repetitions, set a total duration (in which case the last loop "alias" may be truncated if the target duration for the entire set of loops isn't an exact multiple), or allow the clip to continue looping until it reaches either the end of the session's Timeline or the next clip boundary within the track. You can also specify a crossfade time between adjacent loop repetitions. However, as always with crossfades, there must be enough additional material before and/or after the boundaries of the clip within its parent file to fill the desired crossfade duration. Crossfading can often produce smoother transitions, especially when cymbal decays or reverb at the end of the loop might otherwise be abruptly cut off at the splice point.

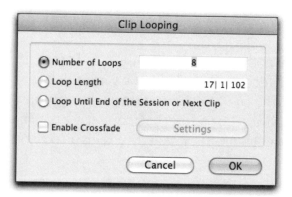

Figure 12.1 Options for looping a selected clip (or clip group). The crossfade option doesn't apply to looped MIDI clips.

Loop *aliases* are created, following the original source clip. The entire series of loop repetitions can be dragged, copied, and so on, much like a single clip or clip group. If you drop some other clip somewhere within an existing looped clip (as seen in Figure 12.2), the topmost clip sounds, and then the underlying loop repetitions continue. Clip loops are very useful when you're building up an arrangement from a simple repeating beat, for example.

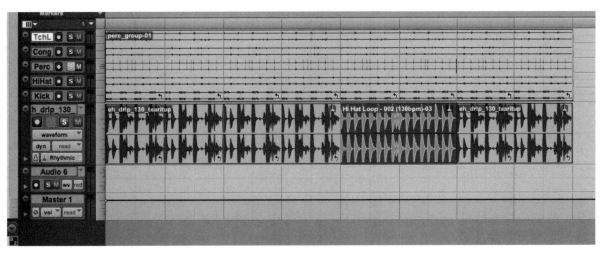

Figure 12.2 Loop icons appear in source clips or clip groups and their loop aliases. Shown here: a multi-track percussion assemblage that has been made into a clip group and looped, plus a looped audio clip with another clip dropped amongst its loop repetitions.

Using the Trim tool on looped clips allows you to increase or decrease the number of repetitions. The last repetition may be truncated by this operation, for example, if you want to shorten it to a lesser number of bars of beats to make room for a fill or transition. If you hold down the Control key (Start key in Windows) while trimming looped clips (but not necessarily clip groups), the total duration changes by even multiples of the source clip's length. This is one of the quickest ways to create additional repetitions of the entire loop.

The dialog box that appears when you execute the Clip > Unloop command (shown in Figure 12.3) lets you either revert back to a single instance of the source clip or clip group or flatten the current looped set into separate clips. Unless you've used the Loop Trim tool—see the next section—the result is similar to having used the Edit > Repeat command in the first place; however, if the last loop repetition was truncated to match the desired duration, a separate clip definition is created for it.

Figure 12.3 Options for unlooping a selected clip (or clip group).

Of course, the usefulness of clip looping isn't limited to musical applications. In audio post, background ambience, or walla, wind, water, or traffic sounds pulled from sound-effect libraries, are often not long enough to fill the required duration. Using clip looping (instead of the Edit menu's Duplicate and Repeat commands) provides a more convenient method for building a base over which you can layer other background sounds.

Loop Trim Tool

You can select the Trim tool's Loop mode to simplify creation of clip loops. This tool enables you to directly create loop aliases as you trim the left or right boundary of a single existing clip within a track without having to use the Clip Looping dialog box. The function of the Loop Trim tool changes according to its position in the clip, as indicated by the cursor icon. When in the upper portion of a clip or clip loop, it trims by adding (or removing) clip iterations; again the Control-key combination (Start key in Windows) constricts the trim length to whole loop iterations. When in the lower portion of a clip loop (where the loop icon appears in the clip), trimming affects the length of each loop iteration. For example, you might use this in Grid editing mode to change a clip loop consisting of four 2-bar loop iterations to eight 1-bar loop iterations, without affecting the overall length of the clip loop. The number of loop aliases adjusts accordingly (exactly double, in this case) to maintain the same total duration for the clip loop. Note that this operation does *not* apply time compression/expansion; it merely redefines the boundaries for the looped iterations. If you *do* use the TCE Trim tool on looped audio clips or audio clip groups, a single, consolidated clip will be created that contains the results of the time compression/expansion operation, including the effects of any fades on the source clip(s).

Duplicating Automation in Your Loop Aliases

Any automation data associated with your source clip or clip group is *not* copied into the loop aliases. The idea in Pro Tools is to provide flexibility for creating automation that may extend across multiple loop repetitions. If needed, you can copy and paste automation (once you have changed the track view to display the desired automation parameter). Submenus for Cut Special, Copy Special, and Clear Special provide options for applying these operations to all automation types, pan data only, or plug-in automation only. After you copy automation data to the clipboard with the Cut Special or Copy Special commands, you can paste it elsewhere with the normal Paste command without affecting any overlapping clips at the track destination, even if no automation parameters are currently visible in that track.

The Paste Special submenu provides several functions that are especially relevant for building grooves from clips and clip loops. The Merge command combines any MIDI data from the clipboard with any existing MIDI notes and/or continuous controller data on the track. The To Current Automation Type command allows you to paste automation from one automation parameter to another; for example, you could paste pan automation into a reverb send. Of particular interest when working with loops, the Repeat to Fill Selection command allows you to paste copies of a segment of automation data (or audio or MIDI) to fill a larger duration. If you need to include automation with a source clip when using it for a clip loop, you can copy the automation from the source clip (Edit > Copy Special > All Automation), create the clip loop, and then use Edit > Paste Special > Repeat to Fill Selection with the clip loop selected. The automation graph from the source clip will repeat for each loop iteration.

Using the TCE Trim Tool for Adjusting Durations

When you change the Trim tool to TC/E (Time Compression/Expansion) mode, its cursor changes to the TCE Trim tool. In this mode, as you trim any audio or MIDI clip, its contents are adjusted to fit into the new duration. For instance, using this mode to reduce a MIDI clip from a duration of four bars to two bars produces a double-time version. Using the TCE Trim tool on audio clips applies the time compression/expansion AudioSuite plug-in—for example, Time Shift, X-Form, or another time-stretching plug-in installed in your system—using the default settings specified in the Processing tab of the Preferences dialog box.

The TCE Trim tool can be useful for matching a clip to your session tempo. Suppose you import a four-bar vocal file that doesn't match the current session tempo. Using the TCE Trim tool, you can easily to conform the clip to the equivalent number of bars in your session. Simply switch to Grid mode and then trim the clip to exactly four bars at the current session tempo.

When used on tracks that are not Elastic Audio enabled, each application of the TCE Trim tool creates a new audio file with some degradation to the audio quality. Naturally, with more extreme time compression or expansion, and with additional applications of TCE Trim, more artifacts will be heard in the results. To maximize quality, if your first TCE adjustment isn't quite right, undo the change and try again to ensure a first-generation result.

The TCE Trim tool can also be used on Elastic Audio–enabled tracks. In this case, the selected Elastic Audio plug-in will be used to process the clip. The Elastic Audio plug-in can be changed at any time to try a different algorithm or switched to the X-Form plug-in for a high-quality rendered result. As an added benefit, the TCE Trim tool can be used repeatedly on the same clip on an Elastic Audio–enabled track with no additional degradation in quality. Elastic Audio always references the original source audio for both real-time and rendered processing.

Working with REX and ACID Files

Both of these formats are optimized for time-sliced loops—that is, audio files that have been analyzed and broken down into their rhythmic components. The REX/REX2 format (which uses a .rex or .rx2 file name extension) was developed for the ReCycle program, by Propellerhead Software. The ACID format (.wav files containing additional metadata about tempo, time slices, and other parameters) comes from the ACID program, originally developed by Sonic Foundry and now owned by Sony Creative. Many loop-savvy programs—including Reason, ACID, Ableton Live, FL Studio, Logic, and Cubase—support REX and/or ACID files and can play these loops at any tempo without pitch changes. Pro Tools can also import these time-sliced audio file formats. As with files analyzed by Beat Detective in Pro Tools, having individual rhythmic components automatically sliced up within the file makes it much easier to rearrange them into new rhythmic patterns.

Importing REX/ACID Files into Pro Tools

You can import REX and ACID files into Pro Tools by dragging them directly from the Workspace browser window (or from the Mac Finder, Windows Explorer, or the desktop) into the Clip List or onto an existing track, which should usually be tick-based for this purpose. If you want to create a new track automatically, drag the files directly into the Track List or into an empty area of the Edit window itself. As you preview each of these files in the Workspace browser using the speaker icon, its tempo can be automatically adjusted to match that of the current Timeline position in your session. When you create a new tick-based track by dragging REX and ACID files into the Track List (or to an empty space in the Edit window), the result depends on your settings in the Preferences dialog box's Processing tab (see Figure 12.4). Using the default preference, time slices in imported REX/ACID files are consolidated for use by Elastic Audio, and any newly created tick-based Audio track will have Elastic Audio enabled (with the default Elastic Audio plug-in).

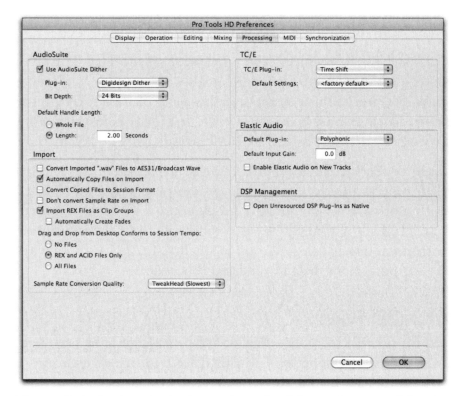

Figure 12.4 Settings in the Processing tab of the Preferences dialog box affect how REX and ACID files get imported into Pro Tools.

Using REX Clip Groups in Your Tracks

If you enable the Import REX Files as Clip Groups setting in the Preferences > Processing page (as shown in Figure 12.4), a new clip group will be created in the Clip List, reflecting the name of the original audio file whenever you import a REX file. In this case, you have the option of subsequently ungrouping those time-slice clips and reordering them. (For the time-slice clips to appear in the Clip List, the option to view auto-created clips must be enabled in the Clip List pop-up menu.) A check box in the same Preferences page enables you to choose whether fades are automatically created when REX files are imported as clip groups.

When placing a clip group created from a REX onto an *existing* Audio track, make sure the timebase for the track is set to Ticks. That way, if you create any tempo changes, the locations of the time slices within the clip group will automatically adjust to maintain their bar|beat locations. (Nothing *prevents* you from placing them onto a sample-based Audio track, but tick-based tracks are more convenient and flexible for most musical applications.) You will also generally want to enable the Conductor button in the Transport window to follow the Tempo Ruler rather than using manual tempo settings (unless you are experimenting with tempo).

You can cut, copy, paste, trim, or loop these clip groups, just as you would any other clip in Pro Tools. If you want access to the individual slices within the clip group in order to rework the beat itself, use the Clip > Ungroup command. (If the REX loop's tempo has increased to match the current tempo in your Pro Tools, some of these time-slice clips may overlap.) Among other things, you can use the Clip > Quantize to Grid command to pull the time slices into a more rigid rhythmic alignment (or to apply a swing, a Groove template, and so on) and then use the Clip > Regroup command to put it back together.

Using REX/ACID Files with Elastic Audio

By default, dragging REX or ACID files into the Track List or an empty area of the Edit window will create a new tick-based track with the default Elastic Audio plug-in enabled (unless the aforementioned Import REX Files as Clip Groups setting is active). When sliced REX and ACID files are imported onto Elastic Audio tracks, the slices they contain are interpreted with 100 percent confidence, so the Event Sensitivity setting in the Elastic Properties dialog box for those clips has no effect afterward.

Building a Better Groove

Once you've chopped out enough good phrases to build a basic arrangement, and perhaps even overdubbed a few additional MIDI and audio parts (maybe some vocals and an instrumental part or two), you may want to add some nuances to the rhythmic arrangement. Up to this point, you may have kept the arrangement fairly repetitious, stringing the same few phrases together many times, almost like a click track or drum loop. What are your options for making it sound less mechanical? Here are just a few ideas:

- Use some of the drum sounds in your MIDI modules, especially small percussion such as shakers, maracas, cabasa, and so on, to layer more variation into your drum groove. Unless you're deliberately seeking a full-blown Latin or world-music groove, try mixing this down underneath the drum track's level for just a hint of flavor. The idea is to add some varying patterns, changing up velocities and swing factors, to create some longer phrases overlaid on the repetitive four-bar base. Even better, if you have a microphone and some hand percussion (and enough rudimentary technique to not just make matters worse), you can perform some of these subtle texture parts yourself for a guaranteed human feel. As a general note, you may be surprised to see how much difference just *one* human-played part, even mixed at a very low level, can make toward a good groove feel—*especially* with quantized MIDI arrangements!

- Use AudioSuite functions to process some of the existing phrases in your groove (using the Create Individual Files option so that your original file is unaffected). For example, you might use the EQ to perform some radical adjustments to the frequency content of some phrases or extreme compression/gate settings. You can then drop fragments of these processed clips into an additional Audio track, trimming their beginnings and ends to create effect fills in fiendishly clever locations.

■ Use the AudioSuite menu's Expander-Gate function on a rhythm phrase selection, activate the External Key function, and choose one of your other Audio tracks (or busses) as the sidechain input. This sidechain signal will control the opening/closing of the gate during your selected phrase, activating it simultaneously with the signal on the other track/bus. (In other words, you're imposing the gain/envelope changes of the sidechain's source audio on your selection.) Depending on where you do this, what source you select, and of course how extreme your Expander-Gate settings are, you can create some interesting rhythmic effects. Again, a new audio clip is created for your results, and you can trim out bits and pieces to use as rhythm accents over your basic groove.

■ Take advantage of Pro Tools' ability to automate sends (and plug-in parameters, of course). Create a send (at send position C, for example) from your drum track; route its output to an internal Pro Tools bus. Then create an Aux Input, with the same bus set as its input, and drop a reverb plug-in on the track. Choose a nonlinear or gated reverb setting (or small room, snare room, and so on). Now, change the Track View selector on the drum track to Send C > Level. In Grid mode, set at perhaps 1/8-note increments, use the Grabber to create breakpoints that outline 1/8-note spikes in the send level right on the snare backbeats—for example, 2 and 4 of each bar (or wherever amuses you). Remember, when viewing break-point automation in Pro Tools, you can hold down the Option key (Alt key in Windows) and click a breakpoint with the Grabber tool to delete it. Don't bother drawing your shapes in every single bar; get it right in a couple of bars and then copy and paste into the rest! Also remember that you can trim automation data to scale it up or down. You're sending an entire drum mix to the reverb, which could sound pretty rude if enabled all the time. But by keeping the volume of your Aux Input fairly low (and by occasionally using an EQ plug-in on the insert prior to the reverb to reduce high and low frequencies so that the hi-hat and kick drum aren't overly prominent), these rhythmic shots to the reverb can blend into the track, creating subtle dynamic pushes on certain beats. Of course, if subtlety is not your intention, the technique is equally applicable for changing dramatic, dub-style shots into a delay or reverb.

■ Try routing some of your percussion grooves (drum loops or entire drum set mixes, for example) through a second channel with extremely aggressive dynamics processing applied. For example, create a send from your drum loop track, choose one of the bus pairs in Pro Tools as a secondary destination, and route it to a new Aux Input track. Use plug-in inserts to apply very large amounts of compression or limiting to that Aux Input track (plus some EQ, if you choose). You can now blend this with the main, unprocessed version of that per-cussion groove, having it drop out or enter at key points in your arrangement. An even larger number of these *mults* or alternate submixes could be used for creative effect. Also consider applying this "iron fist in a velvet glove" approach with lead vocals when you want them to sound more powerful or aggressive than your singer may be capable of delivering naturally. A solid, dynamics-processed backbone may be just the thing you're looking for.

Thinking outside the Bar Lines A common problem when stringing together rhythm phrases is that they contain events that should hang over the bar lines at the beginning or end of the phrase. For example, if the drummer hits the crash cymbal on the fourth beat of the last bar, it sounds unnatural for this cymbal sound to cut off abruptly when the following phrase begins. The Fades dialog box is your best ally for dealing with these situations. A post-splice crossfade after the boundary between the two adjacent clips allows you to smoothly extend the cymbal's decay across the beginning of the next phrase (as long as it's similar to the preceding one—remember that the two clips will overlap during the crossfade). To do this, select the two adjacent clips with the Grabber; then select Edit > Fades > Create (Command+F in Mac, Ctrl+F in Windows). In the Batch Fades dialog box (see Figure 12.5), set the Link option to None so that you can select the Fade In and Fade Out shapes independently. Then select the Post-Splice option under Placement, Preset Curve 1 for the *in* shape of the second clip (so that it starts immediately, with no fade-up), and one of the more gradual curves for the first clip's *out* shape. Select about 200–300 milliseconds for the fade's initial length; you can always adjust this fade duration later with the Trim tool.

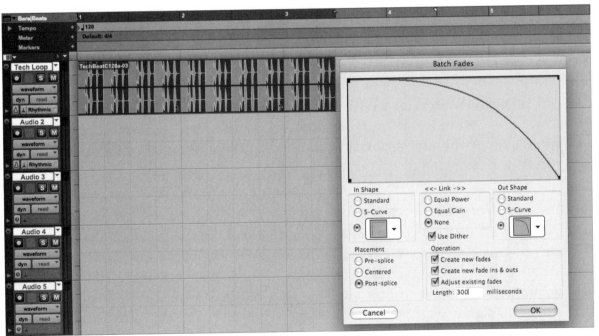

Figure 12.5 Creating a 300-millisecond, post-splice fade between all the selected clips. At each boundary between clips, the second clip begins immediately at full volume, while additional material *after* the end of the first clip fades out over it.

Elastic Audio

Elastic Audio was introduced in Pro Tools 7.4. Essentially, Elastic Audio is a set of software tools that enables *warping* of events within audio clips, allowing you to conform them to the tempo and rhythmic feel of your Pro Tools session and to each other. As shown in Figure 12.6, various

Elastic Audio analysis modes can be selected via the pop-up Elastic Audio plug-in selector in the controls for each Audio track: Polyphonic, Rhythmic, Monophonic, Varispeed, and X-Form (rendered-only processing). Elastic Audio uses a unique plug-in selector available in the Edit window only; it has nothing to do with the track insert plug-ins you use elsewhere in Pro Tools.

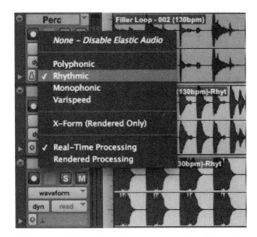

Figure 12.6 The Elastic Audio Plug-in selector on Audio tracks.

Elastic Audio analysis looks at the transients (momentary attacks) within the source audio file to determine where the most significant audio events are located. When an audio clip gets stretched or squeezed to match the current session tempo, the Elastic Audio processing applies time compression or expansion based on these significant transient events. The Clip > Conform to Tempo command adjusts the total duration of the clip to match the session tempo on both sample- and tick-based tracks. If you use Event > Event Operations > Quantize after conforming to tempo, the transients within the audio clip are intelligently adjusted to the appropriate subdivisions of the beat, based on your quantize settings.

Event Markers and Warp Markers

Elastic Audio analysis creates Event markers for the detected transients in the source audio. When you switch the track view to Warp or Analysis view, these Event markers are visible as vertical gray lines over the audio waveform (see Figure 12.7). In contrast, Warp markers anchor a given event within an audio waveform to a specific location in the Pro Tools Timeline (usually a Bar|Beat location on a tick-based track). Warp markers appear as vertical black lines with a triangle at their base. You can add Warp markers to a clip on an Elastic Audio–enabled track using the Grabber tool. This can be useful for a variety of purposes. For instance, you may have identified a snare backbeat in an imported drum loop that you want to anchor to the second quarter note of the bar; adding a Warp marker to the snare hit ensures that, no matter how other audio events in the clip are moved around to match the rhythmic subdivisions or swing factor of the session, this backbeat stays firmly in place. As stated in the *Pro Tools Reference Guide*, you can think of audio clips as rubber bands, the Timeline as a ruler, and Warp markers as pushpins attaching points on the rubber band to the ruler.

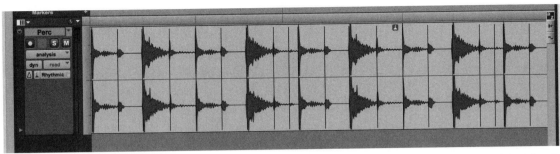

Figure 12.7   An Audio track in Analysis view, showing the Event markers detected by Elastic Audio.

On tick-based tracks, the Warp markers are anchored to the Bars|Beats Ruler. Thus, if you change the session tempo, the Warp markers will automatically shift to retain their current Bars| Beats locations. Time compression or expansion will be applied to the audio between Warp markers to maintain a continuous audio file, using the algorithm of the Elastic Audio plug-in you currently have activated on the track.

Editing Event and Warp Markers

Two track views are specifically related to Elastic Audio: Analysis and Warp. In Analysis view, you can view and edit Event markers. Analysis view lets you add, remove, or reposition Event markers to ensure that the right transients get adjusted to beat subdivisions when quantizing. Sometimes marker positions need to be adjusted, especially if a sound has a relatively long attack or if background sounds are interfering with proper transient detection. In other cases, you might add or delete Event markers to avoid false triggers. In Warp view, you can view and edit Warp markers, which pin an individual audio event within the clip to a specific time location (a relative Bar|Beat location on a tick-based track or an absolute time position on a sample-based track). One of the most typical applications of Warp markers is to adjust the time of individual audio events, perhaps to make specific drum hits or notes on an instrument align more precisely to the nearest 1/8 note, for example.

To use Warp markers to manually correct the timing of an event, do the following:

1. Click the Elastic Audio Plug-in selector in the Edit window and select an appropriate Elastic Audio plug-in.

2. Using the Track View selector, switch the track to Warp view.

3. Enable Grid mode and select an appropriate Grid value.

4. Locate the event that is too early or late.

5. Using the Grabber tool, double-click the Event markers for the transients on either side of the event to anchor them in place. The Event markers will change to Warp markers.

6. Click and drag the Event marker for the out-of-time event to move it to the proper grid subdivision. This Event marker will also change to a Warp marker, and the audio event will adjust with the marker.

Tip Here's a shortcut for correcting the timing of a single note or drum hit. Shift-click on the Event marker for the transient you need to move to activate Individual Warp mode. This automatically converts the neighboring Event markers on either side into Warp markers, anchoring the associated transients in place. Individual Warp mode lets you quickly correct an out-of-time event without affecting the audio on either side.

Creative Sound Manipulation with Event Markers If you're mangling drum and rhythm loops with Elastic Audio while the track is in Warp view, one trick you will want to explore is squeezing or stretching a single event (that is, the area between one Event marker and the next in the audio waveform) to a different duration as a special effect. For instance, if you isolate a single kick or snare hit (that doesn't include any intervening hits on the hi-hat) and stretch it to twice or four times its original duration, you might find this to be an interesting accent or variation to work into your groove.

Elastic Audio Plug-In Window

You can open the Elastic Audio Plug-In window, shown in Figure 12.8, by clicking on the current Elastic Audio plug-in on a track. The parameters available in the Elastic Audio Plug-In window depend on which analysis mode is active on the track. Here we provide some general guidelines for these parameters. You will quickly discover, however, that with a given audio loop (and depending on how aggressively you are stretching and squeezing things), you may need to experiment with more than one mode and adjust parameters according to your own ears.

Figure 12.8 The Elastic Audio plug-in window for the Polyphonic plug-in. Shorter analysis window sizes generally work better for drums and percussion. The Follow button enables an envelope follower to retain more of the original acoustics, especially with extreme time stretching.

- **Polyphonic.** This plug-in is useful for loops with harmonic or melodic elements, especially polyphonic instruments such as piano or multi-instrument mixes (although it's sometimes useful for more complex rhythm loops). A single parameter, Window, is available for Polyphonic mode. As a general rule, Avid recommends starting from the default range of

30–40ms, increasing to as much as 60ms for pads and other legato material or decreasing toward 20ms for more percussive material.

- **Rhythmic.** This plug-in works best on drums, percussion, and similar material with distinct transients. Decay Rate is the only parameter for Rhythmic mode. It controls how much of the audio following each detected event will be audible. In particular, this adjustment can be useful when slowing a clip down to avoid unnaturally long decays on a tambourine, clap, or cowbell sound, for example. At the 100% setting, audio between detected transient events is stretched to fill the gaps completely.

- **Monophonic.** Monophonic Elastic Audio processing is suitable for bass lines, single horn lines, and so on. There are no adjustable parameters for Monophonic mode.

- **Varispeed.** In this mode, the playback pitch of the affected clips changes in proportion to the amount of time stretching or compression applied, as with tape-speed manipulation and traditional samplers. There are no adjustable parameters for Varispeed mode.

- **X-Form.** This plug-in mode is available only for rendered processing (which creates new audio files). It provides the highest quality of the Elastic Audio plug-ins; however, it does so at the expense of speed—X-Form processing can take a *long* time to complete. The plug-in window provides two adjustable parameters. Quality is self-explanatory, but keep in mind that the maximum setting increases processing time as the new file is generated, which can be a significant consideration for longer files. When the Formant button is enabled, the processing algorithm attempts to maintain the characteristic resonances of the original sound after Elastic Audio processing. As you can imagine, this is more likely to be a concern with vocal, brass, and woodwind samples, for example.

> **Elastic Audio and Tempo Events**   If you have tempo events in your session (which can be seen in the Tempo Ruler and its Graphic Tempo Editor), Elastic Audio will warp the clips on tick-based tracks to correspond to the tempo changes. For instance, if you have used a tempo curve to create a *ritardando* (a gradual slowing of the tempo) at the end of a song or phrase, the timing of Elastic Audio–processed events will follow this slowdown. In the process, Tempo Event–Generated Warp markers are created within the affected audio clips; these Warp markers cannot be edited manually.

Elastic Properties Window

The real-time elastic properties of each audio clip in an Elastic Audio–enabled track can be adjusted in the Elastic Properties window (shown in Figure 12.9), which can be opened for a selected clip from the Clips menu. Even easier, just right-click on an audio clip and choose Elastic Properties from the pop-up menu or press Option+5 (Alt+5 in Windows) on the numeric keypad. In this window, on tick-based tracks, you can change the settings for the source length in bars and beats, source tempo, and source meter (time signature). The Event Sensitivity setting enables you to adjust the threshold at which transients within the audio will trigger Event markers for

Elastic Audio processing. (False triggers can be counterproductive and can cause quantizing errors or artifacts.) The Meter field enables you to make corrections for loops that are in a different meter: 3/4 or 7/8, for example. (Elastic Audio *always* analyzes clips using 4/4 time.)

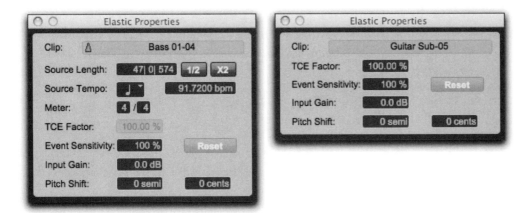

Figure 12.9 The Elastic Properties window for an audio clip on a tick-based track (left) and on a sample-based track (right).

Backward Compatibility of Elastic Audio with Pro Tools Sessions Prior to 7.4   If you disable Elastic Audio processing on an Audio track, a dialog box appears, allowing you to optionally revert audio clips to their original durations and timings or to commit the changes, generating new audio files (in the session's Audio Files folder) for every audio clip currently residing in the track. The Commit option incorporates the effects of Elastic Audio processing currently applied to the clips. For subsequent flexibility, each newly created file will include an additional two seconds of audio pad on either side of the clip boundaries from their underlying original source files, if available. After committing the changes, you can use the File > Save Copy In command to save the session in an older Pro Tools format while retaining the changes you made using Elastic Audio.

Using the DigiBase Browsers with Elastic Audio

Assuming that the tempo of your Pro Tools session has already been established (perhaps from an existing drum loop or various tracks already recorded by live musicians), when you preview rhythmic loops and other audio files in the Pro Tools Workspace (or Project) browser window, you can automatically audition them at the correct tempo for your session. Here is a typical workflow.

1. In the Pro Tools Workspace browser window, locate the audio file(s) for the loops you might like to import (perhaps from a sampling CD that you have purchased).

2. Enable the Conform to Session Tempo button (shown in Figure 12.10); it looks like a metronome and is located in the upper toolbar portion of the browser window.

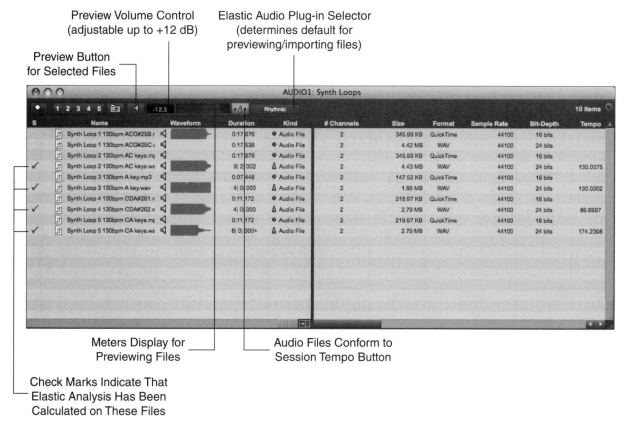

Figure 12.10 Elastic Audio tools and related features in the Workspace browser window.

3. Select the Elastic Audio plug-in you want to use for previewing files in the browser. If you're mainly interested in drum loops, choose Rhythmic.

4. Click on an audio file that you want to audition so that it becomes selected.

5. Click the Audition button (the speaker icon) to preview the file. Pro Tools will analyze the file for Elastic Audio processing. If the analysis is successful, the file will play back at the session tempo. For successfully analyzed files, a check mark will appear in the column to the left of the file name, a metronome icon will indicate that the file is tick-based, and the file's native tempo will appear in the Tempo column.

6. To use a file, simply drag it into the Track List area at the left edge of the Edit window. Pro Tools will automatically create a new tick-based Audio track with Elastic Audio enabled, convert the audio file as needed, and place it on the track.

7. In the new track, the new audio clip for your loop is automatically adjusted to the session tempo. You will also note a Warp indicator icon on the clip waveform, indicating that it has been processed by Elastic Audio.

8. If you are using any swing factor in the session (or if you would like to apply it to the loop you have just placed into the track), open the Quantize page of the Event Operations window (choose Event > Event Operations > Quantize or press Option+0 [Mac] or Alt+0 [Windows]). Most of the same options are available for quantizing Elastic Audio events

as are available for MIDI events, including quantization to a Groove template. Apply quantization as needed.

9. You may want to experiment with how the audio is processed and played back. The Elastic Audio plug-in selector in the Edit window lets you select other real-time algorithms—for example, try Polyphonic (sometimes useful even for rhythm loops without melodic or harmonic elements) or Varispeed (which changes the pitch in proportion to the duration, as on tape and traditional samplers).

Simple Tricks with Pro Tools Automation   The Pencil tool in Pro Tools has several interesting drawing shapes that can be applied to automation, as seen in Figure 12.11. In particular, Triangle, Square, and Random modes can provide some interesting results when drawing automation. Each shape creates steps (individual automation breakpoints) whose spacing is determined by the current Grid value and whose amplitude is determined by your vertical mouse position. For example, say your Grid value is set to 1/2 notes, you're viewing a track's Pan automation playlist, and you've selected the Triangle mode for the Pencil tool. As you click and drag rightward in the track, repeating triangle shapes occur every two beats; the distance between their upper and lower apexes (the *amplitude* of the triangle shape) is determined by how far you drag the mouse up and down as you draw. This is one way to create automation that is synchronized to the beat. The spacing between the resultant breakpoints is determined by the current Grid value. The Square mode works the same way, as does Random. (The *range* of random values also depends on the vertical movement of the Pencil tool as you draw.) And remember: You can always scale automation up or down later with the Trim tool. This technique might be a little radical for a classical piano recording, but it could be just what you need when trying to create an unusual mix.

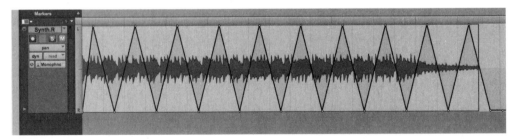

Figure 12.11 You can use the Pencil tool's drawing shapes to create automation. In this example, we set the Grid value to 1/4 notes and drew pan automation using the Pencil tool's Triangle shape.

Beat Detective

The Beat Detective window (shown in Figure 12.12) can be accessed via the Pro Tools Event menu. Beat Detective can be used to automatically identify the transients in the current selection for a variety of purposes, based on the selected mode. Choices include generating Bar|Beat markers in the Tempo Ruler; separating the selection into multiple clips based on the detected beats (beat triggers); *conforming* (moving) separated clips to the session's tempo; or, after conforming separated clips to the tempo, eliminating gaps or clicks between separated clips with crossfades and so on. Beat Detective works best with rhythmic material, at steady tempos, and with well-defined attacks on the beats (drum loops and mixes with rhythm sections, for example).

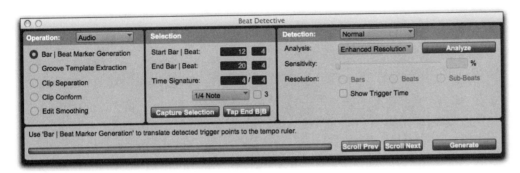

Figure 12.12 The Beat Detective window.

Using Beat Detective

To use Beat Detective, you first select the desired operational mode from among the five mode buttons in the Operation area. (See the upcoming "Beat Detective Modes" section.) Then you indicate the starting and ending Bar|Beat locations and the time signature for your selection in the Selection area. It's extremely important that your initial selection be *exact*! Before applying Beat Detective to a four-bar phrase, for example, use the Zoom features while adjusting the beginning and end of your selection precisely to the correct downbeats.

Next, you select a detection algorithm using the Analysis pop-up selector in the Detection area. The detection algorithm can be used to focus Beat Detective on low frequencies (Low Emphasis, useful when kick drum is the main defining element of the beat, for example) or high frequencies (High Emphasis, useful when hi-hats, acoustic guitar arpeggios, and so on are the key elements of beat subdivisions). The default algorithm is Enhanced Resolution, which typically provides the best results for full mixes and loops.

With the desired algorithm selected, you then click the Analyze button so that Beat Detective examines the selected audio data. After analyzing the selection, you can adjust the Sensitivity slider and other parameters in the Detection area to fine-tune the results.

The Sensitivity slider adjusts how Beat Detective reacts to dynamics. Raise the Sensitivity slider until all significant transients are represented by Beat Triggers with no false triggers. If you see that the bar or beat lines in the display are improperly located, adjust the Sensitivity slider—it's possible, for example, that a softer snare or tom accent on Beat 4 1/2 is falsely triggering Beat Detective, causing it to misidentify the downbeat. For greater control, especially when working with higher sub-beat resolutions such as 1/16 or 1/32 notes, you can also manually adjust Beat Triggers with the Grabber tool to precise locations in the waveform. (Option-click, or Alt-click in Windows, to delete a Beat Trigger. Command-click, or Ctrl-click in Windows, to promote a Beat Trigger from a subdivision to a main Beat or Bar Trigger.)

Elastic Audio has largely overshadowed Beat Detective for making quick rhythmic fixes or quantizing audio to a grid or Groove template. One of the operational advantages of Beat Detective that cannot be duplicated by Elastic Audio, however, is in the generation and manipulation of time slices in audio files with the Clip Separation mode. This makes it very easy to break a beat down into its rhythmic components, enabling you to reorder them as you wish.

Beat Detective Modes

The various Beat Detective modes are as follows:

- **Bar|Beat Marker Generation.** Generates Beat Triggers based on transients in the audio waveform and uses them to create Bar|Beat markers in the Tempo Ruler. This can be useful to create a tempo map from a freeform recording. As with other modes, you start by defining the length of your selection (by specifying start and end bars), the time signature, and the note values that generally make up the smaller subdivisions of the beat. (This helps Beat Detective generate Bar|Beat markers at the right locations.) Next, you select a detection algorithm and click the Analyze button in the Detection area. Then fine-tune the Beat Triggers using the Sensitivity slider, as shown in Figure 12.13. (Setting this to 0% will generate only a single tempo event in the Tempo Ruler, functioning like the Identify Beat command.)

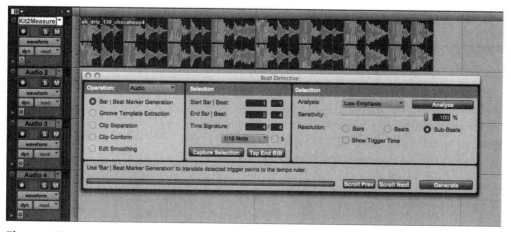

Figure 12.13 In Bar|Beat Marker Generation mode, raising the Sensitivity slider increases the number of Beat Triggers that will be detected in this drum loop.

- **Groove Template Extraction.** This function creates a Groove template, based on the current Beat Trigger analysis of your selection. The Groove template can be either stored temporarily in the Groove Clipboard or saved to disk (as seen in Figure 12.14), where you could use it with the Grid/Groove Quantize function for MIDI data—a great way to impart the feel of one audio or MIDI part to other MIDI parts.

- **Clip Separation.** Based on the Beat Triggers you've defined using the analysis and detection parameters, this function splits the audio selection into multiple clips.

- **Clip Conform.** In Standard mode, Clip Conform adjusts the location of the multiple clips created by the Clip Separation command ("quantizes" them) according to the session's

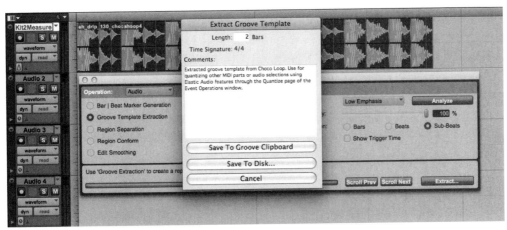

Figure 12.14 Saving a Groove template that was extracted from an audio selection to disk.

current tempo settings. Further options include Strength (less than 100% retains some of the original feel by not moving the separated clips all the way to the nearest grid increment in the session's Timeline), Exclude Within (if already within a certain distance of the nearest grid increment, the event won't be moved), and Swing. You can also conform clip locations either to one of the predefined Groove templates in Pro Tools or to the current contents of the Groove Clipboard. Prior to the introduction of Elastic Audio, this was the most practical method for matching the feel of the current selection to existing MIDI parts or to a groove you've extracted from another audio selection (so that two drum loops sound tighter when played simultaneously, for example).

■ **Edit Smoothing.** This mode applies trimming and crossfades to eliminate gaps left between the clips at their new locations after they've been conformed. Otherwise, after the separated clips are repositioned, you may hear some clicks or choppiness caused by silence between clips or overlaps in clip boundaries. You can specify the length of any required crossfades.

■ **Collection mode.** With Bar|Beat Marker Generation and Clip Separation modes, Collection mode allows you to apply Beat Detective to multiple tracks—with individual detection settings—to build up a composite Beat Trigger map. This is useful for analyzing multitrack drums, for example.

You can also use Beat Detective with MIDI tracks. You can generate groove and tempo information from MIDI tracks and apply it to Audio tracks or vice versa (although Elastic Audio also provides the capability to apply Groove templates to quantize the events within audio clips). For example, you could extract a Groove template from a drum loop and then apply this to a MIDI part you created through step input. MIDI chord recognition parameters included among the options in the Analysis pop-up menu (shown in Figure 12.15) enable you to control how Beat Detective interprets the location of beats in relation to the Timeline positions of the various notes that make up a chord. (In a real-time performance, these are rarely identical.) You can establish the Beat Trigger according to the first, last, lowest, highest, loudest, or average note position in the chord.

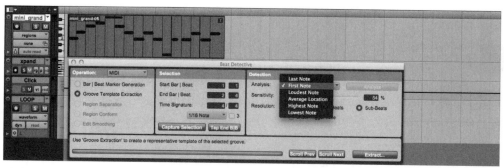

Figure 12.15 When analyzing MIDI with Beat Detective (or extracting a Groove template as shown here), options in the Analysis pop-up menu allow control over how notes within chords are interpreted.

If you're a beat mixer using loops and other "found" audio to build grooves, it will be well worth your while to explore Beat Detective. Although this chapter provides only a superficial overview, the *Pro Tools Reference Guide* PDF document dedicates an entire chapter to Beat Detective.

Working with Effects

Adding effects processing to your tracks can be an essential part of building up a good groove. You can use various types of effects plug-ins to add rhythmic elements to your mix, including tempo-based processing.

Tempo-Based Timing

Sometimes, you might want to set an effects parameter to correspond to a specific note value (say, an 1/8 note or a 1/4-note triplet) in relation to the current tempo of the music. Although you can automatically sync the DigiRack delays included with Pro Tools (and some other third-party delay plug-ins) to the session's tempo, it's also fairly easy to accomplish this manually. You might also try using tempo-based time settings for pre-delays on reverbs, LFO (low-frequency oscillator) speeds on flangers and chorus effects, tremolos, auto-panners, and so on. Setting these time factors in a mix to correspond to the tempo can sometimes help avoid clutter, *especially* with delay repeats.

The Mod Delay III (included with Pro Tools 10) provides delay times ranging from 0.1ms to 5000ms. You can sync the Mod Delay III (and older DigiRack Mod Delay II delays) to the current Pro Tools tempo using the options in the bottom part of the plug-in window (see Figure 12.16). This makes it easy to set repeat times to some rhythmic value without needing to make any calculations. The tempo-syncing feature is enabled or disabled by the Sync button in the plug-in window (in the older Mod Delay II plug-ins, this button looks like a metronome). The Meter and Tempo fields are disabled when Tempo Sync is active; otherwise, you can use these to manually specify delay times in terms of a musical tempo and time signature. The Groove slider is useful for adding some swing factor to delay repeats; that is, each offbeat is progressively later or earlier as you increase/decrease the amount of swing.

Figure 12.16   The Mod Delay III supports setting delay times in relation to musical tempos.

Some older delays and other effects (especially the external, hardware variety and some third-party plug-ins) may only allow you to specify delay times in milliseconds, not note value/BPM, and so on. Here's a method to calculate delay in milliseconds within Pro Tools:

1. Change the Main Counter (either in the Transport window or at the top of the Edit window) from Bars|Beats to Min:Secs.

2. Switch to Grid mode and use the Grid Value selector to choose Bars|Beats as the grid time units and the desired note value as the grid increment. The increments of the grid (at your specified Grid value) now appear as blue vertical lines in the Edit window.

3. Use the Selector tool to highlight a duration of only one increment anywhere within a track. The Length field now displays the duration of your selection in milliseconds.

4. Open the Plug-In window and enter that number into the field for the parameter you wish to affect. In 4/4 time, for example, with the tempo cranked up to 180 BPM (beats per minute), an 1/8 note would be 166ms and a 1/4-note triplet would be 222ms.

Note   Min:Secs timings are only accurate to the nearest millisecond, although delay times can often be adjusted as fine as hundredths of a millisecond. You may need greater precision when using high Feedback values in a delay so that a large number of repeats will stay in time to the tempo without drifting. In this case, you can take your measurement in samples and then divide this by your sample rate to calculate a precise duration in seconds. For example, if a 1/4-note selection measures 15565 samples at a sample rate of 44.1 kHz, you would divide 15565 by 44100 to get 0.35295 seconds, or 352.95ms.

Aside from helping your mix sound less cluttered when multiple delays are used, synchronizing your effects to a subdivision of the musical beat has another advantage: When bouncing out loops from selections that contain delays (for example, for an interactive CD-ROM background, sampler, or loop-based audio program), you'll get smoother loops from your selections, since they won't end randomly between two delay repeats.

BPM: The Not-So-Secret Formula   Dividing 60 seconds by your tempo (in BPM) will give you the duration of each beat in seconds. To calculate the duration of each beat in milliseconds, divide 60,000 by the BPM instead. This provides an alternate way of calculating the length of a 1/4 note (in 4/4 timing). If your tempo is 120 beats per minute, each 1/4-note beat equals 60,000/120, or 500ms (meaning each 1/4 note is a half second, each 1/2 note is a full second, and each 1/8 note is a quarter second, or 250ms). If your tempo is 150 BPM in 6/8 time, each 1/8-note beat equals 60,000/150, or 400ms.

Taking this one step further, we can calculate the duration of individual ticks. Pro Tools divides every 1/4 note into 960 ticks…or every 1/8 note into 480 ticks if you're in 6/8 time, for example. The actual duration of each tick depends on the tempo setting. The formula is the same as above divided by 960 ticks (in 4/4 timing), or 60,000/BPM/960. At a tempo of 120 BPM, each tick represents 500ms/960 ticks, or about .520833ms.

To calculate the duration of a given number of ticks, you would multiply that number by .520833.

Summary

The suggestions in this chapter barely scratch the surface and don't approach the subject of how sampler instruments (including the AIR instrument Structure) can be extremely useful for creating grooves and manipulating audio samples. The power is there to create remarkable mixes, and as you surely know, thousands of hit records have been created in Pro Tools. Get in there and start working!

13 A Multitrack Music Session

This chapter takes a look at using Pro Tools with multiple live musicians in the studio as opposed to working alone in your project studio. This presents some particular challenges—for example, providing multiple cue mixes for performers (because they won't all want to hear the same headphone mix), dealing with monitoring latency issues on host-based Pro Tools configurations, and configuring the Pro Tools mixer to easily switch modes from tracking to editing to mixing. (Unlike the analog recording process, in Pro Tools, you're often doing all three things at once.) This chapter also provides a brief overview of strategies for live recording with a basic Pro Tools system (that is, without a VENUE configuration). Note, though, that it doesn't exhaustively explore all the aspects of music production with Pro Tools…that's a topic to fill an entire book!

Your own studio projects will of course be varied, but for the sake of discussion, let's assume we're running a session with the input source requirements shown in Table 13.1.

This band wants to record all at once rather than layering tracks one by one, although they will later overdub a replacement vocal and perhaps some backing vocals or a solo. Let's assume that we do have a MIDI interface on our Pro Tools configuration and that our audio hardware allows recording 16 simultaneous analog audio inputs.

Let's also assume that we have sufficient microphone preamps for recording all the microphone sources. Most of Avid's HD-series audio interfaces accept only line-level signals, and most non-HD interfaces have insufficient analog inputs for our needs, so assembling a rig that would work for this project would likely require some amount of add-on gear. For example, a 003 Rack+ or M-Audio ProFire 2626 could be supplemented with an external preamp via ADAT Lightpipe input (PreSonus' DigiMax, M-Audio Octane, or similar); a 16 × 16 analog HD I/O would require dedicated multichannel microphone preamps, such as the Avid PRE (see Figure 13.1).

Track Setup and Click Track for Recording

To get started, we need to create a new session with Audio tracks for all the sources we are going to record. We'll also create a click track via the Track > Create Click Track menu command. In addition, we'll need a stereo Instrument track that will not only record the MIDI performance from the keyboard but also monitor its audio while recording. We'll create additional Aux Inputs

Table 13.1 Sample Input Source Requirements

Input	Instrument	Description	Location
Audio inputs 1–8	Drums	Eight microphones: kick, snare, hi-hat, two rack toms, floor tom, plus left/right overheads	In drum booth
Audio input 9	Bass	Direct mono signal from bass preamp	In main room
Audio input 10	Electric guitar	Microphone on amplifier	In main room
Audio inputs 11–12	Acoustic guitar	Microphones on guitar: one on the bridge of the guitar, another over the fingerboard where it meets the body (angled slightly back toward the sound hole)	In isolation booth #1
Audio inputs 13–14	MIDI keyboard	Two direct audio outs for monitoring only (because you're recording this MIDI performance data on a Pro Tools Instrument track, to facilitate subsequent sound selection and editing)	In main room
Audio input 15	Saxophone	Microphone	In isolation booth #2
Audio input 16	Lead vocal (reference track while recording)	Microphone	In isolation booth #3
MIDI input	MIDI In from keyboard		

Figure 13.1 The Avid PRE, an eight-channel high-end microphone preamp, can be controlled from within the Pro Tools software (via MIDI). Its settings are recalled when you reopen the session.

to use as send destinations for effects (even during recording, to provide a less sterile-sounding headphone mix for the performers) as well as several Aux Inputs for use during the recording phase of the project to provide different cue mixes for the performers. This will require multiple headphone amplifiers (let's assume we have those, too); we'll use them to feed different mixes to various performers using output pairs on our Pro Tools audio interface.

Track Setup for Recording

One of the great benefits of working with a digital audio workstation is being able to configure your mixer with exactly the number of tracks and effect sends that the project requires—no more, no less. You can even reconfigure the mixer during different phases of a single project—for example, recording, editing, and mixdown.

Create Audio Tracks and Aux Inputs

For the recording phase of this project, let's create Audio tracks to record input signals and an Instrument track for the external keyboard. Aux Inputs will also be used to provide effects in the performers' headphone mix. The initial positions of new tracks will reflect their order in the New Tracks dialog box. Although we can change track order at any time, we'll try to create them in a logical order to avoid having to move them around later. We'll use the following steps to create the tracks we need:

1. Create a new Pro Tools session. Then choose Track > New (Command+Shift+N on Mac, Shift+Ctrl+N on Windows) to open the New Tracks dialog box.

2. Use the pop-up selectors to specify six mono Audio tracks (in Samples timebase, for now—this can be changed later) for the kick, snare, hi-hat, rack tom, mid tom, and floor tom. Then click the plus sign (+) button to create another row in the New Tracks dialog box. (As we create the remaining tracks, we will repeat this process for each new row while still within the dialog box.)

3. Create a single stereo Audio track for the drum overheads.

4. Add four mono Audio tracks—one for the bass, one for the electric guitar, and two for the acoustic guitar microphones. (Even though the two acoustic guitar microphones will be panned hard left and right, they will be recorded to two separate mono tracks so that we can apply different EQ, compression, and so on to each.)

5. Add one stereo Instrument track to record the keyboard player's performance. (It will default to Ticks timebase.) The Instrument track will serve a similar function to an Aux Input, allowing us to monitor the keyboard as an external audio source. At the same time, we will use the Instrument track to record the MIDI output from the keyboard, giving us flexibility to edit or expand this part later.

6. Add two more mono Audio tracks, for the saxophone and lead vocal.

7. Finally, add a stereo Master Fader (let's assume output pair 1–2 will be the source for our stereo mix). The configuration in the New Tracks dialog box is shown in Figure 13.2.

Figure 13.2 Multiple track types configured simultaneously in the New Tracks dialog box.

8. Click the Create button to close this dialog box and create the new tracks.

9. Select the Track > Create Click Track to create a click track for a metronome sound.

10. Open the Options menu and verify that Pre-Fader Metering is selected. This lets us look at the level of the signal as it enters Pro Tools. If the level in the meter hits red, we can lower the audio level from the source or adjust the preamp gain to avoid creating a clipped, distorted recording of the signal.

11. Save the session. We'll make it a habit to save often so we don't lose our work.

12. Choose Setup > Preferences and verify that the Auto Backup feature is enabled in the Operation page. Most operators prefer to keep 5 to 10 backup sessions and to have Pro Tools create a backup every 3 to 5 minutes.

Keyboard Shortcuts for the New Tracks Dialog Box   As you start to get comfortable in Pro Tools, you can really speed up the setup for new Pro Tools sessions by learning the following shortcuts for each row in the New Tracks dialog box:

■   To toggle a row between mono and stereo (and multitrack, on systems with Pro Tools HD or Complete Production Toolkit), hold down the Command key (Ctrl key in Windows) and press the Left/Right Arrow keys.

■   To toggle between track types (Audio, Aux Input, Master Fader, and so on), hold down the Command key (Ctrl key in Windows) and press the Up/Down Arrow keys.

■   To toggle the track timebase between ticks and samples, hold down the Command+Option keys (Ctrl+Alt in Windows) and press the Up/Down Arrow keys.

■   To add a new row, hold down the Command+Shift keys (Ctrl+Shift in Windows) and press the Down Arrow key. (If you press the Up Arrow key instead, the current row will be deleted.) Alternatively, you can hold Command (Ctrl in Windows) and press the plus (+) or minus (−) keys on the numeric keypad to add or remove rows.

- As in other Pro Tools dialog boxes, you can use the Tab key (or Shift+Tab) to toggle through the Number of Tracks fields in successive rows.

Name the Tracks; Select Their Input Sources

Next, we want to edit all our track names. Not only will this make it easier to see what's going on in our mix, it will also affect how clip names are created when we start recording. Here are the steps to rename our tracks:

1. Double-click the Audio 1 track nameplate to open the Track Name dialog box. Name this track Kick. Click the Next button at the bottom of the dialog box to advance to the Audio 2 track.

   Tip You can hold down the Command key (Ctrl key in Windows) while pressing the Right or Left Arrow key to activate the Next and Previous functions in this dialog box from the keyboard.

2. Rename the Audio 2 track Snare; then click the Next button again. Continue renaming each of the next four Audio tracks for the drums: Hi-Hat, Rack Tom, Mid Tom, and Floor Tom, respectively.

3. Advance to the Audio 7 track (this is our stereo Audio track) and rename it Overheads. Click the OK button to close the dialog box for now.

4. If necessary, switch to the Mix window. Use the input selectors of the mono drum tracks to select inputs 1–6 for each track, respectively.

5. Using the input selector for the stereo Overheads track, choose input pair 7–8 as its input source for recording.

   Tip The following order is fairly typical for mic inputs in drum tracks: kick, snare, hi-hat, toms from higher to lower pitch, and then overheads, left-right. At any point in the recording and mixing process, you can rearrange the drum tracks into any order that's convenient, regardless of their input assignments.

6. Rename the next track (currently called Audio 8) to Bass and select input 9 as its source.

7. Rename the remainder of the Audio and Instrument tracks as follows: E. Guitar, Acoustic 1, Acoustic 2, Keys, Sax, and Lead Vox.

8. Select the appropriate inputs for the recording sources on each Audio track (inputs 10–14). (Skip the Keys track for now.)

9. Pan the two acoustic tracks hard left and right. (Again, we're using two mono tracks for the stereo-miked acoustic guitar instead of a single stereo track so that we can place different EQs and such on the signal from each microphone.)

10. Select input pair 15–16 as the audio input source for the Keys Instrument track. (This is where we'll connect audio outputs from the MIDI keyboard out in the studio.)

11. Enable display of the Instrument section of the Mix window via the View > Mix Window > Instruments command and select the MIDI input and channel where the keyboard is connected to our MIDI interface. Because we are using only one MIDI instrument, we can leave this set to All. Figure 13.3 shows the Mix window after all inputs have been configured.

Figure 13.3 The Mix window for our recording session.

Name Your Tracks Early   Naming tracks before you begin recording is *important*. In Pro Tools, all the audio clips created by recording inherit the name of their source tracks. In a large session, having cryptic names such as Audio 6_01 for original audio files and auto-created clips in the Clip List (and within the tracks, for that matter) *will* lead to confusion.

---

12. Save the session. We're now ready to start record-enabling Audio tracks and checking input levels. Remember that input levels have to be adjusted *at the source* (the line output, the mic preamp, and so on) if any tracks are clipping. Also keep in mind that performers tend to hold back a little while checking levels. Inevitably, when the record light is on, they sing a little louder and play a little harder. So we'll want to leave ourselves some headroom.

Tip Don't stress about recording the absolutely hottest possible levels in Pro Tools—especially when you're recording at 24-bit resolution. You're not fighting to overcome hiss or other limitations of analog tape, and digital clipping *always* sounds very nasty—not at all like the warm tape saturation that's sometimes a desirable effect. Also remember that volume faders on Audio tracks have no effect on the audio signal level being recorded to disk!

---

13. While checking input levels, adjust the tracks' main volume faders to obtain an approximate mix for the song. We will use this later as the basis for our cue mixes; see the section "Setting Up a Cue Mix with Effects" later in this chapter.

Click Track

The band wants to record this song with a click track (which, incidentally, is going to make it very easy to edit in Grid mode afterward), so we need to set this up before recording. Some people opt for using an external MIDI source for click sounds. Others who want to conserve DSP resources and/or ensure extremely precise metronome timing—a legitimate concern in complex sessions with many tracks—will either record the output of the Click plug-in to an Audio track or use repeated audio clips on a track as their click sound. In our case, we'll use the Click plug-in on an Aux Input track as the source for the metronome sound. The options in the Click plug-in window are shown in Figure 13.4.

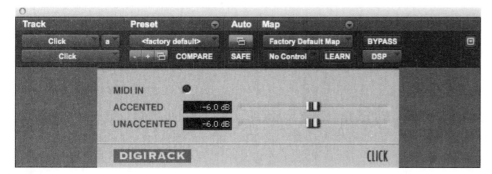

Figure 13.4 The Click plug-in lets you choose from a variety of metronome sounds. Multiple Click plug-ins can be active simultaneously on separate tracks, each with its own metronome sound.

If you prefer, the metronome click from Pro Tools (based on the current tempo and meter settings) can also be transmitted as a MIDI note event so that some external MIDI drum machine or synthesizer produces the click sound (which would then need to be monitored and possibly recorded into the Pro Tools session). Most users will opt to use the Click plug-in, however.

Here are the steps we'll use to configure the click for our session. For the sake of simplicity, let's assume the entire song is in 4/4 time (Pro Tools' default time signature) and the musicians want 1/4-note clicks.

1. In the Transport window, double-click the Metronome button to open the Click/Countoff Options dialog box, shown in Figure 13.5.

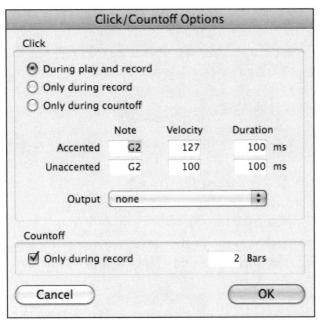

Figure 13.5 The Click/Countoff Options dialog box.

2. Verify that the click is set to sound during play and record and to provide two bars of countoff while recording only. Because we'll use the Click plug-in's metronome click sound, we'll leave the MIDI output selector in this dialog box set to None (instead of selecting any other MIDI destination).

3. Click OK to close the Click/Countoff Options dialog box.

4. If necessary, click the Transport window's Metronome button to enable the metronome click sound.

5. Press the spacebar to start playback in Pro Tools. Verify that the click is audible (from the plug-in in the Click Aux Input). In the pop-up Presets selector within the Click plug-in window, select the desired metronome sound.

6. Adjust the tempo, with the assistance of the performers. Because musicians' perceptions of appropriate click tempos are notoriously unreliable while they are not actually playing, we'll have the band run through the song until they get into a groove. Then, with the

Tempo Ruler disabled (Conductor button off in the Transport window), we'll click in the Current Tempo field and use the T key on the computer keyboard to tap in the tempo as the musicians play.

Tip An alternate way of entering a tempo is to enable Use MIDI to Tap Tempo in the MIDI tab of the Preferences dialog box and then use a MIDI keyboard controller—such as a key on a keyboard or pad on a drum module—to tap in a manual tempo.

---

7. After determining an appropriate tempo, re-enable the Tempo Ruler and double-click the red marker at the start of the Tempo Ruler in the Edit window to enter this value for the session's default tempo.

Grooves on Tap When setting click-track tempos for musical groups, tapping in a manual tempo is often the most reliable method. Have your musicians simply play through the song a couple of times while you set an appropriate tempo—before you even let them hear a click track. Be aware, however, that bands with less studio experience often lose the sense of appropriate song tempos when they're in cold and unfamiliar studio conditions, typically playing slower than when under the adrenaline rush of live performance. Sometimes having the band bring a tape of any good live performance or rehearsal version will provide a more reliable reference for tapping in your manual tempo setting. (Sound quality doesn't matter for this purpose; a cassette or MP3 recording is fine.) Even if you *do* end up backing off the tempo slightly (because live tempos are sometimes too fast for studio recordings), everyone will be happier in the long run!

In the Beginning, There Was a Drum Fill... Once you calculate the proper tempo and enable the Count Off button in the Transport window, you're generally all set to record; the musicians can jump in at the beginning of the session Timeline, at Bar 1, Beat 1. But what if the drummer plays some pickup notes to lead into the first bar? When recording bands to a click track in Pro Tools, you should learn how to use the Event > Renumber Bars command (see Figure 13.6) to establish some point farther into the Bars|Beats Timeline (Bar 5, for example) as Bar 1. That way, you're sure to capture any pickup notes (or studio chatter that you may later decide to leave in the final mix) at the beginning of the session Timeline. More importantly, the bar numbers you see in Pro Tools will make sense in terms of the song structure you discuss with the musicians. You can also use the Move Song Start command in the Time Operations window for this purpose. If the Tempo Ruler is visible in the Edit window, another method is to enable Grid edit mode and simply drag the Song Start Marker to the desired position.

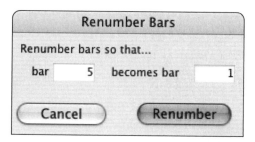

Figure 13.6 The Renumber Bars dialog box enables you to establish some point farther into the Timeline as Bar 1 to allow for pickup bars, anticipated notes, intro fills, and so on.

Creating Effects and a Drum Submix

As discussed in previous chapters, reverb and delay effects are commonly placed on an Aux Input track whose input is set to one of the internal mixing busses in Pro Tools. You then use sends from individual tracks to add their audio to the input bus for the Reverb Aux Input, for example. Another typical use of Aux Input tracks is to create submixes that combine the outputs from multiple source Audio tracks. For our recording, we're going to bus the outputs of all the drum tracks to a single, stereo Aux Input. This simplifies the adjustment of the overall level of the drum mix and also allows for the placement of effects on the entire drum submix rather than on each individual drum track. Here are the steps we'll use:

1. In the Mix window, create two stereo Aux Input tracks. Name them Reverb and Drums. Option-click (or Alt-click in Windows) on their volume faders to set them to 0 dB.

2. Set the input of Reverb to bus pair 1–2 and the input of Drums to bus pair 3–4.

3. If needed, display Inserts A-E in the Mix window (View > Mix Window Views > Inserts A-E). Also display Sends A-E.

4. Place the D-Verb plug-in on Insert A of the Reverb Aux Input track so that sends from any track to bus pair 1–2 pass through its Reverb plug-in.

5. Use the output selectors of the seven drum tracks to change all their current output assignments to bus 3–4, which is the selected input source for the Drums Aux Input track we just created. While we're at it, we'll also choose Setup > I/O and rename stereo bus pairs 1–2 and 3–4; we'll call them RevSend and DrumSub, respectively. Now we can control the overall volume of the drums in the mix with a single volume fader on the Drums track (see Figure 13.7).

Tip You can also right-click on any send label or input/output selector and choose Rename from the pop-up menu to rename an I/O path without using the I/O Setup dialog box.

Figure 13.7 The outputs of all drum tracks assigned to the DrumSub bus pair (3–4), the selected input source for the Drums Aux Input. Any plug-ins we add on this Aux Input track will affect the entire the drum submix.

6. Create a stereo send to the RevSend bus pair (1–2) on Send A of the Lead Vox track. We'll probably end up creating additional sends to the Reverb Aux Input from other tracks as the musicians request it.

Tip Pro Tools 9 and later allow you to assign a send or output directly to a new track. Using this method, you can simplify the process of creating a reverb return for the Lead Vox track by clicking on Send A and selecting New Track from the pop-up menu. In the resulting New Track dialog box, configure a new stereo Aux Input track and name it Reverb. Pro Tools will create the track and route a mix bus from the send on the vocal track to the input on the Reverb track. This eliminates the steps of creating and naming the Aux Input track in advance, assigning its input to a mix bus, and renaming the mix bus.

---

7. (Optional) Rearrange the track order as needed by dragging on the track nameplates so that the Drums Aux Input track appears after the Overheads track and the Reverb Aux Input track appears just before the Master Fader track.

Don't Smoosh Your Crashes! In our example, we've assigned all drum tracks to a single stereo Aux Input track, mainly for the convenience of having a single volume fader (and Mute/Solo buttons) to control the entire drum submix. The other advantage of doing this is that we can apply a single stereo effect to the entire drum submix—for example, a Compressor plug-in on this Drums Aux Input track. Be careful, though; you may not like what a large degree of compression does to the sound of your cymbal crashes. You may prefer to submix everything *except* the stereo overhead microphones (presumably your primary source for cymbals) to a stereo Aux Input when heavy stereo compression is applied. You could always assign the output of this Aux Input (and that of the stereo overheads) to yet *another* stereo bus/Aux Input if you still want a single volume fader to control the entire drum submix. A different approach to drum compression would be to use sends from individual drum tracks (but not the cymbals, perhaps) to a stereo Aux Input where heavier compression is being applied and then blend that together with the main stereo drum mix.

Recording Modes Pro Tools' destructive recording mode is discussed in Chapter 8. You can toggle this mode on and off by choosing Options > Destructive Record. Unlike the default non-destructive recording mode—which creates new clips for each additional take, leaving previous ones intact—destructive recording mode erases any previously recorded audio data in the area of the track being recorded. When recording rhythm sections, for example, you may occasionally work in destructive recording mode to conserve disk space; if you know that you have limited available disk space for a multitrack project, it doesn't always make sense to retain numerous false starts, especially at higher resolutions and 16 or 24 tracks each! (Of course, you can always use the Select Unused and Clear Selected commands in the Clip List submenu at any point to eliminate unwanted audio files and recover disk space.) When recording vocal and instrumental overdubs, however, non-destructive recording mode offers more flexibility and the very useful possibility of compositing an ideal version from several takes at some later point in the process. Always using non-destructive recording also allows for the possibility of rediscovering some brilliant earlier take that no one recognized as a "keeper" at the time. Loop Recording mode (also described in Chapter 8) and the Takes List pop-up menu are other invaluable tools available during the overdubbing process; be sure to learn about these.

Setting Up a Cue Mix with Effects

At this point, we've created Audio tracks for every input and created Aux Input tracks to monitor the Click plug-in and external MIDI keyboard (whose audio output is not currently being recorded, although that certainly would be an option). We can hear all the tracks and adjust the volume and panning for each (without affecting the levels recorded to disk) to get an idea of how the mix will start to take shape. We're almost ready to record—but we still need to provide a cue mix so that the musicians can hear each other in their headphones as they play. Not only does the cue mix need to be unaffected by our volume changes, mutes, solos, and so on as they're recording, but different musicians are going to require different mixes to be comfortable during the recording process.

Let's assume we have three stereo headphone amps out in the studio, so we can provide up to three distinct cue mixes (from three different stereo output pairs on our Pro Tools audio interface). Here's the scenario for this group:

- The guitars, keyboards, sax, and trumpet want essentially the entire, balanced mix in their headphones. In our case, the source for this mix will be outputs 5–6 on the audio interface, but it could be any output pair other than the one you're using for your main stereo mix output.

- The vocalist wants to hear the vocals a little louder than in the band's mix and would like plenty of reverb. The source for this cue mix will be outputs 7–8 on the audio interface.

- The bass player and drummer want lots of their own instruments so they can lock up a groove; they also want the click track extra loud in their headphones. The source for this cue mix will be outputs 9–10 on the audio interface.

We're going to create Aux Input tracks for each of the three cue mixes and then use sends from source Audio tracks so that we can create distinct mixes for each group of instrumentalists. As with many things in Pro Tools, there are many ways to accomplish this; the options presented here may or may not be appropriate for your working style.

One simple method would be to use multiple output assignments for each Audio track and Aux Input. For example, while using physical outputs 1 and 2 for monitoring in the control room, we could create an additional output assignment from all individual Audio tracks and Aux Inputs to outputs 3 and 4 (where we've connected the headphone distribution amplifier, providing an identical mix for all the performers).

Creating Multiple Output Assignments on Audio and Aux Input Tracks   As you know, the Output selector for each Audio, Aux Input, and Instrument track determines the main destination for its audio. To create an *additional* routing assignment for a track's main output, hold down the Control key (Start key in Windows) as you reopen its Output selector. Afterward, a plus sign (+) in the Output selector indicates any tracks that have more than one output assignment. If you also hold down the Option key (Alt key in Windows) as you select an extra output assignment for a track, it is simultaneously added to all tracks. Incidentally, you can also assign each send on a track to multiple destinations using the same Control key (or Start key in Windows) technique.

This method (using multiple output assignments from tracks) isn't very practical for our control room/studio situation, however; we can't solo/mute tracks or change levels during recording because doing so would affect what the performers hear in their headphone mix. In most recording situations, it's preferable to create a separate cue mix for the performers' headphones that won't be affected by changes you make to the control-room mix while recording (for example, soloing a bass track during recording because you think you're hearing a buzz from the instrument's pickups).

Creating Multiple Cue Mix Sends

This is the classic approach, most similar to the method used on traditional mixing boards. It can be very effective and offers maximum flexibility for adjusting the level and pan position of individual instruments in each separate cue mix. Here are the steps we'll take to set up the cue mix sends for our session:

1. Create three stereo Aux Input tracks. Name them CueMix, CueVox, and CueRhythm.

2. Set the input of CueMix to bus pair 5–6, the input of CueVox to bus pair 7–8, and the input of CueRhythm to bus pair 9–10.

3. Create a stereo send from Send C on each Audio track *except* the individual drum tracks to bus pair 5–6. Click the Pre button in the Output window for each send as it is created to make them all *pre*-fader sends; that way, they will not be affected by the source track's main volume fader or Mute button. In other words, we're routing all these pre-fader sends to the input of the CueMix Aux Input via bus 5–6.

4. Right-click on a send selector set to bus pair 5–6 and rename the bus CueMix.

5. Create a similar stereo send from Send C (to the CueMix bus) on the Keys stereo Aux Input that we're using to monitor the keyboards, on the Click mono Aux Input, on the Drums stereo Aux Input (our submix for all the drum tracks), and on the Reverb stereo Aux Input so that these can also be heard in the cue mix.

Creating Sends on All Tracks, Copying Sends and Plug-Ins   If you hold down the Option key (Alt key in Windows) while creating a send on any track, the same send is created in that position for all Audio tracks as well as all Aux Input (and Instrument) tracks. This can be a real timesaver, but in our example, we would then have to *un-assign* some of these sends because we don't want both the original drum tracks and their drum submix to go to the same send, nor would we want to create a send from the CueMix Aux Input to itself. One alternative is to select all the tracks that you wish to affect (and only those tracks) and then hold down Option+Shift (Alt+Shift in Windows) while creating the send. Option+Shift (Alt+Shift in Windows) generally functions as a "Do To Selected" modifier combination in Pro Tools. Another possibility is to Option-drag (Alt-drag in Windows) on an existing send to copy it from one track or position to another.

---

6. Switch to Single Send view for Send C to quickly adjust the pans/levels of the stereo sends to the CueMix bus. Ordinarily, all sends appear as buttons, and you click any one of them to open the Send window. By choosing View > Sends A–E and selecting Send C, the send's Pan, Level, Mute, and Pre/Post buttons will be visible on all tracks simultaneously. (Figure 13.8 shows Send C in Single Send view.)

Figure 13.8 The View menu lets you choose to show individual controls for one send position (globally, on all tracks), including Level, Pan, Mute, and Pre/Post.

7. Mute all Audio, Aux Input, and Instrument tracks, but not the CueMix Aux Input, in order to manually adjust send levels from each track to the cue mix. Because all sends are pre-fader, they're unaffected by track Mute buttons. While the band runs through the song, adjust the mix for the first headphone output.

Tip   Command-click (Ctrl-click in Windows) the Solo buttons for Aux Inputs to "solo-safe" the tracks—this prevents the tracks from being muted when you solo an Audio track.

---

8. Return the sends to Assignments view (View > Send A–E > Assignments) and repeat Steps 1–7, using Send D to create a mix to the CueVox track from the same source tracks using bus 7–8 (rename the bus CueVox); repeat again using Send E to create a mix to the CueRhythm track using bus 9–10 (rename it CueRhythm). Once all three cue mixes are set up, we'll route each to a separate Pro Tools output.

Copying Track Volume and Pan Settings to Sends   If you're working on a system with Pro Tools HD or the Complete Production Toolkit, you could select all the Audio tracks for which you've created a send and choose Edit > Copy to Send. (This command isn't available in standard Pro Tools.) Specify send C as the destination for copying each track's current main volume and pan values (then D, then E). Of course, you would fine-tune these levels and pan positions afterward.

---

9. Set the output of the CueMix track to outputs 5–6 on the audio interface. Set the CueVox track to outputs 7–8 and the CueRhythm track to outputs 9–10. Figure 13.9 shows the Mix window after configuring the three different cue mixes.

10. Un-mute all tracks and have the band do another run-through with headphones to confirm input levels and to accommodate any requests for changes in the cue mixes.

Figure 13.9 Three cue mixes configured in the Mix window.

One last issue remains to be addressed: The output assignments from each of our cue mix Aux Input tracks are now set directly to the output path where the headphone distribution boxes for the performers are attached, so how do *we* hear a cue mix in the control room if we ever need to make adjustments? Because we are not routing through an external mixing board in the control room on the way out to the studio, we'll need to create a stereo send from each cue mix Aux Input to the main stereo output. We'll normally keep those sends muted, except when we need to hear a particular cue mix; in that case, we'll Option-mute (Alt-mute in Windows) to mute all of the tracks and then unmute the send from the desired cue mix's Aux Input.

Markers and Selections   As mentioned in Chapter 8, Pro Tools allows you to create two types of Memory locations: *markers* and *selections*. Markers identify *single points* in time and can appear in the Edit window's Markers Ruler. Selections identify a *range* within the Timeline, such as the bridge of a song, the points where a guitar solo will be punched in/ out, and so on.

Both markers and selections can be either *absolute* (a specific Minutes:Seconds reference) or *relative* (a location in Bars|Beats, whose absolute position depends on the current Pro Tools Tempo setting). For music recording sessions with a click track governed by the Pro Tools tempo, relative Memory locations will be the most useful because discussions with the musicians will generally refer to bars and beats rather than minutes and seconds.

You can drop markers on the fly any time, even while recording; just press the Enter key on the numeric keypad. If you find it cumbersome or distracting to negotiate the New

Memory Location dialog box while doing so, choose the Editing tab of the Preferences dialog box and enable the Auto-Name Memory Locations When Playing option. Marker 1, Marker 2, and so on will automatically be created without requiring you to open the dialog box. You can always double-click a marker to change its name or properties, or drag it within the Markers Ruler to change its position. In Grid mode, marker movements will snap to the nearest grid increment.

You can use markers to set the playback point for Pro Tools; just click a marker in the Memory Locations window or the Markers Ruler. (Choose View > Rulers > Markers to make the Markers Ruler visible in the Edit window.) If you click one marker and then Shift-click another, the Transport window's Start and End values are set to those positions. (This can be very useful for overdubs or to perfect mix parameters while looping a specific section of the song.) For example, to select the entire second verse for playback or punch-in recording, you might click the marker Verse2 and then Shift-click Chorus2. If Link Edit and Timeline Selection is enabled (either via the Options menu selection or the button in the Edit window), not only are both the Edit and Timeline (play) selections set, but the contents of the current track are also selected between these markers. This makes it quick and easy to copy entire sections (holding down the Option key—Alt key in Windows—as you drag with the Separation Grabber) or to make other edits on a selection.

Making the Most of Available Tracks

On large sessions with many source Audio tracks, you may reach the limit of available playback voices in your Pro Tools system. In music projects, this can happen sooner than you think, especially on high sample-rate sessions. If you are a Pro Tools|HD user, you may be able to use Pro Tools' voice allocation (as explained in Chapter 2) in a way that works to your advantage. On Pro Tools|HD systems, if audio clips on two tracks never coincide (for example, a saxophone track used for a solo in the middle of a song and a backing vocal track used only at the end), they can share the same voice assignment; the effects, sends, and output assignments of one track are still completely independent of the other.

On all other Pro Tools system, when your tracks exceed the number of available voices, the highest tracks beyond the available voices will appear grayed out, as shown in Figure 13.10. Remove any voiced tracks (or make voiced tracks inactive via the Track > Make Inactive command), and the corresponding number of grayed-out unvoiced tracks will become fully voiced and active.

Thinking Ahead: Arm Yourself for Editing When recording drums, once you have your basic levels set up, ask the drummer to give you one clean, solid hit on each drum and cymbal. Record these and be sure to rename and keep these clips in your session. You can use them later as replacement hits, if needed. You don't have to make a big deal to the performers about possibly needing these to fix something in the mix—but it certainly helps to have options.

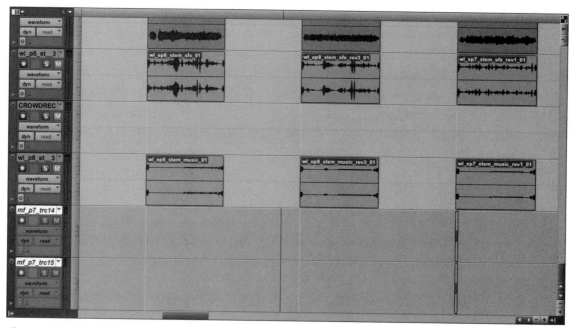

Figure 13.10 The bottom two tracks in this Pro Tools session have no free voices available to them. They are grayed out to show that they will not play back.

Tips for Remote Recording with Pro Tools

Recording live ensemble performances with Pro Tools is indeed a practical possibility. Naturally, you will want to have as compact a setup as possible, potentially rack-mounting most of your gear for quick load in/out. Here are a few tricks you might want to try:

- **Mixing board.** It can be very cost effective to use a conventional mixing board with multiple microphone inputs and individual line outs on the input channels. Obviously, the mixer's microphone preamps need to be high quality to get acceptable results. Fortunately, a number of economical small mixers fit the bill and might also be ideal for your Pro Tools project studio—not only providing additional microphone inputs, but also allowing you to monitor multiple sources in your studio configuration. If your mixer is rack-mountable, that's also a benefit, because you can cable its channel outputs to your audio interface inputs (and cable the main output pair of your audio interface to a mixer channel to monitor the Pro Tools mix output) before you even wheel your rig into the venue.

- **Microphone preamplifier.** Another way to go is a dedicated, multichannel microphone pre-amplifier. Options range from the high end (for example, the Avid PRE) to more economical midrange units for professional applications from PreSonus and others. Again, the fact that these are generally rack-mountable can be very attractive because you can arrive at the performance with all the cable connections between the microphone preamplifier and your rack-mounted audio interface already in place.

- **Compression/limiting.** Levels can be very unpredictable in live performance! When you're recording a live performance (or conference), you can't risk an unexpected peak in level ruining the recording that you're being paid to capture. Be conservative with input levels. Although you might try to maximize input levels in a relatively controlled studio situation, it would be foolhardy to be overly aggressive about this in a live performance situation! That said, good compression/limiting on your microphone inputs can also give you peace of mind—and maybe even save your skin on occasion. Because you have compression in Pro Tools, the idea isn't to use compression to shape the sound, consistently clamping down on the signal; instead, you want to avoid the occasional "rogue" peak from producing a horrific digital distortion sound that would mar an overall good-sounding recording. You can always correct low levels in the mix afterward, but the clipping distortion produced during recording will be there to stay.

Recording Live Theater   If you record live theater, you may find that performer levels onstage are even more unpredictable than a rock band's club performance (which is saying a lot!). At any point, an actor is likely to step right up to your PZM microphone and scream at the top of her voice, even if her mark during rehearsal was several yards away; it's just part of the natural performance flexibility they require. But unlike a rock band, where the vocalists are close to the microphone and therefore the dynamic range has reasonable limits, in theater, each microphone is required to capture sounds anywhere from several yards to as close as a couple of feet away. It's a great idea to have compression or limiting in place for microphones that might be subject to unexpected extreme levels (front-of-stage microphones in theater productions, lead singers, lead guitar amplifiers, and so on).

- **Snake.** A snake gives you a lot of XLR connectors (and usually some 1/4-inch connectors) at one end of a single long cable. These connectors are mirrored at the other end as either a fan of separate cables/connectors or a stagebox with jacks. That's how you get all those microphone and line inputs from the stage back to your mixer and recording rig. (These should be balanced, by the way, to avoid transmission loss in longer cables; use a direct box and so on if required.) If you're sharing microphones and other input sources with another person mixing sound for the house system, you should use a splitter snake; double outputs at your end allow both you and the house mixer to get your input directly from the snake's channels. Figure 13.11 shows a typical live-recording configuration with Pro Tools.

- **Paranoia.** Many people simultaneously record performances in stereo to a DAT recorder directly from the mixing board (rather than from the Pro Tools main L–R output). If someone kicks out your power cable or your computer freezes, at least the performance will be intact as a live stereo mix on the DAT tape. An uninterruptible power supply (UPS) may also save your reputation, kicking over to battery power in the case of an AC power failure.

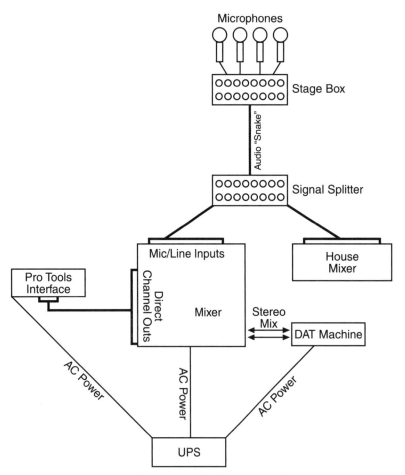

Figure 13.11 A possible setup for live recording with Pro Tools. A splitter snake provides both the recording rig and the house sound mixer with direct microphone (or line/direct box) feeds from the stage. A clean portable mixer provides multiple mic-level inputs and direct outputs from each channel to a multichannel Pro Tools audio interface. This can simultaneously feed a rough stereo mix directly from the mixer to a DAT recorder as a precaution. Everything is powered through a UPS (uninterruptible power supply).

Recording a DAT mix directly from the mixing board also guarantees that you'll have documented whatever portion of the performance transpires if you have no alternative but to restart your computer.

- **Headphones and earplugs.** As the recordist, the usefulness of headphones for you is obvious. You will usually want a design that covers the ear fairly well to isolate outside sounds (often called *circumaural*, *closed-back*, or something similar, as opposed to open or semi-open). This is not only so that you can hear what's coming through the headphones in a noisy environment, but also to protect your ears when recording extremely loud performances. Along the same lines, a set of musician's earplugs is highly advisable (or at the very least some cheap foam ones that you can buy in a drugstore). If the opening bands or even the house music system blows out your ears beforehand, you may miss defects or make errors while recording—not to mention incurring lasting ear damage. Don't forget to bring along an extra set for any assistants, especially if you will be sending them onstage to make adjustments during a loud performance.

Monitoring Latency with Pro Tools Any digital audio system incurs some small degree of delay, or *latency,* as an analog audio signal enters the system, gets digitized, is routed within the system's internal mixing environment, and is then converted back to an analog audio signal on an output of your audio hardware. Even on HD systems, whose dedicated DSP cards provide mix/routing latency times so low that for practical purposes they're usually not an issue while recording, there is still a small amount of delay required for the A/D/A (analog>digital, digital>analog) converters themselves to do their work.

For all native or host-based digital audio workstations that rely on the computer's processing power for their mixing/routing tasks, the large input buffer required produces monitoring latency that can be several milliseconds or more, depending on audio resolution and other factors—enough to produce a noticeable delay. This latency can be enough to disconcert or affect the timing of your performance if you don't deal with it properly. Using a mixing board as the front end for recording microphone sources into Pro Tools and monitoring input audio directly from the board (and not via Pro Tools) is one way to bypass this problem.

Within standard Pro Tools software, you can also reduce latency by using the Playback Engine dialog box to lower the Hardware Buffer Size (try a setting between 64 and 256 samples) while recording tracks. If you have an extremely fast host computer, you may be able to use a low buffer setting all the time. If you're using a slower CPU, however, beware: Lower buffer sizes can reduce how many simultaneous Audio tracks can be recorded and may affect playback of sessions with complex plug-in processing and routing. In that case, set the buffer to 512 or 1,024 samples when editing and mixing, especially when using processing-intensive plug-ins, such as certain reverbs and software instruments.

In Pro Tools 10, the Low Latency Monitoring option in the Options menu provides the lowest-possible latency on outputs 1–2 of supported hardware, including Core Audio and ASIO audio interfaces that have a built-in mixer (such as the RME Fireface or the MOTU 828). (In this case, you might have to use outputs 1–2 not only as the single cue mix send for your performers out in the studio but also for monitoring in the control room, because Pro Tools automatically bypasses all plug-ins and sends on any tracks assigned to outputs 1–2 while Low Latency Monitoring mode is active. Also, remember to disable Low Latency Monitoring mode once you start mixing; otherwise, when you bounce to disk, none of the audio from any Aux Input tracks will be included in the bounced audio file!)

Some audio interfaces, including the Mbox Mini and older Mbox 2 and Mbox 2 Mini, offer another alternative for overcoming the latency issue. A Mix knob on the front of the interface itself allows you to adjust what is heard on its analog outputs between its analog inputs and playback from Pro Tools. While recording, you could simply mute the track to which you're recording (so that its delayed signal doesn't interfere with the timing of your performance) and set the Mix knob around midpoint. The Mix knob adjusts how much of your (dry) signal at the input(s) goes directly into the stereo mix output from the interface (or its dedicated headphone output) for zero-latency monitoring. However, when recording from a mono source—for example, one microphone on a guitar, voice, or wind instrument—be sure to also press the Mono button on the front panel so that this source will be heard in both left and right channels of your control-room monitors or headphones.

Several of the M-Audio interfaces also offer a similar feature via internal routing options in which selected inputs can pass directly to other outputs on the interface itself (including headphone outputs, if available) without first being routed through the Pro Tools mixing environment. This is configured via the control panel software provided with these interfaces, which can also be opened from the Pro Tools Hardware Setup dialog box.

Summary

Every musical project is different. Some classical musicians record together as an ensemble and don't require individual cue mixes or headphones—let alone a click track. Many bands don't (or won't) record with a click track. You can still edit later in musical bars and beats, after applying the Identify Beat command or using Beat Detective to create a tempo map. Many bands don't record all at once, of course. Instead, they layer up tracks, perhaps starting from only the most basic rhythm section in the initial recording session.

In many cases, a single cue mix is acceptable for all the simultaneous performers. If so, you can dispense with the more complex setup described here and instead use a single pre-fader send from each track to a single output pair that feeds your performers' headphone mix. Even in this case, though, it's usually convenient to route these sends through a stereo bus to an Aux Input or Master Fader track, where you can apply a compressor or limiter to keep headphone levels under control.

Be sure to enable the Auto Backup feature in the Operation tab of the Preferences dialog box. And one last reminder, especially important with paying clients and any group of performers out in the studio: *Save your session often as you work!* Good performances are ephemeral moments. If you lose a performance due to a system (or human-operator) error or power outage, musicians may find it difficult to forgive you! Indeed, make the File > Save shortcut Command+S (Ctrl+S in Windows) a second-nature reflex at least once a minute.

14 Post-Production and Soundtracks

This chapter explores some of Pro Tools' capabilities for film and video soundtracks. Chapter 11 provides a general background on the technical aspects of SMPTE time code and an overview of synchronization methods and peripherals for a Pro Tools configuration. The focus here is on basic production strategies, tips for collaborating with users of nonlinear video-editing systems (Avid Media Composer, Media 100, Apple Final Cut Pro, Adobe Premiere, and others), and basic post-production methods, including a cursory overview of how you can use Pro Tools for surround mixing. This chapter (along with Chapter 11) is merely a primer for using Pro Tools in post-production; the particulars vary immensely according to each production facility and the immediate task at hand. Indeed, entire books are dedicated to the subject of post-production alone.

Synchronization Setup

As discussed in Chapter 11, many options are available for synchronizing Pro Tools to SMPTE time code. These range from simple trigger sync setups (after playback starts at the correct point, Pro Tools no longer references the time-code information to maintain speed) to external reference sync (for example, house sync or black burst, providing a common reference for both Pro Tools and the video gear), and continuous resyncing/resolving Pro Tools to the time-code master (via a Sync HD or a similar device). If you principally deal with short-duration projects such as 30-second spots, your requirements may not be as stringent as for creating, say, 30-minute programs or feature films, where even a small amount of drift creates real timing problems.

Figure 14.1 shows Sync HD, a high-end synchronization peripheral from Avid with continuous resync/resolving capabilities for locking Pro Tools hardware with external time code or video sync. It also translates SMPTE to and from VITC (video) or LTC (audio) format. More importantly, it can continuously adjust the sample clock of your audio hardware to keep Pro Tools in sync with incoming time code over extended periods. This external, rack-mounted synchronization peripheral can slave to an external video reference (for example, black burst), an industry-standard word clock, or Loop Sync. Its dual Sony 9-pin serial ports can link Transport functions of Pro Tools to external video/audio devices via the MachineControl option.

If your synchronization peripheral is a standard SMPTE interface (which translates incoming time-code location information from its audio or video format to MTC and then routes it into

Figure 14.1 Avid's Sync HD is a high-end synchronization peripheral for Mac or Windows computers.

your computer, perhaps via the USB port), you can use the Synchronization tab of the Setup > Peripherals dialog box to tell Pro Tools the device type—for example, a generic MTC reader versus a Sync I/O—and the port to which it is connected. (See Figures 14.2 and 14.3.)

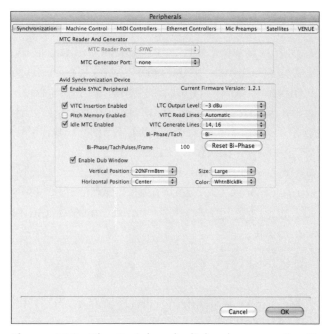

Figure 14.2 The Peripherals dialog box on a Pro Tools|HD system, using the Sync I/O, which can add a time-code window to video signals passing through it.

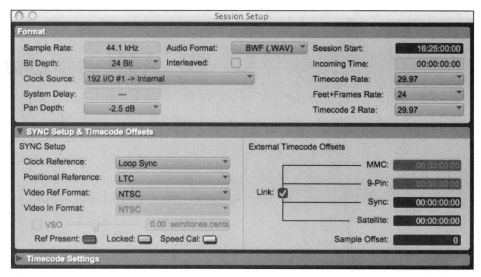

Figure 14.3 Settings in the Sync Setup section of the Session Setup window include the positional reference (the time-code source) for your synchronization peripheral.

MachineControl

MachineControl is an option for Pro Tools HD that enables you to link the Pro Tools transport functions with professional video decks or other compatible devices via their Sony 9-pin serial ports or V-LAN, either as a master or a slave. You can also remotely arm tracks on the device for recording from within Pro Tools (using the Machine Track Arming window).

MachineControl uses a serial connection to external devices. The Avid Sync HD features Sony 9-pin serial ports. Because the HD Accel cards include the DigiSerial port, users who *don't* have a Sync peripheral can also use that DigiSerial port for the MachineControl option; otherwise, they would use the 9-pin serial port(s) on the synchronization peripheral itself. Both positional (SMPTE) and clock references are required for MachineControl to synchronize Pro Tools with other devices. A third option for MachineControl is to use MOTU's MIDI Timepiece AV (connected to the USB port) for position and clock reference and the DigiSerial Port on the HD Accel card for serial MachineControl communication with other devices.

A pop-up Transport selector in the Pro Tools Transport window lets you specify the master device (Pro Tools, the MachineControl device, an ADAT with an optional interface, or a MIDI Machine-Control device). When Pro Tools and an external video or audio deck are linked by MachineControl, they can be scrubbed together, meaning you can review picture and audio in tandem.

When you select Pro Tools as the master, in Online mode, all devices connected via Machine-Control respond to transport and playback functions from Pro Tools (in Offline mode, they don't). Naturally, tape-based devices such as video or audio decks may require some time to rewind or fast-forward to the appropriate location (with the amount of pre-roll specified in the Peripherals dialog box) before playback actually commences. Using Pro Tools as the master with an analog tape machine, ADAT, DA-88, or some other digital multitrack causes more wear and tear on these transports (and slows you down) as they chase the Pro Tools Transport. For this reason, it is more common to designate these machines as the master; because access to audio material is nonlinear in Pro Tools, it will instantly jump to the correct playback position once the external tape transport is ready.

When you select Machine as the master, Pro Tools follows and locks to the Machine master when in Online mode. In Offline mode, the Pro Tools Transport still controls the machine, and as you move the video master to different locations, the playback cursor in Pro Tools reflects its position.

Note that in addition to many professional video decks, several audio DATs and the Tascam DA-88, DA-98, and HS-8 digital multitrack audio recorders are also compatible with the Machine-Control option. The first time you enable MachineControl, it polls the serial ports to automatically detect what device types are connected. You can also configure devices manually, from a pop-up menu.

AVoption|V10 (Discontinued)

Digidesign's AVoption|V10 is a legacy product for Windows XP systems. AVoption|V10 consisted of a single rackmountable interface which connected to the host computer via FireWire.

This video subsystem supported the playback of Avid video media (including 24p/25p resolutions) within Pro Tools and provided video output for an external PAL or NTSC monitor.

AVoption|V10 allowed users to see Avid video edits and various simultaneous clip resolutions within the enhanced Video track in Pro Tools, to use a unique Scrub Movie window, and even to spot video clips to new locations within the Avid Movie track. It also provided a record-enable button for Video tracks in Pro Tools, as well as an I/O View for selecting among the available video-input sources, outputs, and disk volumes for video recording.

Avid Mojo SDI and Mojo DX

The desktop Avid Mojo SDI video interface connects to the host computer via FireWire. It offers DV video I/O plus analog I/O for video conversion to/from DV format, and supports many of the same software features provided by the AVoption|V10 system. It allows Pro Tools systems to play back video via an external monitor, open video sequences created with Avid Media Composer systems in Pro Tools, tabbing from cut to cut and then exporting finished audio for reintegration into an original Avid sequence. Mojo supports uncompressed MXF or JFIF, DV25 and DV50, OMF, AAF, plus several 24P/25P progressive-scan resolutions. The Component Video I/O option for Avid Mojo allows you to connect component video sources to its built-in S-video and composite BNC video jacks.

Avid Mojo DX is a newer version of the Mojo offering faster processing and full 1920 × 1080 HD resolution in addition to standard-definition video. However, the Mojo DX is not currently compatible with Pro Tools.

Using Video Files in Post

As mentioned in Chapter 11, a QuickTime movie, an AVI video file, or an MPEG video file can be used as the video reference for post-production work (as well as VC-1 video on Windows 7) without requiring a video deck in your audio studio at all. If you are collaborating with video editors who use nonlinear systems, they can export a QuickTime movie for use as your master while posting the project in Pro Tools. (*Nonlinear* systems refer to computer and hard disk–based editing systems—not only high-end systems using specific manufacturers' hardware, such as Avid and Media 100, but also software-only solutions, such as Apple's Final Cut Pro and Adobe Premiere. These may require only a FireWire input from a DV camera.)

You will generally want to use video files sized down to DV25 720 × 480 pixels or smaller. This minimizes the load on your system, especially if you don't dedicate a separate hard disk for video playback and/or have a video transcoder such as the Grass Valley ADVC110 to view the video on a separate monitor. (Both are highly recommended, especially for long durations, sessions with many tracks, complex signal processing, or high-resolution audio.) Remember that even though the frame *size* of the video should be reduced, the original frame *rate* must be maintained. Likewise, if you are going to import 48-kHz stereo Audio tracks from the video original, their audio bit depth and sample rate should be maintained. Sometimes you *won't* want to import audio from the video—for example, if an Avid video editor is separately providing an OMFi file (and/or audio files) for the project, discussed later in this chapter.

The video plays in real time within the Video window, and individual frames are displayed in the Video track right alongside your audio waveforms, MIDI, and automation, as seen in Figure 14.4. As you jump around in the session (using the Transport buttons, Memory locations, the Selector tool, and so on), the Video window immediately reflects the new position; no waiting for rewinds, time-code lockup, and all the other encumbrances. In short, using a digital video file as your master provides most of the advantages of VITC, without requiring you to use a video-tape transport while you work in Pro Tools.

Figure 14.4 The Video track can display thumbnails of individual frames, allowing precise placement of audio in relation to video. Use the plus (+) and minus (−) keys on the numeric keypad to jog forward and backward through the Video track by the current Nudge value. Hold down either key to simulate shuttle mode.

Resizing the Video Window To resize the Video window, simply drag an edge or corner of the window to the desired size, regardless of the actual size (in pixels) of the source video file. You can also right-click anywhere inside the Video window to choose from a selection of preset sizes.

Tips for Recording Voice-Overs

First, whether you apply some compression in real time prior to the Pro Tools input or you apply it 100 percent afterward via Pro Tools plug-ins, a healthy amount of compression and/or limiting (dynamics processing, to limit the range of variation in the signal level) is essential to producing quality voice-over (VO) recordings. Especially if the narration is for a book on tape, a radio spot, or a live event, the amount of compression will be a lot higher than what is conventional for vocal recordings in a music project, for example. Appendix D, "Power Tips and Loopy Ideas," provides some additional tips, but here are a several technical pointers:

■ Be aware that large amounts of compression can sometimes darken a voice's timbre because many of the momentary peaks may be mid/high-frequency sibilance—"s," "t," and "ch" sounds, for example. As a general rule, try putting the EQ insert after the compressor in the VO channel first, but don't be afraid to reverse the order if the voice strikes you as sounding somewhat weak.

■ Destructive Recording mode in Pro Tools is handy for recording very long narrations—for example, a 30-minute infomercial or industrial video, and *especially* books on tape that may be many hours long. Aside from using less disk space, it can make file and Clip List management much simpler on these extremely long projects. Just be careful to check where the current insertion point is before you resume recording. It's called "destructive" for a good reason! Even if you don't use Destructive Recording mode, it's often useful to enable Timeline Insertion/Play Start Marker Follows Playback, in Preferences > Operation (which can be toggled on and off with the N key while Commands Keyboard Focus mode is enabled). Each time you stop, the next playback/recording will resume from the point you left off instead of from the same place you started previously (the default mode in Pro Tools).

■ When punching new takes into existing voice-over recordings, provide a few seconds of pre-roll for the voice talent so he or she can match the timbre of the immediately preceding audio. For example, if you're going to pick up recording at 1:30, place the playback cursor there and enable perhaps four seconds of pre-roll before pressing Record and Play. Remember these keyboard shortcuts: To start recording, hold down the Command key (Ctrl key in Windows) and press the spacebar. (Also keep in mind the handy F12 shortcut.) Press the spacebar again to stop recording or playback. To stop the recording currently in progress *and* discard the take, press Command+period (Ctrl+period in Windows).

■ If you have a third-party multiband compressor (or limiting) plug-in, experiment with it on your voice-over tracks (in addition to its more conventional use on the overall mix or submix). Aside from the obvious advantages for gain optimization, this offers a completely different approach for shaping vocal timbre as you alter the crossover points and dynamics settings for each frequency band.

■ Along with a pop filter, a professional-quality microphone is required (not a $100 rock 'n roll model) to record great-sounding voice-overs. Likewise, provide a good copy stand for your voice talent (even if it's just a music stand); some pens, pencils, and highlighters; a great-sounding room (not too dead, not too noisy); some decent lighting; a comfy but quiet chair if desired; and a glass of water!

Shuffle Lock Mode Shuffle Lock mode disables the Shuffle Edit mode. Command-click (Ctrl-click in Windows) on the Shuffle mode button to toggle this function on/off. Not only will the Shuffle button itself be disabled while locked, but all keyboard shortcuts and control-surface switches for this mode are also disabled. Because deleting, cutting, or trimming events in Shuffle mode causes the positions of ensuing events in the track to shift, it can help to disable Shuffle mode to prevent editing mishaps.

Spotting Techniques, Sound Effects

Options for spotting sound effects and other audio events to video obviously depend on your synchronization method. If you are using an imported video file or VITC as your timing reference (time code embedded into each frame of the video signal), then you can spot sound effects to precise locations, even when the video is stopped on a single frame. In contrast, if you're using LTC (time code location information conveyed within an audio signal) to receive SMPTE position data, the master video deck (or other device) must be in Play mode to send the audio signal containing this encoded SMPTE location information.

Spot Edit Mode

As explained in Chapter 6, whenever you click a clip with the Grabber tool (or Trim tool) in Spot mode, the Spot dialog box opens (see Figure 14.5). Time values entered here determine where the clip's start, end, or Sync Point will be moved when you click OK. (See Chapter 8 for a description of how Sync Points can be used to spot sound effects.) You can type the desired start time for currently selected clip(s) or click the Current Time Code field to automatically capture that value. If you're using a VITC synchronization peripheral such as Avid's Sync HD with an external video source or MachineControl, you can simply move the master to the correct frame while stopped (using the jog/shuttle wheel on the video deck, for instance). Then, click Current Time Code (or press the =, or equals, key) to automatically enter that location into the currently selected field.

Figure 14.5 The Spot dialog box is essential for post-production in Pro Tools. Clicking the Current Time Code field or pressing the = key captures the time code value if SMPTE time code is being sent to Pro Tools, entering it into any currently selected field in this dialog box.

Even if you are using LTC to synchronize to your time-code master (where an audio signal contains the encoded SMPTE timestamping information), you can still use this capture feature on the fly as the video master plays. Of course, if the video editor provides you with a window dub video copy with a numerical time-code window, you could crawl the tape to locate precise frame locations and enter time-code values manually. In either case, do your back a favor: Move your video deck close enough to the mouse and keyboard of your Pro Tools rig so that you can comfortably reach both at once. Also, note that although the Spot dialog box supports subframe precision (1/100 of a frame), time-code values can only be *captured* to the nearest whole frame.

Snap to a Start Location   Regardless of whether you are in Spot mode, you can always snap a clip to the current playback cursor position (when nothing is selected within the Edit window) or to the start time of your current Edit selection. With the playback stopped, position the cursor or make a selection; then Control-click (Start-click in Windows) on a clip with the Grabber tool. This shortcut is handy, for example, for forcing the start of one clip to coincide with the start of another selected clip.

Here's a related trick: Make a selection in the Edit window and then hold down the Control key (Start key in Windows) as you click and drag clips from the Clip List into tracks. The beginning of each clip will snap to the same Timeline position as the beginning of your current Edit selection. You can use this technique to replace a selected sound on a track or to align a new sound with it on another track.

Auto-Spotting Clips

The Auto-Spot Clips feature is especially useful when you're using an imported video file, VITC, or the MachineControl option. In these cases, the time-code information is available even when the master is stopped. To use this feature, enable Options > Auto-Spot Clips, enable Spot mode, and click on any clip with the Grabber (or drag a clip onto a track from the Clip List). The clip will automatically move so that its start point (or Sync Point, if it contains one) aligns to the current movie, time-code, or machine location.

Replacing All Occurrences of a Clip   On systems with Pro Tools HD or the Complete Production Toolkit, it is easy to swap all instances of a certain sound effect (or perhaps a drum sound, in musical applications) throughout a session. Just select the audio clip you want to replace within a track, then Shift-Command-drag (Shift-Ctrl-drag in Windows) a substitute clip out from the Clip List. The Replace Clip dialog box will appear, allowing you a choice to replace this single occurrence with the new clip, to replace all occurrences in the same track, or to replace all occurrences in *all* tracks. As you can see in Figure 14.6, other options in the Replace Clip dialog box let you restrict matches even further to occurrences of the clip that start and/or end at exactly the same positions in the Pro Tools Timeline.

For post-production, the Fit To options are of special interest. Original Clip Length is the most commonly used. As the new clip is swapped in to replace the previous one, its length is trimmed to match if it is longer, and any excess from the old clip is removed if it's shorter. Original Selection Length also trims the replacement if it is longer but doesn't remove any excess from the old clip if it's shorter. The last option, Replacement Clip Length, is the simplest: If shorter, the new clip replaces the old one without retaining any excess length from it; if longer, the replacement clip doesn't get trimmed to match the old one's length.

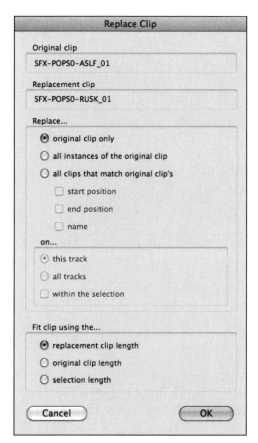

Figure 14.6 The Replace Clip dialog box (Pro Tools HD software only).

VocALign

VocALign is available as an AudioSuite plug-in from Synchro Arts. It is useful for automatic dialog replacement (ADR), among other things. VocALign Project for Pro Tools (shown in Figure 14.7) was included in certain bundles for earlier Pro Tools systems; VocALign Project can also be purchased separately for current Pro Tools systems. VocALign Pro is an advanced version that adds support for multichannel alignment (versus stereo/mono only), longer alignment length, and transfer of alignment path between different signals.

You can use VocALign to automatically align the timing of one audio signal (the *dub*) to another (the *guide*). Not only are the leading edges of each detected segment within the source audio file aligned to the guide, but time compression and/or expansion are also applied to align the waveforms. This is extremely useful for doing dialog replacement while maintaining proper lip sync as well as for quickly aligning Foley and other sound effects to original sync sound from a video shoot. Music mixers also appreciate this automated time alignment for achieving extremely tight tracking of doubled lead vocals and stacked-up backing vocal parts.

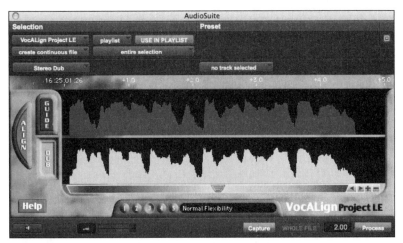

Figure 14.7 VocALign Project (in its AudioSuite plug-in window).

Surround Mixing

After a multichannel Audio track, Aux Input track, Instrument track, or Master Fader has been created, its level meters in the Mix window display multiple channels, as does the metering within any of its Plug-In windows—for example, six channels in 5.1 format. For a 5.1 mix, for example, the output path might typically be the first six outputs on your audio interface (leaving outputs 7 and 8 free for an alternate stereo mix, if you wish).

Point One   Surround format names with a .1 indicate that there is one separate LFE (low-frequency effects) channel dedicated to the subwoofer. If any surround format with two LFE channels were to become an industry standard (such as 10.2), it would consequently have a .2 suffix.

The multichannel paths that you create in the I/O Setup dialog box are essential to surround mixing. A 5.1 main path would consist of six mono subpaths: the five surround speakers and the

LFE subwoofer feed. You can also use multichannel paths for purposes other than surround mixing, however. For example, you might create a multichannel path consisting of simultaneous stereo cue mix, monitoring, and master recorder feeds to three distinct pairs of physical outputs on your audio hardware. The I/O Setup dialog box (shown in Figure 14.8) also enables you to create multichannel paths incorporating multiple stem mixes—for example, spoken dialog, effects, or music that is fed to separate outputs (subpaths).

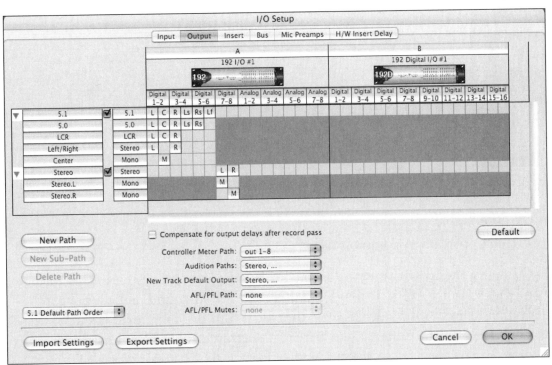

Figure 14.8 In the I/O Setup dialog box, a matrix allows you create main paths—logical groupings of inputs, outputs, inserts, or busses that consist of individual mono signal paths. The paths created in your configuration (mono, stereo, or multichannel surround) determine input and output options for Audio tracks, sends, Aux Input tracks, Instrument tracks, and Master Faders.

For multichannel tracks, an X/Y panner (as seen in Figure 14.9) facilitates positioning of sources within the surround field. Unlike with the standard Pan sliders for stereo tracks, the X/Y panner allows you to position a point within a grid. An additional Divergence parameter for the X/Y panners determines how much the sound source will spread from its designated position into adjacent speakers. Naturally, the Surround Mixer plug-in must be installed in your Plug-Ins folder for these features to be available. The Output window for each multichannel track offers choices for alternative panning methods: X/Y panning, plus knobs for front/rear percentage, center percentage, divergence, LFE feed for the subwoofer, and other surround controls. These also appear separately when you view the panning automation data on multichannel tracks in a surround format.

Figure 14.9 X/Y panners facilitate positioning of sources within the surround field.

Surround Formats Overview

There are several surround formats in common use:

- **Dolby Digital.** Currently the most common format for home-surround systems. This format was formerly known as Dolby AC-3. Dolby Digital is used for surround encoding most DVDs, high-definition television broadcasts, and theatrical film presentations. It's a 5.1 format (full-range channels for left, center, right, left/right surround, plus a dedicated LFE channel for sending low frequencies to the subwoofer from 3 to 120 Hz). Not all DVDs actually incorporate the five discrete channels (plus subwoofer channel). They may have only the Dolby Digital 2.0 soundtrack (stereo or Pro Logic compatible; this Audio track is mandatory) and can additionally have Dolby Digital 1.0 (a mono Audio track) and/or the full Dolby Digital 5.0 soundtrack, of course.

- **DTS (a.k.a. DTS Digital Surround).** A competing 5.1 format to Dolby Digital. This format is also used for theatrical film presentations and sometimes as an alternate surround-track option on consumer DVDs. DTS uses higher data rates for its audio stream than Dolby Digital (either 1.5 Mbps or 754 Kbps versus 448 Kbps or 384 Kbps in Dolby Digital); in other words, a lesser degree of "lossy" audio data compression is applied to the original audio. On consumer DVDs supporting both surround formats, the lower DTS data rates are generally used due to space considerations. Like Dolby Digital, while the majority of titles are 5.1, other channel configurations are also supported by the DTS format, including 4.1 and 4.0.

- **Dolby Surround Pro Logic.** The precursor to Dolby Digital and still the surround format used in hi-fi tracks of VHS videocassettes, LaserDiscs, and most analog television broadcasts. This is a four-channel format—left, center, right, plus a single channel for both rear surround speakers—and is backward compatible with stereo-playback systems. All four channels are matrix-encoded into a stereo Audio track (and then decoded back into their individual components during playback). Dolby Pro Logic is also known as LCRS. Dolby Pro Logic II is similar but incorporates two separate full-range audio channels for the surround speakers. In contrast, the classic Pro Logic specification uses a single band-limited channel (containing only frequencies from 100 Hz to 7 kHz) for both surround speakers.

- **THX Surround EX (a.k.a. Dolby EX).** This is an extension of Dolby Digital 5.1 and was jointly developed by Lucasfilm THX and Dolby Laboratories. In theatrical settings, the two surround speakers for Dolby Digital 5.1 are actually placed at the sides of the cinema. THX Surround EX (Dolby EX) adds two additional surround-back channels for speakers located behind the audience. For that reason, this is sometimes called a 7.1 format (because there are seven speakers plus a subwoofer). Technically, though, in the implementation of this format for home theater, the two surround-back channels are matrix-encoded into the left and right surround channels of a 5.1 setup, so these EX formats might more correctly be called extended 5.1. Thanks to the use of this matrix-encoding method, EX formats are backward compatible with Dolby Digital just as Dolby Surround Pro Logic is backward compatible with stereo systems.

- **DTS-ES Discrete 6.1.** Another extended format. Unlike THX Surround EX (see the preceding bullet), this format truly adds a discrete channel to the DTS 5.1 format for the surround-back speakers. This format is backward compatible with standard DTS decoding systems.

- **SDDS.** A 7.1 format, using seven full-range speakers plus a low-frequency effects channel: left, left-center, center, right-center, right, left surround, right surround, and LFE (subwoofer) channel.

Software and Hardware Accessories for Surround

A Surround Panner option is available for the Avid D-Control work surface that includes a touchscreen interface (which can be used for both parameter control and panning moves), dual joysticks, rotary encoders, and dedicated buttons for surround parameters. J.L. Cooper also offers a standalone surround panner peripheral that can be used with Pro Tools HD via MIDI. It is specifically designed to complement the D-Command work surface, but could be used with any HD configuration. In addition to the joystick, it includes various rotary knobs and switches for real-time parameter adjustment on surround channels.

The Dolby Surround Tools TDM plug-ins (shown in Figure 14.10) not only include a surround-panning interface and support the Pro Tools surround panner but also provide complete surround encoding and decoding matching the industry-standard SEU4/DP563 and SDU4/DP564 hardware equivalents that support sample rates up to 96 kHz. Mono/stereo and surround switching is provided, as well as a delay parameter for the surround channel. Surround Tools supports the Dolby Pro Logic Surround format (LCRS), where information for four channels (left, center, right, plus a single channel for the two rear surround speakers) is matrix-encoded into a single stereo-compatible file. While it does not support Dolby Digital 5.1 surround mixing, templates and detailed instructions are provided for performing downmixes of 5.1 sessions to LCRS for Dolby Surround encoding.

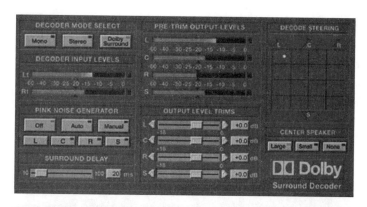

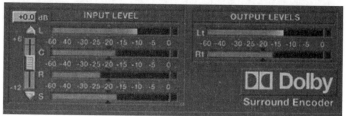

Figure 14.10 Dolby Surround Tools is an LCRS surround encoder/decoder for Pro Tools|HD systems.

If you're serious about mixing in surround, you should also consider the use of surround reverb plug-ins. After all, if the purpose of reverb effects is to simulate characteristics of an acoustic space and you're mixing in 5.1 surround, how much sense can it make to use a reverb that operates in only two channels (left/right)? Avid's ReVibe reverb plug-in is very impressive for this purpose, as is their TL Space plug-in. Waves also offers the 360° Surround Tools plug-in bundle, including a reverb, a compressor, a limiter, a panner, a low-pass filter for the LFE channel, an encoder plug-in for quad and LCR mixes, plus other tools.

Apple's Compressor 4 software for Macintosh users not only supplies tools for creating DVD-Rs that can be played in any standard video DVD player (and includes MPEG-2 encoding) but also allows multiple mono WAV, AIF, or SDII file *stems* bounced out from Pro Tools to be dropped into the appropriate channel slots for encoding into a single AC-3 (Dolby Digital) surround file.

Monitoring in Surround on a Budget

Here's a very economical alternative for surround monitoring: Many current surround receivers used for home DVD viewing and Dolby Digital surround offer component audio inputs for each 5.1 surround channel. This enables you to configure six outputs from your Pro Tools audio interface as the surround output bus and connect these to your receiver to monitor your surround mixes in realistic conditions. Be aware, though, that audio inputs on consumer gear are generally referenced to –10 dBV, so if your audio interface is pumping out +4 dBm (the more common professional standard), you will be too hot for the inputs! (Some audio interfaces support switching analog output levels to –10 dBV reference levels.)

Various manufacturers (including Mackie, Genelec, Blue Sky, Alesis, ADAM, and JBL) offer 5.1 powered monitor packages that can be connected directly to your audio interface's outputs (or patchbay). Naturally, when you are using multiple outputs from your Pro Tools audio interface for the surround mix, many more professional options are available for dedicated surround-sound monitoring.

Stereo Compatibility

Dolby Pro Logic matrix-encodes all four channels of its surround mix into a single stereo-compatible signal. You may be using the Dolby Surround plug-in (and a Pro Logic decoder or even a common surround-compatible receiver) to properly route the four channels of audio out to your speakers (LCRS: left, center, right, plus one channel to both rear surround speakers). Before committing to a mix for Dolby Pro Logic, be sure to switch into ordinary stereo mode to make sure there are no drastically inappropriate shifts in levels or imaging when playing back the mix through only left and right speakers. Phase problems are the most common issue here, and the Leq(A) meter of the PhaseScope plug-in included with Pro Tools can be a useful tool.

Similarly, playing a 5.1 mix back as stereo (commonly known as *downmixing*) can be an important compatibility check. The Waves M360° Surround Mixdown plug-in (part of their 360° Surround Tools bundle) permits the derivation of mixes in stereo, mono LCR, and other formats when placed on your multichannel surround (5.1) Master Fader output path. Similarly, the Avid DownMixer plug-in included in Pro Tools 10 can be used for this purpose.

SurroundScope for Pro Tools HD   SurroundScope is included with Pro Tools in both TDM and RTAS formats. Because this plug-in can be instantiated only on multichannel tracks, it is not available for standard Pro Tools systems without the use of the Complete Production Toolkit. SurroundScope provides monitoring and analysis tools for the multichannel surround mixing process through visualizations of level, phase, and surround positions of multiple channels in the surround field. Supported surround formats include LCR (left-center-right), quad, LCRS (left-center-right-surround; Dolby Surround/Dolby Pro Logic), 5.0, 5.1 (used on video DVDs), 6.0, 6.1, 7.0, and 7.1.

The plug-in's Surround display shows the position of the current track's signal in the surround field. Input level meters show levels for each surround channel. The Lissajous meter reflects amplitude and phase of stereo signals to help you optimize stereo imaging. The Phase meter monitors phase coherency of the left and right channels (only) in the surround mix. As with the stereo PhaseScope plug-in, various metering behaviors can be selected for displaying levels in your surround channels, such as Peak, RMS, Peak + RMS, VU, BBC, Nordic, DIN, and VENUE.

Audio Editing for Avid-Based Video Projects

Digidesign merged with Avid Technology in 1995, one of the world's most important manufacturers of nonlinear (computer- and hard disk–based) video workstations. Even before that, by participating in the development of the OMF interchange format, Digidesign positioned itself as an important audio-editing platform for video projects and for Avid in particular. Avid offers several lines of video-editing systems and software, including Avid Media Composer, Avid DS, Avid Mojo SDI, Avid Media Composer Mojo DX, Avid Media Composer Nitris DX, and Avid Symphony Nitris DX, as well as NewsCutter systems for the news industry, Deko systems for broadcast graphics, and Pinnacle Studio packages for the consumer market. New products are regularly introduced, so for up-to-date information be sure to check www.avid.com.

High-Speed Networking for Production Facilities   If you routinely transfer projects between multiple Pro Tools suites and nonlinear video-editing systems in your facility, you'll find that standard Ethernet-based local area networking is *not* fast enough. You may want to check out some of the Fibre Channel–based networking alternatives. All these require a separately purchased networking card in your computer. Some solutions even include a high-speed file server or disk array (perhaps in a centralized machine room), which facilitates sharing files with other workstations as you collaborate on projects.

File Formats

Nonlinear video editors can commonly import or export AIF and WAV audio files for their soundtracks. An audio-only QuickTime is essentially an AIF file as well, but it offers additional resources for playback by Apple's QuickTime Player. Remember that you can also bounce a mix directly into a copy of the current QuickTime movie in your Pro Tools session. In any case, a 48-kHz sample rate is standard for most current industrial and broadcast-video applications (as opposed to the 44.1-kHz sample rate used for audio CDs), and 16-bit audio files are still more common than 24-bit. Be sure to ask the video editor, however; 24-bit files are becoming increasingly prevalent.

All Avid video-editing systems understand audio files in AIF formats (AIFF-C, to be precise, even though Avid systems do *not* compress audio data within these files). In years past, Macintosh-based Avid systems supported SDII files. Windows-based Avid editing systems and all current versions of Media Composer support WAV audio files. Broadcast WAV files are becoming a digital audio standard (particularly for higher sample rates); the AES/EBU recommends this as a standard delivery and interchange format.

OMF and AAF

OMF and AAF are file-format standards developed in collaboration by various manufacturers (especially Avid) to promote a common format for interchange of data between different computer-assisted, nonlinear editing systems for video and audio. The OMF Interchange file format (OMFi, or simply OMF) allows all the original Audio tracks from an Avid Media Composer project, for example, to be translated for use in a Pro Tools session. OMF stands for Open Media Framework. The Advanced Authoring Format (AAF) standard was introduced in 2001 and is directly supported by current Pro Tools systems; it encompasses both OMF and many other source formats.

Note The terms OMF and OMFi are more or less synonymous, though OMF more properly refers to the entire enabling technology and a body of standards.

OMFi/AAF files can be imported/exported and shared between Pro Tools and other programs, including video editors and other digital audio workstations, such as Digital Performer, Logic Pro, and Cubase. You can import OMFi/AAF files from other video and audio workstations directly into Pro Tools via the same File > Open Session command used to open an existing Pro Tools session. Similarly, you can convert Pro Tools sessions to OMFi format for use with these other programs.

The File > Export submenu allows you to export tracks as AAF/OMF files. (See the Export to OMF/AAF dialog box in Figure 14.11.) Similarly, the File > Open Session command allows you to import tracks from an AAF/OMFi file to a new session. Rendered effects, clip-based gain, and volume breakpoint automation created in Media Composer can be imported to Pro Tools or disabled/ignored entirely. RTAS plug-in data from Media Composer–generated AAF sequences can also be imported into Pro Tools. Plug-in type, order, and control settings are preserved.

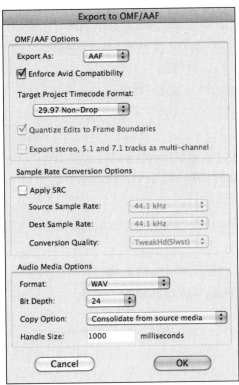

Figure 14.11 The Export to OMF/AAF dialog box for sharing Pro Tools sessions with other video or audio workstations via OMF or AAF interchange formats.

Here's the basic procedure for AAF/OMF interchange: The Avid video editor exports the current project in OMFi format. (Generally, you would not export video into the OMFi file, only audio data.) The OMFi Audio Only option incorporates duplicate copies of all audio files in the Avid project into the OMFi file; it therefore requires considerable disk space. The OMFi Compositions Only option incorporates only the audio playlist information into the OMFi file; with this option it would be necessary to provide the source audio files separately for the Pro Tools system—perhaps on a shared network drive. (The Avid video editor could first run the Consolidate Audio Files command. It's similar to Compact Audio in the Pro Tools Clip List, except it creates an entirely new folder to store compacted files, containing only audio clips actually used in the Avid project rather than their entire source audio files. The editor can then export the sequence with the OMFi Compositions Only option and give you the OMFi file plus this folder of compacted audio files created with the Consolidate command.) After that, you can import the OMFi file directly into Pro Tools using the File > Open Session command.

Media Composer Terms   Good communication with video editors can start with learning a few key words from their language:

- **Bin.** A database where master clips, subclips, effects, and sequences are organized for a project. Somewhat comparable to the Clip List in a Pro Tools project. Media Composer projects can have *multiple* bins, however, and the feature set is larger because video editors deal with more varied source media types: audio, video, animation sequences, still images, and so on.

- **Dissolve.** Strictly, a video fade to black or a mix through to another image, but video editors often use the term for audio fades to silence and crossfades between two audio segments.

- **Gang.** The approximate Media Composer equivalent of an Edit group. Edits performed on one track are mirrored in the others, such as tracks that are grouped together in the Edit window of Pro Tools.

- **Master clip.** The Avid equivalent of a whole-file audio clip. (In Pro Tools, audio clips that correspond to entire files usually appear in boldface within the Clip List but won't when a project is imported from OMF/AAF.)

- **Media data.** The actual audio or video data contained in the source files. This is the largest portion within most OMF or AAF interchange files.

- **Metadata.** Information within the source project or session file itself that can be included in the OMFi or AAF format. This includes pointers to files and information about their sample rate, bit depth, source reel, timestamp, and so on. Metadata also includes all the information about where parts of these files are placed in the Timeline and about automation.

- **Segue.** Occasionally used as a synonym for an audio crossfade.

- **Sequence.** The Avid video-project equivalent of a Pro Tools session document.

- **Stem.** In the film/video production industry, stems can be compared to the signal paths you define in the Pro Tools I/O Setup dialog box—a logical grouping of inputs, outputs, or busses treated under a single name. In a film mix, source tracks might be grouped into a smaller number of stems according to type—for example, dialog, sound effects, Foley, music, and so on. Just as you might use an Aux Input or Master Fader as the overall volume control for a group of tracks or output channels, having a large number of source tracks grouped into stems simplifies the adjustment of overall levels in complex film mixdowns.

- **Subclip.** The Avid equivalent of an audio clip within a larger source audio file. A subclip represents a smaller section within a master clip, just as many audio clips represent smaller sections within whole-file audio clips.

When you use OMFi or AAF files to move audio from Media Composer to your Pro Tools system, all the original tracks and names, fades, and various other parameters are retained. (Video editors frequently use multiple tracks—for example, slugging in music cues and sound effects under the camera soundtracks, which you might refine later. They also create fades or edits on audio to correct dialog, remove extraneous noise, match video fades to/from black, and other audio operations. You get all these when the project is imported into Pro Tools.) Of course, the editor on *any* nonlinear video-editing system could also mix Audio tracks to stereo and export an audio file for you or simply incorporate the full-resolution 48-kHz audio into a QuickTime movie provided as your editing reference (instead of a tape). In fact, if the editor hasn't added Audio tracks to the original sync sound from the video shoot, either of these methods can frequently be just as practical as exchanging OMFi or AAF files. (One drawback is that you won't have any additional audio available at clip boundaries to correct clicks or artifacts at their edit points using crossfades, and so on.)

When opening an OMF/AAF file, the Import Session Data dialog box will appear. This dialog box provides options for how metadata from the original project will be interpreted upon import into Pro Tools. For instance, you could choose to ignore rendered audio effects (to discard the results of real-time EQ, for example, that has been applied in the source video project), to ignore clip-based gain, and/or to ignore volume automation. You can also choose to copy the source media files, convert them to your session's audio format, and/or consolidate (compact) the source files during the import. The Handle Size value is applied with the consolidate option (this is similar to the Padding parameter used in Pro Tools when compacting files in the Clip List); it leaves extra time around each clip boundary so that you have the option of lengthening these for fades and so on. When deciding on the length of the handles, it is always better to err on the side of caution and account for more handle than you might end up needing.

Avid Export Templates for Pro Tools Current versions of Avid's Media Composer, Symphony, and other software include *export templates* for many programs, including Pro Tools, which appear in a pop-up list in their Export dialog box. This can save you a lot of discussion (and/or confusion) when collaborating with Avid video editors. The External options leave audio files in a separate folder, while the Embedded option incorporates the Avid composition and all the audio into a single large file, most practical for short-duration spots and when transferring OMFi files over a local network.

Gain Optimization for Video

When delivering a mix for a video project, ask the video producer for the level specs with which the audio must comply. For resolution and fidelity purposes, logic would tell you to deliver the mix as close to full-scale as possible, but rarely if ever is that allowed for professional video projects. Obviously, the best thing is to understand the project needs and then watch levels on the Master Fader for the output path used for your main mix; the PhaseScope plug-in included with current Pro Tools systems will be very useful here. Gain-optimization plug-ins, such as Maxim (included with Pro Tools) or other third-party alternatives, are extremely useful in audio for video because they enable you to transparently limit peaks within your audio program.

Normalization

Normalization changes the audio level of a sound file or a selected clip within it. Typically, this process finds the peak signal level and either automatically increases it to 100% (0 dB, or *full code*) or adjusts it to a specified number of decibels below 0 (which in some cases may cause the peak audio level to actually *decrease*). The amplitude of the rest of the audio changes proportionally. Most Avid video editing systems have the same AudioSuite normalization function as Pro Tools; you will discover that many video editors don't bother to use it, however.

Normalization is rarely used in professional video for adjusting the level of final mixes, but is frequently used for individual sound files with low levels included in the mix program. Often, an audio mixer working with an OMF or AAF file exported from a video editor will find that a portion of field-recorded files have levels so insufficient that adjusting the track volume can't compensate for the weak level. This is where normalization comes in handy. With the AudioSuite Normalization plug-in, you can select all the sound files that need the level adjustment and batch-process them all at once. You can even normalize the audio file directly in the Clip List with the AudioSuite plug-in (see Figure 14.12).

Figure 14.12 Normalization adjusts the loudest peak in a selection to a specified level, which increases or decreases the sound's volume (depending on the settings in this dialog box).

The RMS mode (as opposed to the traditional Peak mode) for the normalization process is also useful because it generally gives a better idea about *apparent* loudness of multiple sound sources. Instead of the traditional normalization approach, where a single peak determines the maximum amount a selection's gain can be increased, the RMS (Root-Mean-Square) method enables you to specify an average target level. Be conservative, however; depending on the dynamic range within the selected material, clipping can result.

The Gain plug-in (another AudioSuite plug-in) also features an RMS mode. Unlike the Normalization plug-in, it provides the useful ability to detect the current RMS (or peak) level in the current selection. This makes it much more practical to make RMS gain adjustments (more like an average level, enabling you to more accurately adjust the apparent loudness of a selection).

Compression

The general practice is to compress video mixes pretty hard. This is especially true for industrial videos, be they training videos, marketing and product videos, or video modules for live events. Single-band compression (such as the DigiRack compressor provided with Pro Tools and the Focusrite D3) is very effective on single audio sources—for example, the voice-over and/or background music in a video program. Many excellent single-band options are also available for compressing entire mixes, including Avid's Impact and Smack! plug-ins. Multiband compressors (such as Waves' C4, iZotope Ozone, PSP's Vintage Warmer, and McDSP's MC2000 plug-ins) can often be more transparent when compressing entire mixes; they simultaneously apply differing amounts of compression in three or more frequency bands. With multiband compression, the entire mix doesn't necessarily get clamped down if there is some momentary peak exclusively in the low- or high-frequency end of the spectrum. This often produces more natural-sounding results at higher compression ratios.

Don't Forget to Duck (A Side Order of Compression, Please) *Sidechaining* is a classic dynamics-processing technique in which the audio signal from one track determines the amount of gain change to apply to the signal on another track. Consider the example of applying compression to a music underscore for a video project: level changes in the music itself would normally determine the amount of gain reduction applied (per the compressor's current ratio and threshold settings). Sometimes, though, you might want the music's level to drop whenever the voice-over is present, rising back up between phrases (a technique called *ducking*).

To duck your music underscore, create a stereo send from the VO track routed to any unused Pro Tools bus pair. Option-click (Alt-click in Windows) on the Send fader to set it to 0 dB. Insert a compressor plug-in on your music track (preferably before any subsequent EQ inserts in the track) and use its Key Input pop-up (called Sidechain Input in the Focusrite D3 compressor) to select the bus pair carrying the voice-over track's signal. This becomes the key audio source for the compression process. When you enable the external key, the changes in the voice-over level control the amount of gain reduction applied to the music track. Adjust the compressor's Level and Ratio parameters for the desired amount of ducking on the music. Also, bear in mind that the Release parameter affects how quickly the music comes back up after each voice-over phrase.

Rock 'n rollers: Small amounts of compression applied on rhythm guitars and other backing instrumental parts, which are keyed (sidechained) by your lead vocal, can also be very effective. Both will seem to be in your face at the appropriate times and can give the impression that the vocal has a little more power to cut through an aggressive mix. Conversely, using the kick drum as the sidechain input for an expander plug-in on a loosely played bass track can help tighten up a groove.

The Maxim peak-limiting and gain-optimization plug-in (see Figure 14.13) is very effective when applied to entire mixes. Try placing Maxim on the Master Fader for your stereo mix. Lowering the Threshold to flatten out isolated amplitude peaks (keeping in mind that extreme settings will distort the sound) will produce greater overall levels for your bounced mix. Adjust the Ceiling slider to set a maximum output level (–0.5 dB, for example). Unlike conventional hardware limiters, Maxim can read ahead so that limiting is applied with no *latency*, or reaction time, yielding more transparent results.

Figure 14.13 The Maxim gain-optimization and peak-limiting plug-in.

The T-RackS mastering plug-in suite from IK Multimedia also includes a three-band limiter that is very effective on stereo mixes. You can adjust the input drive as well as the crossover points, threshold, and output levels for each of the three frequency bands. PSP's Vintage Warmer is a compressor plug-in that can operate in either single or multiband mode.

Several limiting plug-ins are available from Waves, including L1, L2, and L3. These are even more sophisticated tools for optimizing gain and bit-depth conversions in your Pro Tools projects. They offer single-band peak limiting and other functions, including Waves' proprietary IDR dithering algorithms for high-quality gain optimization and conversion to lower bit depths. As with Maxim, you might typically insert these plug-ins on a Master Fader, although you could also use them on a vocal track, for instance. The L3 Multimaximizer (shown in Figure 14.14) provides peak limiting in five separate frequency bands, with adjustable crossover points and a linear phase crossover to avoid phase distortion between bands. The brick-wall limiting in individual bands can be completely independent or progressively more linked up to the point where, at 100%, L3 functions like a single-band limiter. A variety of dithering options are also included, and up to 12 dB of post-limiting boost or cut in each frequency band. The Waves Suite of limiters has become a standard in national broadcast audio production.

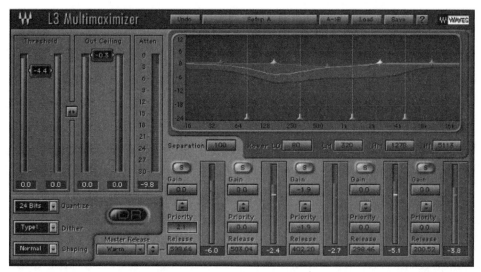

Figure 14.14 L3 Multimaximizer is a powerful gain-management and dithering TDM plug-in.

One last reminder about these gain-optimization processors: The harder you slam your mix against a limiter to obtain maximum loudness, the less dynamic range is retained in the original material. For some applications, this may be just what you want—for example, multimedia, on-hold or background music, live events such as awards banquets, or aggressive-sounding television commercials. Keep in mind, though, that this can quickly become overbearing and will fatigue listeners (especially at louder playback levels). The effect is similar to someone shouting all the time, making each and every syllable hit maximum volume—how long would you put up with *that*? As brilliant as these tools are, applying them in excess leads to the legitimate complaint that dynamics are being sacrificed for the sake of being loud. This phenomenon can certainly be heard in many current movie soundtracks and *especially* digital music releases.

Audio Editing for Linear (Tape-Based) Video Suites

In this situation, you typically play back your audio with the Pro Tools Transport in Online mode, recording from the selected outputs of your Pro Tools hardware to a master video deck.

Sometimes you will perform this layback directly to the video master tape you've been using in your audio suite. In other situations, you may use tie lines to send audio directly to the video-editing suite (slaving Pro Tools to the video master as the SMPTE synchronization source), where your audio is recorded directly to the video edit master. This is preferable especially when using professional video decks with analog-only audio inputs (for example, BetaCam), because it eliminates a tape generation.

Digital Video Decks Professional digital video decks (such as D2, D4, D1, the Digital BetaCam family, and the HDCam family) generally also have digital audio inputs and outputs. (The Audio tracks of a BetaCam SP deck are digitally *recorded*, but the audio I/O is strictly analog.) If your Pro Tools audio interface has AES/EBU digital I/O, this is definitely preferable for audio layoff and layback. Digital audio I/O on professional video gear is almost always in AES/EBU format, with XLR connectors. Manufacturers generally recommend that digital cable lengths not exceed 30 feet, although many people successfully run greater lengths. You should use 110-Ohm digital-type cable and *not* ordinary mic/line cable for all AES/EBU connections—especially for longer runs.

Audio Transfer from Tape Master

When dealing with linear (tape-based) video-editing suites, the first step in the audio post-production process is to record existing audio from the original video into Pro Tools while synchronized to SMPTE time code. Ideally, this comes directly from the video master itself, even if afterward you use a second-generation tape in your local deck as the time-code master while editing. Audio could also be transferred directly from a work tape copy; but if it's an analog copy (onto BetaCam, for instance), you're already one analog generation removed from the master's audio quality.

Here's a typical sequence for pulling the audio from a supplied video master tape into your Pro Tools session:

1. Connect the video master's stereo outputs (analog or digital, as mentioned in the note preceding this section) to one of the input pairs on your Pro Tools audio hardware.

2. Connect the video deck's time-code output (audio if you're using LTC, video if you're using VITC) to your synchronization peripheral.

3. Create a Pro Tools session (typically at a 48-kHz sample rate). Set the appropriate frame rate and session start time in the Session Setup window. Typically, the video program itself will be preceded by color bars and tones. Recording these tones is handy to confirm that consistent levels are maintained when you eventually lay your audio back up to the video master. In this case, if the video program starts at 1:00:00, your actual session start time might be 0:59:00 (if the facility follows the common practice of laying down 30 seconds of tone followed by an additional 30 seconds before program start).

4. Create one or more Audio tracks for recording from the video. Set their input selector to the appropriate input path for the incoming audio from the video deck. Next, either record-enable the track(s) or temporarily switch to Input Only Monitoring, under the Track menu.

5. Put Pro Tools in Online mode; then press Play on the video master. Confirm that Pro Tools locks to time code, starting playback at the appropriate location.

6. Meanwhile, if you're connected via an analog input, adjust input levels to the Pro Tools hardware.

7. Press Record in the Pro Tools Transport and then press Play *on the video master's Transport*. Because Pro Tools is in Online mode, it should drop into Record/Play mode automatically. Press Stop on the video Transport after the layoff is completed.

Specifications: Audio Tracks on VTRs

Digital (a.k.a. *PCM*) audio tracks on professional video-tape recorders most frequently use a 48-kHz sample rate. BetaCam SP is an extremely common video-tape format for industrial video (local television spots; training, product, marketing, and corporate videos; and video modules for playback during live events). BetaCam SP offers two PCM audio tracks (digital audio tracks, also known as *hi-fi* on these machines) plus two analog/longitudinal tracks that are not generally used for professional audio applications. As mentioned elsewhere in this chapter, D2, D5, D1, and Digital BetaCam offer multiple digital audio tracks and feature digital I/O for audio.

DVCAM (Sony), DVCPRO (Panasonic), DV (known as DVC when launched in 1995), and mini-DV also feature digital audio tracks (usually only two, at a 48-kHz sample rate and 16-bit resolution). When using an IEEE 1394 digital connection (commonly known as FireWire, the Apple name for this specification, or i.LINK, a proprietary Sony name) to transfer video from cameras or decks to your hard disk–based video-editing application, the audio is also transferred digitally as part of the DV codec QuickTime file created from the DV source.

Pull-Up and Pull-Down Sample Rates

These specialty sample rates are sometimes employed when film and NTSC video are used in the same project. For video- or audio-only projects, pull-up and pull-down are not a concern (unless you select one of these sample rates by accident).

Film is shot and projected at 24 frames per second (fps), while NTSC color video (the American broadcast standard) uses 29.97 fps. When using Pro Tools to post audio for a film, it is convenient and cost-effective to use a video copy as the image source during the editing process. Transferring each frame of a film at 24 fps to videotape at 29.97 fps presents a problem, however; the math becomes difficult. To make life easier, transfers from film to NTSC videotape use a frame rate of 30 fps (the original frame rate for black-and-white television).

To do a little math, 24 is divisible by 6, and so is 30. Thus, the ratio 4:5 is associated with this transfer because there are four frames of film for each five frames of video. To simplify the process, when the film is transferred to video (referred to as the Telecine process), the video records at the 30 fps standard so that 24 frames of the video can be evenly divided over the video frames. Telecine devices convert each four frames of film into five frames of video. (Each frame of video consists of two interlaced fields, while each film frame contains a complete image. The second and fourth film frames are repeated over three video fields, rather than two, producing one additional video frame for each four original film frames.)

To make the production tracks match the slower video played at 29.97 fps, the audio is recorded at standard sample rates, which is then *pulled down* during playback (perhaps using an Avid Sync HD, Rosendahl Nanosyncs HD, or Apogee Big Ben) while synchronizing to the video. During the transfer process back to film, the audio gets pulled back up. Therefore, the 44,100-Hz sample rate can be pulled down to 44,056 Hz, and 48,000 Hz can be pulled down to 47,952 Hz. Again, unless you're working on projects involving film transfers to video for editing, you probably won't deal with these sample rates (and will generally use 48,000 Hz for most industrial and broadcast video projects).

Synchronized Layback

After you've edited the audio for a video project, you must transfer it back to the video master—in perfect synchronization, of course. Just as Pro Tools has to stay tightly in sync during the initial layoff and throughout the edit process, it naturally must maintain the correct time relationship with the image as you record your audio back to the video master. You will therefore keep Pro Tools in Online mode while the video operator enables the master video deck for audio recording (unless you're laying the audio directly back to the videotape in your own audio suite).

Sync Issues: House Sync

As explained in Chapter 11, house sync (a.k.a. black burst) is a stable video signal that provides a common timing reference for an entire production facility. With appropriate peripheral hardware, the audio clock of a Pro Tools hardware interface can also be resolved to this external timing reference. This eliminates drift between Pro Tools and the video master, especially important for long-duration projects. It also improves Pro Tools' lock-up time to SMPTE. Devices that can accommodate house sync for Pro Tools include the Avid Sync HD, the Digital Timepiece by Mark of the Unicorn (MOTU), Lucid, Aardvark, Apogee, and others. (See Appendix B, "Add-Ons, Extensions, and Cool Stuff for Your Rig," for descriptions of some of these units.)

Analog versus Digital

As mentioned, professional digital video decks generally use AES/EBU digital I/O for audio. If your Pro Tools hardware supports it, this is a preferable way to transfer your audio back to the video master for all the obvious reasons. But digital audio inputs on professional video gear are notoriously finicky about syncing to external digital audio sources, including Pro Tools. If you experience difficulties, by all means troubleshoot the situation—but it may turn out that you're not doing anything wrong.

When a video deck is recording audio via *analog* input, you must provide reference levels for the video operator (and have the courtesy to confirm beforehand that your mix's peak levels are actually reaching maximum).

Reference Levels and Tones from Pro Tools   For years, many Pro Tools operators have kept audio files of *tones* (100 Hz, 1 kHz, and 10 kHz) handy on their system so they could drop them into a Pro Tools session as a level reference for external devices with analog inputs. The Signal Generator plug-in provided with Pro Tools makes this largely unnecessary, especially if you simply need a momentary reference for a video deck's analog input. Create a new, empty Audio track; then place the Signal Generator on it as an insert. In the Plug-In Settings window for Signal Generator, specify a frequency and waveform (sine waves are preferable for this purpose); be sure to set this plug-in's level slider to the appropriate reference level for the project (typically –20 dB). If the main volume fader for your Master Fader is also set to 0 dB, all the video operator has to do is adjust his or her input level to match the reference level, and everybody will be in agreement. On the other hand, if the video editor provides tones in the video master (brought into Pro Tools via either analog or digital input), you should also return these same tones when you lay your Audio tracks back onto the video master so that level consistency can be easily confirmed.

Summary

Post-production professionals will recognize that we've only scratched the surface here. It's a huge field, and synchronization, tape formats, mix formats, and work processes vary tremendously from one facility to another. For the most part, we hope to have provided a little perspective on the process for more audio-oriented Pro Tools users. If you want to be involved in soundtrack work, probably the most important thing is to just go out and do it. You don't have to wait for the plum assignment at a top-flight video or film house to start getting your feet wet. There are tons of independent film and video producers out there—and the advent of high-quality DV cameras with 24p resolution, plus programs such as Adobe's Premiere, Sony Creative's Vegas, and Apple's FinalCut Pro, have immensely increased their numbers. Also, interactive media developers often seek out Pro Tools collaborators for voice-over recording and post-production of video files used in their applications. (See the next chapter for more information about these opportunities.) If the developer or editor provides a small QuickTime or other video file type for you to use, you can post video projects on any reasonably capable computer. It's a credit, it's a learning process, and it just might be the start of something big.

15 Sound Design for Interactive Media

P ro Tools is an excellent platform for creating music and voice-over narrations for use in interactive applications on CD-ROMs, web pages, DVD-ROMs, kiosks, and so on. It's also quite useful for creating sound effects associated with buttons and other hyperlinks— for example, while the cursor hovers over an object or when the user clicks the button or link. You can use many different programs to create media-rich interactive content that prominently includes audio and video files at a decent resolution. The file formats and constraints for audio usage vary for each program and situation; you will need to ask the authors/programmers many questions up front before starting to design sounds for an interactive project.

The unfortunate truth is that, for educational and business-oriented interactive presentations (such as CD-ROMs and broadband web pages with Flash content on the Internet or intranets within organizations), the budget for professional-quality, original audio is often very small. Among other things, this reflects the fact that many interactive authors come from graphic-design backgrounds rather than from video or audio. They may be less cognizant than you might expect of just how much good audio enriches the texture and quality of the interactive experience. That's why so many pieces are in circulation with noisy, poorly compressed narrations, generic button sound effects that were included with the authoring program or harvested from enthusiast websites, and other unfortunate audio. Indeed, you may have to *sell* these people on the benefits of using your services for professional sound design and recording. As always, the best approach is to lead by example. Bring your examples of killer button sounds, background loops, clean and present-sounding voice-overs with small file sizes, and so on.

In contrast, sound design for the gaming industry has grown, becoming a vital part of the audio industry with its own protocols and workflows. The same can be said for music programming and composing for games, which involves specific use of MIDI and loop-oriented production that is very different from conventional music production.

At any rate, it's not enough to simply be the hottest Pro Tools jockey in town or an all-around studio professional (although this certainly will help). You need at least a rudimentary idea of what interactive authors actually *do* when incorporating sound files into their programs—the restrictions, the bottlenecks, and so on. If you're new to all this, one of the best things you can do is get together with a friend who works in Flash, Director, Visual Basic, ToolBook, Author-ware, Adobe Presenter (formerly known as Breeze Presenter), Icon Author, PowerPoint, Keynote, and so on. Have that person show you the exact steps required to place a looping sound file as a background for a page, assign button-click sounds, play a sound while the cursor is over a button, trigger graphic events or advance to the next frame based on audio playback location, and perform other operations for handling audio. Get a good look at the file import dialog boxes in that program so that you know exactly which audio file formats are supported.

As a general rule, with Flash being a notable exception, *you* will need to perform the conversions to lower sample rates or compressed audio file formats. That way, all the audio files you deliver will be ready to plug directly into the authoring environment. Figure 15.1 shows one of the third-party options for Macintosh. If you instead deliver everything at uncompressed 44.1-kHz stereo, leaving it up to the interactive folks to perform audio file format conversions according to their needs, you will almost certainly not be pleased with the results. Also, be sure to ask about the desired durations for sound effects (and be prepared to have to adjust these later in the process). As mentioned later in this chapter, it's also extremely important to be organized and consistent about file-naming conventions for the audio files you deliver. If possible, try to establish the conventions with the authors in the earliest phases of the project, as you're defining the list of required audio.

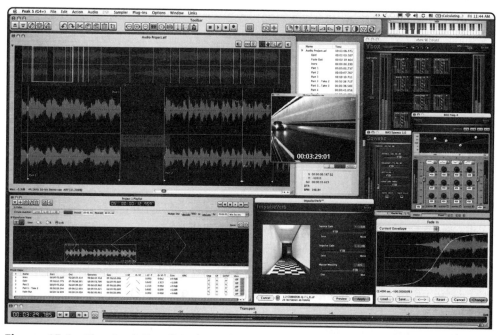

Figure 15.1 Bias Peak Pro (Mac) can be a useful companion program for Pro Tools, as can Sound Forge or WaveLab (Windows). These programs assist with supplemental file conversions and allow for the creation of cue points/markers within audio files for use by interactive programs, as well as loops.

Sound-Effects Libraries, Synths/Samplers, Sound Creation

General video-oriented sound-effects libraries on CD can provide some useful source material for interactive sound creation. Bear in mind, though, that licensing agreements and intellectual-property rights apply as much to an interactive CD/DVD or web page as to any book or video program. If the sound-effects library is not a *buy-out*, where the purchase price of the CD includes the right to use its contents as part of any other program without paying any additional royalties, you could get yourself into trouble. Read the fine print!

Obviously, when creating button sounds and so on, you only use a small portion of generally longer sound effects provided in these libraries. Unless you're creating a specific stereo effect (and the constraints of the project allow you to do so), button sounds are typically mono. The sound designer's craft makes use of all the tools that Pro Tools provides for sound manipulation: pitch shifting, time compression/expansion, and dynamic and filtering effects. For best results, use source sound effects as just one layer in a more complex sound that you build up on multiple tracks (yes, even for a single button) rather than as solutions in and of themselves.

Synthesizers and samplers (including the software-based variety) can also be quite useful for creating interactive sound effects. Aside from the obvious benefits of a more flexible sound palette, you can shape sounds with filtering and layer sounds on multiple MIDI channels in order to build a texture. Using software instruments also makes it very easy to produce groups of related sounds with consistent durations and dynamic levels. For example, this can be useful when creating a series of ascending tones for five or six similar buttons on a page. On audio clips, you can also apply one of the pitch-shifting functions available in Pro Tools (using the AudioSuite menu or Elastic Audio properties) to achieve a similar purpose.

Encourage your interactive collaborators—who wouldn't dream of using clip art in professional projects—not to use "clip sounds" either! Original sound is more creative, giving their programs a much more distinctive feel—there's an obvious analogy to cinema here. Professional results require a professional approach.

The Envelope, Please The *envelope* of a sound describes the contour of its changes in amplitude, pitch, or timbral characteristics over time. When creating interactive button sounds from existing audio files (for example, sound effects from a CD library or from other sources you've recorded), one of the common problems is that the initial *attack* of the sound may not be pronounced enough to make a satisfying impact when the user clicks the button. One solution is to add another layer (an additional sound in another Pro Tools track) with a heavier attack on the front end that quickly fades out. First, however, try switching the track view to Volume and simply *drawing* the loudness contour you'd like for this button sound: a full-volume spike at the beginning, ramping down to a more general level after a couple hundred milliseconds (see Figure 15.2). (In Pro Tools 10 and later, you can achieve the same effect using the Clip Gain Line; this is generally a better approach for modifying a sound's envelope than using volume automation and has the added benefit of providing immediate visual feedback in the waveform.) For simple button sounds, a similar effect might also be achieved by using a compressor plug-in set to a high ratio but with a very long (>100 millisecond) attack.

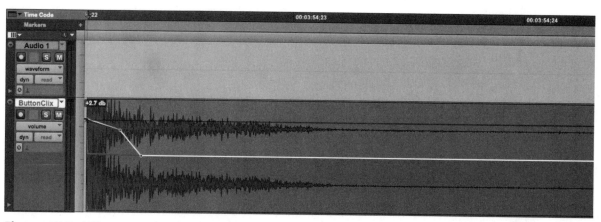

Figure 15.2 When creating button sounds for interactive media, you can use automation or clip gain to create the desired volume envelope. Here, we're increasing the level of the sound's initial attack.

Common Multimedia File Formats

Common audio file formats are discussed in Chapter 1. Here's some additional information, specific to providing audio for interactive developers:

- **WAV and AIF.** WAV was originally developed jointly by Microsoft and IBM, while AIF (sometimes known as *AIFF*) was originally developed by Apple Computer. This probably explains the relative abundance of these audio file formats on each platform. Their characteristics are fairly similar. Both WAV and AIF files are supported audio-recording formats for Pro Tools sessions (earlier Mac versions also supported SDII, discussed in a moment), but WAV format is *required* for recording at sample rates higher than 48 kHz on *any* Pro Tools system. (Technically, Pro Tools uses Broadcast WAV format for recording; however, this format is backward compatible with WAV and uses the same extension.) Bouncing or exporting audio from Pro Tools to WAV format is standard for many Windows audio programs (some of which do not accept AIF or especially the obsolete SDII file format), and AIF files are supported by almost every audio-capable Mac program. However, current versions of most interactive applications on both platforms can accept *either* WAV or AIF.

- **Sound Designer II.** Also known as SDII or SD2, this format was originally developed by Digidesign for its Sound Tools stereo audio workstations. It was also the native file format for early Mac versions of Pro Tools, but it is no longer directly supported in current versions of Pro Tools. SDII files are limited to 48 kHz or less, and SDII isn't supported by any current interactive program. Even on older Mac versions of Pro Tools, it should *not* be used as the audio file format for sessions unless compatibility with much older versions (such as Pro Tools Free 5.01 for Macintosh OS 9) is a specific concern.

- **MP3.** MP3, short for MPEG Audio Layer-3, is part of the MPEG compressed audio/video data standards. It uses a perceptual encoding technique to reduce the size of audio data. When you encode an MP3 file (MP3 encoding is included with all current Pro Tools versions), you choose *a bit rate* for the resulting file. The smaller the bit rate, measured in Kbps (kilobits per second, also abbreviated Kbit/s), the more digital *artifacts* may be noticeable in the result. You can also embed title, author, and copyright information into MP3 files. This format became popular for exchanging music over the Internet because of the small file sizes it can produce (at the expense of a compromise to the audio quality). It is also very attractive for interactive developers because it produces better-sounding audio in smaller files compared to limiting files to a 22,050-Hz sampling rate (a common strategy a decade ago). Be aware, though, that MP3 is not universally supported, especially in older versions of interactive authoring software. For example, some game-authoring programs still don't support MP3 at all. Apple's Keynote presentation software supports MP3 (and AAC) files, as do current versions of Microsoft's PowerPoint. Current versions of the Director and Authorware programs support MP3 files, as does the Adobe Presenter and Adobe Connect Training software for online course development. Flash (by Adobe, originally developed by Macromedia) also frequently uses MP3 files given its common use in low-bandwidth Internet environments. Longer MP3 files can even be streamed as part of a Flash piece. Note that for looping sounds, such as musical phrases and button roll-over sound effects, MP3 conversion may introduce a very small amount of silence at the beginning and end of the waveform. This will cause a loop to hiccup in Flash. In these cases, you may be obliged to deliver WAV or AIF instead, and allow audio compression to be applied when the final Flash project is saved out (which usually will not cause these audio looping problems). As with all audio for computer playback, you will generally apply generous amounts of audio gain compression and maximize the level of your original audio in Pro Tools. Be aware that even at low levels, low-frequency noise—especially pops and breath noises—can cause problems for encoding algorithms that compress audio data (and incidentally, this is *especially* problematic for time-expansion and pitch-shifting processes). Be sure to monitor your material with good speakers and listen to it at a reasonably loud volume. If necessary, try dropping a high-pass filter (using one of the DigiRack EQ plug-ins included with Pro Tools, for example) on the offending track. Prior to delivery, however, be sure to actually *listen* to your MP3 files on inexpensive computer speakers! Unexpected differences in the apparent dynamic range or the prominence of various background and instrumental elements in your mix can often require bouncing out a new file.

- **AAC.** Short for *Advanced Audio Coding*, AAC, like MP3, was developed by the MPEG Group. It is used by Apple in its iTunes Music Store. Version 7 of Apple's QuickTime Pro can also save AAC audio files. AAC is actually part of the MPEG-4 audio spec and uses signal-processing technology from Dolby Laboratories to apply more complex compression algorithms to audio data. These not only reduce the data size more efficiently than MP3 but also produce better-sounding results at any comparable data rate—*especially* for music. To put it another way, AAC encoding can obtain the same quality as an MP3 file that would be 30–35 percent bigger.

- **WMA.** Short for *Windows Media Audio* and introduced by Microsoft in 1999, this compressed audio format is common on the Windows platform and can be played on Mac systems with appropriate add-in software, such as the Flip4Mac component for QuickTime. It is also the default destination format when ripping files from CD in Windows Media Player (although this preference can be changed to MP3). The WMA specification also includes alternate codecs: WMA Pro (supports higher resolutions and multichannel audio), WMA Lossless, and WMA Voice (optimizes voice content at lower bit rates).

- **RealAudio.** This streaming, compressed audio file format, often used on the Internet, was developed by Real Networks. The RealPlayer free download also supports streaming video files—and is notorious for invasively altering playback defaults for various media file types to make itself the default player. It is also very difficult to completely remove from a Windows system. You can reduce audio to various throughputs according to the requirements, with audible compression artifacts resulting from more extreme compression levels. Real Networks' SureStream technology incorporates several different versions of the audio into a single file link. The appropriate density is selected for playback according to the available bandwidth when a user starts playing the file over the Internet. Not all interactive authoring programs support RealAudio, and some require the purchase and/or licensing of a separate plug-in. RealAudio is mostly effective for spoken-word projects because the level of audio artifacts is rather high at typical Internet bandwidths.

- **AU.** Also known as mu-law or Sun/NeXT, this is the audio file equivalent of an audio data-compression standard developed for telephony. 16-bit source audio is reduced to 13 bits (thereby discarding the three least significant bits and increasing quantization error) and then encoded into an 8-bit format. AU is an older standard (prior to MP3, for example) and is frequently used with an 8-kHz (8,000-Hz) sample rate. As you might imagine, from an audio engineer's perspective, this represents a pretty drastic reduction in sound quality compared to current alternatives for audio data compression. However, AU sound files are still occasionally requested by Internet developers when the methodology or programs specifically require this format. A separate program is required to convert bounced mixes from Pro Tools to AU format.

- **QuickTime.** This is principally a video format, although audio-only QuickTime files can be created. On Windows computers, QuickTime file names must end in the .mov extension to be automatically recognized by QuickTime Player. One reason for using audio-only QuickTime files, for example, would be for using the movieTime property in the Director program. This allows other events to be triggered at certain positions while the QuickTime file plays. Playback can be initiated from specific positions within the QuickTime file—for example, when the user clicks a button to hear a specific section.

Great-Sounding Compressed Audio within QuickTime Movies   If you have any influence on how the Audio tracks you contribute for QuickTime movies will be processed later, encourage the interactive authors to consider choosing the MPEG-4 codec for the soundtrack. (Figure 15.3 shows some of the export options from Apple's QuickTime Pro, a $30 upgrade to the free downloadable player for Windows or Mac.) Other traditional and extreme methods (stereo to mono, reducing sample rate, and other compression codecs) exist for drastically reducing the data rate and overall file size for Audio tracks in QuickTime movies. However, you'll likely find that among the current alternatives, MPEG-4 does the least damage to your audio.

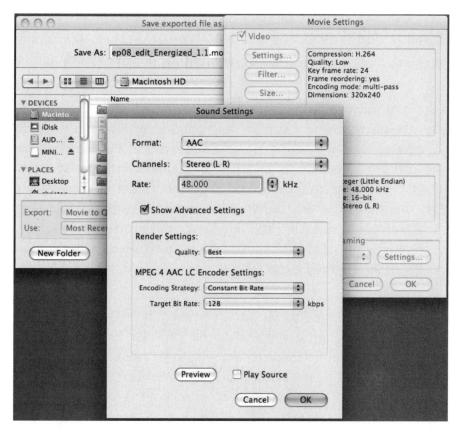

Figure 15.3 Options when using QuickTime's File > Export command and selecting Movie to QuickTime Movie include compressing the soundtrack using MPEG-4 (AAC).

How Audio Is Used in Interactive Media

Terminology varies greatly from one interactive authoring program to another, but some conventions are common for typical uses of audio. Things that can be clicked on (whether buttons or simply linked text or graphics) should make noise when they're clicked to provide user feedback. Often, screens within a presentation or game will play longer audio pieces or loop a smaller audio segment to conserve disk space and reduce competition for disk access between the graphics and audio. Graphic events are frequently scripted to specific locations within a narration (that is, an audio file you've provided). Loading of graphics, animations, and other data competes with the audio files being played for disk access (hard disk, CD, or DVD) and for the computer's resources in general. So you need to be adept at getting good-sounding results at low file sizes. It's pointless to create luxurious, high-bandwidth audio if in actual use it takes too long to start playing or skips during playback.

Voice-Overs

Voice-overs are narrations or phrases other than those spoken by an onscreen character. This is one of the most frequently requested services for interactive media projects. The general technique is similar to voice-over recording for worst-case video scenarios; you should use compression and other dynamics processing to ensure solid, consistent audio levels that overcome all the intrinsic obstacles to intelligibility during computer playback (cheap speakers—including extremely tiny speakers on laptops and LCD displays—noisy computers, low playback levels, and so on).

Remember: Good audio does make a difference in any interactive project. Voices should be recorded in a relatively noise-free environment, using a quality microphone with a pop filter. In typical interactive development scenarios, the two worst noise offenders are computers with their hard disks and fans, and air-conditioning/heating systems in the building. Noisy voice recordings—even for projects that will never be played on anything but computer speakers—will come back to haunt you later. For this reason, even though it's critical to reality-check your audio files on cheap computer speakers before releasing to the client, make *sure* you monitor your audio work on good-quality speakers and headphones. Some end users have better audio-monitoring systems on their computers than you may expect.

Audio for PowerPoint　Audio file formats supported by Microsoft's PowerPoint presentation software include WAV, AIF, and MP3. Although a single audio file can play through a sequence of slides or an entire presentation, for voice-overs that sync to graphic events on each slide (for example, revealing bullet-text points as they are mentioned in the voice-over), it's more common to provide your PowerPoint collaborator with a series of sequentially numbered audio files—for example, Slide01, Slide 02, and so on. Apply plenty of compression/limiting to these voice-over files and make sure they are very close to maximum levels; the audio playback conditions for this kind of presentation are usually far from ideal.

Buttons/Links

Two basic functions commonly trigger sounds with buttons or links. First, when the user rolls the mouse cursor over the "hot" area, a sound file can be triggered (either a single pass or a looping sound created for this purpose). These are called *rollOvers* in the Director and Flash programs, *mouseovers* in JavaScript, or *focus states* in some other programs. The idea is to attract the user's attention to the fact that something will happen once the screen object is clicked. Often, roll-overs also incorporate a graphic effect—for example, a glow around the button, a color change, or an animation effect. When you create a looping sound in Pro Tools, be sure to check it afterward in another program that can seamlessly loop audio selections. (The QuickTime Player does *not* loop audio seamlessly.) In some situations (especially when creating MP3 files), excess data may appear at the beginning of a bounced audio file—just enough to interrupt the seamless loop you were hearing in Pro Tools.

The second sound trigger occurs when the user clicks the button, providing positive auditory feedback. This could be a click sound, a whoosh, or whatever cool audio effect you come up with. This is called a *mouseDown* event in Director and Flash and an *onClick* event in Java-Script. The mouse click might also trigger some graphic effect along with your sound effect. In practice, however, it is more customary for actions, sounds, and graphic effects on a button to occur on mouseUp—that is, when the user *releases* the mouse button. This allows users to roll back off the button before releasing the mouse if they really didn't intend to click there.

Generally, audio levels for background and button sounds (both mouse-click and roll-over sounds) should be lower than first-order content, such as voice-over narrations, the contents of video files, and so on. Start by setting their peaks to about –10 to –12 dB (a little over 30 percent of full code—remember that decibels are logarithmic, not linear). Whatever the level you set for background and button sounds, be consistent unless there's a specific reason for making an exception. (Sometimes a particular sound still *sounds* louder even after it has been normalized down to the same peak level as all the others. Apply compression via the Dynamics3 plug-in within Pro Tools, or more sophisticated gain optimization using Maxim or Waves' L1, L2, and L3, to even out levels by eliminating transients in the pre-normalization level.)

It's difficult for developers to deal with dozens of button sounds with no consistent levels. In short, when creating sound effects for interactive projects, you can't just normalize everything to full code (100 percent maximum volume) and figure you've done your job.

Creating Cue Points   In interactive applications, one very common technique is to create cue points (also known as *markers*) within audio files. A simple handler script (on exitFrame in Director, for example) tells the interactive program to wait until a specific cue point is reached in the audio file before advancing to the next frame in the sequence. By using cue points or simple time references, graphic events can be triggered when specific locations within the audio are reached during playback. This makes it possible to do things such as bring up titles, bullet points, or graphics as certain words are spoken in the voice-over.

Cue points must be created in separate programs—such as Bias Peak Pro, Steinberg WaveLab, or Sony Sound Forge—usually by the authors themselves, although you may occasionally be asked to assist in this process. Contrary to what you might imagine, the marker Memory locations you create in Pro Tools are *not* reflected as cue points within bounced audio files.

Music/Effects Backgrounds

When you create music or ambience backgrounds for scenes in an interactive CD-ROM, DVD-ROM, or website, be aware of what *else* will be going on while your audio is playing. If a great deal of animation and graphics interaction is occurring simultaneously, this can severely affect the throughput available for playing your audio. In this situation, if you don't reduce the size of your audio background file (for example, by reducing from stereo to mono, by reducing sample rate, or ideally by using data compression), it may skip on playback—especially on slower computers, on slower CD drives, or when insufficient RAM is available (which affects the program's ability to preload graphics and other content for timely playback).

Interactive applications often loop playback of audio effects or music as a background for scenes. There are pros and cons to this technique. For one thing, it is an art to create musical loops that are both interesting enough and adequately nondescript so as not to become annoying after a couple of repetitions. There are also technical considerations. Obviously, one of the main reasons for using audio loops is to save disk space (or download time). Instead of a full four to five minutes of audio for the time a user may spend in each screen, 20 seconds worth of well-looped audio might be equally effective. However, in the Director program, looped audio files must be entirely loaded to RAM. (Normally, longer audio files stream directly from disk.) Depending on the RAM and CPU requirements your interactive authors can demand of their potential audience, looped audio can sometimes impose more strict limitations on duration, number of channels, and resolution than would apply for simply playing back a longer file directly from disk.

Some programs, such as the current versions of 3D GameStudio and Flash, can only loop the entire audio file. In contrast, Director will recognize any loop definitions found *within* an AIF file. You must create the loop definition with some program other than Pro Tools, such as Peak, Sound Forge, or WaveLab. As a music and sound designer for Director projects, you can include a header or intro that precedes the looping portion of the file. This is useful not only for music (an eight-bar intro that eventually settles down to a four-bar loop, for example) but also for looping roll-over sounds on buttons and other objects.

In Flash, interactive authors can specify how many times an audio file should loop. They can also create fade-in and fade-out envelopes for that sequence of loop repetitions. If the Flash piece will be playing from a website, however, bear in mind that audio-file sizes are usually reduced drastically to avoid inconveniently long download times. Another pitfall to be aware of is that Flash developers often create loops over a certain range of frames in the Timeline itself and then simply stretch your loop audio across that duration. In these cases, find out what frame rate they're using! If it's 15 frames per second, make sure your loop's duration corresponds exactly to a 1/15 of a second subdivision—even if this means applying time compression/expansion afterward in Pro Tools or some other program. Otherwise, there will be a distinct hiccup each time this looping portion of the Flash Timeline repeats.

Squash Your Loops   It can take a while to get the knack of creating smoothly looping musical/ambient backgrounds for interactive applications. When the loop needs to repeat seamlessly (for example, a humming, glowing sound or a funky groove), here's a trick that can sometimes be useful: Apply relatively extreme amounts of compression (basically, limiting) on the looping selection. This increases the possibility that the end of the loop and the beginning will have similar levels, which is at least one step toward a smoother loop.

In Pro Tools, you can use the Options > Loop Playback option as you perfect selections that will be bounced out as looping audio for interactive applications. If the sound sources for a loop include MIDI instruments (either external devices or software synths), it is often preferable to record these to an Audio track before defining your looped selection and bouncing it out. Otherwise, the instrument's delay or reverb effects from the end of the looping selection may sustain across the beginning, giving a false impression of how smooth the loop really is. Don't forget to save your bounced selection as a Selection Memory location before closing the Pro Tools session in case you have to bounce it out again! Chapter 6 contains some specific hints and shortcuts for fine-tuning your selection by nudging.

Don't Assume!   Audio selections that loop smoothly at 44.1 kHz within Pro Tools may not do so after they've been converted to 22 kHz (more precisely, 22,050 Hz) or especially when converted to a compressed data format, such as MP3. Also, if subsequent normalization on the bounced loop files increases their gain, some clicks at the loop point may become audible. (Beginning and ending your loops at zero crossings can help avoid this.) Be sure to check your loop files (for example, in Peak, WaveLab, or Sound Forge) before turning them over to your interactive clients and collaborators! By the way, looped playback in Apple's QuickTime Player and Windows Media Player always *pauses* slightly between repetitions of the audio file, so they are not useful for verifying loops. Be aware, too, that even non-looping audio files that don't begin or end at zero amplitude crossings can produce an audible click when triggered if a large gain increase is applied by normalization. Be sure to check your normalized files!

For the Sake of Good Order...   Think through the naming conventions you will use *before* starting to bounce out files for interactive projects! For the most part, multimedia authors will import your files via a standard File Open dialog box (see Figure 15.4). If the audio files you provide naturally appear in the proper order, you will greatly reduce the potential for confusion. For example, when you have more than 10 similarly numbered files, use leading zeroes so that file10.AIF doesn't appear between file1.AIF and file2.AIF!

When providing both roll-over and mouse-click sounds for the same button, make the first part of their file names similar so they are automatically sorted together in the file list: QuitRoll.AIF, QuitClik.AIF, and so on.

Figure 15.4   The Flash program can import various audio file formats. Audio waveforms can be viewed within its Timeline in relation to graphics and animation events.

Sharing Well with Others: About Bandwidth

At higher bit depths and sample rates, file sizes are much larger. This is an important consideration for interactive media. High-resolution audio files obviously occupy more disk space or cause longer download times from the Internet. Most importantly, as an interactive application runs, audio playback shares the computer's (and disk's) throughput capacity with the other graphic files and animation. You may get killer sound quality by maintaining your audio files at higher resolutions, but if they're going to skip during playback because animation and graphic files are loading from the same disk, it defeats the purpose, right? So you need to be aware of how and when your audio files are going to be used (and especially what else is happening while they're played) and what the target system requirements are for the application. For example, if the authors still have to support 12x CD-ROM playback on older (slower) computers with limited RAM, this imposes much more drastic limitations on audio file sizes than if they require 18x SuperDrives, a 2-GHz processor, 2 GB of RAM, or a more powerful current computer configuration.

If your source material isn't stereo, you shouldn't create stereo files for the interactive application. Believe it or not, people do this all the time—for example, using stereo files for simple voice-overs! Even if your source *is* stereo—for example, music—when you find yourself obliged to make drastic reductions in audio file sizes, consider whether it's a greater loss to lose the stereo image or to lose high frequencies by reducing sample rate (for example, losing frequencies above ~10 kHz at a sample rate of 22,050 Hz). Either option reduces the file to half of its former size. Listen to each; trust your ears! Again, if the interactive application supports compressed audio file formats such as MP3, this is usually the preferable method for reducing file size and throughput requirements.

Sample Rate

Audio file size is directly proportional to sample rate (doubling the number of samples per second also doubles the file size) and to the number of channels (stereo files are twice the size of mono). As discussed in Chapter 1, under the "Digital Audio Basics" heading, higher sample rates allow the recording/playback of higher audio frequencies. For interactive applications, the two most commonly used sample rates for linear (uncompressed) audio are 22,050 samples per second and 44,100 samples per second (often shortened to 22K or 44.1K in digital audio parlance), although 11,025 (11K) is sometimes used when bandwidth available for audio is extremely limited—for instance, when an application needs to run smoothly on much older computers or on the Internet.

Converting audio down to 22K/16-bit can actually sound okay on typical computer speakers, especially for voice-overs and button sounds (some of which can even be knocked down to 11K if high-frequency components aren't crucial). Remember that, unlike reducing bit depth (which is discussed in the following section), reducing the sample rate to 22,050 Hz does not make your audio files any noisier; it simply eliminates high-frequency information (above about 10 kHz). One of the tricks employed by standalone file-conversion applications such as Autodesk's Cleaner (Mac) or Cleaner XL (Windows) is to augment the apparent brightness of lower sample rate files by adding a slight equalization peak just below the cutoff frequency. Even if you don't have these tools at your disposal, you can approach the same effect. For example, place an EQ plug-in on the Master Fader/output pair that is the source for your bounce. Then use the high-shelf filter to add several decibels of boost from about 9 kHz upward.

Bit Depth

Bit depth describes the size of the digital word representing each audio sample. The number of bits (binary digits) used to capture the input audio signal's voltage for each sample period determines how many discrete amplitude levels can potentially be represented. Like the vertical spacing on graph paper, the fewer increments that are available (the fewer bits per sample), the less accurate the representation, compared to the continuous variations in the original waveform. Early computer multimedia and computer games often used 8-bit audio files (256 possible amplitude levels); the noticeable *quantization error* in 8-bit files gives them their characteristic fizzy sound quality. Incidentally, if the project really does require you to bounce 8-bit files from Pro Tools, be sure to enable the Use Squeezer check box in the Bounce dialog box. This slightly increases the quality of the resultant 8-bit audio, especially for voice-overs, by applying some proprietary gain processing prior to the conversion.

16-bit audio files are currently the norm for CD-ROM interactive applications. This is the same bit depth used on standard audio CDs (which are stereo, of course, and use a 44.1-kHz sample rate). 24-bit audio (often with higher sample rates) is the current norm for the most demanding professional audio recordings but is rarely used in interactive applications.

Managing Audio Levels

Generally, you want to ensure that the dynamic range in audio files intended for computer playback consistently remains near the specified maximum level. For example, you will almost always use a compressor plug-in (and/or limiting) on voice-over narrations to smooth out any variations in volume. As an added benefit, this generally makes voice-overs more intelligible (punching through the general noise of a computer's fan and disk drives, for instance). That way, if you normalize an audio file you've bounced from Pro Tools, the peak level used by the normalization process as the benchmark for adjusting its gain will be closer to the overall levels in the rest of the file (see Figure 15.5). Another more sophisticated technique is to use gain optimization plug-ins, which apply other techniques to produce good-sounding audio at very consistent, in-your-face levels (that is, with very little variation in their dynamic range).

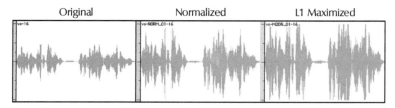

Figure 15.5 The effects of gain optimization: The first waveform was compressed during recording, prior to the Pro Tools input. The second was normalized to 100 percent. (Its peak level corresponds to full code.) The third was processed with L1, by Waves. Note that its amplitude is more consistently near the maximum level.

As mentioned in the "Buttons/Links" section earlier in this chapter, normalization is a key tool for preparing audio for use in multimedia. Even though any experienced Pro Tools operator keeps a careful eye on Master Fader levels in all original Pro Tools sessions (always the primary method for managing levels), in the interactive-development scenario you frequently have to maintain extremely consistent levels throughout dozens or even hundreds of similar audio files because the end user may switch rapidly between them while navigating from section to section. Despite the common misconception that normalizing always increases peak audio levels to 100 percent (and to be sure, in some very rudimentary audio programs, this *is* the only option), Pro Tools and most professional batch-conversion programs support normalization to any level. For example, if the main voice-over files are at nearly 100 percent, your entire collection of backing music loops and button effects might be normalized to peak levels of –6 dB or –10 dB (50.1 or 31.6 percent of full code, respectively). That way, the various categories of audio files you deliver come into the authoring program pre-mixed instead of depending on the interactive author's skill level with handling audio levels—or occasionally confronting severe practical limitations for such adjustments in the authoring program itself.

For music and ambient backgrounds especially, the RMS mode of the Gain plug-in (under the AudioSuite menu) will be very useful. Adjusting the RMS gain of diverse sounds to an identical level can be a more reliable way to make them *seem* to be of similar loudness. In contrast, when using the ordinary Peak mode of Normalization (or Gain) processing, isolated transients and other variations in the dynamic range of the source audio can still leave you with files that appear to be of unequal loudness, even if their peaks are all carefully adjusted to, say, –10 dB.

Audio Data Compression

Data compression reduces the size of the data representing the original audio waveforms. It is always a lossy process—some of the original information is lost. Among the various methods for reducing the size of audio data, some are more effective with certain types of sounds than others (for example, for spoken word versus a music file). Of course, it's important not to confuse data compression with audio *gain* compression (which reduces the dynamic range, or volume variations, within an audio signal).

MP3 encoding (discussed earlier in this chapter) is a compression method for audio data that takes advantage of the characteristics of human hearing. We tend to hear mainly the loudest sound in each of a series of critical bands of frequency, so other sounds within the same band are converted to lower bit depths with little noticeable deterioration of sound quality. MP3 encoding also compresses redundant data that is present in both channels. (This is, of course, a gross oversimplification of the MP3-encoding method, designed to give you a general idea.) MP3 really does provide spectacular reductions of file size before obvious digital artifacts appear. If an interactive application supports MP3 files for longer audio files (and doesn't require cue points to trigger events), this is a *much* more attractive option than reducing sample rate (let alone reducing bit depth), preserving as much as possible of your original sound quality at a smaller file size. MP3 audio is especially prevalent in Flash-based Internet applications. SWA, the Shockwave audio format associated with Director, also generally uses MP3 compression. By all means, offer to do the MP3 audio encoding yourself rather than leaving it in the hands (and ears) of the interactive designers. They will, however, need to provide you with guidelines for the target bit rate (audio data density, measured in kilobits per second, or Kbps) according to their design requirements. Otherwise, it's all too likely that they will use some general compression preset from their host program (see Figure 15.6 for an example) that can drastically compress audio in favor of retaining graphic quality.

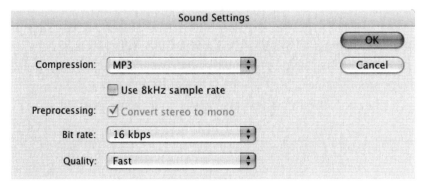

Figure 15.6 The default settings for audio quality (unless changed by the user) when publishing a Flash presentation from Adobe Flash CS3 Professional.

Make Some Noise about Audio Quality!   As shown in Figure 15.6, the default settings for handling audio in Flash are drastic, to say the least. Most Flash developers will request that you submit uncompressed WAV (or AIF) files. So far so good. But when they publish the completed presentation to create a Flash SWF file that can be run within a browser, the default sound settings will severely degrade the quality of your audio if you don't intervene. Ask them to open the Flash tab of the Publish Settings dialog box and change the Audio Stream and Audio Event properties to a 128 Kbps bit rate and, if necessary, to disable the Convert Stereo to Mono checkbox.

AAC and MPEG-4 audio (in some ways, two aspects of the same thing) are newer, more efficient methods of compressing audio data. By all means, *if* the target application supports this codec for audio (many, including Flash and Director, do not), it is one of your best choices. For example, for a comparable quality level, MPEG-4 audio files can be as much as 30 percent smaller than MP3 (which is already far smaller than uncompressed, or linear, audio). QuickTime video files now also support MPEG-4 encoding in their audio tracks (not to be confused with MPEG-4 encoding in their video track, a different matter). In fact, if you own QuickTime 7 Pro, you can convert the audio tracks within QT movies you've bounced from Pro Tools (see the next section) into MPEG-4 and/or AAC. The sonic results are impressive, considering the huge reduction in file size.

You Need Some Low-Grade PC Speakers!   If you create music and sound effects for the average computer, a cheap set of computer speakers is a *necessity*. Your tiny near-field studio monitors are *too* good, as are the speakers on an Apple iMac, for that matter. Always reality-check everything on the mediocre sort of mini-speakers included with the average PC (price limit $20, if you're buying them separately). Those way-low bass and percussion sounds you spent so much time on might disappear entirely (or come back in some exaggerated and unpleasant form when played on PC speaker setups with a subwoofer). The general prominence of parts within musical arrangements can change radically—occasionally an issue when files are heavily compressed to MP3 and similar formats. Even more importantly, the apparent levels of voice-overs and dialog versus background music or sound effects can change drastically on these setups compared to even modest studio monitors. It is not amusing when a bumpin' rave bass line becomes completely inaudible or when an apparently innocuous timbre, after suffering from data compression and playback through cheap computer speakers, turns into some sort of flatulent buzz.

Creating Audio for Digital Video Files

Sometimes, animations created in other programs will be converted to QuickTime, MPEG, or AVI files to facilitate playback within an interactive application. You can add audio from Pro Tools into new copies of existing video files via the File > Bounce to > QuickTime Movie command. Here's how:

1. Select File > Import > Video. In the File Open dialog box that appears, locate and double-click the digital video file. If the video file includes audio that you want to bring into your Pro Tools session, be sure to enable the Import Audio from File checkbox in the Video Import Options dialog box. The video image will appear in the Video window of Pro Tools, and a Video track will be created that shows thumbnails of the individual frames in the QuickTime movie.

2. Using the Video window (which plays the file in real time within Pro Tools) and the Video track as a guide, create your soundtrack. If you find that redrawing of the video thumbnails within the Video track slows down the editing operation, switch it to Blocks view.

3. When you are ready to bounce your audio mix back into the QuickTime movie, select File > Bounce to > QuickTime Movie. This will not affect the video from the source video file; it's simply cloned into the new copy.

4. In the Bounce dialog box (shown in Figure 15.7), choose mono or stereo for the bounced audio, keeping in mind that stereo requires twice as much throughput for playback in the target program. Consult your interactive authors about data-rate guidelines for the QuickTime file. The Squeezer option appears in this dialog box if you're forced to convert down to 8-bit audio within the QuickTime file. (You should be prepared to compress

audio data, sacrifice stereo, and/or reduce sample rate before ever resorting to 8-bit audio.) If your source Pro Tools session is 48 kHz or higher, you may also want to convert the audio to a 44.1-kHz sample rate for playback within interactive applications. If required, you can perform data compression on the soundtrack of the resultant video file afterward, using QuickTime Pro (via its File > Export command), Peak Pro, WaveLab, Sound Forge, or another audio-editing program that supports QuickTime video files. As a matter of fact, QuickTime Pro supports a good selection of audio-compression codecs (including MPEG-4/AAC) that can produce smaller video files that are still excellent sounding and compatible with most interactive authoring environments.

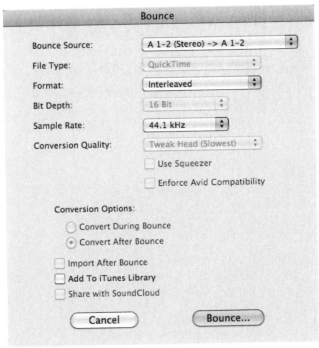

Figure 15.7   The dialog box for bouncing to a QuickTime movie. This is similar to bouncing audio files to disk, but incorporates the audio output from Pro Tools as the soundtrack within a QuickTime copy of the video file currently being used in the session.

Summary

How the audio you provide is used within an interactive piece varies widely between programs, as well as from one author to the next. It's crucial to plan things out with the developers before starting to create sounds and bounce files. Among other things, you must know what file formats and resolutions the developers require, the bandwidth limitations on the target computer platform (this determines your options for sample rate or audio data compression, for example), what file-naming conventions they prefer, whether voice-overs and music underscores can be long durations or must be broken up scene by scene, whether the host program can loop audio smoothly, and whether Standard MIDI Files (SMFs) are among the preferred media types.

Pay special attention to maintaining consistent levels among all the voice-overs, button and background sound effects, videos, and music that you create for an interactive project. It is not especially convenient for interactive authors to make individual volume adjustments as they play back your sound files; in fact, it's usually a pain in the neck. So it's up to you to ensure that all the sounds you create in a given category have consistent levels (normalization is an invaluable tool for this), usually with distinct levels for each category of sounds—for example, buttons, background audio, and voice-overs.

The basic concepts explored in this chapter should give you a start, at least for asking the right questions when you are approached to produce audio for interactive projects. Although almost any current Pro Tools system is well equipped for this kind of work, the more firsthand knowledge you have about how the authors will actually use the audio you provide, the better your chances of getting the assignment.

16 Bouncing to Disk, Other File Formats

As discussed in earlier chapters, a Pro Tools project consists of a session document plus many additional audio files that are referenced by the session. You will commonly create additional files using Pro Tools' bouncing functions.

When you're mixing a stereo project, you would typically listen to your audio via two outputs on your audio hardware. In fact, for those who record their mixes in real time to a video master or some external two-track recorder, this may be all that is required. On the other hand, you may need to create *reduction* mixes from your Pro Tools project as a submixing strategy or to create *mixdown* files that can be used by other programs. To cite a common example, you will frequently create stereo mixdown files from Pro Tools so that you can write an audio CD (using another program) or so that a video editor or multimedia programmer can use the finished mixdown in a project. Pro Tools provides many powerful options for exporting audio files to standard formats. This chapter provides some guidelines for producing files to be used by other programs.

Bounce to Disk

The File > Bounce To > Disk command creates a new audio file containing the result of all the audio clips, automation, processing, and other MIDI/audio or mix data contained in your session (or the current Timeline selection). What you hear through the selected Pro Tools output pair (unmuted tracks, real-time sources on Aux In or Audio tracks, plus all the inserts, plug-in processing, automation, and signal routing) is exactly what will be incorporated into the bounced file. Pro Tools always bounces files to disk in real time, so external sends/returns and inserts can be incorporated, as well as any software-based instruments and effects or external sound sources connected to the audio interface (monitored through Aux Input tracks).

The Bounce dialog box (shown in Figure 16.1) also allows you to apply file conversion, either during the bounce or afterward. For highest accuracy in the rendering of plug-in automation, Avid recommends converting *after* the bounce. Regardless of the audio file type used for the original Pro Tools session, you can always choose among other supported formats for the bounced mixdown file. The Import After Bounce option brings the bounced audio file back into the Clip List. This option will only be available, however, if the file format, sample rate, and bit depth are directly compatible with the current session.

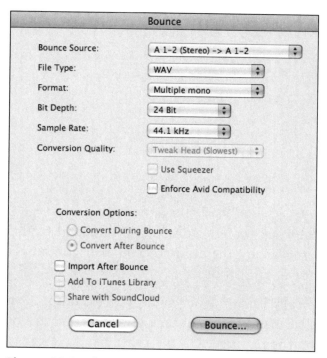

Figure 16.1 The Bounce dialog box for exporting a mix of either the entire session Timeline or the current Timeline selection.

Don't Get Your (Reverb) Tail Caught in the Door!   When selecting events to bounce to a file from Pro Tools, be aware that delay repeats, reverb decays, and amplitude envelope decays from virtual instruments may extend beyond the end of the current Timeline selection. If your selection extends only to the end of the last clip in the session, the final delay repeats or reverb decay may get abruptly cut off. Be sure to add enough space at the end of your selection for these to fade out naturally.

Likewise, when bouncing audio files to be looped (for example, backgrounds for a CD-ROM or webpage), remember that as you're listening to looped playback of a selection within Pro Tools, the decay of any reverb and delay effects from the selection's end overlaps the beginning of the next repetition. You may be surprised later by a significant drop at the beginning of your bounced loop due to missing delay repeats from the previous repetition. To work around this problem, *duplicate* the selection to be looped and bounce two full repetitions. Then reimport the file into Pro Tools and trim the new clip down to only the smoothly looping second half. (This *will* include the delay repeats from the previous repetition.) From Pro Tools, you could then use the Export Clips as Files command in the Clip List pop-up menu to save the trimmed audio clip from Pro Tools as a new file for looping.

When bouncing a mix file that uses reverb or delay at the end, again remember that the reverb tail or delay repetitions may last longer than the actual program material. One way to deal with this is to create a fade-down using the volume automation on the Audio or Aux Input tracks that host the reverb or delay plug-ins. Create the volume fade to coincide with the end of the program, and use your ear to judge how long the fade-down should be. Another possibility is to create a volume-automation fade on the Master Fader track. Remember, though, that all plug-ins are post-fader on the Master Fader track; listen carefully to the effect of the volume fade after its creation.

Converting to Common Audio File Formats

The Bounce dialog box allows you to select AIF, WAV, audio-only QuickTime, and MP3 files from Pro Tools. Mac versions can additionally bounce to Sound Designer II (SD II) files, while Windows versions can additionally bounce to Windows Media Audio (WMA) files. You can also bounce out MXF files from any current system. Chapter 1 provides brief descriptions of the characteristics of each of these audio file types. Each may offer additional parameters (especially in the case of MP3 and WMA) during the process of bouncing to disk from Pro Tools. You can also choose the bounced file's sample rate—for example, reducing to 44.1 kHz from a higher session sample rate to burn a standard audio CD.

You can choose from among various bit depths for the resultant file. Even if your source session is 24 bit, for example, you may frequently reduce bounced files to 16 bits to burn audio CDs with more consumer-oriented programs. If you should need to convert audio to 8 bit (for telephony or older interactive programs), a Squeezer checkbox will appear, which allows better quality during that conversion. Make sure you've considered all other options first, however, including audio data compression and lower sample rates.

For *surround* mixing, you will often need to deliver files in DTS or AC3 multichannel formats (for DTS and Dolby Digital 5.1 formats, respectively). You'll find additional information about surround mix formats in Chapter 14.

About MXF Files   All current Pro Tools systems enable bouncing directly to Material eXchange Format (MXF) files. This file format has been described as a wrapper format that facilitates interchange of audio and video material in the content-creation process. The MXF file structure is built upon the AAF data model and contains clips of *essence* (audio and MPEG/DV video, for example) plus MXF metadata that provides information about duration, required codecs, and other details that can include shot location, production company, crew or talent information, and so on. The MXF standard is becoming more prevalent not only in exchange of post-production content but also for real-time streaming of content in broadcast networks. MXF is principally described by SMPTE standard 377M. It was promoted by the Pro-MPEG forum with a coalition of manufacturers and professional organizations including SMPTE, the EBU (European Broadcasting Union), and the AAF Association.

Tips for Mac Users   Macintosh files generally include a *resource fork*. This section of data within the file header indicates the file type so that the operating system launches the appropriate program when you double-click a file in the Finder. When you burn a data CD-ROM for Windows users using Toast, choose the Mac OS and PC (Hybrid) CD option. This ensures that, as seen from the ISO partition (for Windows, Linux, and UNIX), the aliases of your audio files will have the Mac resource fork stripped out. (This is also what people mean by *flattening* a QuickTime file or saving it as "self-contained." A data header that is specific to the Mac operating system is stripped out.) Mac-only (HFS) data CDs are problematic for most Windows users—except for those who have purchased a utility to read directly from HFS volumes.

Bounce to QuickTime Movie

The File > Bounce To > QuickTime Movie command bounces the session's audio mix (or currently selected range) in real time into a new copy of the digital video file currently being used in the session. The resulting file will be in QuickTime format regardless of whether the original video file was MPEG, AVI, or some other format. As shown in Figure 16.2, many of the options in the dialog box for bouncing to QuickTime are the same as those in the dialog box for bouncing to disk. Within the new copy of the video file, your mono or stereo audio mix is combined with the Video track.

Interactive authors will often request a lower sample rate for the audio in their QuickTime movies (such as 22,050 Hz or even 11,025 Hz) to keep file size and throughput requirements to a minimum. When audio throughput is a concern, however, be sure to ask about using one of the

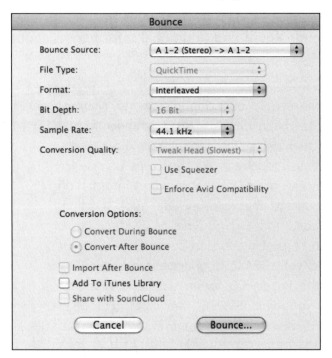

Figure 16.2 The File > Bounce To > QuickTime Movie command opens the dialog box shown here. Your audio mix will be the soundtrack within a new copy of the digital video file.

current audio codecs for data compression instead, like MP3 or MPEG-4. These will sound a *lot* better than reducing the sample rate! The most common sample rate for professional video applications is 48 kHz; use this if the QuickTime movie itself is your method for returning a soundtrack to the video editor.

Another Way Out   Another method for exporting audio clips from Pro Tools is the Export Clips as Files command in Clip List pop-up menu. The Export Selected dialog box, shown in Figure 16.3, provides options for the output file format that are similar to those in the Bounce dialog box, and allows you to combine split stereo clips into a single interleaved stereo file. This command exports selected clips as is; in contrast, bounced audio files created by the Bounce To > Disk command incorporate real-time plug-in processing or automation applied within the selected Timeline range. On the other hand, because the Export Clips as Files command can be used on *multiple* selected clips, it can be useful for batch exporting files to disk.

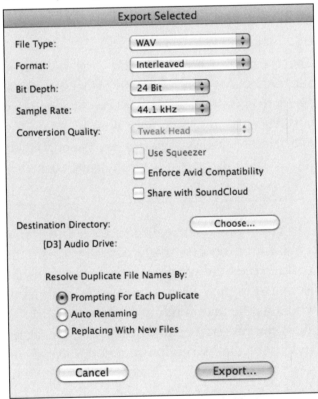

Figure 16.3   The Export Selected dialog box appears when you choose the Export Clips as Files command from the Clip List pop-up menu.

Normalization and Gain Optimization

As explained elsewhere in this book (including Chapter 8), the normalization process locates the peak level within an audio file and, if required, increases the entire file's level to bring that peak to the level you specify using the Level slider in the Normalize AudioSuite plug-in window. If your original peak levels are lower than this setting, levels throughout the rest of the audio file will increase proportionately as the peak levels are increased to the specified value (including background noise, if any). This ensures that a bounced mix file will peak at exactly the level you want. (This can be useful for optimizing bounces when you need to burn a quick audio CD.) It is a good idea to normalize to less than full scale (–1 dB to –3 dB) to leave some headroom and reduce the potential for digital "overs" occurring as the digital audio is transferred from one digital device or program to another.

If you're recording a bounced file from a Pro Tools analog output to another device, such as a video deck, normalization helps you ensure that the reference level you provide actually represents the peak level within your audio program. On the other hand, for commercial CD and DVD mastering, unless you have knowledge and experience of the mastering process, have very high-quality mastering and metering plug-ins, and so on, you would be well-advised to leave this final step to the experts at a good-quality mastering house (who always prefer that you do *not* apply normalization or any other dynamics processing to your bounced mixes). It also bears repeating here that your first area of attention for ensuring optimal levels in your bounced mixes should always be the Master Fader levels for the selected output path, assisted by the PhaseScope plug-in provided with Pro Tools or some other third-party alternative.

Peak/RMS Mode Selectors in Plug-Ins   The choice between RMS and Peak calibration modes for the Normalization function (also available for the Gain and Signal Generator plug-ins) was introduced with Pro Tools version 7. Normalization in all previous versions worked in Peak mode only. The RMS (Root-Mean-Square) mode normalizes based on the effective *average* level of the current audio selection and is therefore most useful when normalizing to levels significantly less than 100% and especially when trying to match apparent loudness levels between multiple mixes or selections.

Contrary to what you might think, it's also very common to normalize to some *other* value than 0 dB (100% full code). In some cases, the normalization process might actually *reduce* the audio levels within files if the peaks in the original audio exceed the specified level for the normalization function. For example, when creating a collection of sound effects for use in multimedia, you might establish –10 dB (about 31.6% of full code) as the maximum level for normalizing all button sounds so that these automatically come into the interactive authoring program at relatively lower levels. Figure 16.4 shows the plug-in window for the Normalize function, located under the AudioSuite menu.

Figure 16.4 The Normalize AudioSuite plug-in window in Pro Tools.

When creating mix files for professional audio CDs and video projects, it can be *undesirable* to normalize to 0 dB (100%). When bouncing out mix files to be used directly for burning one-off audio CDs, this will generally not be an issue. If, however, you're recording a normalized mix output digitally to another device (for example, to a DAT or real-time CD recorder) or especially when creating your own CD duplication master, it's prudent to hedge a little on your definition of "full code." Most professionals will normalize their mixes to some lower value (–1 dB or even –3 dB) just to be on the safe side. Otherwise, in certain situations, a digital audio signal that does not actually exceed 0 dB at any point can produce audible clipping when played back or recorded to a target digital audio device that has some discrepancy in its clipping threshold, including some consumer CD players.

And, of course, you should always *listen* to any audio files that you bounce or normalize. Likewise, if you record in real time to another device, listen to what you've recorded, *especially* at the points within the material where you know peak levels occur. The few extra minutes spent on quality control are nothing compared to the years it may take to regain a client's confidence if a problem occurs!

Normalizing within Pro Tools

You can apply the AudioSuite > Normalize command to any Audio track selection in the Edit window or directly to audio clips/files within the Clip List. Like many other AudioSuite functions, you can choose either to destructively (permanently) overwrite the contents of the currently selected file(s) or to create a new file or files containing the result of the processing. Bear in mind, of course, that many plug-ins increase the *level* of the audio passing through them—for example, when you boost one of the frequency bands in an EQ or increase the Gain parameter in a compressor. If normalizing clips in a track results in such a gain increase, be sure to check that any subsequent plug-in processing in the track's signal chain won't push the level into clipping.

Normalizing Bounced Mixes

When you reimport a bounced mix into Pro Tools, the audio file appears in the Clip List. If you wish, you can directly normalize any file or clip there using the AudioSuite > Normalize command. If you imported a disparate collection of stereo mixes into Pro Tools to assemble a one-off audio CD, for instance, one strategy might be to normalize them all in the Clip List (leaving yourself a little headroom for gain increases as a result of EQ, for instance) before dragging them onto Audio tracks to apply EQ, limiting, or whatever other processing is required.

Aside from applying normalization to files within Pro Tools, you can use a variety of other programs to apply normalization and gain optimization, including all the additional audio-editing programs mentioned later in this chapter. Some standalone programs can apply normalization as part of batch file format conversions.

PhaseScope and Signal Tools   All current versions of Pro Tools include a stereo metering plug-in called PhaseScope. This plug-in can be used on the stereo Master Fader for the output pair that is the source for your bounced mixes. The behavior of its level meters can be toggled between Peak, RMS, Peak + RMS, VU, BBC, Nordic, DIN, and VENUE. A Phase Meter display is available, which can also be switched to Leq(A) mode to display the weighted average of the power level passing through the channel. A Lissajous display reflects the amplitude and phase relationship of the audio. As has been mentioned elsewhere in this book, optimizing the gain structure in your Pro Tools sessions and maintaining consistent levels in bounced mixes should primarily be accomplished by keeping a close eye on the levels in your Master Faders for the selected audio output path. You will retain more audio quality by adjusting levels here in the Pro Tools mixing environment than by normalizing a mixdown file that has already been truncated or dithered down to 16-bit resolution.

Avid Dither Plug-Ins

Especially for music applications, you should generally place dithering plug-ins, including the POW-r Dither plug-in, on the Master Fader for the outputs you will be bouncing whenever performing a bit-depth reduction—for example, when bouncing from a 24-bit session to a 16-bit stereo mix. Dithering reduces the prominence of quantization error (distortion) at low signal levels when audio files are reduced to a lower bit depth. (Bit depth is also known as *word length* because it's the length of the binary number used to represent the amplitude value of each audio sample in the file.) Dithering should always be the *last* plug-in on the Master Fader for your mix output; get in the habit of placing the dithering plug-in in its last insert slot right from the start. As shown in Figure 16.5, the POW-r dither plug-in has only two parameters:

- **Bit Resolution.** When bouncing a file, the resolution should be set to the bit depth of the target bounced file. When recording from digital outputs of Pro Tools, set this to the resolution of the target device—for example, 20 bits if you're recording to the digital input of an older digital multitrack, such as the ADAT XT 20. Dithering should not be used when recording from the analog outputs of current audio interfaces, whose digital-to-analog converters offer full 24-bit resolution. When bouncing to an 8- or 16-bit file or when recording to the digital input of a 16-bit DAT recorder, it would still be appropriate to insert a dithering plug-in on the Master Fader for that output pair.

- **Noise Shaping.** This setting applies specialized filtering to reduce the prominence of quantization distortion in the critical 4-kHz frequency band, where it is most apparent to human hearing. POW-r Dither supports three different types of noise shaping: Type 1, Type 2, and Type 3. The type that works best for each project depends on the nature of the material and your personal taste. In general, Type 1 is the flattest and is often best suited for solo instrument recordings or voice-overs, while Type 3 has the most pronounced noise shaping and is typically preferable for material with a wide stereo image and extended frequency range. But trust your own ears on this and experiment with the different types to see what works best for each recording.

Figure 16.5 The POW-r Dither plug-in optimizes results when reducing the bit depth of your audio. 16-bit dithering is appropriate when bouncing a 16-bit file to disk for burning to an audio CD.

Other Dithering Options

Various plug-ins for mastering and dynamics processing also include dithering. Master X^3 by TC Electronic (shown in Figure 16.6) is a mastering plug-in for Pro Tools|HD and VENUE systems that includes 3-band dynamics processing, soft-clipping, fine gain adjustments, and dithering. The iZotope Ozone plug-in is a Native mastering plug-in that includes multiband dynamics and a harmonic exciter, parametric EQ, mastering reverb, stereo image control, a loudness maximizer, and dithering. The L3 Ultramaximizer from Waves (included in its Diamond and Platinum bundles) also includes dithering and noise shaping, along with its sophisticated multiband limiting.

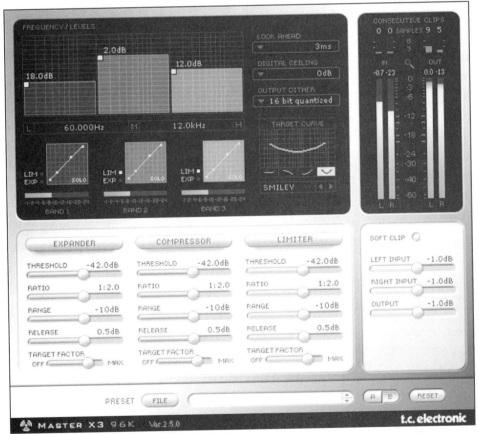

Figure 16.6 The Master X^3 plug-in from TC Electronic is derived from the company's Finalizer hardware unit. It combines several types of processing often used on vocals or stereo mixes: 3-band compression, EQ, limiting/expansion/soft clipping, gain adjustment, and dithering.

Although this chapter is mainly concerned with dithering as an aspect of bouncing audio files to disk, it is worth mentioning that there are also many excellent professional *hardware* devices available for real-time conversion of digital audio signals from one bit depth or sample rate to another. These can be handy, especially when exchanging digital audio signals between multiple units in your studio (digital mixers, keyboards, effects, Pro Tools, digital multitracks, and others). The z-3src from Z-Systems Audio Engineering is an external digital audio device that provides real-time conversions for bit depth and sample rate in a variety of formats. The TC Electronic Finalizer (available in Express and 96K versions) provides these functions plus other useful mastering features, including limiting, gain optimization, and multiband compression. The aforementioned Master X^3 plug-in is based on that renowned piece of studio hardware.

Sample Rate and Bit Depth

Regardless of whether your current Pro Tools session document is 16 or 24 bits, the Bounce dialog box allows you to choose 24-, 16-, or 8-bit bit depths for the bounced file. If you plan to burn a standard audio CD, for example, your source files should be dithered down to 16 bits (although some CD-burning applications offer their own dithering options for reducing from 24 to 16 bits during the CD-writing process). Audio files at 8-bit resolution have a characteristic fizzy or crunchy quality, much associated with older computer applications, inexpensive video games, and toys. This is due to the high degree of quantization error—a kind of angular, digital distortion of the original waveform due to its amplitude variations being rounded off to fit the 256 possible values. If you are ever required to create 8-bit files, make sure that you maximize your gain first by using compression or some other dynamics processing. You should also select the Squeezer option in the Bounce dialog box to optimize conversions to 8-bit resolution, especially if your source is a voice-over file.

Compressed File Formats (MP3, AAC, MPEG-4, RealAudio, and So On)

Audio data compression (which should not be confused with *gain* compression of audio signals) is supported for Audio tracks within QuickTime movies and is an essential part of how the aforementioned audio file formats and MPEG (.mpg) video files are structured. QuickTime, WAV, and AIF audio files support the older Adaptive Delta Pulse Code Modulation (ADPCM) method for compressing audio data. ADPCM exists in two mutually incompatible variants:

- **IMA-ADPCM.** Standardized by the International Multimedia Association, this option typically appears as IMA 2:1 or IMA 4:1 in file-conversion dialog boxes. Now largely outmoded, it was the most prevalent audio data compression format for AIF files for some years.

- **MS-ADPCM.** This is Microsoft's take on the format.

ADPCM used *companding* as well as frequency-selective bit-depth reduction to reduce the size of audio data. Like the more advanced MP3 and RealAudio compression methods discussed below, this is a *lossy* process; some of the original audio information is lost. For spoken-word recordings in particular, ADPCM-compressed files can be relatively acceptable for computer playback. Some music files and loops adapt better to this type of compression than others; it is definitely worth a few minutes of experimentation if the project requires large reductions in audio file size (bearing in mind that you must do this in a program other than Pro Tools). But unless the authoring or telephony application for which you're bouncing audio files doesn't support any of the more contemporary methods for audio data compression, you'll find that the sonic results of IMA and MS versions of the older ADPCM codec are decidedly inferior to MP3, MPEG-4/AAC, and other current audio-compression techniques.

Pro Tools supports bouncing MP3-compressed audio format and can also create full-linear (uncompressed) audio when you choose QuickTime, (Broadcast) WAV, SDII, or AIF formats for audio bounces. Other audio-editing and conversion programs (including Autodesk's Cleaner XL program, whose main purpose is data compression for digital video files) can create files incorporating ADPCM data compression for audio—a format that may still sometimes be requested for interactive media applications (discussed in more detail in Chapter 15).

Better-Sounding Results with Compressed Audio Data Formats   As a general rule, the compression algorithms used for audio data don't react well to low-frequency noise. Rumble from traffic, air conditioning, and vocal pops, for example, will occasionally produce audible artifacts in compressed audio (just as they do with time-stretching and pitch-shifting processes), especially when file sizes are drastically reduced. To avoid ugly surprises, be sure to listen to your material on a good monitoring system at reasonably high volumes before committing. Naturally, a pop filter is a must for recording voice-overs. To eliminate some of the low-end garbage from recorded audio, try using the Hi-Pass filter provided by the EQ III plug-ins in Pro Tools; adjust its cutoff frequency as high as possible without compromising vocal timbre.

MP3

MP3 is another file-format selection in the Bounce dialog box. Short for MPEG Audio, Layer 3, MP3 is a compressed audio file format that can dramatically decrease file size before severely impairing sound quality. It is, of course, "lossy"—that is, something is lost in the compression process. The selected bit rate for the resultant file (measured in kilobits per second, or Kbps) determines the amount of compression that is applied. (Lower bit rates create smaller files, but with consequently greater deterioration of the sound quality.) A second dialog box allows you to enter title, author, genre, and copyright information. For sending approval mixes via the Internet (as well as finished audio, such as voice-over recordings for corporate clients, radio spots, and so on), MP3 can be an excellent choice, as it often reduces file size such that you can send the file as an e-mail attachment (perhaps choosing a bit rate of 128 Kbps or less). If you are producing audio files for interactive developers, whose throughput requirements are more restricted to ensure smooth playback alongside the interactive graphic content, be sure to ask whether MP3 audio files are supported. MP3 is the most common audio file format for Adobe Flash, for instance, although usually this compression will be applied by the developer when the Flash project is published. For high-quality background effects and especially music, you will be much happier with MP3 compression compared to reducing the sample rate to 22 kHz or converting audio files from stereo to mono.

If you create your bounce in a non-compressed audio file format, you can perform an MP3 conversion afterward in another program. For example, Apple's iTunes program provides excellent MP3 conversions. Figure 16.7 shows some of the options in the advanced Preferences for MP3 conversion in iTunes. Remember that lower bit rates reduce audio quality. You will generally find it advisable to specify the sample rate and force the number of channels to stereo if appropriate, and always enable the 10-Hz high-pass filter for MP3 conversions. Joint Stereo mode is highly recommended for all data rates under 128 Kbps. Other professional stereo audio-editing programs, such as BIAS' Peak Pro (Mac), Sony's Sound Forge (Windows), and Steinberg's Wave-Lab (Windows), also provide MP3 conversion, as does Audacity, a freeware program for Mac, Windows, and Linux.

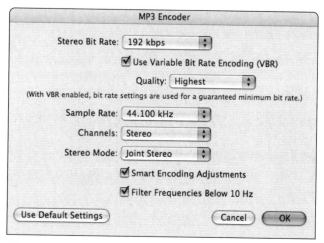

Figure 16.7 iTunes provides conversions from AIF/WAV to MP3 or AAC (a variant of MPEG-4). Seen here: the custom settings dialog box for MP3 conversion.

MPEG-4 and AAC

MPEG-4 is not among the audio file formats you can bounce directly from Pro Tools, but it is well worth knowing about. This is also true of AAC (Advanced Audio Coding), a specific application of the MPEG-4 specification. These formats were developed by the MPEG Group. They are used by Apple in its online service for downloading music, the iTunes Store, and are supported by QuickTime Player, iTunes, and many interactive applications. In these formats, signal-processing technology from Dolby Laboratories applies more complex compression algorithms that not only reduce data size much more efficiently than MP3 but also produce better-sounding results at comparable data rates—*especially* for music. To put it another way, AAC encoding can obtain the same quality as an MP3 file that would be 30–35 percent bigger.

About QuickTime Pro 7   QuickTime Pro 7, in addition to the MPEG-4 export capability already supported in version 6, can save audio files in AAC format. It also supports multichannel audio, real-time video capture from digital video cameras via FireWire, and the very efficient H.264 video codec (part of the MPEG-4 standard) that is also used in Blu-ray and HD-DVD video.

Additional Audio-Editing Programs

Although Pro Tools is a hugely powerful audio program, you may also use other audio-editing programs on occasion, especially for manipulating mono and stereo audio files. We've already alluded to using additional programs for certain types of audio data compression. For multimedia sound design, batch-conversion programs for changing file formats or sample rates, applying normalization, and other transformations can be useful—for example, when you've saved 39 button-click sounds and 39 associated roll-over sounds and you want to normalize all their peaks to 10 dB down. Likewise, when you've created audio files that should loop smoothly in an interactive application, these programs will be useful for double-checking every file—in case you have to adjust loop points after conversion to 22 kHz, for instance.

A program that can edit stereo audio files directly is also very convenient for trimming start and end points of the mix files you've bounced from Pro Tools, adding cue point markers for interactive authoring, applying effects in plug-in formats not available in Pro Tools, editing audio directly within video files, and so on. This section mentions only a few of the most common programs used for professional applications.

Peak Pro (Mac)

This comprehensive audio-editing program for Macintosh from BIAS supports many mono, dual mono, and stereo audio file formats (up to 192-kHz, 32-bit floating-point resolution in the full version). It also offers many file conversions (including import from audio CD, and MP4/AAC and MP3 encoding from source audio files in other formats), DSP functions, looping tools, direct file transfers with various samplers, batch-file processing, and online playback of audio files while locked to external time code (MTC). Peak also supports several real-time plug-in formats, including VST and Audio Units simultaneously, in five insert slots that can be configured in series or parallel signal-routing configurations. You can also use it to insert markers (called *cue points* in some programs) into audio files, used by interactive authoring programs to cue graphic events to locations within an audio file. Peak supports video files in QuickTime, DV, and other formats so that Audio tracks within them can be edited and processed directly without bouncing out a new copy. Peak includes creation of Red Book–compliant audio CDs (including CD-TEXT, PQ editing, ISRC codes, and DDP export), as well as POW-r Dither for reductions down to 16 bit from higher–bit-depth source files. Playlists support using regions from many different source files, either for CD assembly or bouncing out a new audio file, with gain adjustments, crossfades, real-time effects, and other features. In version 6 and later, podcasts can be authored and uploaded as RSS feeds directly from Peak.

Sound Forge (Windows)

Sound Forge—originally developed by Sonic Foundry (also the developers of ACID Pro) and now owned by Sony Creative—is another full-featured audio-editing program. It supports a variety of mono and stereo file formats at sample rates up to 192 kHz and 32-bit resolution and offers MP3, Windows Media, and RealAudio conversions; import from audio CD; DSP functions, including sample-rate conversion; plus support for Direct X audio plug-ins with automation. You can burn audio CDs directly from Sound Forge in track-at-once mode; it also supports file transfer with samplers, editing of audio soundtracks within video files, and non-destructive play-lists of audio regions within a file. Sound Forge also supports video files so that you can process or edit the soundtracks within them, including DV, 24p, QuickTime, AVI, MPEG, RealMedia, and WMV. Like Peak, Sound Forge supports the placement of markers/cue points into files for use by interactive authoring programs. There are also tools for creating ACIDized loops. A more economical, feature-limited version, Sound Forge Audio Studio, is also available. Sound Forge is by far the most widespread program for professional editing of stereo and mono files on the Windows platform. Although somewhat outdated, the book *Sound Forge 8 Power!* by Scott Garrigus (Course Technology PTR, 2005) provides power tips and loads of useful theory that will help you get the most out of Sound Forge. An interactive CD-ROM, *Sound Forge CSi Starter*, by Robert Guérin, is also available.

WaveLab (Windows)

Another professional audio-editing program by Steinberg (developers of Cubase VST), WaveLab supports many audio file formats, including MP3, AIF, WAV, SDII, multichannel surround, and WMA Pro 5.1 and 7.1. It also supports numerous DSP effects and file/sample-rate conversions, looping and sampler tools, plus data CD-ROM and audio CD burning (including non-destructive real-time effects processing and a fully compatible implementation of the Red Book audio CD standard for duplication masters, even directly from 24-bit source files with built-in Apogee UV22 dithering) and authoring and extraction tools for DVD-Audio. Audio playback can be synchronized to external MTC time-code sources, and the Audio-Montage feature offers non-destructive playlist editing with volume/pan automation. WaveLab also supports batch processing of multiple files, including plug-in effects.

Audacity (Mac, Windows, Linux)

This is a free, open-source program for Mac OS X, Windows, and GNU/Linux. While it doesn't offer many of the advanced features in the aforementioned professional programs, Pro Tools users will find it surprisingly useful. It can be just the thing for trimming the start and end of bounced mix files, normalizing and making other gain adjustments, inverting polarity, changing sample rates for interactive projects, exporting MP3 or Ogg Vorbis audio files, adding end fades, or even trimming file lengths so that they loop smoothly. Audacity can also record directly to hard disk. Not too bad, considering it's free! You can download Audacity at audacity.sourceforge.net.

Using Pro Tools Clip Definitions in Other Digital Audio Programs Region Synch is a Windows program developed by Rail Jon Rogut that converts in both directions between the clip definitions exported to source audio files from your Pro Tools session and the region definition format used by Sony/Sonic Foundry's Sound Forge program. (In Pro Tools, clip definitions are contained in the session document, not the source audio files. Use the Export Clip Definitions command in the Clip List pop-up menu to embed pointers for clips into the source audio files.) Because Sound Forge regions are also supported by Adobe Audition, n-Track Studio, Samplitude, and Steinberg's WaveLab—not to mention Sony Creative's own Vegas and CD Architect programs—this can be immensely useful. For example, imagine you're bouncing a long continuous file that will need CD track markers embedded into it (perhaps a live concert or an audiobook CD). Enable the Import After Bounce option, drag the bounced file onto a track, and then use the markers and events already in your session as a guide as you make selections and create a series of contiguous clip definitions corresponding to each CD track. Once you export these clip definitions back to the source file and convert them to Sound Forge regions, you can use Sound Forge, CD Architect, or WaveLab to create audio CD tracks based on the region definitions within this single continuous file. You can download a demo version of this very economical Windows program at http://www.railjonrogut.com.

Audio CD Creation

The requirements for creating one-off audio CDs for clients and promotional use are considerably more informal than when submitting a CD as the master to a commercial CD-duplication house. If you're burning your own CDs for evaluation, for playback in standard audio and computer CD drives, or for your band to sell at local gigs, you'll generally have pretty good compatibility using almost any of the current CD-writing programs. Obviously, given the current fashion, you might want to take the time in Pro Tools to normalize your mixes and possibly apply some peak limiting and other gain optimization so that your CD slams as hard as the other discs in everyone's changer. (Be careful not to overdo this; 100% full-code levels can create digital overs that produce audible distortion on some systems. Plus, relentlessly pushing every mix up against the ceiling of the dynamic range creates a fatiguing listening experience.) On the other hand, if you plan to submit a CD-R that will directly serve as the duplication master for a commercial release, its format must conform to a set of standards called the Red Book, which includes ISRC information and other data in the P and Q subcode channels.

The Red Book Specification for Audio CDs Developed jointly by various manufacturers, particularly Sony and Philips, this specification was originally published in a book with a red cover—hence the name "Red Book." CD-DA (audio) discs permit up to 99 stereo tracks of 16-bit digital audio at a sample rate of 44.1 kHz. The internal timing reference on audio CDs is grouped in hours, minutes, seconds, and frames—at 75 CD frames per second (not to be confused with SMPTE frames). To be acceptable as a Red Book master for commercial duplication, a CD must include all the appropriate subcode data for the P and Q channels, which only certain CD-writing programs provide. This is necessary in order to create a glass master (used for stamping CD copies) directly from your CD-R. Disc Description Protocol (DDP) filesets have been adopted as a common method for optical disc replication. The advantage of DDP filesets is that they deliver both audio data and metadata in an error-protected format. (CD masters can also be submitted on 1630 or DDP tape, which some CD-mastering programs can create.) If your CD-writing program cannot create the additional subcode information, you can still submit your audio on a CD-R, but expect to pay an additional setup fee.

Commercial CDs incorporate eight channels of subcode data (P, Q, R, S, T, U, V, and W), interleaved with audio data at one complete subcode frame for every 588 audio samples. However, audio CD players read only the P and Q channels. The P channel simply indicates when selections are playing. The Q channel incorporates disk and track running times, copy-prohibit and emphasis flags, a TOC (table of contents), error detection, and a UPC catalog code for the entire disk. The Q channel also includes ISRC information (International Standard Recording Code) for each track, identifying the composition's owner, country of origin, serial number, and year of production.

Programs for One-Off Copies

The following are general-purpose CD-writing programs you can use to create audio CDs as well as data CD-ROMs. Some, like Toast, allow you to adjust spacing between CD tracks. Audio CDs created by these programs will generally play just fine in most CD drives. These programs all create Red Book–compatible CDs. However, they don't implement *all* the features of the Red Book specification (UPC, ISRC, PQ codes, and so on) that are required for creating a duplication master for commercial CDs. You might say that CDs created by these programs conform to a *subset* of the features in the Red Book specification.

Toast (Mac)

Manufactured by Roxio, Toast is by far the most prevalent CD-burning program on the Macintosh platform. Audio CDs, enhanced audio CDs (which might include photos or videos in addition to the audio), and MP3 audio CDs can be created from most source audio file formats, and you can adjust the spacing between CD tracks (including zero spacing in disk-at-once mode). CD-Text information can be included on audio CDs created with Toast. This information (stored in the R and W subcode channels of the lead-in area on the audio CD) allows compatible players to display data such as disk title, artist name, and track titles while playing your CD. Toast supports creation of data CD-ROMs (including Mac/Win hybrid format), data DVDs and data on Blu-ray discs, as well as MP3 CDs, video CDs, Super Video CDs, and video DVDs. Toast versions 8 and higher also support plug-ins in Audio Unit (AU) format and various types of cross-fades between tracks.

iTunes

Apple's iTunes software is commonly used on both Mac and Windows platforms, largely due to the popularity of the iPod and iPhone products. iTunes accommodates a variety of source file formats, including AIF, WAV, and MP3. It can rip tracks from audio CDs to MP3 or AAC format (applying compression while creating files of the specified type on your disk) or to AIF and WAV files (creating files with no data compression). Like Toast, iTunes also supports burning audio CDs. It includes a 10-band equalizer that can be non-destructively applied during the CD-burning process, a feature to create crossfades between CD tracks, and rudimentary tools for fine-tuning individual track levels. iTunes also provides excellent options for MP3 or AAC conversion from your source AIF and WAV mixes bounced from Pro Tools.

Roxio Creator (Windows)

Also manufactured by Roxio, Roxio Creator 2012 (and its predecessors, Easy Media Creator and Easy CD Creator) is a CD-burning program for Windows. It supports recordable CDs and DVDs (as well as Blu-ray discs in the Pro version). Like Toast, it supports burning data CD-ROMs and audio CDs from a variety of different source audio file formats (including MP3) and provides a SoundStream normalizer feature to ensure consistent levels on Audio tracks from multiple sources. It supports creating Red Book–compliant ISRC codes, UPC codes, and PQ subcode channel information on audio CDs.

Sound Forge (Windows)

This robust, industry-standard audio-editing program from Sony (originally developed by Sonic Foundry) also includes features for *track-at-once* writing of audio CDs; support of MP3, WMA, and many other audio/video file formats; and support for source sample rates up to 192 kHz and 64-point floating-point resolution. Sound Forge offers loop tuning and ACIDized loop-creation tools, automatable real-time effects including multiband compression, noise reduction, VST, and DirectX plug-in support, as well as support for Flash SWF files, multichannel Dolby AC-3, and Windows Media Audio.

Programs for Creating Duplication Masters for Commercial CDs

As we've said, additional information must be incorporated into a CD master for commercial duplication. Not surprisingly, a CD-writing program included with your CD-R drive isn't necessarily going to support the extra features required to create a Red Book–compliant CD master. However, it *will* produce audio CDs that perform acceptably in most CD players or that a commercial CD-duplication house can use as the basis for creating a CD-duplication master after adding the appropriate data in the Q subcode channel (for a fee). The programs discussed here, however, incorporate the necessary features for professional CD duplication (from a CD-R or in some cases from a tape). As with mastering and gain optimization of your stereo mixes for release (discussed below), if you aren't extremely familiar with all the requirements for assembling a duplication-ready CD master and the particular requirements of your duplication house, it is a good investment to pay an expert to do this properly. In any case, you'll need one of these programs if you intend to create indexes within CD tracks or to create CD track numbers *within* a single audio file (in the middle of a cross-fade or applause in a live performance, for example).

Sony CD Architect (Windows)

This professional CD-creation program from Sony accepts source audio files at sample rates up to 192 kHz and 32-bit resolution and provides high-quality resampling and dithering to standard CD audio. Tools for placement of CD track markers and indexes are provided, along with the requisite information for the P and Q subcode channels, UPC/EAN codes, and many other features required when creating master CDs for commercial duplication. Normalization and non-destructive gain envelopes can be applied to any audio event. More than 20 DirectX plug-ins are also included with the program and can be applied non-destructively during the CD-burning process. A variety of crossfade shapes can be created between adjacent audio regions and across CD track markers between them, and you can create hidden tracks. CD Architect supports Sound Forge regions directly, and you can open audio events from CD Architect into Sound Forge for other types of editing.

WaveLab (Windows)

This audio-editing program from Steinberg (manufacturers of the Cubase audio/MIDI sequencer, Nuendo, and other MIDI-related software and interfaces) includes features for creating audio CDs and data CD-ROMs. Like the CD-writing programs already discussed, WaveLab can also create all the ISRC and other information in the Q subcode channel, create track numbers and indexes within a single audio file, and so on, to produce a CD-R master for direct commercial duplication. Non-destructive, real-time VST plug-ins, multiband compression, parametric EQ, stereo expansion, and other audio processing can be applied during the CD-creation process, as well as UV22 HR dithering (the current "high-resolution" form of Apogee's popular UV22 dithering algorithm used in many audio programs and hardware units). WaveLab also supports source audio at sample rates as high as 384 kHz (!) and 32-bit floating-point resolution in many different file formats. Audio-Montage playlist features include crossfades between separate files and up to 10 simultaneous effects, all of which can be applied non-destructively in real time.

Nero (Windows)

This suite of software from Nero AG (www.nero.com) includes powerful tools for creating audio CDs, DVDs, CD video, and data CDs. Features for audio CD creation include crossfades, CD-Text, copyright information and UPC/EAN codes, copy-prohibit flags, index creation within CD tracks, CD track IDs within a continuous audio file, MP3 CD creation, mixed-mode and CD Extra formats, non-destructive normalization while burning CDs, and disk-at-once or track-at-once writing modes.

Leave Mastering to the "Masters"   When we talk here about creating a CD master for duplication, we mean the physical process of organizing the data—all the IRSC and UPC/EAN codes, indexes, pre-gaps, copy-protection flags, and other data required for a commercial release. This can be complicated; if you're not completely familiar with these concepts, do *not* try it at home! Most CD-duplication houses can handle these details for a reasonable fee—but be sure to thoroughly check the test CD they provide, programming various track orders in your player, skipping between tracks, and so on.

Note, however, that *mastering audio* is an entirely different process, where dynamics processing, EQ, and other adjustments are applied to finished stereo mixes to make them sound better, with more uniform quality. Experienced mastering engineers know how to optimize for CD, vinyl, radio, and other playback scenarios. They also occasionally work miracles, applying corrective measures for any deficiencies in your original mixes or simply making a disparate collection of tracks sound more uniform.

When submitting audio files of a mix to a mastering engineer, provide these at the maximum resolution possible without any intrusive processing, sample rate, or bit-depth conversions on your part. Bounce the mix at your original session's sample rate with no dithering applied and at 24-bit or 32-bit resolution. Don't alter the stereo mix with dynamics processors or normalize it, either. It's better to leave this to the experts—they have much more sophisticated tools (and expertise) at their disposal. Supplying a 16-bit audio CD, 100% normalized or with its dynamic range already modified in some other way, severely curtails a mastering engineer's flexibility. If you'd like, you can provide a second, reference-only CD with your compressed mixes, but be sure to provide your raw, high-resolution mixes as audio files within folders on a separate data CD-R or DVD-R.

Broadcast WAV files (with either the .wav or .bwv extension) are generally the preferred submission format, in part because of AES/EBU recommendations that record companies use this delivery format for audio projects (not only mixes, but source audio tracks in the project). Nevertheless, be sure to check with your mastering engineer first so that you bounce your Pro Tools project to the preferred format.

Summary

The goal of this chapter was to provide some context for sending your audio from Pro Tools out into the world. As always, when you're converting audio to a lower bit depth (with an inferior signal/error ratio) or to a compressed audio data format, you need to manage your gain structure and mix output levels to get the best-possible dynamic range and as few artifacts as possible. When collaborating with others, always ask what file format they prefer and determine all the file formats that their system or program supports, and don't be afraid to make a useful suggestion if another format will fit the bill better.

17 The Score Editor Window

In 2006, Avid acquired Sibelius Software, Inc., a manufacturer of one of the dominant music-notation software programs on the market. Not surprisingly, Pro Tools soon incorporated notation functions built on Sibelius technology. Although it represents just a small portion of the Sibelius feature set, the Score Editor window that debuted in Pro Tools 8 is an extremely useful feature that not only can generate scores for printing but also offers a musically sensible way of editing MIDI and Instrument tracks. The Score Editor window also enables users to export Sibelius-format files that can be opened and modified using the full Sibelius software.

As shown in Figure 17.1, the Score Editor window has many familiar features. Not only does the staff configuration reflect traditional score appearance, but almost all of the Pro Tools–specific controls are similar to what you find in both the Edit window and the MIDI Editor window.

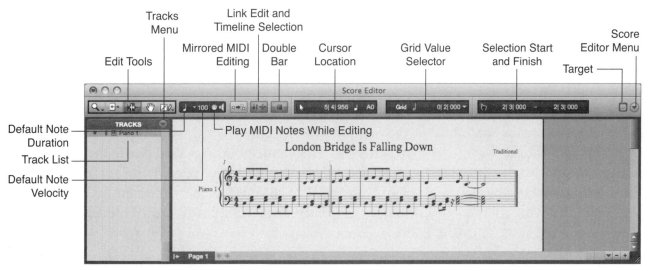

Figure 17.1 The Score Editor window.

If your MIDI sequence begins right at the beginning of your session's Timeline, the Score Editor window reflects this by having the notation start right at the head of the staves. If, however, your project starts the MIDI sequence a number of bars after the start of the Timeline (perhaps the Move Song Start function was applied to move the song start 10 measures ahead), then a corresponding number of empty bars will appear in the Score Editor window. Also, the number of empty bars shown after the last MIDI clip of your sequence is determined by the Double Barline button in the Score Editor toolbar: When enabled, the traditional double-bar notation will appear at the end of the last measure of your score; when disabled, a number of empty measures will appear after the last measure containing any note information. The number of empty measures displayed is determined by the setting in the MIDI tab of the Preferences. (See the "MIDI/Score Editor Display" section on the MIDI Preferences page.)

Using the Edit Tools

To bring up the Score Editor window, simply right-click on a MIDI clip and choose Open in Score Editor toward the bottom of the menu. If you find yourself using the Score Editor window on a regular basis, you can choose to have Pro Tools open it whenever you double-click on a MIDI clip: Choose Setup > Preferences and select the MIDI tab; then select Score Editor from the pop-up menu for the Double-Clicking a MIDI Clip Opens option.

If you are familiar with how the Edit window tools work with the Notes display in MIDI and Instrument tracks (covered in Chapter 10), then you are pretty much ready to start editing notation in the Score Editor window. To recap, the Selector tool, referred to as the Note Selector tool in the Score Editor window, can be dragged over notes in a single staff or across several staves, allowing various menu functions as well as actions by the Grabber tool to then be applied to the selected notes. You can also select multiple notes with the Grabber tool by clicking the first note and Shift-clicking on additional notes. Then drag the notes to a different pitch or time on the staff or staves. You can use the Trim tool to lengthen notes by positioning the tool on a note and dragging to the right. Similarly, positioning the Trim tool on a note and dragging to the left will shorten the note duration. Before trimming notes, make sure you know whether the Allow Note Overlap option in the Notation Display Track Settings dialog box is selected. (This option is explained in the sidebar "Display Quantization and Note Overlap" later in this chapter.)

Editing with the Pencil Tool

The Pencil tool acts the same way in the Score Editor window as it does in Notes view on MIDI and Instrument tracks. Using the Pencil tool in Freehand mode (selected from the Pencil tool menu in the Score Editor toolbar) is especially powerful when working with musical notation for step editing or programming. For musicians who've cut their teeth programming MIDI events using event lists with columns of dry data, the ability to place notes using a graphic representation of music notation is a dream come true.

To get started, you'll want to specify the Default Note Duration and Default Note Velocity settings to the right of the Edit tools at the top of the Score Editor window. As in the MIDI Editor window, you can select from a range of a 1/64 note to a full bar for step-entering notes with the Pencil tool, and a velocity range of 0 to 127. You may also want to set the Score Editor window's Grid value, as this will affect the spacing used for notes and the increment used for lengthening or shortening notes with the Pencil tool and Trim tool. In addition, the Display Quantization setting in the Notation Display Track Settings dialog box can affect the resolution of notes you draw as well as the lengthen- or shorten-increments shown for the Pencil tool or the Trim tool.

By way of example, let's look at the results when using a default note duration of a 1/4 note and a Grid value of a 1/8 note. When we click the Pencil tool in Freehand mode anywhere in a staff, a 1/4 note will be inserted. When the 1/4 note appears, the rest notation for the measure is adjusted to reflect the newly added note. If we click the Pencil tool again anywhere in a staff and drag to the right, the duration of the note will adjust by 1/8-note increments (the Grid value) as we drag—starting with an 1/8 note, then increasing to a 1/4 note, a dotted 1/4 note, a 1/2 note, and so on. Similarly, dragging back to the left before releasing the mouse causes the note duration to decrease in 1/8-note increments. We can also transpose the note by dragging up or down. Transposing can be done while creating a note or afterward, when the Pencil icon changes to a Grabber-like finger icon when placed over an existing note.

Other modes of the Pencil tool can be used to create multiple notes of the same pitch, with variations between the tool modes in note length and velocity. The Pencil tool's Line mode enables you to create a string of notes at the same pitch and velocity (as specified by the Default Note Velocity selector). The length of the notes is determined by the Default Note Duration (or by the Grid value, if smaller), with the note spacing determined by the Grid value. To draw a string of notes, simply click at the desired starting beat on a staff and drag to the right. The Pencil tool's Triangle mode will draw notes the same way, with the velocity of the subsequent notes changing from the default value to 127 and back in a triangle pattern. Likewise, the Pencil tool in Square mode will draw notes with velocities alternating between the default value and 127. The Random mode sets note velocities randomly anywhere between the default value and 127 when you click and drag to draw notes.

Keys, Meters, and Chords in the Score Editor Window

As in the MIDI Editor and Edit windows, you can work with key changes, meter changes, and chord symbols in the Score Editor window. Unique to the Score Editor window is the ability to display chord diagrams used for guitar tabs. Figure 17.2 shows a meter change at Measure 5, from 4/4 to 3/4, and a key change at Measure 9, modulating up a half step to D-flat major. Triad chords accompany the melody and chord diagrams have been added for guitar accompaniment. All of these events appear in the corresponding Meter, Chord, and Key Rulers in both the Edit and MIDI Editor windows.

Figure 17.2 Examples of meter and key changes as well as chord diagrams and symbols used in the Score Editor window.

Meter Change

To insert a meter change, right-click with the Pencil, Note Selector, or Grabber tool and choose Insert > Meter Change or open the Event menu and choose Time Operations > Meter Change. In the Meter Change dialog box (see Figure 17.3), you can choose the location for the meter change event, specify whether the event corresponds to the exact start of a bar (with the Snap to Bar selection), and set the new time signature. You can also choose the note duration of the click, which is handy when choosing meters such as 6/8, where a dotted 1/4-note click may work better than straight 1/8 notes. If ever you want to edit the meter or its location, simply double-click the meter event with the Grabber tool and make your changes. If you need to delete a meter change, choose the Grabber tool and Option-click (Alt-click in Windows) on the time signature display to delete it.

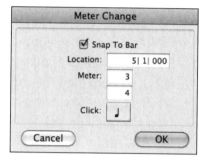

Figure 17.3 The Meter Change dialog box. Inserting a new meter in the Score Editor window will add the event to the Meter Ruler in the Edit and MIDI Editor windows.

Key Signature Change

With key-signature changes, you can apply the methods described for meter changes to create, edit, and delete key events. The Key Change dialog box (see Figure 17.4) presents a choice of keys; you determine the mode by selecting either the Major Keys or Minor Keys radio button in the

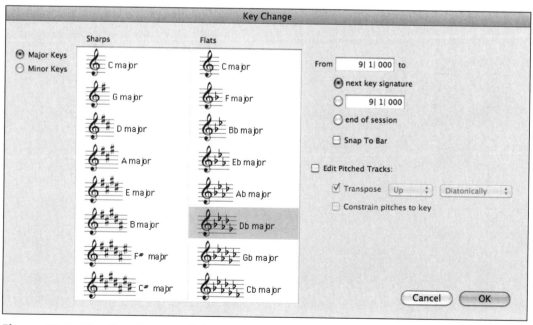

Figure 17.4 The Key Change dialog box.

upper-left corner. You then choose a starting location for the key change event and specify how long the newly chosen key will be in effect: until the next key signature, to a specified location, or to the end of the session. As with the Meter Change dialog, you can make sure the event lines up with a bar start via the Snap to Bar selection. You also have the option of having Pro Tools intelligently transpose the notes included in the start and end location with the Edit Pitched Tracks checkbox. With this option selected, you can transpose note pitch up or down either diatonically or chromatically. Most of the time, you will want to use the Constrain Pitches to Key selection, unless the performance includes notes that intentionally fall outside of their key, such as chromatic progressions or blue notes. In these cases, the diatonic option will allow you to transpose between major and minor keys while preserving notes that fall outside of the new key.

Chord Change

Unique to the Score Editor is the ability to display chord symbols and diagrams in your composition (although Chord Change events can be added on the Chords Ruler in either the Edit window or a MIDI Editor window). Creating, editing, and deleting chord changes follows the same methods used for meter and key changes. As shown in Figure 17.5, the Chord Change dialog box lets you choose the chord's tonic with the Chord selector, the chord mode with the Chord Quality selector, and the chord inversion with the Bass selector. It then displays in guitar notation the resulting options from your selection; choose one by double-clicking its chord diagram or single-clicking the desired diagram and then clicking OK. If you choose an inversion of the chord, the chord symbol in the Score Editor window will list the root and mode of the chord, and then the bass note to the right above the chord diagram. A corresponding event is placed on the Chord Ruler, which can be displayed in either the Edit window or the MIDI Editor window.

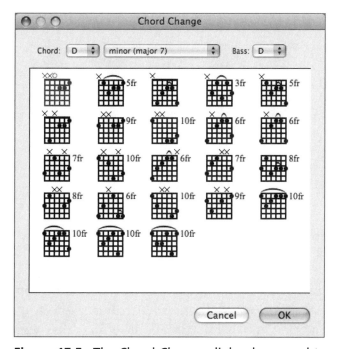

Figure 17.5 The Chord Change dialog box, used to create both chord diagrams and symbols in the Score Editor window and chord change events in the Chord Ruler found in the Edit and MIDI Editor windows.

Settings and Setups

The display of all elements in the Score Editor window is determined by two groups of settings: the Notation Display Track settings and the Score Setup settings. Both can be accessed via the Track List pop-up menu in the Score Editor window or by right-clicking anywhere in the notation portion of the window. Consult these two dialog boxes to establish general settings for spacing, to specify what information is actually shown within the notation, and to configure transposition settings for band and orchestral instruments.

The Notation Display Track Settings

Upon opening the Notation Display Track Settings dialog box, shown in Figure 17.6, make sure the correct track is chosen with the selector menu at the top of the dialog box. Directly below the track selector is a pop-up menu for setting the appropriate clef for the instrument that the selected MIDI or Instrument track represents. Choices in this menu include Grand Staff, Treble, Bass, Alto, and Tenor. To the right of the Clef selection is the Display Transposition setting, which enables you to alter the notation to represent instruments that transpose from concert pitch. For instance, if you want a MIDI or Instrument track to represent a part for a trumpet, which would need to play a C to represent concert pitch B flat, simply choose B flat from the Key pull-down menu and choose +1 with the Octaves slider.

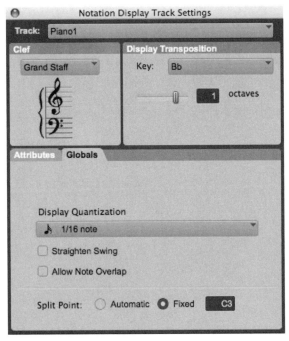

Figure 17.6 The Notation Display Track Settings dialog box, with a transposition setting appropriate for a concert B-flat instrument, such as a clarinet or trumpet.

The lower-half of the Notation Display Track Settings dialog box deals with the note-duration resolution used to display the notation and provides two tabs—Globals and Attributes—both of which have the same controls. Think of the settings in the Globals tab as default settings that you can choose initially or revert back to if desired. In the Attributes tab, you will notice the Follow

Globals selection; that chooses the settings currently found under the Globals tab. Deselect the Follow Globals selector to apply the settings you make in the Attributes tab. Also note that your Attributes tab settings will not change if you choose the Follow Globals selector; they will merely not apply to the notation. Also present are selectors for Straighten Swing as well as Allow Note Overlap. In addition, when Grand Staff is selected as the clef, you can choose what note separates the treble and bass staves or let Pro Tools do the job. The Fixed button applies the note specified in the field to the right of it, and the Automatic button lets Pro Tools analyze the MIDI or Instrument track for note groupings and logically divide them between the two staves.

Display Quantization and Note Overlap   A couple things are worth highlighting regarding the Notation Display Track Settings dialog box. First, if you ever notice that your notation is peppered with 1/32 grace notes in the Score Editor window for a MIDI or Instrument track containing a pastoral melody of 1/4 and 1/8 notes, you will want to check out your Display Quantization settings. A good rule of thumb is to start by setting the duration one shorter than the shortest note length in the performance. In the case of the pastoral melody, try a 1/16-note duration and take a look at how the notation in the Score Editor window has changed. If you're not satisfied, try selecting an 1/8-note duration. Note that this setting affects only how the performance is displayed in the Score Editor window, not the performance itself. Also, if you are planning to step-program in the Score Editor window, set the Display Quantization amount before starting, as its setting will override what is selected as the MIDI Note Duration setting at the top of the Score Editor window (for display purposes).

If you find yourself hitting a wall when using the Trim tool to extend certain notes' durations in the Score Editor window, most likely the Allow Note Overlap function in the Notation Display Track Settings dialog box needs to be selected. This enables you to create slurred or tied notes to signify their overlap of the next performed notes. Again, settings for Display Quantization will affect the minimum duration increment used as you extend a note with the Trim tool.

The Score Setup

The Score Setup dialog box, shown in Figure 17.7, lets you choose the settings for the general appearance of the page. Like the Notation Display Track Settings dialog box, you can access the Score Setup box by right-clicking in the notation portion of the Score Editor or through the Track List pop-up menu. Starting with the Information section, you can add a name to the score, which appears top center, and include the name of the composer of the score, which appears top right. Immediately below the Information section is the Display section, which lets you toggle on or off elements in the Score Editor window, including the title and composer, track names, page numbers, chord symbols, bar numbers, and chord diagrams. The Spacing section allows you to adjust the spacing between staves and stave systems, to add space below the title and composer text, and to add space below any printed chord diagrams and symbols, separating them from the staff underneath. Lastly, the page and staff size as well as the page margins and orientation are set in the Layout section of the Score Setup dialog box. You can choose between Letter, Legal, Tabloid, and A4 page sizes in either Portrait or Landscape mode. The staff size and margins can be set in inches or millimeters.

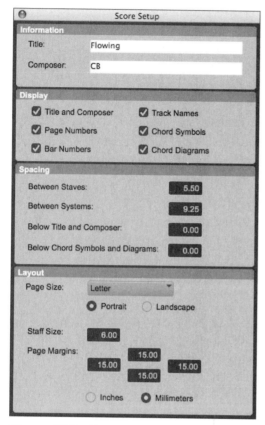

Figure 17.7 The Score Setup dialog box, which allows you to insert both title and composer information, as well as choose the general appearance and orientation settings.

Summary

The Score Editor window provides key functionality for the music-making aspects of the Pro Tools platform, especially for composers and arrangers. You can perform a piece of music in Pro Tools using MIDI and Instrument tracks, edit and arrange the resulting performance, play the sequence for the intended musicians, and then print out the score for a live performance, all within Pro Tools. Even if the original performance is intended to be kept within Pro Tools, the ability to edit and step program in the Score Editor window—especially combined with the editing choices in the MIDI Editor window—offers time-saving flexibility for creating music. With these tools at your disposal, Pro Tools comes one step closer to being the ultimate one-stop shop for electronic music making.

18 Pro Tools Power: The Next Step

The learning process never stops. Not only is Pro Tools constantly evolving with new software features, new audio hardware, and so on, but your own ambitions will no doubt increase as you gain more experience with audio production (and Pro Tools features), which means you'll need to continue learning to accomplish more advanced goals.

This chapter briefly reviews typical upgrade paths for the current generation of Pro Tools hardware. (Appendix B, "Add-Ons, Extensions, and Cool Stuff for Your Rig," discusses other peripheral equipment and accessories for Pro Tools systems.) In addition, this chapter provides some basic suggestions for deepening your knowledge and enhancing your career possibilities.

Upgrade Path: For Your System

One of the things that makes a digital audio workstation like Pro Tools so attractive is that you can upgrade it as your requirements and budget dictate. You can incrementally increase the power of your production system: bigger and faster hard disks, more plug-ins, more RAM, additional or higher-resolution audio hardware, more sophisticated synchronization and MIDI connections, a faster computer…the list goes on.

Naturally, because Pro Tools is largely software based, the creative environment itself evolves over time. In contrast, your options for expanding and updating the system configuration are more limited with most hardware-based alternatives for editing audio and MIDI.

Inevitably, as your use of Pro Tools becomes more sophisticated and you tackle more ambitious projects, more demands are placed on your system. The options for expanding the Pro Tools hardware itself depend on which system you're using. Pro Tools|HD and Pro Tools|HDX hardware is modular by nature. Pro Tools|HD Native systems can be expanded with up to four HD-series interfaces. Systems built around an interface from the Mbox family, the older Mbox 2 family, or the 003 family offer more fixed I/O configurations, as do systems with M-Audio interfaces (although you can still enhance some of these systems via external preamps equipped with Lightpipe or S/PDIF digital outputs, as discussed in this chapter). In addition to the audio hardware itself, with the rapid advance of technology, there will always be more powerful computer platforms available for Pro Tools—but be sure to do your homework before making any upgrade. The program may not be compatible with brand-new motherboard chipsets, computer models, and other hardware without requiring an upgrade. Be sure to check the compatibility documents in the Support area of Avid's website before proceeding. Also, the Avid Audio Forums known as the Digi User Conference (DUC) is an excellent place to learn about other users' real-world experiences; you may even find parts lists and suppliers for putting together your own custom rig. In particular, with more sophisticated plug-ins, higher track counts and audio resolutions, and increased use of software instruments, you may constantly crave more memory, storage, and processing power from your host CPU. The following sections review some of the typical options (and a few potential pitfalls) for expanding your rig.

Pro Tools Hardware Upgrades

Older audio interfaces for Pro Tools|HD systems include vacant bays where you can install an expansion card for more analog or digital I/O plus a Legacy Peripheral port for connecting audio interfaces from the long-discontinued 24|Mix family, such as the 888|24 I/O, 882|20 I/O, 1622 I/O, or 24-bit ADAT Bridge I/O. You can further increase the number of audio inputs and outputs by adding a second interface to your configuration. Among the current generation of HD-series interfaces—the HD OMNI, HD I/O, and HD MADI—only the HD I/O offers expansion bays (not available in the 16 × 16 analog configuration, as all four bays are occupied). HD I/O option cards are available to install in any empty bay.

You can also increase the DSP capacity of a Pro Tools|HD or Pro Tools|HDX system by adding HD Accel cards (Pro Tools|HD) or HDX cards (Pro Tools|HDX). Among other things, this adds processing power, increases voice count, and allows you to use more simultaneous plug-ins. A larger number of simultaneous tracks, sends, inserts, and so on may also be supported. Adding HD Accel cards or HDX cards to your system also enables you to increase the number of hardware I/O channels available to your system by connecting additional audio interfaces.

Pro Tools|HD systems support daisy-chaining two HD-series interfaces—from the current generation of interfaces or the older 96 I/O, 96i I/O, 192 Digital I/O, or 192 I/O interfaces—on the Core card and each HD Accel card (each card supports up to 32 channels of I/O). Therefore, even on the entry-level Pro Tools|HD 1 system, adding a second audio interface will increase your physical I/O from 16 to 32 channels without requiring any additional cards.

Current Mac Pro models from Apple have four PCIe card slots, one of which is occupied by the graphics card. Expanded configurations beyond an HD 3 required an external PCI expansion chassis, connected via a single PCIe card in one of the computer's internal slots.

Caution: PCI versus PCI Express (PCIe)   Current Mac Pro models (and all Macintosh G5 computers since the end of 2005) use an expansion slot specification known as PCI Express, or PCIe. Cards in the older PCI format are incompatible with PCIe. Similarly, PCIe cards are not backward compatible with PCI slots. The Magma PE6R4 six-slot external PCI expansion chassis allows you to use older PCI cards for Pro Tools|HD with a host computer that offers only PCIe slots. It is connected via a PCIe card installed in the computer.

Although you can still find HD Accel cards for sale on eBay and elsewhere, they are no longer distributed by Avid. The official upgrade path for all Pro Tools|HD systems going forward involves an exchange for Pro Tools|HDX hardware. (Avid also offers a very affordable path to Pro Tools|HD Native hardware.) A single Pro Tools|HDX card provides up to 256 voices and supports up to four HD-series interfaces, for a total of 64 channels of simultaneous I/O. Pro Tools|HDX systems can be expanded with up to three cards total, for a maximum voice count of 768 voices and up to 192 channels of I/O.

Computer Hardware and Operating System Upgrades

One significant computer hardware upgrade for Pro Tools is the addition of a second monitor. When you're working long hours, especially with larger Pro Tools sessions, a second monitor can make a huge difference in your productivity. Adding a second monitor lets you view the Mix and Edit windows on separate monitors and keep various plug-in and Output windows anchored and visible. Many currently available graphics cards support dual monitors and provide excellent results with Pro Tools. Another option is a single mega-monitor, such as an Apple 27-inch Thunderbolt Display. These large, high-resolution monitors provide enough room to spread out both the Edit and Mix windows side by side or to have one conveniently long Edit window.

Adding more RAM to your computer can also improve the operation of Pro Tools. Standard Pro Tools 10 software requires 2 GB of RAM, while Pro Tools HD 10 software has a 4-GB minimum. Additional RAM is strongly recommended in most cases, especially to take advantage of the new Disk Cache feature in Pro Tools HD and Pro Tools with Complete Production Toolkit. (As discussed elsewhere, this feature allows you to load audio files used in Pro Tools sessions into RAM for cached playback.)

Generally, the faster your disks, the more channels of audio you can record and play back reliably. (7,200-RPM drives are recommended for all but the smallest configurations; 10,000 RPM drives are also worth a look.) Users who work with large sessions should consider expanding to multiple drives, especially to support higher track counts and/or higher sample rates and bit depths. Aside from installing an additional internal SATA drive, external USB 2.0 (Windows 7), FireWire 400 and 800 (Mac), and eSATA drives can also be good options for Pro Tools—just confirm that any drive you buy meets the requirements posted on Avid's website. Aside from causing general performance issues, incompatible drives can actually cause error messages in Pro Tools. Note, however, that the new Disk Cache feature on compatible systems makes it possible to record and play back from drive configurations that were formerly unsupported by Pro Tools, including Avid Unity MediaNetwork and ISIS shared storage systems.

When it comes to operating-system upgrades for your computer, make absolutely *sure* the new OS is compatible with your current version of Pro Tools. The same applies for new motherboard chipsets and computer models. Avid maintains current compatibility documents in the Support area of its website (www.avid.com).

Audio production is a demanding real-time application, and you will find that Avid is fairly conservative about certifying new operating systems and hardware. If the contacts at your

Avid dealer are technically qualified regarding computer hardware and operating-system issues, seek their advice. Otherwise, contact Avid Sales and Support via email. You can also find the latest information and read up on other users' experiences in the Avid Audio Forums (a.k.a. DUC) at duc.avid.com. Keep in mind that, as with all online forums, posts on the DUC can range from helpful and technically impeccable to pugnacious and histrionic.

In short, if your Pro Tools system is currently working, don't be stampeded into the latest operating-system upgrade until you've done adequate research. And if you must experiment with unsupported configurations, don't beat up on Avid if you experience unpleasant side effects.

Pro Tools Software Upgrades

Avid regularly releases new versions of the Pro Tools software. Registered users are generally entitled to upgrades at a reduced price and can download minor customer-service updates for free. Be sure to verify that each software upgrade is appropriate for your hardware, though. Sometimes, an incremental version exists simply to support new hardware and may not be required by—or even compatible with—a current configuration.

As is common with other software manufacturers, Avid offers a series of maintenance updates between major upgrades of the Pro Tools software. Again, some of these exist merely to support new hardware options. Be sure to check out all the Read Me information on Avid's site (and the compatibility documents, of course) before downloading and installing any upgrade. And *be sure to register your Pro Tools system* so that you are informed of important upgrades and new products; likewise, let Avid know if you change your address (you can do this on the Avid website).

Secondhand Pro Tools Systems   If you've purchased a secondhand Pro Tools system, you can still register with Avid, which entitles you to service and future upgrades. (You can download the PDF version of the Transfer of Ownership form from the Support section of Avid's website; it must include serial numbers, be printed, and be signed by both you and the seller.) Make sure you understand exactly which computer models and operating systems are supported by the used Pro Tools hardware you intend to buy, however. Also, for your own records, make sure to get the original sales receipt for any used Pro Tools system that you purchase, if possible.

Pro Tools Peripherals

Upgrading from a simple MIDI interface to a multiport model is a typical upgrade path for many users, as is adding sophisticated SMPTE synchronization (with reference sync, if your hardware supports it). Adding an external control surface is another upgrade option. (See Appendix B for more information.) Rackmountable high-performance hard drives from Glyph and others are also attractive options; unlike most hard drives, their performance level specifically with Pro Tools is guaranteed, and they're also designed to be relatively *quiet*. As noise is often a concern, another common Pro Tools add-on is an acoustical housing of some sort to isolate the fan noise from the computer and hard drives from your critical control-room listening environment. (USB and DVI/VGA extenders can also be an attractive option, allowing you to move the computer and drives out of the control room altogether; see Appendix B.) If working in a home studio, a well-ventilated closet with some soundproofing may be a good solution.

Audio Hardware

Certainly, a lot of great microphones and microphone preamps are available that you can add to your system; the sky's the limit! As mentioned elsewhere in this book, Avid's PRE, an eight-channel mic preamp, is attractive not only because its microphone preamps sound good, but also because you can remotely control its settings directly from the Pro Tools session via MIDI. Each time you reopen a session document, the previous settings on the PRE are restored. This is a huge help for maintaining consistency in your levels and overall sound throughout multiple songs, recording dates, and overdub sessions. Many other high-quality microphone preamps are available; each has a unique sound (and often additional options for processing or otherwise coloring the sound prior to the Pro Tools input), and many even offer digital outputs that can be connected to your audio interface.

Combining a multichannel Pro Tools system with external reverbs, compressors, and other effects is simple using sends or hardware I/O inserts (routed through the inputs/outputs of your audio interface). As a Pro Tools user, though, you're more likely to build up the majority of your arsenal for effects processing via plug-ins rather than stacking up boxes in your studio racks.

If you have multiple digital audio devices in your studio, you might also investigate the master audio clock generators that are available (also known as *word clock* or *word sync*). Slaving all your Pro Tools audio hardware, multitrack digital recorders, DAT recorders, digital effects and patchbays, and so on to a single clock source can make life much simpler, facilitating digital transfers and phase-accurate playback. As when using a synchronization peripheral to slave your audio hardware to a house sync (black burst) video signal, having the playback speed of all your playback and recording devices precisely slaved together at the hardware level reduces lock-up times and facilitates the maintenance of sync over extended periods of time. Extremely high-quality clock sources can also audibly improve sonic quality, especially on older hardware and less expensive audio interfaces.

Avid periodically offers hardware upgrades at a reduced price for existing users, especially when introducing new hardware. Be sure to check out the available exchanges for Pro Tools|HD hardware, older (blue) HD-series interfaces, and older control surfaces when considering an upgrade.

Also, be sure to consider what *other* equipment upgrades may be required by any Pro Tools system upgrade. For example, your existing hard disk setup for an older Pro Tools 24|Mix configuration with a single eight-channel interface may be entirely inadequate for 32 simultaneous channels of 24-bit, 96-kHz audio with a current system.

Pro Tools|HD Native

Pro Tools|HD Native is a powerful and relatively inexpensive option for Pro Tools users looking to upgrade to the power of Pro Tools HD. A Pro Tools|HD Native system is comprised of a Pro Tools|HD Native PCIe card and one or more Pro Tools HD-series audio interfaces. The HD Native card supports up to four audio interfaces, for a maximum of 64 channels of simultaneous I/O. Only one HD Native card can be installed in a system at any time.

Pro Tools|HD Native systems utilize the processing power of the host computer (host-based processing) for all mixing operations and plug-in processing. As such, the HD Native card does not provide on-board DSP processing power for Pro Tools. However, the card does include a single, high-powered FPGA processor to handle real-time routing and low-latency monitoring. The FPGA provides a high-speed data path to and from HD-series interfaces, which allows for extremely small buffering between the I/O and the host computer and also provides a low-latency mixer path inside the card itself.

Pro Tools|HD Systems

Pro Tools|HD systems are comprised of a single HD Core card with one or more optional HD Accel cards and one or more Pro Tools HD-series audio interfaces. The HD Core card supports up to two interfaces for up to 32 channels of simultaneous I/O. Each additional HD Accel card also supports up to two interfaces. Audio interfaces can be connected to each HD Accel card in a system, up to a maximum configuration of 160 channels of I/O.

Each Pro Tools|HD card (HD Core and HD Accel) includes nine DSP chips (200 MHz processors) that provide processing power and voices for the Pro Tools mixer and TDM plug-ins. A Pro Tools|HD 2 system, which includes an HD Core card and a single HD Accel card, provides up to 192 voiced tracks for the software (the maximum for Pro Tools|HD hardware systems).

Pro Tools|HDX Systems

Pro Tools|HDX systems are comprised of one or more Pro Tools|HDX cards with one or more Pro Tools HD-series audio interfaces. Each HDX card supports up to four audio interfaces, for up to 64 channels of simultaneous I/O. Each additional card adds support for four additional interfaces, up to a maximum configuration of 3 cards, 12 interfaces, and a massive 192 channels of I/O.

Each Pro Tools|HDX card includes 18 DSP chips with 350-MHz processors, providing five times the processing power to Pro Tools as the older Pro Tools|HD cards. A Pro Tools|HDX system with a single HDX card provides up to 256 voiced tracks for the software. A maximum configuration of three HDX cards provides up to an astounding 768 voiced tracks.

Pro Tools HD-Series Interfaces

HD-series audio interfaces include the older blue audio interfaces from Digidesign (192 I/O, 192 Digital I/O, 96 I/O, and 96i I/O) as well as the current Avid HD interfaces (HD OMNI, HD I/O, and HD MADI). Any of these interfaces can be used with any Pro Tools|HD Native, Pro Tools|HD, or Pro Tools|HDX system.

Among the HD-series interfaces, the older 192 I/O, 192 Digital I/O, and 96 I/O as well as the current HD OMNI and HD I/O each have an Expansion port, where you can directly connect a second HD audio interface via DigiLink cable. The primary port on the interface connects to the appropriate card on your HD system (Pro Tools|HD Native card, HD Core or HD Accel card, or Pro Tools|HDX card).

96 I/O. The 96 I/O provides 16 simultaneous channels of I/O (from the 20 available I/O connections). For each channel pair, you can select among eight analog ins/outs, ADAT Lightpipe I/O, AES/EBU digital I/O (XLR connectors), and S/PDIF digital I/O (coaxial or optical). This audio interface supports sample rates of 96, 88.2, 48, and 44.1 kHz.

96i I/O. The 96i I/O provides 16 analog inputs and two analog outputs (all with 1/4-inch TRS jacks) and S/PDIF digital I/O with RCA jacks only (no AES/EBU or ADAT Lightpipe). The gain on inputs 1–4 can be continuously varied via software (Hardware Setup) between –12.0 dBV and +4 dBu, while inputs 5–16 can be switched via software between –8 dBV and +4 dBu.

192 I/O. The 192 I/O also supports a maximum of 16 channels of simultaneous I/O and sample rates up to 192 kHz. It features an I/O card bay, where you can install eight additional analog inputs, analog outputs, or digital I/O. This would allow you to use up to 16 analog, ADAT, or TDIF inputs or outputs simultaneously. The basic interface includes eight channels of analog I/O via DB-25 connectors; these require separate breakout cables. It provides up to 16 channels of 48-kHz ADAT Lightpipe digital I/O (two sets of eight, the second of which can alternatively be configured for optical S/PDIF at even higher sample rates), eight channels of Tascam TDIF I/O, eight channels of AES/EBU digital I/O (accessed via a second 25-pin D connector, identical to that used for TDIF), plus two additional channels of standard S/PDIF or AES/EBU digital I/O. The 192 I/O also offers real-time sample-rate conversion on incoming digital signals and includes a soft-clip limiting feature. Again, any 16 of the ports on this interface can be active simultaneously. If you have both the 192 I/O and a 96 I/O on your system, the 192 1/O should always be the first interface connected to the Pro Tools|HD card. A DigiLink cable connects from the Expansion port on the first interface to the Primary port of the second interface.

192 Digital I/O. The 192 Digital I/O is similar to the 192 I/O, without the eight-channel analog input and output sections and with a second digital section. The base unit has two sets of ADAT Lightpipe inputs/outputs (16 channels), plus two TDIF connectors (another 16 channels), plus two additional channels of standard S/PDIF or AES/EBU digital I/O. It additionally provides 16 channels of single-wire AES/EBU I/O (or up to eight channels of dual-wire AES/EBU I/O at a 192-kHz sample rate) via two 25-pin D connectors. DB25 connector breakout cables are available for the AES/EBU channels from these interfaces to standard XLR AES/EBU digital connectors.

HD OMNI. The HD OMNI audio interface features 4 channels of analog input, 8 channels of analog output (perfect for surround mixing), 24-bit converters, and sample rates up to 192 kHz. In addition to its analog I/O, HD OMNI provides 8 channels of ADAT I/O (supporting S/MUX II and IV), 2 × 8 channels of AES/EBU I/O, and 2 channels of S/PDIF I/O.

HD OMNI is unique among the HD-series interfaces in that it includes a compact built-in pre-amp, allowing you to record from microphone sources without requiring a separate preamp peripheral. The interface also provides monitoring controls, Main and ALT speaker selections, and a dedicated cue path for artist headphone mixes. Its built-in, customizable monitor mixer allows you to monitor external sources independently from your recording setup—even when Pro Tools isn't running. This is great for hooking up a CD or DVD player, or an external instrument such as a keyboard or drum machine. HD OMNI provides an attractive and affordable I/O solution for music production/recording and post-production studios.

HD I/O. The successor to the 192 I/O, Avid's HD I/O is a multichannel digital audio interface featuring 24-bit converters and supporting sample rates up to 192 kHz. HD I/O is available in one of three standard configurations: 8 × 8 × 8 (8 analog in, 8 analog out, and 8 digital in and out), 16 × 16 analog in and out, and 16 × 16 digital in and out. The interface also provides standard digital I/O in all configurations, with built-in sample rate conversion. The I/O configuration can also be expanded by installing an HD I/O option card into any empty bay or customized by replacing cards for a desired configuration.

All configurations include two channels of AES/EBU I/O (supporting 192 kHz single-wire), two channels of S/PDIF I/O, and eight channels of ADAT I/O (supporting S/MUX II and IV).

HD MADI. HD MADI is a 64-channel digital audio interface that supports the Multichannel Audio Digital Interface (MADI) format at sample rates of up to 192 kHz.

HD MADI provides simplified connectivity between Pro Tools|HD systems and MADI-compatible audio equipment, such as routers, digital mixing consoles, VENUE systems (with the MADI option), and converters.

Slave Clock Connections on Your Audio Interfaces   When Pro Tools configurations have multiple HD interfaces, they are cabled together via their Loop Sync ports. This aligns their audio sample clocks to maintain sample-accurate synchronization between them at the hardware level. The Loop Sync output of the primary interface is connected to the Loop Sync input of the secondary interface, and so on through the others. (Like most word-clock ports, these have BNC connectors.) Finally, the Loop Sync output of the last HD audio interface is connected back to the Loop Sync *input* on the first device.

Alternatively, as mentioned previously, you could also slave the Pro Tools audio interfaces—and all the other digital audio gear in your studio—to a centralized clock source in a star configuration. Ideally, this clock source would be a standalone unit, such as the highly accurate clock generators available from Lucid Audio and others, although an extra-stable sample clock output from certain high-end devices or an add-in card on several digital mixers might also serve this purpose.

One last note about HD-series interfaces: In addition to the 12-foot DigiLink cable supplied with each card and the 18-inch DigiLink cable supplied with each HD audio interface, you can also order cables in 25-, 50-, or even 100-foot lengths. This enables you to move one or all of your audio interfaces into the studio or soundstage, eliminating long runs of analog cabling (and the associated potential for noise, hum, and RF interference) from the input path to the analog-digital converters on your HD audio interface. The maximum length for 192-kHz operation is 50 feet, while at 96-kHz operation, 100-foot DigiLink cable lengths are supported.

DSP Plug-Ins   One of the most attractive features of Pro Tools is the ability to expand its functionality through additional plug-ins and other auxiliary software. Developers are constantly introducing new software, plug-ins, and upgrades for their Pro Tools–compatible products.

Since the introduction of Pro Tools|HD, an entire generation of plug-ins has emerged that take advantage of the TDM processing architecture and DSP chips available on HD cards. Here are a few notable effects-processing examples:

- **ReVibe (Avid).** This room-modeling reverb supports 5.x surround formats, with independent reverb, early reflection, and level controls for the rear channels.

- **Impact (Avid).** This compressor plug-in supports surround formats up to 7.1. It's mainly designed for applying console-style compression on the mix bus (that is, on the Master Fader track for your mix output path that is the source for bouncing your mixdown to disk), although it also supports sidechaining and has many other applications. Impact's sound and the simulated ballistic characteristics of its onscreen gain-reduction meters emulate classic compressors used on mixing consoles.

- **Smack! (Avid).** This compressor/limiter plug-in supports multichannel formats, offering controllable harmonic distortion and sidechaining, with many tonal coloration possibilities that are especially useful for music applications.

- **Massenburg Design Works Hi-Res Parametric EQ.** This plug-in offers five fully adjustable bands of EQ, each of which can function as a boost/dip, low-pass/high-pass, or low-shelf/high-shelf filter. All bands offer 6-dB/octave slopes for the low- and high-pass filter mode; band 5 also supports 18- or 24-dB/octave slopes. Frequency selections are available from 10 Hz to 41 kHz. This EQ plug-in can be used on mono, stereo, or multichannel tracks. It emulates the constant-shape reciprocal filter curves of Massenburg's own GML 8200 parametric filter, a high-end stereo hardware unit. Many parametric EQ plug-ins are available for Pro Tools, but when the *inventor* of the parametric EQ (not to mention award-winning producer, engineer, and sound designer) puts one out, it's worth a listen!

- **Forte Suite (Focusrite).** This plug-in emulates a channel strip on Focusrite's high-end Forte recording console from the mid-1980s, using physical modeling to simulate the vintage ISA 110 EQ, plus the expander, gate, de-esser, and surround compressor from the 130 series (with sidechaining capability) for multiple effects in a single plug-in instance.

■ **TL Space TDM (Trillium Lane Labs).** Among other things, this convolution reverb simulates reverberant spaces as well as well-known digital, spring, and plate reverbs. It can use up to eight DSP chips to accomplish its extremely processing-intensive tasks without latency, including multichannel surround configurations. Based on an impulse response (derived from a recording of the ambient space or similar device), TL Space convolves the incoming signal, imposing that space's characteristics upon it. Of particular interest is its online library of impulse responses to simulate new spaces.

■ **Phoenix (Crane Song).** This suite of TDM plug-ins emulates analog tape compression as one more mastering tool for increasing apparent loudness without increasing gain. Five separate plug-in components are included: Luminescent, Iridescent, Radiant, Dark Essence, and Luster. Each provides diverse characters and degrees of coloration and is based on Crane Song's proprietary Harmonically Enhanced Digital Device (HEDD) technology.

■ **Eventide Anthology II bundle (Eventide).** This plug-in suite provides 15 classic Eventide effects, including two channel-strip modules, EQ45 parametric EQ, EQ65 filters, H3000 Band delays, Quadravox, H949 and H910 harmonizer pitch shifters, phaser, flanger, and dynamics. Also included are reverb algorithms from Eventide's DSP4000, Eclipse, and Orville hardware units, with 3-band parametric EQ provided both before and after the reverb.

■ **Sonic NoNOISE (Sonic Solutions).** This extremely powerful tool for audio restoration (removal of broadband noise, peak distortion, clicks, crackling, hum, and buzz) can also be used as an AudioSuite process, but it requires Pro Tools|HD hardware for real-time operation.

With the introduction of Pro Tools|HDX hardware and the new AAX plug-in format, DSP plug-ins will need to evolve to take advantage of these newer, more powerful standards. The DSP chips on Pro Tools|HDX cards will run AAX plug-ins but not the older TDM plug-ins. On the other hand, the DSP chips on Pro Tools|HD cards are not compatible with the new AAX plug-in format.

Time will tell how exhaustive third-party developers are in porting their existing TDM plug-ins to the AAX format; however, the new format offers compelling advantages. A great many HDX-compatible AAX plug-ins are likely to emerge in the coming months.

003 and Digi 002 Systems

Although both of these product lines have been discontinued, the 003 and Digi 002 family audio interfaces continue to be fully supported in Pro Tools 10. The audio interfaces offer enough inputs for recording up to 18 channels simultaneously: eight mic, line, or D/I analog channels; eight ADAT Lightpipe channels; and two S/PDIF digital channels (see Figure 18.1). For many musical applications, however, eight analog inputs may not be enough.

Figure 18.1 Analog and digital audio connectors on the 003 Rack.

Standalone mic preamps with digital outputs can be used to expand your analog input capacity (budget permitting), through either the S/PDIF or Lightpipe input sections on a 003 or Digi 002 interface. Mono, stereo, and eight-channel models are available, according to your requirements and budget. Here are just a few examples:

- **ART Digital MPA.** Dual channels with hardware inserts, S/PDIF, AES/EBU, and Lightpipe digital output, sample rates up to 192 kHz.

- **dbx 386.** Part of the "silver" series. Dual pre channels with a tube preamp section. Includes S/PDIF and AES/EBU digital outputs and supports sample rates up to 96 kHz.

- **Joemeek TwinQ/OneQ.** Dual or single channel, with 4-band EQ, enhancer, de-esser, compression, analog inserts, and digital output in AES/EBU or coaxial/optical S/PDIF format, supporting sample rates up to 96 kHz. A word clock input is also provided.

- **Aphex 1788A.** High end. Eight-channel microphone preamp with optional digital output card for ADAT Lightpipe, TDIF, and AES/EBU supporting sample rates up to 96 kHz (although 48 kHz is the highest sample rate supported for Lightpipe). A word clock input is also provided. Includes a built-in limiter for the microphone inputs. Can be remote-controlled via MIDI from Mac/Windows software or from Aphex's optional 1788RC hardware controller to keep analog cable runs from microphones as short as possible. (Also controllable from D-Control and D-Command.)

- **PreSonus DigiMax D8 and DigiMax FS.** Mid to high end. Both models feature eight class A XMAX mic preamps and 24-bit ADAT digital output. While the D8 supports 44.1- and 48-kHz sample rates, the FS can support up to 96 kHz. The FS model also offers word-clock input and output as well as direct outputs and inserts on every channel, while the D8 offers the choice of using external sync via a BNC word-clock input and direct outputs on every channel but no inserts.

- **Focusrite ISA 220 (mono) or ISA 430mkII (dual) with optional digital output board.** High end, with parametric/shelving EQ, compressor, de-esser, and optional 430mkII ADC digital output card supporting S/PDIF (optical or coaxial), AES/EBU, word-clock and Digidesign SuperClock output, and sample rates up to 192 kHz.

- **Focusrite OctoPre/OctoPre LE.** The OctoPre provides eight channels with compression/limiting and word-clock input/output, plus S/PDIF and AES/EBU, via an optional digital output card (plus optional Lightpipe digital outputs) that can be installed in the back panel, supporting sample rates up to 96 kHz. The OctoPre LE is a more economical version that also supports the digital output option for Lightpipe.

- **Focusrite LIQUID4PRE.** Four-channel physical modeling unit for more than 40 mic preamps (with more downloadable online), with Lightpipe and AES/EBU digital I/O and BNC connection for word-clock sync, controllable from within the Pro Tools software (and/or with the D-Command, D-Control, and VENUE control surfaces) via an included RTAS or TDM plug-in, which also allows storing up to 99 presets and locking the front panel against unwanted alterations to this preamp's settings. Supports sample rates up to 192 kHz.

On a 003 Rack or Digi 002 Rack system, you can use an Avid control surface to have physical faders and transport controls plus knobs/sliders for controlling the volume and pan controls, send levels, plug-in parameters, and so on within the Pro Tools software.

You can also add a high-quality digital word-clock source to a 003 or 002 system. (Options from Apogee, Lucid, and other companies are listed in Appendix B.)

Pro Tools Mbox Systems

The Pro Tools Mbox family represents the third generation of the Mbox platform for Pro Tools. The Mbox family includes the Mbox Mini, Mbox, and Mbox Pro. The Mbox Mini provides two channels of analog audio input, one of which includes a microphone input option, and two channels of analog output. This unit does not include digital inputs and thus its I/O cannot be expanded. The Mbox also provides two channels of analog audio input and output; however, both input channels include microphone input options. Additionally, this unit includes two channels of S/PDIF digital input and output, which are available independent of the analog inputs and outputs (see Figure 18.2). As such, this unit's I/O can be expanded using appropriate digital devices. Similarly, the Mbox Pro provides six analog inputs (four of which include microphone input options) and six analog outputs, supplemented by two channels of independent S/PDIF digital input and output.

Figure 18.2 You can use the analog and digital connections on the Mbox independently for 4 × 4 operation.

For audio interfaces with a digital input, one attractive option is a high-end mic preamp with digital output. While recording or monitoring a digital input, the internal sample clock of the audio interface can be slaved to an external mic preamp. Some MIDI modules and guitar/bass preamps also offer S/PDIF digital outputs. Using digital audio connections wherever possible can reduce accumulated background noise in your projects—especially after you layer up many tracks—and makes managing input levels much simpler.

Mbox 2 Systems (Discontinued)

The Mbox 2 offers up to four simultaneous channels if you use both the stereo analog and digital inputs simultaneously (see Figure 18.3). However, its S/PDIF digital *output* always mirrors analog outputs 1–2. The Mbox 2 Pro can record six separate inputs: Channels 1–2 can be switched between two combo XLR/TRS microphone inputs on the rear panel or two DI instrument-level inputs with TS jacks on the front panel. The Aux In inputs on the rear panel can be switched between line-level TRS jacks or a phono preamp with RCA jacks, and appear as channels 3–4 in Pro Tools. It also has stereo S/PDIF I/O that is independent of the other inputs. In contrast, the Mbox 2 Mini offers only stereo analog I/O (TRS connectors for both channels 1–2, which can be switched between line and instrument, plus an XLR mic input that can alternatively be selected for channel 1). All Mbox 2 family interfaces are still fully supported in Pro Tools 10.

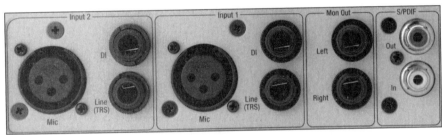

Figure 18.3 Analog and digital connections on the Mbox 2.

Similar to the Pro Tools Mbox and Mbox Pro interfaces discussed above, the Mbox 2 and Mbox 2 Pro can be expanded by adding a mic preamp with S/PDIF digital outputs.

The Original Mbox

The original (first-generation) Mbox is no longer supported in Pro Tools. This interface was limited to two simultaneous inputs and two simultaneous outputs—from either the combo connectors for analog input *or* the S/PDIF connectors (RCA) for stereo digital I/O.

M-Audio Systems

Many of the M-Audio interfaces that are compatible with Pro Tools include S/PDIF digital inputs. For these, the options discussed above for high-quality mic preamps with digital outputs also apply. The ProjectMix I/O (which, like the NRV10, incorporates a control surface) and ProFire 2626 also offer ADAT Lightpipe I/O, so any of the previously listed multichannel mic preamps with Lightpipe digital output would also be an excellent complement to these units. In addition to the capability to slave the interface's sample clock to a selected digital input (shared by all M-Audio interfaces that have an S/PDIF and/or ADAT Lightpipe input), the ProjectMix I/O also includes BNC connectors exclusively dedicated to word-clock input and output.

Upgrade Path: For Your Mind

In Appendix A, "Further Study and Resources on the Web," you'll find a few suggestions for further study, including websites, CD-ROM training, magazines, and books. Regardless of what further study you undertake, the most important thing is to try to make some time in your schedule to explore Pro Tools. Experiment with unusual mixing effects and other offbeat ideas to build up your arsenal of techniques. Also, take advantage of opportunities to work on projects with your Pro Tools system that are completely outside your daily routine. If your audio-engineering work with Pro Tools mainly involves video post, take on a CD-mastering project for a local band. If you're mainly a music mixer, record a spoken-word piece—perhaps a narration for a training piece, a local poet reciting her work, a family history, a radio spot, or what have you. The out-of-left-field requests from clients can take you into areas of Pro Tools—not to mention into effects applications and signal-routing techniques—that you may not have explored before. You're guaranteed to learn something along the way that will prove useful in your regular work.

Career Options

Pro Tools is used in music-production studios, video-production houses, film studios, radio- and television-broadcast stations, film and historical archives, record companies, multimedia development houses, and audiobook publishing houses. If you are trying to establish yourself as a Pro Tools operator, don't wait around for the perfect job to materialize. Get out there and visit the production houses in your community—even if no positions are currently available. Ask to see their installations and inquire about how they operate. Remember that *any* job that keeps you working in Pro Tools on a daily basis will help you hone your skills with the program. Even if your ambition is music production, many of the Pro Tools techniques you master while posting industrial videos or recording spoken-word bits for web and CD-ROM projects will carry over into subsequent phases of your career.

If you are a musician using Pro Tools in your own home-project studio, consider working for some other local clients. Take out an ad out in the local paper and offer to record singer/songwriter demos at a fixed rate for a fixed number of hours, including a CD copy at the end of the session. Of course, you will have to fix the parameters of the services you offer according to your system's capabilities; if you have only one or two microphones, you can't have a whole steel-drum band trooping into the basement or spare bedroom! Be aggressive in your initial pricing. If you do a good job, a fair percentage of these people will book additional hours and subsequent sessions. Even with a single microphone, any Pro Tools system is perfectly equipped to record oral histories or any other spoken-word piece, such as an author or poet reading her work or corporate-training and motivational presentations.

With many of the more portable systems (for instance, an Mbox interface with a current Mac or Windows laptop), you can go on site to record, making your service even more attractive. Again, you're guaranteed to learn something along the way, improving your Pro Tools chops. For that matter, if you have a high-quality matched pair of microphones, you can even record local music and theater performances on location with your luggable Pro Tools rig. If you have a high-quality handheld digital recorder or DAT, you can take that out instead for on-location recording and then transfer the recording to Pro Tools for editing and mastering of the CD.

As another option, offer to record demos of friends or associates looking for voice-over work. Interactive media developers are increasingly contracting voice talent directly. If your collaboration with the talent can deliver finished voice-over files in immediately usable formats (see Chapter 15 for more information), you both stand to make some money.

Maintaining a Learning Attitude and Finding Additional Resources

This book has pursued two objectives: first, to provide a quick start for novice Pro Tools users, condensing the most essential concepts, features, and techniques in order to help you become productive with Pro Tools in the shortest time possible; and second, to provide useful suggestions for people already using the program, including insights that will be helpful even for experienced operators.

This is just a start, however. If you've spent some time with the excellent manuals and PDF documentation Avid provides with Pro Tools, you've surely noticed many additional keyboard shortcuts, tool modes, parameters, dialog-box selections, and other application-specific information that are not covered in the pages of this book. Of course this book doesn't provide space for a truly exhaustive discussion of all things Pro Tools, but beyond that, we've deliberately sought to narrow the focus somewhat. Building on the essential facts, this book aims to walk you through typical situations for applying Pro Tools features rather than taking the one-size-fits-all, purely descriptive approach that a technical manual necessarily follows.

You will find it worthwhile to read the Avid documentation. Take a printout of the *Pro Tools Reference Guide* home or out to lunch with you (after you've finished *this* book, of course). Print out the *Keyboard Shortcuts* document, make notes to yourself about shortcuts and features you want to remember, and post them around your keyboard and monitor.

Make time to experiment with features and techniques; try something excessive! Seek out other Pro Tools users and spend time with them as they work. You can always pick up something—even from users who, in theory, are less technically grounded in Pro Tools than you are. If your Pro Tools work is routinely in a single field (such as audio for video, for example), you can pick up some great ideas by collaborating with other Pro Tools operators who use the program for something completely different, such as music production or multimedia.

Many learning resources are available out there. A few suggestions are collected in Appendix A. The Avid website includes the Digi User Conference online forum, plus an excellent technical-document library with downloadable reference guides for its software and hardware add-ons for Pro Tools. The Avid site also sells books, DVDs, and online Pro Tools training, and includes past copies of the free online *DigiZine*. Other learning options for Pro Tools users include courses and certification options offered by Avid Learning Partners. In Appendix A, you will also find suggestions for further study.

Summary

As a Pro Tools user, you're involved with one of the most popular and powerful audio tools available. If you're just breaking into the business, make some calls to local production facilities—not only to network, but also to learn how they work with Pro Tools. Collaborating with many Pro Tools users over time will illustrate that there's rarely a single best way to do things. Every time you sit by and observe while another Pro Tools user works (at any level), you have a chance to learn something new. Don't stop there, though; find an opportunity to teach someone *else* how to use Pro Tools. Not only is this a swell thing to do, but as anyone who has ever taught will tell you, in the process of clarifying your ideas for someone else's benefit, you will attain a higher level of knowledge yourself.

The following appendixes provide additional technical information, tips (be sure to check out Appendix D, "Power Tips and Loopy Ideas," if you're already an experienced Pro Tools user), resources for further study, plus information about archive and backup.

Thanks for reading. Here's to your success with Pro Tools 10 and beyond!

Appendix A: Further Study and Resources on the Web

You may wish to dig deeper into digital audio, sound recording in general, or MIDI, depending on your interests and immediate requirements. Even those who have been at this for years can find something new and interesting to study. What follows here is a very brief overview of resources for learning more about subjects related to Pro Tools.

Books about Audio

When you're ready to read more about digital audio in general and Pro Tools in particular, use this list as a starting point:

- *Digital Audio Explained: For the Audio Engineer* by Nika Aldrich. Published in 2004 by Sweetwater Press, this is one of the best sources for practical information about digital audio. The author provides in-depth, clearly written explanations about sample rate, bit depth, digital filters, ADC/DAC design, sample clocking, dithering, and other key concepts. If the rudimentary digital audio concepts in Chapters 1 and 2 of this book were all news to you, this is a great place to start. A key chapter—and required reading for experienced digital audio workstation cosmonauts—is "The Myths of Digital Audio."

- *Pro Tools 101: An Introduction to Pro Tools 10* by Frank D. Cook. Published in 2011 by Course Technology, this is the latest edition of Avid's official Pro Tools 101 book and represents the first course in the Avid Learning Series supporting Pro Tools certification. This book takes a comprehensive approach to the fundamentals of Pro Tools systems and includes hands-on exercises and projects utilizing media on the included DVD-ROM.

- Earlier editions of *Pro Tools Power!* by Colin MacQueen, Steve Albanese, and Christopher R. Burns. Editions of this book for Pro Tools 5 (2001), Pro Tools 6 (2004), Pro Tools 7 (2007), and Pro Tools 8 (2010) by Course Technology PTR are predecessors to this book and serve as the foundation upon which this book has been built. Users on older systems will find these earlier editions to be useful.

- *Digital Audio Dictionary* by Colin MacQueen and Steve Albanese. Published in 1999 by Howard W. Sams & Co., this is a large glossary in book form.

- *Principles of Digital Audio,* Sixth Edition by Ken C. Pohlmann. Published in 2010 by McGraw-Hill and first published in the 1980s, this is still a respected source for a technical, theoretical grounding in digital audio.

- *Sound Recording Handbook* by John Woram. Published in 1989 by Financial Times Prentice Hall, this book provides in-depth information about recording in general—analog *and* digital audio—at a rewardingly technical level.

- *Practical Recording Techniques,* Fifth Edition by Bruce and Jenny Bartlett. Published in 2008 by Focal Press, this book provides information on all aspects of recording. This book is commonly used in college audio recording programs.

- *Audio Production Techniques for Video* by David Miles Huber. This book was published in 1987 and again in 1992 by Butterworth-Heinemann. It provides in-depth post-production information, including all the "old school" techniques.

- *Modern Recording Techniques,* Seventh Edition by David Miles Huber and Robert E. Runstein. Published in 2009 by Focal Press, this is an excellent reference for digital audio and for audio recording in general. This book is used in many schools and universities.

- *Handbook of Recording Engineering,* Fourth Edition by John Eargle. Published in 2002 by Springer, this is a comprehensive reference work about general audio recording.

- *Handbook for Sound Engineers,* Fourth Edition edited by Glen Ballou. Published in 2008 by Elsevier, this is the current version of a series descended from the Audio Cyclopedia. This book is a massive and authoritative reference resource, providing deep, detailed technical information on a wide range of audio topics.

- *The Art of Mixing,* Second Edition by David Gibson. Published in 2005 by Course Technology PTR, this is a thought-provoking book about mixing from a visual perspective; a little offbeat, but applicable to any analog/digital mixing environment.

- *The Art of Digital Audio Recording: A Practical Guide for Home and Studio* by Steve Savage. Published in 2011 by Oxford University Press, this book provides a practical and comprehensive introduction to today's recording environments, including both technical and non-technical, aesthetic considerations.

- *Mastering Audio: The Art and the Science,* Second Edition by Bob Katz. Published in 2007 by Focal Press, this is an excellent discussion of both analog and digital audio principles, dithering, jitter, bit-depth and sample-rate issues, noise reduction, equalization, metering, and other good stuff.

- *Pro Tools for Video, Film, and Multimedia,* Second Edition by Ashley Shepherd. Published in 2008 by Course Technology PTR, this book covers mixing/sync and delivery formats, and describes Pro Tools editing and mixing techniques in general.

Magazines

- *Electronic Musician*
- *Keyboard*
- *Mix*

- *Recording*
- *EQ* (now merged with *Electronic Musician*)
- *Sound on Sound*
- *Tape Op*
- *Computer Music*
- *Future Music*
- *Music Tech*

www.avid.com

Be sure to thoroughly investigate the Support & Services section on the Avid website, where you will find links for the Avid Knowledgebase, downloads, support plans, and training. The Training section is especially useful for learning about the worldwide training and certification options offered through Avid Learning Partners.

Avid also posts a majority of the manuals and Read Me files for their hardware and software products on their website. These resources can be extremely useful when you're trying to figure out if an expansion option or upgrade is suitable for your system. Information is also provided about technical support and customer service, as well as hardware exchange offers for users upgrading to newer or more powerful systems.

DAE Errors   If you ever get an error message from Pro Tools citing a DAE error number, you can research this problem on Avid's website. Go to the Avid Knowledgebase and type the error number into the Search field to see possible causes and remedies for your problem.

Other Useful Websites

In addition to the Avid website, you'll find scores of other useful websites for the audio engineer:

- **duc.avid.com.** The Avid Audio Forums, known as the Digi User Conference (DUC), are free forums hosted by Avid, with sections for Pro Tools 10, Pro Tools 9, Pro Tools|HD Systems, Post and Surround, Live Sound, and more. New users may find it useful to lurk here for a while—it's a great forum for Pro Tools users at any level. Aside from the occasional user rants and squabbles found on any online forum, you'll find some pretty smart folks here offering productive advice and opinions. The forum is also very active on nights and weekends; the advice you obtain from other users might get you out of a jam sometime. Just be sure to include an actual question or topic in the subject line of your post (as opposed to, say, "Help!") and specify exactly which version of Pro Tools software you're using so that people can help you. Even veteran Pro Tools users find good content here.

- **www.harmony-central.com.** Topics here range from gear-related, technical, and music business to just plain silly (not that there's anything wrong with that!). Of particular interest to Pro Tools users: the Recording forum; Phil O'Keefe's In the Studio Trenches forum; Craig Anderton's Sound, Studio & Stage forum; and Nuestro Foro (en español).

- **www.musicplayer.com.** This site includes forums related to music and audio. Of particular interest to Pro Tools users: Ethan Winer's Acoustics forum, the Project Studio forum, and the Keyboard Corner.

- **www.synthzone.com.** This site has a little bit of everything: links to manufacturers, to sites dedicated to MIDI instruments, to dealers, to MIDI software, to alternate tunings, to information about soundcards and audio hardware, and to digital audio workstation software.

- **digitalprosound.digitalmedianet.com.** This site features a collection of information about products and techniques related to professional digital audio. The Tutorials section includes articles about podcasting, noise reduction, voice-over techniques, various audio and video programs, ADR looping, soldering, and building portable sound booths, to name just a few.

- **www.recording.org.** This general audio website includes forums about digital audio workstations and other topics. Within the DAW area, you may find occasional posts about Pro Tools, Avid hardware, and related topics. As with all online forums, the experience and maturity level of members here run the full gamut.

- **www.gearslutz.com.** In these online forums, you will find both project studio folks and industry heavy-hitters, with threads about studio gear, digital audio, mastering, and post-production, as well as discussions about many computer-based audio/MIDI programs, including Pro Tools.

- **www.tapeop.com.** This is the companion website for a bimonthly magazine (available by free online subscription) about music recording, with tips and gear reviews plus excellent interviews with engineers, producers, and artists. *Tape Op* maintains a refreshingly practical focus, placing more emphasis on how-to's and how-they-did-it than on glamour profiles of the latest electronic gizmos. Online forums can also be found on this site.

- **www.aes.org.** This is the Audio Engineering Society's website. Although you must be a member to access the online journal and some other areas, the technical articles in PDF format are available to anyone visiting the site, as are most of the standards documents (including the society's *Recommended Practices* documents). For digging deeper into technical aspects of audio production, this is one of the most reliable sources available. Pro Tools audio professionals especially should read the 2003 document AESTD1002.1.03-10, "Recommendation for Delivery of Recorded Music Projects," found in the Technical Documents section. Among other things, this document suggests Broadcast WAV Format (BWF) as the standard delivery format for digital audio files; lists recommended sample rates; provides printable forms for recording, mixing, and duplication notes; and provides track sheets, delivery labels for analog and digital media, and an excellent (albeit brief) technical glossary.

- **www.midi.org.** This official website of the MIDI Manufacturers Association provides technical information on the MIDI Specification itself, plus proposed and forthcoming standards, much of which is available in downloadable form. A comprehensive About MIDI section includes educational articles about MIDI basics, General MIDI, Standard MIDI Files, and XMF (eXtensible Music Format) files, at both beginning and more-advanced technical depths.

- **www.kvraudio.com.** This website is devoted to news about audio plug-ins, various plug-in hosts, and press releases and announcements of newly released or updated plug-in products. This site is invaluable to those Pro Tools users who have invested in the VST to RTAS Wrapper from FXpansion, which opens up the world of VST plug-ins to Pro Tools users. With a loyal and vast user base, KVR also features extensive forums, as well as cooperation from manufacturers for a database of online support for many products.

- **www.macosxaudio.com.** This site is a massive resource for all things audio for the Macintosh. Pro Tools is duly represented here in the forums, as are many other platforms. In addition to the forums on effects, instruments, and hardware, the site hosts forums delving into the topics of the business of music and audio, music theory, and the development of software.

Schools

Avid Learning Partner schools offer Pro Tools courses and certification. Available courses include Pro Tools 101 (Introduction to Pro Tools), Pro Tools 110 (Pro Tools Production I), Pro Tools 201 (Pro Tools Production II), Pro Tools 210M and 310M (music production techniques), Pro Tools 210P and 310P (post-production techniques), and Pro Tools 310I (ICON mixing techniques). Additional courses that are available through select Avid Learning Partners include Pro Tools 130 (game audio) and Pro Tools 205 (Cl24 or Artist Series control surfaces) as well as VENUE 110V and 210V courses (Live Sound Production I and II). Certification options include Pro Tools User, Pro Tools Operator, and Pro Tools Expert certification; ICON Expert certification; and VENUE Operator certification.

For more information about certification courses and training centers, check out the Training area of Avid's website (www.avid.com/US/support/training). There, you'll also be able to view information on all Avid certification options, review the courses offered in Avid's authorized curriculum (including Pro Tools and VENUE), search for an Avid Learning Partner in your area, view web tutorials, and more.

Appendix B: Add-Ons, Extensions, and Cool Stuff for Your Rig

Tons of options are available for expanding a Pro Tools configuration—through both hardware and software add-ons. Given the number of software plug-ins available for Pro Tools and how quickly they are updated, you should always start by referring to the Avid website for information and confirm the absolute latest versions on each plug-in developer's own website. Accordingly, this appendix concentrates on *hardware* enhancements for various Pro Tools system configurations. Avid offers multiple audio interfaces, additional cards and I/O, the MachineControl option, control surfaces, and so on. Many of the available options are discussed in Chapters 3 and 18. Here are a few other ideas you may find useful.

External Control Surfaces

Using a mouse or trackball to control all the functions in Pro Tools is perfectly practical. Indeed, this is how the vast majority of Pro Tools users operate. Nevertheless, it is often convenient and far more productive to use an external device with dedicated buttons, faders, and so on for hands-on control. For one thing, multiple physical faders allow you to automate mixes on the fly, moving several faders simultaneously and independently. (With a mouse or trackball, of course, you can only drag one slider at a time.) External control surfaces can vary in size and can be placed in the control room for access from various positions by various people if necessary. Having large, tactile transport buttons and illuminated buttons for record-enabling and muting tracks facilitates a more heads-up relationship between the Pro Tools operator and performers or other collaborators. The larger controllers for Pro Tools provide illuminated level meters and illuminated parameter displays for track names, levels, pan, and many other features similar to standalone digital mixers, plus dedicated controls for functions that are specific to Pro Tools. In short, they facilitate rapid, two-fisted operation of Pro Tools, which can dramatically increase productivity—especially when you have a roomful of clients or performers.

ICON Integrated Console Environments

The ICON family of integrated console solutions centers around two control surfaces (or *work-surfaces*, as they have become known) that can be used with Pro Tools: the large-format D-Control (see Figure B.1) and the medium-format D-Command. Both of these offer motorized faders, buttons, rotary encoders, transport control, and signal-routing options. ICON systems also both use the rack-mounted XMON monitoring/cue mix module.

Figure B.1 The D-Control tactile worksurface consists of a main module plus one or more 16-channel fader modules. It can be expanded up to 80 channels/faders.

D-Control

The core D-Control *tactile worksurface* consists of a main module, plus a single 16-channel fader module that can be mounted on either side of the main module. In fall of 2007, D-Control was updated to feature a darker color scheme. Referred to as D-Control ES, this model also includes higher-contrast text and graphics and a new switch LED color layout. Up to four additional fader modules can be added to the base D-Control configuration for a maximum of 80 channel strips/faders.

D-Control provides dedicated LED displays for the Main/Sub time indicators and for the Start, End, and Length fields of the Pro Tools software on the main unit. Dedicated switches activate windows in the Pro Tools software, such as Mix, Edit, Transport, Memory Locations, MIDI Operations, Beat Detective, and others. Additional dedicated switches for Pro Tools functions include the four Edit modes, track height up/down, and Edit menu commands such as Undo, Redo, Cut, Copy, Paste, and Repeat. A Focus channel strip is available in the center main module for editing any selected channel's parameters without leaving the center of the console. In addition, D-Control has dedicated EQ and Dynamics panels on the main module that you can use to control any channel on the fly. D-Control has a built-in alphanumeric keyboard, a two-button trackball, and a shelf for an optional computer monitor or a swinging arm for mounting a flat-panel display. A built-in talkback microphone and switch are also included, with a dedicated monitoring section for internal/external talkback, listenback, input source selectors for the control room, separate level controls for main and near-field monitors, dim and mute buttons, input selection, and separate controls for three cue mixes, as well as level controls for headphone outputs and a feed to loudspeakers out in the studio room. D-Control connects to the Pro Tools system's host computer via Ethernet (10BaseT, with RJ45 connectors).

In addition to touch-sensitive motorized Penny & Giles faders, each channel strip on the fader module has six touch-sensitive multifunction rotary encoders with LED rings to indicate current parameter values or metering. LED meters are provided for each channel strip, plus eight channels of metering for the master section. Each channel strip provides 29 illuminated switches for changing channel modes, attributes, and so on. LED displays indicate channel names or the currently selected editing parameter for each channel strip.

An optional surround panner module is available for D-Control that includes a color LCD touchscreen, two touch-sensitive joysticks, two touch-sensitive rotary encoders with LED rings, and six mode switches for each panner. You can move sources in the surround field by touch using the onscreen icons within the LCD display or by using the joysticks. An AutoGlide function allows programming smooth transitions from one point to the next.

In addition to supporting surround mixing, the included XMON Monitor System provides dedicated outputs used for three separate stereo cue mixes, talkback, listenback, studio monitors, and headphones. XMON connects to D-Control via a single 15-pin cable.

D-Command

D-Command (shown in Figure B.2) is described by Avid as a "mid-format" console. Like the D-Control, D-Command has been updated with the new ES color scheme and improved text and graphics displays. The D-Command main unit features a central control section with monitoring and communications controls and eight touch-sensitive, motorized 100mm channel faders. D-Command communicates with the host Pro Tools computer system via Ethernet. Each channel strip has two rotary encoders with LED rings to show either the current parameter setting or metering. It is expandable up to 40 faders via up to two 16-channel fader modules.

Figure B.2   The D-Command tactile worksurface consists of a main unit with eight channel strips and can be expanded with up to two 16-channel fader modules.

On each channel strip, one six-channel LCD beneath the rotary encoder displays information about the current parameter while another serves as a display strip. Each channel can function independently, in a separate mode from the others. D-Command provides illuminated switches and meters on each channel, plus eight more meters in the center section. The center section has dedicated control panels for EQ (with 12 rotary controls) and dynamics plug-ins (with six rotary controls and dedicated output, gain reduction meters). The Transport controls include a jog/shuttle wheel and dedicated switches for Loop Playback, TrackPunch, QuickPunch, MachineControl, and other functions. D-Command includes the same XMON remote, rack-mounted analog I/O audio monitoring and communications system as D-Control. The monitoring section on D-Command provides control for up to two 5.1 surround inputs, three stereo inputs, and two cue sends.

MC Pro

The compact and ergonomic MC Pro control surface (shown in Figure B.3) came into the Avid family by way of the 2010 Euphonix acquisition. MC Pro connects to a Pro Tools system using EUCON Ethernet control. MC Pro provides programmable SmartSwitches, allowing you to perform complex tasks/keystrokes with a single button press.

Figure B.3 MC Pro control surface.

The MC Pro controller includes a high-resolution touchscreen for easy access to features and operations, an integrated USB keyboard/trackball and jog wheel, high-resolution faders and rotary encoders, 56 programmable SmartSwitches with individual LCD displays, and 9 softknobs for processor and plug-in control. MC Pro provides direct access to Pro Tools functions and commands via the Application Sets installed with Pro Tools and the EuControl software.

System 5-MC

Based on the System 5 digital console and the MC Pro controller, the Avid System 5-MC control surface (shown in Figure B.4) provides tightly integrated, hands-on control of Pro Tools and Pro Tools HD software via the high-speed EUCON Ethernet control protocol. System 5-MC provides a modular architecture that can be expanded to include up to 48 channel strips, each with 8 rotary encoders and a motorized fader.

Figure B.4 System 5-MC control surface.

The System 5-MC controller includes all of the features of MC Pro, plus the benefits provided by System 5 channel strips. Each channel strip features touch-sensitive, motorized faders; dual high-resolution LED meters; 4-character LEDs for track and rotary encoder displays; 8 touch-sensitive rotary encoders; and a high-resolution TFT display showing metering, processor graphs (for EQ and pan), routing, and 12 to 14 character channel names. Like MC Pro, System 5-MC provides direct access to Pro Tools functions and commands via the Application Sets installed with Pro Tools and the EuControl software.

Control|24

Control|24 (shown in Figure B.5) is no longer produced but is still in use in many studios and is fully supported in Pro Tools 10. This unit combines a control surface for Pro Tools with 16 phantom-powered Class A mic/line preamps engineered by Focusrite. The first two channels also include an instrument-level direct box setting. The Control|24 features a surround monitoring section and a built-in talkback microphone for communicating with performers in the studio or onstage. It also includes a dedicated 8 × 2 analog line mixer, which can be useful for submixing multiple keyboards, live feeds from a mixing board, or other outboard devices. Also provided are 24 touch-sensitive 100mm moving faders as well as dedicated EQ and dynamics switches on each channel; illuminated switching for mute, solo, record enable, channel select, and automation buttons for each channel; plus dedicated transport keys with a scrub/shuttle wheel.

Figure B.5   Control|24 control surface (discontinued).

The back panel of the Control|24 has numerous analog connectors, including 16 line/microphone inputs with phantom power, slate and dual aux inputs and outputs, and two DB-25 connectors for connection to Pro Tools audio interfaces via DigiSnake cables (eight output channels each). A third DB-25 connector provides eight outputs for speakers (via a DigiSnake breakout cable). Control|24 communicates with Pro Tools via a 10BaseT Ethernet connection.

C|24

The C|24 control surface (shown in Figure B.6) was introduced in fall of 2007 as an update to the Command|24 model. It includes the features listed above for Control|24 in a redesigned format. The faders are arranged in three banks of eight each, and the LED display strips have two lines of six characters each. The mic input section is a newer design that includes high-pass filters and –20-dB pads on each channel. These mic preamps are based on the 003 design. The 8×2 mixer section can be routed directly to the monitoring section. C|24 also includes an updated 5.1 analog monitoring section with individually trimmable outputs (in 0.5-dB increments) for convenient calibration. Soft keys are also provided for controlling various functions.

Figure B.6   C|24 control surface.

Artist Series Controllers

As discussed in Chapter 3, Avid's Artist Series control surfaces for Pro Tools include the Artist Control, Artist Mix, and Artist Transport. The Artist Series controllers connect to the computer via Ethernet on both Mac and Windows platforms. Artist Series controllers provide tactile control of Pro Tools and Pro Tools HD software as well as direct access to software functions and commands via Application Sets installed with EuControl software. See Chapter 3 for more information on these control surface options.

Mackie Control Universal Pro (MCU Pro)

This control surface by Mackie Designs communicates with Pro Tools via MIDI using the HUI protocol (see Figure B.7). The MCU Pro directly supports a number of other DAW programs, including Logic Pro, Cubase, Nuendo, ACID, SONAR, Digital Performer, and others. Overlays are included for the master section of the unit, showing the program functions for Pro Tools, Cubase, Nuendo, SONAR, and so on.

(Photo courtesy of Mackie.)

Figure B.7 Mackie Control Universal Pro (MCU Pro).

The MCU Pro includes nine motorized, touch-sensitive 100mm faders (eight channel faders plus a master fader), V-pot rotary encoders, and dedicated record, solo, mute, and select buttons on every channel. There are also dedicated Transport buttons, a jog/shuttle wheel for the transport or for scrubbing audio within tracks, a backlit LCD display showing metering and track names, and a dedicated seven-digit display for time code. When used with Pro Tools (and as printed on that overlay for the unit), the MCU Pro has dedicated zoom controls; buttons that directly open the Mix, Edit, Transport, and Memory Location windows; and other buttons for Enter (OK) and Cancel, Undo, and other functions. A Plug-In button switches the LCD display to that view, and V-pots 1–4 control values of plug-in parameters in the currently active plug-in window. The pan button assigns V-pot knobs to that function on all channels. You can also select Pro Tools automation writing modes from dedicated buttons. Additional Mackie Control Extender fader expansion packs (eight channel strips each) can be added to the base unit.

Synchronization Peripherals

As explained in Chapter 11, if you need to synchronize playback and recording of Pro Tools to an external SMPTE time-code source, you must add an external synchronization peripheral to your core Pro Tools configuration. Avid offers the Sync HD, with features to resolve audio-playback speed over extended periods of time to a clock or video reference or to incoming time code. Many third-party peripherals also offer excellent synchronization options at a variety of performance levels and price points. Just a few are mentioned in this section, and new models continually appear, of course. In addition to starting playback or recording at the appropriate time according to *location* information received from SMPTE (or MIDI) time code, all the options listed here offer the additional ability to *slave* (resolve) the internal sample clock of Pro Tools hardware to an external source.

Avid Sync HD

The successor to the Sync I/O, Avid's Sync HD is a high-end synchronization peripheral that connects to Mac or Windows computers via USB (see Figure B.8). It translates SMPTE time code to and from VITC (video) or LTC (audio) format and can resolve (continuously adjust) the sample clock of your audio hardware to keep Pro Tools in sync with incoming time code over extended periods. Alternatively, the Sync HD can resolve the sample clock of the Pro Tools hardware to an external video reference (black burst/house sync), industry-standard word clock (1× the audio sample rate), or SuperClock (a timing reference for audio hardware operating at 256× the sample rate). The Sync HD can *burn* a time-code window into video signals passing through it. Dual Sony 9-pin serial ports can be used to link Pro Tools transport functions with external video/audio devices, if the optional MachineControl software is installed in Pro Tools. The word clock supports up to 192 kHz, as well as standard video and film pull-up or pull-down rates.

Figure B.8 Avid's Sync HD.

MOTU MIDI Timepiece AV (USB)

The MIDI Timepiece AV connects to the host computer via its USB port (see Figure B.9). This rack-mountable interface features eight independent MIDI ins/outs for 128 total MIDI channels, all of which are individually accessible from within Pro Tools (via Audio MIDI Setup on Mac or the supplied MOTU drivers on Windows). This unit includes hardware synchronization outputs (9-pin ADAT sync and word clock), plus a video-sync input. (The video-sync input and the word-clock output have BNC connectors.) You can switch the word clock output between 1× and 256× the sample rate used to slave your Pro Tools hardware to the MTP AV, which in turn you can *genlock* (slave to match frame rates) to the black burst/house sync video signal at its video-sync input. The MTP AV also supports LTC at any SMPTE frame rate, and can convert this to hardware sync (ADAT or Pro Tools SuperClock) for resolving your audio hardware's sample rate to this time-code reference. The MTP AV is also a full-featured MIDI patchbay, merger, and processor. You can access all its features from the front panel during live performance or, more importantly for Pro Tools users, via the included software.

(Photo courtesy of Mark of the Unicorn.)

Figure B.9 MIDI Timepiece AV, a multiport MIDI interface from MOTU, which also offers LTC synchronization.

Word Clock and Sync Generators

As mentioned elsewhere in this book, in studios with multiple digital audio devices, it can be very useful to synchronize the audio sample clocks of all these devices to a single, central source (similar to the way house sync is used in video studios to synchronize frame rates). Obviously, this source's clock must be extremely stable. For some situations—such as recording from a digital source or playing Pro Tools back in sync with a digital multitrack—it may be sufficient to simply lock devices together via word-clock connections on the audio interfaces or use the Clock Source option in the Hardware Setup dialog box to synchronize Pro Tools to the digital input. Some devices generate a stable clock reference as part of their standard features (such as the Finalizer, from TC Electronic, and the Avid Sync HD). Some digital mixers offer an optional card that can provide a stable clock reference to Pro Tools and other digital audio devices. Nevertheless, for larger configurations and especially for demanding, high-resolution audio, professional users will opt for a higher-quality standalone word clock/sync generator to effectively eliminate jitter (sonic artifacts caused by minute variations in the sample clock) that can degrade the sonic image. Here are just a few examples.

Lucid Audio GENx-192

This device from Lucid Audio (see Figure B.10) acts as an extremely stable master clock source for digital audio configurations, at sample rates up to 192 kHz. In addition to 1× word clock, it also directly supports the 256× SuperClock format. This is an amazingly accurate master clock for the price.

(Photo courtesy of Lucid Audio.)

Figure B.10 The GENx-192, by Lucid Audio.

Rosendahl Nanosyncs HD

The Nanosyncs HD supports 1× word clock, 256× SuperClock, AES/EBU sync, and video black burst/house sync, at sample rates up to 96 kHz (see Figure B.11). It incorporates USB connection to a host computer that can generate MIDI time code or provide it to the DAW software by converting it from incoming LTC time code. The Nanosyncs HD has six video outputs (supporting both NTSC and PAL, including high-definition frame rates and Tri-Level Sync), AES/EBU and S/PDIF sync outputs, and eight separately configurable word-clock outputs with BNC connectors.

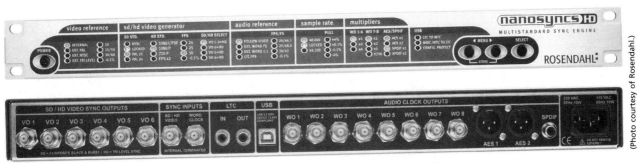

Figure B.11   Front and back panels of the Nanosyncs HD, by Rosendahl.

Apogee Big Ben

This high-end, extremely low-jitter digital clock source from Apogee Electronics supports sample rates up to 192 kHz (see Figure B.12). Inputs/outputs include two AES/EBU digital with XLR connectors, S/PDIF on both coaxial and optical connectors, ADAT Lightpipe, S/MUX II or IV, and six BNC connectors for word clock (1× only for highest sample rates, up to 2× at 96 kHz or 88.1 kHz, or up to 256× at 48 kHz and 44.1 kHz). The SureLock feature maintains steady clock adjustment if there is any interruption (and subsequent reestablishment) of an incoming clock source. With the optional X-Video card, incoming video sync (black burst) or video-sync generation is also supported in PAL or NTSC, with pull-up and pull-down sample rates. The Big Ben also includes a front-panel LCD display for the exact sample rate. When using the Big Ben on HD systems with multiple audio interfaces, attach each directly to the Big Ben via its Ext In word-clock input (with BNC connector) rather than connecting these interfaces together via their LoopSync ports in the usual fashion. Then open the Pro Tools Session Setup window and select Word Clock as the clock source for each of your HD interfaces.

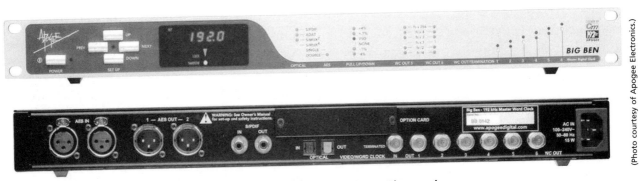

Figure B.12   Front and rear panels of the Big Ben, by Apogee Electronics.

Ergonomics, Rackmounting, Extenders

Let's face it: You spend long hours working at your Pro Tools rig. Whatever helps you to not hunch, stretch, strain, hunt, or squint so much will improve your quality of life! Standard office furniture—and for that matter, typical computer workstation furniture—doesn't always provide the most ergonomic setup for the way you work in Pro Tools. Just how many times a day are you willing to stand up, bend down, step across the room to adjust a mic preamp or effect, arm a DAT for recording, and so on, before it's worth investing a little time and money in improving the *efficiency* of your working style? After all, the less wear and tear the work itself inflicts upon your patience and concentration, the more creative you can be. Besides, it just looks and feels better to have all your gear neatly racked, your system components readily accessible at convenient angles, and your cables organized.

Pro Tools Custom USB Keyboard

This USB keyboard, available for Macintosh or Windows computers, has color-coded sections (see Figure B.13). Text for standard Pro Tools key commands is printed on each key, as well as the standard QWERTY characters. Because this represents an additional expense (and costs more than conventional replacement keyboards), many users have been skeptical about the value of this option. But this keyboard really does shorten the learning curve in many cases. An added benefit is that it may help you become accustomed to using keyboard shortcuts instead of onscreen controls and menu commands.

Figure B.13 Pro Tools Custom USB keyboard for Macintosh.

Rackmounting, Workstation Furniture

You can certainly build your own studio furniture (in some rooms this is a necessity) or perhaps adapt some existing computer workstation furniture for your project studio. Alternatively, various manufacturers provide work surfaces and rackmounting systems that are specifically tailored to the needs of digital audio workstation users.

Omnirax

Omnirax offers various lines of furniture, including workstation desks for Pro Tools (with rackmounting systems to accommodate numerous rack spaces of gear). Omnirax was the first company to address the special needs of digital audio workstation users, especially with the ProStation line. The Synergy S6C24 XL (see Figure B.14) was designed to house the Control|24 control surface. Numerous other designs are available for control surfaces of different sizes, including ICON worksurfaces. This is a solid company that has supported Pro Tools since the earliest days, and it really stands behind its products. Features specifically aimed toward digital audio workstation users include bridges for mounting computer monitors and near-field audio monitors, various configurations of rack mounting both above and below the work surface, cable channels, heavy-duty casters, and a sliding shelf for easy access to the computer.

(Photo courtesy of Synergy.)

Figure B.14 The Synergy S6C24 XL, designed to house the Control|24, is flanked by 12-space rack bays.

Argosy Console

Argosy's studio furniture includes slanted bays for computer monitors, plus rack mounting and work surfaces for computer keyboards, trackballs, or mouse pads, and so on. The company's consoles include a variety of models that are custom-fitted for Pro Tools control surfaces, including the Mirage DC-24, specifically designed for the D-Command (see Figure B.15). It includes a padded armrest, a pullout tray for a computer keyboard and mouse, and two 19-inch rack spaces, each six units high.

Sterling Modular

The Sterling Modular "Pro Series" line provides seamlessly integrated solutions for Avid and other manufacturer's mixing consoles. Constructed from a tubular steel leg set that is custom-sized to best fit your console and studio, the frame can be expanded as your future component

(Photo courtesy of Argosy.)

Figure B.15   Argosy's Mirage DC-24 is designed for the D-Command worksurface.

needs grow. You can choose from pre-configured patch bays, rack buckets, and producer desks, or get a custom configuration that reflects your preferences. Sterling Modular also provides numerous customization options for Avid C|24, D-Command, D-Control, and other control surfaces through their mixer conversions (see Figure B.16).

(Photo courtesy of Sterling Modular.)

Figure B.16   Sterling Modular mixer conversion furniture designed for the D-Command worksurface.

Noren Products

This company's AcoustiLock acoustic isolation enclosures for your computer, hard drives, and rackmounted gear (various sizes are available) enable you to place your Pro Tools system in the control room without creating a noise problem. Of particular interest to Pro Tools users is the ACL-16TD model, with up to 16 units of rack mounting, plus three more units on top that slide to the rear for access to cabling patchbays and other frequently accessed devices. Their sealed enclosures provide cooling while requiring no fans, as well as providing equipment noise reduction factors of 99% (from 71 dBA down to 33 dBA).

Sound Construction and Supply

This company manufactures Isobox Studio and Isobox Post acoustic isolation enclosures for your computer, hard drives, and rackmounted gear (various sizes are available) so that your Pro Tools system can remain in the control room. The Isobox line includes thermostatically controlled fans with digital intake/exhaust temperature displays, thermal alarms, efficient sound traps, and intake HEPA filters for the fans. Sound Construction and Supply also offers custom workstation furniture, including consoles specifically for the D-Command, ProControl, C|24, Artist Series controllers, and Control|24.

Extenders

When things don't quite reach in your studio configuration, you may be able to solve the problem with a simple trip to your local audio or computer store. Slightly longer cables for balanced audio connections, MIDI, monitors, FireWire devices, and so on are readily available. Avid's DigiLink cabling system supports very long runs of cable—up to 100 feet (50 feet at 192-kHz sample rates)—which conceivably allows you to put your audio interfaces and Avid PRE microphone preamps out in the studio or even on stage, minimizing the length of analog cabling in your setup. Sometimes, however, you need to separate things in a different way—for instance, when your CPU and peripherals need to be in an equipment room or closet, far from your monitor and keyboard. Without the proper equipment, this separation can be impractical or degrade the display quality, which certainly won't make it any easier to work for extended periods of time.

Gefen

This company offers some interesting products for removing noisy computers from the control room entirely. Gefen's CAT5•1000 system (one sender, one receiver) permits the separation of a standard VGA monitor (analog video at resolutions up to 1920×1200) and USB keyboard/ mouse from a Mac/Windows computer by up to 330 feet, using a single Category-5 (CAT-5) cable. Numerous other products offer DVI and USB extenders in different configurations. The CAT5•5000 system (depicted in Figure B.17) uses two CAT-5 cables to support two monitors connected to independent video outputs from the computer, and is ideal for dual-screen Pro

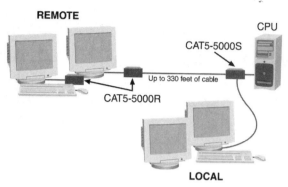

Figure B.17   The CAT5•5000 system, by Gefen.

Tools users. Gefen also offers a variety of USB-only extenders, FireWire repeaters and extenders (including models that support fiber-optic cable runs for extremely long runs), audio distribution amps using CAT-5 cable, monitor converters, and other extremely clever accessories for physically extending a computer or video configuration.

Appendix C: Archive and Backup

Digital audio data occupies *large* amounts of disk space. As seen in Table 3.1 in Chapter 3, even at 16-bit resolution and a 44.1-kHz sample rate (used on standard audio CDs), each stereo minute of audio consumes 10 MB of disk space. If you're recording 24-bit audio at 192 kHz, each minute on each stereo track occupies 68.8 MB!

The large size of Pro Tools projects means that some of the more common methods for backing up and archiving data can become inconvenient. A graphic designer, for example, might make daily backups to rewritable CDs or DVDs or a USB drive, and copy completed projects to recordable CDs or DVDs for long-term storage. But Pro Tools projects with multiple takes on multiple tracks (let alone higher sample rates) can easily exceed the capacity of these storage formats. An extra level of complexity is introduced when multiple disks are used for audio recording with Pro Tools, both for space considerations and to spread the recording/playback load for better performance. To effectively back up or archive your projects, you need to understand exactly how Pro Tools handles the audio files referenced in a session.

Where Pro Tools Stores Session Data

The principal file in Pro Tools is the session document. It contains all track and clip names, clip definitions that are pointers to the parent audio files (and video files, if applicable), the automation and mixing/signal routing, plus all MIDI data used in the session. Session documents contain no audio data, so they are relatively small (generally well under a megabyte, even including a fair amount of MIDI data). As explained in Chapter 8, the File > Save As command allows you to create successive iterations of your session document, all of which will continue to reference the same Audio Files folder and use it for any new audio recordings. If you instead create a copy of the current Pro Tools session using the File > Save Copy In command, you can create a separate copy of your audio files in a new Audio Files folder, which will then be used for any subsequent files. If you *don't* copy all the audio files, new session copies can end up using both the previous session's Audio Files folder and their own Audio Files folder for any audio files created subsequently. To make a backup or archive copy of that new session, you would therefore need to copy *both* Audio Files folders to be sure you're including all the source audio files it references.

A session's Audio Files folder contains all new audio recordings made within this session. In addition, audio files created as a result of processing functions in the AudioSuite menu are also stored here (such as Pitch Shift, Time Compression/Expansion, Normalization, and other functions). When you copy source audio files in the Import Audio dialog box (rather than simply adding them as a reference to their original location), copies are also placed within the session's Audio Files folder. Lastly, any audio files on Audio tracks whose Elastic Audio mode is set to Rendered Processing (as opposed to Real-Time Processing, which requires more CPU power) are placed into a Rendered Files subfolder in the main session folder. If you disable Elastic Audio on an Audio track and choose the Commit option in the Commit Elastic Audio dialog box, the temporary rendered file is deleted, and the resultant file is written into the Audio Files folder.

The DigiBase browser windows help keep track of which files are being used in the current session document and where they reside. The Workspace browser shows all disk volumes on your system, what folders and media files they contain, which drives are designated for audio recording and/or playback, and, most importantly, how much free space is currently available. When preparing for backup or archive, though, you will find the Project Browser window (shown in Figure C.1) especially useful. Among other helpful information about the audio files used in the current session, the Path column allows you to quickly confirm the disk and folder locations where these files reside prior to backup or archival.

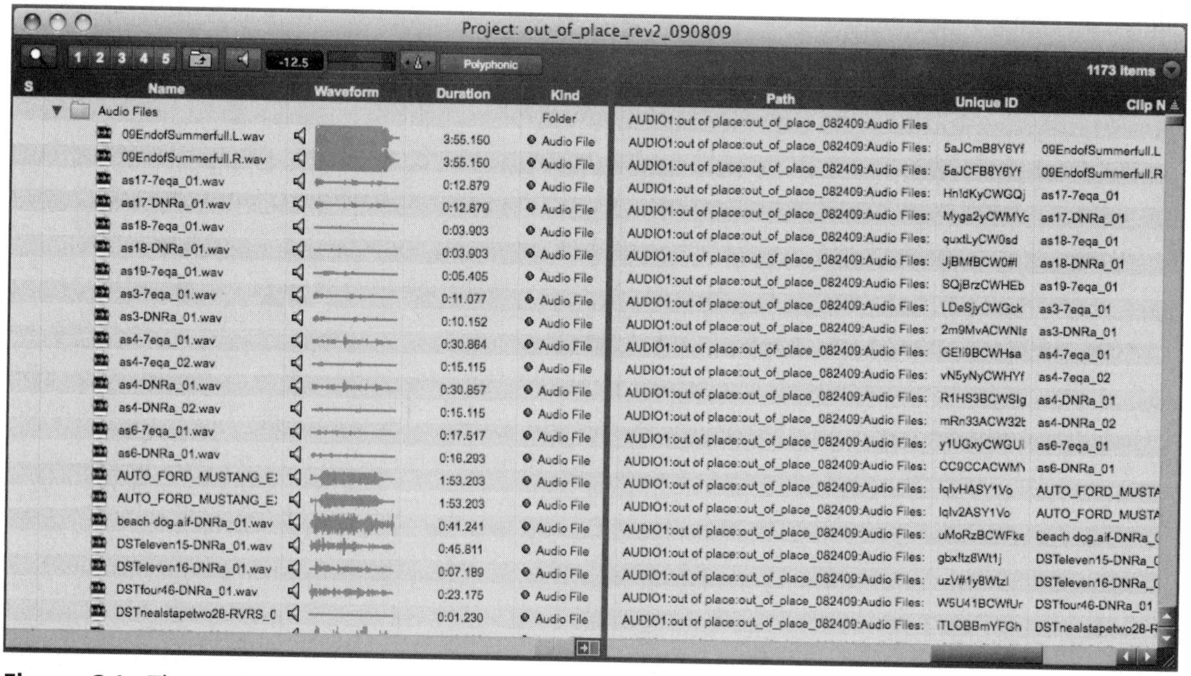

Figure C.1   The Project Browser window helps keep track of the disk locations for audio and video files used in the current session.

Using *multiple disks* for audio recording, however, makes the backup and archive scenario a little more complicated. In Setup > Disk Allocation, you can select a specific disk for recording from each Audio track. Alternatively, using round-robin allocation, Pro Tools will cycle to the next eligible audio drive for storing audio files with each new Audio track you create. (In either case, only disks that have been designated as Record volumes—as opposed to Playback or Transfer only—in the Workspace browser window are eligible.) Whenever multiple disks are used for recording audio, a folder with the same name as your session folder is automatically created on each disk, containing Audio Files folders that are used for any tracks allocated to that record drive. So if you're using multiple disks for audio recording and playback—which is common when working with large sessions at high sample rates—these additional folders on the other disks must also be backed up to ensure you've included all that session's source files.

Lastly, bear in mind that not all audio files used in a Pro Tools session necessarily reside in the Audio Files folder. When an existing audio file being imported into your Pro Tools session *doesn't* require any conversion to the current session's settings, that file remains in its original location—unless you intentionally use the Copy button instead of the Add button in the Import Audio dialog box. For instance, you might keep a folder of standard sound effects for use in multiple projects, or use mixes bounced from other programs or Pro Tools sessions. These may be used in Pro Tools directly from their original location.

In this case, you will generally still want to archive the referenced audio files along with each session where they are used (to ensure a complete, self-contained archive).

Preferences for Importing Audio   In the Processing tab of the Preferences dialog box, you can enable the Automatically Copy Files on Import option. When enabled, audio files imported into Pro Tools are *always* copied into the Audio Files folder of the current session, even if their audio format would have permitted them to be used from their original location. Although this increases your usage of disk space, it has several advantages. First, when making nightly backups or archiving the finished project, you know for sure that all source audio files reside in the Audio Files folder (or several Audio Files folders, if you're using multiple disk allocations for the session). Second, it can be less dangerous! The Clip List's Compact Selected command (like the Delete option for the Clear Selected command) permanently alters or deletes the original audio files. Likewise, any destructive processing applied with AudioSuite options will alter the audio files. If you use the same audio files in multiple sessions (and especially if several people use the same Pro Tools system), a careless moment can have catastrophic consequences for other Pro Tools session documents. Having each session contain new copies of all imported audio files reduces the risk of this occurring.

In a professional studio setting, it can be a good idea to keep track sheets and project logs for your Pro Tools sessions, indicating what audio files are used and their disk locations. This makes archiving and retrieving multiple sessions easier. The Project Browser window and the File > Export > Session Info as Text command make this much simpler. You can save these tab-delimited text files, print them, or include them in word-processing documents. Alternatively, you could build a simple database (in FileMaker Pro, for example) with a database record for each archived session and paste this text data exported from Pro Tools into a text field. While you're at it, create additional fields for the project name, client, session sample rate, bit depth, microphones used, account rep, talent phone numbers, or whatever other information about the session you think could be useful.

Why and When Should You Save Your Data?

Backup and archiving are performed for different reasons, as explained later in this appendix. In any case, as a Pro Tools user, you are dealing with very large amounts of data. Learn how to use the Select Unused, Clear, and Compact commands in the Clip List's pop-up menu. By eliminating unused takes and compacting longer audio files from which you've used only a few small segments, you can free up considerable disk space and make your backup/archive smaller. Just be sure you take the time to think through what you're doing; don't get ahead of yourself eliminating unused clips if you will be compositing a track from multiple takes afterward, for example.

Backup

Backup is a precaution. You must regularly make safety copies of all your important data (like, say, your client's projects) so that if some disaster (disk malfunction, smoke damage, computer virus, or operator error) causes it to be lost from your computer, you can go back to these copies instead of losing the entire project. It's like what dentists say about your teeth: You don't have to take care of all of them, just the ones you don't want to lose! Ideally, you should make backup copies every work day if you have a fast, convenient means of doing so. Using a separate hard drive for mid- and end-of-session copies is gaining popularity in the industry. Also, backup copies should be stored in a different room—or, ideally, in a different building. After all, what good will it do to back up your work to CD/DVD backup copies that sit in a box next to the computer if there's ever a fire in the studio? At the very least, you should perform a fairly thorough backup of all your important data once a week—assuming that you don't mind potentially losing an entire week's worth of work and/or feel you can explain to your clients how you've lost several days' worth of recordings.

You should also periodically back up your entire computer. The bottom line? The faster and more convenient it is to back up the huge amounts of data you generate in Pro Tools, the more often you will do it! And while we're on the subject of data security, consider investing in a bank's safe deposit box. Keep all your original Pro Tools disks and registration information in this single location. With insurance, new computers and audio hardware can be purchased, but all the installation materials will be a real hassle to get again. (Not as bad as losing the actual *work* you've done in Pro Tools—and possibly your client—if you aren't backing up your project data on a regular basis, but you get the idea.)

Archive

Archiving is more long-term storage and should be performed on finished projects or seldom-used files that you don't wish to keep on your system for space considerations or other reasons. As with backing up, when archiving, you should take a moment to carefully eliminate any unused audio clips and compact the remaining audio files in your Pro Tools session (being extra careful to confirm they aren't also being used in other sessions) before archiving the session folder and its related files (for example, bounced mixes). For most Pro Tools users, recordable CDs are simply too small and inconvenient for anything but very small projects; recordable

DVDs and/or Blu-ray discs are much more practical, even for mid-sized and project studios, and have a much longer projected lifespan than CDs do.

Create and Maintain a Database of Your Archived Work! Once you've been at this for a while, you'll likely have a very large number of archived disks. Locating and retrieving specific sessions or projects can become unwieldy if you don't get yourself organized. Many solutions are available for this, but here is a method that has proven successful: Number each archive disk and give it a meaningful volume name when it is burned. Then build a simple database. As you archive each disk, enter all the information about the project files it contains into this database, the date of archive, the disk number, who performed the archive, and so on. This makes it easy to find things among the hundreds of archive discs you may accumulate. If you prefer to purchase a solution, have a look at Studio Suite by AlterMedia (www.studiosuite.com). This studio-management application for Mac and Windows includes an archive database. It also prints labels (with bar codes) for media; does time tracking for booking and billing your studio rooms, equipment, and people; generates invoices; organizes equipment inventory and barcoding; keeps maintenance logs; and creates patchbay labels.

CD-R, DVD-R

A standard data CD-ROM holds around 700 MB of data. This may seem like a lot, but for backing up or archiving audio (and even worse, video data), 700 MB suddenly isn't so spacious after all. A continuous recording of 16 channels for four minutes, at a bare-minimum 16-bit, 44.1-kHz resolution, will consume 364 MB, and that's before applying any AudioSuite functions, rendering Elastic Audio, or bouncing mix files—let alone recording multiple takes or recording overdubs!

If you *have* to archive or back up such a project to CD-R, a program such as Retrospect can automatically split it to multiple discs. However, this makes it more difficult to retrieve just one or two files from this session without reloading the entire project to your system. Alternatively, you could take the time to split up your project files into folders that are smaller than 700 MB each and then burn each of these to a separate CD—but this is burdensome and takes a surprisingly long time. In short, unless you exclusively do short-duration sessions with a small number of tracks, a DVD backup solution for your computer will be much more practical.

A 4.7-GB recordable DVD (either DVD+R or the somewhat less popular DVD-R format) actually holds about 4.3 GB of data. On a Macintosh computer with a recordable DVD drive, you can use either Roxio's Toast Titanium program or the Finder to record data to DVDs and CDs, while Nero, Media Creator, and other programs are practical choices on Windows systems—as well as the operating system itself, of course. Recordable DVDs are frequently a good choice for archiving Pro Tools projects because many of them *will* fit into 4 GB or so—if not, they can perhaps be split between two discs rather than, say, nine or ten CDs.

The DVD capacity can still be rather small for Pro Tools sessions with a large number of high-resolution Audio tracks, however. Splitting large sessions onto multiple DVDs can be unwieldy and time-consuming. Double-layer DVD formats offer capacities up to 8.5 GB on a single-sided disc (DVD+R9 media). When using current double-layer (also known as *dual-layer*) models to write to conventional DVD-R and DVD+R media, 8× and 16× write speeds are supported. For users who record at higher sample rates, longer durations, or higher track counts, a double-layer drive for backing up data to DVD can be a good option.

Blu-ray Disc

The Blu-ray disc format is quickly gaining support. The name derives from the fact that disc drives for Blu-ray use a blue-violet laser to read and write data at higher densities rather than the longer-wavelength red laser in current DVD drives and recorders. While a 36.5-Mbps transfer rate is the current 1.0 specification (useful for recording and playback of HDTV at full quality, among other things), the Blu-ray Disc Association (BDA) has been working on a 2.0 specification that will double this transfer rate. A single-layer Blu-ray disc (also known as BD-25) offers 25-GB capacity, while dual-layer versions (BD-50) reach 50 GB. In addition to the BD-ROM format used for video and other prerecorded content and the BD-RE format for HDTV recording, of special interest to users of media workstations are the BD-R (recordable) and BD-RW (rewritable) Blu-ray disc formats. As this format becomes more widespread, it will be of great interest to those of us who manage large quantities of media data.

What about Rewritable Media?

Users often wish to use rewritable media (CD-RW, CD+RW, DVD-RW, DVD+RW, and the older DVD-RAM format) for backup and archive. Rewritable media undoubtedly has a place in the backup/archive strategy for any Pro Tools system, but always in conjunction with write-once media. First, some older CD players and drives won't play rewritable CDs at all, so these are potentially problematic for burning audio mixes to CD. If the CD players you have support rewritable CDs, these could be used for burning trial mixes for listening on home stereos, boom boxes, automobile stereos, and so on.

At any rate, given how inexpensive recordable CD and DVD media has become, you might as well use write-once media for trial audio mixes anyway. Even for backup and archive, there's also a cost issue to consider. You can buy a large number of write-once disks for the price of a single rewritable disc, so for long-term archival, write-once disks (CD-R, DVD-R) are generally the way to go. Write-once CD-Rs can even be a practical choice for daily/weekly backup of smaller sessions—not to mention all the other non-audio files that are essential to running a studio (billing, archived databases, and correspondence, for example). The price disparity is especially dramatic for recordable CDs (CD-R); bought in spindles of 50–100, they're currently well under 20 cents each, versus up to three or four times more per CD-RW. The price differential for DVD-R versus DVD-RW is similar. So you could potentially save various incremental archive/backups onto write-once media as your project progresses for the same price as a single backup on a rewritable disc. (Some of the more rudimentary CD/DVD writing programs don't support creating multisession discs on rewritable media, so each previous backup on the recordable disc must be erased in order to write a new session.) Generally, writing data is also significantly slower on rewritable media than write-once media. Furthermore, if your projects are important (and your clients just might think so), you definitely need more than one generation of backup. Otherwise, you can find yourself in an uncomfortable position if the last session version you backed up has been damaged in some way.

All this being said, many Pro Tools users will still find rewritable discs to be a very practical part of their daily backup routine. For example, at the end of each day you could back up your session onto a rewritable DVD (or several, if necessary), rotating through two or three different daily discs as a safety precaution. When the project is finished, it would then be archived off the system onto conventional write-once DVDs or a tape backup system.

Rewritable DVD Formats

The DVD+RW rewritable DVD format can be read by most standard DVD drives (either in computers or in standard video DVD players). DVD+RW uses 4.7-GB media and is currently the most common rewritable DVD format among computer users. The DVD-RW format developed by Pioneer is similar but lacks the built-in media defect–management features of the DVD+RW format. If you're buying a DVD-recording drive, you can cover your bets by choosing a model that supports both these "plus" and "minus" (sometimes called "dash") rewritable formats. By all means, get the fastest drive you can afford; given their larger capacity, the difference between a 16× DVD burner and a 2× model is considerable.

Toast Titanium (Mac)   This disc-burning program from Roxio supports a variety of disc formats, including CD-R, CD-RW, DVD-R, DVD+RW, and Blu-ray. For manual backup, it can often be sufficient (as long as *you* know the folder and disk locations where all the files used in your Pro Tools sessions reside). Among the CD formats Toast supports are audio CD; CD-ROM in Mac (HFS), Windows (ISO), or hybrid Mac/Win formats; Video CD; CD-I; MP3 CD; and Enhanced Music CD.

Current versions support writing multiple sessions onto a single DVD+RW disc. (In other words, the previous day's backup doesn't have to be erased from the recordable DVD before you back up today's data.) With the data-spanning feature, large data sets are automatically split across multiple disks while creating archive CDs or DVDs. Restoring from these multi-disk archives (either the entire set or a single file) is equally easy. Current versions also support automatic cataloging for the contents of burned discs. Also, most of the features of Roxio's Jam program for Red Book CD mastering are included in current versions of Toast.

Removable Disk Options for Data Backup

As the price per gigabyte of hard-disk storage continues to plummet, many Pro Tools users have found external or removable hard drives to be an excellent option for daily backups. Given that compact external FireWire drives are available in capacities of 1 TB or more for around $150, for example, this can be your ideal "removable media" for backing up large sessions on a daily basis. And because these are full-performance hard drives, the transfer rates are also faster than DVD, tape, or older removable disk drive systems. Before walking out of your studio at the end of the session, you can just drag your session folders (and supplementary Audio Files/Fade Files folders, if the session's disk allocation spans multiple disks) onto the FireWire drive. After unhooking that drive from the computer, drop it into your briefcase or backpack and take it home with you for safekeeping. If you spend just a little more for an external FireWire drive that also meets the performance requirements for Pro Tools, you can simply open this session directly from that disk attached to some other Pro Tools system if a disaster ever occurs in your own studio.

Inexpensive FireWire caddies (enclosures into which you can swap a drive mechanism) are also widely available. Not only are these useful for accessing your data on another system, they're also great for swapping various disks into a single enclosure as projects come and go in the same studio.

More sophisticated removable hard drive systems are also available for Pro Tools. For example, Glyph offers the rack-mountable GT 103 unit with bays for up to three hot-swappable GT Key FireWire hard-drive cartridges, with capacities up to 2 TB each (7,200 RPM mechanisms using the Oxford 911 chipset, which is required for FireWire disks used as audio drives by Pro Tools). Not only does this facilitate using hard drives as a backup medium, it also allows the same Pro Tools system to be used simultaneously for many large sessions because each one could use a completely separate set of removable hard disks, if necessary.

Yet another backup strategy is the use of disk imaging or mirroring systems or backup software backup. Having a mirror image of an audio drive is obviously a useful function. Programs such as Carbon Copy Cloner and Super Duper for Mac or Paragon Drive Copy for Windows, however, can also image the disk where the operating system and all your program files reside. Should these ever become corrupted or lost due to media defects, a virus, operator error, or loss of the computer itself, having this snapshot of the previous system state to go back to will be hugely important, saving downtime and possibly avoiding the loss of a client.

Of course, once a project is complete and you want to permanently *archive* the session, you will want to look at one of the other more cost-effective data-storage formats discussed here (Blu-ray, DVD, or tape archive, for example).

Respect for the Older Generation   If your projects are mission critical, you should take a serious attitude toward backup. Consider this scenario: You faithfully back up your Pro Tools session at the end of the day (or night), turn out the lights, and go home. In the dead of the night, a fire breaks out, or your nitwit partner or intern throws your session in the trash, or a virus trashes your entire system in spectacular fashion, or a thief breaks in and steals your system. After dealing with the insurance company, firing your intern, repairing your computer, or making other necessary repairs or replacements, you'll need to reload your session and audio files from the backup copy (cleverly stored in a different room and unaffected by the disastrous occurrence). Much to your dismay, though, you discover that your session file or audio files were damaged (or "corrupted") when you backed them up. To avoid anguish, embarrassment, and everlasting torment, you will need to be able to work through successive previous generations of backup. For example, if you use rewritable media (CD-RW, DVD-RW, Blu-ray, tape, and so on), backups should be rotated between two or three different disks on subsequent days. That way, if yesterday's file copies were damaged when backed up due to a bad disk, you can always go back to the day before yesterday, or the day before that.

Tape Backup Options

A decade ago, when the largest removable disk solutions were 1 GB or less, tape drives were the only practical way to back up or archive large media projects. These days, tape drives remain a good option. Common tape formats for data currently include LTO, DLT, AIT, and others. Many of these are supported by various backup programs (see the next section), and you will find them in numerous production facilities. Current high-capacity tape drives offer excellent data-transfer rates and are a great choice for professional facilities, especially when large projects need to be archived on a regular basis and when the size of the data sets to be archived will necessarily span multiple tapes.

Currently, Linear Tape-Open (LTO) drives are available from various manufacturers, in capacities per cartridge of up to 1.5 TB (native capacity of LTO-5 media). Library or jukebox configurations with multiple cartridge slots allow many terabytes of data to be archived in a single operation.

Expensive as these tape cartridges are, for facilities that archive a large number of copies during the course of a year (daily incremental backups and weekly full backups), tape backups are cheaper than using large-capacity disks for backup and data storage. The economics of your own situation will determine the best solution; if you generally work with mid-sized or small Pro Tools sessions at 48-kHz sample rates or less and only 12–32 channels of I/O, then some combination of recordable-rewritable DVDs, large-capacity removable disk systems, or external FireWire drives may be more than sufficient for your backup and archive requirements.

The backup software applications used with these tape drives allow for incremental backups; only files that have actually changed since the previous backup are copied off to tape. This not only greatly decreases the storage capacity required for nightly backups, but also makes the operation much quicker (because unchanged files aren't being copied to tape). For large facilities with multiple users and projects, intelligent, incremental backups are the most reliable solution—even when data is being copied to disk media.

One last observation about removable data storage, either on tape or disk: These systems often have a limited commercial existence. It is entirely possible that, in seven or eight years, a given data-storage format that everybody is using right now may be (a) no longer manufactured, (b) hard to find media for, or (c) incompatible with current computers and operating systems. Be conservative when selecting your backup solution; take a good hard look at who manufactures the solution and how widespread it is beyond the media-production industry. Consider what you would do today if someone handed you a 44-MB SyQuest cartridge (a once *de facto* standard for transporting "large" quantities of data between computer systems) containing a Sound Designer file to be remastered. Because of the rapid cycle of obsolescence for data-storage media, commercial production facilities often must take the time and expense to periodically transfer their vaults to more current storage formats or otherwise maintain older computer systems and antique storage peripherals for the sole purpose of retrieving archived projects when necessary.

Backup Software

One of the essential techniques for data security is performing daily incremental backups to disk or tape. The backup software looks at modification dates for every file on the disk volumes selected for backup, copying only files that have been modified since the last full or incremental backup. This saves time and avoids wasting tape space by writing redundant copies of files that haven't changed. Many excellent backup programs are available; only two are mentioned here—because they're ubiquitous and also perform admirably.

- Retrospect is a widespread and highly reliable backup program for Windows and Macintosh. Retrospect can perform incremental and full backups from multiple disk locations (including other networked computers), which can be stored and repeated later and programmed to occur at specific dates and times. The software supports a wide variety of storage devices as the destination for backups, including hard drives (both direct- and network-attached), tape drives and libraries (connected via FireWire, SCSI, iSCSI, or Fibre Channel), and removable disk drives. The latest version can also back up to and restore from offsite cloud storage. Retrospect doesn't have any intrinsic understanding of how Pro Tools projects are structured, however. It is your responsibility to understand that a Pro Tools session may use files and folders on multiple disks and to make sure these are all included in the selected data for backup.

- Nero 11 includes the NeroBackItUp 11 utility for programmed backup operations (either full or incremental). The Nero suite of software also provides excellent tools for creating data CDs and DVDs and labels, a drive-imaging utility, and, among other things, robust capabilities for creating audio CDs.

Appendix D: Power Tips and Loopy Ideas

The information in this appendix is a potpourri of cool tricks and clever workarounds for Pro Tools. Also, for good measure, we cover a few good keyboard shortcuts that too many users overlook.

Mixing and Processing Tips

The tips in this section concern the Mix window, general mixing techniques, and a few pointers for routing and signal processing.

Pro Tools in Living Color

In current versions of Pro Tools, you can change the fill colors of the mixer strips for all tracks (as well as track views displayed in the Edit window) from plain gray to whatever color is assigned to their color strips. First, double-click a track's color strip to open the Color Palette window. Then, click the Apply to Channel Strip button next to the pop-up selector and adjust the Saturation slider to set the amount of color desired. Not only will this brighten up your life, but it can truly be useful in larger sessions. For example, assigning all drum or backing vocal tracks the same color will facilitate navigating a large number of tracks.

Invert Polarity

Many Pro Tools users overlook the fact that many plug-in windows (including the DigiRack EQs, dynamics processors, and delays) have a Phase Invert button, usually to the right of the plug-in's main input, gain, or threshold slider. When this button is enabled, the polarity of any signal passing through the plug-in is inverted. This is useful, for example, if you ever place microphones on both the front and back of a combo guitar amplifier or the top and bottom of a snare drum. If one of these paired tracks is pulling air while the other one is pushing, you're not going to be happy with the sound.

I Want My Backward Reverb!

In the analog days, we did this by turning the tape around and recording reverb backward. Creating *preverb* in Pro Tools is also easy. For the sake of argument, let's say you're creating this effect for the lead vocal track. Here's what you can do:

1. Make a copy of the vocal track by right-clicking on the track nameplate and choosing Duplicate. Include the main playlist in the duplicate track.

2. In the Edit window, select the entire duplicate vocal track, starting from the beginning of the session's Timeline and extending a few seconds past the end of the last clip in the track (to be sure you can record the entire reverb decay *after* the end of the reversed selection).

3. Apply the AudioSuite menu's Reverse function to the vocal selection, creating one continuous file for the reversed result of the entire selection.

4. Apply an AudioSuite reverb plug-in to the reversed vocal, creating another new audio file.

5. Apply the AudioSuite menu's Reverse function to the selection a second time.

6. On playback, you should now hear the backward reverb ramping up before each peak in the vocal track.

7. If you want to get a little more clever (especially because backward reverb often sounds sloppy within vocal phrases), insert a compressor on the backward reverb track and side chain it with an external key whose source is a send from the dry vocal track. (Set the ratio of the compressor very high and its threshold low.) Whenever the vocal track is present, it will duck down the backward reverb.

Pro Tools 10 makes this process even easier. A new Reverse button in the AudioSuite plug-in window for Reverb and Delay plug-ins lets you easily render reverse delay and reverb effects with a single click. Clicking the Reverse button provides three processes in one:

1. It reverses the Edit selection.

2. It processes the reversed Edit selection with the current plug-in settings.

3. It reverses the processed Edit selection.

Squeaky-Clean Acoustic Guitar and Electric Bass

For reducing string squeak on acoustic guitars and especially electric bass (caused by fingers sliding along the strings as they shift positions), you can sometimes get results with a de-esser plug-in. Just lower the de-esser's key frequency way down into the range of 4–5 kHz or lower. Activate the Key Listen feature as you slide around the de-esser's frequency parameter (which defines the center of the narrow frequency band that determines when compression will be applied) to focus on the offending squeaks. Then, adjust the Threshold setting as far down as possible before noticeably altering the instrument's timbre. (There's more latitude on an electric bass; because its fundamental frequencies are lower, harmonics up in the squeak zone are spaced farther apart.)

Adjusting Individual Volume Levels in Grouped Tracks

Ordinarily, after you create a mix group, adjusting the volume level of any of its track faders will move all the faders up or down, maintaining their relative positions. This can be very convenient, for example, for seven or eight drum tracks, several backing vocal tracks, and so on. But what if you want to individually adjust the volume of a single track in a group? Of course, you could use the Mix Group List (in the lower-left area of the Mix window) to temporarily disable the group, adjust the track's volume fader, and then re-enable the group. (Groups in this list are active only when they're highlighted.) But there's a quicker way: While holding down the Control key (Start key in Windows), you can individually adjust any fader in an active group.

Manual Delay Compensation with Time Adjuster Plug-In

Generally speaking, each plug-in introduces a small amount of delay in a track's signal path. For example, in Pro Tools HD, this delay is about four samples for many DigiRack plug-ins, while it can be significantly greater for some third-party plug-ins that perform more complex processing. This can cause problems for tracks that need to be phase-aligned when they are subjected to different types of processing. Take the example of a drum set recorded with multiple microphones and tracks. If you insert various plug-ins on the snare track but not on other tracks (such as the hi-hat, overheads, toms, and so on), the snare bleed-through on those other tracks will be misaligned with the signal on the snare track, causing phase-cancelation and smearing in the higher frequencies.

The Time Adjuster plug-in provides an option for manually correctly for processing delays between tracks, providing up to 8,195 samples of delay-compensation adjustment. It also provides positive and negative gain adjustment and a Phase (Polarity) Inversion function. You don't have to get crazy trying to adjust for plug-in delays on every single mono track, but in cases like the one outlined here, where the same signal is present in two different tracks, maintaining alignment is an important issue that can improve the overall sound of your mix—if you're willing to do the math.

Of course, the Automatic Delay Compensation feature in Pro Tools automatically takes care of plug-in processing delay adjustments for you. (The maximum delay-compensation limit varies according to the session sample rate and type of Pro Tools system you are using.) When Delay Compensation is active, manual adjustments with the Time Adjuster plug-in are generally not necessary.

You can also use one of the Long Delay plug-ins (with its Mix value set to 100%) to compensate for longer track delays, such as those caused by microphone placement. While you can also use the Time Adjuster plug-in for this purpose, its maximum delay amount may be insufficient for some applications (especially in live situations), and it's frequently more convenient to work in milliseconds than samples. If you already know the distances involved in the microphone placement that cause the time-alignment problems in the first place, you can use well-known and simple formulas for calculating the corresponding delay times.

Setting Tempo-Related Delays by Ear

Pro Tools enables you to set the timing of delay repeats to note values (in relation to the current session tempo) in all the DigiRack delay plug-ins except for Short and Slap. Chapter 12 discusses a manual method for setting delays to 1/8 note, 1/4 note, or other musical values with certain third-party delay plug-ins. Here's yet another way to do it, which doesn't even require calculating a tempo map for the session:

1. Assuming you have a snare backbeat or perhaps a reasonably steady kick figure during some portion of the song that you can loop for a moment, create a send from this track to the delay—even if that's not the sound to which you ultimately want to apply the delay.

2. Increase your Feedback parameter enough to generate several repeats—perhaps to about 35% or so.

3. Solo the snare/kick track and the Aux Input track where this delay plug-in is instantiated.

4. While listening to playback, adjust the delay time until the repeats are in time with the 1/4 notes. This setting gives you the length of each 1/4 note, which then becomes your timing reference for calculating 1/8- and 1/16-note delays (one-half or one-quarter the delay time, respectively), 1/4-triplet delays (two-thirds the delay time), and so on.

Groovy Pre-Delays

One typical novice mistake in cluttered-sounding Pro Tools mixes is sloppy timings on multiple delays that clatter around in a nonmusical fashion. Setting delay times to specific musical note values, relative to the song's tempo, usually helps create more natural and open-sounding mixes. Most *reverb* plug-ins also feature pre-delay times; adjusting these to 1/16 notes or some other short, tempo-related value can also help create a better-sounding mix.

EQ: The Zero-Sum Game

Beginning engineers always seem to attack every equalization problem by boosting frequencies. Bass guitar or kick drum doesn't have enough edge? Crank it up! Not enough buzz-saw aggression on the crunch guitar part? Lash on some 2,500 Hz! The problem is, maximum level (*full-code*, or 0 dBFS) for the mix never changes. Consequently, because EQ is a *gain* change in the affected frequency range, boosting one instrument's level (or range within that instrument's frequency spectrum) produces more or less the same effect as *reducing* the gain of all others proportionately.

With this idea of a fixed ceiling in mind, experienced mixers often apply the technique of carving out frequency bands for instrumental parts, using gain *reductions* in specific, relatively narrow frequency ranges on other instrumental parts so that they compete less for those ranges of frequencies. On many great mixes, for example, if you were to solo perhaps the bass guitar part, you (or the bass player) might think it could really use a lot more clack in the low midrange. But by slightly notching out these frequencies in the bass part, the engineer has created a space for the corresponding clack of the beater striking the kick drum, which consequently comes forward in the mix—exactly what the song *as a whole* required.

Here's another example: For competing keyboard and guitar parts, instead of radically boosting that frequency range somewhere around 2–2.5 kHz, to give edge to crunchy rock guitar parts, try notching this same range downward in the keyboard or bass part. You may find that the guitar really didn't need much more level or EQ at all—once it's no longer getting shouted down in this important frequency band.

Bear in mind that it can be very misleading if you make all your EQ adjustments on individual tracks while they are soloed (especially if a performer is standing at your shoulder, obsessing about his or her sound). Instead, when adjusting EQs, try to think in terms of the entire mix and the key places where each part needs to fit into the overall frequency spectrum to complement vocals and other instrumental parts. As far as overall volume adjustments are concerned, remember that the maximum level for the mix is always the same; so to put it simplistically, *boosting* one instrument's level (or one frequency range) is like turning *down* all the others!

EQ and Stereo/Surround Panning

Where you pan a sound in a stereo or surround mix will also affect your decisions about EQ. Among other factors, two sounds might not conflict as badly in a given frequency range if they are panned to widely separated positions. Furthermore, on a simple perception level, the timbre of a sound can seem to change according to its position in relation to others. However, as with delays, reverb, and other time parameters, relying on the inherent separation in your stereo or multichannel surround mix can come back to bite you later. Even if you aren't using stereo delays, chorus effects, and so on, it's very important to listen to your stereo mix in mono (or your surround mix in stereo, and so on) before making any final decisions about EQ. You may be surprised at the logjam of conflicting frequencies present in your mix that weren't apparent in your controlled monitoring environment. To optimize mixes for unpredictable real-world playback situations, experienced engineers frequently switch between stereo and mono (and/or surround) as they make decisions about levels and EQ.

Path Meter View in Output Windows

A surprising number of experienced Pro Tools users overlook this feature. To the right of the Close button in the upper-left corner of Output windows (either for tracks or sends) is another button for the Path Meter view. Click this button to open an additional right panel in the Output window that displays a level meter for the track or send's assigned path.

One great use for this feature is to monitor the destination bus level when many sends are assigned to it (for example, a bus that is the source for an Aux Input track with a reverb or delay plug-in). Just as you can produce clipping and distortion on audio tracks, Aux Input tracks, Instrument tracks, and Master Faders, the summed signals from multiple sends can produce clipping on a bus on their way to an effect.

After opening the Output window for any of the sends assigned to a bus, click the Path Meter View button to keep an eye on the levels on the bus. Like other level meters in Pro Tools, the path meter in an Output window has red clipping indicators in its top segment. You can clear these indicators by clicking them or by using the Track > Clear All Clip Indicators command (or keyboard shortcut Option+C on Mac or Alt+C on Windows).

Gimme More in the Cans, Man!

This tip reviews yet another way of setting up a cue (headphone) mix in Pro Tools, using a multichannel audio interface. The headphone mix provided to performers is a crucial aspect of any recording session, especially when multiple performers are physically isolated from each other and are depending on the headphone mix to hear each other. Here's what to do:

1. In the Mix window, set up your basic mix in Pro Tools as the performers run through the song. You will base the initial headphone mix on the mix you are monitoring in the control room.

2. Create a stereo send (using Send A, for example) for the headphone mix so that you can adjust its balance separately from the control room mix. Hold down the Option key (Alt key in Windows) as you create this send on any Audio track (using the pop-up selector) so that the same send is simultaneously created from *all* Audio tracks (or use Option+Shift/Alt+Shift to create the send on all selected tracks).

3. Choose an internal mix bus pair in Pro Tools—for example, bus 3–4—as the destination.

4. Use the Track > New command to create a stereo Aux Input and name it Cue Mix. Select the mix bus you used for the sends (such as bus 3–4) as the input for this track.

   Using an Aux Input provides you with a single volume fader for the headphone mix. It also gives you the flexibility to apply compression, reverb, and so on specifically to the musicians' cue mix.

5. Set the output assignment of this Aux Input to the output pair on your audio interface that is connected to the performers' headphone amplifier—for example, outputs 3–4. Also, to prevent this Aux Input from being muted when soloing other tracks in the project, Command-click (Ctrl-click in Windows) the Solo button on the Aux Input track to activate Solo Safe mode. Now, when auditioning tracks individually, you are assured that their signal will always be sent through the Cue Mix headphone feed.

6. Choose View > Sends A–E and change the send display option from Assignments to Send A, where you created the send from all Audio tracks in Step 2. You now see mini faders and panners in the send portion of each Audio track in the Mixer window; these control send A.

7. Hold down the Option key (Alt key in Windows) as you click on the P button in any of these sends (or the Pre button in a Send window) to switch them all to pre-fader. Their level and mute status will be unaffected by the settings on the track itself, allowing you to make changes in the control room without affecting the headphone mix.

8. If you are using standard Pro Tools software, you must set each send level separately. Remember that as a starting point, you can Option-click (Alt-click in Windows) each send's level slider to set it to 0 dB. If you are using Pro Tools HD or Pro Tools with the Complete Production Toolkit, however, you can copy the current main mix to all of the sends in a single operation. Select all applicable tracks and then select Edit > Automation > Copy to Send. The Copy To Send dialog box will open.

9. In the dialog box, choose the options to copy the current value for the main Volume and Pan to Send A and click OK.

After you've established this cue mix setup, here's one easy way to switch to monitoring the headphone mix in the control room to make adjustments (assuming that outputs 1–2 on the interface are the source of the control-room monitoring mix):

1. Option-click (Alt-click in Windows) any Audio track's Mute button to mute them all. (Your pre-fader sends to the cue mix are unaffected by their tracks' Mute button.)

2. Create a stereo send (using Send E, for example) from the Cue Mix Aux Input to outputs 1–2. Option-click (Alt-click in Windows) on the send level slider and set it to 0 dB.

3. When you're finished making adjustments, mute this send and then Option-click (Alt-click in Windows) a Mute button as before to unmute your source Audio tracks.

By setting your cue mix as described here, you could even automate this mix going out to the performers' headphones or use additional sends to route reverb and effect outputs to its bus, providing a near-finished product mix for the talent—which will be especially appreciated during last-minute overdubs. All this takes much less time than manually dialing in a headphone mix on an analog mixing console, leaving you more time for creative aspects of the production.

A Change of Venue

This is really more of a general tip for novice mixers. If you only listen to your mix in one room and always on the same playback system, upon subsequent listening elsewhere you will almost certainly discover room for improvement. Before you bless any mix, burn a quick CD and/or copy it to your iPod to play through a few home stereos, boom boxes, and car stereos. The prominence of vocals, delays, and reverbs—and especially the character of the low end—really does change radically according to the playback situation. Performing this reality check early in the mix process is guaranteed to make you happier with the final results.

Editing Tips

In addition to the many editing tips throughout the book, here are a few more ideas—both simple reminders and more advanced techniques.

Shortcuts in the New Track Dialog Box

So you've learned the Shift+Command+N shortcut (Shift+Ctrl+N in Windows) for opening the New Track dialog box. That's a good start. However, the New Track dialog box provides a host of additional keyboard shortcuts. Let's recap them here:

- Press the Left/Right Arrows while holding down the Command key (Ctrl key in Windows) to switch the current row of tracks between mono, stereo, and multichannel (on systems with Pro Tools HD or the Complete Production Toolkit).

- Press the Up/Down Arrows while holding down the Command key (Ctrl key in Windows) to cycle through the possible track types—Audio, Aux Input, Instrument, Master Fader, or MIDI.

- While holding down the Command+Option keys (Ctrl+Alt keys in Windows), press the Up/Down Arrows to switch between the track timebase options for the current track entry field—Samples (absolute) or Ticks (relative).

- Press Command+plus/minus (+/−) on the numeric keypad (Ctrl+plus/minus in Windows) to add or delete rows for additional track entry fields.

Additionally, tracks can be created, duplicated, moved, or deleted during playback, as can sends and inserts. These mixer configuration changes are not permitted during audio recording, but they are possible when recording MIDI only.

Warning, Warning, Warning!

Pro Tools is really good about warning you when an operation will be irrevocable, destructively modifying (or eliminating) audio data. This is a wonderful thing, and it has saved many inexperienced and veteran users from making mistakes. Sometimes, though, you are sure about what you're doing, and you don't want to click through a second alert box to confirm it (such as when you're clearing unusable Audio tracks and deleting them from disk). In these cases, hold down the Option key (Alt key in Windows) as you click the first OK button to bypass the confirmation dialog boxes. But please, think before you click!

Export Clip Definitions for Use in Other Sessions

This isn't so much a cool tip as a friendly reminder: Unless you're in Destructive Recording mode, each time you record on a Pro Tools Audio track, a new audio file is created. A single clip appears in the Clip List that represents the entire audio file for that take. As you edit the audio in your tracks, additional clip definitions are created automatically by Pro Tools, and of course the commands in the Edit menu's Separate Clip submenu also create new clip definitions (pointers to segments within the audio files residing on disk). By default, these clip definitions are contained only in the originating Pro Tools session document, not in the audio files themselves. If you try to import clips from one of these audio files into another Pro Tools session, only the whole-file clip appears in the Import Audio dialog box—not all the other clip definitions within it that you created in the first session.

At times you will want to use clip definitions from a session in other Pro Tools sessions, other audio programs, or even in a sampler program or plug-in. For example, if you create multiple clips within a drum track to build up new grooves, you might want to use these bits and pieces in other sessions. The Export Clip Definitions command in the Clip List pop-up menu does this for you. Clip definitions from the current Pro Tools session are exported into their parent sound files and are subsequently visible in the Import Audio dialog box from any other Pro Tools session.

Cycling through the Edit Modes and Tools (Edit Window)

Pressing the single open quote (`) key—the unshifted equivalent to the tilde ~ key on U.S. English keyboard layouts—cycles between the four Edit modes (Shuffle, Slip, Spot, and Grid).

Pressing the Esc key (Mac) cycles between the Edit tools (Zoomer, Trim, Selector, Grabber, Smart Tool, Scrubber, and Pencil).

Making Selections with the Timebase Ruler (Edit Window)

To make selections with the Timebase Ruler in the Edit window, do the following:

- Double-click anywhere in any of the Timebase Rulers to select the entire session (from the beginning of the session Timeline, including all clips—and/or automation breakpoints—in all tracks).

- Option-click and drag (Alt-click and drag in Windows) within any Timebase Ruler to make an Edit selection on all tracks *and rulers* simultaneously. Selecting the Link Timeline and Edit Selection button in the Edit window will accomplish the same thing when dragging in a Timebase Ruler but will not include any Conductor Rulers.

You can also use the Markers Ruler to make selections. First, position the edit cursor and/or make a track selection either by clicking an existing marker or by using one of the Edit tools within a track. Then, Shift-click on a second marker to extend your current selection to that point.

Extending the Current Selection with the Tab Key (Edit Window)

You can use the Tab key to extend the current selection in the Edit window. Here are your options:

- **Shift+Tab.** This extends the selection to the next clip boundary (end of the current clip or beginning of the next clip).

- **Option+Shift+Tab (Control+Shift+Tab in Windows).** This extends the selection to the previous clip boundary (beginning of the current clip or end of the previous clip).

- **Control+Shift+Tab (Start+Shift+Tab in Windows).** This extends the selection to include the entire next clip.

- **Option+Control+Shift+Tab (Control+Start+Shift+Tab in Windows).** This extends the selection to include the entire previous clip.

More Tab Key Tricks (Edit Window)

Here are yet more Tab key shortcuts in the Edit window:

- **Tab.** Each press moves the playback/edit cursor forward in the current track to the next clip boundary (beginning or end), Sync Point (if a clip contains one), or fade beginning/end.

- **Option+Tab (Ctrl+Tab in Windows).** Same as Tab, except the cursor location moves backward.

- **Control+Tab (Start+Tab in Windows).** Selects the next clip or fade in the current track.

- **Option+Control+Tab (Ctrl+Start+Tab in Windows).** Selects the previous clip or fade in the current track.

■ **Tab to Transients.** When this button is enabled in the Edit window, pressing the Tab key moves the playback/edit cursor forward to the next transient attack in the current Audio track. To move back to the previous transient, press Option+Tab (Ctrl+Tab in Windows).

Lengthen/Shorten the Current Selection with the Plus/Minus Keys (Edit Window)

To move the end of the current selection by the current Nudge value, hold down the Command+ Shift keys (Ctrl+Shift on Windows) as you press the +/– (plus/minus) keys on the numeric keypad. To move the *beginning* of the current selection by the current Nudge value, hold down the Option+Shift keys (Alt+Shift on Windows) as you press the +/– (plus/minus) keys on the numeric keypad.

Power Scrubber (Edit Window)

Many users underestimate the usefulness of the Scrubber tool for editing. Here are a few tricks you should know:

■ While using the Selector tool, you can hold down the Control key (Start key in Windows) to temporarily switch to the Scrubber tool.

■ If you add the Shift key as you scrub, the current edit selection is extended to the point where you stop scrubbing. This makes it easy to locate audio events by ear! (The Shift key selection technique also works when using the Scrubber tool itself.)

■ To drag at extra-slow speed for finer precision, hold down the Command key (Ctrl key in Windows). Try using this in combination with the previous two modifier keys!

■ For extra-*fast* scrubbing (Shuttle mode), hold down the Option key (Alt key in Windows). Shuttle mode is also available when temporarily switched to Scrub mode while using the Selector tool, and you can also use it with the Shift key to make edit selections.

■ In current versions of Pro Tools, scrubbing applies to both audio and MIDI events.

Use Your Scroll Wheel

The wheel on your mouse scrolls vertically in the Mix and Edit windows. Learn these additional modifier-key combinations for scroll-wheel techniques that will boost your productivity.

■ To scroll the Mix or Edit window back and forth horizontally, hold down the Shift key as you scroll the wheel.

■ To zoom in/out horizontally in the Edit window, hold down the Option key (Alt key in Windows) as you scroll the wheel up and down.

■ To zoom the vertical (amplitude) scale of all audio waveforms in the Edit window up/down, hold down the Option+Shift keys (Alt+Shift keys in Windows) as you scroll the wheel up and down.

- To scroll the vertical (pitch) display of MIDI data in on a track up/down, hold down the Control+Option+Command keys (Start+Alt+Ctrl keys in Windows) as you scroll the wheel up/down with the cursor over the track.

- To zoom the vertical (pitch) display of all MIDI data in the Edit window up/down, hold down the Option+Command+Shift keys (Alt+Ctrl+Shift keys in Windows) as you scroll the wheel up/down.

The Three-Button Quickstep for Switching Windows

If you are using a mouse or trackball with three buttons, consider assigning a macro to the third button—for example, the Command+= (equal sign) shortcut (Ctrl+= on Windows) to switch between the Mix and Edit windows.

Nudging and Grid Mode

You don't always have to open the pop-up selectors to change between the Grid and Nudge preset values! Here are a couple of shortcuts that will save you some mouse travel, plus some very useful nudging techniques.

- To toggle through the preset Grid values for the time units currently in use (for example, to select between whole bars and various note values when in Bars|Beats mode), hold down Control+Option (Start+Alt in Windows) as you use the +/- (plus/minus) keys on the numeric keypad.

- To toggle through the preset Nudge values for the time units currently in use, hold down Command+Option (Ctrl+Alt in Windows) as you use the +/- (plus/minus) keys on the numeric keypad.

- To nudge selected clips, MIDI notes, or automation breakpoints left or right, use the +/- (plus/minus) keys on the numeric keypad.

- To extend or shorten the *left* edge of the current selection by the current Nudge value, press Option+Shift (Alt+Shift in Windows) as you nudge. To extend or shorten the selection's *right* edge, hold down Command+Shift (Ctrl+Shift in Windows) instead.

- To nudge the *contents* of a clip without affecting the left-right boundaries of the clip itself, hold down the Control key (Start key in Windows) as you nudge.

Keyboard Focus Modes

Many Pro Tools users never explore the utility of the little A-Z button in the upper-right corner of the Edit window, which activates Commands Keyboard Focus mode. Activating this mode enables many single-keystroke shortcuts that can really speed up your editing in Pro Tools. To name just a few, you can execute commands such as Cut, Copy, Paste, or Undo by pressing only a single letter key: X, C, V, or Z, respectively—no need to hold down a Command modifier key (Ctrl in Windows). The A and S keys trim the start/end of the current clip to the insertion point, 1–5 on the alphanumeric keyboard select the five zoom preset buttons, and F creates a default fade type without requiring you to open the Fades dialog box. The P and ; (semicolon) keys move the edit cursor or Edit selection up and down one track, respectively, while pressing Shift+P or Shift+; (semicolon) extends the selection upward or downward.

Incidentally, Pro Tools provides other keyboard-focus modes for one-keystroke operations—each of them even more underused than Commands Focus! The Clip List and Track List each have their own A-Z buttons. When Clip List Keyboard Focus is enabled, you can select a clip by typing the first few letters of its name. With Group List Keyboard Focus enabled, Mix and Edit groups can be enabled or disabled by typing their group ID letter. Both the MIDI and the Score editors also have their own keyboard-focus modes that mirror the functions of the Edit window Keyboard Focus mode.

Using Key-Signature Events on a Looping Ostinato Figure

This example is just one creative application of key-signature events in Pro Tools. Suppose you want to make a complex 1/16-note ostinato figure shift tonalities so that it will match a chord progression playing underneath it—for example C-D7-Ab-G7, two bars each. One approach is to alter the accidentals at each key-signature event in the ruler like so:

1. Create a MIDI or Instrument track. Use that track's Playlist selector to ensure that it is set to Pitched so that it will be affected by key-signature events. In Notes view, create a fiendishly intricate 1/16-note C major arpeggio that you want to repeat as a two-bar ostinato figure. To increase your fun quotient, make this arpeggio span at least two or three octaves or perform this whole exercise simultaneously on two or more MIDI tracks that contain intertwining arpeggios.

2. Switch the track to Clip view and activate Grid mode with a Grid value of one bar.

3. Using the Loop Trim mode of the Trim tool, trim this two-bar clip to the right until you have four repetitions totaling eight bars.

4. If it is not already visible, use the View > Rulers > Key Signature command to show the Key Signature Ruler. You will note that the default key signature of C major already appears at the beginning of the Timeline, which will work fine for the first chord, C major.

5. Click to position the edit cursor at bar 3, where the underlying chord changes to D7. Click the plus sign at the end of the Key Signature Ruler to create a new key-signature event. (Disclaimer: A little bit of music theory is going to be required here, since you'll need to choose relative key signatures to produce scale modes that are most compatible with the chord progression.)

6. The Key Change dialog box appears. In this case, a D Mixolydian scale would sound nice against this second chord, so you can choose G major (one sharp) as the key signature.

7. Before closing the dialog box, enable the Edit Pitched Tracks checkbox. Make sure the Transpose checkbox is disabled, but enable the Constrain Pitches to Key checkbox. Then click OK.

8. Move the edit cursor to bar 5, where the A♭ chord occurs. Create another key-signature event, again enabling the Constrain Pitches to Key checkbox only. This time, we will choose C minor (three flats) to get the equivalent of an A♭ Lydian mode.

9. Finally at bar 7, repeat this process, choosing C major (no flats or sharps) for the equivalent of G Mixolydian mode over that G7 chord.

10. Click the Return to Zero button (in the Transport window or at the top of the Edit window) and then press the spacebar to start playback. You will hear the notes in your looped 1/16-note ostinato changing as each key signature event is crossed in the track.

General Tips

What follows is an assortment of techniques, advice, options, and other cool stuff that might come in handy as you continue to use Pro Tools.

Calculators for Tempos and Note Values to Milliseconds

Several websites offer calculators for tempos and note values. Here are a couple:

- **www.macmusic.org/software.** Check out the freeware application called Music Math (for either Mac OS X or OS 9), written by Laurent Colson. It converts between beats per minute (BPM) and equivalent millisecond settings for your delay (or other effects—LFO modulation rate on a flanger, perhaps?). It also converts between sample durations and tempos, MIDI notes and frequencies, as well as transposition and time-stretching values.

- **www.analogx.com/contents/download/audio/delay.htm.** For Windows users, AnalogX offers the free downloadable Delay Calculator, especially useful for reverb pre-delays, hardware delays, and delay plug-ins that don't allow adjusting delay times per musical values.

That Lock-Step Don't Dance

Quantization and Groove templates are incredible tools, especially when used in conjunction with the Elastic Audio features in Pro Tools. They can also be the death of a groove when applied in excess, however. The Restore Performance option for MIDI clips (in the Event Operations window) can undo quantization even after the session has been saved many times or return a MIDI selection to the state it was in the last time you applied the Flatten Performance command. This is great if you realize late in the creative process that an instrumental part that seemed way too loose early on really works fine after additional parts have been added to the session. You should also have a careful listen to many of your favorite tracks; often, the tension between two different rhythmic feels is exactly what makes those grooves sound so great. To cite a famous and extreme example, check out the contrast between the straight 1/8-note feel in the guitar part and the laid-back swing feel in the bass and drum parts, in Chuck Berry's "Johnny B. Goode." Now, imagine how much *worse* this would sound if all those audio events had been quantized to precisely the same 1/8-note swing factor!

Things That Make Pro Tools Cranky

Everyone's system has its own set of peccadilloes, but here's a short list of things that can be problematic on almost any Pro Tools system:

- Energy-management, power-saver, and energy-saver features of the operating system (usually enabled via the Control Panel in Windows or System Preferences on Mac)

- Screen savers (also enabled in the Control Panel or System Preferences)

- Background disk optimizers, system-monitoring software, and the like

- Network/web activities (such as serving up MP3 files to the Internet)

- Fragmented hard drives

- Extremely full hard drives (over 90% is always a problem)

- Not repairing disk permissions from time to time with the Disk Utility—especially after installing updates to Pro Tools or its plug-ins (Mac)

More Tips for Recording Voice-Overs

Here are a few tidbits that you might find useful with regard to recording the spoken word:

- Lip smack and cottonmouth can be the bane of your existence. And the more you compress a voice-over to squash everything right up to a consistent level, the worse it gets. To avoid having to maniacally edit out these extraneous noises, try this old trick: Offer the narrator a few bites of a nice, crispy apple. (Fuji or Granny Smith work well, but anything fairly tart will do the trick.) If you don't have any apples handy, bring apple juice instead. This works!

- When editing voice-overs recorded in noisy environments (for example, from on-location interviews, around office or industrial ventilation systems, or anywhere near a computer), after chopping them up into keeper segments, you may find that the background noise popping in and out with each audio clip is bothersome. Use the Batch Fades dialog box to create fade-ins and fade-outs on individual clips so that these transitions will at least be a little smoother. This technique can be equally useful for guitar fills played through a noisy amplifier, vocal lines, drum hits that you've split into individual clips using the Strip Silence feature with a healthy amount of start and end pad, or just about anything that's intermittent within a track. Select all clips in the track and then press Command+F (Ctrl+F in Windows). In the Batch Fades dialog box, select the fade-in/out shapes you want (Standard is a good place to start). In the Length field underneath the Create New Fade Ins and Outs checkbox, try an initial setting of 50 milliseconds or so. If you've already trimmed the beginning of each VO clip too tightly and the attacks on initial words are overly softened by the fade, repeat the operation using a fade-in shape with a steeper slope.

- Professionals who do character voice work may cringe at this heretical suggestion, but when you're using the same voice talent for many different characters (as in cartoons or simulation scenarios for training videos), a very small amount of pitch shift up or down can be surprisingly effective. The idea is not necessarily to apply some extreme amount as a special effect (not that there's anything wrong with that!), but instead to work in ranges of perhaps a semitone or two at most that listeners won't identify as pitch-shifted. The reason this works so well is that, no matter how adept actors may be at pitching their voices, the characteristic resonances or formants of each individual's vocal tract remain more or less constant. Pitch shifting can also shift these formants, and a very small amount can help sell the idea that it's a different person. Notice that the Pitch Shift dialog box has a Fine slider for adjusting pitch shift in increments of 1/100 of a semitone, called *cents*. A few tenths of a semitone can make all the difference between the pitch-shifted audio sounding processed or natural. The Transpose field in the Time Shift dialog box can also be adjusted in fine increments if you hold down the Command key (Ctrl key in Windows) as you adjust its value. The monophonic mode of the Time Shift plug-in also allows you to shift formants independently of the pitch shift amount.

Creating Your Own Session Templates

Most users will repeatedly work on certain kinds of projects, creating many sessions with similar configurations. To save time, you can create your own templates. These serve as starting points for new sessions, with a Mix window configuration, including plug-ins, inserts, and sends; track names; Edit window display format; window arrangements; zoom presets; session sample rate and bit depth; SMPTE start time; and so on. Here's a brief how-to, assuming you want to use an existing, finished session (containing audio and/or MIDI clips) as the basis for creating a blank template:

1. Use the File > Save a Copy In command to save this session under a completely new name and in a different location (perhaps onto your desktop, where it will be handy later). Give it an obvious name, such as "30-second spot template." Do *not* enable any of the other copy options in the Save dialog box (Copy Audio Files and Session Plug-In Settings Folder, Copy Root Plug-In Settings Folder, or Copy Movie/Audio Files). Close your current session and then open the copy you just created.

2. In the Clip List pop-up menu, use the Select All and then Clear Selected commands to remove all existing clips from the new session copy. (Caution: Click the Remove button, not the Delete button, which would permanently eliminate these source audio files from disk, trashing your previous session!) Delete any existing memory locations. If you were using a Video track, delete that from this session copy as well.

3. If necessary, clean up your track names, track views, and other settings until they are exactly how you want them to appear in newly created sessions based on this template.

4. Choose Save as Template under the File menu. Choose whether you want to save the template in one of the previously made categories, in a new category you create, or in a new location on your computer setup (which also prompts you for a new name). Also choose not to include any media in the template.

Transferring Sequences from MIDI Workstations into Pro Tools

Suppose you or your clients have songs already recorded into a standalone MIDI sequencer, drum machine, or standalone MIDI workstation (a keyboard synthesizer that includes an internal sequencer for MIDI recording). You'd like to bring this MIDI data into Pro Tools to start adding vocals and other Audio tracks. Unfortunately, the device in question can't save a Type 1 Standard MIDI File (SMF) file; otherwise, you would simply use the File > Import > MIDI to Track command, which creates MIDI tracks as necessary for each MIDI channel within the source file that contains data. An alternative is to record the device's MIDI output in real time. But you have a challenge: The only MIDI source that Pro Tools can synchronize to is MIDI Time Code (MTC—a variant of SMPTE time code, which is an *absolute* time reference), while the MIDI sequencer can only generate or synchronize to MIDI Beat Clock (also known as MIDI Sync—a *relative*, tempo-derived time reference, based on 24 clocks per 1/4 note). Don't despair; it can easily be done!

1. Use the Setup > MIDI > MIDI Beat Clock command to enable generation of this data on the appropriate MIDI output port connected to your external MIDI sequencer.

2. Go into the setup of the external MIDI sequencer and change its synchronization mode so that it slaves to an external MIDI Beat Clock rather to than its own internal tempo setting. For example, on a Roland keyboard workstation, change the sequencer's Sync mode from Internal to Slave. Your external sequencer should now start/stop playback as you click Play/Stop in Pro Tools.

3. Set an appropriate tempo in Pro Tools because its MIDI Beat Clock output now controls the playback tempo of the external MIDI sequencer. (Of course, you can connect the audio output from the external MIDI device to your Pro Tools hardware and monitor it within Pro Tools through an Aux Input or Instrument track.)

4. Create 16 MIDI or Instrument tracks in Pro Tools (or fewer, if you already know exactly which of the sequencer's tracks/channels contain MIDI data). Set their input selectors to channels 1–16 on the appropriate MIDI input/device.

5. Arm all these MIDI tracks for recording by holding down the Option key (Alt key in Windows) as you enable the Record button on any one of them.

6. Click Record and Play in the Pro Tools Transport to record the multichannel MIDI output of your external sequencer into Pro Tools.

7. Afterward, remember to assign appropriate device/channel *output* destinations for each of the MIDI or Instrument tracks, and also to take your external sequencer out of Slave Sync mode (and/or disable MIDI Beat Clock output from Pro Tools)!

Appendix E: Signal Flow in Pro Tools

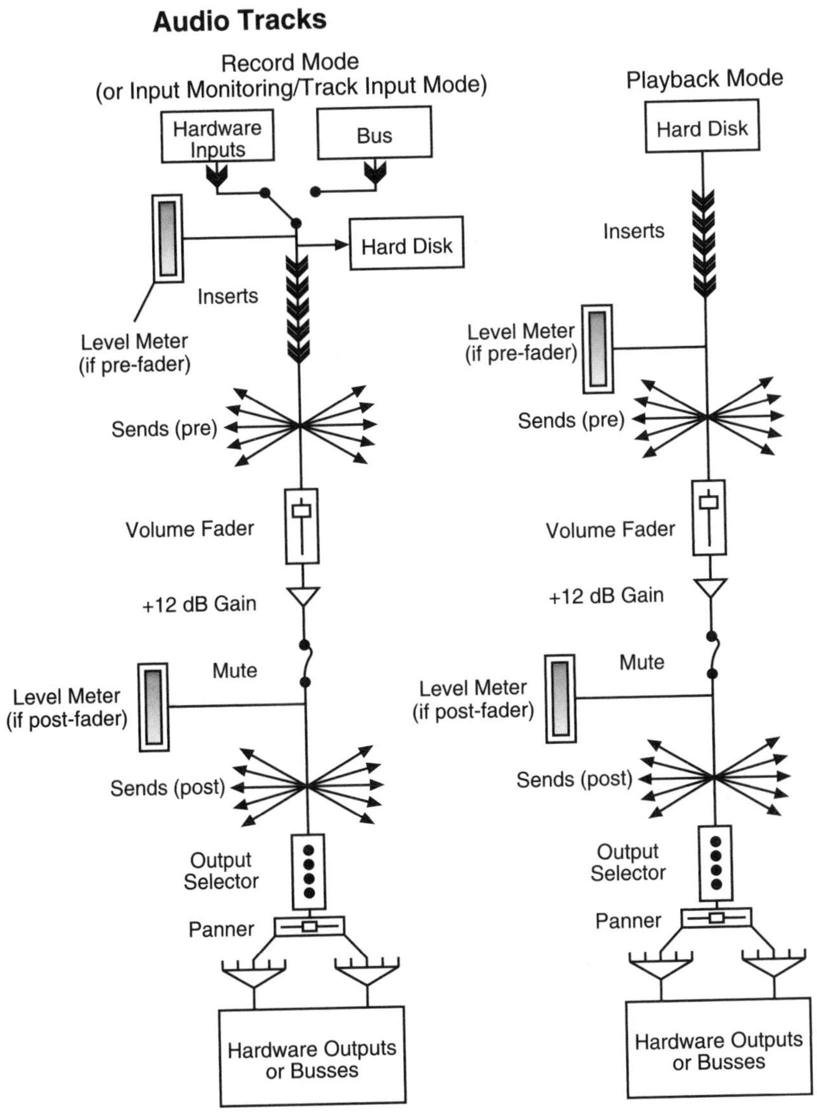

Audio Tracks

Figure E.1 Signal flow for an Audio track during recording (as well as when Input Only Monitoring is enabled or the TrackInput button is enabled on systems with Pro Tools HD or Complete Production Toolkit) and during playback. Notice that the main volume fader is located just before the output stage (and any post-fader sends); therefore, it has no effect on input recording levels!

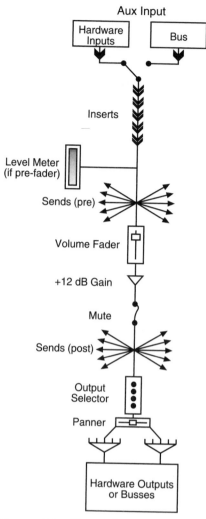

Figure E.2 Signal flow for an Auxiliary Input track. Its input source can be either a physical input on the audio hardware or one of the internal mix busses in Pro Tools. Notwithstanding their MIDI functionality, from a signal-flow perspective, Instrument tracks are identical to Aux Inputs (and could actually be used as such). In practice, on either type of track, the actual signal source might originate from a plug-in on one of its inserts—a software instrument or the Click and Signal Generator plug-ins, for example.

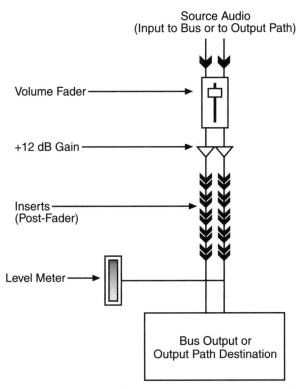

Figure E.3   Signal flow for a Master Fader track. Master Faders have no sends. Unlike Audio tracks, Aux Input tracks, and Instrument tracks, the Insert section on a Master Fader is always post-fader.

Index